2-6-70

The Movement Toward Latin American Unity

LATIN AMERICA
(PROPOSED AND ESTABLISHED ECONOMIC BLOCS)

MEXICO

GUATEMALA
EL SALVADOR
HONDURAS
NICARAGUA
COSTA RICA

JAMAICA
ST. KITTS – NEVIS
ANTIGUA
MONTSERRAT
DOMINICA
ST. LUCIA
BARBADOS
ST. VINCENT
GRENADA
TRINIDAD & TOBAGO
GUYANA

CARRIBBEAN
FREE TRADE
ASSOC.
(ESTABLISHED IN
1968)

*VENEZUELA

*COLOMBIA

*ECUADOR

*PERU

BRAZIL

*BOLIVIA

PARAGUAY
PARANA
PARAGUAY
PARANA
PARANA
URUGUAY

URUGUAY

CHILE *

ARGENTINA

RIO DE
LA PLATA

RIVER PLATA
BASIN GROUP
(AGREED UPON IN 1968)

CENTRAL AMERICAN COMMON MARKET
(ESTABLISHED IN 1960)

LATIN AMERICAN FREE TRADE ASSOC.
(ESTABLISHED IN 1960)

* **ANDEAN GROUP**
(A SUBGROUP OF L.A.F.T.A. PROPOSED IN 1966)

PRAEGER SPECIAL STUDIES IN
INTERNATIONAL ECONOMICS AND DEVELOPMENT

The Movement Toward Latin American Unity

Edited by
Ronald Hilton

**Published in cooperation with
The California Institute of
International Studies**

FREDERICK A. PRAEGER, Publishers
New York · Washington · London

The purpose of the Praeger Special Studies is to make specialized research monographs in U.S. and international economics and politics available to the academic, business, and government communities. For further information, write to the Special Projects Division, Frederick A. Praeger, Publishers, 111 Fourth Avenue, New York, N.Y. 10003.

FREDERICK A. PRAEGER, PUBLISHERS
111 Fourth Avenue, New York, N.Y. 10003, U.S.A.
5, Cromwell Place, London S.W.7, England

Published in the United States of America in 1969
by Frederick A. Praeger, Inc., Publishers

Library of Congress Catalog Card Number: 75-87827

Printed in the United States of America

PREFACE   **1525831**

The present volume on the movement toward Latin American unity, and more precisely toward Latin American economic integration, developed out of a conference about which details are given in the Introduction. We wish to thank the institutions whose support made the conference possible, especially the Inter-American Development Bank, the Bank of America, and Stanford Research Institute. We are also indebted to the Bank of America for the map and tabulation at the beginning of the volume. All the participants expressed their ideas with complete freedom, and neither the California Institute of International Studies nor any of the organizations mentioned is responsible for the statements made in the collection of studies. Every author speaks for himself. No attempt has been made to force a consensus out of these papers, yet, as we have tried to show, there was a significant agreement on many general points.

This symposium reflects the present unglamorous state of inter-American relations. The times call for candor, and the U.S. Government has in effect issued a call for the American states to face reality and avoid slogans. In his Pan American Day speech in Washington on April 14, 1969, before the Organization of American States, President Nixon pointed out that the rate of growth in Latin America is "less than the rate of growth in non-Communist Asia, and it is less, even, than the rate of growth in Communist Eastern Europe." He described this situation as intolerable and warned that, despite the hopes created by the Alliance for Progress and Latin American economic integration, the future looks grim: If the rates of growth in the United States and in Latin America remain the same until the end of the century, the per capita income in the United States will be fifteen times as high as in Latin America.

President Nixon warned: "This is a result which we cannot tolerate. We must do better." The feeling is shared by Americans of different political affiliations. Ambassador Sol Linowitz, who resigned on May 1, 1969, as U.S. representative to the Organization of American States, has expressed similar sentiments. We should not, however, allow the world to assume that the responsibility for this failure lies with the United States alone. At least half of the burden must be assumed by Latin America, where some governments have recently indulged in a xenophobic nationalism, refusing to listen to others or to submit to any kind of world order, and holding that each nation is a law unto itself.

The smoke screen of demagoguery should not obscure the real issues: the development of a viable world order and the adoption in economic and social fields of sane policies which will make this possible. Is the movement toward Latin American unity, and in particular the development of economic integration, making a positive contribution, or is this but another illusory attempt to hide reality?

Ronald Hilton

v

CONTENTS

Chapter

PART III: ECONOMICS AND BANKING

Chapter

PART VII: SCIENCE AND CULTURE

Chapter

PART VIII: REGIONAL STUDIES

Chapter

LIST OF TABLES AND FIGURES

TABLES

FIGURES

ABBREVIATIONS

AOT	Associated Overseas Territory
BID	Banco Interamericano de Desarrollo (Inter-American Development Bank)
CABEI	Central American Bank for Economic Integration
CACM	Central American Common Market
CARIFTA	Caribbean Free Trade Association
CCITT	International Telegraph and Telephone Consultative Committee
CED	Committee for Economic Development
CELAM	Consejo Episcopal Latinoamericano
CGT	Confederación General de Trabajadores
CIAP	Comité Interamericano de la Alianza para el Progreso (Inter-American Committee of the Alliance for Progress)
CIES	Consejo Interamericano Económico y Social (Inter-American Economic and Social Council)
CITEL	Comisión Interamericana de Telecomunicaciones
CLASC	Confederación Latinoamericana de Sindicatos Cristianos
CODECA	Corporación de Desarrollo Económico del Caribe
COMECON	Council for Mutual Economic Aid
COMTELCA	Comisión Regional de Telecomunicaciones
ECLA	Economic Commission for Latin America
ECSC	European Coal and Steel Community
EEC	European Economic Community
EFTA	European Free Trade Association
ERP	effective radiative power
ETV	educational television
FAO	Food and Agriculture Organization
GATT	General Agreement on Tariffs and Trade
IA-ECOSOC	Inter-American Economical and Social Council
IBRD	International Bank for Reconstruction and Development
ICAD	Inter-American Committee for Agricultural Development
IDB	Inter-American Development Bank (Banco Interamericano de Desarrollo)
INCAE	Instituto Centroamericano de Administración de Empresas
INTAL	Instituto para la Integración de América Latina
ITN	Inter-American Telecommunications Network
ITU	International Telecommunications Union
JPM	Joint Planning Mission
LACM	Latin American Common Market
LAFTA	Latin American Free Trade Association
MCC	Mercado Común Centroamericano
OAS	Organization of American States (See OEA)
ODECA	Organización de Estados Centroamericanos
OEA	Organización de Estados Americanos (See OAS)
ORIT	Organización Regional Interamericana de Trabajadores
PAHO	Pan American Health Organization
ROCAP	Regional Organization for Central America and Panama
SIECA	Secretaría de Integración Económica de Centroamérica
SUDAM	Superintendência para a Amazônia
SUDENE	Superintendência do Desenvolvimento do Nordeste
UNCTAD	United Nations Conference on Trade and Development
VHF	very high frequency

INTRODUCTION

Latin American Economic Integration

The leaders of Latin America have been re-examining the fundamental obstacles to economic development that must be overcome. There is a growing realization that (1) economic development is a complex, long-term process and (2) the creation of a meaningful market system is the best known framework in which to promote economic growth. To speed up the formation of strong markets, Latin American nations have been trying to unite into regional economic units.

They know that too many economic development schemes have been proposed that imply that Latin America could, in a few years, reach desired standard-of-living levels. "Easy" solutions to the complex problems confronting Latin American nations have been suggested. Some have frequently claimed that rapid economic growth would be assured if the United States would provide enough foreign aid or if extensive land reform programs were implemented. Businessmen and the general public have supported various programs to foster accelerated economic growth, only to be disappointed in the results. Fortunately, the direction of thought has changed and economic development is now seen as the composite product of many interrelated elements. Among these elements, economic integration plays an important part.

Summary of Major Latin American Economic Integration Efforts

Central American Common Market (Established in 1960)	Costa Rica, El Salvador, Guatemala, Honduras, and Nicaragua.
Latin American Free Trade Association (Established in 1960)	Argentina, Bolivia, Brazil, Chile, Colombia, Ecuador, Mexico, Paraguay, Peru, Uruguay, and Venezuela.
Andean Group (Proposed August 1966 but not yet established) *	Bolivia, Colombia, Chile, Ecuador, Peru, and Venezuela.
River Plata Basin Group (Agreed upon in 1968. Efforts of this group are expected to revolve around specific development projects.)	Argentina, Brazil, Bolivia, Paraguay, and Uruguay.
Caribbean Free Trade Association (First proposed in December 1965, but not officially established until May 1, 1968)	Antigua, Barbados, Guyana, Jamaica, and Trinidad and Tobago. The Associated States of Dominica, Grenada, Montserrat, St. Kitts-Nevis, St. Lucia, and St. Vincent.
Latin American Common Market (With a hoped-for establishment date of 1985)	A proposal to merge the Central American Common Market and the Latin American Free Trade Area.

*The Andean Subregional Group, with the exception of Venezuela, reached an accord in May 1969. For accounts of the state of the various groups at the beginning of 1969, see two publications of the Office of External Research of the U.S. Department of State: Andrew B. Wardlaw, *Achievements and Problems of the Central American Common Market* (February 1969, pp. 46) and Edward G. Cale, *Latin American Free Trade Association: Progress, Problems, Prospects* (May 1969, pp. 64).

CHAPTER **1** INTRODUCTION

By Ronald Hilton
Stanford University
California Institute of International Studies

The movement toward Latin American unity is part of a worldwide trend toward the reorganization of the world into continental systems which would supersede to some degree the traditional sovereign states. It was the subject of a conference held in Palo Alto, California, under the auspices of the California Institute of International Studies. The conference papers were subjected to the careful scrutiny of the 250 invited specialists present and revised in the light of their comments. The resulting volume gives us an assessment of the "state of the Latin American union" as of 1969. This introduction attempts to single out some of the conclusions and to buttress them with recent data about Latin American economic developments.

The mood of the group was mixed. While sympathetic to the general idea of Latin American integration, it was not euphoric. The European community appeared to face an impasse created by de Gaulle, and grandiose conceptions such as "The Great Society" had proved to be illusory. The second United Nations Conference on Trade and Development (UNCTAD) held in New Delhi in 1968 had ended in dismal failure. About 1,600 delegates had met for eight weeks and achieved virtually nothing. There were loud demands that Raúl Prebisch resign as secretary general of UNCTAD; at first he stubbornly refused to do so, but later he quietly abandoned the post. The participants at the Palo Alto conference reflected the widespread concern that statesmen convene with fanfare at international conferences and achieve little of substance.

After the roseate dawn of common markets, a protectionist trend seemed to be setting in everywhere. On March 17, 1969, U. S. Secretary of Commerce Maurice Stans said that "the entire world seems to be going protectionist." The psychological climate of the world is at least momentarily not propitious for Latin American economic integration.

In Latin America it is hard to discern progress. The goals of the Alliance for Progress are not being met. It is calculated that 250 million Latin Americans are getting less food than they used to. On the eve of the Palo Alto conference, the Economist Intelligence Unit published a special report entitled The Crisis in Latin American Integration. At the Punta del Este meeting in April 1967, the heads of state of practically all the American governments, including President Johnson, pledged very vocally to

3

work for Latin American development and economic integration, but in the two years since then inter-American meetings have been generally unproductive. Both the Seventh Extraordinary Conference of the Latin American Free Trade Association (LAFTA) and the Eighth Ordinary Conference disbanded without in any way reaching the prescribed goals. Admittedly, it is hard to find a middle ground between the pessimism of independent observers and the optimism of LAFTA officials, who assert that negotiations conducted during 1968 were very successful.[1] The long-range trade picture of Latin America does not appear encouraging. Between 1950 and 1968 Latin American participation in world trade declined more than 50 per cent.

Despite the criticism of Marxist, Catholic, and nationalist groups, the consensus of specialists is that whatever gains may be achieved through economic integration and by the Alliance for Progress are offset by the failure of Latin America to face its population problem. Figures released early in 1969 showed that, especially in Mexico, the population percentage increase, far from declining, had jumped unexpectedly. In Central America it was 3.5 per cent. On March 15, 1969, the Agency for International Development reported to Congress that the goals of the Alliance for Progress were neither realistic nor attainable until the people of Latin America took steps to control population growth. Economic integration should allow the free passage of surplus populations across national boundaries within Latin America, but there are few signs that the barriers are being lowered. Meanwhile, Latin America is suffering from a brain drain, as many of its most qualified people emigrate to the United States and Europe.[2]

While the Palo Alto conference held that it would be ill-advised to attempt to repeat in Latin America the success of the European Common Market, the consensus was that careful moves toward economic integration should be encouraged. Vast inputs of capital would not necessarily promote economic integration and would in part be counterproductive. There were fears that the repayments on foreign loans would largely offset the amounts received in new loans. Indeed, it has been calculated that, since the Alliance for Progress came into being, the cost of servicing the region's debts has doubled. About 75 per cent of the bank funds now coming into Latin America is used to pay the interest on old loans.

The participants in the Palo Alto conference felt that the economic integration of all of Latin America might be premature and that the integration of subregions could be a realistic first step. However, the journey of President Johnson to the Central American capitals in 1968 revealed the inner tensions in the Central American Common Market, which had generally been described in glowing colors. In early 1969 the Central American Common Market was struck by a major crisis. President Somoza of Nicaragua reimposed import duties on goods from other Central American countries, alleging that Nicaragua had an unfavorable balance with the other market members and that Costa Rica had failed to ratify the protocol calling for a 30 per cent surcharge on luxury

4

goods coming from outside the market area. The other Central American countries retaliated by removing Nicaragua's duty-free privileges. It is too early to assess the impact of this. Barclays Bank Survey of March 1969 still spoke optimistically of CACM, but Granma of March 23, 1969, said CACM was on the verge of collapse. Fidel Castro's newspaper was indulging in wishful thinking. It did not mention that Central American intraregional trade increased from $213 million in 1967 to $260 million in 1968.

The Andean subregional group was created in a truncated form in May 1969; Venezuela, economically the most powerful member of the group, refused to join, for fear of endangering its high-cost industries. There remained a faint hope that the government of President Rafael Caldera, which had abandoned the Betancourt doctrine of nonrecognition of regimes such as that of the Peruvian junta and had special ties with the Christian Democratic government of President Frei in Chile, would seek to cooperate with the group, which is held together largely by fear of the Colossi of the East, Brazil and Argentina.

Obviously, the Caribbean faces almost insurmountable obstacles to integration. Castro's Cuba remains scornful of a movement to integrate countries which it regards as colonies of the United States. No one can take seriously talk of integrating Haiti and the Dominican Republic. The Caribbean Free Trade Association (CARIFTA), bringing together the Commonwealth countries in the area, was at the beginning of 1969 still little more than a gleam in the planners' eyes.

There was especial support at the Palo Alto conference for the attempts to integrate natural areas, such as the River Plate Basin, but here again the obstacles were all too apparent. The failure of the Hylean Amazonian Institute showed how difficult it would be to plan the future of that vast basin, while the decision of the Argentine Government to give priority to the Chocón-Cerrillos project in Patagonia would clearly slow down the integrated development of the River Plate area.

The old question "Cui bono?" constantly recurs in discussions about LAFTA. Economic integration should prove profitable for U.S. and Latin American industrialists seeking large markets, but its benefits would not necessarily reach the common people. Indeed, prices might increase if economic integration led to a rise in tariff barriers between Latin America and the rest of the world. The economic integration of Latin America has been attacked in Marxist publications emanating both from the Soviet Union and Cuba as a U.S. plot to create a vast market for goods produced by U.S.-owned factories employing workers earning much less than their American counterparts. [3] This criticism was muted at the conference, and even the representatives of Communist countries were discreetly silent on this point, but there was a marked feeling that much of the support for, as well as the opposition to, Latin American economic integration came from industrial groups whose income would be affected favorably or adversely.

5

While the Marxists denounce Latin American economic integration as a U.S. capitalist plot, it is evident that the Latin American movement toward unity has anti-American overtones.   They
could be heard in the convocation of the first meeting of the Special
Latin American Coordination Commission in Santiago de Chile from
March 31 to April 5, 1969. Shortly after the Peruvian junta in
early 1969 expropriated the International Petroleum Corporation
properties, the Brazilian Government voiced support for Peru,
and the Brazilian Minister of Foreign Affairs addressed an invitation to the other governments of Latin America proposing that their
ministries of foreign affairs meet to formulate a common policy
vis-à-vis the United States. Galo Plaza, secretary general of the
OAS, and members of the Nixon administration expressed approval
of the proposed coordination of Latin American policy, but such approval could not change the fact that the intent of the proposal was
clearly to support Peru in its fight with the United States.   Since
the Andean Group was supporting the Pacific Coast republics' claim
to sovereignty over a 200-mile strip of coastal waters, it seemed
inevitable that this also would bring the group into conflict with both
the United States and international law.   The refusal of the group to
respect international law in this regard threatened to bring chaos
into maritime affairs and suggested that the Latin American integration movement may prove a negative force in U.S. attempts to
produce an orderly world.

The Peruvian Aprista Andrés Townsend Ezcurra, secretary general of the Latin American Parliament, spoke fervently at
the Palo Alto conference of the movement toward Latin American
political unity, but the consensus of the group was that such unity
was, at least for the present, illusory, since military dictatorships
have been sweeping parliamentary regimes aside throughout Latin
America. Not only does the Latin American Parliament seem like
a dream, but even APRA's hopes of coming to power in Peru by
peaceful democratic means have been shattered by the military
coup which removed President Fernando Belaúnde. Indeed, as
things are going at present, if Latin America is to achieve unity,
it may be by the "Alliance of Swords," as Latin Americans call it.

In the field of communications the prospects are mixed.
Surface communications, which are essential to heavy industry,
show little sign of improving, but aviation and satellites can be especially useful precisely because of the difficulty of surface communications.   Certainly, the development of communications will
speed the movement toward integration. Apart from ambitious
plans for satellite communications, there have been only modest
steps forward, such as the 1969 agreement on the route for the Pan
American Highway across the Darien Gap.

Economics does not function in a human vacuum, and there
was much discussion at the conference of what might be called the
psychological integration of Latin America. Spanish America has
a sense of unity. The liberators such as Simón Bolívar gave expression to this feeling of unity, but in the nineteenth century Spanish Americans generally were conscious primarily of their own na-

tionality and had practically no continental loyalty. Now the improvement of communications is bringing Latin America closer together not only materially, but also intellectually and spiritually. However, "Latin America" is a very arbitrary label, even though it has now been accepted officially as designating all the member states of the Organization of American States except the United States. This would imply that Cuba is not a Latin American country, while Jamaica and Barbados are. The fact is that there is a psychological gap between Brazil and Spanish America, between Negroes, Indians, and whites. The expression "Latin America" suggests a unity which in human terms scarcely exists.

Indeed, the crisis in the hitherto cordial U.S.-Peruvian relations suggests that there is a recrudescence of a nationalism which is much more powerful than any "Latin Americanism." A demagogic appeal to the nationalism of an illiterate mob produces primitive howls, while the same mob would look blankly at any speaker proposing Latin American integration unless it were implicitly reinforcing nationalism. In varying degrees this phenomenon occurs throughout Latin America and indeed throughout much of the "Third World." The only difference in Cuba is that Fidel Castro uses the Soviet bloc rather than Latin American integration to back up the xenophobic nationalism which has developed in the island. A campaign against a foreign enemy remains the most convenient instrument of government for those who have seized power illegally or who find it difficult to run their own countries and to appease their own subjects.

We may regret this acute nationalism, but it can be explained. One reason is that the Latin American countries have not yet integrated their own territories, and Peru, cut in three by the high Andes, is an excellent case of this. There is a greater sense of urgency to integrate one's own country than to integrate a whole continent. Given this urge, the best the outside world can hope for is that the republics will not integrate their own territories in such a way as to make international integration difficult or impossible. Our experience to date suggests that this will not be an easy task.

National integration is difficult not only because of the geography of most of the countries, but also because of the history of Latin America. Most Latin American countries derive from colonial administrative units, and the doctrine of Uti possedetis has been a prime factor in establishing the geographical configuration of the republics. Really this makes little more sense than the new political divisions of Africa, which also go back to the arbitrary divisions of colonial administrators. This is commonly admitted in discussions about Africa, but only a few brave Latin Americans, such as Juan Bautista Alberdi, have dared to question the principle of Uti possedetis. It would be a good thing if Uti possedetis were given a decent burial, but the force of tradition, the professional deformation of international lawyers and the archivistic tendency to look to the past rather than to the future make this unlikely. The economic integration of Latin America would remove some of the absurdities inherited from the colonial period, but unfortunately

7

politics, especially international politics, belongs to the theatre of the absurd.

Latin American politicians and diplomats usually pay lip-service to the idea of integration, and this is a good thing. Despite Hamlet, words, words, words may become, if they are repeated often enough, facts. Yet perhaps the basic question is one of historical determinism. Latin American theoreticians love to speak of "irreversible" historical phenomena. Is the movement toward Latin American integration irreversible? Putting it in more positive terms, we may repeat the adage that nothing can stop an idea whose hour has arrived or, as Sarmiento is reputed to have scrawled on a rock: "On ne tue point les idées." That the Sarmiento tradition has not fared too well in Argentina should, however, give us pause.

It is then difficult to give a simple answer to the question: Can Latin America unite? We cannot even state baldly that Latin America should unite. We fear that this volume will disappoint those who are looking for simple or even clear answers. The world is an extremely complex place, and a failure to realize this is one of the sources of international problems. Yet this realization should not lead to discouragement. Despite misgivings about the details of the Latin American integration movement at the Palo Alto conference, no one suggested that it should be halted. In this at least the consensus was positive. The Inter-American Development Bank was commended as a competent institution working in difficult circumstances.

NOTES

1. The Mexican publication *Comercio Exterior* in its February 1969 issue (p. 101) gave an optimistic report of these negotiations. The economist Albert O. Hirschman is more receptive to official optimism than many of his colleagues, and has warned against what he has dubbed "fracasomanía," i.e. the tendency to stress the failures of such negotiations.

2. An ECLA survey still in process in 1969 gives alarming figures on unemployment in the region. The figures show that about 40 per cent of Latin America's active work force suffers from either total or partial unemployment.

3. There is a considerable Soviet literature attacking U.S. economic "imperialism" in Latin America and denouncing the economic integration of Latin America. See Страны Латинской Америки в современных международных отношениях, Moscow 1967.
Б. И. Гвоздарев Союз ради Прогресса, Moscow 1964.
З. И. Романова, Проблемы экономической интеграции в Латинской Америке, Moscow 1965.

PART I

HISTORICAL BACKGROUND

2

POLITICAL THEORY AND
REGIONAL INTEGRATION:
THE FIRST TEN YEARS

By   Roger D. Hansen
National Planning Association
Washington, D. C.

The appearance of major studies by Karl Deutsch and
Ernst Haas in the late 1950's won for integration theory a prominent position among the contemporary approaches to the study of
international relations. [1] A decade later its achievements are very
much a matter of debate. While disappointment with results have
led many students of integration theory to focus their attention on
smaller and, hopefully, more manageable units such as local communities and city-suburb relations, others continue investigations
at the international level. [2]

Ernst Haas is one of those who has continued to work at
the supranational level, and a recent contribution of his (co-
authored by Philippe Schmitter) attempts to construct a theoretical
framework applicable to the study of international integration in
both industrialized and underdeveloped regions of the world. Europe was the focal point for most of the early works on regional
integration, and the application of integration theory to Latin America,   Africa, and Asia is a more recent phenomenon. Since Haas
has studied the integration process in both industrial and non-industrial settings and has attempted to devise a theoretical approach
applicable to both, an investigation of some of the limitations entailed in his approach provides a fairly accurate picture of the
general state of regional integration theory at the present stage in
its development. This is true for two reasons: Haas is one of the
most thoughtful and sophisticated theorists of regional integration;
and most, though not all, of his major concepts and conclusions
complement and confirm those of other leading students in the
field. [3]

A MODEL OF REGIONAL INTEGRATION

"Does the economic integration of a group of nations automatically trigger political unity? Or are the two processes quite
distinct, requiring deliberate political steps because purely economic arrangements are generally inadequate for ushering in political unity?"[4] The Haas-Schmitter model is specifically addressed to the question of the automaticity of the link between economic and political integration; so, too, is this essay. The thesis
proposed by the above-named authors is that "under modern conditions the relationship between economic and political union had best
be treated as a continuum. "[5] Why? In order to portray the Haas-

Schmitter views most fully and fairly, their answer is presented with no intervening interpretation:

> Linkages between economic objectives and policies, on the one hand, and political consequences of a disintegrative or integrative nature, on the other, are of a "functional" character: they rest very often on indirection, on unplanned and accidental convergences in outlook and aspiration among the actors, on dialectical relations between antagonistic purposes. . . Integration can be conceived as involving the <u>gradual</u> <u>politicization</u> of the actors' purposes which were initially considered "technical" or "noncontroversial." Politicization implies that the actors, in response to miscalculations or disappointment with respect to the initial purposes, agree to widen the spectrum of means considered appropriate to attain them. This tends to increase the controversial component, i.e., those additional fields of action which require political choices concerning how much additional autonomy to delegate to the union. Politicization implies that the actors seek to resolve their problems so as to upgrade common interests and, in the process, delegate more authority to the center. It constitutes one of the properties of integration—the intervening variable between economic and political union—along with the development of new expectations and loyalties on the part of organized interests in the member nations.[6]   [Emphasis added.]

The authors define a successful political union as a regional entity upon which actors bestow "a significant portion of their loyalties." They posit that a successful union implies an end to threats of revolt or secession even though the scope of central control continues to be extended. "In other words, a political union can be said to exist when the politicized decision-making process has acquired legitimacy and authority."[7]

Having developed the dynamic of "politicization," Haas and Schmitter construct three sets of observable variables "which seem to intervene more or less consistently between the act of economic union and the possible end product we label political union."[8] They consist of <u>background variables</u> (size of member-units, rates of inter-unit transactions, extent of social pluralism within the units, and elite complementarity), <u>variables at the moment of economic union</u> (degree of shared government purposes, and powers delegated to the union), and <u>process variables</u> (decision-making style, post-integration rates of transactions, and the adaptability of governments in situations of disappointment and crisis). High, mixed, or low ratings are to be determined for each set of variables as they are applied to the study of any regional grouping. The "higher" the scores, the more likely it is that an economic union will "automatically" be transformed into a form of political union. "Because a spillover is likely to occur in these cases [i.e., cases of high scores for all three sets of variables], the functional adaptation to its implications is likely to be 'automatic' in the sense that the participating actors will make the kinds of decisions which will safeguard their collective economic welfare..."[9] The "lower" the scores, the less the automaticity and the more difficult the move from economic to political union.

With the exception of the final variable — adaptability in crises — all are familiar in the literature of regional integration and need not be discussed at this point. A further word should be said about the adaptability measurement, however, because it involves an issue of some importance to our following analysis of the Haas-Schmitter scheme and Haas' original theoretical observations upon the course of European integration. Haas has consistently maintained that economic integration will have more "spillover" into a broad range of political issues than any other functional approach, i.e., that economic issues and policies are less "autonomous" than others. The process of spillover from economic integration will not only lead to gradual politicization, but also to crises. "Crisis is the creative opportunity for realizing [the] potential to redefine aims at a higher level of consensus."[10] Thus, the degree of "autonomy" which characterizes modern industrial economic sectors, and the propensity for economic integration to engender crises in advanced economies are crucial assumptions in Haas' "expansive logic of economic integration," and will be analyzed below.

A final element in the Haas-Schmitter model should be noted — the concept of the "functional equivalent." The authors argue that in Western Europe "the element of automaticity to which we have called attention is provided by the internal logic of industrialism, pluralism, and democracy... Industrial society is the setting in which supranationality and a lively spillover process are able to flourish... [However,] specific regions may well possess unique cultural or stylistic attributes which are able to serve as functional equivalents for important traits isolated in [Western Europe]."[11] [Emphasis added.] Much of the article in which this model appears is devoted to a study of the functional equivalents in the Latin American scene which may help to overcome the otherwise "low" scores that the authors attribute to their integration variables in the case of the Latin American Free Trade Association (LAFTA).

A CRITIQUE

The theoretical weaknesses in the model delineated above may best be illustrated by applying it to the process of integration first in Western Europe, and then in less developed regions of the world. The Haas treatment of European integration might be summarized thus: limited sectoral economic agreements so increase trade flows and mutual problems connected with them that a supranational bureaucracy develops, and an everbroadening number of economic activities are touched by growing supranational jurisdiction. Industrial groups as well organize on the new regional level in order to influence the emerging power centers. Over time these centers of jurisdiction are granted increasing powers; and political loyalties, following in the wake of economic interests, come to focus on the new supranational entities. The end result: political union.

The major question which has arisen with regard to the Haas analysis (and prognosis) is the necessary extent of the political ramifications of economic union in the Western European case. As Etzioni suggests, "how far [spillover] carries unification before it is exhausted is a question whose answer is as yet largely unknown."[12] Much criticism of the dialectic of spillover simply points to the obvious fact that the pace of European integration has diminished dramatically, if not completely. To the extent that the "logic of economic integration" as expounded by Haas and other functionalists suggested an inevitability about the eventual political unification in Europe of the Six, this type of criticism appears to have at least temporary validity; however, it generally contributes little to a better understanding of the integration process in industrially and politically developed regions. Of much greater relevance, and therefore considered in some detail below, is a theoretical critique developed by Stanley Hoffmann and others. The degree of relevance attributed to it will inevitably be conditioned by the individual scholar's propensities to accept or reject "historical sociology" as an enlightening approach to the study of international relations.[13] In addition, economic theory and economic events in the Western European setting suggest some limitations to the spillover thesis which may well have been heretofore ignored or overlooked.

Economic analysis, both theoretical and empirical, is most helpful, however, in calling into question the relevance of the Haas-Schmitter model for understanding the connections between economic and political integration in Latin America and other semi- and nonindustrial regions. One perceptive student of regional integration in African and Latin American settings has suggested that in many underdeveloped areas

> much that in the European context would be simple welfare politics becomes tinged with emotive and symbolic content that is usually associated with national security politics. One consequence ... is that there is less opportunity for autonomous bureaucrats to go quietly about the business of integration in "noncontroversial" spheres... If the problem in most underdeveloped areas is one of premature "overpoliticization," then it is not helpful for comparative study to conceive of the integration process as "gradual politicization."[14]

A discussion of the theory and practice of economic integration in such unions as the Central American and East African common markets will both substantiate the objection raised by Nye and

14

suggest the necessity of some major revisions in present integra-
tion-theory constructs as applied to economically less-developed
regions.

WESTERN EUROPE

Stanley Hoffmann recently wrote of Europe of the Six that

the failure (so far) of an experiment tried in apparently ideal conditions tells us a great deal about
contemporary world politics, about the chances of
unification movements elsewhere, and about the
functional approach to unification. For it shows
that the movement can fail not only when there is
a surge of nationalism in one important part, but
also when there are differences in assessments of
the national interest that rule out agreement on the
shape and on the world role of the new, supranational whole. [15]

He argued that

functional integration's gamble could be won if
the method had sufficient potency to promise a
permanent excess of gains over losses, and of
hopes over frustrations. Theoretically, this might
be true of economic integration.   It is not true
of political integration (in the sense of "high politics "). [16]

In treating the distinction between "high politics" and
economic welfare issues in this manner, Hoffmann's analysis is
sharply contrasted with the Haas-Schmitter model, which insists
that "economic and political union had best be treated as a continuum, " and Haas' view that "the advent of supranationality [within
the EEC institutions] symbolizes the victory of economics over politics, over that familiar ethnocentric nationalism which used to
subordinate butter to guns, reason to passion, statistical bargaining to excited demands. "[17] Hoffmann's major criticism of the Haas
theory of integration is not that it is logically inconsistent, but
rather that it is incomplete. "As long as the process [of integra-
tion] is not completed, we must analyze the building of the political
community as an incipient instance of 'interest group politics, ' of
'domestic politics of the community, ' and as a continuing example
of traditional interstate politics. "[18] [Emphasis added.]

This line of reasoning leads Hoffmann into an exercise in
concrete systems analysis of the international setting in which the
European integration experiment has been undertaken. He argues
that the failure of the unification movement among the Six to progress into "high politics" via economic spillover can be traced to
the interaction of three factors in the present international system —
"one of which characterizes every international system, and the

15

other two only the present system. "[19]   The universalistic factor
is "the diversity of domestic determinants, geo-historical situations, and outside aims among its units; any international system
based on fragmentation tends, through the dynamic of unevenness,
to reproduce diversity. "[20]   Of the two unique features, one is
that today's is "the first truly global international system; the regional subsystems have only a reduced autonomy; the 'relationship
of major tension' blankets the whole planet... "[21]

Combining these two features of the international system ,
Hoffmann argues that intra-Six relations have inevitably become
"subordinated to their divergencies about the outside world; the
'regional subsystem' becomes a stake in the rivalry of its members about the system as a whole. "[22] At this point Hoffmann
traces the mounting disagreements between the units of the Six —
France and Germany in particular — with regard to the world role
of Europe, its relationship with the United States, etc. The third
system feature — the nuclear age and the present "stability of a
bipolar world" — supports and expands the operations of national
diversity. "Damocles' sword has become a boomerang, the ideological legitimacy of the nation-state is protected by the relative
and forced tameness of the world jungle. "[23]

One might add that the legitimacy of the European states
of the Six in recent years has been supported not only by the operation of nuclear deterrence, but also by their effectiveness in the
areas of economics and welfare. Experiencing some of the world's
most rapid growth rates, the Six emerged from their weakened national situations of the immediate post-war years with a renewed
capacity to sustain popular approval. Paradoxically enough, economic integration played a major role in strengthening these national capacities for independent action in other policy areas. Thus,
the very effectiveness of economic cooperation in stimulating economic growth within the EEC expanded the margins for political
conflict among its members on a broad range of foreign and defense policy issues. One of the reasons for the contradictory outcome of the functional approach to regional integration is that the
"spillover" from economics into politics was far more limited than
that which Haas had projected, a point which will be developed
below.

With regard to the present theoretical literature on regional integration the Hoffmann analysis raises one fundamental
issue which might best be put in its starkest form: given the present
state of the art (or science, if you will) does regional integration
theory represent a useful endeavor? The answer is, of course,
conditioned more by one's particular interest in and approach to
the study of international relations than by the inherent merits or
demerits of regional integration analysis itself. For those who
value the insights provided by historical sociology, or by concrete
systems analysis, regional integration theory in its present state
has obvious limitations. Most analyses of this genre — Hoffmann's
included — stress an international system characterized by universality of scope and diminishing (if not demised) regional autonomy.

It naturally follows that regional integration analysis must become much more macro-system-oriented if it is to escape the kinds of distortion into which it has been led by its present subsystem orientation.

Had Europe of the post World War II era been possessed of more regional autonomy than was the case, the Haas analysis and prediction of eventual political union would surely have been of greater relevance than has proven to be the case.[24] In retrospect, it is probably not an accidental happening that most successful instances of African integration occurred under colonial rule, which imposed a type of subsystem autonomy, and that the United States' experiment in federation was undertaken during a period when the Atlantic Ocean implied isolation rather than involvement at the center of world politics. In fact, Europe's intimate connection with the macro-system engendered Hoffmann's "logic of diversity" which soon challenged Haas' "logic of integration" (i.e., spillover) in the race for Europe's future. And even if the race should eventually be won by integration, the issue raised by Hoffmann is still pertinent. Regional analysis which remains as compartmentalized as it is at present will suffer from a serious theoretical inadequacy: an inability to isolate and measure the impact of those external factors which affect the integration process.

Haas himself has recently recognized that "something is missing" in his exploration of the integration process in Western Europe.[25] But he does not view the inadequacy of his original theory as a product of its disregard for external factors. Rather he continues to focus exclusively on aspects internal to regional integration experiments, and concludes, with regard to Western Europe, that he underestimated the "built-in-limits" of pragmatic interest politics concerned with economic welfare.

> Pragmatic interests, simply because they are
> pragmatic and not reinforced with deep ideolog-
> ical or philosophical commitment, are ephem-
> eral... And a political process which is built
> and projected from pragmatic interests, there-
> fore, is bound to be a frail process, susceptible
> to reversal. And so integration can once more
> develop into disintegration. [26]

The reversal in the move toward political union in Europe occurred when de Gaulle's EEC partners rejected his bid for a common foreign and defense policy. At this point the General blocked the scheduled advance to decision by majority voting in the Council of Ministers, effectively restraining the move toward supranationality within the Six. Thus the integration movement, based on "pragmatic politics," was stalled by the opposition of one member state whose government viewed increased supranationality as detrimental to its own conception of proper European foreign policy and defense posture.

Haas develops the following matrix to encompass his amended views of regional integration:

Aims of Non-Governmental Elites

		Dramatic-Political	Incremental-Economic
Aims of Statesmen	Dramatic Political	Integration either direct and smooth; or impossible	Integration erratic and reversible
	Incremental-Economic	Integration erratic and reversible	Integration gradual but automatic

The trouble with Haas' amended approach is that it suggests many possibilities without <u>accounting</u> for any. What situations, events, pressures produce the dramatic-political integrative leadership of a Bismarck, a Cavour? When will similarly motivated elites appear? To say, as Haas does, that "The reliance on high politics demands either a statesman of this calibre or a widely shared normative elite consensus"[27] and that "in most actual situations in which regional integration is desired, neither ingredient is present in sufficient quantity"[28] may tell one something about the general distribution of an integration effort's basic ingredients. However, these static observations are of limited value in explaining either the initial "mix" of the variables or the dynamic process itself.

The appearance of a de Gaulle remains a mystery within the context of the Haas approach, and he still refers to France as the "deviant case"within the Six.[29] Whereas, in terms of the Hoffman approach, international system pressures on European integration suggest the inevitability of such "deviance," on the part of one actor or another. Thus, while Haas' amended theory is surely strengthened by his recognition that "integration and disintegration as two rival social processes are simultaneously at work,"[30] regional integration theory still seems too isolated from external pressures that may well help to account for the variety of outcomes which are observed.

The second issue which Hoffmann raises—more indirectly—concerns the Haas view of the "victory of economics over politics" in the New Europe — the "subordination of guns to butter." According to Haas, "<u>Grosspolitik</u> is merely a phrase left over from a pre-industrial setting, national grandeur and national destiny conceptions which the upward mobile citizen weighs distrustfully against the new 'telly,' Renault, or that trip to the blue Adriatic."[31] This view led Haas to predict the ultimate triumph of welfare politics over "high" politics. Critics have countered that the broader the spectrum of "welfare" functions conceded by the units to supranational regulation and control, the more those units would resist further transfers of effective authority.

Under what conditions might the Haas prediction of political unity resulting from such a victory of economics over politics take place? First, if man were the homo economicus which Haas seems to suggest in some of his writings, democratic governments might be compelled to concede increasing authority to supranational institutions whose member units together represented a market theoretically capable of optimizing all the advantages of size. [32] However, homo economicus is a model which even the economics profession employs with apologies for its obvious psychological inadequacies. Second, if few of the economic advantages of a European Common Market could be attained without political unity, governments might be pressured to concede the requisite authority even by constituencies somewhat differently motivated than the model economic man.

An analysis of the economic achievements of the EEC to date, however, reveals two characteristics which have helped to weaken the logic of spillover. The first is that the Common Market can operate so as to produce major economic gains without moving from customs union to political union. The second is that the benefits of economic integration in the Common Market have been rather equitably spread among the member units, thus avoiding to a considerable extent a series of "distribution crises" which might well have aided the spillover process.

Expanding the size of the market open to producers within the EEC has permitted the achieving of economies of scale resulting from mass production and product specialization; it has also induced greater competition. Further, increased rates of regional investment, both domestic and foreign, have been engendered by the move toward free trade within the Six. A recent Brookings study of the Common Market concludes that its economic achievements have been very substantial.

> The conditions requisite for a successful customs union are all present: the members are advanced countries at an almost equivalent level of industrialization; they have long been major trading partners and have common geographical borders; they are all heavily engaged in international trade and some of them had high tariffs originally, allowing much scope for rationalization. Furthermore, the EEC began during a period of economic prosperity, which made the required economic adjustments easier. In turn, because the EEC was successful, economic prosperity was prolonged and enhanced. Thus there has occurred an interaction between income growth and international trade in a "virtuous circle" often sought but seldom achieved. [33]

Intra-EEC trade "grew at a truly remarkable compound annual

rate of 17.0 per cent between 1958-59 and 1965."[34]   Investment
rates rose substantially in each country, as did GNP growth rates
and the inflow of foreign capital.

Of vital importance in understanding the limitations to the
logic of spillover in this setting is the recognition that these very
substantial benefits have been achieved without much movement
toward greater supranational jurisdiction.   Economists have long
recognized that customs unions among developed countries can
deliver a substantial economic payoff for a very limited price in
terms of the surrender of national sovereignty.   In a theoretical
work written in 1960 Bela Balassa concluded that "an intergovernmental approach appears to be sufficient to ensure satisfactory
operation of an economic union without a unification of the institutional structure..."[35]   Krause, in his new study of the EEC, con-
firms the Balassa view:

> Economic integration requires coordination of
> many economic policies and this involves essen-
> tially political decisions, but formal political in-
> stitutions may not be needed to bring this about.
> Governments do not need to be told, for instance,
> that excessive inflation in an open economy quickly
> leads to difficulties for themselves and their trad-
> ing partners.   They can see for themselves the
> rapidly deteriorating balance of payments, and
> pressures immediately arise for corrective ac-
> tions.   A "hidden hand" toward policy coordina-
> tion is directed by the market mechanism and
> it has proven to be very effective with the EEC. [36]

And Krause's analysis of the workings of the Common Market led
him to a conclusion unsettling to the logic of spillover: "What is
certain is that political integration will occur only as a result of
a positive political decision to bring it about, not as a result of
economic pressures alone."[37]

The final observation to be made with reference to the
workings of the EEC and the process of spillover is that the gains
from economic integration were spread among the Six in such a
way that no "distribution crises" arose, thus depriving the spillover process of opportunities in which to "redefine aims at a
higher level of consensus." While one might characterize the
bitter contest over a common agricultural policy as a problem of
distribution of benefits — French agricultural gains balanced
against German manufacturing gains — this particular issue had
its origin in the Messina negotiations. It did not arise as an unexpected crisis resulting from integration; rather, like the ghost of
Hamlet's father, it appeared in the first act and never ventured
far from the stage. The other major crisis faced among the Six,
involving various British bids for membership in the EEC, has
almost nothing to do with economic issues.

Economic theory suggests why the "hidden hand" of the

marketplace helped to minimize the problem of an equitable distribution of economic gains from free trade among the EEC countries. It is worth investigating because it also provides us with a frame of reference for understanding the contrasting experience with economic integration among less developed countries.

Economists have noted that economic integration is generally accompanied by two contrasting types of results; Myrdal has labeled one set "spread effects," and the other "backwash effects."[38] Spread effects are those which tend to minimize income disparities within a market area, and include such factors as increased demand in more developed centers for the products of the less developed periphery, and the transmission to the latter of technological knowledge, improved skills, and capital. Backwash effects include the movement of capital and skilled labor toward the more advanced centers, and the concentration in them of new industries, thus tending to exacerbate regional disparities in levels of economic development.

For the purpose of this essay, the relevant point of these theoretical observations is that spread effects, which are likely to reduce regional disparities on the average, predominate in a union of developed economies..[39] Highly developed price systems permit the exploitation of cost differences; existing industrial structures in each country allow each to benefit from the effects of increasing intra-industry specialization; infrastructure similarities discourage the concentration of foreign investments in any single member unit; and the existence of highly developed transport and communications facilities promotes interregional exchange. Factors such as these have often been cited as contributing, for example, to the decline of interregional disparities in income in the United States. They have undoubtedly helped to minimize potential crises in the EEC and, in doing so, to limit the opportunities for an active spillover process.

In contrast, backwash effects play a far greater role in unions of underdeveloped countries; the more marked the initial disparities in such a union, the more the backwash effects tend to predominate.

> With an imperfect price system, primitive trans-
> portation facilities, and an uneven distribution of
> social and economic overhead in these areas, ag-
> glomerative tendencies assume importance. These
> are related to the availability of overhead capital,
> skilled labor and linked industrial processes, when
> the latter not only provide ready markets and low-
> cost inputs but also contribute to future improve-
> ments through the exchange of technological infor-
> mation and induced technical change.[40]

In retrospect, it seems that three factors led to an overestimation of the expansiveness of functional integration with regard to the Europe of the Six. They were, first, a failure to relate

21

the theory of regional integration closely enough to the international system; second, an overemphasis on the homo economicus model in calculating human motivation; and third, a failure to recognize that sizable   (and equitably distributed) economic gains would result from a common market coordinated by sovereign states rather than managed by ceaselessly expanding supranational authorities.

REGIONAL INTEGRATION AMONG LESS DEVELOPED COUNTRIES

Backwash effects and their tendency to exacerbate disparities in levels of development in Latin American, African, and Asian regional economic integration experiments provide an insight into the major criticism   thus far leveled against the Haas-Schmitter model as it applies to these areas of the world. As Nye points out, integration involving less developed countries seems to produce not "gradual politicization," but "overpoliticization"; empirical evidence suggests that at the very least the result is instant politicization. A brief discussion of the two most comprehensive economic integration attempts among such countries at present — the East African and the Central American common markets — will substantiate this observation.

The East African common market originated with a customs union including Kenya and Uganda in 1917; Tanganyika became the third member in 1927. Despite its longevity, the common market was in a state of collapse by 1965. The severe frictions among the three newly independent African states arose over the issue of the distribution of the benefits from economic integration. Uganda and Tanganyika argued that all the gains were going to Kenya, and cited the following indicators: Kenya was supplying well over 60 per cent of the interregional exports; its trade surplus with the other members was substantial and growing; and it was increasing its position as the industrial center of the union. Kenya was producing 70 per cent of the manufactures of the common market, and exporting a growing percentage of them to the two relatively less developed member countries. By 1958, 404 of the 474 companies registered in East Africa were located in Kenya. By 1960 the country's manufacturing sector accounted for 10 per cent of Kenya's GNP, in contrast with 4 per cent figures in the other two member states. [41] Various attempts to ease the resulting frictions failed to halt the progressive deterioration in economic relations; in 1965 Tanzania began to restrict regional imports over the heated protests of Kenya. Growing trade restrictions,together with the decision to dissolve the region's monetary union and establish three national central banks "provoked a general fear that the common market and common service agreements might be completely destroyed." [42]

The crisis produced a final attempt to resolve the existing disputes arising over the issue of balanced economic growth in the regional union. In East Africa, as in Central America, the concept of balanced growth refers not so much to GNP growth rates as to an increasingly "equitable" distribution of industry throughout the union, and generally balanced increases in inter-regional trade. The results of the Philip Commission efforts to reach a compromise settlement were the signing in June 1967, and the implementation as of December 1, 1967, of the Treaty of East African Cooperation — "an ingenious effort to eliminate the causes of past frictions among the member countries."[43] Whether or not the scheme succeeds, its intricate and comprehensive na-ture is a living monument to the political sensitivity in less de-veloped countries to the problem of "equal distribution," and es-pecially to the insistence of each on the right to an "industrial sector," however, limited.[44] For such countries today the fac-tory is a symbol of independence and modernity which will not be relinquished for reasons of economic efficiency. Such reasoning in these instances is approximately as productive of a change of policy as lecturing de Gaulle on the disutility of the force de frappe.

The Central American Common Market is less than a decade old, but the explosive political issue of "balanced economic development" (desarrollo económico equilibrado) surfaced as soon as the freeing of internal trade and the formation of a uni-form external tariff began to affect trade flows and the location of new industry in the region. In Central America the two "less developed" member-countries are Honduras and Nicaragua; the latter qualifies only in the sense that its manufacturing sector is somewhat smaller than those in the three "advanced" member countries — Guatemala, El Salvador, and Costa Rica. The issues raised and the demands made by Honduras and Nicaragua are the same as those of Uganda and Tanzania: the backwash effects of their membership in the Central American Common Market are limiting and retarding, not benefiting, their economic develop-ment. And their evidence is the same: growing trade deficits with the more advanced member countries, loss of tariff revenues due to free trade, and the increasing concentration of industry in the more advanced industrial centers of Guatemala City, San Sal-vador, and San José (Costa Rica). Again the issues are charged with "high politics." For example, at the September 1966, meeting of the regional Economic Council both Nicaragua and El Salvador announced their decision to withdraw from the Market should their mutually exclusive demands be denied. The Nicara-guan Minister of Economy stated that his country would withdraw if it were not granted certain forms of preferential treatment within the Common Market. To which the Salvadorean Minister of Economy replied that, if Nicaragua were granted preferential treatment, El Salvador would withdraw from the integration scheme. A compromise is still being sought.[45]

Nicaragua and Honduras: Trade with Central America
(in millions of dollars)

Commercial Balance

	1960	1961	1962	1963	1964	1965	1966
Nicaragua	-$0.2	-$1.1	-$1.8	-$2.6	-$7.9	-$11.0	-$13.3
Honduras	3.4	2.7	3.8	-0.5	-1.3	-4.3	-6.5

Source: Roger D. Hansen, Central America: Regional Integration and Economic Development (Washington, D.C.: National Planning Association, 1967) pp. 55-57.

The Central Americans, like the East Africans, have attempted to cope with the issue of balanced development through a regional development bank which lends generously to the less-developed members, through licensing arrangements which encourage domestic and foreign investors to locate new plants in the less industrialized member states, and various other forms of preferential treatment. However, all such attempts are hard-pressed to overcome the agglomerative tendencies, detailed above, associated with the backwash effects of economic integration in less developed regions. This is true even in regions like Central America where the disparities in the economic structures are not very pronounced, and for at least three reasons. First, the more advanced member countries are too short on resources for their own development programs to do much by way of aiding fellow members. Second, the more developed countries often do not wish to do so; nor are the vested interests in those countries particularly receptive to any such channeling of resources or to agreements granting others preferential treatment. Third, the factors contributing to the lagging performance of a member country in these unions are often of such a nature that financial resources cannot restore anything resembling a balance except, perhaps, in the very long run. In the case of Honduras, for example, impediments to development are more political and administrative, more "human resource" oriented than are those of her neighbors; only years of slow and marginal improvements at these levels of development will permit Honduras to benefit from the advantages of economic integration on anything like a par with other member countries.[46]

The East African and Central American experiences confirm the observation that "instant politicization" characterizes economic integration in the less developed world. The findings sharply limit the relevance of the Haas-Schmitter model — one which would have us view economic and political union as a continuum, and gradual politicization as the mode of movement along that continuum. It can, of course, be claimed that despite the heated frictions and "high politics" of these two common markets, both continue to operate, and generally at increasingly comprehensive levels of economic integration. This is quite true, and it will be argued below that the odds in favor of their continued

24

functioning may be somewhat better than recent crises suggest. However, such a conclusion is derived from a line of reasoning which has virtually no relation to the Haas-Schmitter model, a model which can hardly incorporate in its present form the "high politics" of industrial development discussed above.

Two further criticisms of the Haas-Schmitter approach have been raised. One is that while the model directs our attention to many of the relevant variables, no attempt has been made to weight them in order of importance. Nye concludes from his studies that the relation among member-country elites is by far the most important variable, and suggests that this follows naturally from both the highly political atmosphere of new African states, and their domination by very narrow elites. [47] Events in Central America tend to support his conclusions.

The criticism is, of course, one that has been raised against several of the newer theoretical approaches to international relations. Many have objected to decision-making theory on the same grounds: endless lists of variables without a proper weighting for each may lead to endless research with limited results. With regard to the Haas-Schmitter model, however, the variables are kept to a manageable number, and further research might allow the development of refinements to deal with this limitation.

A second complaint is that the list of variables diverts attention from factors not incorporated within them — another familiar criticism. One author suggests the need to include the concept of an outside catalyst, while recognizing that if such a catalyst proves to be a relevant variable, "automatic politicization" a la Haas-Schmitter would have little meaning. [48] This suggestion is a step in the right direction, though it does not seem to go far enough. The idea of a deus ex machina as a necessary concept in the theory of regional integration can only attain its proper analytical significance if it is incorporated in such a way that relevant "external" variables cannot be ignored. As suggested in our earlier discussion of Europe, this might be done through a systems analysis approach which would bind regional integration theory much more tightly to the international system in recognition of reduced regional autonomy. However it is accomplished, the need is evident.

THE FUTURE OF REGIONAL INTEGRATION IN LESS DEVEL-OPED AREAS: THEORY AND PRACTICE

Thus far we have dealt with some of the theoretical limitations involved in the literature on regional integration, and, with regard to less developed areas, not upon its prognostications for the future of present and pending experiments. These concluding comments will alter our focus in an attempt to answer two questions. How does the current theoretical literature on regional integration assess the probabilities for success of integration

schemes in Latin America, Africa, and Asia? Do the present
concrete examples of such regional integration confirm these
theoretical conclusions, or suggest the need for alteration in
them?

Virtually all of the present literature is pessimistic with
regard to the future of integration schemes among less developed
countries. Etzioni, for example, tentatively suggests that limited
horizons, lack of administrative and political skills, and preoccupation with domestic modernization problems all represent
major barriers to successful integration schemes. [49] Hoffmann
regards fully integrated units ("political communities") and plu-
ralistic social structures within them as essential requisites for
successful regional integration, and observes that the lack of
such structures in many Latin American countries reduces the
possibilities of integration to "a chimera."[50] Deutsch's "capabilities" approach also produces pessimistic observations on regional integration among underdeveloped nations. In most of
them domestic "loads," derived from as well as necessitating
social, political, and economic change, are already outdistancing
capabilities. In such circumstances it is difficult to imagine that
"responsiveness" among member units to each other's needs will
expand at a pace adequate to balance the increasing burdens imposed by integration schemes. [51] Finally, Haas argues that

> because the modern "industrial-political" actor
> fears that his way of life cannot be safeguarded
> without structural adaptation, he turns to integra-
> tion; by the same token, political actors who are
> neither industrial, nor urban, nor modern in
> their outlook.... seek refuge in national exclu-
> siveness. Thus, countries dominated by a non-
> pluralistic social structure are poor candidates
> for participation in the integration process. Even
> if their governments do partake at the official
> level, the consequences of their participation are
> unlikely to be felt elsewhere in the social structure.[52]

The Haas-Schmitter studies of LAFTA seem to confirm
this pessimism. Applying their scheme of variables, they conclude that the area is "an unlikely candidate for international community formation..."[53] They account for the fact that LAFTA
has not entirely collapsed by the appearance of two "functional
equivalents" — the bargaining principle of "reciprocity," and the
role of Latin America's técnicos. The reciprocity principle entails the willingness of parties to recognize duties as well as
rights; specifically in the LAFTA case the willingness to see that
benefits from integration are equitably shared. The técnicos, the
region's economists-civil servants, are portrayed as playing a
role in LAFTA similar to that undertaken by integration-oriented
civil servants in Western Europe. [54] The Haas-Schmitter prediction, however, remains generally pessimistic with regard to
the prospects for Latin American integration.

Here a final observation on the Haas-Schmitter approach
is in order. In developing the "functional equivalent" of "reciprocity" they draw on the writings of the sociologist Alvin Gouldner.
He has suggested that the norm of reciprocity is a rule "which defines certain actions and obligations as repayments for benefits
received."[55] "The norm minimally demands that people should
help those who help them, and that people should not injure those
who have helped them."[56] Haas and Schmitter conclude that
"abstract sociology seems to describe the LAFTA system very
accurately,"[57] and much of their following analysis is devoted to
describing how the norm of reciprocity may prove to be an important variable in the course of efforts toward Latin American
integration.

It is difficult to avoid questioning the value of the authors'
"necessary... excursion into sociology."[58] Does Gouldner's
suggestion that "the norm of reciprocity may operate to maintain
a social system characterized by an absence of formal institutions
and a paucity of well developed status duties"[59] add anything to
present understanding — theoretical or pragmatic — of the behavior
of national actors in the international system? Is there anything
novel in the suggestion that in the present international system of
independent nation-states an equitable distribution of benefits from
cooperative endeavors will play an important role in the maintenance of those forms of cooperation?

In addition to presenting an old truth in new wrapping,
the sociological excursion raises a serious methodological problem. The original nine variables in the Haas-Schmitter scheme
reveal that LAFTA is a "possible-doubtful" candidate for "automatic politicization"; "reciprocity" then becomes their crucial
"functional equivalent" in measuring possible outcomes. Surely,
however, in situations where the dominant mode of inter-state
behavior is the kind of cooperative bargaining implied by reciprocity, results from the application of integration theory will
have a very limited payoff. For we are once again closer to the
traditional realm of " 'strategic-diplomatic behavior' with its own
rules of the game."[60] With regard to the inter-state arrangements like LAFTA it is probable that equilibrium analysis would
reveal more about the organization's mode of operation and its
significance for the study of international relations than would
integration theory in its present forms; at least Liska's demonstration of the uses of equilibrium analysis suggests that it would
ask more relevant questions and provide more relevant answers
in such a case.[61] This suggestion will, of course, be rejected
by the quantifiers who emphasize the difficulties of measurability
inherent in equilibrium analysis as applied to the study of international relations.[62] However, at the present stage in the discipline's search for theoretical underpinnings, apparent adaptability
to methods of quantification does not appear to be the most judicious test of promise.

Returning to the major issue of this section, are the pessimistic conclusions concerning the prospects for successful re-

gional integration in underdeveloped areas confirmed by today's concrete examples? In general, the answer seems to be in the affirmative. Etzioni's study of two such instances that failed, Nye's analysis of the failure to achieve political union in East Africa, and the lack of progress toward political union in Cental America all highlight the barriers to political integration among less developed nations. 63

Against this general background, however, the continued functioning of the East African and Central American economic integration schemes poses an interesting question: how have they managed to survive in the face of the difficulties suggested by both political and economic theory? At the level of economic theory we have noted the probability that a union of underdeveloped countries will suffer from backwash effects which promote an un-balanced distribution of gains unless the member countries are very evenly matched in levels of economic development. Given the "high politics" of new industrial location, disparities in infra-structure and pre-integration levels of industrialization will be particularly productive of "distribution crises." And in actual practice, we observed that such conflicts have in fact emerged in both regions. At the level of political analysis, we noted the tendency of distribution crises to "politicize" issues raised by economic integration very rapidly, without allowing the "gradual politicization" approach to operate. A final problem posed by theory for these two economic unions has been expressed by Etzioni: " Unions that try to maintain a medium-level integration, e.g., economic only, or economic with a minimum of political integration, are unstable, not because they are likely to disinte-grate but because their capacity to form consensus is out of bal-ance with the need for it: they are likely to become more inte-grated or regress to a lower level of integration. "64

The first point to be made is that either of the economic unions under consideration might collapse at any moment; both are operating in atmospheres of constant crisis. In 1965 the East African common market was on the verge of collapse; in 1966 two Central American member-states openly threatned withdrawal. In both cases, however, economic integration was preserved; in East Africa the crisis had produced by the end of 1967 a far more complex scheme of coordination than ever before undertaken in the region. Thus, while recognizing the fragility of both common markets, the reasons for their continued operation are worth con-sidering.

Several relevant factors emerge as we shift our atten-tion from an exclusively regional focus to the interaction between these two regional groupings and the international system within which they are functioning. An approach which analyzes the structure of the international system and the transnational forces of change within it indicates why these particular states have turned to economic integration rather than seeking "refuge in na-tional exclusiveness. " It has long been recognized that a high degree of external "compellingness" can promote integration, that external threats lead to a corresponding tightening of cooperative bonds. We have already noted that the degree of international stability inherent in the bipolar balance which emerged in the 1960's lessened the external pressures for European integration. France on the one side and China on the other could better afford the risks of reasserted national autonomy within the interstices of the super-power confrontation. In contrast, two elements in the present international system enhance the degree of compellingness for economic integration operating upon the countries of Central America and East Africa.

The first involves a particular characteristic of the present international economic system — generally referred to as "sluggish" world demand for many primary commodities — and its effect upon the prospects for economic growth in small countries whose economic performances are heavily dependent upon the export of such items. The Central American case is illustrative of the problem.

For many years prior to the formation of the Common Market, and as late as the 1950's, over half of the region's income was obtained from agriculture, and four crops — coffee, bananas, cotton, and cocoa — accounted for approximately 90 per cent of Central American export earnings. They also represented close to one quarter of the total income of the region. The exportation of a few commodities weighing so heavily in the total value of a country's production can be viewed in two ways. It is often portrayed as a significant advantage. World trade allows a country to maximize its national income, concentrating its resources in the production of those commodities wherein its comparative advantage lies and exchanging them for goods produced less expensively abroad than they could be domestically. This, in highly simplified form, is the essence of the static argument for free trade. In contrast, a pattern of production which concentrates so heavily on a very few export commodities can also be viewed as a problem of dependence upon the unpredictable vagaries of world demand and supply conditions, which severely restricts a country's capacity to influence its own economic performance. After World War II, as conscious policies directed toward economic development assumed increasing priority in the underdeveloped world, the latter view became predominant.

Two specific complaints have been developed with regard to such dependence. The first concentrates on the fact that primary commodity trade has historically proved particularly vulnerable to marked short-term price and earnings fluctuations. Where these products represent a substantial portion of national income, the effect of such fluctuations on economic performance can be significant. Furthermore, when countries are implementing development programs in which foreign exchange is a limiting factor, sudden shortfalls in export earnings can, by restricting imports, produce major bottlenecks and thus retard development.[65]

A second — and much more important — complaint focuses not on fluctuations in primary commodity export earnings, but on the long-term trends for such commodities. It argues that growth in demand for many primary commodities will be slow, and therefore unreliable as an impetus to economic development. Future trade prospects for Central America's traditional exports are discouraging, underlining the applicability to Central America of arguments that stress the perils of undiversified export dependence. In 1966 the three major export crops — coffee, bananas, and cotton — accounted for 80% of the area's export earnings. Prospective world demand and supply conditions for these crops suggest that Central America's export sector is likely to grow in the medium-term future at no more than a 3% rate per annum. Since the region's annual population growth rate — among the highest in the world — is close to 4%, traditional exports will make no contribution to raising Central American per capita income from its present, rather modest base of $300.

In general there are two explanations for the slow growth in world demand for agricultural products of the underdeveloped countries. The first involves the low income-elasticity of demand for foodstuffs; as one's income increases, a diminishing proportion of it is spent on food. The second explanation is that the industrialized countries are becoming more and more self-sufficient with regard to agricultural products. This development is due both to great productivity gains in developed-country agricultural production and to increased levels of agricultural protection. The slow growth in world demand for the raw-material exports of the underdeveloped countries can again be traced to two developments in the industrialized countries: productivity gains, and the increasing replacement of raw-material inputs by synthetics in industrial production.

The years between 1950 and 1962 illustrated the problem. The volume of underdeveloped country exports rose slowly — 57 per cent over the period, or about 4.5 per cent annually. In addition, the terms of trade for the underdeveloped countries deteriorated; that is to say, the prices they received for their exports fell sharply in relation to the prices they had to pay for their imports. For Latin America, the drop was 21 per cent and, for the most part, reflected adverse movements in coffee prices. [66]

The issue of sluggish demand for many traditional exports of the less developed countries has been analyzed in detail on many occasions, and the effort to separate fact from fiction need not be repeated here. What is relevant for our purposes is that elites in countries like those of Central America have been convinced by some overstated economic arguments that their continued dependence upon the export of a few primary products condemns them to economic instability and slow rates of growth. Furthermore, even a most judicious weighing of the evidence leads to the general conclusion that "the limited possibilities of expanding the exports of primary products would appear as a constraint to the acceleration of economic growth in the less developed coun-

tries. "[67]   This is particularly true for traditional Central
American exports, while it would not be true for other primary
products like fruits, certain vegetables, and beef. As these
countries seek to diversify their economies through industrialization, major impediments to efficient production imposed by the
size of their domestic markets on the one hand and the difficulties
of exporting manufactured goods on the other most often result in
inefficient structures of production, balance-of-payment difficulties, and economic stagnation. [68]

Problems posed by export dependence, and the limitations of their microscopic domestic markets were major "compelling" factors in the Central American decision to attempt economic integration. And in less than a decade the results are impressive: over 95 per cent of the items listed in the Central
American tariff schedule are entitled to free trade within the region; over 98 per cent of those items are covered by a common
external tariff; regional trade has grown by close to 400 per cent,
rising from 6 per cent of total Central American imports to close
to 20 per cent. It is interesting to note in the face of this impressive effort that more than twenty official attempts at political
unification of the region have failed dismally since the disintegration of the original Central American Federation over a century ago.

In East Africa a major attempt at political unification in
1963 failed as well; yet economic union persists despite regional
dissension. Here the explanation is similar, but with a variation:
economic union was a pre-independence achievement. When
faced with the realization that the common market was disintegrating (1965-66), elites in each member country recognized the
"compellingness" of the situation. For Kenya, it lay in the fact
that her protected access to Tanzania and Uganda provided the
Kenyan manufacturing sector with its major foreign markets;
without them Kenya's economy would face mounting structural
difficulties. For the other two members, "compellingness" involved not present markets for manufactures so much as potential markets. They, even more than Kenya, needed the protection
of the union's common external tariff to foster incipient manufacturing sectors. The bargain struck in June 1967 and made
operative in December may not be comprehended in its entirety
by this single "economic" issue; without it the course of events is
inexplicable.

The pressures which the international system exerts
upon economies like those under consideration should not be understood to imply an absolute economic necessity for integration;
they are more subtle. Economists studying underdeveloped countries speak of "demonstration effects";   political scientists talk
about the "crises" of legitimacy, participation, and distribution
arising in many of these countries in unison rather than sequen-
tially. [69] Both disciplines are noting aspects of the same phenomenon — the broad social and psychological impact of the economically and politically "developed" world on other regions. Modernizing elites in most less developed countries have identified

industrialization with development; to the extent that it is viewed as synonymous with modernity, industrialization has become a goal which transcends cost-benefit analysis.

This impact, too, is a transnational pressure which is especially "compelling" to the smallest, or least-developed countries. The greater the limits to the development of an industrial sector in one of these countries imposed by lack of domestic purchasing power, and the more vulnerable its present economy to the problems of export dependence, the more compelling are the pressures to resolve domestic problems through various modes of economic integration, and the less possible is a retreat into "national exclusiveness." This "model" must be qualified by the recognition that a certain learning period may be needed to convince such nations of the difficulties which exclusiveness implies. Contrasting Latin America with Africa, it is probable that the economic lesson is better understood where the "political kingdom" is of an older vintage. It may also be that Latin American nations are more prepared for differing forms of economic integration because the commitment of a substantial segment of their governing elites (and other politically relevant actors) to industrialization is a phenomenon with a half-century history.

If a final illustration of the interaction between international system and regional integration is needed, the issues raised at UNCTAD provide us with one. A major impediment to rapid economic growth within many less developed countries is that their domestic markets are too small to support efficient industrialization. If they were able to export their industrial products to the West, this bottleneck could be overcome. However, as many recent studies have shown, the levels of effective tariff protection in the United States and Western Europe are generally very high for just those industrial products which the less developed countries are now manufacturing in quantity. This, then, is another important sense in which the international economic system is compelling Latin America and other regions toward various patterns of integration. And if the West were to abolish the tariffs in question — for example those on textiles, sporting goods, etc. — or to grant significant trade preferences to the less developed countries, movements toward regional integration in Asia, Africa, and Latin America would probably experience a major setback. Faced with the lure of the West's markets, less developed countries would probably conclude that the costs of regional integration far outweighed its benefits. Thus, transnational forces — in this instance trade patterns and the process of industrialization — can be both integrating and disintegrating in nature. Viewed another way, the regional disintegrating aspects of freer world trade are also integrating at the global level.

The use of the word "model" two paragraphs above should be disclaimed immediately. This essay has presented a critique of current theories of regional integration; it has not attempted to construct a comprehensive alternative. In this sense it has been the easy approach to the problem. The difficult — and hopefully, in the long run, the most productive — work is being done by those who do produce the theoretical constructs, and begin to test them. The Haas-Schmitter model which has provided the focus for much of the preceding discussion represents a valuable contribution to the advancement of our understanding of the integration process, and a number of the criticisms raised may prove inconsequential as the model is refined in the process of empirical investigation.

An examination of present regional integration literature does, however, suggest that major attention be paid to two unresolved sets of questions.

First, what really is involved in "the logic of economic integration?" Theoretical and empirical issues raised in this essay suggest that the "hidden hand" of the marketplace in economic integration schemes among advanced economies with increasingly competent monetary and fiscal policy tools may operate to minimize distribution crises, limit "spillover" into politics, and promote the coordination of national policies rather than the emergence of supranational institutions. Conversely, the "logic of economic integration" among less developed countries, suggested by economic analysis and confirmed empirically, may generally prevent the appearance of gradual politicization.

Second, what is the theoretically appropriate manner in which to relate regional integration theory to the international system? The lower the degree of regional autonomy in an international system which is finally global in scope, the more necessary will it be for present theoretical approaches which concentrate on what we might call endogenous regional factors — or variables, in the Haas-Schmitter sense — to incorporate exogenous factors in a systematic manner. Events in the European, Latin American, and East African cases considered above reflect a dynamic interaction between an internal regional dialectic, analyzed by present theory, and macro-system pressures relatively unexplored in the current literature. Resolving the problem may prove theoretically and empirically formidable; ignoring it will minimize productive research.

In this context, are there not some advantages to examining in far greater detail the concept and ramifications of "compellingness"? Would it not lead to a better understanding of the dynamics of economic unions like the Central American and East African common markets than does an emphasis on political culture, present rate of transactions, elite complementarities, etc. ? Would it not suggest that such economic integration schemes may be increasingly "compelled" to function — perhaps for decades — with rather minimal implications for political integration? Might it not shed new light on the monumental difficulties facing LAFTA, where some large member countries with sizable internal markets are far less "compelled" than others ?[70] May not Argentina and Brazil be more able, but perhaps less willing, to engage in endless LAFTA negotiations whose payoff, given the minimal amount of trade involved, may be quite marginal? May they not choose in favor of bilateral — rather than continental — integration arrangements? The emerging subregional Andean bloc viewed in this context also suggests that states in Latin America may organize groupings which would be better analyzed in terms of "external" pressures than "internal"variables.

One interesting effort toward a closer interrelating of endogenous and exogenous variables has recently been undertaken by Karl Kaiser with regard to the United States and the EEC. He attempts to reconcile an empirical systems analysis approach with integration theory by considering regional integration "as a special case of system transformation. Hence, 'unification,' 'community building,' 'sector integration,' or 'functional integration' can be researched as part of manifestations of system change."[71]

The difficulties of such an approach are obvious. The more comprehensive one's scope becomes, the more apparent it is that all aspects of international and regional change are a part of a "seamless web of social reality" which defies exhaustive treatment. Thus, the advantages of regional integration theory which is partial and selective in scope; and thus, unfortunately, its present limitations.

NOTES

1. See, for example, Karl Deutsch et al., *Political Community and the North Atlantic Area* (Princeton University Press, 1957), and Ernst Haas, *The Uniting of Europe* (Stanford University Press, 1958).

2. For some of the recent trends in the literature on political integration, see Philip E. Jacob and James V. Toscano, eds., *The Integration of Political Communities* (Philadelphia: J.B. Lippincott Company, 1964), *passim*.

3. See, for example, the various writings by Deutsch, including his several essays in *The Integration of Political Communities*; by Amitai Etzioni, including *Political Unification: A Comparative Study of Leaders and Forces* (New York: Holt, Rinehart and Winston, 1964); and the essays collected in *International Political Communities: An Anthology* (New York: Anchor Books, 1966).

4. Haas and Schmitter, "Economics and Differential Patterns of Political Integration: Projections about Unity in Latin America " (in *International Political Com-*

munities: An Anthology, pp. 259-99.)

5. *Ibid*, p. 261.

6. *Ibid*, pp. 261-62.

7. *Ibid*, pp. 265-66.

8. *Ibid*, p. 266.

1525831

9. *Ibid*, p. 274.

10. *Ibid*, p. 273

11. *Ibid*, pp. 284-85.

12. Etzioni, *op. cit.*, p. 54.

13. For various applications of "historical sociology" to international relations see, among others, Raymond Aron, *Peace and War: A Theory of International Relations* (New York: Doubleday & Co., Inc., 1966), and Stanley Hoffmann, ed.,*Contemporary Theory in International Relations* (Englewood Cliffs, N.J.: Prentice-Hall, Inc., 1960).

14. J.S. Nye, Jr., "Patterns and Catalysts in Regional Integration," *International Organization*, Autumn 1965, pp. 870-84.

15. Stanley Hoffmann, "The Fate of the Nation-State," *Daedalus*, Summer 1966, p. 867.

16. *Ibid*, p. 882.

17. Haas, "Technocracy, Pluralism, and the New Europe," in Stephen Graubard, ed., *A New Europe?* (Boston: Houghton Mifflin Co., 1963).

18. Hoffmann,"Discord in Community: The North Atlantic Area as a Partial System," reprinted in Francis O. Wilcox and H. Field Haviland, Jr., eds., *The Atlantic Community: Progress and Prospects* (New York: Frederick A. Praeger, 1963), p. 11.

19. Hoffmann,"The Fate of the Nation-State," *loc. cit.*, p. 864.

20. *Ibid*, p. 864.

21. *Ibid*, p. 864.

22. *Ibid*, p. 865.

23. *Ibid*, p. 865.

24. Or, on the contrary, had the international system represented a greater degree of "compellingness," political unity might have been induced. The issue of compellingness will be discussed in a following section.

25. Haas, "The Uniting of Europe and the Uniting of Latin America," *Journal of Common Market Studies*, V, No. 4 (June 1967), 315-43.

26. *Ibid*, pp. 327-28.

27. *Ibid*, p. 328.

28. *Ibid*, p. 328.

29. *Ibid*, p. 319.

30. *Ibid*, p. 315.

31. Haas, "Technocracy, Pluralism, and the New Europe," *loc. cit.*, p. 71.

32. For a discussion of the economic literature on the effects of market size, see Bela Balassa, *The Theory of Economic Integration* (Homewood, Ill.: Richard Irwin, 1961) chaps. vi-viii.

33. Lawrence B. Krause, *European Economic Integration and The United States* (Washington, D.C.: Brookings Institution, 1967) p. 20.

34. *Ibid*, p. 21.

35. Balassa, *op. cit.*, p. 272.

36. Krause, *op. cit.*, p. 24.

37. *Ibid*, p. 24.

38. See Gunnar Myrdal, *Economic Theory and Under-Developed Regions* (London: Duckworth, 1957), chap. iii.

39. On this point see Balassa, *op. cit.*, p. 204.

40. Bela Balassa, *Economic Development and Integration* (Mexico City: Centro de Estudios Monetarios Latino-americanos, 1965), p. 123.

41. See Nye, "East African Economic Integration" in *International Political Communities: An Anthology*, pp. 405-36; Miguel Wionczek, "La Comunidad Económica de Africa Oriental," *Comercio Exterior*, October 1967, pp. 837-40.

42. Wionczek, *loc. cit.*, p. 839.

43. *Ibid*, p. 840.

44. See *Ibid* for one of the few accounts available as yet on the recent events in East Africa.

45. For a detailed account see Roger D. Hansen, *Central America: Regional Integration and Economic Development* (Washington: National Planning Association, 1967), chap. iv.

46. See *Ibid*, chaps. iv-v for a more detailed discussion.

47. Nye, "Patterns and Catalysts..." *loc. cit.*, p. 881.

48. *Ibid*, p. 882. Haas also considers the relevance of "external environment factors" in his essay "International Integration: The European and the Universal Process," reprinted in *International Political Communities*, pp. 93-129. But his writings make no attempt to systematize their relationship to regional integration.

49. Etzioni, *op. cit.*, pp. 318-21.

50. Hoffmann,"Fate of the Nation-State," *loc. cit.*, pp. 904-5.

51. See in particular the Deutsch essays in *The Integration of Political Communities* for an extended treatment of these concepts.

52. Haas, "International Integration: European and Universal Process," *loc. cit.*, p. 106.

53. Haas and Schmitter, *The Politics of Economics in Latin American Regionalism: The Latin American Free Trade Association after Four Years of Operation*, Monograph Series in World Affairs, III, No. 2 (University of Denver, 1965-66), p. 7.

54. *Ibid*, chap. v.

55. Quoted in *Ibid*, p. 53.

56. *Ibid*, p. 53.

57. *Ibid*, p. 53.

58. *Ibid*, p. 53.

59. *Ibid*, p. 53.

60. Hoffmann,"Discord in Community," *loc. cit.*,p.9.

61. See George Liska, *International Equilibrium* (Cambridge: Harvard University Press, 1957).

62. For such criticism see Hoffmann, *op. cit.*, p. 51.

63. See Etzioni, *op. cit.*; Nye, *op. cit.*; Hansen, *op. cit.*

64. Etzioni, "The Dialectics of Supranational Unification," reprinted in *International Political Communities*, p. 143.

65. A recent study by Alastair MacBean, *Export Instability and Economic Development* (Cambridge: Harvard University Press, 1966) concludes that, with regard to the underdeveloped world as a whole, the problem of instability of export earnings has been overstated. The study does not deal with the second problem, that of longer-term trend prospects for primary commodity earnings.

66. All measurements of terms-of-trade trends are heavily influenced by the base period chosen; different time periods would yield significantly different results. The years discussed above are chosen not because they are particularly representative of longer-term trends, but rather because they do illustrate the problems which concerned Central American officials.

67. Balassa, *Economic Development and Integration*, p. 67. For a general discussion of the degree of primary commodity export dependence in Central America, see Hansen, *op. cit.*, chaps. i-ii.

68. See Harry Johnson, *Economic Policies Toward Less Developed Countries* (Washington, D.C.: Brookings Institution, 1967), for a discussion of tariff structures in Europe and the United States and their effect upon the export possibilities for manufactured products from the ldc's.

69. See various essays in *Political Parties and Political Development*, Joseph LaPalombara and Myron Weiner, eds. (Princeton University Press, 1966).

70. Other elements are of course important in determining attitudes in the larger member-countries. Mexico has often been LAFTA's strongest proponent, principally because Mexican products are thought to be highly competitive in a LAFTA-wide market.

71. Karl Kaiser, "The U.S. and EEC in the Atlantic System: The Problem of Theory," *Journal of Common Market Studies*, V, No.4 (June 1967), 410.

CHAPTER **3** LATIN AMERICAN ECONOMIC
INTEGRATION: SOME HISTORIC
GUIDEPOSTS

By James H. Street
Department of Economics
Rutgers University

In the recent discussion of economic integration, whether
related to Europe or to Latin America, the tendency has been to
emphasize political and legal aspects rather than the underlying
causal forces, which are essentially technological. The focus on
the creation of new institutional arrangements is readily understandable, since excessive reliance on nationalism and its attendant instruments of economic exclusivity — trade restrictions,
monetary controls, and the like — have been major impediments
to regional free trade and economic harmonization. Modifications in existing institutions will clearly be necessary if economic
integration is to come about, and the forces of inertia as well as
of active opposition that stand in the way are well known.

Yet the role of institutions is essentially secondary.
Institutional change alone is unlikely to ensure the success of
integration, since institutions are rarely more than permissive.
They cannot compensate for missing functional elements. Writers
who emphasize institutional barriers and the means of their
removal imply that there is an inherent dynamism in Latin America simply waiting to spring forth once the fetters of outmoded
systems are released. Obviously forces of change are at work
in Latin America, but many are the result of externally induced
pressures, such as the effect of recently introduced health measures on the death rate. Whether the basic internal forces will
lead strongly toward growth and integration, as appears to be
happening in Europe, or in some other direction, is far from
clear. Recent trends suggest that the dominant pressures are
toward further structural maladjustments rather than toward
integration.

Underlying the process of economic co-ordination there
must be a set of technological circumstances and functional opportunities that lead toward integration, or that are at least compatible with it, if the process is to gain momentum. It is advis-
able to assess as realistically as possible what these circumstances and opportunities are, since they dictate the feasibility
of development policies directed toward integration.

Historical example, though they may be over familiar
and at the same time subject to wide variation of interpretation,
offer useful guides to the integration process because they enable
us to distinguish broad underlying forces. The outstanding histor-

ical case of successful integration of a large regional unit is, of course, that of the United States. Significantly similar to it, even though the major components of the system were not geographically contiguous, was the formation of the economic network represented by Great Britain during her maximum imperial expansion. At the risk of reiterating elementary concepts, this study will examine aspects of these successful systems that seem to have been given inadequate attention in much of the recent discussion of integration for Latin America.

It must be conceded at the outset that both systems have enjoyed singularly permissive institutional environments in which to carry out the integration process. The United States began with a constitutionally established customs union embracing internal free trade and a common outer tariff, and although it took a major civil conflict to subordinate the strong neocolonial orientation of the Cotton South, the direction of growth policy during the nineteenth century was steadily toward internal integration. Despite temporary constrictions during periods of business concentration and depression, this process has continued in a generally favorable institutional climate.

In the British case, the chief institutional factors contributing to integration were the triumph of the policy of Free Trade, the solidification of colonial control, and the development of the sterling system of international money and credit. Even in the waning days of empire and after the shocks of disruptive wars that forced the liquidation of overseas investments, the British system retains much of the vitality of the organizational rationale under which it once flourished.

Nevertheless, in both the cases that have been cited, the organizing principles that were laid down do not explain the extraordinary growth and co-ordination that were attained. They were facilitating factors; they were not the causative agents of achievement. These causative agents were principally the abundant availability of complementary resources, technological initiative and versatility in the use of these resources, the development of appropriate transportation networks, and the inclusion in the financial framework of devices to promote the transfer of real capital (technology) to the less developed but promising parts of the region.

I

It is needless to comment on the abundance and diversity of natural resources that provided the material basis for the American system. The British Isles were also exceptionally endowed with the essential resources for an industrial revolution, and when swelled by the riches of empire had access to a prodigious flow of raw materials in great variety. In contrast, the position of Latin America with respect to resources is elusively difficult to assess. One does not have to be as pessimistic as

Simon G. Hansen, when he says, "In natural resources Latin America is among the least favored of the major regions of the world,"[1] to recognize that Latin America is deficient in the amount and location of good coking coal and other mineral requisites for a solidly based industrial system. Likewise, because the region lies so preponderantly in the tropic zone, the possibilities for complementarity in agricultural products are rather limited. All of this has been said before, and it is basic.

On the other hand, it can be argued that just because Latin America possesses limited complementarity in its natural resources, it is all the more important to organize them for more effective use within the region. We are also reminded by the relative recency of discoveries such as the rich iron deposits of Venezuela that Latin America is still in many respects an unknown frontier whose resources are almost certain to expand with development.

What is required in Latin America is a shift in the orientation of complementarity. Like Latin America in more recent times, the United States was originally oriented toward overseas metropolitan markets. During this period, external complementarity assisted internal growth as agricultural products, chiefly cotton and wheat, earned the foreign exchange that was used to finance the early stages of railroad construction and industrial development. Eventually, however, the United States directed its attention inward and increasingly substituted internal for external complementarity.

The same process was begun, on a lesser scale, in Argentina in the latter part of the last century and later in Brazil, but it never took hold as a concerted effort for internal development. (Possibly the Vargas period in Brazil should be excepted from this statement.) Much of the industrial investment at this stage remained under foreign direction, and the dominant social classes in Latin America apparently did not recognize the need to assume control of the development process, nor had they the capacity to direct it toward a fuller exploitation of domestic resources. In a number of instances important accumulations of foreign exchange reserves and other financial resources were misapplied by irresponsible governments and allowed to become dissipated. Belatedly, and on a regional scale, the integration movement now seeks to undo these mistakes. The reorientation will probably not be easier for the delay, but its urgency has come to be better appreciated. Latin America must discover its own frontier, in more than the romantic sense.

II

An effective integration movement in Latin America requires a vastly more adequate internal transportation and communications network. Again, the historic examples are instructive. The internal development of the United States was

41

promoted by the creation, and from time to time the obsoles-
cence, of successively more effective means of overland transport. The early turnpikes, canals, and river systems, including
the powerfully influential Mississippi and its tributaries, were
supplemented and eventually overtaken by the railroad. It is a
commonplace of economic history that the transcontinental trunk
railroads, largely completed and reconstructed after the Civil
War and enlarged by extensive feeder systems, tied the continent
together economically and made the United States a nationally
integrated unit. The construction of roads, highways, and
airways has elaborated the system but has not changed its essential character.

The British system was, of course, based on cheap and
efficient water transport, and, while it had the effect of integrating
the Commonwealth, it also tied the periphery countries more
securely to the neocolonial system by assigning them a role in
the "network of world trade."[2]   Argentina was one of the countries that benefited most by this relationship, since without
falling under direct political control she obtained the use of the
refrigerated ship and thus access to the desirable European market for chilled beef. The Argentine railway system, the only
system approaching a national network in Latin America, was
but an extension of the sealanes radiating from Europe. It is
unfortunate that through a gross investment miscalculation by
the Perón government, the country lost the opportunity to trans-
form its railroads into a domestically dynamic network and perhaps an expanded multinational system that would have had great
functional significance for integration.

In other parts of the region the absence of basic transportation links is even more crucial. When Frank Tannenbaum,
an acute observer, remarks that "There is no St. Louis, Chicago,
Minneapolis, Denver, or Salt Lake City in the center of South
America,"[3] he is not only calling attention to the heavy cluster-
ing of population along the seaboards, but to the paucity of interior
development centers and the nonexistence of regional transportation hubs which such cities in the United States represent. While
the causes for population concentrations with a coastal orientation are long-standing and complex, the limitations of internal
communication have bound the scattered indigenous communities
and the more recent settlement areas, such as there are, in
enforced isolation. Thus, they presently lack promise as expanding market areas.

Unquestionably the terrain has posed major obstacles
to transcontinental surface routes — the wall of the Andes and
the great wasteland of the Amazon basin are formidable barriers.
Yet it is an illusion to suppose, as some do, that Latin America
will be economically integrated by air transport. Integration
requires the movement of freight, much of it of low value, and
ultimately of masses of people, and this necessitates extensive
surface routes: trunk roads, feeder roads, penetration roads,
and local urban networks. In tonnage hauled, the railroad loco-

motive is still the world's prime mover, pulling two-thirds of
all freight and rivaling ocean shipping in ton-mileage in carrying
the world's cargoes.[4]

Has Latin America skipped the railroad era? Probably,
by default. While the World Bank has recently financed the completion of important rail links in Colombia and Mexico, the private financing of new tracklaying seems to have evaporated before the increasing costs of right-of-way, the unprofitability of
operating under public regulation, and the probability of ultimate
nationalization. The same considerations apply to the construction of privately financed toll highways and turnpikes, sometimes
recommended as an alternative.

While the costs of distance haulage are substantially
lower by rail than by road for the country that already has its
rail system, the motor truck and the autobus have the advantages
for newly developing countries that they can be introduced piecemeal, relatively inexpensively, and with greater flexibility for
both long and short hauls. However, for the purposes of integration, they require a network of highways. Experience during the
period of the Alliance for Progress has shown that governments
will have to devise more effective means of underwriting the
counterpart costs of major highway construction. It is not generally feasible for foreign government lenders and international
banks to meet such local currency costs as the acquisition of
right-of-way and the hiring of domestic labor, and some countries have failed to take advantage of outside assistance because
of their inability to meet local costs. Until a higher priority is
assigned to basic transport, regional integration will remain
correspondingly difficult.

III

A third distinguishing feature of the North American and
British integration systems was the technological initiative and
versatility in the use of resources, which, in contrast, has been
conspicuously lacking in Latin America until very recent times.
The technological lag, in this instance, is of historic dimensions,
and will not be easily overcome. It is characterized not simply
by the retarded stage of industrialization that has been achieved
in Latin America, but by a deep-seated cultural apathy toward
invention and discovery, or what has now become organized
research and development, that has only recently been recognized
as having severe consequences for the attempt to accelerate
growth in the region.

Great Britain has "grown up with" technological innovation for at least two centuries and the United States for more than
a century and a half, so that it has seemed normal to treat natural
resources as social resources, subject to manipulation and control.
This process has proceeded at many social levels and has involved
the entire population to some degree. Hence agriculture, ordinar-

43

ily a backward sector, early participated in the advance, and much of the ordinary working population became accustomed to seeking the technical short-cut that did not diminish production but actually increased it. This is more than a set of skills; it is an acquired outlook on life that has often been deprecated as unduly material-istic, but that has led to continual adaptive adjustments to circum-stances. It has impelled people to look for opportunities within an internally expanding economy and has constantly resulted in more intensified use of resources. Thus, it has contributed to integration.

How can such attitudes be implanted in a society that in large part tends to reject technological in favor of institutional solutions?[5] The principal ways are through direct experience with tools, machines, and effective managerial practice, and through education which emphasizes such experience. Education in Latin America must not only be expanded, but must become more pragmatic. Unfortunately at the higher level much that is currently being borrowed from the advanced economies is over-refined and unrelated to the present developmental needs of the region. Thus, there is the danger of perpetuating an educated elite that is culturally estranged from its environment. Popular education is not simply a social adornment; it is an essential requisite to economic growth and to effective political organiza-tion.

Latin Americans would do well to study examples of successful educational innovation wherever they have occurred, both as to method and philosophy. The land grant college move-ment in the United States, Horace Mann's program for popular education, and John Dewey's revolution in educational concepts, as well as the workers' education program sponsored by the Fabians in England, all have relevance for present-day Latin America. Similar movements within the region, such as those of Sarmiento in Argentina, and of Rébsamen and Vasconcelos in Mexico, should inspire efforts to build into the popular education movement a philosophy that will stimulate increased technological awareness and resourcefulness. At the vocational level, the SENAI system of industrial training established a quarter century ago in São Paulo by industrialists who sought to fill their own manpower needs has much to commend it.[6]

IV

A fourth element that contributed greatly to the British and U.S. integration systems was the development of devices to promote the transfer of real capital, that is to say, the fruits of modern technology, to the less developed but nevertheless promis-ing parts of the region. These devices were in large degree financial and supported by a legal framework, hence institutional, but it is their functional significance in transferring technology that is directly relevant to integration.[7]

During the growth period of the British and North American systems such transfers were largely carried out in private hands by individuals and enterprises that assiduously sought exploitable opportunities. Today, because of the changed climate affecting private investment, new development ventures, which are inherently risky, must be carried out by governments under foreign aid programs and by international lending agencies such as the World Bank and the Inter-American Development Bank that operate in large part with revolving funds. These institutional changes have generated a new set of problems that threatens to impede the flow of further technological transfers.

In the heyday of British overseas investment, new ventures were often undertaken with great audacity, but proved successful because they were based on industrial and commercial skill that was made effective through close managerial supervision on the site of the investment. (In contrast, many foreign investments by Americans that first became significant in the 1920's resulted in failure because they were not so supervised.) Yet the private financial system embodied safety valves that prevented the accumulation of excessive debt burdens when risky ventures failed or fiscal crises affected the recipient countries. For one thing, long-term capital loans to finance development projects were clearly distinguished and separately held from short-term commercial credits granted to promote the sale of consumer goods exports. Thus, a tendency for overseas customers to over-import was corrected by adjustments in commercial credit that did not necessarily affect the flow of long-term capital. In recent times, because of the large role played by government assistance in foreign investment and because responsibility for the balance-of-payments problem has been increasingly assumed by recipient governments, there has been a tendency to blur the functional distinction between long-term and short-term credits. Long-term funds intended for development have sometimes been diverted to the maintenance of excessively high and ultimately unsustainable levels of imports, and governments have been forced to renegotiate short-term credits that become ever more burdensome.

Another safety feature in the system of private credits was the provision for the liquidation of unsuccessful loans, both long- and short-term, through default or bankruptcy of private borrowers, without thereby endangering the entire credit of a government and its economy. Today we see the massive accumulation of external public debt that hangs over the developing countries as the result of a few short years of well-intentioned assistance by outside lending agencies. Among these, the international banks cannot accept large defaults without injuring their own credit standing and future effectiveness.

The seriousness of this situation, in financial terms, for Latin America was described by the Inter-American Development Bank in its annual survey:

During the years of the Alliance for Progress, the accumulation of external public debt by the region has expanded rapidly. From an outstanding balance of U.S. $ 6.58 billion at the close of 1960, it increased to U.S. $ 11.9 billion in 1965 and U.S. $ 12.6 billion in 1966.

...it is estimated that service on the external public debt is currently absorbing about 75 per cent of the gross capital inflow included under the heading, and tends to expand. This means that Latin America could be approaching a virtual bottleneck in its foreign financing in which the net transfer of external real resources to aid the economic development of the region would become impossible. In such a case, either the gross inflow would have to increase on a large scale, or the terms of indebtedness should be substantially improved with respect to terms and interest rate. [8]

It is clear that institutional means will have to be devised to prevent this impasse in the flow of technology from materializing. Since it is unlikely that private capital transfers of the traditional type will prove sufficient, public lending agencies will, with the consent of the recipient countries, have to establish closer technical and administrative supervision and "follow through" on the riskier investments to insure against excessive waste and consequent defaults.

It must also be recognized by the lenders that despite all precautions, investment failures are bound to occur. There must therefore be provision for the systematic liquidation of bad debts without interrupting the entire credit flow. In the end, it will have to be recognized that what is involved is a world redistribution of income and of transferable real resources. A system of outright grants scaled to the capabilities of the advanced countries would be the obvious solution, but aside from the unequal willingness of nations to share their wealth in this manner, problems would remain of preventing investment-stimulated inflation in the recipient countries and excessive balance-of-payments drains on the lending countries. In this connection, John H. G. Pierson has recently made an imaginative proposal for solving the drain problem in conjunction with the expansion of international liquidity which has become a prime concern of the principal trading nations. Pierson proposes that the balance-of-payments difficulty in providing sufficient aid to the developing countries "should be met head-on by building into the new international monetary system a permanent arrangement for neutralizing development aid as, inherently, an adverse balance-of-payments factor. Such an arrangement would in effect place at the disposal of any country additional reserves or special drafting rights (S.D.R's) commensurate with its deficit on foreign-aid account."[9]

The suggestion, as Pierson acknowledges, entails a number of complex institutional changes that will not readily find acceptance. However, it goes to the heart of the problem, if foreign investment is to continue to be the principal means of effecting international transfers of technology. Pierson's proposal recognizes that the means of payment, which are after all paper instruments, are secondary to the real flow of development goods, and should be adjusted accordingly.

V

History does not repeat itself, invariably and in all respects. If it did, and the advanced countries with their functioning integration systems served as precursors, we could depend on the forces of inevitability and have little to worry about. Yet there is little reason to think that economic integration will emerge strongly and automatically from the "inherent dynamism" of present-day Latin America.

However, history reveals some essential ingredients in the integration process which, if not present, may be developed or substituted for. These ingredients include, as a minimum, internal complementarity of resources, an appropriate regional transportation network, a naturalized cultural receptivity to technological innovation, and a sustained means of transferring technology to the less developed zones. Leaders of the integration movement should address themselves consciously and persistently to the liberation of these underlying forces while they initiate adjustments in the institutional superstructure which can facilitate, but only facilitate, the regional growth process.

1. *Economic Development in Latin America* (Washington: Inter-American Affairs Press, 1951), p. 36.

2. The organizational symmetry of this system, as well as its breakdown was effectively described in the classic study, *The Network of World Trade* (Geneva: League of Nations, 1942).

3. *Ten Keys to Latin America* (New York: Alfred A. Knopf, 1964), p. 12.

4. For a comparison of the cost structure of different transport media and their effect on the dispersion of economic activity, see Richard S. Thoman, Edgar C. Conkling, and Maurice H. Yeates, *The Geography of Economic Activity,*2nd ed. (Boston: McGraw-Hill, 1968), Chap. 7.

5. Technological interest has not always and everywhere been lacking in Latin America. The pre-Columbian civilizations were highly innovative until truncated by the Conquest and reduced to subsistence cultures. And there are centers of industrial development such as Medellín, Córdoba, and Monterrey, as well as the larger complexes centering in São Paulo, Buenos Aires, Santiago, and Mexico City, but they have tended to remain cultural islands in their own countries.

6. The acronym stands for Serviço Nacional de Aprendizagem Industrial (National Industrial Apprenticeship Service).

7. The current interest of the Inter-American Development Bank in international transfers of technology is indicated in the titles of two papers presented at the ninth annual meeting of the bank in Bogotá, Colombia, on April 22-26, 1968: P. N. Rosenstein-Rodan, "Problems of Multinational Investments within the Context of Latin American Economic Integration. Philosophy of Regional and Foreign Investment and its Relationship to the Absorption of Modern Technology "; and Pierri Uri, "Access to Technology: the European Experience. Foreign Private Investment and Technological Progress."

8. *Socio-Economic Progress in Latin America.* Social Progress Trust Fund Seventh Annual Report, 1967. (Washington: Inter-American Development Bank, 1968), p. 25.

9. Letter to *The New York Times,* April 21, 1968.

<table>
| CHAPTER | **4** | LATIN AMERICAN HISTORY AND INTEGRATION |
</table>

By   Frédéric Mauro
University of Paris-Nanterre

INTRODUCTION

In asking ourselves how history permits us to understand the problems of Latin American integration better, we do not pretend to ask lessons from history. The modern school of history knows very well that it cannot give them, that there is no "moral" of history, that nothing ever repeats itself or, if invariables and repetitions occur, it is very difficult to discern them. On the other hand, we believe in useful history, and since here we are dealing with economics, we believe in useful economic history. For economic history is the economics of the past. It is retrospective, whereas economics is prospective — this is their only difference. To a large extent, they speak the same language, and they nourish each other. One is impossible without the other. These points of view are now admitted by economic historians.

Here we must show how they can be put to work in the case of a specific economic problem: that of Latin American integration.

As Bela Balassa[1] recently reminded us, the term "integration" implies various meanings. Mainly, two categories: those which define a zonal integration (regional integration) among several countries and those which define a national integration. Let us consider them successively.

REGIONAL (OR CONTINENTAL) INTEGRATION

Economic history is both the study of business cycles and the study of economic structures, even though the distinction between the two is in large measure artificial. But both contribute a great deal to the comprehension of problems which relate to the integration of the Latin American continent.

The Role of Business Cycle Analysis

Henri Hauser thought that it was particularly the short-run business cycle which interested the historian, because it permitted him to explain events. On the other hand, historians after the war wanted to show that economics concerned itself with the short run, and economic history with the long term.[2] In fact, both are useful to our research.

Short-Run Business Cycle. It is interesting to know the
latest developments of business cycles in order to formulate,
specify or adapt the policy of integration. This task can be accomplished by the historian. He, more easily than others, can present the latest fluctuations in the prolongation of the oldest. A
comparison will be possible in time — over a very long period —
in the interior or exterior of the Latin American continent. The
shifts between business cycles are interesting to observe and to
use in applying policies of harmonization in the interior of the
zone. So, also, are the variations of intensity of short-run fluctuations. Let us take the example of wholesale prices between
1950 and 1960. We shall compare Costa Rica and Chile.

Index Base 100, 1950

	1950	1955	1960
Costa Rica	100	94	96
Chile	100	555	2237

We see that it is hardly possible for two countries to
live together whose short-term fluctuations are so different. We
see also that the other countries of Central America are comparable to Costa Rica. On the other hand, Brazil (index 602 in 1960)
and Paraguay (index 1776) are closer to Chile. These figures
surely justify the efforts to create a Central American Common
Market (CACM) and show that a union of the three South American
countries mentioned is possible.

However, the short-run business cycle is interesting for
another reason. It is characteristic of a certain structure. It
is by knowing the short-term business cycle that we can classify
the corresponding structure. We shall see that a knowledge of
structures is indispensable in solving the problems of integration.
In the preceding example regarding Costa Rica and Chile, it is
certain that a more continuous and thorough study of short-run
business cycles would show that they are very different, because
the mechanisms of economic life in the two countries obey different necessities and conditions with, in particular, a primary
sector and a tertiary sector in which the structure and composition resemble one another very little. In the same way, a historical study showed that short-term fluctuations in Mexico were for
the most part "presidential cycles"[3] tied to bargaining negotiated
by the state — something which is more difficult to conceive in
Paraguay or even in Argentina.

Long-Term Cyclical Fluctuation. This is the pre-eminent
domain of the historian, the trend, whether it has to do with the
multisecular trend, the secular movement, the long-term
Kondratieff cycle or even the Hoffmann-Kuznets cycles astride the
long term and the short period. It is obvious that by the graphs
of moving averages, of least squares method or other adjustments,
the system of long-term fluctuations — the history of business

cycles — of each Latin American country must be constructed in such a way as to permit two types of comparison:

a. <u>Some Comparisons Among Latin American Countries</u>
More significant even than the comparison between short-run and long-term fluctuations is the extent to which countries can unite in terms of their economic structure. We are struck, for example, by the difference which exists in history between the economics of great cycles of a country such as Brazil, which experienced succes - sively the cycles of wood, sugar, gold, livestock, coffee, industrialization, without mentioning those of cocoa, rubber, precious stones — and that of Mexico, deeply penetrated from the beginning by extractive activity and where the slowing down of this activity brought about, first of all, economic suffocation (a closed economy) and secondly, agrarian reform and industrialization.

Long-period study being that of the dynamics of structures, and each long-term fluctuation bringing a modification to these, the study of the long-term business cycle joins that of the growth and development stages which we must examine later.

b. <u>Some Comparisons Between Latin America and the Rest of the World</u>
We note in passing that these comparisons, which are already interesting and revealing for the short-run business cycle, are even more so for the long term. On the one hand they permit us to specify better the nature of Latin American economies as opposed to more developed European or North American economies (and the case of Canada is every bit as interesting as that of the United States), or even less developed economies such as Africa and Asia (with the exception of Japan). On the other hand, they permit us to see which countries it will be most suitable to associate with the Latin American Common Market or which will be the most useful to its development. Let us take an example. Between 1873 and 1896, products, capital, and European emigrants poured into Latin America, because Europe was experiencing a "b" phase of the Kondratieff fluctuation: the rate of interest had fallen, and unemployment was the natural consequence of the serious problem of marketing. The slump was less severe in Latin America. The inflow of these factors of production and consumption reactivated the pump in several of the continent's countries perhaps faster than in Europe. Consequently, the knowledge of the differences between the long-term variations of interest rates allows us to predict where it is easiest to find capital. The same reasoning is valid for labor and markets.

In any case, these remarks lead us to conclude that the

study of economic movements of each of the Latin American countries and of the world, in their dynamic evolution, is necessary in order to shed light on the problems of Latin American continental integration.

Role of Structural Analysis

First of all, let us recall certain definitions. Economic phenomena can be broken down in simple mechanisms, which one finds in every age and place. These elementary mechanisms combine with each other in quantity and according to variable proportions to form complex mechanisms which present a certain permanence which we call structures. An aggregate of structures within a geographical, socio-cultural framework forms a system. In a certain economic context this system results in an economic "regime." Regimes, systems, and structures evolve imperceptibly under the effect of short-period fluctuations and, in a very appreciable manner, lead to new structures, new systems, and new regimes under the effect of long-period fluctuations.

It is possible to study Latin American structures in two ways: statically and dynamically.

In a static study, the geographical, anthropological, and social framework appropriate to each national system can be traced: for this a proper model is then constructed, that is, an aggregate of interdependent quantitative relationships. The models can be compared to show how the differences between them stem from the differences existing in their frameworks. One arrives inevitably at a classification where these frameworks will play a determing role. The geographical framework, for example, will compel us to distinguish between the economies of Andean countries and Atlantic countries, those of temperate or subtropical countries, and those of tropical or equatorial countries. The anthropological framework will require us to distinguish the economy of Indian countries from those of "white" or "black" countries.

Nevertheless, all these classifications, as useful as they are for the fusion or federation of the various national economies or for the regrouping in medium-sized units of certain among them (the Central-American Common Market for instance), will be incomplete and unreliable as long as they fail to consider the future behavior of these economies and their orientation. These aspects are apparent only by means of a dynamic study.

In a dynamic study, we can trace dynamic models in the interior of national geographical, anthropological, and social frameworks, taking into account both national economic developments and relationships between them or with the exterior world. Thus, to borrow an expression used by Víctor Urquidi, each economy will be examined and understood in its "trajectory." Knowing where it comes from, we can then determine which stage

of growth it is in and which stages it must yet cross. We can
then classify the countries according to the stage or substage at
which each one has arrived. For this, we can use either the
general dynamic model of Walt W. Rostow or any other more developed model, better adapted to Latin American reality. It is
obvious that it will be easier to unite countries which have
arrived at about the same stages of development than countries
which are still chasms apart from this point of view —unless the
more developed country feels it is already capable of assuming
the burden of the development of the less developed country, which
is rarely the case in Latin America.

Obviously, knowledge of structures even in their dynamics
will not help us in our action in the same way as will knowledge
of business cycles. The latter will allow us to know the oppor-
tune moment when steps toward union, fusion, co-operation are
to be taken. The harmonization and co-ordination of economic
politics must carefully take into account fluctuations in which they
are submerged and on which they must act. The dynamic knowledge of structures will permit us to decide which measures of
interpretation it is necessary to take and between which countries.
It is through this interpretation that one can arrive, for example,
at a precise definition of what are called "countries of relatively
less economic development." It is through this interpretation
that one can make an inventory of the possible agreements of
"complementarity." This interpretation will facilitate the study
of the "integration of border regions" such as that undertaken
between Colombia and Venezuela. It is precisely history which
can teach us that certain limits between states, which are the
consequence of particular historical circumstances, do not necessarily correspond to modern economic realities. The Argentine
Alberdi stated as early as 1844:

> America is badly constructed, gentlemen, if I may
> express myself thus. Its politico-geographic map
> must be redrawn. It is an old edifice built accord-
> ing to a faulty design. Formerly it was a Spanish
> factory in which the departments devoted themselves
> to particular tasks divided according to the indus-
> trial plan necessary to the manufacturer. Today
> each department is an independent nation burdened
> by the universality of social elements and working
> for itself according to its own inspiration. In this
> new existence, the nation no longer finds its geo-
> graphic situation suitable and well adapted to its
> multiple and varied functions, and it needs to have
> its construction modified, but it clashes with limits
> established by the parent state monarchy and re-
> spected by republican America. [4]

These remarks lead us to the consideration of two problems for which the role of history is again enlightening:

Total Integration or Partial Integrations?

If integration of the aggregate of the Latin American countries seems difficult or virtually inaccessible, partial regional integrations are possible and perhaps more effective. Several projects have been outlined and even initiated: Central American Common Market, Greater Colombia (regrouping of Colombia, Ecuador, Venezuela), the West Indies Federation, "Southern Cone," ABC (Argentina, Brazil, Chile). In another connection, big plans for international regional development have been envisaged: development of the basins of the Amazon and of the River Plate. These projects are founded not only on geographic proximity but also on economic similarities, which only can be appreciated, as we have said, by the dynamics of structures. But at the same time, history will show why in the past national frontiers were stronger than these possibilities of regional aggregations. Knowing them better, one can then more effectively combat centrifugal forces. The study of the independence period (1800-1825) is revealing in this regard.

Comparison With the European Common Market?

It is already possible to devote oneself to the historical study of the European economic communities and to the results they have obtained. This requires a resetting of the phenomena within the economic, political, and social framework of Europe and a knowledge of the structures and of the European short- and long-run business cycles since the beginning of the Industrial Revolution or even of commercial capitalism. Such studies should allow fertile comparisons with Latin America. As one can imagine, these comparisons show the considerable differences existing between integration problems in Europe and the same problems in America. In the one case, we have highly-developed economies, with important and competitive heavy and light industries which must be made to work together and complement one another. In the other case, we have a ridiculously weak industry in comparison with the needs of the mass population. In the one case, we have an integrated society with a high level of consumption. In the other, a society which, if not always dualistic, is poorly integrated or not at all, representing a restricted market for many products. In the one case, we have a very strong capital coefficient; in the other, it is very weak. In one case, a confined space, perhaps too confined; in the other, an immense space, often still empty. In the one case, economies accustomed to dominate; in the other, those used to being dominated. Consequently, it is futile to want to do for America what was done for Europe; this is the first conclusion of such a comparison. The second is that on certain precise points, and in particular in the realm of institutional organization, [5] the experience of one can be helpful to the other. Now, all this is only possible by means of a precise historical study of the integration of each.

NATIONAL INTEGRATION

This is more urgent than the other, for national integration is a sign of the economy's health and development. The policy of integration at the national level can be based on historical research according to two plans, just as for the continental level:

The Business-Cycle Plan

Historians can supply the statistical series permitting us to define the fluctuations of national economy from the colonial period up to the present day — short- and long-term fluctuations. Above all, they can do this for each region of a country and especially for cities which serve as poles of development to these regions and which furnish given statistics in a more liberal fashion than for the country or small towns. Work of this nature is presently being undertaken in Brazil and in various countries of Spanish America. It permits interregional comparisons. It shows whether all regions live by the same rhythm, are on the same time — a favorable condition for appropriate integration. Naturally, other comparisons are possible: variations of city-country consumption, variations in standards of living or consumption of different social groups.

The Structural Plan

Integration measures must rely on a precise knowledge of data concerning geography, economy, demography, anthropology, sociology, and politics. However, these social sciences lack principles of explanation if deprived of their historical dimension. The weakness of certain branches of social anthropology is due to their neglect of this historical dimension. Many phenomena or the form they take are tied to the persistencies of the past and often can no longer be justified. Historical research helps us take this into account and explain them. On the other hand, a structural analysis of different regions, of different social and economic groups, emphasizing the stage of their growth, will allow us to realize more successfully national internal "complementarities." It will permit us to discover what are the stimuli and permanent obstacles (and not only those of the present) to the development of such and such a region. An important investigation is being carried out on the role of cities in the regional development of Latin America.[6] Based on the choice of a certain number of samples, it does not neglect historical study. What was the nature of the regional urban network in the past? What in the past did the city contribute to its region and the region to its city? Such are the questions which the historian seeks to solve in the framework of this investigation.

One arrives in this way at a national or regional accounting and at regional and national quantitative dynamic models. It is a new way to write history, making it understandable to the economist.

History, apart from this, is interested in the rest of the world and provides us with theoretical diagrams supported by actual experience. It allows us, for example, to consider the process by which the disappearance of dualism can be effected in an economy which has gone beyond the "take-off."

In Europe the transformation of rural structures was brought about by a migration to foreign parts or to the cities. Toward the cities went those in tertiary employment, except where there were local or regional possibilities of development of a secondary sector. In this way, the peasant-townsman dualism gave way little by little to an integrated society of townsmen or farmers working as manufacturers and living as townsmen. "The return to the land" seemed generally difficult   inasmuch as it signified returning to peasantry for people who had tasted city life. In the same way we can see that in Latin America it is difficult to create a peasant class where none exists. At most, that which exists might be arrested on condition that sufficient security be guaranteed, as well as modern means of living and production. More often than not, the future, even in South America, will go to large agricultural exploitations of the industrial type in the form of capitalistic enterprises or co-operatives with an agricultural manpower mechanically well-equipped and well-paid, rather than to a landowner-grower peasantry whose rudimentary work-implements will place them well under the average wage level. [7]

History places us, then, in the presence of an irreversible process in which the irreversibility does not depend on ordinary fatality but on geographical and technical conditions. It permits us to understand that to act against or in spite of these conditions condemns us to ineffectiveness. However, we must insist on the need for a serious study of history and on the danger incurred if history is used superficially. In the multiple comparisons which have been made between the Latin American Common Market and western experiments of the nineteenth century,[8] some are more adequate than others. The customs union such as that   established   in Germany in the Zollverein has little in common with the Mercomún, for it developed during a period when states intervened infrequently in economic life and when one of their only means of intervention was through customs tariffs. Now, as Raymond Barre[9] recently pointed out, states today have many other means of intervention in economic life, and to condemn a common market to be only a customs union is to change hardly at all the existing situation. On the other hand, in spite of appearances, the comparison with the Thirteen Colonies which broke away from England at the end of the eighteenth century seems more accurate, to the extent that, just as in the case of the Thirteen Colonies, we have, south of the Rio Grande, economies dominated by the great Western giants (except for Cuba, which is dominated by the Soviet giant). They seek their autonomy; their union is being effected not so much by the solution of traditional rivalries as by the need to escape from external control.

Can one go back even further into the past and compare the efforts of Latin American integration to those of French, Spanish or English kings to break down the interior barriers of their kingdoms and form those great metropolitan economic areas which dominated the world in the sixteenth and seventeenth centuries? Here again, one could dig out the notion of economic space, its relationship with the state of technology, and ask oneself if an optimum space for each stage of technological development can be calculated. But history teaches us that purely incidental circumstances have made of Brazil a unique empire and of Spanish America a balkanized continent. The size of Brazil, badly adapted to the nineteenth century, appears particularly suited to the techniques of the twentieth. Ultimately, the solution seems to lie not so much in an integrated Latin America as in a certain number of regroupings similar to the pre-existent Brazilian grouping.

Finally, a historical reflection leads us to think that the opportunity for Latin America in the twenty-first century lies not so much in that it possesses a temperate zone such as the one where industrial Europe developed (following the Mediterranean climate of the ancient civilization) but rather in that Latin America is mainly tropical in a period when techniques have made possible a highly-developed civilization in the tropical zone. This view in the perspective of history must make optimists of us.

1. Bela Balassa, "Toward a Theory of Economic Integration," in Miguel S. Wionczek, ed., *Latin American Economic Integration* (New York: Frederick A. Praeger, 1966), p. 22.

2. Henri Hauser, *Recherches et documents sur l'histoire des prix en France de 1500 à 1800* (Paris, 1936). See also Introduction to Papers and Proceedings of the meeting of the American Economic Association in December 1955, *American Economic Review*, May 1956.

3. See article by Frédéric Mauro in *Caravelle* (Toulouse), 1964, No. 2.

4. Juan Bautista Alberdi, *Conveniencia y objetos de un congreso general americano*.

5. Raymond Barre, member of the Commission of Fourteen in Brussels, has urged sociologists to undertake a study of the European economic communities—that is, a study of the new behavior of the civil servants employed by these community organizations.

6. RCP No. 147 of the Conseil National de la Recherche Scientifique (Paris).

7. Caio Prado Junior, *A revolução brasileira* (São Paulo, 1966).

8. Wionczek, *op. cit.*, p. 5.

9. In a lecture on "The Common Market in 1968: Balance and Perspectives," given at the Faculté des Lettres et Sciences Humaines de Paris, Nanterre, February 16, 1968.

PART **II**

GENERAL PROBLEMS

CHAPTER **5** OBSTACLES TO LATIN
AMERICAN INTEGRATION

By Sidney Dell, Director
New York Office of UNCTAD

It seems quite clear that Latin American integration is in
trouble. What is less clear are the reasons for this.

The most obvious evidence of the troubles that have arisen
is the failure of the Latin American Free Trade Association to
reach agreement in 1967 on the second stage of drawing up the
"Common List" of products to be unconditionally freed of trade restrictions at the end of the transition period in 1973. Strictly speaking, the failure to reach agreement by the end of 1967 means that a
basic provision of the Treaty of Montevideo has not been fulfilled.

The commonly accepted view of the reasons for the breakdown of negotiations is that the Latin American countries are bent
upon protecting their own national markets under the pressure of
vested interests in existing industries. What is lacking, according
to this view, is the political will to set in motion a serious program
of economic integration, involving categorical commitments to the
automatic reduction of trade barriers over a fixed period of years.
It thus appears that the declaration of intent by the Latin American
heads of state at Punta del Este in April 1967 to establish a common
market is being undermined by the persistence of a narrow nationalistic approach to development problems.

While there is a good deal of truth in this view of the matter, there is a tendency in North America and Europe to draw too
precise an analogy between LAFTA and EEC. It is assumed that
the main objective in Latin America, as in Europe, is the lowering
of trade barriers and that success or failure can be judged largely
or entirely by the progress made in reducing intraregional tariffs
and other restrictions.

It has been said repeatedly in this context that the real
difficulty with the Treaty of Montevideo is that the process of regional tariff disarmament is not automatic, but has to be negotiated painfully year by year and product by product. Once the easy
reductions in tariffs had been completed during the early years of
the integration program, it became more and more difficult to go
ahead with new reductions of trade barriers, and the failure to
agree on the second stage of the Common List was only one manifestation of the slowing-down process.

The point that is usually overlooked, however, is that

"integration" in any real sense of the term cannot come about in Latin America, or any other underdeveloped region, simply by a process of reduction of trade barriers. The analogy with Europe is an exceedingly poor one because the countries comprising the European Economic Community and the European Free Trade Association were already trading extensively with one another even before the treaties of Rome and Stockholm were signed. Western Europe was already highly industrialized, and the problem was to promote greater efficiency and productivity by taking advantage of the economies of specialization and exchange that could be generated by the lowering of trade barriers.

The problem in Latin America is a quite different one. The concern there is not merely to bring about specialization within the small amount of industry that already exists but, more importantly, to promote a massive expansion of industry overall. This cannot be done simply by lowering the barriers to trade. Industrial development in any underdeveloped region calls for the deliberate mobilization of resources to this end, so as to overcome the forces of inertia which have held back the development of these countries over the past century. The liberation of market forces within a large economic area may be conducive to more rapid growth in a region such as western Europe, where a large industrial base is already in being. But if the liberation of market forces through the reduction of trade barriers were all that Latin America needed to develop, the region would have developed a long time ago, before the present era of trade restrictionism began.

One could easily imagine a state of affairs in which Latin American countries dismantled their trade barriers vis-à-vis one another, without thereby generating an integrated process of development for the region as a whole. One would still have highly developed enclaves within a generally depressed continent, and there might even be a tendency towards retrogression if the stronger units in the relatively more advanced countries tended to overwhelm the weaker units elsewhere.

Even in Central America, where differences in levels of development are somewhat less pronounced than they are in South America, it is still far from clear what contribution to the growth of the region will be made by the lowering of trade barriers per se. The Central American integration program has frequently been referred to in recent years as a model of what can be accomplished when a group of underdeveloped countries get together and undertake a really serious program of tariff disarmament. Progress under this program has indeed been impressive, and within a space of five years, the five countries participating in the integration program were able to eliminate restrictions on about 95 per cent of the tariff items. This encouraged a rapid growth in the trade among these countries, and the share of transactions with one another in their total trade is now of the order of 20 per cent.

The objective of trade liberalization was, of course, much easier to achieve in Central America than in South America. For one thing the intercountry differences in per capita levels of income and development are much smaller in Central America than in South America. In addition there are fewer industries in Central America, and therefore fewer vested interests in industrial protection. Nevertheless, the success of the trade liberalization program in Central America has been striking, and much can be learned from it.

It is, however, far from clear as yet how significant a contribution this liberalization will make to the development of Central America. Much of the trade that has been generated reflects relatively little by way of added production in the region itself. The following statement from the 1966 Annual Report of the Central Bank of Nicaragua is of particular interest in this connect connection:

> The share of trade among the Central American countries in their total external trade has been increasing in recent years: intraregional imports accounted for 16.2 per cent of the total imports of the Central American countries in 1966, whereas in 1960 this share had amounted to only 6.4 per cent. It is nevertheless worth pointing out that the process of import substitution which has been taking place in the Common Market is not as extensive as the above figures might appear to suggest, since the manufactured products traded within the area have a high import content in the majority of cases.

If, of course, the domestic content of the manufactures traded increasingly within the region is low, the expansion in intra-trade in relation to total trade may to a significant extent be a purely statistical phenomenon, resulting from the fact that exports are valued gross rather than in terms of domestic value added.

There does not appear to be any analysis of the growth of the regional trade of Central America that would throw light on this matter. Obviously, however, there is a danger that the types of industry established in Central America under a relatively laissez-faire system of regional free trade would be selected on a rather haphazard basis from the standpoint of development, and would not necessarily lead to a balanced program of mutually supporting industries for the region as a whole.

There is even a possibility that the industries established could conflict with the immediate priority needs of the area for industrial development. This could happen, for example, if a relatively high common external tariff were established for certain types of luxury imports, while manufacture within the area was encouraged by levying relatively low duties, or no duties at all, on the machinery, raw materials and components required for producing the luxury goods in question within the area. From the standpoint of its development, it might be much better for the region to continue importing such luxury goods in the relatively limited quantities that would result from the imposition of high tariffs on the finished product instead of going into production itself and dissipating valuable exchange and capital resources on domestic production of luxuries that could hardly contribute to the long run growth of the region.

Thus, successful as the Central American tariff reduction program has been, the region is still lacking a serious industrial policy or program. The benefits of the tariff reduction program seem to have accrued mainly to the big foreign companies that have had the strength and resources to move in and take advantage of the program. Local enterprise appears to have gained very little. [1] Moreover, new industry has tended to gravitate to the more advanced centers in El Salvador, Costa Rica and Guatemala, bypassing the two less developed countries, Honduras and Nicaragua.

Originally it had been intended that Central America should have a system of planned integration industries. Each country was to be allocated certain specific industries, and plants established in accordance with this allocation were to enjoy access to region-wide markets, as well as certain advantages over any competing plants that might be established elsewhere. The scheme ran into difficulties because it was made clear to the participating countries that external finance would not be made available either directly or indirectly for setting up regional monopolies. Insufficient account was thereby taken of the need to secure an equitable distribution of the benefits of industrial development among the participating countries, and of the fact that in a region comprising only 13 million people, it was inevitable that the size of the market would in many cases not allow more than one firm to operate efficiently at a satisfactory rate of utilization of capacity. This being the case, to leave the distribution of industry entirely to market forces was to perpetuate the backwardness of Honduras and Nicaragua and destroy their interest in the union.

Some effort was made to achieve equitable results by other means, notably through the provision of special financial assistance to the backward areas to encourage their development. But it can hardly be said that a coherent program of region-wide industrial development has yet emerged.

Tariff reductions thus do not in themselves provide sufficient motive power to promote the economic interdependence of underdeveloped countries. Indeed, under certain conditions regional tariff reductions may tend to militate against regional economic integration, properly defined. By regional economic integration one means, or should mean, the process whereby a group of countries establish more and more intimate economic ties with one another by developing intercountry specialization and complementarity, by setting up multinational enterprises and so forth. But in the absence of deliberate action, to stimulate indigenous enterprise it can happen that the main effect of regional tariff reductions may be to encourage foreign enterprise to set up subsidiaries in the area concerned, taking advantage of the larger market provided, without doing much either to promote local enterprise with a region-wide orientation, or to strengthen the economic links between the participating countries. In so far as this occurs, the lines of integration would appear to run much more strongly from the subsidiaries to the parent companies than between the countries participating in the tariff reduction program.

At all events it seems quite clear that tariff reductions and economic integration are by no means one and the same thing, and that the elimination of restrictions on intraregional trade may not in itself create a sufficient basis for regional economic integration. What is needed for this purpose is a deliberate distribution of industry policy, accompanied by agreements on the means of carrying out that policy. It is significant that the Chase Manhattan Bank, in an analysis of the Central American Common Market, came to the conclusion that "Regional industrial policy poses a major challenge to continued merging of the five economies."[2] Unless Central America makes significant progress in the near future in setting up policies along these lines, it may find that the hopes created by the rapid growth in regional trade during the past ten years will be frustrated, and that integration may not get much further than the circulation of foreign consumer goods which have been subjected to a rather modest degree of processing within the area. Such trade could not create the basis for a cumulative process of growth and integration. It would provide the appearance of integration without the substance.

Very similar considerations apply in LAFTA. It was inevitable that the process of reducing trade barriers should grind to a halt so long as no agreement was reached on a distribution of industry policy for the region. The lack of such a policy means that the weak countries in the region have no assurance that their own infant industries will not be overwhelmed by the more advanced industries of their stronger neighbors; and still less do they have any assurance of a fair share of any new industrial capacity, whether financed out of external or local resources.

Thus the problem is not, at its roots, a problem of tariff-cutting techniques. Nor is it simply a question of introducing automaticity into the process of reducing tariffs. If, of course, governments are prepared to commit themselves in advance to an automatic system of tariff-cutting across the board, it goes without saying that the objective is more likely to be realized than if they insist on bargaining over every item. But this is purely a question of method, and is not the fundamental issue at all. The question one has to ask is—why were the EEC and EFTA countries prepared to lower their trade barriers across the board according to a pre-agreed timetable while the LAFTA countries were not?

This question cannot be answered simply by talking of political will, for the question then arises—what was it that created the political will in the one case and not in the other? Certainly not a conviction about economies of scale or specialization.

65

Economies had very little to do with the political will of Western European countries to units. As Professor Walter Hallstein pointed out: "We are not in business at all. We are in politics."[3]

It must also be remembered that while the EEC and EFTA countries were sufficiently close to one another in levels of income and industrial development to feel that they could all gain from an opening up of region-wide markets, no such assurance could be provided in the much more heterogeneous economy of the Latin American continent. For in Latin America it would be quite possible and even likely that regional free trade would not merely distribute gains unequally, but might confine the gains to some countries while inflicting actual losses upon others. To ask a country to agree to the unchecked operation of market forces on an automatic basis in such a context is to ask it to abandon its own interests in the interests of the region as a whole — which no country can be expected to do even if the regional benefit is substantial.

Thus pressure for automaticity is likely to fail in its purpose unless it is accompanied by clear provision for satisfactory rates of growth and of industrial development for each of the participating countries. What is required is not a hypersophisticated or overambitious regional plan, but a modicum of agreement among countries on a distribution of industry policy in the light of the best economic criteria available. This could be reinforced by the use of national and international assistance to promote and finance the establishment of industries catering to region-wide markets on a basis of fair shares for all constituent countries, consistent with economic rationality. This may mean more assistance per capita to Bolivia, Ecuador, and Paraguay than to Argentina, Brazil, and Mexico, but that is indispensable if regional cohesion is to be maintained, and if Bolivia, Ecuador, and Paraguay are to retain a stake in the integration program.

In fact, of course, LAFTA has provided special treatment not merely for the least developed group—Bolivia, Ecuador, and Paraguay—but for an intermediate group as well—Chile, Colombia, Peru, Uruguay, and Venezuela: the latter are not considered to be as vulnerable as Bolivia, Ecuador, and Paraguay, but nevertheless do not feel able to face the full strength of Argentina, Brazil, and Mexico.

Cutting across two of these three groups is the group of Andean signatories of the Declaration of Bogotá—Bolivia, Chile, Colombia, Ecuador, Peru, and Venezuela. The Declaration, signed in August 1966, significantly puts the need for industrial cooperation and complementarity ahead of the process of lowering trade barriers; and provides that the latter process should be programmed so as to take into account the various intersectoral differences in levels of development. More specifically, the Declaration indicates the need for:

coordinating industrial development policy with a
view to establishing complementarity agreements

which would avoid the duplication of projects
and which would permit the establishment of
new industries or the expansion of old ones,
so as to provide for the needs of the enlarged
market comprising our countries. This co-
ordination should preferably concentrate in
the following fields:

1. Basic metallurgy
2. Nonmetallic minerals
3. Chemicals and petrochemicals, with
   special attention to fertilizer
4. Wood, cellulose and paper
5. Metal manufactures, especially motor
   vehicle components and capital goods
6. Electric and electronic industries
7. Food industries.

These are the industries which the Andean countries are
anxious to foster. And the question arises here—as in Central
America—whether external resources will be denied to the Andean
countries on the grounds that they are trying to establish regional
monopolies (the avoidance of "duplication of projects"). For example, the Andean countries have given notice of their intention
to enter into a complementarity agreement in the field of petro-
chemicals. The stated objectives of the agreement include the
balanced development of the petrochemical industry through the establishment of plants of optimum size catering to the needs of the
participating countries as a whole, and specializing so as to secure the available economies of scale.

To this end, the investment plans of the participating
countries are to be coordinated, and particular plants are to be
assigned to particular countries. Moreover, under article 4 (a)
of the complementarity agreement, member countries are required to discourage or prohibit the establishment, within their
own borders, of plants similar to those assigned to other participating countries. Other LAFTA countries may subscribe to the
agreement provided that they comply with its terms, including the
distribution of industry policy which it lays down.

Will external assistance be available to carry out the
terms of agreements of this type? When national and international
lending agencies think of providing assistance for integration, they
usually do so in terms of regional infrastructure—river basin development, large power complexes, international highways, transport and communications, and so forth. There can be no doubt of
the importance of large projects of this type. But there is only a
limited amount of this sort of thing to be done, and the more important policy questions, ultimately, are those that arise in relation to external financing of investment undertaken in accordance
with a regional policy for industry. This may involve the creation
of local monopolies either because of the small size of the market
and the need to avoid proliferation of uneconomically sized units,

or because of the need to provide a temporary inducement to new investment. Obviously, such monopolies should be closely regulated in the interests not merely of the country in which they are located but of the region as a whole. And the weapon of reducing tariffs on imports from third countries should always be held in readiness to discourage inefficiency or excessive profits. But granted such regulation, there is a case for reconsidering the standards hitherto applied by national and international lending agencies in this context, which may have contributed significantly to the failure of efforts towards industrial cooperation and complementarity in Latin America.

Alternatively, the onus is on those with objections of principle to regional monopolies to indicate how the same basic objectives of industrial cooperation could be achieved in a different way. Otherwise there is bound to be an uneasy feeling that the objection is not so much to monopoly as such, but to a monopoly created by local interests. The fact that bilateral or multilateral lending agencies will not make resources available for the establishment of a locally based regional monopoly will not in the least prevent the big American or European companies from coming into the area and establishing de facto monopolies of their own. Thus denial of resources to local enterprise may be tantamount to weighting the scales still more in favor of large-scale foreign capital than they already are, even though this may not be the deliberate intention. It is considerations of this type that have made Latin American labor and business wary of the danger that what goes under the benign name of "integration" may in reality be a means of opening up new opportunities for foreign enterprise to take over the most profitable investment outlets in the region. Any program that concentrates on trade liberalization on an automatic basis without regard to these more fundamental issues is not likely to get very far in Latin America either now or in the future.

That is not to say that private foreign investment has no role to play in the development of Latin America. On the contrary, the resources and technical know-how that foreign capital can make available are obviously of great potential importance for the region. The problem is not to prevent the inflow of foreign capital, but to channel it into the sectors where it is most needed, and to create the conditions in which such inflow can make its contribution effectively without displacing Latin American enterprise. It should be the aim of any regional coordination of investment to seek coherence and consistency not only as between the investment programs of the various participating countries, but also as between local and foreign investment. In industries where techniques are well known and adequate local resources are available, there may be a case for limiting the participation of external capital so as to encourage local enterprise. Where, however, the establishment of new industries is planned, there may be decisive advantages in offering incentives to foreign capital, although even here consideration may be given to local participation in ownership and control, where possible, or to arrangements whereby ownership and control can ultimately be transferred, partially or wholly.

Finally, how far does the subregional approach offer prospects for overcoming some of the obstacles that have held back the progress of LAFTA? Does the approach of the Andean countries, taken together with the bilateral arrangements envisaged between Argentina and Brazil, hold out the promise that a subregional attack on the problem of integration may be more successful than the approach of the Treaty of Montevideo?

Referring to the bilateral discussions between Argentina and Brazil the Buenos Aires review Análisis has commented as follows:

> In reality, these bilateral discussions represent a realistic method of advancing integration, one of the principal merits of which is that there appears to be no other method available, unless one resorts to supranational decisions, which do not exist outside the speculation of theoreticians either here or in any other part of the world. It is well-known that the delays and difficulties involved in the process of Latin American integration in general and LAFTA in particular are principally the result of the different levels of development of the various countries (in fact, a different level for each country)... Consequently, multilateral agreements of the sort which led to the establishment of the European Common Market cannot achieve continental integration in Latin America except very slowly and with great difficulty. Integration will rather have to come about through a system of poles of attraction—that is to say, subregional agreements which could serve as pivots to the system unifying markets and seeking to bring about complementarity between various productive activities. [4]

It is a factor of considerable importance that the concept of continental solidarity has not thus far gained much support in Latin America, notwithstanding the considerable cultural and linguistic affinities of the constituent countries. The difficulty is that there is an inherent conflict between the nationalism of the developing countries and the objectives of regional integration.

Yet nationalism is an important force in the development process which should not be underestimated. Indeed, historically the process of industrial development in Europe and North America was accompanied and facilitated by strong forces of nationalism. Nationalism gives a sense of common purpose, and creates both the morale and the discipline needed for making sacrifices in the present so as to invest in the future. Many of the Latin American countries are scarcely integrated at the national level, and it is not altogether surprising that people who have difficulty in identifying themselves with their own country should see even less sense in identifying themselves with a continent of which they know little or nothing.

While the sort of view expressed in Análisis is therefore perfectly comprehensible, it does not follow that a new formula for integration has been found. One sees the possibility of a somewhat chaotic proliferation of bilateral, trilateral and polilateral agreements in various industries, the membership and provisions of each agreement being quite different. Whether such a hodgepodge could lead ultimately to serious economic coalition or interdependence may be open to doubt. Although the Andean group of countries may be able to avoid the encroachment of stronger or more efficient industries in Argentina, Brazil and Mexico, they can scarcely escape other problems. Indeed the Andean group is itself not so homogeneous that it will necessarily be able to get so very much further than the region as a whole—witness the fact that already a dispute between Ecuador and Venezuela has prompted the two countries to defer the mutual application of concessions under the Montevideo Treaty until 1969.

It will also be extremely difficult to achieve a balance of advantages among the participating countries on the basis of a purely industry-by-industry approach. In other words, even if the Andean countries were to succeed in negotiating, say, twenty industrial complementarity agreements, how would any one of them decide whether it was getting a fair deal out of these agreements, taken as a whole? And it is this very question of the equitable distribution of benefits that has threatened to wreck the larger group of which the Andean countries are only a part.

Thus the problems facing the Andean countries are not essentially different from those encountered by the LAFTA group as a whole. The case for Andean cooperation rests mainly on the possibility that the smaller group will develop more cohesiveness and a greater willingness to act jointly than the larger group. Against this, however, there is the danger of setting one part of Latin America against another, and of creating new sources of regional friction that do not exist at present.

Above all, the establishment of smaller subregional groups within Latin America does not overcome the conflict between nationalism and continentalism to which reference has already been made.

A country that is anxious to get on with the job of development may have the greatest hesitation in holding back in the hope that two, three, or five years from now it may do better if it can agree on some division of labor with its neighbors. A project that is only 20 per cent efficient may bring greater benefits if it can be set in motion immediately than a better project that would be twice as efficient but which would have to wait five years for intergovernmental agreement and action. Time is of the essence in the development process, and one cannot blame governments for being a shade skeptical as to their ability to reach effective agreements with their neighbors. It remains the duty of those who see the economic advantages of integration to do all in their power to secure greater recognition of those advantages in the developing countries.

Whether the art of international negotiation and accommodation
has reached the point at which these economic advantages can be
realized in practice remains a moot question.

NOTES

1. See Francisco Oliveira, "Integración y econo-
mías de escala," in CEMLA, *Boletín Mensual,* November 1967,
pp. 632-633.

2. Chase Manhattan Bank, *World Business,* January 10,
1968, p. 15.

3. Address to Joint Meeting of Harvard University
and M.I.T., May 22, 1961.

4. Banco Nacional de Comercio Exterior, *Comercio
Exterior,* Mexico, December 1967, p. 969.

6

SOCIO-ECONOMIC PERSPECTIVES FOR A LATIN AMERICAN COMMON MARKET

By   Robert W. Bradbury
Department of Economics
University of Florida

On April 12 to 14, 1967, the presidents of the countries of Latin America (with the exception of Cuba and Bolivia) and the President of the United States met at Punta del Este, Uruguay, for a summit meeting in order to revitalize the Alliance for Progress and to make other significant changes in the "inter-American system." In order to extend the scope of the Latin American market, one of the significant agreements was that which pledged a continuing effort to establish a Latin American Common Market. This agreement was signed by all of the Latin American presidents who participated in the meeting with the exception of President Arosemena of Ecuador.

The proposal of a common market was not a new idea but one which had been studied since shortly after World War II. Prior to World War II, Latin America had been predominantly an exporter of agricultural products and other raw materials and an importer of manufactured goods. This does not mean that there was no manufacturing within Latin America, as important industrial complexes already existed in the vicinity of Mexico City, Mexico; São Paulo, Brazil; and Buenos Aires, Argentina. These major centers, plus centers of lesser importance in other Latin American countries, supplied a rather wide range of consumer goods, but the general observation that the Latin American countries were not highly industrialized when regarded in relation to other more advanced industrial areas of the world is obviously true.

During the war years of 1941 to 1945, there were many new industries established in Latin America because of the shortage of supplies available from the United States and from the other belligerent nations. These new industries were not always well established and were still operating at high cost and consequent uneconomic competitive advantage at the end of the conflict. They continued in existence largely because of various protective devices, i.e., high tariffs, import permits, import quotas, and exchange controls.

ECLA

In order to help create a viable economy in Latin America, the United Nations established the Economic Commission for Latin America (ECLA). ECLA was located in Santiago, Chile.

The most influential economist in ECLA was the Argentine, Raúl Prebisch, who influenced the economic thinking of a large majority of the economists in Latin America, particularly those employed in governmental development and planning. Dr. Prebisch's main contention was that the Latin American countries, as exporters of raw materials, would continue at a disadvantage relative to the developed countries under the present economic conditions. In his opinion, the Latin Americans would have to give more and more of their raw materials in return for the manufactured goods which were imported from abroad because the demand for raw materials (and particularly for foodstuffs such as sugar and coffee) was inelastic, while the demand for imported manufactured goods was highly elastic.

According to Prebisch, the solution to this dilemma of an unfavorable trend in terms of trade was to industrialize to the extent that the Latin American countries would no longer be dependent on foreign sources for the major portion of their manufactured consumer goods. It was thought that domestically produced consumer goods would in the near future substitute for the imported consumer goods. The demand for imports would thereby be lessened and the Latin American countries might then find it possible to use the proceeds of their exports to buy capital equipment.

Prebisch believed that one important stimulus to economic development was a widening of the market so that firms of the most efficient size could be established. Thus an integrated market of most or all of the countries would permit economies of scale and, therefore, a great increase in industrialization.

LAFTA

As a result of the studies made at Santiago, Chile, committees representing the various countries were appointed during the 1950's to try to form a common market for Latin America. It proved to be impossible to get a majority of the countries together at any one time, but in 1960, eight nations met in Montevideo, Uruguay, to discuss the formation of a common market. These eight included the three countries with the greatest industrial development and, therefore, with the greatest interest in the establishment of a common market. These three were Mexico, Brazil, and Argentina. In addition, three others with certain established industries, Uruguay, Chile, and Peru attended and were quite enthusiastic, while the remaining two, Paraguay and Bolivia, were industrially underdeveloped by any criteria.

The discussions led to the rejection of a common market but to the establishment of the Latin American Free Trade Area (LAFTA). Some of the countries felt that establishing a common external tariff would involve an impairment of their national sovereignty. While the countries agreed to a gradual reduction in tariffs among themselves, this reduction was to take place only over a period of twelve years.

73

The reductions of the intraregional tariff barriers were to be accomplished by two different devices. First, each year the representatives of the countries would meet and agree bilaterally to a reduction of 8 per cent on their intraregional trade. Second, every three years they were to meet and agree to a multilateral reduction of 25 per cent.

The agreement included many escape clauses and, for each reduction, it was required that agreement be reached at these periodic meetings. Bolivia and Paraguay argued that they should be given special dispensations because of their underdevelopment, and special escape clauses were therefore included for their protection. In spite of this, Bolivia did not join LAFTA at that time, but the other seven signed the agreement in 1960. By 1961, the seven had ratified and LAFTA started operations. Since then Ecuador and Bolivia have joined under the same escape clauses as did Paraguay, and Colombia and Venezuela have become members.

These eleven countries, which comprise the bulk of the population and of the gross national product (GNP) of Latin America, have been co-operating for almost six years. Their intraregional trade, however, constituted less than 10 per cent of their total international trade at the time that LAFTA was initiated. This intraregional trade has increased by about 100 per cent during the life of LAFTA but still constitutes only a small fraction of their total international trade.

During the first three years, many substantial tariff reductions were granted on a bilateral basis. However, the organization ran into difficulties when unanimous agreement on the multilateral agreements was attempted. The Chase Manhattan Bank, in its publication, World Business, estimates that the regional tariffs have been reduced to about 50 per cent of the level applicable to non-regional imports. Thus it would seem that LAFTA has been reaching its goal and would at this rate eliminate tariff barriers in the twelve years specified.

The tariff reductions made so far, however, have generally affected items which are not produced by the countries granting the concessions. Thus there have been no domestic producers who might oppose the tariff concessions. When the attempt is made to generalize these bilateral agreements, opposition appears. Almost 60 per cent of the intraregional trade is accounted for by trade between Argentina and Brazil, and the major bilateral concessions were between these two countries. Thus an erroneous feeling of success may be conveyed by viewing the results on a percentage basis which obscures specific detail.

The many uses of escape clauses and the long discussions involved in obtaining the multilateral reductions have contributed to a sense of discouragement among the members regarding the future of LAFTA. To try to revitalize LAFTA, President Frei of Chile asked four leading Latin American economists, Felipe Herrera, Raúl Prebisch, José A. Mayobre, and Carlos Sanz de

Santamaría to serve as a committee to recommend changes in LAFTA. These four gentlemen met and recommended certain changes which were largely in line with the successful development of another experiment in economic integration that had taken place in Central America.

CACM

The Central American Common Market (CACM) was established at almost the same time as was LAFTA. CACM was composed of the five republics; Guatemala, El Salvador, Honduras, Nicaragua, and Costa Rica. Panama was not included, but indicated in August of 1966 a desire to join. The successful integration of CACM, which contributed materially to an increase of intraregional trade of approximately 400 per cent in the Common Market area may be traced to the following four factors.

First, the five countries of Central America had been part of a federation during their first 15 years of independence. Thus, even after their separation into unaffiliated, independent countries, a tradition of co-operation continued. For this reason, the spirit of nationalism and the possible consequence of mutual suspicion is not as pronounced politically as among some of the countries of LAFTA. In the 1950's, the five Central American countries organized ODECA, which is the agency for political co-operation and which may result in an actual political union of the five countries at some time in the future.

In the case of the LAFTA countries, the traditional rivalry between Argentina and Brazil for the position of leadership may have diverted constructive effort and ability from a co-operative effort. The historical enmity of Bolivia toward Chile because of the loss of Bolivia's Pacific coastline (which resulted from the War of the Pacific in 1879) is a hindrance to present co-operation. As a result of the same conflict, Peru lost part of its southern coast which is valued for its rich deposits of nitrates. Bolivia and Paraguay also fought a war over an expanse of plains called the Chaco in the thirties, and Ecuador lost territory to Peru in the early forties.

It is recognized, therefore, that for the LAFTA countries to co-operate as closely as the CACM countries would require the settlement of long-standing political disputes and a willingness to co-operate more fully. It has been true in the experience of other common market experiments that economic co-operation does lead to closer political co-operation.

Second, it is easier to form an economic union of countries that are in the same stage of economic development and with approximately equal gross national product per capita. These conditions are met by the countries of CACM but not by the countries of LAFTA. In the case of Central America, none of the countries had an outstanding industrial complex and their income per capita was fairly uniform. Costa Rica has the highest gross national product per capita, approximately $400, while Honduras has the lowest with slightly over $200, and the other three countries are all clustered around a $300 gross national product per year per capita.

In the case of LAFTA, there is a great disparity both in economic development and in regard to GNP per capita. From the standpoint of economic development, Mexico, Brazil, and Argentina have already established many industries. From the standpoint of GNP per capita, Venezuela and Argentina have several times the income per capita of countries such as Paraguay and Ecuador.

The third factor affecting the potential for economic integration has great importance. Monetary stability is conducive to the development of intraregional trade and in this respect CACM has an outstanding record. The five countries have exchange rates that are stable in the international money markets. Guatemala's quetzal is equal to the American dollar; the monetary unit of Honduras is 50 per cent of a quetzal; El Salvador's unit is 40 per cent of a quetzal; Nicaragua and Costa Rica have units that are approximately equal to one-seventh of a quetzal. For bookkeeping purposes, the Central American peso, which has been established as equal to the Guatemalan quetzal, is used in all intraregional transactions for clearing all balances of payments.

An example of the close co-operation among the five countries is illuminating. The presidents of the five central banks have organized a committee whose executive secretary is a past president of the Central Bank of Costa Rica. This committee, with headquarters in San Salvador, meets monthly with a different central bank serving as host and discusses such matters as exchange clearings, internal price movements, and external exchange pressures. A long-run possibility that might result from this co-operation is the actual introduction of a common monetary unit in the five countries. However, the introduction of a common monetary unit would involve the adoption of common monetary and fiscal policies by the five countries. This degree of co-operation will probably not come about before the adoption of closer political ties.

On the other hand, some of the countries of LAFTA have experienced extreme inflation, which hinders intraregional monetary stability. Chile, Uruguay, Argentina, and Brazil have all endured extreme and continuing inflation. Paraguay and Bolivia had an inflationary period during the early 50's, but in recent years these countries have been successful in stabilizing their currency. The price rise in Brazil has been as much as 89 per cent in one year, and while it has been lowered it is still quite high.

Several of the Latin American countries have attempted to maintain stable exchange rates with the outside world while undergoing internal price inflation. It is nonetheless true that such internal economic conditions are highly disruptive to the development of intraregional trade within a common market. If goods were permitted to move freely under a system of reduced or eliminated trade barriers, these goods would tend to move toward the country with the highest rate of internal inflation. This would inevitably lead to periodic devaluations of the inflated currencies with its disruptive effect on the growth of intraregional trade.

Fourth, ease of transportation is another essential for the continued growth of a large integrated market economy. While Central America is not outstanding from the standpoint of transportation, the Inter-American Highway does connect the capital cities of the five republics by paved roads. Therefore, goods manufactured in one country can be delivered by truck to another country with little delay.

On the other hand, between some of the LAFTA countries the movement of goods can be slow and very costly. From Ecuador to Argentina the only effective route is by water by way of the Panama Canal, which places Buenos Aires at a much greater distance from Ecuador than from the major ports of the United States or Europe.

THE FUTURE

The four economists who were engaged in the effort to revitalize LAFTA recommended that a sincere attempt should be made to establish a Latin American Common Market with a common external tariff; that CACM be permitted to join as a unit; and that those countries of Latin America that were outside the two groups be urged to join the common market. The economists recognized that a willingness to co-operate must be fostered among the Latin American nations and that outstanding political difficulties must be resolved. They also recognized that inflation was a drawback and urged the nations suffering from chronic inflation to try to stabilize their currency. The necessity of improving the transportation systems between the countries was also given due weight.

It had been urged that the proposed Latin American Common Market be placed on the agenda for the summit meeting of the Presidents, which had been originally scheduled to be held in 1966 in Buenos Aires. It was not, however, included on the original agenda, and it seemed to have been omitted from the agenda of the re-scheduled summit meeting at Punta del Este in April, 1967. President Johnson took the initiative in March of 1967 in a special message which urged that the subject of the common market be given a high priority on the forthcoming meeting of the Presidents. In the writing of the final agenda for the meeting, the Latin American Common Market was included.

77

The proposal was for all of the countries of Latin America to agree that by 1970 they would join the common market and that the necessary international agreements would be signed and ratified by that date. The proposed common market would then gradually eliminate intraregional barriers to trade and would adopt a common external tariff. The proposal was that this should be fully accomplished within 15 years of the ratification, or by 1985. If this is successful, at that date a Latin American Common Market will come into existence with a viable economy and with a population which is more than 50 per cent greater than that of the United States.

The Latin American Common Market would evolve from a merger of the Latin American Free Trade Association and the Central American Common Market. Because of the recent lack of success of LAFTA, it was felt that it would be unwise merely to adopt minor proposals whose only purpose would be to strengthen the present organization. It was considered far more judicious to make a more dramatic proposal for the common market. The new common market would involve much more co-operation and would require the adoption of a uniform tariff against nonmember imports. To be worked out in the next three years will be agreements to permit the free movement of labor and capital among the member countries and the co-ordination of monetary and fiscal policies. Of vital importance will be the elimination of the high rate of inflation now existing in some of the Latin American countries.

It is the hope of the founders that there will be a gradual reduction in the feeling of nationalism and an accompanying growth in the spirit of co-operation not only at the level of economic interchange but also in the realm of political co-operation. It is hoped that Latin America will co-operate in other fields such as the interchange of technological advances, including improvements in agricultural technology, and that the new common market may follow the lead of Central America in many other co-operative adventures such as the Joint Tariff Commission and the Council for University Co-operation.

One of the most promising ways that these countries may co-operate is in the improvement of transportation. In this project, the United States may well participate for the national as well as the regional and continental advancement. Also neighboring countries can co-operate in the development of grids for the distribution of hydro-electric energy to centers of population which are located in two or more co-operating countries.

A danger in developing a common external tariff is that the Latin American countries may be tempted to adopt a high tariff toward goods which are produced outside of the common market. Such a program, while it might give an initial stimulation to any industries within the market, might potentially lead to long-run stagnation. It is hoped that the external tariff will be relatively low and subject to later reductions.

The success of the Kennedy round of GATT negotiations in Europe (which may lead to an estimated reduction of 35 per cent in trade barriers) as an incentive, led to the hope that this pattern might eventually be followed by Latin America. Latin America must continue to depend on the outside world for much of its heavy machinery and equipment, as well as quite a few raw materials which are needed in its developing industries and which are not found within the confines of the Common Market.

The development of a common market in Latin America will change the present pattern of international trade but will not reduce the volume of trade between Latin America and the rest of the world. The total of trade of the European Common Market with the rest of the world expanded very rapidly in spite of the close economic integration of that area. As a region becomes more prosperous, demands increase and a larger amount of imported goods are purchased.

While the summit meeting of April, 1967, set the guidelines, there are many stumbling blocks that will appear in the future that may slow down or even prevent progress. The meeting of the foreign ministers at Asunción in August, 1967, did agree to the general statement that the CACM should be allowed to join LAFTA as a unit, but the meeting was a disappointment in other respects in that the plans for the Common Market were not advanced as much as had been hoped. One new development that was approved was the recognition of the newly established regional cooperation among the Andean countries of South America. While such regional integration can move forward at a more rapid pace than the common market for all of the countries, the very success of subregional groupings may slow the progress toward the ultimate goal. True statesmanship will be required in order to eliminate some of the political frictions that exist between the nations, and a less nationalistic attitude must be engendered if nations are to make the concessions necessary to make the whole project viable. It will also be necessary for individual businessmen to face the unhappy fact that certain special advantages must be relinquished in order to promote the general good.

A Latin American Common Market will increase the economic and political bargaining power of the area when negotiating for fairer treatment from the EEC and the United States and should in the long run bring about closer ties, both economic and political, between nations and groups of nations which are more nearly equal in size and in economic strength.

CHAPTER 7 LATIN AMERICAN ECONOMIC
INTEGRATION: ITS BENEFITS
AND OBSTACLES

By   Alfredo Roldan
     Department of Economics
     University of Nebraska

The economic effects of integration have been analyzed
from the point of view of world welfare vis-á-vis the welfare of
the economies participating in the integration and from a static
vis-á-vis a dynamic point of view.   Moreover, there has been a
tendency to defend the world interests in a static framework, and
those of the integrating economies in a dynamic one.   The former
may be identified as the "free trade" and the latter as the
"protectionist" approach to economic integration. [1] The latter approach has been adopted by a number of Latin American economists
centering around Raúl Prebisch and the Economic Commission for
Latin America (ECLA). [2] Prebisch's ideas on international trade,
repeatedly expressed since 1949, [3] provide the core to this approach
which, strongly pragmatic, falls short of theoretical analysis.   The
interested reader can fill this gap by going through the contributions of Balassa, [4] Scitovsky, [5] and Tinbergen. [6]

In this study world welfare will be disregarded.   In the
first section the case for economic integration will be summarized
exclusively from the point of view of the participating economies.
This will require a review of both static and dynamic arguments.
In the second section the causes of the Latin American lack of integration will be explained.   The analysis of these two sections
will make it possible to draw some conclusions about the steps to
be taken to promote integration, which will be done in the third
section.

I

Within a static framework, the removal of obstacles to
trade would bring about a change in the allocation of productive
resources.   Provided that there is no rise of the tariffs with respect to the rest of the world[7] this would bring the integrated
union closer to its transformation curve in the sphere of production, and to its utility frontier in the sphere of consumption. [8] If
there is a rise in these tariffs, there will be two forces acting in
opposite directions: the deletion of intraregional tariffs will pull
towards the production possibility and utility frontiers, whereas
the rise of external tariffs will push away from those frontiers.
The final result will depend on the relative strength of these forces.
If there is a tendency towards those frontiers, say within the first
possibility (no rise of external tariffs), the union as a whole will

experience a gain; but this does not mean that every participant will necessarily have a share in that gain. This point will be taken up in the next section.

For a dynamic analysis, the problem is no longer the impact of the integration on the relative position of the union with respect to a given pair of production possibility and utility frontiers; it is rather the impact of such integration on the frontiers themselves. Given the subjective nature of the utility frontier, it is difficult to apply to it the dynamic analysis, and we will confine ours to the production possibility frontier or transformation curve. To do this we will follow Balassa's argument.

Basing his analysis, among other things, on a fairly well developed theory of internal and external economies, as well as on empirical findings with respect to technological development and market structure, Balassa rightly claims that integration will result in a push outwards of the transformation curve. The process would work as follows:

1. By enlarging the market the integration would permit an adequate use of internal economies which are closely related to indivisibilities of plant and equipment, managerial and technical abilities, techniques or methods of mass production, technological research, and the like. [9] In contrast with Balassa's views, it may be argued that an adequate use of these indivisibilities would imply a mere reallocation of existing resources with no change of the production function, hence a displacement of the previous position along the production function, towards the pre-existent transformation curve, with no displacement of the curve itself. [10] In other words, it may be argued that the internal economies involved in such adequate use of the indivisibilities should be more correctly treated in a static than in a dynamic framework. The following consideration, however, would justify the inclusion of indivisibilities in the dynamic setting. The possibility of a more efficient use of those indivisibilities, by giving a greater range of choice to an economy, would permit the establishment of industries with greater Hirschman "linkage effects, " and so an unbalanced approach to development.

2. With respect to external economies, we first have to observe that, very obviously, third party benefits (whether through the market say, in the form of better prices, or independently from it, in the form of a better industrial atmosphere, e. g.) cannot be reaped if the third parties are not there. [11] In the case of small countries, with limited markets and resource endowments, the simultaneous appearance of several productive units is rather difficult. If, on the other hand, several small countries get together, by enlarging their markets and pooling their resources, they permit such simultaneous appearance, the use of external economies, a reduction of costs, a greater independence from foreign markets, and so Rosenstein Rodan's balanced approach to development.

Secondly, technological research is ordinarily characterized by high costs (we may say, by an indivisibility of costs) and presence of external economies, the latter with the restrictions arising from secrecy and patent laws. Technological development, the product of research, is one of the main factors responsible for the displacement of the production function. Furthermore, displacing that function may very well be a better development strategy than trying to enhance the resource endowment. Let us examine this more closely.

The findings of Abramovitz, [12] Bruton, [13] Nelson, [14] Solow, [15] and others [16] strongly suggest that in advanced countries, (where the factor endowment is rich to begin with, and the rate of savings and investment is high) the growth of output is due much more to technological progress than to capital formation. This should be even more so in underdeveloped countries, with poor resource endowment and low rates of savings. True, we have to admit that research is costly, in other words, that technological progress is not inexpensive; that poor countries may benefit from some of the research conducted in advanced countries, part of these benefits arising from the external benefits already mentioned, partly from international co-operation. But we have to bear in mind that the bulk of the research conducted in advanced countries corresponds to their own problems and needs, which are substantially different from those of the underdeveloped countries. The latter need a technology suitable to their natural and structural problems. That these countries have failed to develop such badly needed ad hoc technology has been repeatedly recognized, and the Bruton study has the merit of putting this technological gap in the foreground by means of a statistical analysis showing that the growth of output in Latin America is not due either to technological progress or even to capital formation, but rather to excess capacity, uneconomically created as a consequence of overprotectionism, or because precisely the lack of an ad hoc technology has forced these countries to use foreign technologies ill-adapted to the domestic factor endowments. [17] The failure of the Latin American economies to respond with growth of output to the substantial capital inflows of the Alliance for Progress [18] provides a confirmation of Bruton's findings.

The absence of an indigenous technology in the underdeveloped countries can be explained, to a large extent, by the high cost of research, and by the fact that much of the benefits do not accrue to the undertaker of the research but to his neighbor. However, if several of such countries share in the costs, the burden becomes more tolerable and the distribution of costs and benefits more equitable. These considerations permit one to assert that even if the Latin American countries do not achieve any formal integration, they still must get together to promote research on a large scale. The existence of such regional agencies as Organization of American States (OAS) and ECLA considerably enhances this endeavor.

Whereas in the case of external economies, social are greater than private benefits, in the case of external diseconomies,

social costs are greater than private ones. The vagaries of foreign markets do create extra social costs and so external diseconomies. As Balassa aptly contends, the existence of risks of
foreign markets requires a premium that "creates a divergence
between private profitability and social productivity"[19] which does
not permit the volume of production to be carried to the extent that
is socially desirable.

3. With respect to market structure, a larger framework
is conducive to smaller business concentration.[20] Balassa's empirical information does not permit him to draw any precise conclusions, and in connection with Latin America this writer is more
skeptical than with respect to Europe. This skepticism is
strengthened by the policy of "complementarity agreements" which,
for want of a more elaborate supranational planning system, consist of earmarking industries to geographical areas in a rather
arbitrary fashion. This is also a point that will be taken up later
in the study.

4. Another important point is that economic integration
reinforces the bargaining power of the participants. This reinforcement is two-fold: on the one hand the reciprocal demand
curve of the union gains elasticity; on the other hand the curve of
the rest of the world loses elasticity. In a free trade world, this
would have no importance, because, although the difference of elasticities and so of bargaining power would be there, there would
not be any bargaining, at least not in the form of tariffs and other
hindrances to trade. But the world being what it is, the bargaining power argument is important, as will be seen later.

5. Closely related to points 2 (last paragraph) and 4
above is the ECLA's thesis of the "trade gap," which can be summarized as follows: the growth process requires acquisition of
capital goods which are not produced in Latin America, hence they
have to be imported. The erosion of the comparative advantage of
the area in primary (especially agricultural) production because of
the low income-elasticity of the world demand for such products, and
because of the discriminatory policies practiced by industrial countries,[21] is a serious limitation to the importation of such capital
goods. The difference between the import needs[22] and the capacity to import makes up the "trade gap." One possible solution is
to produce those goods domestically. This implies industrialization, which is very anti-economic if carried along within narrow
national boundaries.[23]

II

From the preceding section we can see how strong is the
case for Latin American integration. Paradoxically, the reality
is of a dismal lack of integration. Moreover, after striving for
integration for almost a decade, the achieved success has been
modest, whether measured in terms of intraregional trade volume,
or of degree of development; whether in the case of the Central

American Common Market or in the case of the Latin American Free Trade Association (LAFTA). There must be an explanation for this, and in this section we will try to find it.

1. It has been argued that integration is not feasible among economies that are more competitive than complementary. This argument makes sense at best in a static framework of underdevelopment, for it is true that trade cannot be carried very far based on absolute advantages in items of primary production rather than on comparative advantages in items of secondary production. In fact, trade between two countries becomes altogether impossible if competitiveness is so great that both countries produce the same goods at the same costs. This situation is unlikely when secondary production is involved, but it is more likely if only primary production, especially if of the same type, is at stake. If the participating economies are sufficiently advanced, however, they may remain competitive and still achieve a fruitful integration, because the very competition would promote further efficiency and, therefore, more "trade-creation" than "trade-diversion," to use Viner's terms. This is the case of the European countries, whether among the "inner six" or the "outer seven."[24] Moreover, in a dynamic framework, the aim may be precisely the change of the productive structure. If the problem is not simply one of promoting trade on the basis of pre-existent production patterns, however, but one of creating trade pari passu with the productive substratum, it is like starting from scratch, and the progress is bound to be slow. Hence, it seems relevant to ask: Is Latin America prepared to launch a joint undertaking of integration and change of production patterns? Since there is a great deal of interdependence between these two objectives, it appears that it should be more efficient to pursue them simultaneously rather than successively; and granting that especially at the beginning the pace should be slow, steps must be taken to avoid traps of stable equilibrium at low levels of income.[25]

2. Another explanation has to do with the sufficiency of the transportation system of the area. This problem is a complicated one and requires more attention.

To begin with, the topography of the region is responsible for high costs of both construction and maintenance of inland transportation media.[26] To this we must add that much of the Latin American transportation system was constructed with the idea of serving a foreign trade oriented, in the last century, especially towards Europe, and more recently towards North America. There was little concern for the creation of strong national, let alone regional economies.[27] Matters grew worse because vested interests led to uneconomic planning and operation of the facilities, either by unduly lengthening the routes, by wastefully duplicating them, or by allocating the resources more with political than economic criteria. The history of the Latin American highways and railroads is plagued with this kind of shortcomings. With respect to railroads, they were constructed with no concern for uniformity: within a single country, Argentina, there are railroads with narrow, wide, and extra-wide track gauges. [28] Although intercountry comparisons are not very meaningful, the following figures are illustrative. Disregarding quality and duplication of facilities, the total length of the Latin American highway system (including Cuba) in 1963 was about one-fifth of the U.S. counterpart; the railroad system about one-third as long; the number of freight cars about one-eighth, and the freight carried about one-twentieth. [29]

The gap left by the highway and railroad systems has been partially filled by air transportation, thanks to its spectacular progress in the postwar period; unfortunately, this costly method cannot be entirely substituted for surface transportation.

With respect to inland waterways, it is well known that the world's largest river is in South America. In addition to the Amazon, there are in the area a number of other large rivers, the most important of which are the Plata, Orinoco, and Magdalena. There are about 25 thousand miles of navigable rivers, out of which 15 thousand are in the Amazon watershed. Except for the Plata system, however, the volume of freight moving through them is negligible. The Plata is of considerable importance for the neighboring countries, especially Paraguay. Utilization of the other rivers requires much improvement of the waterways and comprehensive area development plans.

These considerations explain the overwhelming dependence of Latin American foreign trade on ocean transportation, [30] the dependency ratio being of the order of 90%. Unfortunately, the area does not have a good domestic merchant fleet. As recently as 1961, over 90% of the cargo corresponding to the Latin American foreign trade was carried in vessels of non-Latin American flags. [31] Matters are aggravated by the noncompetitive structure of the shipping industry, a fact that was admitted by the Joint Economic Committee of the U.S. Congress in 1965. [32] This structure accounts for the way that shipping lines are admitted in the international conferences, in which only four Latin American companies are represented. [33] But when a company is invited, failure to accept the invitation brings about retaliatory measures. [34] It is not strange that the Latin American lines have little weight in the decision-making process of such conferences in matters as important as determination of freight rates and sailing schedules. To complicate matters even more, the Latin American port facilities are very poor, [35] and the cargo volume at each port is frequently low and almost always irregular. In summary, the ocean transportation system on which the area depends primarily for its foreign trade, including the intraregional, is extremely inadequate. The following quotation further illustrates such inadequacy. "Merchandise sent from Pôrto Alegre to (next door) Montevideo arrives sooner if routed through Hamburg... Uruguayan wool consigned to the U.S. goes first to Hamburg, despite the presence in port of domestic vessels that make direct runs to New York."[36]

Under these circumstances the promotion of a merchant fleet is essential simultaneously with the improvement of harbor facilities. It is necessary, however, to be aware of the fact that even in countries like the U.S. the shipping industry requires substantial subsidization by the government.[37] An infant Latin American fleet would require even greater protection. Both the international conferences and the governments of industrial countries, however, strongly oppose this, and past attempts to give some kind of protection to Latin American lines have failed.[38] Therefore, the countries of the area cannot be very optimistic about gaining, in isolation, their independence from great shipping powers. On this ground, their unification appears indispensable, although it may not be sufficient.

3. Next we must consider the inadequacy of the payments system. As we have seen, the "trade-gap" problem is essentially one of shortage of convertible currencies, and one of the ideas behind integration is to save such scarce resources. If intraregional transactions have to be paid with these currencies, however, as has occurred up to now, this purpose of integration is not satisfied. For an underdeveloped country, the need to import from fellow underdeveloped countries manufactures produced under "infant industry" circumstances, foregoing the possibility of buying from cheaper sources, is already a burden; if, in addition, the payment has to be done with scarce[39] foreign exchange, the burden becomes intolerable. As Vanek[39] puts it, for a country with scarce foreign exchange reserves, the need to use those reserves paying for imports from other high-cost fellow-underdeveloped countries is the worst that can occur.[40]

The constraints put to intraregional trade by the absence of payment agreements has worried ECLA for a long time;[41] and although both the International Monetary Fund and the U.S. government have opposed the formation of a Latin American payment system based on currencies not used for ordinary international transactions (which is tantamount to saying on currencies other than the dollar), there is a growing sympathy in the academic community towards the Latin American point of view.[42]

The simple adoption of some convenient currency to settle intraregional transactions, however, would not prevent the possible emergence of trade imbalances. To prevent them, some provisions have been adopted by LAFTA along the lines of the reciprocity principle. In essence, this principle calls for promotion of trade flows from deficit to surplus countries, or vice-versa, for a reduction of flows from surplus to deficit countries, if the former alternative proves unfeasible. It has been acknowledged that the unfortunate implication of the second alternative is a holdback of the integration process, and so it has been accepted as a sort of necessary evil. Let us now clarify that trade-gains or losses are not the same thing as growth-gains or losses, and the reciprocity principle takes care only of the former. If promotion of trade is the main objective of the integration, as may be the case of Europe, we can ignore growth-gains or losses, but this is not the case of Latin America. Now consider the case of a country exporting exclusively raw materials to another country in the region that utilizes those materials in the manufacturing sector. It is perfectly feasible that the former will develop a trade surplus with respect to the latter. If we think of Venezuela vis-à-vis Brazil, this situation is not only feasible but imminent. According to the reciprocity principle, Venezuela should be in the case of promoting further imports from Brazil, which amounts to saying, further deviations of imports from cheaper sources to Brazil. If growth is tied up with industrialization, Brazil would be receiving all the gains and Venezuela none. It may be said that it is not the purpose of the Latin American integration to promote trade of primary products, but it is rather unreasonable to expect that Venezuela fail to specialize in mineral exports to the rest of the region. We can thus see that a payments agreement offers only a partial solution to the problem of trade imbalances. Later in this section we will see how the reciprocity principle has been supplemented.

4. In the first section a question was left open regarding the possibility that not all the participants will share in the growth gains arising from the integration. This point should be analyzed.

Along the lines of reasoning initiated by Heckscher[43] and Ohlin[44] and later followed by Stolper[45] and Samuelson[46] liberation of trade in the commodity market (which is the essence of free trade areas and customs unions) should tend to equalize factor prices. As a consequence of this, if any party is going to be hurt, it certainly cannot be a low income one. Simple observation of actual trade developments, however, whether in the international or in the interregional sphere, casts doubts on this equalizing tendency. A classical and often cited illustration is the case of Italy: the liberation of trade between the North and the South, brought about by the political unification of the country, has shown a polarization rather than an equalization tendency. In the Latin American framework a close counterpart is the Brazilian case where there is a marked divergence in the development paths of the backward Northeast and the advanced South. Trying to explain this contrast between facts and theory, we may first think of the very restrictive type of assumptions on which that theory is based: equal number of factors and products, constant returns to scale, absence of external economies, perfect competition. Strictly within the commodity market, another explanation has been offered in terms of the factor endowments of the countries practicing commercial intercourse. If the factor proportions with which two countries are endowed are sufficiently similar to preserve similarity, also, in the factor intensity of the products object of their trade, the liberation of this trade will result in the equalization tendency. But if the proportions of such initial endowments are so different as to permit reversals in the factor intensity of the products, no general statement can be made with respect to the tendency of the relative factor prices.[47] Given the ambiguity of these results in spite of the narrowness of the assumptions (essentially the same as those of the original theory) Johnson aptly asserts that this argument shows how little can be said! It indicates, however, some instances in which the polarization tendency may appear.

Let us now examine what happens when not only products but also factors are free to move, as occurs when we shift from customs unions to common markets. Although intuitively we may expect a distinct equalization tendency (factors, being free to move, they should go from places where their prices are low to places where they are high), this tendency has not appeared in Italy or Brazil. Myrdal observes that even in the U. S. it was not general until the government stepped in with huge area development programs. Why? Myrdal offers his explanation in terms of perverse factor movements. Those countries, or regions, which for some reason got started first so much advantage with respect to the others that they became poles of attraction for much of the capital and human resources of the latter.[48]

Acknowledging the existence of the problem, the steps that have been taken to solve it have been of two types: granting special privileges to countries at lower and intermediate levels of development[49] along the lines of the reciprocity principle already mentioned; and formulating complementarity agreements.[50] These agreements, arrived at by means of negotiations, consist of assigning specific industries to specific countries with the commendable purpose of avoiding wasteful duplications but, otherwise, with little or no attention to economic criteria of resource allocation. This measure, if short of a sophisticated planning discipline, would prevent the displacement of the union towards its production possibility and utility frontiers. In the absence of careful planning, there is no guarantee either that such agreements would permit an efficient use of internal and external economies. In fact, since the aim is to prevent geographical agglomeration of business, it is almost by necessity that external economies will be wasted. The earmarking of industries to geographical districts would let the producers feel that they had acquired rights to such districts. This would freeze the degree of monopoly, creating an atmosphere less favorable to undertake costly research to increase efficiency.[51] Few of the benefits of integration would remain. A union created along the lines of unplanned complementarity agreements would be a monster.

III

In the first section we have found that the case for economic integration arises from: (1) the welfare gains, both from the production and consumption points of view, inherent in a better resource allocation; (2) a better use of internal and external economies; (3) the emergence of an atmosphere more conducive to the creation of an indigenous technology; (4) a likely lower degree of monopoly; (5) a strengthening of the bargaining power; (6) enabling the union to close the trade gap.

In the second section we have found the following among the obstacles to Latin American integration: (1) the need to create a productive substratum (which is tantamount to saying industrialization) pari passu with the promotion of trade; (2) the deficiency of the transportation and payments systems; (3) the danger of an inequitable distribution of costs and benefits.

With respect to the first of these three points, we have seen that its inevitable consequence is a retardation of the process. Without ignoring this outcome, steps must be taken to avoid traps of stable equilibrium at low levels of income. Although capital formation is called to play an important role, there are indications that displacing the production function may be a better strategy than moving along it. This displacement requires, however, a technological revolution that cannot be achieved with an unprepared labor force; hence, a substantial upgrading of the human resources of the region appears indispensable.

With respect to the second point we have found that, given the scarcity of railroad, highway, and inland waterway facilities, Latin American international and intraregional trade depends primarily on ocean transportation, which, unfortunately, is not free from tremendous obstacles. As a consequence, the transportation problem should be simultaneously tackled on several fronts. Especial attention should be paid to highway development because: (1) it is more independent than ocean transportation from the interference of foreign powers, (2) Latin America has a considerable excess capacity in the automobile industry[52] which could be economically utilized promoting automotive transportation.

With respect to the third point, we have seen that the reciprocity principle adopted to take care of it at best disposes only of the trade losses accruing to some countries, and that at worst it not only retards the slow-moving integrating process, but may even enhance the divergence in rates of growth. Finally, we have seen that provisions of the type of complementarity agreements simply prevent the attainment of many of the benefits of integration. If the problem is one of attaining these benefits subject to the constraints analyzed in the second section, it does not make sense to propose patterns of integration ignoring the existence of such obstacles; but it makes even less sense to remove the obstacles in a way inconsistent with the attainment of the benefits. A good solution has to pay attention to both sides of the problem. There are two ways to achieve this purpose: one along a dirigistic approach, the other along a free trade approach. Both have been summarized by Balassa,[53] and each has pros and cons. Probably the main shortcoming of the former is that it requires a complicated planning machinery, for which Latin America is ill prepared either technically or politically. The main disadvantage of the free trade approach seems to be that, if left alone, it would result in the inequitable distribution of costs and gains we have discussed. However, it is possible to avoid this difficulty along the compensation principle of welfare economics.[54] As is frequent, the case may be of a compromise between the two approaches: go ahead refining the devices of supranational planning already started in the region but without disregarding the second approach. The creation of a compensation fund,[55] with all its difficulties, should be far simpler than the creation of an efficient planning machinery.

The writer is greatly indebted to W. E. Kuhn, Professor of Economics, and E. S. Wallace, Director of the Bureau of Business Research, both at the University of Nebraska.

1. See Jacob Viner, *The Customs Union Issue* (New York: Carnegie Endowment for International Peace, 1950), ch. iv. Free traders are interested in world welfare, without making any dynamic considerations. Protectionists are willing to accept some present sacrifices for the sake of future domestic welfare, i.e. for the sake of growth. Hence in the latter approach are implicit, if not explicit, dynamic considerations.

2. See, e.g., ECLA's *The Latin American Common Market,* 1959.

3. Raúl Prebisch, *The Economic Development of Latin America and Some of its Principal Problems* (Economic Commission for Asia and the Far East, 1949).

4. Bela Balassa, *The Theory of Economic Integration* (Homewood, Ill.: Richard D. Irwin, 1961).

5. Tibor Scitovsky, *Economic Theory and Western European Integration* (Stanford University Press, 1958).

6. Jan Tinbergen, *International Economic Integration* (Amsterdam: Elsevier, 1954); and "On the Theory of Economic Integration" in *Selected Papers* (Amsterdam: North Holland Publishing Co., 1959).

7. This is perfectly feasible in a free trade area, but becomes complicated in more advanced forms of integration (customs unions, common markets) because then the external tariffs have to be unified. Of course, if this unification takes place at the lower level, this condition is amply satisfied; however, this solution is rather unrealistic. If the unification takes place at the higher level, the condition is amply violated. Somewhere between these extremes the condition would be just exactly satisfied.

8. The mechanism is well-known and need not be repeated here. The interested reader may find it in Balassa, *op. cit.,* ch. ii and iii, or if more detail is wanted, in James E. Meade, *Trade and Welfare* (Oxford University Press, 1955), Parts II and III.

9. For a comprehensive treatment of indivisibilities see Abba Lerner, *The Economics of Control* (New York: Macmillan, 1944), ch. xv and xvi.

10. For purposes of a diagramatic illustration of
the above, suppose i) the existence of two products Y_1 and
Y_2 and two factors X_1 and X_2; ii) that the production of
both goods is subject to indivisibilities of the technological variety and that the smallness of the market creates a
monopolistic situation in both industries. In the average-
and-marginal-cost-curve diagram, this situation can be represented in Fig. 1. The quantities produced will be $\bar{y}_1$, of
Y_1 and $\bar{y}_2$ of Y_2. In the Edgework diagram, with dimensions
determined by the availability of factors X_1 and X_2, output
volumes $\bar{y}_1$ and $\bar{y}_2$ are represented by the levels of the isoquants correspondingly labeled. The economy will locate
itself on either of the intersections a or b. Since these
points lie off the contract curve (the locus of the tangency
points of the isoquants corresponding to the two industries),
in the transformation-curve diagram either of them will correspond to a point like c lying inside the curve of Fig. 3.
Suppose, now, that the enlargement of the market destroys
the monopolistic situation in both industries and that the
output volume can be carried to the points of minimum aver-
age cost. These outputs volumes will now be $\bar{\bar{y}}_1$ and $\bar{\bar{y}}_2$ The
new situation will correspond to point e on the contract
curve dd of Fig. 2 and on the transformation curve of Fig. 3.

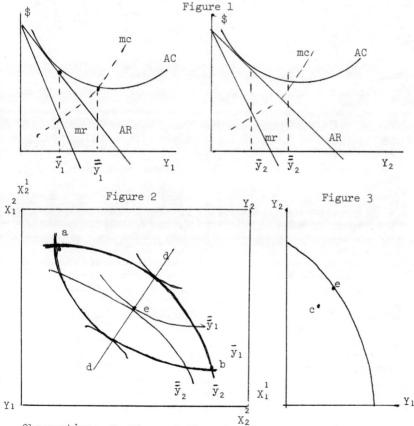

Figure 1

Figure 2

Figure 3

Observation: In Figure 2 the subscripts of the X's correspond to factors, whereas their superscripts correspond to
products.

11. Here, Scitovsky's external pecuniary economies are in point. Suppose that the opening of a new factory raises the price of its inputs and lowers the price of its output. Suppose, also, that both inputs and output are intermediary products that are going to be produced and used, respectively, by some other productive units. These other productive units will benefit, indeed, from the higher prices paid for their outputs or from the lower prices they have to pay for their inputs. These outer productive units are the "third parties" of my argument.

12. Moses Abramovitz, "Resources and Output Trends in the United States Since 1870" in *Occasional Papers,* No. 52 (National Bureau of Economic Research, 1956).

13. Henry J. Bruton, "Productivity and Growth in Latin America," *American Economic Review,* December 1967, pp. 1099-116.

14. Richard R. Nelson, "Aggregate Production Functions," *American Economic Review,* September 1964, pp. 576-606.

15. Robert Solow, "Technical Change and the Aggregate Production Function," *Review of Economics and Statistics,* 1957, pp. 312-20.

16. Abramovitz, Nelson, and Solow worked exclusively with U.S. figures. Bruton, insofar as advanced countries are concerned, worked with U.S., Western European, Canadian, and Japanese figures; his emphasis, however, is on Latin America.

17. It is true that investments are capital formation regardless of the excess capacity that they may be creating. Moreover, some excess capacity is inevitable even when investment is performed with maximum care. But this is hardly the case of the excess capacity existing in Latin America. See, e.g., Sidney Dell, *A Latin American Common Market* (Oxford University Press, 1966), pp. 19-24 and 134-36. We must recognize that on this ground, among others, for the same quantity of investment there are differences in quality.

18. The regional rate of growth, measured in terms of the growth of the per capita gross domestic product, has shown a steadily decreasing tendency over the period 1950-1965 (see OAS, *La Alianza Para el Progreso y las perspectivas del desarrollo de América Latina, Examen del primer quinquenio,* 1967, Table 1.1), which the Alliance, launched in 1961, was unable to neutralize. Correlating average rates of growth of individual countries during the period 1961-65 (extracted from the same source) on the one hand, with net dollar inflows in the same countries between 1961-64 (extracted from a mimeographed document prepared by the

Department of Economic Affairs of the OAS for the 5th meetings of the Inter-American Social and Economic Council) on the other, a (slightly) negative index was found.

19. Balassa, *op. cit.*, p. 183.

20. As Lerner puts it,"If the size of the indivisibilities is greater than the size of the market, perfect competition with free enterprise is doomed...If the size of the market is greater than the size of the indivisibility, so that the output of the firm is sufficient to reduce the indivisibility to insignificance, perfect competition is possible." Lerner, *op. cit.*,pp. 180-81.

21. The U.S. policy of subsidizing domestic farming; the E E C policy of discriminating in favor of former African colonies.

22. Professor Kuhn has called my attention to the theoretical meaninglessness of the phrase "import needs"; however, it is possible to assign to it an operational content with respect to some predetermined rate of growth, for example. The critical reader may still feel somewhat uneasy with the "trade-gap" notion.

23. For a summary exposition of the "trade gap" theory, see Dell, *op. cit.*, pp. 9-11.

24. Balassa, *op. cit.*, pp. 25-35.

25. For analysis of these equilibria see Richard R. Nelson, "A Theory of the Low Level Equilibrium Trap," *American Economic Review*, Dec. 1956, pp. 894-908 and Robert Solow, "A Contribution to the Theory of Economic Growth," *Quarterly Journal of Economics*, Feb. 1956.

26. Simon Hanson, *Economic Development in Latin America* (Washington, D.C.: Inter-American Affairs Press, 1951), pp. 341-45, cites the case of a U.S. project to construct about 1,000 miles of the Inter-American Highway across Central America. Although the initial attempts related to it date back to the 1930's, formally the project was started only in 1941, and abandoned after two years of work, frustrations, and completion of only 347 miles at a cost of $36 million. This gives an idea of the magnitude of the Latin American transportation problem.

27. Hanson, *op. cit.*, ch. xi.

28. Robert T. Brown, *Transportation and the Economic Integration of South America* (Brookings Institution, 1966), pp. 188-94.

29. OAS, *América en cifras, 1965: Situación eco-nómica: 3 Comercio, transporte, comunicaciones y turismo,* (1966); for the highway figures, Table 333-11 for the rail-road figures, Tables 333-01 to 333-02.

30. ECLA, *Economic Survey of Latin America,* (1963), pp. 95-96. Also Brown, *op. cit.,* p. 44.

31. ECLA, *Latin America and the United Nations Conference on Trade and Development,* pp. 128-134, cited by Enrique Angulo, "Transportation and Intra-Latin American Trade," in M. L. Wionczek, ed., *Latin American Economic Integration* (New York: Frederick A. Praeger, 1966), p. 178. Also ECLA, *Economic Survey of Latin America,* p. 101.

32. Dell, *op. cit.,* p. 103.

33. *Ibid.,* p. 102. The exact number of Latin American lines cannot be mentioned, but the Latin American Shipowners Association of LAFTA countries started in 1963 with sixty members. See Angulo, *op. cit.,* p. 181, who cites *Comercio Exterior,* XIII (December 1963), pp. 920-21.

34. Angulo, *op. cit.,* p. 186, mentions this type of invitation extended by the European River Plate Conference to Uruguayan shipowners.

35. OAS, *Informe sobre actividades portuarias,* doc. 18-E (July 1962), cited by Dell, *op. cit.,* p. 102.

36. Angulo, *op. cit.,* p. 186.

37. Dell, *op. cit.,* p. 107, citing again the Joint Economic Committee, states that the amount of the subsidy received by the U.S. shipping industry is of the order of $350 million a year.

38. Angulo, *op. cit.,* pp. 187-189, and Dell, *op. cit.,* pp. 105-108, cite a number of illustrative cases.

39. Jaroslav Vanek, "Las uniones de pagos entre países de menor desarrollo, eficaz instrumento de integración económica," *El Trimestre Economico,* July-September 1965, pp. 524-29.

40. Vanek's argument is based on two assumptions. One is the (artificial) undervaluation of convertible currencies in both the import and the export countries. The other is that the economic rent that corresponds to the scarce foreign exchange (scarcity arising from its under-valuation) is reaped by someone, whether the government or the importers. Suppose that the beneficiary is the government; then, what the procedure amounts to is an ad valorem tax on the use of the foreign exchange. From the point of

view of exports, there is no tax because there is no use of foreign exchange; however, the overvaluation of the domestic currency works its way, as is well known by the theory of international trade, raising the prices of exports. Thus, as long as undervalued foreign exchange is used, if one good is going to be the object of (interregional) trade, its CIF cost has to be lower than the domestic cost by at least the sum of the overvaluation of the two domestic currencies. Given the rather high rates of such overvaluation predominant in underdeveloped countries, and particularly in Latin America, the former consideration implies that there must be a sizable difference in production costs (of the order of 100% according to Vanek), which is another serious constraint for trade among those countries. Of course, this difficulty disappears if the scarce currency is not required to pay for this kind of imports. This is why Vanek's main conclusion is that even in the absence of any formal integration, the simple establishment of a payments union would tremendously enhance trade among underdeveloped countries.

Professor Vanek has further clarified his views, in a letter to this writer, as follows: "exchange scarcity tariffs are only a device to extract part of the scarcity rent in the sense that if intra-(customs)-union tariffs were completely eliminated without a payments union, only income distribution would change, but the inefficiency of regional resource allocation would remain, unchanged in degree. Thus it can be concluded—within the neoclassical general equilibrium—that with region-wide overvaluation significant benefits for the region can be derived from a regional payments union. Of course, both unions in combination will be preferable to either union undertaken separately."

41. See, e.g., ECLA, *Multilateral Compensation and International Trade* (Santiago, 1949).

42. See, e.g., Raymond F. Mikesell, "Algunos problemas y posibles formas de abordar la solucion del problema de pagos dentro de la ALALC," in CEMLA, *Cooperación financiera en América Latina* (Mexico City, 1963); Robert Triffin, "Una cámara de compensación y unión de pagos latinoamericana," in CEMLA, *op. cit.*; and Vanek, *op. cit.*

43. Eli Heckscher, "The Effects of Foreign Trade on the Distribution of Income" in H. S. Ellis and L. A. Metzler, eds., *Readings in the Theory of International Trade* (Philadelphia: Blackiston Company, 1950).

44. Bertil Ohlin, *Interregional and International Trade* (Harvard University Press, 1933).

45. Wolfgang Stolper and Paul Samuelson, "Protection and Real Wages," in Ellis and Metzler, *op. cit.*

46. Paul A. Samuelson, "Prices of Factors and Goods in General Equilibrium," *Review of Economic Studies*, 1953-54, pp. 1-21.

47. See Harry G. Johnson, *International Trade and Economic Growth* (Harvard University Press, 1961), pp. 25-28.

48. See Gunnar Myrdal, *Rich Lands and Poor* (New York: Harper, 1957), especially ch. iii, where the theory is presented with respect to regions, and ch. xi, where it is applied to international trade. It is possible to recognize in Myrdal's argument a strong similarity with the "agglomerative tendencies" of location theory.

49. See Dell, *op. cit.*, chap. vii.

50. *Ibid.*, pp. 64-68 and 129-36.

51. Along a Schumpeterian line of reasoning, it may be argued that monopoly is not necessarily bad, because it enables research, technological progress, and innovation. This is true when there is freedom of entry in the industry, freedom to come out with new ideas and products that may displace the old ones; in other words, when there is potential, if not actual, competition. This is not true if both potential and actual competition are killed by what I have termed "frozen degree of monopoly."

52. Dell, *op. cit.*, p. 19.

53. Balassa, *op. cit.*, pp. 7-10, where the word "dirigistic" is used.

54. For a compact but comprehensive discussion of what I am terming "compensation principle" see J. Henderson and R. Quandt, *Microeconomic Theory* (New York: McGraw-Hill, 1958), pp. 219-20. A discussion more closely connected with our case in point can be found in Lerner, *op. cit.*, p. 363.

55. Alfredo E. Roldan, "Una nota sobre integraciones económicas," *Económica* (Universidad Nacional de la Plata), May-August, 1965. The proposal presented in this study is a straightforward application of the "compensation principle": if the benefits of integration accrue only to some of the participants, but not all, the privileged parties should give up part of their gains for the benefit of the others, which otherwise would not have any inducement to remain in the union. The "compensation fund" is only a scheme to channel those benefits from one group to the other.

CHAPTER **8** A COMPARISON BETWEEN
EUROPEAN AND LATIN
AMERICAN INTEGRATION

By Antonio R. Sarabia, Partner
Lord, Bissell and Brook
Chicago

GENERAL

This study compares some aspects of the integration of
the present European Economic Communities[1] and the proposed
Latin American Common Market.[2] Most of the Latin American
countries are members of the Latin American Free Trade Association or of the Central American Common Market.

Today the word "integration" is much used. I use it here
in the sense of economic integration, as exemplified by a common
market. A common market "goes beyond the removal of internal
tariffs and the creation of a common external tariff to the elimination of barriers to mobility among the member countries of workers and managers, of capital, and even of enterprises. It thus
not only promotes specialization in countries within the region,
but also encourages cooperation or unification in industrial and
other production, and in the structure of business organization.
As the common market proceeds, moreover, its increasing ir-
revocability encourages the businessman to commit investments
sooner and on a longer term than would be the case with less
complete forms of integration."[3]

The present members — the original members for that
matter — of the European Economic Communities (EEC) are
Belgium, West Germany, France, Italy, Luxembourg, and The
Netherlands.

The members of the Latin American Free Trade Association (LAFTA) are Argentina, Bolivia, Brazil, Chile, Colombia, Ecuador, Mexico, Paraguay, Peru, Uruguay, and Venezuela.
The members of the Central American Common Market (CACM)
are Costa Rica, El Salvador, Guatemala, Honduras, and Nicaragua.

The Latin American countries are those with Spanish,
Portuguese or French background.[4] Panama, the Dominican
Republic, Haiti, and Cuba are not members of LAFTA or CACM.
Cuba has gone the way of communism and has been expelled from
the Organization of American States (OAS).

Cuba, so long as it retains its communist affiliations, is
out. Haiti and the Dominican Republic, as parts of an island in
the West Indies, present special problems. The former British

West Indies, now independent, such as Jamaica, Barbados, Trinidad and Tobago, as well as Guyana, on the north coast of South America, are not "Latin American."

If we think in terms of continental Latin American integration, starting with Mexico at the north and ending with Argentina and Chile at the extreme south, the only non-member of either LAFTA or CACM is Panama. We are talking then about a proposed Common Market among 17 independent nations, as compared to six in the EEC.

In the EEC, we have four different languages.[5] In Latin America, except for Portuguese-speaking Brazil, all the others speak Spanish. Both groups follow the Civil Law system. Both groups form part of Western Society. The broad cultural backgrounds are those of western man. The traditions of Portugal and Spain — as part of Western Europe — became implanted in Latin America.

SOME COMPARISONS

The countries of Europe prior to World War II were industrialized. There was a tradition of looking overseas for export markets. The possibilities of world trade were well known.[6]

Because of regional isolation, different local conditions and rates of political development, the legal systems, while having a common Civil Law cornerstone, have tended to develop in divergent manners.[7] National pride and the legal profession's pride in its own institutions, inhibit development and changes in the law, and make difficult the goals of unification of the law. The one great step was the adoption of the Código Bustamante in 1928.[8] Thus, the difficulties in the way to the attainment of a treaty similar to the Treaty of Rome, which established the European Economic Community in 1958, can be clearly seen.

As I stated some years ago: "The execution of the treaty creating the European Common Market in 1957 can compare in scope with the execution of the Constitution of the United States in 1787. In the history of western man, each represents a bold new concept and a great step forward in the legal and economic organization of society."[9]

As stated by Eric Hoffer in his book The Ordeal of Change [10] it is human nature to fear and resist any change. There is a saying in Spanish which epitomizes this: "Más vale malo por conocido que bueno por conocer."[11] It takes a great crisis to have society accept the "radical" changes suggested by scholars and men of vision.

Thus, the Industrial Revolution which started in England about 1750 and the French Revolution of 1789 were sufficiently unsettling to break the molds of tradition. Something similar can be said for the Mexican Revolution of 1910 and the Russian Revolution of 1917.

After World War II, Europe, realizing the need for economic unity in order to be able to compete with the economies of the United States and Russia, which indicated that mass production and mass consumption, unhampered by restriction, were important factors in economic development, took the steps which culminated in the EEC of the Six. Thus, the Treaty of Rome[12] which became effective on January 1, 1958, stated as its main purpose in Article 2:

> It shall be the aim of the Community, by establishing a Common Market and progressively approximating the economic policies of Member States, to promote throughout the Community a harmonious development of economic activities, a continuous and balanced expansion, and increased stability, an accelerated raising of the standard of living and closer relations between its Member States.

We are all familiar with the great progress made since January 1958, as well as with the difficulties which the EEC faces. It is interesting to note that the difficulties have tended to increase as stability and prosperity have increased, and as the threat of Soviet power has tended to be obscured. The economic threat of the United States has also tended to diminish during these years, although there are those, such as Jean-Jacques Servan-Schreiber, [13] who point out the challenge presented by American managerial and technological development.

We should also keep in mind that the Rome Treaty was, in a sense, the culmination of the plan presented on May 9, 1950, by the French statesman Robert Schuman, with the aid of, among others, Konrad Adenauer, Alcide de Gasperi, Jean Monnet, and Paul Henri Spaak. [14] This plan, presented to the Six, resulted in a new organization, the European Coal and Steel Community.

Thus, if we take the LAFTA Treaty of Montevideo[15] and the CACM Treaty of Managua[16] as representing some of the early European efforts towards economic unification[17] we can then see that the Presidents' Declaration of Punta del Este of April 1967 — although it sets 1970 as the starting date and 15 years later as a completion date — marks the specificity and urgency which were present when Robert Schuman presented his plan of May 1950 for the European Coal and Steel Community.

THE DECLARATION AND THE TREATIES

The Montevideo Treaty and the Presidents' Declaration both make reference to a common market for Latin America. [18]

Declaration of the Presidents

        Section I of the Declaration states:

     The Presidents of the Latin American Republics resolve to create progressively, beginning in 1970, the Latin American Common Market, which shall be substantially in operation in a period of no more than 15 years....

     The President of the United States of America, for his part, declares his firm support for this promising Latin American initiative.

     Section II, Chapter I, states:

     Section 1.d.:   The Latin American Common Market will be based on the improvement of the two existing integration systems: [LAFTA and CACM]
...
In 2.a. it is stated that the Council of Ministers of LAFTA is instructed to adopt the measures necessary to "accelerate the process of converting LAFTA into a common market."

     In 2.b.: To coordinate progressively economic policies and instruments and to harmonize national laws to the extent required for integration...

     In 2.c.: To promote the conclusion of sectoral agreements for industrial complementation... , and

     In 2.d.: To promote the conclusion of temporary subregional agreements...

     With respect to CACM, the Presidents commit themselves to:

        3.a.   To carry out an action program that will include...:

             1. Improvement of the customs union and establishment of a Central American monetary union;

             2. Completion of the regional network of infrastructure;

             3. Promotion of a common foreign-trade policy;

             4. Improvement of the common market in agricultural products, and implementation of a joint, coordinated industrial policy;

5. Acceleration of the process of free movement of manpower and capital within the area;

6. Harmonization of the basic legislation required for economic integration.

Under Section 4, the Latin American Presidents commit themselves:

a. Not to establish new restrictions on trade among Latin American countries, except in special cases, ...

b. To establish, by a tariff cut or other equivalent measures, a margin of preference within the region for all products originating in Latin American countries, ...

c. To have the measures in the two preceding paragraphs applied immediately among the member countries of LAFTA, ...

g. To have a committee established composed of the executive organs of LAFTA and CACM to coordinate implementation of the foregoing points...

In 5: The Presidents of the member states of the OAS agree:

a. To mobilize financial and technical resources within and without the hemisphere to contribute to the solution of problems in connection with the balance of payments, industrial readjustments, and retraining of the labor force that may arise from a rapid reduction of trade barriers during the period of transition toward the common market, ...

e. To make available to Central America, with the Alliance for Progress, adequate technical and financial resources, ... for the purpose of accelerating the Central American economic integration program.

f. To make available, within the Alliance for Progress and pursuant to the provisions of the Charter of Punta del Este, the technical and financial resources needed to accelerate the preparatory study and work involved in converting LAFTA into a common market.

There are also chapters on "Multinational Action for Infrastructure Projects"; "Measures to Improve International Trade Conditions in Latin America"; "Modernization of Rural Life and Increase of Agricultural Productivity, Principally of

101

Food"; "Educational, Technological, and Scientific Development and Intensification of Health Programs"; and "Elimination of Unnecessary Military Expenditures."

No one can quarrel with these declarations or these goals. The serious question is whether they portray the millennium or a practical program. Strictly speaking, these are expressions of the Presidents present at Punta del Este. This is not a treaty requiring ratification, nor is it a self-executing document.

Managua Treaty

The Managua Treaty states in its Article 1:

> The Contracting States agree to set up among themselves a common market which should be fully established in not more than five years from the date of the entry into force of this Treaty. They also undertake to set up a customs union among their territories.

There are provisions for free trade rights for all products of national origin with transitional arrangements (Art. 3), equalization of excise and similar taxes (Art. 6), on violation of export subsidies and unfair business practices (Chap. III), freedom of transit of goods (Chap. IV), industrial integration (Chap. VI), establishment of the Central American Bank for Economic Integration (Chap. VII), and fiscal incentives to industrial development (Chap. VIII).

Article 31 provides for a duration of the Treaty of 20 years from date of entry into force, and for indefinite renewal. At the end of 20 years, any member may resign, but only effective five years after giving notice.

Montevideo Treaty

The Montevideo Treaty provides in its Article 1 for the establishment of a Free Trade Area over a period of "not more than 12 years from the date of the Treaty's entry into force."

The Treaty provides for "National Schedules" and a "Common Schedule" (Art. 4), as well as for Economic Complementarity (Chap. III), Most-Favored-Nation Treatment (Chap. IV), Equal Treatment with Respect to Taxation (Chap. V), agricultural provisions (Chap. VII), special treatment for countries "at a relatively less advanced stage of economic development" (Chap. VIII), for a review of the provisions at the end of the original 12-year period (Art. 61), unlimited duration for the Treaty (Art. 63), and provisions for resignation (with a five-year saving clause) (Art. 64).

Even a brief examination of these three documents shows the cautious and mixed feelings represented therein.

In the Presidents' Declaration, the unique position of the United States is apparent. In spite of the elegant language, it is implicit that somehow the United States is expected — or it is hoped that it will — finance a good chunk of this. Aside from the explicit references to the OAS and the Alliance for Progress, the very fact that the Declaration was under the auspices of the OAS, which is largely financed by the United States, makes the implication clear.

The Montevideo Treaty and the Managua Treaty are similar in the obvious reluctance to a firm commitment.

Rome Treaty

Contrast this with the manner of treatment in the Rome Treaty. Article 2 which gives the "aim of the Community" has been quoted above. Still under Part One we have a list of "the activities of the Community" (Art. 3); the "Institutions," namely, the Assembly, the Council, the Commission and the Court of Justice (Art. 4).

Part Two provides for the free movement of goods, agriculture, free movement of persons, services and capital, and transport.

Part Three establishes the "Common Rules" for competition, antidumping, fiscal provisions, restrictive trading practices, as well as the "Economic Policy," "Social Policy," and "The European Investment Bank."

More important, the Rome Treaty as the source of Common Market law contains two types of provisions. [19] The first, following the usual form of international agreements, lays down certain obligations which are binding on the member states alone and are not directly applicable to their nationals. This type of provision is not self-executing. It binds the member states to take the necessary measures under their own municipal (local) law for the fulfillment of these obligations. The majority of the provisions concerning the customs union are under this classification. The other type of provisions consists of a code of common rules which are self-executing. Such rules are directly applicable without the need for any further action by any member states other than the ratification of the Treaty. An example is Article 85 which prohibits certain agreements in restraint of competition between "enterprises." [20]

COMMENTS

The Presidents Declaration calls for action on the part of the Latin American nations represented there, leading to the

103

first steps toward   a Latin American Common Market.   Part Two, Chapter I, Section 4g calls for a committee composed of members of the executives of LAFTA and CACM to "coordinate implementation" of the steps to be taken by the Latin American countries. This committee has been organized and has begun its work.

The Rome Treaty states that any European State may apply to join (Article 237).   The Managua Treaty states that it shall remain open to any Central American State (Article 33). The Montevideo Treaty states that it shall remain open to other Latin American States (Article 58).

The Rome Treaty establishes a transitional period of 12 years during which a complete customs union will be organized (Article 8).   The Managua Treaty establishes no time limit for the creation of a customs union.   The Montevideo Treaty establishes a term of "not more than 12 years" for the complete establishment of the Free Trade Area (Article 2).

The Rome Treaty established the European Investment Bank to assist in the development of the Common Market (Title IV).

The Managua Treaty did not provide for such a Bank. However, the Central American Bank of Economic Integration was established as a financial organ of the Common Market by a separate agreement; it, with the Central American Clearing House,serves as the basis of the regional financial system.[21]

The Commission under the Rome Treaty, subject to certain controls by the Council and the Parliament, is the executive body representing the communities (Part Five, Title I).   The Managua Treaty has an Executive Council and under that, really performing the functions of the executive, the Permanent Secretariat.   The Economic Council is the representative body (Chap. IX).   The Montevideo Treaty has an Executive Committee, with the Conference of the Contracting Parties as the representative organization (Chap. IX).

For the settlement of disputes, the Rome Treaty provides for the Court of Justice (Part Five, Title I).   The Managua Treaty provides for arbitration (Article 26).   The Montevideo Treaty has no specific provisions for the settlement of disputes.

Thus, the Rome Treaty has been more concerned with unity and less concerned with safe-guarding national sovereignty It provides for a relatively simple relation between the Commission, the Council and the Parliament.   The Council can issue directives to the individual members (Article 100) where required for the approximation of the laws of the Member States. Further, the Court of Justice has comprehensive jurisdiction, being at the same time an international court to regulate disputes between the Member States, and a constitutional court to interpret the Treaty and define the powers of the other Institutions.   It also has the functions of an administrative court to supervise the legality of the acts of the Common Market and acts as a civil court in respect to breaches of contract or torts committed on behalf of the Common Market. [22]

Implicit in the structure of these three different Treaties is the greater self-sufficiency existing in the Rome Treaty. The Rome Treaty represents the intent of the Six to form a union. The other two treaties represent the misgivings and attempts to safeguard, at all costs, national sovereignty. It is evident that, if any such union is to work, a good deal of "national sovereignty" will have to yield to the greater interests of the whole.

However, it can be fairly said that the members of LAFTA and CACM, considering the realities and the legal structure of their respective treaties, have accomplished just as much, if not more than the members of the EEC. If we consider the starting point — the point of departure — as of the date of entry into force of each Treaty, taking into account the political social, economic, educational differences and other divisive forces, we must stand in admiration of LAFTA and CACM.

It is a mixed blessing for the Latin American countries that the road to be traveled is so long and the goals to be reached immediately are so great. And yet, if a man does not dream big dreams, how can he ever accomplish them?

Sometimes nations and peoples need the tempering of adversity to realize their potential. It may be that the current balance of payments difficulty being experienced by the United States along with the problems of the Viet Nam war and the Negro in U.S. society, may turn out to be a great benefit to the Latin American countries, since it will force some U.S. disengagement from "foreign aid."

The latest book by Gunnar Myrdal, Asian Drama. An Inquiry into the Poverty of Nations, has a principal theme: "Economic development... among the less developed countries, must be generated and achieved mainly from internal sources..."[23] This reflects "realism in economic studies."[24]

It is in this area where the United States, under its Protestant proselytizing ethic, has gravely misled all the developing nations, and particularly Latin America. We have acted toward Latin America as if it were a wayward child. And, unfortunately, Latin America has acted as a delinquent teenager. We are both at fault. It is time we stopped our paternalism and it is time the Latin American nations grew up. All the energy which is spent envying and hating the United States can better be spent in working and creating their own affluent society. It is to be hoped that the United States and Latin America can produce the type of leadership required at this crucial time. In a way, the kind of leadership that each country produces is but an extension of the worth of its own people.

105

Implicit in this is the value judgment that the western way of life and standards are the desirable ones. Even Marxism — which in its modern interpretation under Russia and communist China exalts hard work as a desirable goal — can be said to be an offshoot of capitalism.[25]

What this comes to, is that the Latin American nations have to make their own choice and effort to move up this western ladder. Given the world situation today, this will come from a "capitalist democratic revolution" or from a "communist totalitarian revolution." I see only one choice for us.

I have great faith in the ability of the Latin American nations to move forward. I am very optimistic.

The urgency for the need for action as individual nations and as members of the Latin American Common Market has to be grasped by Latin America. It can be, if the benefits to be derived from a common market — along with some of the sacrifices involved in creating it — are understood.

NOTES

1. Under the Treaty Establishing a Single Council and a Single Commission of the European Communities, signed at Brussels, April 8, 1965. Under the Treaties of the European Coal and Steel Community, The European Economic Community and the European Atomic Energy Committee a Single Council and a Single Commission of the European Communities were established. Thus, the Six under these three separate Treaties are now known as The European Economic Communities (4 *International Legal Materials* 776, July 1965).

2. The formal proposal for a Latin American Common Market was made under the Declaration of the Presidents of America. Organization of the American States, *Official Document, OEA/Ser. K/XIV/1.1,* Doc. 4 (English), April 14, 1967.

The signatories of the Declaration were: The Presidents of Argentina, Brazil, Colombia, Costa Rica, Chile, El Salvador, United States of America, Guatemala, Honduras, Mexico, Nicaragua, Panama, Paraguay, Peru, Dominican Republic, Venezuela, and Uruguay in that order. Also signing was the Representative of the President of the Republic of Haiti and the Prime Minister of Trinidad and Tobago. Trinidad and Tobago became a member of OAS in 1967 and in December of that year, Barbados also joined the OAS. The President of Ecuador was present but did not sign and Bolivia was not represented.

3. *Regional Integration and the Trade of Latin America*, Committee for Economic Development, supplementary paper No. 22, January 22, 1968, p. 22 (hereafter cited as CED).

4. See definition of "Latin America" e.g. in *Webster's New World Dictionary* (World Publishing Co., 1957).

5. The European Economic Communities have four languages: French, German, Dutch, and Italian. See e.g. Art. 248, Rome Treaty.

6. "The two areas differ markedly in such basic factors as topography, physical facilities, social organization, and political traditions, as well as such economic aspects as the structure of their industries, their trading patterns, and their financial and other institutions. The obstacles to economic integration in any of its major forms are much greater in Latin America than in Europe. Whereas Europe had achieved a highly developed transportation and communications network long before the signing of the Treaty of Rome, a dominant characteristic of Latin America is the relative isolation not only of one country from another but of regions within countries, the result of the physical barriers and distances in Latin America as well as of its traditional 'colonial' orientation toward Europe and the United States. Also, the lack of diversification, especially in agriculture — where several countries concentrate on the same product, for example, coffee, and meat — does not provide a broad basis for trade with their neighbors." CED, p. 27.

The isolation and lack of incorporation into the national life of large segments of native Indian populations in such countries as Peru, Mexico, Guatemala, and Colombia are well known.

7. Those of us who have occasion to work with the legal systems of Latin American countries are acutely aware of these not-so-fine differences.

8. This is a complete codification in 437 sections, including the entire international private law in 295 sections and in the remainder, criminal and procedural conflicts law... This Code of International Private Law was adopted at the Sixth Pan-American Conference in Havana on February 20, 1928, and has been ratified by 15 Latin American States. Rabel, *1 The Conflict of Laws: A Comparative Study* (University of Michigan Press, 1945).

9. Sarabia, "The European Common Market," *Journal of Accountancy*, May 1963, p. 54.

10. Hoffer, *The Ordeal of Change* (Harper & Row, 1963).

11.   Paraphrased: "No matter how bad the known is, it is better than the unknown."

12.   "Treaty establishing the European Economic Community and related documents" published in English by the Publishing Services of the European Communities.

13.   Servan-Schreiber, *Le défi américain* (Paris: Editions Denoel, 1967).

See "U.S. Business Taking Over Europe?" *U.S. News & World Report*, November 20, 1967, p. 103.

14.   "The enthusiasts inside the Six... came to the conclusion that the success of the Coal and Steel Community justified further efforts on the economic side... They decided to set up a committee of government representatives under the chairmanship of M. Spaak... The result... was the Spaak Report... which set out very clearly the essential elements which would have to be incorporated into the treaty in order to achieve the declared aim of the Six... after much hard bargaining the Rome Treaty was signed on March 25, 1967." Campbell and Thompson, *Common Market Law* 6 (1962).

15.   Latin American Free Trade Association, Montevideo Treaty, February 18, 1960.

16.   General Treaty of Central American Economic Integration, Managua Treaty, December 13, 1960.

17.   Campbell and Thompson n.14 *supra*, 2 and ff.

18.   The Montevideo Treaty states in its preamble: "Determined to persevere in their efforts to establish, gradually and progressively, a Latin American Common Market..."

The Presidents Declaration states e.g., Part Two, Chapter I: "1a. Beginning in 1970, to establish progressively the Latin American Common Market..."

19.   "The Rome Treaty is a unique document because it is at once a multinational agreement, a constitution and a law." Sarabia, n.9 *supra*, p. 55.

20.   Gaudet, *The Common Market and the Law*, 5 (1961).

21.   Simonds, "The Central American Common Market," *International and Comparative Law Quarterly*, XVI (1967), p. 918.   The Peso Centro-americano ($CA), at par with U.S. dollar, was set up in 1964 for clearing house purposes, n. 16, *Ibid*.

22. Sarabia n. 9 *supra*, p. 57.

23. Saulnier, Book Review of "Asian Drama," *Wall Street Journal*, April 4, 1968.

24. *Ibid*.

25. "And if Communism seems likely to become a vehicle for the transmission of Western achievement to non-Western countries it is due partly to the fact that Communism is a Western, and particularly a Capitalist, heresy which the West rejected." Hoffer n. 10 *supra*, p. 23.

CHAPTER **9** THE CASE AGAINST LATIN
AMERICAN INTEGRATION:
ECONOMIC AND POLITICAL
FACTORS

By   Donald Solar
Department of Economics
C. W. Post College
Long Island University

INTRODUCTION

At a summit meeting held in April, 1967, at Punta del
Este, Uruguay, the presidents of countries belonging to the Organization of American States gave "concrete expression to the ideals
of Latin American unity" by agreeing to create a Latin American
Common Market.

The Common Market will be based on the development
and convergence of the two existing subregional trading systems,
LAFTA and CACM, with provision for the entry of Latin American
countries not yet affiliated with either grouping.

Although the Action Program signed at Punta del Este
defines economic integration as a "collective instrument" for accelerating the over-all growth of the region, [1] provisions are included for insuring a balance of benefits among all of the member
countries. Thus, the relatively less industrialized countries are
to receive preferential treatment in matters of trade and technical
and financial co-operation, and with respect to the construction of
the physical infrastructure of the region. [2]

It is generally recognized that genuine economic integration among underdeveloped countries involves regional co-ordination of economic policy as well as the elimination of intraregional
trade barriers. The degree of integration may go as far as united
political action and the acceptance of some sort of supranational
planning authority.

While it is clear that the Common Market envisaged by
the OAS presidents goes beyond the simple pooling of markets,
the Punta del Este document does not specify the degree of "completion of Latin American integration" sought by its signers.

In 1960 the United States reversed its policy of resisting
the trend toward economic regionalism in Latin America and since
then has actively encouraged economic and political co-operation
among the OAS countries. The United States was not only a signatory of the Punta del Este agreement, but also pledged financial
support for the Latin American unity movement. Although no
major initiative has emerged for establishing a formal relationship
between a Latin American Common Market and the United States,

110

the possibility of such a development has been discussed in official circles. [3]

The first section of this study reviews the historical and intellectual sources of the development policy embodied in the Punta del Este agreement.

The following section analyzes the possibilities for national equalization policies as an alternative method of giving impetus to industrial development.

The final section attempts to explain why the current emphasis on regionalism will tend to reinforce existing obstacles to progress in Latin America.

I

Prior to the Great Depression, economic growth in the Latin American countries followed the traditional pattern of colonial economies producing mineral, agricultural, and raw materials for export to the more industrialized countries from whom they imported the manufactured goods they needed. This process of "externally induced development" ceased to operate after the crisis in 1929. [4]

The disruption of world markets which occurred during the early 1930's and the changing patterns of international supply and demand caused a drastic reduction in Latin America's terms of trade. Since then additional factors have tended to slow down the rate of growth of exports of agricultural products which have made up a large proportion of total exports. The most important markets for the exports of Latin America have populations which are not increasing rapidly and which have a low income-elasticity of demand for farm products.

It is those same countries, moreover, that have been most successful in expanding agricultural productivity, and have begun producing at home a number of foodstuffs they would otherwise have had to import. In the sphere of tropical products, Latin America has been faced with increasing competition from Africa and other areas.

Faced with a declining rate of increase in the demand for their agricultural and livestock products, the countries of Latin America turned to import-substituting industrialization (ISI) which became the driving force of economic development in that area under the intellectual leadership of Raúl Prebisch, former Executive Secretary of the Economic Commission for Latin America (ECLA). In brief, the implementation of the policy of ISI involves (1) the investment of capital, made available by domestic savings and transfers from advanced countries, in the construction of domestic facilities for the production of goods formerly imported; and (2) protection from previous suppliers abroad. Within Latin

111

America, ISI seemed to follow logically from the demonstrated existence of a national market for the previously imported product and from the need to devote foreign exchange to the purchase of technologically advanced capital goods. [5]

The official espousal of protectionism in Latin America aroused much criticism in Western academic circles. The desirability of a liberal system of international trade has been taken for granted by most Western economists since the classical economists produced the principle of comparative advantage: Freedom of trade permits each country to specialize in the production of those goods which it can produce most efficiently, and to avoid wasting resources on producing goods that it can produce only inefficiently, instead of importing such goods from countries that can produce them more efficiently and paying for them by exports of the goods that it can produce efficiently. [6]

The arguments for a liberal economic order capable of optimally allocating given world resources were derided by young Latin American economists who took the position that "static" efficiency conditions are not relevant to the problem facing the underdeveloped countries. When "dynamic" considerations of economic growth and development are taken into account everything becomes different. Liberal international economic policies are to blame for the condition of economic stagnation, and protectionism is an obvious remedy for that condition. [7]

The classical conceptual apparatus has been defended and refined by economists in the advanced countries. According to Harry Johnson, for example, the argument for a liberal economic order is even stronger in the dynamic context of growth and development than it is in the static concept of efficiency:

> ...the process of international competition even if it
> is allowed to operate only imperfectly contains two
> automatic mechanisms that tend to transmit the proc-
> ess of economic growth from the advanced countries
> to the underdeveloped or developing countries: the
> growth of demand for natural resource products, and
> the growth-induced upward trend in the price of labor
> in the advanced countries. [8]

The first aspect of the transmission process refers to the growing pressure of demand on natural resources which would stimulate exploration for and exploitation of new sources of supply, and the development of other parts of the world possessing such resources with the aid of capital, technology, and trained labor supplied by the center. [9]

Balassa has analyzed the process by which Britain's economic growth was transmitted to her suppliers of grain, cotton, timber, and meat during the nineteenth century. His findings indicate Britain's desire to forego agricultural protection, coupled with her increasing need for raw materials and the need of the industrializing continental countries, "goes far to explain the attainment of rapid rates of growth, and high living standards in several primary-producing countries in the temperate zone."[10]

The second important aspect of the transmission process relates to the rising demand for labor in the developed center and to the general tendency of technical progress to raise real wages if the supply of labor is not governed by the Malthusian population principle. The growing disparity between real wages in the center compared with the periphery makes it increasingly profitable to establish production facilities in the latter areas. Such facilities would be designed initially to service markets in the periphery formerly supplied from the center, and later, once the cost advantage outweighed the transport costs back to the center, to export to the center itself.[11]

Notwithstanding the impressive credentials and impeccable logic of the orthodox model of international development, the protectionist policy of ISI rapidly gained adherents in Latin America and by the 1950's had captured the imagination of the region's intellectual elite among economists and technicians. The traditional analysis was rejected in Latin America on the grounds that changes in the structure of the world economy had invalidated the notion of the international transmission mechanism. Rather than explaining the international diffusion of growth, the classical trade theory had been used to rationalize economic backwardness as the natural result of the international division of labor.

The gradual change in the intellectual atmosphere has been succinctly described by Hirschman:

> The phase of export-propelled growth (crecimiento hacia afuera) in Latin America lasted roughly from the middle of the nineteenth century until the Great Depression; and it took another twenty years, from 1929 to the Prebisch manifesto of 1949, before the end-of-export-propelled-growth became official Latin American doctrine.[12]

At about the same time that the limitations of free trade were becoming an important basis in Latin America for the belief in the need for deliberate policy interference in the allocative functions of international competition, the process of protected import-substitution began encountering an increasing number of difficulties. There was a growing awareness of the limitations and disadvantages of ISI as a route to economic development.[13]

The major difficulties encountered by ISI were attributable to the facts that the substitution of those types of manufactured consumer goods and capital goods which were easy to produce had been largely completed and that the national markets for these types of products were relatively restricted given the existing economic and social structure. The economic limitation of internal markets has been stressed by Jacques Chonchol:

Approximately one-half of the population of the region, those depending for a living on agricultural activities, together with appreciable sectors of the urban lumpenproletariat, hardly constitute a good market for manufactured consumer goods: their income is too low and there is no hope of improving it under present conditions.

In a message to UNCTAD I (in 1964), Prebisch explained that the "simple phase" of ISI had reached, or was reaching, its limit in the underdeveloped countries "where industrialization had made most progress." Criticizing the "inward-looking industrialization" of which he had been a prominent proponent, he recommended instead an outward-looking industrialization policy based primarily on the region-wide pooling of national markets as a means of combining scale economies with the advantage of international specialization. [14]

Until about 1956, theoretical literature on regional trade groupings was dominated by the thinking of classical and neoclassical economists from the advanced countries. [15]

From that analytical viewpoint customs unions are said to be beneficial to the extent that they lead to trade creation rather than trade diversion. Trade creation occurs when the elimination of customs duties between members in the union leads to the extinction of inefficient producers who could survive only behind tariff walls. When such tariff walls are eliminated, there will be a new trade flow into the country; there will also be a new outflow of commodities produced by those industries which, in the country in question, have proved more efficient than their competitors in other member nations.

Trade diversion, on the other hand, is what happens when goods formerly imported from countries outside the union are brought in from a member country in response to the new element of discrimination. Since the new source of imports is more expensive, trade diversion is detrimental. Trade creation leads to an improved allocation of existing resources, whereas trade diversion leads to an inferior allocation of existing resources. [16]

The application of this analysis to underdeveloped countries leads to the conclusion that preferential regional groups of these countries would divert more trade than they would create and for that reason should be avoided. This result was all the more certain, given the policy of deliberately interfering with the market allocation of industry among the member countries. [17]

The ECLA-school of economists and "técnicos" were not overly impressed by the negative implications of the conventional wisdom on unions of underdeveloped countries. From their point of view it was not most important to ask whether the regional removal of trade barriers would lead to a more-or-less efficient use of resources in the participating countries or throughout the world. They focussed instead on the prospect of realizing dynamic gains through new investment and a change in the pattern of investment and rested the economic case for Latin American integration on the belief that these dynamic gains will more than offset the net increase in trade diversion associated with the shift from national to regional protection. [18]

To recapitulate: The structural changes which convulsed world markets during the early 1930's ushered in a new phase of Latin American development, "crecimiento hacia adentro" or growth via the domestic market. The predominant mood of public policy during this period favored import-substituting industrialization within protected national markets and reflected the extent to which Prebisch's thesis had been accepted by the planners-technicians who administer national governments in Latin America.

After gathering strength during the Depression and during World War II and flourishing briefly during the early 1950's, the policy of ISI came up against the hard fact that efficiency and growth of industrial production in underdeveloped countries is dependent on, and limited by, the extent of the market open to producers.

As a way out of the "dilemma of seeming to have too little industrialization in development terms and too much as judged by static criteria of efficiency, "[19] the vanguard of Latin American economists were prompted to emphasize increasingly the need for the elimination or reduction of barriers to intraregional commerce. The trend toward economic union, as a method of broadening the market for industrial output and facilitating, thereby, the combination of scale economies with intra-area specialization, gave rise to LAFTA and CACM and found its broadest expression in the Punta del Este agreement of 1967.

Meaningful evaluation of a given policy for expanding industrial markets requires a knowledge of substitute approaches. For this reason the following section of this study analyzes a major policy alternative to regional economic integration.

II

There are at least three methods by which the market for industrial output can be expanded in Latin America. The first is the expansion of exports to world markets. The second is the increasing economic integration of the countries in the region in order to expand intraregional trade among them. The third method is the enlargement of the national market of the country itself through appropriate internal economic policies. [20]

The third alternative, which is the subject of this section, refers to the possibility of incorporating the rural masses of Latin America into the consumer markets of the national economies and implies a need for drastic change in the rural/agricultural sectors.

The basic features of Latin American agriculture are the great concentration of land in the hands of a few owners and the landlessness of great masses of the rural population. [21] While space prevents a review of the available data on wealth inequality in Latin America, it will suffice to consider the results of a recent study of Industrialization and the Distribution of Wealth in Peru published by the Land Tenure Center of the University of Wisconsin.

Besides documenting the existing high degree of inequality in the ownership of real estate, Chaplain, the author of the paper, attempted to test the hypothesis that wealth inequality in Peru increases during the process of industrialization by analyzing land concentration ratios in sixteen political units as related to various indices of industrial growth. He reported a correlation of .50 between "urbanism" and land concentration and a correlation of -.57 between "per cent of work force in agriculture" and land concentration — among other coefficients suggesting a direct relationship between degrees of industrialization and wealth inequality. [22]

Chaplain also indicated that the city of Lima ". . . probably has seen an over-all increase in inequality since 1930, if only due to the excessive numbers of migrants added on at the bottom."[23] The dimensions of the inequality problem in Peru is suggested by Chaplain's tentative conclusion that "Such an increase in class, regional, and international inequality may be more than the current evolutionary political system can bear."[24]

The main effects of land concentration in Latin America on the potential for agricultural progress and general development may be briefly summarized. Among the most negative consequences in terms of productivity is the inefficient use of land and labor associated with single-crop cultivation relied on by the large traditional estates and by many of the large modern plantations. [25] As Jacques Chonchol points out, "With the use of only small amounts of effort and capital — apart from land — and very little risk, it is possible to obtain a personal income which is more than satisfactory from the point of view of the owner's economic and social requirements and for his exercise of political influence."[26]

Due to a plentiful labor supply unorganized and not in possession of land or any immediately available alternative employment, wage levels are determined by the few leading landowners. In many instances, the total value of wages paid on large traditional-type estates equals less than 10 per cent of their gross product. [27]

Under these conditions, incentives for modernizing agriculture are weaker than the desire to accumulate land" . . . which by virtue of the political influence of the owner pays only a minimum in the way of taxation."[28] As a result of this system the value of land is greater as a source of personal income, social

116

prestige and political power than as a factor of agricultural production.[29]

Useful land is also kept unproductive for speculative purposes by absentee owners of large tracts in the more remote areas and, to a lesser extent, by many owners of the large, modern plantation-type enterprise.

Apart from its effects on productivity and the supply of agricultural products, land concentration is the cause of a very unequal distribution of agricultural income which itself is — on a per capita basis — significantly lower than the income obtainable in other sectors of the economy. The domestic agricultural product of Latin America was $558 per person engaged in farming for the 1963-65 period contrasted with $1,769 in the non-agricultural sector.[30]

The facts of income inequality within the agricultural sectors of the individual countries have been documented by several studies. The FAO, for example, has found that "in one important Latin American country" 60% of the families in agriculture received $210 or less in 1960; the average family income for this group was $175 or $2 to $4 per person per month. At the same time the upper 1% of the 9 million persons in this country's agriculture reported an average family income of $3,400 per year or 20 times the average of the lowest 60% (ignoring the unreported income received by this group).[31]

Mitchell and Schatan have attempted to estimate the quantitative impact of a rise in the earnings of the low income segment of the rural population on the demand for the output of traditional industry. According to their calculations, a 150% rise in the income of that group could be expected to quadruple their expenditures on textiles, footwear, apparel, wood, and furniture by 1980 at constant prices and assuming a rural population growth rate of 2% per year. This would represent a 40 to 60% increase over the total gross value of output sold by those branches of industry in 1950.[32]

Agrarian reform on the scale necessary to overcome demand deficiency in the domestic markets of Latin American countries raises issues that many generations of economists have sought to avoid. According to Gunnar Myrdal, economic theory was developed in such a way as to facilitate the formulation of problems in ways that avoid the equality issue.

Since Mill's sharp division between the sphere of production, on the one hand, and the sphere of distribution on the other, this device has been utilized by economists for the purpose of directing their analysis almost entirely to production and exchange, with relatively little attention being devoted to questions of income and wealth distribution and the need for distributional reform.[33]

Even Ricardo, whose primary interest was the relative

117

prices of the three productive factors — as well as the writers after him who came to represent the classical line in economic theory —were, on the whole, sympathetic to the doctrine of laissez-faire even with respect to income distribution. Their position on the latter issue was derived from Ricardo's theory of wages and the Malthusian population principle which together doomed to failure any "artificial interference" aimed at increasing the standard of living of the workers.[34] While the advent of birth control pulled out the props from under this motivation for opposing redistribution, a variant of Ricardo's wage theory still has theoretical relevance in the poorer nations.

In this connection, it is worth noting that the average annual growth rate of food production in Latin America has been approximately 2.5% in the last decade much less than the 3% (approximate) average annual growth rate of the area's population. Thus, Escobar Cerda, executive director of the IBRD, in an evaluation of the recent Caracas conference on "Population Policies in Relation to Development, " opined that the participating experts "undoubtedly" had in mind the impossibility of achieving the economic surplus necessary for the take-off towards development in societies where new beings continually use up this surplus.[35]

Apart from the Malthusian population trap, a concern about the impact of redistributional reforms on productivity levels has also been a dominant theme in discussions of the equality issue. Alfred Marshall wondered whether the desirability of economic equality "would . . .justify changes in the institution of property, or limitations of free enterprise even when they would be likely to diminish the aggregate of wealth."[36] The fact that the thinking of the great economists was permeated with bases for tolerating inequality has made it easier for propertied classes to resist demands for wealth redistribution with better consciences. Thus, at a recent round table on "Agricultural Development in Latin America" sponsored by the IDB, several representatives of the land-owning interests warned against the adverse productivity effects of redistributing land from large, well-managed going concerns to small, uneconomic, family-operated farm units. The secretary general of the National Society of Agriculture (of Chile), for example, asserted that". . .where agrarian reforms are presently being carried out, it is precisely the more efficient enterprises that are being most threatened."[37]

The productivity argument against land redistribution is weak at two points. First, with respect to the identification of small-scale farming with agrarian reform, it should be noted that land fragmentation is not a necessary concomitant of the equalization process. Land redistribution can be carried out in various forms of enterprise including a large economic undertaking composed of small farmers in association.[38]

In the second place, the results of recent investigations conducted by the Inter-American Committee for Agricultural

Development (ICAD) indicate that small-scale farming cannot be condemned on the basis of the productivity criterion. The ICAD found that agricultural production "per hectare in farms" and "per hectare cultivated" tended to be highest on small farm units (in Brazil, Argentina, Chile, Peru, Columbia, Ecuador, and Guatemala), for selected years during the 1950-60 period.[39] As Mitchell and Schatan have noted:

> . . .with the exception of poultry products, all of these high value foods can be produced just as economically on family-sized farm units as they can on large units. . . This fact is too little understood by economists, who simply assume without studying the actual situation that large-scale production is always more economic than medium- and small-scale production.[40]

The widespread tendency in Latin America to equate size with agricultural efficiency has been reinforced by the "functionalist" school of development theorists. These economists observe that unequal wealth and economic development have coexisted and assume therefore a positive virtue in economic inequality. Their model of dynamic causation has been briefly summarized by Chaplain:

> Beginning with a feudal agrarian society of high over-all concentration among all who own any real estate . . .the process of population growth and commercialized economic development would bring about an even greater concentration of property than already existed. The function of this increasing inequality . . .is to transfer sufficient wealth into the hands of entrepreneurs so that large-scale capital investments required for sustained economic growth can be made . . . Subsequently . . .equalization of income should occur in time to enlarge consumption sufficiently to soak up the increased productive capacity.[41]

The contemporary relevance of the functionalist model, as a basis for opposing equalization policies, is open to question on several counts. First, while it is true that large concentrations of wealth in a few, progressive hands could be effectively invested to promote industrial development, there is no assurance that the propertied elite is interested in forming domestic capital. A case in point is Peru where the overwhelming majority of the entrepreneurs in the industrial sector have been foreign immigrants. It has been demonstrated that hardly any Peruvians used their wealth to develop the country's textile industry.[42]

More important, however, in evaluating the "functionalist" model is the fact that after several decades of industrialization in Latin America no process of equalization has been set in motion. Indeed, as indicated above, the evidence suggests a trend toward greater inequality within most Latin American countries.

Before attempting to interpret and evaluate public action
aimed at broadening markets for Latin American industry, it is
appropriate to consider the potential impact of agrarian reform
on an equally significant objective of contemporary development
policy: the ability of industry to absorb an adequate share of the
rapid growth in the labor force, especially in urban areas.

The rate of growth in industrial employment in the countries of Latin America, with only a few exceptions, has not even
kept pace with the rate of population and labor force expansion.
It is roughly estimated that industry absorbed only a little more
than 23% of the 23 million persons added to the urban labor force,
and 15% of the 36 million persons added to total employment between 1925 and 1960.[43]

The limited labor absorption capacity of the industrial
sector is reflected in the rapid growth of service employment.
While the more productive services (power, water supply, transportation, etc.) have provided relatively rapid expansion in new
jobs, usually above the growth rate of over-all urban employment,
the most rapid expansion has taken place in the residual other
services that are characterized by low productivity and disguised
unemployment. The service sector in Latin America, observes
Griffin, "is largely a sponge which absorbs the excess population
of the rural areas and its growth represents virtually no increase
in economic welfare."[44]

Knowledge of the causes of the labor absorption problem
facilitates an assessment of the relative employment effect of
agrarian reform as compared with regional integration. As a
point of departure, it might be noted that the amount of employment created by a given volume of investment depends on the product mix and the technology chosen to produce the various goods
and services in the product mix.[45] Thus, a major factor holding
down the labor absorption capacity of industry in Latin America
has been the changes in the structure of manufacturing which
typically result in a relative increase in the share of the more
capital-intensive industries at the expense of the more labor-intensive traditional branches.[46]

If the desired increase in market size is attained through
the integration of existing industrial sectors, the product mix and
the technology orientation of industry will continue to shift away
from the more labor-intensive traditional branches.[47]

On the other hand, as indicated above, a sweeping redistribution of aggregate agricultural purchasing power would have a
significant impact on traditional industries which have the greatest
potential for labor absorption. In other words, for a given increase
in the size of the market for industrial output, the redistributive
approach to market expansion will bring about the absorption of a
higher percentage of the displaced rural population than would the
integration approach.[48]

Apart from this indirect effect of agrarian reform on industrial employment, considerable scope for increasing employment opportunities in agriculture itself would also result from the implementation of that approach. To quote Mitchell and Schatan:

> At present, one third to one half of the entire agricultural labor force in Latin America is "redundant" —either unemployed or underemployed. The most likely reason for this redundancy is the land tenure situation. A farm family restricted to three or four acres of poor land. . .simply cannot utilize its own labor force more than a small fraction of the year. . . Furthermore the renters, sharecroppers, or laborers on the large latifundia where the land is extensively exploited at a level far below its productivity, can do little or nothing about improving the utilization of their own labor . . . [49]

III

Since 1930 the political economic activity of the Latin American state was primarily concerned with measures to "nationalize" the economy, to reduce the vulnerabilities of over-dependence on the world market for participation in modern economic life. The major thrust of economic policy has linked the developmental aspirations of the region to import-substituting industrialization and tariff protection.

It has already been said that during the 1950's it became apparent that the continued momentum of ISI was being impaired by the "growing and damaging disequilibrium between urban/industrial advance and rural/agricultural backwardness."[50] Between 1951 and 1960, industrial production for Latin America as a whole increased 97% while agricultural output rose only 47%. Allowing for the differential in demographic growth, this meant that on a per capita basis, industry grew about five times faster than agriculture during the decade.

The preceding sections of this study described the emergence of the "integration ideology" as a response to the diminution of growth impulses from import substitution and analyzed the implications of an alternative approach to the same problem. The present section reviews and evaluates the trend of public action, with respect to this issue, since the Alliance for Progress was created in 1961 at Punta del Este.

When the Alliance was set up in 1961, it was hoped that the end of the decade would see substantial gains on the most pressing social and economic problems of Latin America. It represented a comprehensive design for development, with a special emphasis on policies for redistributing wealth and income, "initially prescribed as Latin America's quid pro quo for U.S. assistance."[51]

121

If, however, the significant part of the record is that
which governments have done in the name of change, and not what
they initially intended to do, then the Alliance must be counted as
a failure. The accomplishments in actual expropriation or purchasing of land and then the granting or distributing of this land
to the rural populations "adds up to very little."[52]

Several agrarian reform agencies established in the wake
of the Alliance for Progress (for example, Honduras' Instituto
Nacional Agrario) were inaugurated with substantial fanfare and a
broad grant of legislative authority, "then provided with no more
than a caretaker's fee from the national budget."[53] In most countries, distribution is barely keeping up with the annual increase
in the number of rural families, and even this is not true for every
country. In Colombia, for example, 33,071 families were settled
on privately-owned and public lands and awarded titles during the
1962-65 period while the number of rural families increased by
14,000 per year.[54]

The following data indicate the number of families benefiting from land redistribution in the OAS countries, having such
programs, for the period shown:

Bolivia	1953-1965	171,932
Brazil	1967	2,519
Chile	1964-3/67	4,827
Colombia	1961-6/66	36,389
Costa Rica	1962-1965	3,571
Dominican Republic	1962-1965	3,348
Ecuador	10/64-3/66	23,180
El Salvador	1950-1965	6,200
Guatemala	1955-1963	25,174
Honduras	1962-1965	2,588
Mexico	1961-1965	169,577
Nicaragua	1963-1966	1,312
Panama	1963-1965	811
Paraguay	1954-1965	44,750
Peru	1963-1966	26,000
Venezuela	1959-1966	131,250
	TOTAL	653,428 [55]

The figures given above (based almost entirely on official
data) include not only distribution of public, semi-public and expropriated land-holdings, but also the results of the programs of
colonization and of regularization of the precarious tenure of occu-
piers of commonlands carried out in a number of countries. Specifically with reference to colonization, it should be noted that,
despite the tendency of Latin American policy-makers to pose the
"myth of open spaces" as an alternative to agrarian reform through
land redistribution, the evidence indicates that the amount of un-
used land really suitable for modern agriculture is very limited.[56]

The data on families benefited from land redistribution should be interpreted in the light of a recent statement by Mitchell and Schatan: "Such programs would need to benefit between 650,000 and 750,000 rural families in Latin America per year over the coming decade if the problems of agrarian structure are to be adequately met."[57]

The lack of commitment exhibited by the OAS countries with respect to wealth redistribution contrasts sharply with the official enthusiasm during this period regarding the development of regional integration systems. Although LAFTA has not yet fulfilled expectations, it does represent a formal commitment to eliminate, within a specified period of time, customs duties and other intraregional trade restrictions. Since the 1967 Punta del Este meeting, a subgrouping of LAFTA nations "seem to be experiencing great success in ironing out obstacles that have held back progress within the larger Latin American Free Trade Area," — as evidenced by the signing of a tariff reducing treaty on petro-chemicals.[58]

The Central American Common Market has reported more progress than LAFTA: at least 95% of the tariff items traded among countries belonging to CACM have been freed, and steps are being taken to adopt a common external tariff against outsiders. The CACM, moreover, has established a series of institutions and instruments designed to accelerate the integrative process. The Central American Bank for Economic Integration (CABEI), for example, was set up with a capital of more than $40 million to finance projects of regional development and to channel loans granted by the Inter-American Development Bank, the World Bank and A I D.[59] The economic impact of this trade grouping is suggested by the fact that total intraregional imports into CACM countries relative to total CACM imports from the entire world increased from 6.3 per cent in 1960 to 15.0 per cent in 1965.

By the time the presidents of the OAS countries reconvened at Punta del Este in mid-April of 1967, six years after the creation of the Alliance for Progress, it had become clear, as Eldon Kenworthy puts it, "that the emphasis has now shifted from developing the hinterland — 'helping the farmer was high priority' in 1964 — to developing a common market."[60]

This raises an important question: Given the possibility of effectively enlarging the Latin American market through agrarian reform — as an alternative to regional integration — why have the planners - technicians chosen to emphasize the latter approach? What aspect of the técnico's training and/or intellectual orientation is capable of explaining their failure to stress the necessity for wealth redistribution in the rural sectors?

The logic of redistributive reforms can be challenged on at least two grounds: their effectiveness in actually augmenting long-run income, and their effect on the "natural" processes of industrialization. With respect to the first point, it might well be suggested that the persons who direct socio-economic policy in Latin America are haunted by the spectres of Ricardo and Malthus. Could it be that reservations about equalization policies have their roots in the conviction that population pressures in Latin America preclude a rise in the long-run equilibrium earnings of the poor campesino? No! The natural theory of wages must be ruled out as an explanation of the attitude of Latin American policymakers toward land reform as a method of expanding markets. Until very recently in Latin America, the existence of a population problem was not even officially recognized and demography is still neglected in the training of social scientists.

As a result, according to Luis Escobar Cerda, "professionals assume the direction of their countries without ever having considered that population constitutes a problem — except for it being too small — since that is as far as popular 'knowledge' or 'conviction' reaches."[61]

Turning to the second possible basis for avoiding redistribution, it might be thought that the "functionalist" position on the relation of wealth inequality to development has decisively influenced economic thinking in Latin America. It is not realistic, however, to explain policy trends in those terms. As the first section of this study demonstrated, the notion of an automatic transmission mechanism was discredited in the eyes of Latin American intellectuals many years ago as evidenced by their adherence to ISI and tariff protection in accordance with Prebisch's thesis that under conditions of free trade economic inequalities between developed centers and backward areas tend to increase.

Equally significant is the attention paid by LAFTA and CACM officials to the need for special provisions for industrial development in the less developed member countries. The evolving principle of "balanced growth" is a reflection of the planners' attachment to a dynamic concept of distributive justice with respect to the industrial sectors within the integrated area.

The point of the preceding paragraphs is to make clear the fact that current neglect of rural/agricultural backwardness in Latin America cannot be explained in terms of the policymakers' intellectual and theoretical predilections.

Thus, the determinants of policy trends affecting land tenure systems must be sought in the character of the Latin American political process and particularly in the limitations on public action implicit in the way political power is achieved and maintained.

The nature of the political process in Latin America may be analyzed, following C. W. Anderson, in terms of "power contenders" and "power capabilities." A contender for power is defined as any individual or group seeking to have its demands implemented through state machinery; possession of a power capability enables an individual or group to be politically influential.[62] It should be noted, at this juncture, that foreign power contenders must be included in describing the patterns of alliance and conflict that determine the direction of public policy in Latin America. [63]

In terms of these analytical categories, the political process in Latin America may be said to consist of two distinct phases:

> In the first, contenders "outside" of the coterie of elites which habitually take one another into account in planning their political strategies are seeking to demonstrate a power capability that will gain them access to the political process. The second phase may then be described as one of manipulation and negotiation among power contenders with reciprocally recognized power capabilities. [64]

While the terms on which established contenders negotiate for the structuring of power relationships varies among countries, these relationships in general are based on flexible coalitions among diverse power contenders which are subject to prompt revision at any time if the terms under which the original government was formed are deemed violated. Thus, in 1954, when the Arbenz government attempted to carry out an extensive agrarian reform in Guatemala, among other drastic measures, it was overthrown by threatened holders of important power capabilities.

The Latin American political system in other words, permits the admission of new contenders into the "arena of reciprocally recognizing elites" as long as they demonstrate a significant power capability and provide assurances that they will not jeopardize the traditional system of power. With the exception of real revolutionary situations, the normal rule of Latin America is that new power contenders may be added to the system, but old ones may not be eliminated.

In this connection it is worth noting that until recently it was generally expected that the Latin American middle classes were going to play the same role as their European counterparts and carry out the cultural and institutional changes demanded by the growth of industry. However, as the preceding analysis suggests, the power capability of the middle sectors was not so used. "Far from reforming anything," writes Claudio Veliz, "they have become firm supporters of the Establishment; they have not implemented significant agrarian or fiscal reforms but have displayed remarkable energy trying to become landowners or to marry their offspring into the aristocracy."[65]

In this political context it is not difficult to understand why structural changes in the land tenure system have not occurred outside of the four regimes in contemporary Latin America that could be described as revolutionary in nature (Mexico in 1910, Bolivia in 1952, Cuba in 1959, and Guatemala from 1945-1954). Agrarian reform in all four revolutions was designed to eliminate both the power contenders and the power capability represented by the semi-feudal control of land and labor. [66]

The Alliance for Progress grew out of the fear in official U.S. circles that continued neglect of the rural masses in OAS countries would contribute to a rising tempo of revolutionary change. The basis for Washington's concern is explained in a brilliant analysis, by Eldon Kenworthy, of the emergence and significance of the "north-south conflict" in world politics. He compares the governments of the OAS countries, with some exceptions, to "black bourgeoisie trying to make it by cutting themselves off from rural compatriots." In those societies, the north-south conflict manifests itself in struggles between the "northernized" elites who dominate national institutions and whatever opposition can be mustered by power contenders ". . . seeking to demonstrate a power capability that will gain them access to the political process."

Unwilling to support revolutionary movements which might "go communist," Washington placed its faith in the national governments to carry out major social and economic reforms under the Alliance. This expectation was based on Washington's vision of social revolution without political revolution and was backed by a substantial power capability: economic assistance contingent on progress towards the stated goals. [67]

Given a political system whose rules preclude the elimination of historical power contenders, the result of this endeavor was predictable. To quote Kenworthy:

> Anyone familiar with the distribution of power in
> Latin America will realize that existing governments,
> with some exceptions, cannot implement the reforms
> . . . and survive. Even so innocent a measure as
> abolishing illiteracy by 1970 (one of the Alliance
> for Progress' original goals) would decisively alter
> the balance of political power in a country like
> Brazil . . . [68]

Increasingly concerned about rising social unrest and insurgency, and frustrated in its attempt to stimulate changes in Latin America, the United States fell back on the creation and manipulation of supranational institutions as a way of promoting internal stability and guarding against defections within its sphere of influence. The implications of this approach had been visible on earlier occasions, in the 1954 Guatemalan disorder, for example, when the U. S. used the OAS to legitimize its own power capability, and in 1962 when it bought Haiti's support by an offer of a jet airport for Port-au-Prince when it needed a fourteenth vote to expel Cuba from the OAS. [69]

Thus, the process of regional integration, which had been set in motion by ECLA-trained professionals bent on overcoming the problem of insufficient markets without threatening established power contenders, was completely consistent with Washington's need, after almost wrecking the OAS by its role in the 1965 Dominican crisis, for a stronger, more decisive organization to take the lead in inter-American affairs. Viewed in this light, the second Punta del Este agreement represents a technique for system maintenance more than a strategy of development.

Apart from the intended consequences of these politically-inspired and mutually reinforcing trends toward Latin American "unity," certain unintended implications merit consideration. As the results of a recent study by Peter Odell seem to suggest, economic integration will tend to intensify the process of the spatial concentration of nonagricultural activity within the countries of Latin America:

> . . .the existing coast — or near coastal — locations of almost all the centers of economic activity. . .seems likely to act as magnets for the new investment in industrial activities both because these areas are immediately recognizable as industrial growth centers equipped with the kind of economic and social infrastructure required, and because such locations provide access by sea to the main markets for industrial goods located at or near the coast in other member countries of the economically unifying continent.[70]

The point is this: the creation of a Latin American Common Market will have the effects of reducing present levels of industrial dispersion and impeding current efforts to stimulate industrialization at growth points located away from coastal centers of economic activity. Córdoba, for example, among other inland Argentinian cities, may lose its market in the Buenos Aires region because, given the elimination of intraregional trade barriers, products made in Córdoba will have to compete with similar products from a coastally located industrial complex in another member country of the trading zone.[71]

The logic of this analysis applies with even greater force to the smaller countries of the west coast of Latin America. In Peru the position of those groups opposing Belaunde's emphasis on national integration will be strengthened ". . .as the limited supply of public investment funds which Peru has available for infrastructural developments have to go into expanding facilities in the Lima area — in order to attract industry oriented towards the Latin American market — rather than to road-building, etc. in the eastern part of the country."[72]

CONCLUSION

In conclusion, the following points may be enumerated:

1. The rise of import substituting industrialization and protectionism as sources of growth impulses in Latin America has been associated with an increasing acceptance there of modern

economic insights including the thesis that unhampered trade between two regions, one of which is industrialized and the other underdeveloped, normally operates to the cumulative disadvantage of the latter.

2. After the achievement of a degree of industrialization within protected national boundaries, the continued effectiveness of ISI became contingent on releasing a larger part of the population from the limitations on consumption implicit in latifundismo and subsistence agriculture.

3. The failure to deal with the increasing disequilibrium between urban/industrial advance and rural/agricultural backwardness was determined not by the intellectual orientation of the rising class of técnicos but by the nature of the political system of the region: ". . .one that permits new power contenders to be added to the system but is so designed that other political factors are not eliminated."[73]

4. By ensuring the continued and "balanced" growth of capital-city-oriented industrial sectors on the basis of export opportunities outside the national territory, regionalism offers a way out of the socio-political dilemmas associated with the process of creating sufficient new demand among the impoverished masses of the countries concerned.

5. The evolution of this approach has been decisively influenced by the U.S. involvement. Frustrated in its attempts to inspire major social reform — but unwilling to allow defections, à la Castro, from its sphere of influence —Washington has intensified its efforts to promote and shape a "Latin American NATO"[74] capable of effectively legitimizing the use of American power in the suppression of revolutionary change.[75]

6. Broadly speaking, the case against Latin American integration rests on the proposition that "the central problem of development . . . is not the gap between rich nations and poor nations: it is the gap between the rich and poor parts of the developing nations themselves."[76] The process of closing the latter gap involves an awakening of the new nationalism of underdeveloped countries which have long enjoyed statehood, but a form of statehood in which, as Robert Patch has noted, the subjection of the majority depends on the "nonexistence of the nation."[77] The movement toward Latin American "unity" or "continental nationalism," under the aegis of U.S. power, will enhance the ability of existing governments to resist nationalistic forces bent on redistributing rural wealth and restructuring agrarian society in favor of the unrepresented masses. Also it should be noted that production for a continental market will adversely affect industry's ability to absorb an adequate share of the rapid growth of the labor force and will inhibit or preclude the growth of industrial centers away from the capital cities.

1. *Declaration of the Presidents of America,* Punta del Este, April 12-14, 1967, p. 6.

2. *Ibid,* p. 11.

3. "Latin American Development and Hemisphere Trade," Joint Economic Committee, 1966, p. 12.

4. Albert O. Hirschman, "The Political Economy of Import-Substituting Industrialization in Latin America," *Quarterly Journal of Economics,* February 1968, p. 3.

5. Harry G. Johnson, *The World Economy at the Crossroads* (Oxford: Clarendon Press, 1965), pp. 79-80.

6. *Ibid,* p. 8.

7. *Ibid,* p. 10.

8. *Ibid,* p. 76.

9. *Ibid,* p. 76.

10. Bela Balassa, *Economic Development and Integration* (Mexico City: CEMLA, 1965), pp. 44-45.

11. Harry G. Johnson, *Economic Policies Toward Less Developed Countries* (Washington, D.C.: Brookings Institution, 1967), p. 50.

12. Hirschman, *op. cit.,* p. 3.

13. Johnson, *The World Economy at the Crossroads,* p. 81.

14. Raúl Prebisch, *Toward a New Trade Policy for Development,* 1964, pp. 21-22.

15. Miguel Wionczek, "The Latin American Free Trade Association," *International Conciliation,* January 1965, p. 9.

16. Staffan B. Linder, "Customs Unions and Economic Development," in Miguel Wionczek, ed., *Latin American Economic Integration* (New York: Frederick A. Praeger, 1966), p. 39.

17. Sidney Dell, *A Latin American Common Market* (Oxford University Press, 1966), pp. 15-16.

18. Gerald M. Meier, *The International Economics of Development* (New York: Harper and Row, 1968), p. 210.

19. Milton Lower, "Economic Integration in Latin America," in Milton D. Lower, Raymond R. Hannigan, and Rudolf K. Jansen, *Some Aspects of Latin American Trade Policies* (University of Texas, Bureau of Economic Research, 1964), p. 22.

20. Committee for Economic Development, *Regional Integration and the Trade of Latin America* (1968), pp. 14-15.

21. Jacques Chonchol, "Land Tenure and Development in Latin America," in Claudio Véliz, *Obstacles to Change in Latin America* (Oxford University Press, 1965), p. 81.

22. D. Chaplain, *Industrialization and the Distribution of Wealth in Peru* (University of Wisconsin, Land Tenure Center, 1966), p. 12.

23. *Ibid*, p. 21.

24. *Ibid*, p. 21.

25. Chonchol, *op. cit.*, p. 83.

26. *Ibid*, p. 84.

27. *Ibid*, p. 83.

28. *Ibid*, p. 84.

29. *Ibid*, p. 84.

30. Inter-American Development Bank, *Agricultural Development in Latin America: The Next Decade* (Washington, D.C., 1967), p. 64.

31. *Ibid*, p. 65.

32. *Ibid*, p. 107.

33. Gunnar Myrdal, *Rich Lands and Poor* (New York: Harper, 1957), p. 117.

34. *Ibid*, p. 119.

35. Luis Escobar Cerda, "After Caracas: Problems and Perspectives," *Population Bulletin*, February 1968, p. 9.

36. Myrdal, *op. cit.*, p. 122.

37. Inter-American Development Bank, *op. cit.*, p. 227.

38. *Ibid*, p. 78.

39. *Ibid*, pp. 134-35.

40. *Ibid*, p. 55.

41. Chaplain, *op. cit.*, p. 3.

42. *Ibid*, p. 24.

43. Inter-American Economic and Social Council, *Industrialization in Latin America: Priority Problems* (Santiago, 1967), pp. 11-12.

44. K. B. Griffin, "Reflections on Latin American Development," *Oxford Economic Papers*, No. 1, March 1966, p. 2; see IA-ECOSOC, *op. cit.*, p. 97.

45. B. Higgins, *Economic Development* (New York: Norton, revised ed., 1968), p. 380.

46. IA-ECOSOC, *op. cit.*, p. 13.

47. *Ibid*, p. 14.

48. IA-ECOSOC, *op. cit.*, p. 116.

49. IDB, *op. cit.*, p. 48.

50. Hélio Jaguaribe, "The Dynamics of Brazilian Nationalism," in Veliz, *op. cit.*, p. 176.

51. Eldon Kenworthy, "Black-White at Home, North-South Abroad," *Yale Review*, Winter 1968, p. 178.

52. IDB, *op. cit.*, p. 268.

53. C. W. Anderson, *Politics and Economic Change in Latin America* (Princeton, N.J.: Van Nostrand, 1967), p. 144.

54. IDB, *op. cit.*, p. 275.

55. *Ibid*, p. 269.

56. Anderson, *op. cit.*, p. 77.

57. IDB, *op. cit.*, p. 79.

58. Alliance for Progress, *Newsletter*, April 8, 1968.

59. CED, *op. cit.*, pp. 96-97.

60. Kenworthy, *op. cit.*, p. 178.

61. Escobar Cerda, *op. cit.*, p. 4.

62. Anderson, *op. cit.*, pp. 90-91.

63. *Ibid*, p. 91.

64. *Ibid*, p. 101.

65. Claudio Veliz, "Introduction," in Veliz, *op. cit.*, p. 2.

66. Anderson, *op. cit.*, p. 109.

67. *Ibid*, p. 161.

68. Kenworthy, *op. cit.*, p. 178.

69. Nathan Miller, "The OAS under its New Secretary General," *New Republic,* March 2, 1968, p. 11.

70. Peter Odell, "Economic Integration and Spatial Patterns of Economic Development in Latin America," *Journal of Common Market Studies,* March 1968, p. 281.

71. *Ibid*, pp. 281-82.

72. *Ibid*, p. 283.

73. Anderson, *op. cit.*, p. 108.

74. Linda B. Miller, "Regional Organization and the Regulation of Internal Conflict," *World Politics,* July 1967, pp. 582-600.

75. Ricardo Krushnir, "Las bases militares de Estados Unidos en Puerto Rico y su función estratégica," March 1968, (unpublished report).

76. Walt W. Rostow, "Deeper Roots for the Alliance," quoted in Joint Economic Committee, *Latin American Development and Hemisphere Trade,* a report of the Subcommittee on Inter-American Economic Relationships (Washington, D.C.: U.S. Government Printing Office, 1966).

77. Robert Patch, "Peasantry and National Revolution: Bolivia," in K. H. Silvert, ed., *Expectant Peoples* (New York: Random House, 1963), p. 113.

CHAPTER **10** PARTICIPATION AS A COMPONENT
OF INTEGRATION: A RATIONALE
FOR REGIONAL INTEGRATION
CENTERS

By George A. Truitt, President
International Development Foundation
New York

Partisans of Latin American integration have had occasion to rejoice. Anyone familiar with the deep-running Latin American need for national and individual identification derives a great deal of encouragement from the spirit of political unity attained by the Central American Republics. It is a significant event that most of their product labels now proudly add to their national identification "producto de Centroamérica."

Yet it does not take much effort to become downhearted about the prospects of economic integration in South America, especially on the basis of recent trends. The tariff-reduction lists of LAFTA have been getting thinner every year, as countries run out of painless concessions. A truly stunning disappointment occurred recently when the subregional Andean group shied away from the scheduled signing of an accord to eliminate trade barriers. The reasons for this seem to trace to a political weakening in Venezuela.

These are two typical examples of the experience made so far in Latin American integration, typical in that they seem puzzling in their contradictions. The meaning of the evidence appears particularly obscure if one tries to analyze the interplay between political and economic factors as co-determinants of the process of supranational integration. Does economic achievement bring political unity? Or is it rather political unity which makes possible economic achievement?

The Messina conference in 1955 was a milestone in West European integration. Dissatisfied with the slow progress of political federalism, the conferees decided to approach the goal of unity through the economic door, leading to the Common Market. This has become known as the Messina Method. Except for the Latin American Parliament, most efforts for Latin American integration seem to have adopted the Messina Method.

But as Haas and Schmitter pointed out in their admirable study The Politics of Economics in Latin American Regionalism (University of Denver, 1966), "The Messina Method worked because Western Europe possessed three essential attributes: the recognized expertise of the technicians and their secure civil service status; the existence of an institutionalized communications pattern between national ministries and interest groups deeply concerned with their policies; and the presidency of a respected, resourceful and committed advocate of European political unity over the committee which did the drafting."

No Latin American statesman as yet has provided the kind of leadership that Paul-Henri Spaak lent to West European integration. However, President Carlos Lleras Restrepo of Colombia has raised the banner of the Andean subregional group. President Eduardo Frei Montalva of Chile has made a persistent effort to breathe some mystique into LAFTA. And ex-President Fernando Belaúnde Terry's promotion of the Marginal Highway scheme has done much to lend some vision to supranational cooperation on the subcontinent. Thus with regard to top-level political guidance the picture is promising.

It is similarly possible to feel encouraged by the availability of técnicos. While one might question the job security of some of the technicians employed by national governments, there is a strong community of technicians employed by the U.N. Economic Commission for Latin America, the Inter-American Development Bank, and the Pan American Union. In fact, these technicians have constituted the strongest pressure group for integration.

It is in the area of effective communication between government agencies and their interest-group constituencies where the comparison between Western Europe and Latin America falls completely apart. With a few disfunctional exceptions, Latin American republics simply have not reached that level of politization.

No President of Ecuador has been elected by more than four per cent of the people. Even Colombia has had a discouragingly low electoral participation, which President Lleras recently attributed to "the lack of popular leaders and limited communication with the masses." Lack of institutionalized communication between the government and the people was an important theme in President Frei's inaugural speech in November 1964 and still is in his more recent pronouncements.

Instead of being like a pyramid resting on a massive base of local self-government and consisting of successive levels of mutually supportive institutions, many governments in Latin America can be better compared with balloons connected with their country below only by a slender tether of legitimacy. Most citizens do not oppose their governments, but they also do not participate in the business of government. The state-citizen relationship is frequently thought of by both parties as essentially intractable. In the cultural background looms the image of the just and honest Gran Señor dispensing justice to the grateful populace. The idea of the citizen determining the policies and actions of his government through a sustained two-way relationship is only beginning to take hold.

Lack of participation in government means many things

to economic integration. Not all of them are negative, but those that are tend to be the most persistent. Experts negotiating tariff reductions find their task somewhat easier if few pressure groups try to predetermine their negotiations. However, such gains melt away later on when advanced negotiations have to be brought back to the beginning, or promulgated agreements amended or suspended, once the producers and the consumers feel that their pocketbooks are affected, as they inevitably do, and when they start protesting — as they inevitably do.

A government finds it more difficult to negotiate with another in a situation when one or both partners derive their negotiating mandate from a narrow segment of their nation. They know from experience that narrow base means instability — that a narrowly based government can easily be succeeded by another which rests on a different narrow base, or on a broader one. Either way, little policy continuity can be expected. This insecurity has to be discounted in negotiations, hence the focus is likely to shift to the short term — a climate in which economic integration never can truly prosper. This is why co-ordination of industrial development plans has been even much less successful than negotiation of annual tariff concessions. This is also why the tariff reductions are difficult to obtain when they affect significantly traded items to a degree which would bring about shifts in production. In other words, the doubtful prospects of the continuity of some governments denies to Latin America the most significant benefit of economic integration: rationalization of production resulting in low prices of mass produced goods.

The skeptics say, therefore, that all talk of economic integration is premature in Latin America, because the political base on which to make lasting decisions simply is not there. Such a conclusion could be reached only with greatest reluctance. It is, unfortunately, the governments of the poorest nations — which therefore have the greatest need for the rewards of economic integration — that are the most unenduring partners to a treaty. By the reckoning of the United Nations Development Program, 87 per cent of the 32 countries whose per capita income averaged less than $100 per annum have each suffered an average of two major and violent internal upheavals since 1958.

It may well be that some of the economic integrationists have been indulging in wishful thinking. Hearing the hopeful economic projections of the Treaty of Montevideo, one is reminded of earlier attempts to duplicate in developing countries the success of the Marshall Plan in industrialized Europe. Amazingly, it took a long while to discover that below certain levels of human organization capital transfusions alone will not work. Now in the sixties, we may be committing the same error all over again by trying to attain Latin American integration by the Messina Method without having the benefit of the national political and social institutions which were available in Western Europe.

On the other hand, it is not at all indicated by available

135

evidence that we face a black-or-white proposition. The achievements of the Central American Market mentioned earlier are not to be overlooked.

A closer examination of the accomplishments of the Central American Common Market may shed some further light on the subject of our inquiry. W. J. Phair summarizes the comprehensive statistics presented in his paper Economic Integration As a Tool of Development in Central America (University of New Mexico, 1967) as follows: "The overall growth figures during the post-1962 period of accelerated integration have exceeded the expectations of many. Intraregional trade is now a significant portion of total trade, manufacturing production (the main focal point of policy to date) has expanded well beyond pre-1962 totals, and the success of the program in attracting investments has been of an order beyond the most optimistic predictions.

There have also been a number of disappointments. The structural changes needed to sustain growth are not taking place as rapidly as Central American planners had hoped, and the impressive development figures thus far registered are in part a result of an unforeseen expansion of traditional export revenues. Agricultural output for internal consumption is still insufficient, although plans are now being carried out to remedy this shortage. The enlarged volume of imports has brought on a serious current-account deficit without satisfactorily altering the composition of goods purchased away from sumptuary items, and public investments have been too frequently carried out in an inefficient manner."

With the exception of Costa Rica, the Central American republics have a level of internal political participation much lower than most countries of South America. It may be that it was the relative absence of articulate interest groups that enabled the national political leaders and their technicians to achieve a functioning Common Market. At the same time, the structural quality of these achievements suggests that this phase may have reached its limits. It seems that the achievement of the Central American Market, while real, only skimmed the cream off the integration process, pooling existing markets and attracting investment in such traditional crops as coffee, cotton, and bananas. In so doing, they came closer to the development levels of some South American countries, but also perhaps closer to the integration obstacles faced by South American countries because of deficiencies in social structures. The next stage may begin when the institutions created (Central American Bank for Economic Integration and the Central American Clearing House) and the political consensus and psychological uplift achieved will reach deeper into the national socio-economic structures.

The conceptual conclusions from these observations seems inescapable. Economic integration does not necessarily produce political unity (LAFTA), but it may (CACM), depending on the stage of development. The interplay between political and

economic forces does not end when one succeeds the other.
Rather, the development curve travels through successive fields
which alternate with regard to the preponderance or subordination
of economic vs. political determinants. Hence sustained development requires cyclical if not simultaneous attention to both political and economic development. In a fairly homogeneous region
(e.g. Central America) the positions of the national curves coincide. In a heterogenous region (e.g. the Andean group) these
curves are scattered. Integration as a tool of development should
therefore seek to strengthen that of the two components which
seems to represent the bottleneck at a given point in the development cycle of a country or group of countries, and it should seek
to bring the cycles of national development into phase within regions to make joint action practical.

The objectives of economic development are well defined
and known, as are the tools with which they can be furthered by
economic integration. What are the objectives of political development, and how can they be furthered on a supranational level?

As a component of integration, political development
seeks to increase the participation of all citizens in all functions
of society. One of the deficiencies typical of developing societies
is the insularity of progress. Just as production inputs tend to
gravitate towards the established centers of production, political
power tends to accrue at the top of the traditional society. This
elitism brings about a certain ease of decision making, except
that all those who have been excluded from the decision making
process feel equally uninvolved in the implementation of such
decisions. Given an opportunity, the previously excluded majority
tend to reverse the decisions made without them. Hence the
chronic instability of unrepresentative regimes, their inability to
assure long-term implementation of integration treaties and
plans. Such negotiating partners do not inspire confidence. The
preponderance of projections as opposed to policy commitments
in Latin American integration plans stems from the lack of broad
participation in the governmental machineries which undertake
the negotiations. Conversely improved participation should inspire international confidence and resolve to make the important
commitments which depend for their success on predictability of
national economic policies.

The deficiencies of participation abound in Latin America.
Half of the population are peasants, largely non-voting semi-
literates living outside the monetary economy. The urban centers
brim with the underemployed who live not in socially organized
neighborhoods but amorphous slums. The political parties lack
a functioning middle echelon, public administration is archaic,
local government is either appointive or not functioning, the educational system is too often an instrument of escape and privilege
rather than socialization. Enormous human resources thus are
unrealized, both in social and economic terms.

The problems hindering participation are so great that

137

we cannot expect in our lifetime a situation where they could be disregarded. But for the cyclical interplay of political and economic forces it is not necessary to achieve complete success on either front. Each step toward greater participation, however limited, sets the stage for a corresponding economic step forward, apart from having its own social justification.

Broad participation in the decision making processes of a society is a prerequisite of its efficiency, as Communist planners have learned. Participation in public institutions teaches citizens how to function effectively in an organized, mutually supportive relationship. It nourishes the belief that one can influence the pattern of one's life, transcending the environment, and forges commitments to ideas beyond oneself and family. Improved participation in the functioning of public institutions means, from the economist's point of view, greater access of the less efficient producers to capital and technology, resulting in increased productivity. The consequent growth of income means expansion of the domestic market, accumulation of internal capital and tax revenues. Significant national markets and availability of internal private and public capital make in turn supranational integration a dynamic prospect.

Much is being done on the national level to increase popular participation. Eleven Peruvian government agencies have joined together and with IDB help launched a program to integrate the Andean Indian. The same country blazed the trail in organizing the voluntary service of university students in villages under the Cooperación Popular program. Chile has just implemented a revolutionary law facilitating the unionization of farm labor. Colombia and several other countries have successfully maintained industry-supported vocational schools. These are but a few random examples of the recently intensifying national efforts to increase popular participation in the various functions of modernizing societies.

Missing, however, is the supranational dimension of these efforts. A noteworthy but lonely exception is the work of DESAL (Desarrollo Social de América Latina) in Santiago de Chile which has functioned as a source of conceptual, moral, and funding backstopping for Catholic groups engaged in sociopolitical modernization. Other civic leaders, politicians, and professionals engaged in political development have had very little opportunity to exchange experiences, co-ordinate activities, and above all acquire the additional moral momentum that goes with any human effort which transcends national barriers.

The Organization of American States has not been successful in filling this vacuum for reasons comparable with the flaws of LAFTA on the economic plane. The disparities among the individual countries are too great, and their out-of-phase curves of the cyclical interplay of political and economic forces present an overwhelmingly complex scheme. The common denominator being extremely low, action opportunities become extremely rare. Any comprehensive, all-encompassing plan is likely to fare no better than the Felipe Herrera plan of 1965. At the same time, there is a crying need for the type of interlocking action envisioned by the Herrera plan. (It combined integration of LAFTA economic sectors with such features as a Central University Council, a Latin American Information Agency, compulsory secondary education program for urban dwellers.)

Albert Hirschman's concept of "reformmongering" has been critizied as presenting a handy escape device to those who oppose thorough structural reforms. The uninspiring record of Latin American integration as attempted so far on an ambitious scale calls for making use of it. In particular, regional efforts seem to present a more encouraging prospect. The Central American Bank of Economic Integration has accomplished something concrete in Central America — an example that has been noticed apparently by the founders of the Andean Development Corporation.

The time has come to complement these regional banking and economic planning agencies with their equivalents in the field of political development. There should be a Regional Integration Center for Central America and Mexico, one for the Caribbean, one for the Andean group, one for Argentina-Uruguay-Paraguay, and one for Brazil. The objective of the Regional Integration Centers would be to assist internal integration (participation within each member country), and in so doing further regional integration. Each Center would connect, co-ordinate, plan, report, and help fund on-going and new national efforts to improve the quantity and quality of human organization so as to bring about greater citizen participation and institutional continuity. The Centers would link together directors of agrarian reform agencies, leaders of chambers of commerce, university deans, municipal government officers, working journalists, campesino leaders, civic educators, voluntary agency officers, women's organization leaders, urban planners. Through the Centers these leaders could pool their methodological experience, consult on priorities, establish joint training facilities, and co-ordinate their strategies.

The benefits which the planners of economic integration would obtain from the Regional Integration Centers would be several:

1. strengthening of the representativity and hence continuity of governments as partners to an integration plan, resulting in greater mutual confidence and willingness to make specific commitments;

2. bringing the political development curves within a region more into phase, resulting in better ability to negotiate expeditiously;

3. building a political constituency for economic integration;

4. facilitating functional integration (by economic sector).

We should remember that the 1955 Messina breakthrough in economic integration was preceded in Europe by a decade of lively political activity advocating European unity. In the aftermath of World War II, a large number of supranational groups from the Moral Rearmament to the Social Democratic parties to the PEN Club laid the political foundation on which the Common Market was built, engendering in turn, we may expect, greater political unity in the near future.

These functional groups in Western Europe did much to overcome the emotional ravages of war, bridging over century-old chasms of national antagonisms such as the one between France and Germany. Latin American integration is similarly impeded today by a number of ancient grudges and border disputes, often exacerbated and kept alive by vested interests and narrow-minded politicians. It is true in Latin America as in Europe that a professional from one country (say, Bolivia) can communicate better with a fellow-professional from another country (say, Paraguay) than with a campesino (or hacendado) in his own country. Following the lines of this natural affinity among professionals, communication channels can be pioneered which will ultimately connect the entire national societies. Better international communication among the professionals will in turn enable them to better lead and motivate their fellow citizens.

The people of Latin America must first make an inner commitment to the desirability and feasibility of change before they can be expected to become its agents. Their leaders must first feel an indentification with an integration movement before they can be expected to subordinate the actions to the ideals of integration. As in all development planning, we have to recognize the difference between an idea and a motive. An idea is like a die which someone with a motive to do so later puts to use to attain a specific end. In the integration efforts as in development programs in general there has been an apparently idealistic but also depressingly passive belief in the power of ideas. At this point there is much bitter evidence showing that it is not enough eloquently to postulate an ambitious goal; also, that it is not enough to present a reasoned argument in favor of a technical innovation. In addition, it is necessary to motivate people actively to pursue the lofty goals, and to make use of the new techniques available. That involves leadership which is capable of bringing about massive participation in development by stimulating broad involvement in the decision-making processes of modernizing society.

11

THE REGIONAL IMPLICATION OF ECONOMIC INTEGRATION

By Harold A. Wood
Department of Geography
McMaster University
Canada

A QUESTION OF TERMINOLOGY

Before embarking on any discussion related to the word "region," it is necessary to define the meaning which is to be attached to the term. In the present instance, the precaution is particularly important, for the architects of economic integration normally think of a region as a multinational grouping together of entire countries for commercial or other purposes.

Such a broad areal concept, of course, must have a name, and maybe "region" is the right one. Yet it should not be forgotten that multinational regions are quite different from territorial subdivisions at the subnational level which are also properly called "regions." It is with areas of the latter type that this study is concerned.

However, even at the subnational level, one may find areas of many different kinds referred to as regions. Indeed, the various "regional divisions" of a country may be as numerous and varied as there are reasons for carrying out the subdivision in the first place. In the context of the present inquiry, therefore, we must include a statement of purpose. Our regions will be defined as parts of individual countries, which, due to their polarity and/or functional characteristics, provide suitable area units within which to plan the economic, social, and cultural development involved in a program of multinational or binational economic integration.

THE NEED FOR REGIONAL ANALYSIS

The main proposition of this study is that any comprehensive multinational planning program must include carefully executed studies at the regional level if it is to be successful. If only to coordinate the different sectoral objectives within a locational framework; if only to permit each country to evaluate the implications of the program within its own territory; some clear indication must be given, not merely as to what is to go where, but with respect to what services or facilities should be allocated to each location. In other words, it must be recognized that the purpose of development planning — whether national or multinational — is to improve living conditions in specific places or areas. The needs

141

of these areas are the first consideration — and, until the needs
have been defined in really a comprehensive manner, it may not
be possible to judge whether a particular project is desirable or
not. Certainly it would be quite impossible to place in proper order of priority all the projects which might be undertaken.

For the analysis of the development problem, for the planning of various activities, and for the evaluation of the success of
the program, a regional approach is indispensable.

THE REALITY OF REGIONS

A corollary of the statement that regional analysis is necessary is that regions, as defined above, actually exist. This, indeed, is simply another way of saying that all parts of a country
will not have identical development potentials, and will not be iden-
tically influenced by changes in multinational commercial relations.
These areal inequalities in turn will not be randomly distributed
over space but will form distinct patterns, making it possible to
draw boundaries on a map between areas with one response to the
processes of integration and areas with another.

POLITICAL REASONS FOR REGIONAL DIFFERENTIATION

Multinational integration will have different effects on different parts of a country where the new policies may require the reduction or elimination of special privileges which had been accorded
to one part of a nation, but which were either specifically withheld
from other areas or else were inapplicable there. Most clear-cut
is the situation in which interregional differences have been legally
established, such as in the free trade areas which many countries
have set up on or near their borders. Yet, equally significant are
regional differences maintained politically even though not defined
in those terms, as where high import duties on manufactured goods
benefit the domestic industrial areas, while at the same time discriminating against the rural parts of the same country. In either
case, any sudden opening of new trade channels for the nation as a
whole will have an unequal impact on areas which had been unequally
affected by the pre-existing trade restrictions.

ECONOMIC REASONS FOR REGIONAL DIFFERENTIATION

Regardless of political considerations, the regions which
are largely self-sufficient, and participate only to a small degree
in international trade, will be less directly affected by multinational
economic integration than those which are commercially oriented.

Futhermore, among the more developed regions the influence of integration may be either positive or negative, depending
upon the relative advantage each possesses in comparison with other
regions within the new economic union.

142

PHYSICAL REASONS FOR ECONOMIC INTEGRATION

In many cases, economic inequalities will be directly related to the character of the physical environment. Those areas will benefit directly by economic integration which are best suited physically for the efficient production of items which can easily be exported. Where the natural resources do not lend themselves to export production, indirect benefits may ensue if surpluses are available for domestic consumption. But little or no advantage will come to areas which are deficient in almost all natural resources.

WHY MULTINATIONAL PLANNING SHOULD INCLUDE THE PLANNING OF REGIONS WITHIN COUNTRIES

If it is agreed that regions are not all alike, it follows that the use of national averages in comprehension development planning must be accompanied by extreme caution. For the planning process is surely incomplete unless it takes cognizance of the entire chain of events which starts with planning decisions and ends with real improvements in the lives of individual human beings. And, as has been stressed, the over-all environment in which the individual lives differs so greatly from place to place, especially in the so-called "developing" countries, that it can only be properly handled in a regional context. Only at the regional level may one truly assess the effects of any national or multinational development program and judge whether what is being planned is indeed justified—whether what is produced by the plan is what is really needed. Nor can the whole regional picture remain confined within the frame of planning theory, for if the regions are not treated with sufficient special attention to their needs, some may rebel and seek solutions to their problems by the use of procedures other than development planning. A country may be something more than the sum of its regions, but it is also something less, and it ill behooves us to pay greater attention to the former than to the latter.

THE URBAN-RURAL DICHOTOMY

Of all regional differences, the ones which are most striking in Latin America are those between the urbanized regions, with their emphasis on commerce and manufacturing, and the rural regions, dependent upon primary production. Some implications of these differences with respect to multinational integration have already been mentioned, but the matter is of such fundamental importance that some elaboration is necessary.

URBANIZED REGIONS

The argument most frequently quoted in favor of economic integration in Latin America is that a large market area offers econ-

economies of scale, permitting the development of industries which could not profitably operate without ready access to consumers living outside the country in which the industry is located. While the argument is valid enough, it does not follow that the expanded market can be easily served. Because of the vast distances involved, the limited development of long-distance transportation facilities, and the fact that in huge areas the aggregate purchasing power is extremely low, any Latin American industry which depends on a market of continental proportions, will inevitably face very high costs for the transportation of its finished products, and will have to carry out its manufacturing most efficiently if a profit is to be made while, at the same time, the consumer is offered reasonable prices. Hence, only regions with real competitive advantages will see a great expansion of manufacturing if economic integration becomes a reality, and these regions, for the most part, are those which are not only already urbanized but also enjoy the benefits of a location on or near the coast, where advantage may be taken of the economies of water transport, or possess some other assets, such as industrial raw materials, power, or skilled labor.

Perhaps even more significant than the intensification of manufacturing will be its growing specialization, a trend which, again, will act to the benefit of some areas and to the detriment of others. Hence, with respect to urbanized regions and the manufacturing sector, regional differences must be taken into consideration in economic planning. Yet even more important is a recognition of the differences between the urbanized areas which have most of the manufacturing and the rural areas which depend on other activities.

RURAL REGIONS

It is almost universally true in developing countries that the areas depending upon agricultural production may be called upon to pay much of the cost of industrialization, and if it is also true that they will get little new industry of their own, they clearly present planning problems of a type quite different from those of the urbanized regions. Somehow, their gross productivity must be increased sufficiently to achieve three essential objectives:

    (a)   to provide increased surpluses which can be sold abroad, in processed or unprocessed form, to earn the foreign exchange needed by those economic sectors which are more dependent on imports,

    (b)   to provide adequate supplies of food for the expanding urban population, and

    (c)   to permit a very substantial rise in rural standards. The effects of this rise will be two-fold. On the one hand, it will serve to put a damper on the rate of rural-urban migration, which would be greatly accelerated and give rise to critical problems if economic integration brought prosperity only to the cities. On the other, it will provide increased markets for the products of the industrial areas, and thus begin to create the true regional economic integration which is one of the indispensable characteristics of a developed part of the world.

It is evident therefore that the planning of "rural regions" while different in kind from the planning of "urban regions" cannot take second place either in its timing or in the energy devoted to it. Only a comprehensive regional planning program embracing from the outset the needs of these two different kinds of areas can bring real and lasting benefits to either one.

SUGGESTED STEPS FOR THE FORMULATION OF A DEVELOPMENT PLAN BASED ON A PROJECTED MULTINATIONAL ECONOMIC INTEGRATION

To summarize, a set of procedures is suggested which would ensure that regional differences are adequately considered within an over-all development plan based on multinational economic integration. For purposes of illustration, a few examples are taken from the Rio Plate Basin, where the matter of integration is currently under study, but the approach would be applicable anywhere.

1. The first step should be a preliminary study of the growth potentials of all areas within the countries which it is hoped to integrate. In this study, areas would be differentiated on the basis of five criteria:

   i.   their existing economic activities,

   ii.   their existing per capita income (levels of living),

   iii. their potential increase in population carrying capacity,

   iv.   their potential increase in per capita production,

   v.   the "spread effect" which development in the area will have upon surrounding areas. [1]

   In the case of the River Plate Basin, where five countries are involved, it is suggested that this preliminary study should embrace all of Argentina, Uruguay, Paraguay and Bolivia. Because Brazil is so vast, and because its northern and northeastern portions are already in the hands of regional development agencies, it might be sufficient to limit the integration study to the southern and central-west sections of the country. However, the SUDENE and SUDAM should be urged to prepare to take part in a comprehensive national planning program which would include all of Brazil.

2. National targets should be set for the manufacturing and mining

sectors in each country, on the assumption that economic integration will take place, and including a special treatment of industries based on domestic agricultural, pastoral, mineral, fishing, and forest products.

3. (To be carried out simultaneously with step 2.)
National targets should be set for the agricultural, pastoral, forestry and fishing sectors in each country, on the assumption that economic integration is to take place, and that total output must be increased sufficiently to meet the following objectives:

   i. to increase the exports of primary products sufficiently to earn the foreign exchange required to pay for the increased imports of industrial machinery and raw materials,

   ii. to feed the national population adequately,

   iii. to provide raw materials for the new industries which are planned.

At the same time, the per capita productivity and the efficiency of marketing arrangements must be improved sufficiently to permit a substantial increase in the real income and in the living standards of the rural workers.

4. A selection will then be made of the key "growth poles" around which the planned development will be articulated. These poles will include:

   i. some established urban centers,

   ii. new centers in hitherto non-urbanized areas of high agricultural productivity,

   iii. new centers in frontier areas, particularly where important lines of communication are being opened up and where supplies of power are readily available. In the case of the La Plata Basin, one obvious potential "growth pole" in a frontier area would be at Foz do Iguaçu - Puerto Presidente Stroessner, located on oppostie sides of a crossing place on the Paraná River and near Iguazú Falls. Another would be at Salto - Concordia, where a major dam and transport facility across the Uruguay River can be combined to help unite Uruguay and Argentina.

5. In each country, a set of planning regions should then be delimited. For countries, such as Bolivia, Paraguay, and Brazil, containing large stretches of territory which are almost uninhabited and therefore do not yet contribute meaningfully to the national economy, the regions might fall into the following two categories:

   i. regions where the development program is expected to produce changes; these regions will probably include most of the occupied areas as well as those areas not yet occupied but in which development is planned at an early date,

ii. regions in which significant changes are not envisaged until some later date, if at all; most of these regions will be in sparsely populated areas.

Each region should have a measure of functional unity, containing areas which are mutually complementary economically. Regions of the first group will each be built around an existing growth pole or poles, or around poles which are to be established in the initial phase of the program. In the latter group, the growth poles may not be already in existence nor may it appear feasible to create them immediately. Nevertheless, the location of each region should be roughly established so that each one contains a site or sites at which growth poles might suitably be developed as and when the over-all expansion of the national economy makes it desirable to develop these stagnant or frontier zones.

6. A planning body should then be established for each region. In the case of regions for future development, the planning body could be quite small, and have its offices in the national capital.

The programs of all the regional offices would then be coordinated through a national regional planning office, as is done, for example, in Chile. In addition, to the extent that it is necessary, joint binational or multinational advisory committees should be established, to coordinate all the regional planning programs of neighboring countries, and to work out special development details in frontier zones.

7. The many separate physical projects required to meet the over-all development objectives may now be planned, provided with the most appropriate spatial articulation, and executed in the most suitable order of priority, in confidence that sufficient coordination has been achieved to ensure an efficient pattern of progress.

CONCLUSIONS

Any scheme for multinational economic integration requires a previous analysis of the regional implications of the scheme at the subnational level. Such an analysis will serve not only to confirm or deny the desirability of various degrees of integration but will greatly facilitate the design and execution of the integration program. In order to demonstrate the use which should be made of these regional studies, a seven-phase organization of the over-all planning effort is proposed, starting with an examination of areal differences in growth potential and culminating with the organization of regional planning machinery through which specific development projects may be evaluated and spatially coordinated. It is suggested that the omission from a development program of any of the seven phases will result in serious weaknesses. The regional approach is not merely worthwhile; it is an element essential to success.

NOTE

1. Areas of this type, termed "areas of synthesis for planning,"were defined in the First Interamerican Seminar on the Definition of Regions for Development Planning, held in Hamilton, Canada, in September, 1967, and organized by the Regional Geography Committee of the Pan-American Institute of Geography and History. For a more complete discussion (in Spanish) of the concept, see the General Conclusions of the Seminar, published in *Revista de la Sociedad Interamericana de Planificación*, No. 4, (Dec., 1967).

12

THE ROLE OF THE UNITED STATES IN LATIN AMERICAN ECONOMIC INTEGRATION

By William and Helga Woodruff
Department of Economics
University of Florida

In recent years many appeals have been made by the political leaders of the United States for greater economic progress in Latin America. The economic integration of that area has become a major goal of United States foreign policy. Unfortunately, the growing stress placed by the United States government upon economic progress in Latin America overlooks the fact that there are many kinds of progress, not always mutually compatible; and that progress itself is a very unusual and conditional affair.

It is our belief that the present economic policy of the United States towards the countries of Latin America is based upon a wrong diagnosis of their economic ills and a wrong prescription for their cure.

The diagnosis and the cure offered by those who speak for the American government, and for the United Nations Economic Commission for Latin America, might be summarized as follows:

> the overwhelming dependence of Latin American countries upon the demands of the industrialized centers of North America and Western Europe has placed Latin America in an economically weak position (usually the fate of countries which place "too many eggs in one basket"). New strength, so the argument continues, can only be obtained by economic integration, which would lead to greater trade and the promotion of industrialization. On the grounds of equity (as well as economic efficiency) it is now up to the industrial centers of the western world, such as the United States, to assist this movement, not only by financial support but also, and more importantly, by trade concessions. Only thus can the United States obtain more stable neighbors, and, in doing so, provide a sound defense in this hemisphere against Communism.

It seems to us that this is an oversimplification of a most complex historical and economic situation. Worse still, it looks at Latin America's economic problems from the standpoint of the industrialized and largely urbanized communities of the northern hemisphere. But to fasten a European and U.S. pattern of economic growth and development upon twentieth-century Latin America, would be to assume that the United States and European countries have the only rational economic system and that all others are the result of ignorance or error. Nothing could be more absurd or more misleading. The fact of the matter is that there is no norm which Latin American countries have somehow failed to reach, or for that matter to which they should struggle.

The wealth of the United States is not the result of superior economic knowledge, or the application of a rational economic process. It is the result of a unique historical situation. World colonization by the Europeans and North Americans is the crucial and neglected factor explaining economic growth and development in recent times. The idea that all will be well if Latin American countries will only "do as we did" is based upon a misreading of history. Much of the high tide of human progress over the past century must surely be traced to the bringing into cultivation of vast, new fertile regions of the world, to the tapping of enormous new mineral deposits, and to the introduction of new forms of transport and power. It was the wealth thus obtained, and so rapidly put to use to industrialize and to urbanize great parts of the United States, that enabled the American people, however temporarily, to set aside the basic "law" of political economy — diminishing returns. But that was a finite phase of history which did not depend so much upon rational theory as upon historical circumstance and good fortune. During the nineteenth century, it was this new and highly profitable interrelatedness developed between industrializing Western Europe (as well as the northeastern parts of the United States) and the primary-producing lightly-settled areas of the Americas, South Africa, and Australia that provided much of the bounty of Western Europe and North America.

The economic integration of the United States in the nineteenth century (the United States being the first great Common Market) did not precede but followed this movement. The efforts being made towards the economic integration of Latin America today are being made in an entirely different phase of history and in entirely different circumstances. Most Latin American countries are relatively poor and lack an extensive, available frontier of rich natural resources. Nor do they face the same external, political challenge and threat that faced developing countries such as Germany and Japan in the nineteenth century, or Israel today. The manifold historical problems which caused (and still do cause) Latin America to remain divided are not likely to disappear with economic integration.

Moreover, the development of Latin America might well be hindered by a growing nationalism. While a fierce nationalism may encourage the development of a particular country, it will almost certainly militate against the economic integration of the Latin American republics. Regardless of the growing stress placed by economists upon national income and national economic growth today, it is not the political entity that has caused economic growth during the past hundred years, but the interrelatedness of continents. On this score alone twentieth-century Latin America, we believe, is at a serious disadvantage compared with nineteenth-century Europe and North America. With the best of intentions and the most efficient and honest international bureaucracy, one cannot hope to recreate the favorable circumstances that North America and western Europe knew at an earlier stage of their history. No economic prescription can hope to recreate those conditions.

Meanwhile, an air of fantasy dominates present United States policy towards Latin American economic integration. Part of this comes from false historical analogy, i.e., generalizing from the favorable and unique circumstances of United States history and the ready availability of United States wealth. "The miracle of fecundity," which is United States history (and upon which so much of our present economic theory and international planning is based) has in fact encouraged many American economists to extrapolate the extraordinary curve of progress of the last century of the Western world into the future of the whole world. From this springs the idealistic outlook of the economists and technocrats who have had singular power and influence in determining United States policy as well as the policy of the Economic Commission for Latin America and the Latin American Free Trade Area. It is largely their doing that the idea of scarcity, which has always been at the center of economic theory, should have been replaced by the idea of plenty; that the option of difficulties, which is largely what economics is about, should have given way to a discussion of ideal, universal solutions.

It is this lack of historical sense that has led some economists, when speaking of the role of the United States in Latin American economic integration, to place an unjustifiable emphasis upon industrialization and urbanization as the primary and the true source of economic progress. Sometimes with the fervor of Old Testament prophets, the argument is put forward that, "come what may," industrialization must be advanced by the countries of Latin America, and that to facilitate this development, economic integration is essential.

Quite apart from the ambiguity that surrounds this term "industrialization," it seems to us no argument to say that because industrialization became the dynamic factor in the northern hemisphere at one period in history, it must necessarily become the dynamic factor in Latin America today. There is a false assumption that industrialization is the cause and not the effect of economic development. Economists have become so obsessed with the idea of industrialization being the Eldorado of the modern age that they have forgotten that it takes an already rich country to industrialize and eat well at the same time.

151

The trouble is that industrialization has become the new alchemy. It plays the role that chemistry played in the Middle Ages. Because industrialization (numerically at least) shows the most rapid rate of "growth," whereas agriculture (the means by which most of us still live) is referred to in current economic dogma as "the least productive sector of an economy," we are asked to believe that industrialization is a desirable process of change regardless of its relevance to the total economy of a country or that country's historical situation.

The fact is that the circumstances in which industrialization became the dynamic factor in the northern hemisphere and those in Latin America today are entirely dissimilar. The countries which industrialized in the nineteenth century had the wealth to industrialize, as well as the technical traditions and a favorable social environment. They did not become rich because they industrialized; the first countries to industrialized were already relatively rich. And they were rich because of the unique way in which they had become interrelated with the primary producing areas of the nineteenth-century world. For those who appeared late on the international scene in the nineteenth century (we are thinking of Japan and Germany), industrialization could only be achieved by great sacrifice.

In any event, discussions about the industrialization of Latin American countries, which supposedly will be encouraged by economic integration, are carried on remote from the cost of induced development. If we want to know what it costs to develop a country in the absence of those favorable nineteenth-century conditions to which we have referred, we only have to look at Israel, remembering that Israel is minuscule when compared with the whole of Latin America (it is smaller in size and numbers than El Salvador). Now if it has taken such a gifted people as the Israelis — determined as they are — to come as far as they have, with the extraordinary financial assistance they have received, one is prompted to ask (even in narrow financial terms) what fantastic sum is required to obtain an equal advance throughout the countries of Latin America. The United States does not possess the equivalent amount of ready money (measured per head of Latin American population) that it and the countries of Western Europe have made available to the Israelis since 1948. A guess would put the required sum in the region of a thousand billion dollars. Because of this, it is unrealistic, we feel, to expect or even to encourage anything but a very modest increase in the industrialization of most Latin American countries. Economic integration will not begin to solve the problem of the cost of induced development.

Undoubtedly, a degree of industrialization will proceed in Latin America. But its path will be utterly dissimilar from that taken by industrializing societies at an earlier period. It was one thing for the Japanese to make the leap to western levels of industrialization in the nineteenth century (which largely consisted in the mechanization of already present traditional industries) and an entirely different thing for the Latin American countries to make the leap today. Moreover, the Japanese were already poised for rapid development, and, like the Israelis in more recent times, they faced the threat of complete subjugation, and had the advantage of internal unity and a strong central government. In addition, Japan (as well as Russia and Israel) was spared the intrusion of what is called "North American modernization" with its stress upon consumer goods rather than work and sacrifice. If the purpose of private, direct United States business investment in Latin America is to introduce the technology of consumption rather than production, those investments will simply increase rather than reduce the economic problems of Latin American countries. In the United States, industrialization and modernization run together. The manufacture of color television in the United States, for instance, makes economic sense because the Americans can make it and pay for it. Color television in the underdeveloped world (where there is no such parallel development between industrialization and modernization) makes economic nonsense. This is where industrialization (especially if it is concerned with the technology of consumption) might completely distort an economy. Some Latin American countries seem to have the worst of all worlds as far as the strategy of development is concerned. They can neither afford to develop their own industry, nor are they able to isolate themselves from the flood of consumer goods produced by United States capital in Latin America or imported from overseas.

Leaving aside the question of the kind of investment, many Latin Americans wonder whether the price they have to pay to the United States' private investor is not unjustifiably high, even allowing for payments for the risk-bearing enterprise, technical knowledge, and entrepreneurial skill invariably accompanying foreign investments.

Many of those who speak for the United States government have not only tended to disregard the problems surrounding induced development in Latin America, they have also cast their hopes too high in expecting to find relief for Latin American countries through a growth of Latin American trade. Certainly, what trade expansion has taken place thus far gives no basis for such optimism. It simply will not do to point to the success of the Zollverein or of the European Economic Community to prove that "what is not, can be." The Zollverein and EEC were integrating what was. LAFTA, on the contrary, is attempting to integrate what it hopes will be. In this sense, LAFTA is an ideal, far removed from the realities of the Latin American world. Moreover, for economic integration to substantially increase the external trade of Latin American countries, it would be necessary to recreate the special and perhaps nonrecurring trade conditions that existed between parts of the nineteenth-century Western world; conditions on which, alas, so much trade theory is still based. To the argument that the United States ought to provide trade concessions on grounds of equity, we can only say that no matter how laudable equity sounds as a principle, it has never determined the foreign policy of sovereign states. It is one thing to strive for an ideal world, and another thing to assume that the ideal world has arrived. International idealism cannot be the axiom of United States foreign policy.

Economic integration has a role to play in the future of Latin America, but, unless one blinds oneself to certain historical and economic facts, that role must continue to be an unimportant one for many years to come. Not least because the historical developments of Western man in the North Atlantic have created a deep and pervasive interrelatedness with Latin American countries. This is where so much talk about Latin American economic integration or the economic integration of South with North America fails to appreciate the much wider view that must be taken of Latin America's future, as those familiar with the trade patterns of Latin American countries know. That future, it appears to us, will be determined not so much by Latin American economic integration, but rather by the developments within the different countries, and the role that Latin American countries will continue to play in the life of the whole Atlantic community. Unless a fierce nationalism comes to dominate Latin American politics, the external economic ties with Europe and North America will continue to play a greater role in the economy of Latin America than an integrated internal market. Absence of economic integration is not an important source of Latin American economic ills; its growing adoption can only have a most limited effect, and talk about "the tricks of growth" should not be allowed to delude anyone into believing anything else.

Contrary to the ideas held by government economists in Washington, we are convinced that what is needed to obtain greater economic strength in Latin America is not so much economic integration as a satisfactory response to the fundamental challenge from within the different Latin American societies. Falsely, this fundamental challenge is looked upon as largely economic, but it is far more complex than that. Its solution will not depend primarily upon economics, but upon the accumulated reserves of the cultural and religious traditions of these peoples. As a tool of analysis, economic theory has its important place. But decisive economic change will not wait upon it any more in Latin America than elsewhere. Causation is a very much bigger and more problematical thing than theoretical analysis; it is in fact, if one is prepared to learn from history, independent of theoretical notions. After all, if theory were vital to growth one must wonder how it came about that so very much economic development did take place in the world in the nineteenth century independent of theoretical notions. This is where an historian of the economic process does not have to be an economic determinist. Even in dealing with economics, development (something dependent upon the interaction of total forces within a society) is often confused with growth (which is a relatively unimportant statistical concept).

We submit that what is emerging in Latin America is a qualitative new order not a quantitative expression and extension of the nineteenth-century Industrial Revolution. How that order will develop we do not know; and despite the growing art of "long-term forecasting, " that is all we do know for certain. Economic change certainly won't come because someone has proved theoretically that it would be better for all concerned if it did. In any event, the real economic world will carry on under laws indifferent to our forecasting. One is certainly not likely to understand what is happening if it is assumed that Latin America's future must be created in the image of the United States. We are convinced that, the more universal and absolute the theories on Latin American development, the more likely they will be wrong. When Western physicists seek refuge from talk of objective knowledge by introducing relativity and complementarity it behooves economists not to be dogmatic. The United States badly needs economists who, in their traditional role, will remind us of unpleasant economic truths — a difficult role for those who claim to be the children of the Enlightenment. When one is rich it is doubly difficult to understand why other people are poor.

All of which is not meant to advocate a passive attitude or isolationism, or race superiority, or selfishness, or apathy, but purposive action based on an intelligent understanding of the depth of the problems that confront us. No one doubts that there is a long-term sound purpose for some of the aims of ECLA and LAFTA; within limits, a degree of integration is feasible; but it will take time and will. And it can never occupy the role which its present advocates ascribe to it.

We realize that we shall not escape the charge of having been negative in this paper. We can only answer that unless the foreign economic policy of the United States towards Latin American economic integration undergoes a complete reassessment of commitments away from present idealistic, universal solutions, it will result in bitter disillusionment. It is our belief that such a reassessment cannot be made without taking account of the following points:

1. Regardless of American generosity and goodwill, the problem of the economic development of Latin America is too vast and too complex for the action of the United States government to have anything but the slightest effect upon it.

2. Not only does the United States harbor illusions about its role in Latin American development; more specifically, it harbors illusions about the role of integration in Latin America's future. For the United States government to make the economic integration of Latin America a major goal of United States foreign policy is to deal with the periphery of the problem of Latin American development. The foundations of Latin American economic strength

must first be laid in the individual countries, not in grandiose schemes for integration.

3. What is needed in United States policy towards Latin America is a shift in emphasis away from universal, idealistic solutions to indigenous economics.

4. Especially should American economists stop claiming universal validity for industrialization as the key to economic development. Economically and socially, industrialization cannot be considered outside the particular conditions of the country concerned.

5. Because economists do wrongly claim universal validity for industrialization, hopes for the expansion of the internal and external trade of Latin America, especially in industrial products (as a result of economic integration) are unrealistic.

Perhaps the most ominous and regrettable thing about the literature dealing with the economic integration of Latin America is that its authors have lost sight of man. The worship of a totemistic device called GNP and economic efficiency, as well as the increasingly implausible attempts to confine economics to means and diregard ends, has blinded economists to the human context of economic activity and the relation of economics to the whole. Instinctively, the laboring people of most lands are aware, even more than the intellectuals who try to guide them, that forced, rapid economic development cannot be divorced from human sacrifice and social disorder. If economic efficiency is the goal of those United States economists (or their progeny abroad) who advise Latin American countries, we can understand why the leaders of some Latin American nations take advice, impartially, from Peking, Moscow, or Washington.

CHAPTER **13** ECONOMIC INTEGRATION IN
LATIN AMERICA: THE NEXT
FIFTY YEARS

By George Jackson Eder
Washington, D. C.

> "This is not prophecy, just a
> nightmare." E. M. Forster,
> "The Machine Stops," *The Eternal
> Moment and Other Stories*. New
> York: Harcourt Brace, 1928.

Economic integration in Latin America: The next fifty
years — What a risky subject to choose for a talk before so well-
informed an audience as I see before me! We need look back only
a few years to the great predictions of economic development and
boundless prosperity voiced at Bogotá, Punta del Este, and Montevideo to realize the perils of prophecy for, after seven years of
promises, the gap between the United States and the developing
countries of Latin America, and between the richer nations and
the poorer nations in that area, is greater than ever. The hopes
and predictions of only a scant few years ago have proved to be
nothing but empty oratory and idle dreams.

True, it is safer to prophesy the events of the next fifty
years than it is to forecast what is about to happen in the next five.
But I am going to take an even safer course. My foresight is fal-
lible — definitely — but I have found that my hindsight is remarkably
good. So I intend to tell you of the events of the next fifty years
from the vantage point of the year 2018 and, by hindsight, tell you
what has happened to Latin American integration in all those years.

We are now in this year of grace, 2018, trying to put together the jigsaw pieces of the past to form a picture of all that
has happened over the last five decades. Fortunately, we have as
our guide the Forthright Report on United States Aid to Latin America, compiled by the senior Senator from Delaware and his able
staff. In fact, so complete is that report on the events from the
year 1968 to the present time, and so fully have its contents been
debated in Congress and the press, that it would be otiose for me
to go into the statistical and other details that are, of course, so
well known to all of you here.

Instead, I shall confine myself to showing, from my research into the records of the past, how the developments recorded in the Forthright Report, and the conclusions reached from
those facts, were all clearly foreseeable fifty or more years ago,
and were in fact foreseen and predicted by many who had no

personal axe to grind, no reasons of partisan or financial self-interest at stake, and who were not misled by some of the peculiar economic theories of the time.

As shown in the third volume of the Forthright Report, the idea of a Latin American free trade area or common market was developed primarily by the United Nations Economic Commission for Latin America with headquarters in Chile; in fact, it was practically the brain-child of that remarkably persuasive economist and gourmet, Dr. Raúl Prebisch, who saw in the success of the European Economic Community, following the second World War, a solution for most of Latin America's economic problems. The terms of trade, economies of scale, effective allocation of productive resources, absorption of new technologies —terms that mean little to us today—were the slogans of the time. But, as Gottfried Haberler pointed out more than fifty years ago:

> The great disservice of the exaggerated claims of success of the common market is that they have led Latin Americans to try to do the same. . .I am afraid that the conditions in Latin America for integration, the political as well as objective economic and geographic conditions, are much less favorable than in Europe. . . .There are quite a few man-made structural handicaps (such as the various government-owned transportation companies) which operate extremely inefficiently. This is the first reason why Latin-American integration cannot be as effective as European. The second reason is concerned with different degrees of inflation. . .and it is very hard to see how countries which pursue such different monetary policies. . .can really integrate. The third reason relates to the much higher degree of government intervention in the economic process. That again makes integration much more difficult. Fourthly, the whole set-up of the Treaty of Montevideo is very different from that of the Treaty of Rome. The terms of the Treaty of Rome provide for broad tariff categories, while according to the Treaty of Montevideo there is no across-the-board cutting of tariffs.

Dr. Rodrigo Botero, Secretary for Economic Affairs to the then President of Colombia, Carlos Lleras Restrepo, showed why a common market was far simpler for the contiguous countries of Europe than for the widely separated nations of Latin America, and quoted Bela Balassa to the effect that "empirical studies indicate that. . . distance has a considerable effect on economic intercourse" — which is hardly surprising and would seem to apply to other forms of intercourse as well.

It was undoubtedly because of geographical proximity, as well as historical, ethnic and economic similarities, that Raúl Prebisch's ideas first took root in Central America and, as you know from the Forthright Report, integration in that area proceeded

from the bilateral agreements of the early 1950's to the Multilateral Treaty of 1958, which eliminated intraregional duties on
some 200 items and set as its goals an eventual regional free
trade area, the equalization of external tariffs, the harmonization
of fiscal and other measures to promote industrialization, and the
free movement of persons and capital within the area. The Treaty
bogged down in later negotiations for further tariff reductions on a
commodity-by-commodity basis, but business leaders in Central
America, motivated by enlightened self-interest as well as a pa-
triotic public interest, continued to press for a common market,
and in 1960 a Tripartite Treaty of Economic Association was
signed, providing for immediate free trade, except for some fifty
items, and automatic across-the-board tariff reductions for most
of these. This was followed a year later by a General Treaty of
Central American Integration on the same automatic basis, with
total intraregional free trade promised within five years, except
for sugar, coffee, cotton, wheat and flour, alcoholic beverages
which contributed so heavily to government revenues, and petroleum products on which no country cared to jeopardize its own
refinery.

Although the pressure behind this integration movement
came chiefly from businessmen, especially in El Salvador, Guatemala, and Costa Rica, the treaties themselves had to be negotiated and implemented by the governments so, by 1968, there
were 33 different government and international governmental
agencies involved in the scheme, many of them with branches or
representatives in each of the five countries of Central America
and elsewhere in the Hemisphere, and with such a proliferation of
alphabetical names in English and Spanish as to practically ex-
haust the possibilities of the common alphabet. Government planners even contemplated the necessity of overcoming the letter
shortage by turning to the Greek or Hebrew alphabets.

The success of CACM—the Central American Common
Market— was striking, so far as could be judged from the statistical evidence. Intraregional exports, which had been insignifi-
cant prior to integration, rose from 7.5% of the total exports of
the area in 1960 to some 20% in 1967. Exports are taken as the
criterion because import figures were distorted by U.S. aid shipments. This meant a gain of some $180 million, of which perhaps
$130 million can be imputed to integration and the remainder to the
fact that all exports —not merely intraregional exports — doubled
over the period. For the sake of perspective, it may be pointed
out that Central America's entire intraregional sales under CACM
reached less than $220 million per annum at their peak, or about
one-quarter the amount of the annual sales of R. H. Macy and
Company.

The profit on $220 million of exports can at the most be
placed at 5% or $11,000,000. Whether or not this result warranted
the $130 million of Inter-American Development Bank direct assist-
ance to CACM, and the $650 million that the United States and other
international agencies poured into Central America between 1960

and 1967, would be hard to say, and whether or not it resulted in
the creation of new trade, or the diversion of pre-existing trade,
would be impossible to prove. Certainly, consumers in Central
America paid more for manufactured products — and 75% of the
intraregional trade was in manufactured goods — than if they had
purchased them in the cheapest world markets, for, obviously,
if Central America could have manufactured better products or
cheaper products than any other country in the world, there would
have been no need for tariffs or for regional preferences. This
is axiomatic, and applies to any regional associations for discriminatory controls over free commerce. In that sense, there
has certainly been a diversion of trade and an economic loss to
the world as a whole.

On the other hand, from the Central American viewpoint,
CACM meant that the area would be less vulnerable to worldwide
economic pressures and wars, by reason of its increasing self-
sufficiency in manufacturing, and that the new industries could
provide jobs for surplus rural labor displaced by the hoped-for
greater efficiency of agricultural production which was the sine
qua non of any real economic progress in Latin America. And
certainly, manufacturing enterprises — foreign, local, and
jointly-owned — would not have been established in Central America to the extent that they have developed over the past fifty years
had it not been for integration, for reasons which Ingo Walter and
Hans Vitzthum pointed out over fifty years ago.

But the proof of the success of integration in Central
America came with the cessation of U.S. aid, made necessary by
the fiscal and other aberrations of the 1960's. Central America,
left on her own, with pressing balance of payments problems and
many over-expansive projects uncompleted, was desperately
short of funds, and particularly of foreign exchange. Necessity,
the prolific mother of invention, came to the rescue, as the
fuerzas vivas — the entrepreneurs of Central America, the businessmen, the new industrialists, commercial farmers, bankers,
professional men, political leaders and others — cast about for
new sources of revenue. And then the solution struck so many at
once that it is difficult to assign priority for the idea, an idea,
which in any event, had been immanent in the minds of Central
American statesmen for generations — the reunification of Central
America, the fulfillment of the dream of the last of the filibusteros,
William Walker.

A hundred years ago, Andrew Carnegie had erected a
palace in San José to serve as a center and inspiration for Central
American unification, but, as Luis Anderson, one of the wisest of
Costa Rica's international lawyers used to say, the only obstacle
to unification was that then there would only be one President instead of five, one Ambassador to Washington, Paris or London,
and one-fifth as many sinecures for temporarily exiled statesmen.
And then it suddenly dawned upon these fuerzas vivas that the very
multiplicity of foreign offices provided the solution. The six
countries of Central America, including Panama, had embassies

in over eighty countries of the world, eighteen Ambassadors in the United States alone, and close to five hundred embassy buildings ranging from simple mansions to palaces of almost princely opulence.

It was quickly ascertained that if this ambassadorial representation could be reduced to one embassy in each country, the sale of the surplus buildings and of other Central American government edifices abroad, would net over $600 million. With this incentive, and with the prior assurance that Central America would retain her six votes in the UN and the OAS, the Confederation of Central American Republics came into being, with a Constitution modeled on that of Switzerland but adapted to Central American mores.

It might be thought that, with a Confederation, the need for CACM, ODECA, SEC, SIECA, and the other unpronounceable agencies and their branches — 67 of them by that time — would have come to an end, but old bureaus never die and, much to Senator Forthright's indignation, the United States is continuing to support a good part of their expense. So, in answer to the question of how CACM has fared over the past fifty years, it may be said that it and all its progeny are still thriving, and that the Confederation of Central American Republics, while relatively impoverished compared to her three neighbors to the North, is, thanks in part to CACM, far more prosperous than it was fifty years ago.

Of course, this prosperity has not been distributed with an even hand. As Keith Griffin pointed out in the early 1960's, the polarization of investment in the more prosperous regions of a free trade area and the impoverishment of the backward regions is the historical record:

> The union of Ireland and Britain (1800-1921) had disastrous effects on Irish industrial and agricultural production. . . . The formation of Great Britain resulted at least in the relative impoverishment of Wales and Scotland. The creation of unified Italy wrought the destruction of southern Italian industry. . . . The Civil War [was] fought in the United States to prevent the Southern agricultural states from leaving the industrial North. . .

Even during the early years of the Central American Common Market, Honduras and Nicaragua showed practically no gain in exports as the result of integration, while Costa Rica, El Salvador and Guatemala — and later Panama — multiplied their industry and commerce many fold. In compensation, the Central American Clearing House and the Central American Bank for Economic Integration, now continued as the Federal Reserve Board of Central America, were established in Tegucigalpa, the Secretariat for Central American Tourism was located in Managua and, under the Confederation, this policy of decentralization or of rotation has been followed throughout, although — with complete freedom of movement and of enterprise within the Confederation — there has been no attempt to follow the misguided leadership of the United States in subsidizing regions that are economically unviable and that should be restored to the national forest preserves.

The population problem which loomed so large some fifty years ago, not only in Central America but in all of Latin America, when the growth rate ranged from 3.1% to 3.8% per annum in Central America and 2.9% for the area as a whole, has happily been solved. It would be pertinent to quote, in this connection, what Professor Murdock of Yale wrote some fifty years ago:

> Devotees of foreign aid are singularly oblivious to demographic realities. . . . Every innovation in medicine or public health, every improvement in diet or nutrition, every gift of money or surplus agricultural products, serves only to keep alive great numbers who would otherwise have perished from disease, malnutrition or famine. The resulting population increments divide and absorb both the increments in production and the largesse from abroad, with the inevitable consequences of increasing dependency and pauperization and a constantly falling rather than a rising standard of living. Foreign aid, whatever its nature, has thus tragically injured the very ones whom it has sought to assist, and it has no reasonable prospect of ever genuinely helping any society which has not come realistically to grips with its own population problem.

Professor Barlow of Michigan similarly pointed out that the eradication of malaria had been particularly disastrous from the demographic viewpoint, lowering the death rate and raising the birth rate.

The ravages wrought by well-meaning men in combatting disease and reducing the infant mortality rate, while raising the birth and survival rates with food donations and otherwise — what Russell Baker called "the American knack for wrecking, and then making a mess out of the wreckage" — gave promise of a Latin American population explosion from 260 million fifty years ago in 19. ⁻ to 700 million at the present time — a promise of starvation for half a billion human beings! Even in 1967, 180 million in Latin America were undernourished, 50 million starving, and Alberto Lleras, predicting famine, asserted that it was not merely a case of slums and a housing shortage — there were not even enough cemeteries to handle the dead!

Fortunately for Latin America and for the world, the work of the "Nine Wise Men," the "Panel of Five," and of the "Committee of Four," the economists who guided the destinies of Latin America in the 1960's, was overturned in the course of the following decade by the "Four Horsemen," for God in His infinite wisdom and Mercy sent the four horsemen of the Apocalypse —

162

Famine, Pestilence, War and Death — to undo the damage men had done and restore the balance of nature.

No one had every suggested an alternative effective course of action to prevent Latin America from sinking to the lowest levels of economic degradation. Latin American leaders for the most part preferred to sweep the problem under the rug, and the best hope that their economists could offer was that, although every child born into the world brings another mouth to feed, he also brings another pair of hands to work. This two to one truism overlooked the fact that, with the high birth rate and increasing life span, the percentage of Latin America's population in the unproductive age groups of the very young or very old was almost twice that of the United States, a condition aggravated by the then prevailing social security retirement age of 50 to 55. *

Under the Confederation, and compelled to live on its own resources without the demoralizing force of U.S. aid, Central America has raised the retirement age, stabilized its population, and is gradually lifting the level of literacy to the high ratios maintained by Costa Rica.

The "Integration Industries" — the monopolies created under the early CACM arrangements — have given way to moderately protected industries, while undue duplication of facilities has been deterred by sound business practice and competition. With an assured Confederation-wide market, growing in purchasing power but not in population, many foreign investors have been attracted to the area, in some cases working in combination with local entrepreneurs but with no arbitrary government requirement of participation.

With the cessation of U.S. aid, there was no longer the necessity of bowing to U.S. demands for Harvard's tax reforms,

---

*Historians differ on this point. Some contend that it was not World War III and famine that controlled the population explosion, but the $100 bonus for voluntary sterilization introduced at about that time after the failure of more conventional birth control methods. Contraception had been legalized in the late 1960's but, as only the more intelligent were able to employ it with complete success, it soon became the greatest degenerative force that had ever operated in that area. The combination of contraception, abortion, and sterilization that had proved so successful in Japan would have required "a literate, disciplined people, without strong superstitions, or theological principles governing the biology of reproduction," as Stuart Chase had pointed out in a long-forgotten book, The Most Probable World. It was unsuited to the Central American environment, but the bonus for voluntary sterilization, with the slogan "Copulation Without Population" was immediately successful. All historians are agreed that, whether it was the war or the bonus that reduced the population, it was certainly the latter that stabilized the population after the war — and with ameliorative rather than degenerative consequences.

meaning corporate and personal income taxes and other levies so high as to be incompatible with the needs of a developing economy. To foster new industries and the reinvestment of profits, the corporate income tax was placed at a uniform 40% on dividends, compared with the former 60% rate on net income in El Salvador, 30% in Nicaragua and Costa Rica, and 48% in Guatemala. Personal income taxes were reduced, and the old customs duties which ran as high as 200 or 300%, were cut to levels that forced local industry to be competitive and reduce prices. On the other hand, real estate taxes were increased as a spur to the more effective use of land, while more efficient tax administration for all taxes increased government revenues without burdening legitimate business. Monetary stability was maintained, although the Central American peso was devalued at the same time as the American dollar, in order to keep the same parity level.

Thanks to the cessation of U.S. aid and a return to a free enterprise economy, the rate of economic development of the Confederation exceeds that of any period since 1923-29, confirming the accuracy of Lincoln Gordon's contention that there seems to be a high inverse correlation between the amount of per capita aid and a country's rate of economic growth. All in all, the Confederation, and the Central American Common Market before it, have proved their worth, and fulfilled all expectations.

Unfortunately, the same has not been true of LAFTA — the Latin American Free Trade Association. Fifty years ago, Botero pointed out that, in 1954 without tariff preferences, intraregional trade in the LAFTA countries reached 10.3% of their total trade, and ten years later, after three years of multilateral tariff reductions under the LAFTA arrangements, it reached 10.2%. At no time up to the abandonment of the LAFTA scheme, did intraregional trade ever exceed 12% of the total and, in 1967, for example, prior to the disintegration of LAFTA, it amounted to less than $800 million which, for an area of that size, population and wealth, compares not too favorably with Macy's 1967 sales of $759 million a year.

Furthermore, while R. H. Macy and Company made a profit of nearly $20 million on those sales, and paid taxes of over $50 million, it is doubtful whether the LAFTA trade entailed any profit at all, other than to the merchants involved, for it was supported largely by the taxpayers through foreign exchange, export, and other subsidies, and, far from bringing revenues to the governments involved, the LAFTA arrangements were supported by International Development Bank contributions of $200 million, and U.S. aid and other direct contributions of $170 million, this representing only a fraction of the sums poured into the organization by the U.S. and other governments.

The first sign of a crack-up in LAFTA was the drop in the number of tariff reductions for intraregional trade, from 7,600 items in 1961-62 to an average of some 500 items in the succeeding years. These tariff concessions were what the

Colombian Ambassador to the LAFTA conference called "phony reductions" —paper concessions on items not produced in the countries granting them or irrelevant to intraregional trade. Haberler,
Botero, and others, in fact all informed students of the subject,
predicted in the 1960's that LAFTA could never be a success so
long as negotiations were on a commodity-by-commodity basis instead of having the across-the-board percentage reductions on all
items, as in the EEC and CACM arrangements. Even the President of Chile, one of the prime movers in the scheme, admitted
that LAFTA was stagnating. Botero pointed out that, unlike the
situation in Central America, there was no significant, influential
group of men in business or government in the LAFTA countries
who took a regional rather than a national viewpoint; that the most
ardent advocates of Latin American integration were associated
with international organizations or academic institutions, or politicians who were out of power.

The actual split in the LAFTA organization occurred almost exactly fifty years ago, when Bolivia, Chile, Colombia,
Ecuador, Peru and Venezuela formed their own Andean group,
amid loud protestations by the representatives of those countries,
and of the LAFTA authorities, that such regional subgroups, far
from detracting from LAFTA, were actually in furtherance of the
aims of the alliance, and would aid in the ultimate goal of a total
Latin American common market which, of course, never
materialized. The split-off of the Andean group was followed by
that of the River Plate region. By that time, most people were
ready to agree with Arturo Frondizi's comment that Latin American integration was only a Utopian dream.

The reasons for the failure of LAFTA as compared with
the success of the CACM group are not hard to find. Distance
played a part, as did also the disparate ethnic and economic status of the constituent countries, ranging from Mexico, Brazil,
and Argentina with their highly developed industrial complexes,
to Bolivia where manufacturing was embryonic and illiteracy rates
were and still are the highest in South America. Monetary de-
basement in Argentina, Brazil, Chile and, until the late 1960's,
in Colombia, with concommitant exchange controls, subsidies, and
other government interferences with the free market, made true
integration almost impossible, as Dr. Haberler foresaw five decades ago.

But the basic reason why Mexico and the countries of
South America could not agree to integrate in fact is that in each
of these countries, unlike Central America, powerful industries
had been built up— and overbuilt — under the protection of im-
pregnable tariff walls, import controls, and foreign exchange
subsidies. None of these industries— or practically none—was
in a position to face the free competition even of intraregional
trade, and the labor unions combined with the business interests
to prevent any substantial lowering of the barricades. As in the
case of the poor family with twelve children— admittedly too
many for limited resources —the question arises "which baby

should we kill?" and none of the LAFTA countries was prepared to sacrifice its own infant industries.

But, despite the black picture painted by the statistics, and despite the ultimate abandonment of LAFTA, something did come out of it. As anyone who read Jean J. Servan-Schreiber's book, Le défi américain, which created such a sensation fifty years ago, could have predicted, the only enterprises well enough organized from a technical as well as a management viewpoint to take advantage of the opportunities afforded by LAFTA were the American corporations that had proved to be the chief beneficiaries of the European common market, plus a few equally well-organized European corporations and a handful of Mexican and Brazilian entrepreneurs. These companies flocked to the LAFTA area, chiefly to Mexico, Brazil, and Venezuela, and brought new enterprises and new products to the region that might not have come had it not been for the LAFTA arrangements.

In mentioning Servan-Schreiber's book, I must warn that, as one commentator of the period remarked: "Seldom have so many correct conclusions been based upon so many errors of fact and interpretation." In fact, many of his conclusions were equally erroneous, but his major contention, that the success of the American companies in Europe was due to their superior organization, their expenditures for research and development, and their dynamic spirit of innovation, was undoubtedly true, and is a tacit recognition of Joseph Schumpeter as himself one of the great innovators of the past century.

Servan-Schreiber's recommendation to Europe's leaders —and here again he was correct —was not to legislate against the American invasion, for that would condemn the old world to permanent second-rate status and widen the gap between Europe and the United States, but to apply all of Europe's latent talent to research and organization on its own, to profit by what they could learn from the American enterprises established in their midst, and, if possible, to beat America at its own game of technological and managerial innovation. That, substantially, is what has occurred over the past fifty years, with healthy rivalry, not so much between nation and nation, as between one entrepreneur and another in the battle for the consumer's dollar. And it has been a battle in which all — consumers as well as entrepreneurs and capitalists — have come out the gainers.

In Latin America, the response to the American challenge was more direct. As long ago as the 1960's, the Committee of Four had foreseen the likelihood that foreign private initiative, as they put it, with its great technical and financial superiority, might acquire a predominant position in the Latin American common market to the detriment of local entrepreneurs. To counter this, they proposed that the international agencies, and the industrialized countries participating in LAFTA, provide technical and financial support to Latin American industry, and that the LAFTA countries adopt restrictive legislation to curb foreign private enterprises and compel them to share their know-how with Latin American entrepreneurs and government enterprises. As a consequence, the results which Servan-Schreiber had warned against in Europe ensued; the LAFTA countries fell further behind in the race for survival; the economic gap widened; and when it became clear that no further grants and so-called loans could be expected from the United States, the LAFTA countries uniformly defaulted on those obligations, and confiscated the foreign enterprises established under the aegis of the common market. These enterprises, in which the U.S. companies alone had invested over $10 billion, given employment to over one and a half million workers, accounted for over one-tenth of the total Latin American industrial output, and paid one-fifth of all Latin American taxes, were taken over by the governments. Within months, they became hopelessly disorganized under government management and a burden on the economy, as could readily have been foreseen from the experiences of the post-World War II decades. Better to build pyramids, as Keynes had suggested, than for a government to invest in an attempt to manage great industrial and utility enterprises.

As in the case of the CACM agencies, the LAFTA organization, the Bank for Latin American Integration, and all their agencies and subagencies throughout the Hemisphere and in Europe continued to flourish as the green bay tree, their secretariats supported by fully funded pension trusts that should carry them on for another fifty years — all, as Senator Forthright discovered, largely at the expense of the American taxpayer.

All of these developments were fully foreseeable fifty years ago, prior to the period covered by the Forthright Report, provided one had the knowledge of accounting to understand the annual reports of the government and international enterprises and see that, behind the glowing figures of continuing profits, there lay deficits and the steady attrition of capital investment, all concealed by management-dictated accounting practices that, had they been indulged in in the United States, would have sent the perpetrators to jail for life. The auditors carefully reported these facts in their footnotes to the accounts — depreciation rates the same as for comparable industries in the United States, when any intelligent person would know that such depreciation rates were meaningless in a country where the currency had been debased ten to one, or a hundred or a thousand to one, and that paper profits were in reality devastating losses — or a statement that the accounts in Latin American currencies had been translated into dollars at the rates at which the amounts were received or loaned, which any Dutch accountant, or other accountant versed in international transactions, would know was ridiculous. These and other accounting peculiarities were red-flagged by the auditors' opinions that the accounts had been prepared in conformity with generally accepted accounting principles which, except for Dutch accounting, assumes that money has a constant value, giving the impression to a layman that the mathematical symbols used in the accounts do in fact represent the certainty that mathematics would seem to imply.

But the presumption that everyone who reads an annual report knows what generally accepted accounting principles are, is like the legal rule that everyone is presumed to know the law — a necessary assumption but untrue. And the fact is that probably none of the managers or directors of the Latin American government enterprises, and not one in a hundred of the directors of the intergovernmental enterprises, nor one in a thousand of the economists who were presumed to be experts in economic development, had any more than the barest theoretical understanding of modern corporation accounting, much less of Dutch accounting methods. None of these so-called experts seems to have grasped the significance of an income statement or balance sheet, nor would have known the importance of a cash requirements or flow of funds statement, and, as a consequence, no one realized that not a single government-owned public utility in Latin America, and only a scant handful of the government-operated industrial enterprises, were operating in the black. Notwithstanding the paper profits shown in the books, they were operating on a deficit basis, requiring the constant injection of new capital or tax subsidies to keep them going from year to year. Many of them were in fact insolvent and, with few exceptions, far from promoting economic development, they represented a major drain on the economy.

Suppliers' credits, from Japan, Canada, and Western Europe, and, most lamentable of all, from the Inter-American Development Bank, kept them going, and were in themselves proof positive of the utter incompetence of management in relying on two to five year credits for capital investments that could not possibly be paid off in less than ten to twenty years. Fifty years ago, thanks to the attempt at forced-draft industrialization under the Latin American integration program, 48% of the foreign debt of the Latin American governments was due in less than five years; debt service took 20% of the proceeds of all of Latin America's exports, and absorbed 75% of the gross new capital inflow into Latin America. For all this, the only remedy proposed by such organizations as the Inter-American Development Bank, and such leaders as Alberto Lleras, was what they called a revision of the debt structure, and acceptance of the more favorable terms proposed at Punta del Este. What this meant in plain English was that Latin America was unable to meet its obligations and, to tell the truth, never had any intention of meeting them except with a view to obtaining further foreign aid, as was revealed by one researcher some fifty years ago. It was preparing to default on loans granted at interest rates far below the interest rates paid by the United States Government and other lending institutions on their own obligations, and it demanded so-called "soft loans" at 1.25% interest and 20 year maturities that only the grossest hypocrisy or ignorance could characterize as loans. Senator Gruening was right when he told the then Secretary of State Rusk that they were "not loans at all, considering their terms, and in all probability will never be repaid."

When U. S. aid ended, the insolvency of the Latin American government enterprises and their drain on the economy could no longer be concealed and, one by one, most of the LAFTA countries turned to Communism or military dictatorship in the hope that complete socialization would prove more effective than the mixed economies which had wrecked these nations' institutions in the 1960's and '70's. It was not until after the end of World War III that the nations of South America and the Caribbean, in common with the Confederation of Central American Republics, came to the realization that, of all sectors of society, the government sector was the most corrupt, the most theoretical, and the least competent to run the nations' industrial, agricultural, commercial, financial, and public utility enterprises. They learned, as a disillusioned writer in the '60's had foretold, that the surest road to economic development—not perfect by any means, but the best— is a system, not of laissez-faire, but one where the government confines its activities chiefly to the fundamental government functions such as maintenance of law and order, education, sanitation, and other necessary services which cannot or will not be supplied by private initiative, and, above all, providing such regulation and control as is needed to ensure a true, competitive free-market economy, with such safeguards as are essential for the safety, health, and welfare of the general public.

Under this system, and thanks to the natural and other curbs on population that proved so salutary in Central America, the former LAFTA countries have enjoyed an era of material, social, and political development far surpassing even the halcyon years of 1923-29, and historians who look back on the Latin American Free Trade Association recall it only as an unfortunate but noble experiment by well-meaning men.

> But man, proud man,
> Drest in a little brief authority,
> Most ignorant of what he's most assured, . . .
> Plays such fantastic tricks before high heaven
> As make the angels weep.

PART **III**

ECONOMICS AND BANKING

CHAPTER **14** MONETARISM VS. STRUCTURALISM: CONFLICT IN U.S. ECONOMIC AID TO LATIN AMERICA

By   Alvin Cohen
     Department of Economics
     Lehigh University

In April 1967, the Presidents of the United States and of the Latin American countries met in Punta del Este, Uruguay, to discuss possible new directions for the Alliance for Progress and for inter-American relations. One of the most widely publicized decisions was their position favoring a Latin American customs union, a first step toward the goal of Latin America's economic integration. On a smaller regional basis, efforts had already been made. The Central American Common Market and the Latin American Free Trade Association had been functioning for quite some time. The intent of the Presidents' statement was to bring changes in market structures and in productivity to all Latin American countries, not just to the members of the two regional groupings. Subsequently, much of the positive impact of the Presidents' declaration has been lost. Bolivia, Chile, Colombia, Ecuador, Peru, and Venezuela signed an agreement in February 1968 to establish their own trade and development organization, the Andean Development Corporation. As a consequence of this, the goal of Latin American integration seems even further away than it did at Punta del Este in 1967, unless one views the objective as achievable through multiple subregional groups evolving into a single entity.

Undoubtedly, the Presidents' declaration was motivated by a need to reaffirm the Alliance for Progress, by a belief that the goal of economic integration would yield significant structural change in the area's systems of production and distribution, and by an awareness of the need for structural change to bring about social development. Nevertheless, economic integration and structural change have costs. The formation of the Andean Development Corporation suggests that total area integration immediately was politically too expensive. In view of the cost of structural change, one wonders whether or not it is all that important an objective, and furthermore, assuming its importance, whether or not the Latin American policy of the United States has been oriented consistently toward the structural change objective.

As for the importance of structural change to the developmental process, there has been a growing awareness that social change in depth is necessary if the developmental process is to take place. In accordance with this point of view, it is argued that changes in economic variables alone do not stimulate the progress of the developmental process. Rather, the process is one of a continuing interaction of economic variables with the political and

173

social parameters. This interaction moves a society away from its traditional, non-technological value system. Thus, the developmental process means a change in the societal constraints as much as it means an increase in gross national product or in real per capita income. Indeed, some changes in the societal constraints can be considered as developmentally positive even when there has been no change in these aggregate measures of economic activity.

Although of much current vogue, structuralism is not universally accepted. There are dissenters. In economic literature the dissent is evidenced by the controversy between "structuralists" and "monetarists."[1] The nature of the controversy suggests something more than merely theoretical or definitional importance. For example, with respect to economic policy formulation, accepting the structuralist view should facilitate the search for and the proposal of political economy recommendations more appropriate to the developmental process than would be the case under monetarism. Support for this interpretation comes directly from the failure of traditional monetary and fiscal policies to solve the developmental problems of backward societies, and even to solve those problems of backwardness in advanced societies. Were it true that development be essentially economic, then these traditional policies should prove adequate developmental tools. However, the tools have proved inadequate. Backward societies have frequently used these policies unsuccessfully. A typical case is raising reserve requirements to restrict credit as a deterrent to inflation. Results often have been a continuance of, if not an increase in, the inflationary tendencies. As for advanced societies, deficit financing has not corrected structural unemployment.

With respect to the Latin American aid policy of the United States, academic acceptance of the principle of structuralism has preceded political acceptance. It is only recently that the foreign economic program of the United States has come to reflect the importance of structural change. Since the Alliance for Progress does subsume structural change while previous aid programs of the United States did not, the signing of the Charter of Punta del Este, August 1961, may be used conveniently as the date marking the shift from exclusive subservience to monetary stability and private enterprise — monetarism — to, at the very least, a willingness to accept the posture of structural change — structuralism. On the other hand, however, the United States' invasion of the Dominican Republic might well mark a shift back to monetarism. Furthermore, monetarists continue influential in foreign aid policy decisions. Aid-receiving Latin American countries still must demonstrate interest in maintaining price stability and in adopting anti-inflationary policies. This is specifically true of short-term credit obtained from the International Monetary Fund.

Support for monetarism comes from both economic and political circles. Economists are impressed with the efficiency of traditional monetary and fiscal policy tools for maintaining economic stability and insist that economic stability is an essential precondition to a backward society's developmental process. Political circles tend to equate economic stability with political stability and the latter with the containment of communism. It follows logically, therefore, that to achieve economic stability is to deter communism. However, to equate economic and political stability is undesirable. The equation tends to deny that transforming an underdeveloped nation's societal structure is a separate consideration. On the contrary, transformation should be considered separately and of greater importance than communist containment. To believe that a policy of containment by itself would alter the societal structure suggests a lack of appreciation for the economic mechanisms necessary to support an intensive and continuous developmental effort. Furthermore, in the case of Latin America, to equate economic and political stability is to grossly misunderstand the political forces at work in these developing but generally non-democratic countries.[2] Unfortunately, during the 1948-61 period, containment seems to have been virtually the only criterion for United States foreign policy. It appears to have been assumed that any and all policy details appropriate to the objective of communist containment were, simultaneously, appropriate to the objective of facilitating modernization. As a result, United States policy, based on this erroneous notion of mutual appropriateness, had to fail.

In support of this monetaristic-communist containment interpretation it can be pointed out, for example, that there was nothing positive in the position taken by the United States at the meetings of the Council of the OAS, at the meetings of the foreign ministers of American states, and at the meetings of the Inter-American Economic and Social Council during the 1948-1958 period. Then too, once the United Nations Economic Commission for Latin America (ECLA) began to function, the United States opposed ECLA's structuralist interpretation of Latin America's development problems. With respect to ECLA, United States negative reaction was particularly strong when ECLA initiated discussions which ultimately led to the formation of the Latin American Free Trade Association.[3] Additionally, the attractiveness of statism to Latin America's underdeveloped and underprivileged masses was not associated by the United States as emanating out of a desire for development or for structural change. Because of this, it was inevitable that the United States continued firm in its conviction that, one, private investment was the superior mechanism for solving Latin America's growth problems, and, two, that monetary stability was an absolutely necessary precondition to the flow of private investment funds from the United States to Latin America. The aid programs of the United States between 1948 and 1961 have had this private investment.bias. Undoubtedly, at times, this bias has been expressed as part of the necessary strategy to obtain Congressional approval.

Also important as an example of the negativeness of U.S. foreign policy is the resistance of the United States to the establishment of a regional bank for Latin America, until 1958. In terms of the position of the United States vis-à-vis Latin America, this negativeness was wholly consistent with the negative position of the United States during all of the post-War period. For example, in October 1954, the United States rejected a proposal of the United Nations for the establishment of an inter-American loan fund. At that time, the U. S. stressed the adequacy of the lending facilities of the World Bank and the Export-Import Bank. Again, in 1957, at the Inter-American Economic Conference, the Secretary of the Treasury, Anderson, stated that he saw no need for a new lending institution. [4] On both of these occasions the United States might well have thought that a lending institution with control by the Latin Americans would end the ability of the United States to tie economic aid to the principle of monetary stability. By the end of that Inter-American Conference, however, the United States had agreed to consider the proposal of the Conference to establish a regional lending entity. The position of the United States, then was made consistent with both its pre-War position on the establishment of such a bank and with its post-War position on the establishment of special lending institutions for other geographic regions. As for the pre-War position, an inter-American bank, supported by the United States, had been proposed at the Seventh International Conference at Montevideo, 1933. A convention was finally drawn in May 1940 but it failed to receive the requisite number of signatures. As for special lending institutions for other geographic regions, as early as 1956 the United States adopted a position favorable to the establishment of a regional bank for the Middle East.

The shift in the position of the United States with respect to the establishment of a regional bank for Latin America should not be viewed in isolation. In the context of the times, it reflected a slowly growing comprehension of the nature of the developmental process, and with this, the recognition that modernization is more effectively handled when not viewed as synonymous with communist containment. While this comprehension is far from perfect and the recognition still incomplete, the extent to which they do exist suggests the acceptance of several basic conditions. First, since the process of growth tends to interject a note of political instability, and because political instability can be assumed to be a condition unattractive to private investors, the efforts of the private sector at rapid capital accumulation and technological advance are likely to be inadequate. Second, nationalism seems concomitant with growth. Furthermore, nationalism can be either a positive or a negative factor in a country's growth process.

The second condition creates additional problems which, themselves, require special attention and solutions. To mention one, bilaterally arranged aid agreements between the United States and individual Latin American nations equate the public position of the one with the public position of the other, the sovereignty of the one with that of the other. It cannot help but place the aid-receiving nation in an inferior position, and one that is all too obvious relative to multilaterally arranged programs. With respect to the multilaterally arranged programs, the political weakness of the aid applicant is viewed in the context of the weak political position of most of the participants in the same international program. In the case of the bilateral program, the political position of the aid applicant is related directly to that of the United States. Moreover, for multilateral programs, the aid applicant is requesting something to which it is entitled as a participant. In the case of bilateral programs, the aid applicant is requesting a dispensation. Consequently, it could be argued that bilateral programs are more likely to stimulate a country's nationalism into unproductive ventures to improve its international political position than would be the case with multilateral programs. Furthermore, in the bilateral agreement, the aid receiver is bargaining for its "fair share" of United States aid relative to each of the other aid-receiving Latin American nations. Here, again, nationalism and the public position of the aid-receiving nation will receive attention and be a complicating factor. As a special solution, it can be argued that multilaterally arranged programs are superior to bilateral agreements, at least to the extent that multilaterality minimizes the criticism of the United States by one country for the size of the United States economic aid program to any other country. For reasons of national politics, however, the principle of multilaterality in arranging economic aid programs has been difficult for the United States to practice.

In addition to the Inter-American Development Bank, the Eisenhower Administration gave multilaterality, if not structuralism, further support. When President Eisenhower made his good-will tour in 1960, both greater governmental development effort and expanded multilaterality were topics of his conversations with the various heads of state: with Kubitschek of Brazil, with Frondizi of Argentina; and, with Alessandri of Chile. After the Kubitschek-Eisenhower meeting of February, Brazil presented a plan for coordinated development to the Organization of American States. Later in the same year, at the Inter-American Economic Conference, in Bogotá, these themes were taken up again. The Act of Bogotá, drawn in September at this Conference, is a pledge of the OAS member nations for greater developmental cooperation to effect a social and economic revolution.

The change from Republican to Democratic control of the Executive Branch of the U. S. Government in 1961 gave momentum to the increased aid-mutual effort, structuralist movement. President Kennedy, in March 1961, at a White House reception for Latin American diplomats, "unveiled" the Alliance for Progress.[5] In the same month he urged Congress to act hastily to appropriate the $600 million requested by President Eisenhower to implement the Act of Bogotá of April 1960. Congress passed this appropriation in April. Later in the year, at the special Inter-American Economic Conference, Punta del Este, Uruguay, the United States officially presented its Alliance proposal, an inter-American, multilaterally financed aid program. This proposal obtained Conference approval.

As for the functioning of the Alliance, a nine-man committee was created to review and to pass upon Alliance loan requests originating from the member nations of the OAS. The Committee of Nine, as it came to be known, was to be available to review developmental plans submitted by the various Latin American governments and to make any recommendations they felt would harmonize the plans with Alliance goals. However, the Committee was to function in an exclusively advisory capacity and had no authority to make recommendations to any institution or agency which provides financial assistance, not even to the Inter-American Development Bank. In terms of organization, the Committee was responsible to the Inter-American Economic and Social Council of the Organization of American States. Selection of this Committee is done by the World Bank, the Economic Commission for Latin America, and the Inter-American Economic and Social Council of the OAS. Such a selection procedure plus the fact that the Latin American nations should also give financial support to Alliance projects are evidences of increased governmental effort and greater mutuality. In March 1966, the OAS Inter-American Economic and Social Council reduced the size of the Committee to five members. Subsequently, the members of this Committee resigned in protest.

As a further concession to the principle of multilaterality, in 1963 an eight member committee — Committee on the Alliance for Progress but known by its Spanish initials, CIAP — was created. Its function was to give central direction to all Alliance's finances and projects. Seven of this Committee's members are representatives of their governments. The eighth, who serves as chairman, is elected by the Organization of American States. The former Committee of Nine was to serve as an advisory body to CIAP. Since the dissolution of the Committee of Nine, CIAP no longer represents a net gain in multilaterality. At first, the Congress of the United States opposed the establishment of CIAP. It was opposing a further extension, although a weak extension, of multilateral principle. Multilaterality in the Alliance, for example, is supposed to mean that Latin American member nations provide financial help to other member nations, just as the United States does, even though in smaller amounts. In Congress, arguments were given to separate CIAP's political responsibilities from its financial responsibilities in an effort to retain control over the United States contribution to Alliance funds. In practice, CIAP's financial responsibilities are minimized by the Latin American countries' direct application to the U. S. Agency for International Development (AID). Furthermore, CIAP is not in a position to veto any decision made by the U. S. /AID. Because of the direct or bilateral relationship between AID and Latin American countries, CIAP is of little consequence in terms of any real strengthening of the multilateral principle. Nonetheless, it is an expression of intent.

However, the substance of the intent is extremely limited. In 1965, for example, and in 1966, the United States was mildly interested in a Latin American effort to reform the Charter of the Organization of American States. The suggestions of the Latin Americans would have increased multilaterity. Our strongest support was for the establishment of an inter-American peace force, not crucial in terms of the developmental objective of structural change. Furthermore, United States support for the peace force could be explained by U.S. feelings of guilt and its embarrassment at having violated its inter-American agreements by its unilateral intervention in the Dominican Republic. In addition to the peace force, the United States has also supported the formation of an Inter-American Cultural Council within the OAS to parallel the Economic and Social Council. Although this increases multilaterity, the change is obviously in an area not crucial to the national interests of the United States.

These negative considerations aside, the Alliance does encompass fundamental structural change. There is, therefore, in the U.S. support of the Alliance an awareness that growth by capital accumulation and market development is insufficient for achieving a sustained increase in societal well-being.[6] This means there is some recognition that Latin America's growth process will not imitate that of the United States. How does one equate such recognition with the U.S. abortive invasion of Cuba, 1961; with the position of the United States on communism at the San José, Costa Rica, Conference, 1963; and with the intervention of the United States in the Dominican Republic, 1965? These activities indicate a lack of consensus on the mechanisms of the growth process and only some loose agreement as to what should be its results. Lack of consensus on mechanisms and the loose agreement on results reinforce a tendency to failure of United States/Latin American policy to achieve structural change. These inadequacies are not without a set of generally contributing circumstances. For the United States, the conduct of its Latin American policy is complicated by the organization of the Department of State as well as by the variableness of public opinion. Whatever the inconsistencies in the Latin American policy of the United States, the policy evolves in accordance with a group of objectives. It is frequently true that these objectives are neither always clearly stated by the executive branch nor clearly understood by the general public. Furthermore, the attainment of these objectives appears to be predicated upon the erroneous assumption that what is appropriate for containing communism is appropriate for facilitating modernization.

Moreover, there are from time to time miscalculations in foreign policy detail which place the goals further from, rather than closer, to attainment. The intervention of the United States in the Dominican Republic has had exactly this result just as the Alliance for Progress, in like manner, has proved far from perfectly satisfactory. Even in the earlier post-War period, when price stability and preventing further communist expansion in Latin America were objectives of the United States, there were important miscalculations of policy detail. For example, neither U.S. Ambassador Braden in the days of Perón in Argentina nor U.S. Ambassador Loeb in Peru during the Prado administration's last days prior to Peru's presidential election of 1962 were circumspect enough in their statements about those countries' internal political affairs. Both of those host nations asked that the United States recall her Ambassadors. (Their positions as representatives of the government of the United States rather than the correctness of their observations is the point being raised.)

Such foreign policy details are the product of a semi-permanent Department of State staff whose policy actions change much more slowly than the changes in foreign policy direction. After all, while the actual foreign policy direction is influenced by public opinion, the details by which direction will be effectuated are more closely related to, one, a customary way of doing things within the State Department, and two, an inclination on the part of lower level officers to make decisions which would be approved by those above them in the hierarchy. Admittedly, this is less likely to be the case with the staffs of the missions of the Agency for International Development because of the nature of the Agency's hiring procedures. Then, too, detail miscalculation at the national level, as well as policy misdirection, occasionally can be explained by the fallibility of the incumbent Secretary of State. National Security Council and Cabinet review hopefully minimize this factor, all other things being equal. However, with respect to the failure of United States/Latin American policy from 1948-1958, and specifically during the Secretary of State-ship of John Foster Dulles, the Council and Cabinet seem to have been contributing rather than corrective forces.

Since 1961, the Alliance for Progress has been the agreed upon mechanism for achieving structural change in Latin America. However, in the several years of the operation of the Alliance, the United States has become unhappy with its achievements and pessimistic of its future, even while remaining committed to it. Perhaps the reaction is due, in part, to having been over-optimistic of its potential. Certainly this would not be the first time that too mu ch had been anticipated from foreign aid programs and from Latin American relations. Historically, it has been frequently true that the promise of satisfying basic objectives has exceeded accomplishments.

Quite naturally, the previously discussed set of circumstances generally contributing to the failure of United States/Latin American policy are operative upon the Alliance. But, the Alliance also is hampered by its own set of obstacles. While the Alliance seeks structural change, it is unfortunately being carried out without full understanding of the depth of societal change necessary and, with virtually no appreciation for the mechanisms of economic growth applicable to the Latin American environment. Willingness to urge general developmental planning is about as far as the United States has come in the search for new tools to facilitate Latin America's economic development. But this, after all, is nothing more than a recognition of one of the advantages of statism so that the position of the United States is certainly not novel. In support of planning, the United States, under the Alliance for Progress, provides grants and loans to national planning agencies. Additionally, the United States has given indirect support to the formation and the operation of the Latin American Institute for Economic and Social Planning, an agency of the United Nations' Economic Commission for Latin America. [7]

Since the Alliance for Progress has had so limited an

impact and because its instruments for stimulating growth seem
so conservative, it is indeed surprising to find the Alliance being
criticized for lacking conservatism. One academician, for example, has asserted that the appropriate mechanism for economic
growth is private investment and that the poor performance of the
Alliance to date is due to the failure of the United States to emphasize it.[8] This contention, however, is at variance with the actual
practice of the Agency for International Development. AID uses
whatever financing it considers most appropriate and this frequently
has included investment by the private sector, both domestic and
foreign.[9] Moreover, this activity is clearly consistent with congressional intent.[10] Furthermore, given factor mobility, permissive political-economic policy, and a high rate of return relative
to domestic alternatives, private capital will move from the United
States and from other developed nations with lower real rates of
return to Latin America. The investment activities of "Adela"—
Atlantic Community Development Group for Latin America—are
reflective of such capital movements.

More relevant than the presumed lack of conservatism
of the growth mechanisms of the Alliance is the extent to which
Latin America shares interests and to which inter-American homogeneity exists. It has been suggested that the architects of the
Alliance felt that such a program could be as successful for Latin
America as the Marshall Plan had been for Europe.[11] This policy
formulation was based upon the assumption that Latin America,
like Western Europe, was a type of continental community with a
common heritage and a collective sense of responsibility. However, the European community, if indeed it did exist, is not the
Latin American community. At the time of the Marshall Plan,
Europe's problem was the reconstruction of industrial capacity;
Latin America's at the inception of the Alliance was still the evolution of an industrial society. Reconstruction presupposes the
existence of a set of attitudes and institutions appropriate to industrial processes. Modernization requires that they be developed.
(In some Latin American countries, naturally, the development of
these conditions has proceeded rapidly, but in many of them they
are still significantly underdeveloped.)

With respect to inter-American similarity, considerable
heterogeneity exists. For example, Latin America's natural resource base is not comparable to that of the United States, and
there is considerable inter-American variation as well. There
are also language differences— a type of French in Haití, Portuguese in Brazil, and Spanish in most of the other nations. Internal
language differences can also be observed — Spanish, Aymará, and
Qechua in Peru and Bolivia. Then, too, the size of the indigenous
population varies. Furthermore, although Latin America has been
neither culturally isolated from nor culturally ignored by the United
States, the extent of the contact varies widely from country to country, with Mexico and Argentina providing excellent contrast. Finally, while one can talk of the "elites" in Latin America, both
their power and the strength of their traditional orientation vary
significantly. To appreciate the importance of this variation, one

has only to compare the political environment in Colombia to that in Chile. Moreover, the composition of each elite tends to be quite diverse.[12]

These country differences are not always recognized and when recognized their importance is not always properly evaluated. While no pretention is made at having the proper evaluation of their importance, it is true that assumed similarities of Church, language, and cultural origin lead one to think of Latin America as a continental community with shared interests and a common sense of responsibility. Among these nations, however, it would be incorrect to think that the interests are shared and that there is a common sense of responsibility. Furthermore, the natural, physical, and cultural heterogeneity means that growth and behavioral generalizations applicable to Ecuador, let us say, perhaps have less or no applicability to Uruguay. The importance of the heterogeneity is not universally accepted. Victor L. Urquidi, for example, a well-known Mexican economist, feels that the dissimilarities are nothing more than distracting exceptions.[13] The process of generalization to which Urquidi so strongly clings for Latin America is deceptively useful for the derivation of developmental postulates, as has been so well done recently for the case of the agricultural surplus economy.[14] Nonetheless, logically deduced theoretical postulates are translated into effective developmental policy detail only insofar as the theory is applicable to a real world situation. In this respect, the degree of national variation from the assumed homogeneous phenomena is crucial. The combination of all of the heterogeneous elements precludes, for Latin America, the type of capitalistic, industrial growth observed in most western societies. Those in the United States responsible for Alliance policy and, as well, those responsible for foreign policy direction, should keep this in mind.

The assassination of President Kennedy, November 1963, caused grave concern among the Latin Americans as to the future of the Alliance. Even though many Latin American public figures have criticized it, they have indicated that they would like it to continue, at least for as long as no better alternative is available. This concern was minimized by President Johnson's indicating his intention to continue to give the program United States support. As a further indication of this commitment, the United States, at the second Special Inter-American Conference, in Rio de Janeiro, November 1965, pledged itself to contribute to the Alliance beyond its original 1971 termination date.

The position of the Chief Executive of the United States was made along with and, in a sense, in spite of, vocal, domestic opposition. Such opposition, for example, was strong during the presidential campaign of 1964. Furthermore, even within the Executive Branch of the government, there was opposition. In the spring of 1965, there was a proposal to disband the Agency for International Development and to reallocate its activities to other administrative entities in the Department of State. Had this proposal been effectuated, the Alliance would have been weakened since its functioning would have taken on an even stronger bilateral tone. This proposal, like domestic public opposition to the Alliance, is a reflection of the recent resurgence of nationalism in the United States, a force which threatens both the U.S. commitment to the Alliance and its objective of structural change.

Even so, the foreign policy rationale of structuralism, with democratic regimes, is still strong, although that of stability whether with or without structural change is stronger. Nonetheless, the policy details for achieving structural change within a democratic framework and while minimizing inter-American disagreement have not always been appropriate. All other things being equal, however, the United States will continue to aid Latin America for as long as, and if for no other reason than that, it believes poor nations are most susceptible to political systems objectionable to it. Aside from its general willingness to provide growth support to the Latin American countries, the United States still has far to go to accept the Latin American proposition that their growth processes must come about through an absolute freedom to use whatever economic mechanism or system they feel most effective in their cultural and physical environments. The unwillingness of the United States to permit the Latin Americans absolute freedom in selecting their own economic mechanism suggests U.S. insistence that both monetarist and structuralist objectives can and must be pursued simultaneously. Unfortunately for both the future of United States-Latin American relations and the developmental future of Latin America, this insistence indicates that the United States does not recognize the basic contradiction between monetarist and structuralist objectives.

NOTES

1. David Felix, "Industrialization and Stabilization Dilemmas in Latin America," *Journal of Economic History,* December 1959; Joseph Grunwald, "The 'Structuralist' School on Price Stability and Economic Development - the Chilean Case," *Latin American Issues: essays and comments* (New York: The Twentieth Century Fund, 1961), A. O. Hirschman, ed.; Dudley Seers, "A Theory of Inflation and Growth in Underdeveloped Economies Based on the Experience of Latin America," *Oxford Economic Papers,* June 1962; and Victor Urquidi, "Some Structural Problems," *The Challenge of Development in Latin America* (New York: Frederick A. Praeger, 1964).

2. For several excellent efforts to explain these political forces, see: Charles W. Anderson, *Toward a Theory of Latin American Politics,* Occasional Paper No. 2, Graduate Center for Latin American Studies, Vanderbilt University, February 1964; S. N. Eisenstadt, "Breakdown of Modernization," *Economic Development and Cultural Change,* XII, July 1964; Harry J. Benda, "Non-Western Intelligentsias as Political Elites," *Australian Journal of Politics and History,* November 1960.

3. Miguel S. Wionczek, "History of the Montevideo Treaty," *Latin American Economic Integration* (New York: Frederick A. Praeger, 1966), Miguel S. Wionczek, ed., pp. 92-99.

4. *The New York Times,* August 20, 1957.

5. The phrase — "alianza para el progreso" (alliance for progress) — was first used by Kennedy in a campaign speech delivered in October 1960, in Tampa, Florida. See: Arthur M. Schlesinger, Jr., *A Thousand Days: John F. Kennedy in the White House* (Boston: Houghton Mifflin, 1965), p. 194.

6. For the inadequacies of a capital-oriented theory applied to Chile, see: Tom E. Davis, "Changing Conception of the Development Problem: The Chilean Example," *Economic Development and Cultural Change,* Vol. XIV, No. 1, Oct. 1965, pp. 21-32.

7. For the Planning Institute and for progress in planning, see the following issues of the *Economic Bulletin for Latin America,* the publication of the Economic Commission for Latin America: Vol. VII, No. 2, October 1962, pp. 115-122; Vol. VIII, No. 2, October 1963, pp. 129-146; and Vol. IX, No. 1, March 1964, pp. 143-152.

8. William Withers, *The Economic Crisis in Latin America* (New York: The Free Press of Glencoe, 1964), p. 293.

9. *Proposed Mutual Defense and Development Programs,* FY 1966 (Washington, D.C.: U.S. Government Printing Office, March 1965), pp. 25-26.

10. A recent expression of this intent is found in: *Private Investment in Latin America* (Washington, D.C.: U.S. Government Printing Office, 1964), pp. 3-6. A Report of the Sub-Committee on Inter-American Economic Relations of the Joint Economic Committee, 88th Congress, 2nd Session.

11. Peter Nehemkis, *Latin America, Myth and Reality* (New York: Alfred A. Knopf, 1964), pp. 234-235.

12. For the Colombian case, see: Everett E. Hagen, *On the Theory of Social Change,* (Homewood, Ill.: The Dorsey Press, Inc., 1962), pp. 357-358. For the Peruvian case, see: Alvin Cohen, "The Technology/Elite Approach to the Developmental Process: Peruvian Case Study," *Economic Development and Cultural Change,* Vol. XIV, No. 3, April 1966.

13. Victor L. Urquidi, *op. cit.,* p. 1.

14. John C. H. Fei and Gustav Ranis, *Development of the Labor Surplus Economy* (Homewood, Ill.: Richard D. Irwin, Inc., 1964), published for the Economic Growth Center, Yale University.

15

REGIONAL INTEGRATION AND INCOME REDISTRIBUTION: COMPLEMENTS OR SUBSTITUTES?

By   Matthew Edel
Department of Economics
Massachusetts Institute of Technology

Economic equality and international integration are stated aims of the Alliance for Progress. The Charter of Punta del Este cited two objectives related at least in part to equality:

(2)   To make the benefits of economic progress available to all citizens of all economic and social groups through a more equitable distribution of national income, raising more rapidly the income and standard of living of the needier sectors of the population.

(6)   To encourage, in accordance with the characteristics of each country, programs of comprehensive agrarian reform leading to the effective transformation, where required, of unjust structures and systems of land tenure and use, with a view to replacing latifundia and dwarf holdings by an equitable system of land tenure...

Similarly, regional economic ties were posited as a goal of the Alliance:

(11)   To strengthen existing agreements on economic integration, with a view to the ultimate fulfillment of aspirations for a Latin American common market that will expand and diversify trade among the Latin American countries and thus contribute to the economic growth of the region.

Equality and international integration appear in the Charter both as ends in their own right, and as means toward the first goal listed, an annual increase in per capita income of 2.5 per cent. The framers of the Charter must have believed that these objectives could form part of a unified program. The attainment of each would further economic growth, and higher incomes resulting from growth would make the specific goals easier to attain. But were they right? Even if goals are not absolutely incompatible, alternative mixes of policy may lead to the attainment of different goals in greater or lesser degree. There may be a trade-off between progress toward different ends. One example of competition between two goals of the Alliance is the often mentioned "dilemma" between stability of the price level and continued economic growth. In the long run, if a number of structural changes in the economy are accomplished, growth and price stability may be not only compatible but mutually reinforcing. In the short run, however, to try for one may impede the attainment of the other.

This study presents a critical appraisal of the compatibility of international integration along the lines envisioned by LAFTA with the rapid attainment of economic equality. It will be argued that, while the two are compatible if suitable policies are followed, separate instruments will be required for their separate attainment. Although it is often assumed that regional integration itself will reduce inequality in the distribution of income or wealth, the actual impact of integration may be the reverse. What is more, the economic success of a common market might reduce political support for use of the separate redistributive instruments necessary for the achievement of equality. This finding should not be taken as a condemnation of regional economic union, but it does demonstrate that this union must be accompanied or preceded by separately planned social reforms if inequality is to be reduced. As I consider this a valid goal, as well as a necessary condition for the fullest possible economic development of Latin America, I do feel impelled to inject a note of skepticism with regard to what seems to me a tendency to place all of the hemispheric development eggs in the integration basket.

The view that a free trade area or common market will further economic equality is based on elements of several theories. One is that rising levels of national income (fostered in this case by the common market) will naturally lead to more equality. A second is that increased trade, by reducing disparities between factor prices, will help to equalize incomes. And a third is that a common market will create new opportunities, which being new and open to utilization by new investors or entrepreneurs, will lead to a wider spread of wealth. Some of these expectations relate primarily to income distribution within countries, some to international differences. Each of these effects might, if all goes well, develop as posited. But reverse effects are also possible. Each argument is, in fact, double edged.

That income distribution becomes more equal during economic development is something of a tenet of faith among American growthsmen. It is hinted at in Rostow's dynamic of a universal drive toward a mass-consumption economy (although this does not imply universal equality as much as an enlarging of a middle class).[21] A similar view appears in the textbooks, as in this caption from Samuelson's Seventh Edition:

> Advanced economies show less inequality of income distribution than do preindustrial economies—contrary to dire predictions of scientific socialists that the rich get richer and the poor get poorer under capitalism. The mixed economy show greater equality. [24, p. 111]

186

This view can be supported by some factual evidence. There is a less equal distribution of income (as measured by shares accruing to the top and bottom fifths of the distribution) in many underdeveloped countries than there is in Western Europe or the United States, confirming, as Samuelson puts it, "casual tourist observation." But there are exceptions, and these correlations do not prove causality.[14, 15, 19] It may be that the greater equality of wealth in the United States was a cause of growth being more rapid there than in, say, Brazil, rather than being an effect of that growth differential. Similar arguments about the effects of income distribution on growth are also applied, at times, to the explanation of the more rapid growth in the north than in the south in the United States in the nineteenth century.

Time series evidence on income distribution within single countries is less consistent with the hypothesis of increasing equality. There was some narrowing of the gap between the shares of income accruing to the highest and lowest fifths of the size distribution in the United States between 1929 and the end of World War II. Since then, however, relative income ratios have remained approximately constant. In the United Kingdom, concentration of incomes has also decreased over time. However, in Germany following unification, there was an increase in inequality.[14, 15] Since German development was, in a sense, a result of economic integration, this might be the more relevant precedent for Latin America. And what little data has become available on income distribution on currently developing areas seems to indicate that industrialization increases inequality, at least for a time. During the 1950's, income disparities increased in both India and Mexico.[17, 28] It would thus seem premature to expect that equality would, in the normal course of events, be increased automatically by economic growth following regional integration.

The theory of factor-price equalization is a second prop of the argument for the income-redistributing effects of integration. It holds that free trade will equalize between regions the returns to any factor of production.[12, 18, 23, 27] In each trading country, the wage of unskilled labor will, after trade, be equal. Rents of standard-grade land and interest rates must also become equal. This proposition is based on the view that a factor will be more highly remunerated, before trade, in that country in which it is relatively scarcer. In this same situation, goods requiring more intensive use of the scarce factor in their production will have higher relative prices. When free trade is attained, these goods will be imported, reducing the demand for the scarce resource in their domestic production, and forcing its wage or rent toward the international average. Full intracountry equality will be achieved if a number of rigorous conditions, probably not met in Latin America, hold. But even where they are not met—where trade is only partially free, where some factors are specific to one country, etc.—a tendency toward intracountry equalization is predicted.

As an example, think of two countries, A and B. Assume

A has abundant land, but is short of labor. Let country B, on the other hand, be densely populated. If the two countries have roughly similar sizes, levels of income, and patterns of demand, then in the absence of trade, normally country A will have a higher wage/rent ratio than country B. If food production uses land as its relatively intensive factor of production, while clothing is a labor-intensive product, then country A will have relatively cheaper food and more expensive clothing compared to B. If the two countries form a common market, then A will trade food for B's cloth, and this trade will lead to an equalization not only of product prices between the countries, but also factor prices. Wages in A will fall, and rents rise. The reverse will happen in B.

From equalization of factor prices, income equalization may also ensue within each country. Suppose, for instance, that in country B, the land-scarce country, land is held by only a few landlord families. Other families live only by labor. Increasing wages to the many, and decreasing rents to the few, will tend to reduce income inequality. Meanwhile, if A, the land-abundant country, is a nation of family farms, then each family's falling wages will be matched by a rising return to its land, and family income will remain evenly distributed. Income distribution in the entire common market will, in this case, become somewhat more equal. This model seems to approximate nineteenth-century conditions if one thinks of A as North America (or Australia) and B as Britain. Since from the vantage point of the United States it seems likely that abundant land is likely to be evenly-distributed land, it can be predicted that international integration may improve the distribution of personal income (unless a change in the difference between per capita averages in the two countries swamps the first effect—see Appendix).

This need not be so in every instance, however. Suppose that it were country A's land that were monopolized, while B's were evenly divided, even though A was still the more land-abundant country. Then trade would increase inequality in A by raising rents to the few while lowering wages to the many, while leaving family income distribution unaffected in B, although more of each family's income would come from wages than before trade. In this case, income distribution over the entire common market would have worsened. This latter case may actually approximate Latin American conditions more closely than the previous case. As is shown in Table I, there seems to be a slightly positive correlation between the abundance of land and the inequality of its distribution. The evidence is, of course, inconclusive. Land concentration statistics are not reliable, and the example ignores such other factors of production as capital and skills. But it may, at least, serve as a caution against the uncritical use of the more common assumption.

A third manner in which a common market may affect income distribution is through the creation of new opportunities for money-making activities. To the extent that the wider market breaks down monopolies, or creates the possibility of new lines of

production, or removal to new areas of industries formerly restricted to the one country which had enough of a market to support them, it may open new channels of mobility which in the end
lead to greater equality. However, if the opportunities created
are such that only the already advantaged can benefit from them,
then the distribution of income may worsen. The evidence as to
which effect will be strongest particularly concerns the geographical distribution of the dynamic benefits of growth. Geographical
distribution is not the same thing as personal income distribution,
but it is related. If the average income disparity between two
regions (or two sectors of an economy such as industry and agriculture) widens, then so will disparities between the highest and
lowest personal incomes. Indeed, it is even possible for the
overall distribution of incomes by size to worsen while within
each region income distribution becomes slightly more equal, if
the gap between regions (or sectors) widens rapidly enough. [15, 28]
(See Appendix.)

Enthusiasts for integration are prone to assume that the
main effect of a common market will be to provide more opportunities, relatively, to the lagging section. They expect the backward countries to progress relatively most rapidly, as seems to
be the case within the European common market where Italy has
lately been the fastest growing member. It is felt, for example,
that capital, which is normally mobile across borders, will be
drawn to the region in which wages are lowest, thus helping to
reduce the differences. However, these effects are no more
certain than others already considered. There seem, over long
periods in a country or region's development, to be strong tendencies for industry to concentrate in the already most industrialized locations. These effects, often loosely described in terms of
"polarization," "dominance," or "backwash" effects, have not
been fully explored in theory, but they seem to have a basis in
economies of scale in infrastructure, external economies in the
labor market and elsewhere, and mutual support of market demand
created in advanced subregions, when trade throughout the region,
even when free of tariffs, is subject to transport costs.

Statistically, such polarization has often been observed.
Italy's position in the EEC, and Puerto Rico's rapid growth in a
sort of common market with the United States mainland seem to
be the exception, not the norm. Italy after unification—a country
in which, in effect, a common market had been created—is a classic example. The north, probably starting with some advantage
over the south, widened the interregional gap in industrialization
and income levels. [7] Pakistan, Mexico, and Yugoslavia, to name
only a few industrializing nations, have also suffered the effects
of increasing regional disparities. International common markets
have had similar experiences. The East African market was dis-
rupted by disputes arising from Kenya's attraction of a propor-
tionally greater share of industries. The Central American common market has been affected partially by polarizing growth. The
most advanced country, in terms of income levels, has not been
the most rapid in its growth. But if Costa Rica has been growing

more slowly than Guatemala, Nicaragua, and El Salvador, all four of these countries have greatly widened the gap between their level of income and that of the poorest and most slowly growing nation, Honduras. (See Table II.) A more general survey of regional inequality in national development, by Williamson, indicates that increasing disparities are customary throughout at least early phases of development. Only in the more developed countries does regional inequality become stable and eventually fall.[29] For countries at the Latin American level of development, the net effect of economic integration on regional economic growth might be to increase disparities between member nations, at least unless deliberate offsetting provisions were instituted.

Location is, of course, not the only aspect of access to new opportunities. Access to capital, entrepreneurial experience, and contacts with buyers or others who know of opportunities may all help determine who can invest. Those groups of individuals (as well as those regions) with more experience and contacts in advanced economic activities are more able to take advantage of opportunities. In many cases, they are individuals near the top of the income distribution. This effect may be even more pronounced if, due to larger markets, the optimal size of industries or other enterprises is raised. While some small firms may be able to grow, a sudden widening of the market when a tariff-reducing treaty comes into force may create once-and-for-all investment opportunities to pre-empt commanding economic advantages, which only the largest investors can utilize. This factor is usually considered in relation to the fear that foreign businesses may be the only ones able to move in when such opportunities arise. Certainly U.S. and Japanese companies have reason to look on Latin American integration as a benefit to themselves. And just as certainly, appropriation by them of all of the best investment opportunities would lead to a form of inequality which, if not measurable in national concentration indices, would be a serious problem. But even if it is the largest national industries which expand the most rapidly, this will, at least in the short run, involve a widening of wealth differences within Latin America.

This difference might be offset by deliberate policy measures. But will these separate instruments be used? They might, unless either of two factors intervened. The first might be a technical incompatibility, by which income redistribution would be inconsistent with regional trade. The second might be a political incompatibility based not on any technical inconsistency but rather on a loss of interest in equality resulting from the success of an integration program. Technically, there does not seem to be any lack of complementarity between redistribution and regional integration measures, at least as long as the member countries coordinate their reforms. Countries that instituted redistributive programs of the sort contemplated in the Alliance for Progress — land reform, progressive taxation, welfare measures, compensatory education, and the others — would not be incapacitated by this from forming a common market. (There might be a few problems if welfare measures led to overvaluation of some members' curren-

TABLE I

Abundance and Distribution of Land, Latin America

Country	Land Availability	Ownership Inequality
	Hectares agricultural land per rural resident	Gini Index of concentration
Uruguay	4.98	81.7
Argentina	4.44	86.3
Chile	2.09	93.8
Venezuela	1.92	90.9
Bolivia (pre-revolution)	1.19	93.8
Panama	.87	73.7
Ecuador	.73	86.4
Honduras	.69	75.7
Colombia	.65	84.9
Guatemala	.58	86.0
Brazil	.50	83.7
Costa Rica	.40	89.1
Peru	.34	87.5
El Salvador	.33	82.8
Dominican Republic	.32	79.5

Coefficient of correlation = .108 (including Bolivia)
Coefficient of correlation = .131 (excluding Bolivia)

Sources: Land Availability from Schulman[25]; Ownership Inequality from Russett.[22]

TABLE II

Economic Growth Rates in the Central American Common Market
1960-1965 (in 1965 dollars)

Country	Per Capita GDP 1965	Growth Rate 1960-1965 Total	Per Capita
Costa Rica	413	6.0	1.9
El Salvador	274	6.6	3.3
Guatemala	328	6.6	3.6
Honduras	222	4.6	1.1
Nicaragua	333	8.3	4.6

Source: P. N. Rosenstein-Rodan, "Latin American Development: Results and Prospects."[20] The original data source is the Secretariat of the OAS.

cies but a greater emphasis on progressive taxation could ameliorate this inflationary difficulty.) Nor would there be any economic reason why a common market could not be formed between countries which had undertaken Cuban-style income redistribution. (Overcentralized control in such a market could be subject to the bargaining problems that have plagued COMECON, but these, too, can be overcome.) Thus, if there is any obstacle to redistributive programs being undertaken along with integration, to compensate for its possible backwash effects on equality, it must be a political obstacle. Such an obstacle may in fact exist: regional integration may reduce the political feasibility of income redistribution by removing the economic incentive for its support by industry.

Reasons for this incentive must be sought in the economic history of Latin American industrialization, and in the problems of limited markets that have plagued it. Virtually all of the Latin American economies had their origins in what might be termed a "hacienda-export" system. [10] One or two primary product exports provided the bulk of foreign exchange, as well as the basis for a few private fortunes among the exporters, and the taxes for the support of a governmental bureaucracy. Outside of the export sector much of the land was controlled by large estates. A few landowners earned high incomes under this system, but often preferred imports to domestic products. The majority of the rural population, whether living on the estates or owning the small bits of land left over, did not earn enough to afford many consumer goods. In a situation like this, there was little scope for industrialization. The majority could not pay; those who could, earned enough of their income, directly or indirectly, from exports as to be able to import their manufactured products without the economy facing a foreign-exchange crisis.

This situation, with some minor variation, prevailed in Latin America throughout the nineteenth century, and persists to this day in some countries. The dynamic for its replacement was provided by the rapid expansion of exports, beginning in the late nineteenth century with Chilean nitrates and Argentine and Uruguayan wheat and animal products. Coffee, petroleum, copper, fishmeal and some other products have provided similar influences more recently. Each of these products, as its market and its production expanded, created new sources of income for the domestic economy, both through export taxes, and through factor payments and purchases of inputs. Depending on both the nature of the crops or minerals involved, and the relative strength of the domestic government and the foreign companies, these payments might be a larger or smaller share of the export value. In some cases, the incomes were sufficiently great to create a substantial domestic market for manufactured products. The agricultural port and capital city of Buenos Aires was the first of these important markets; others followed. Within each of these markets, in its more buoyant periods, domestic industry began to make its appearance, particularly in the production of textiles, shoes, and other light consumer goods. Protective tariffs aided the growth of these industries, which grew by taking the pre-existing export-originated demand away from imported commodities. And, by the nineteen thirties, it was found that inflation of the currency could keep demand at the same levels, and allow continued industrial growth, when overseas demand slumped, as long as imports could be reduced sufficiently to keep pace with the decline in exports.

Import substituting industrialization led to rapid growth for a considerable period, but not indefinitely. Eventually, industries captured the entire market for a product away from imports, and slowed their pace of growth. Almost none had grown efficient enough, in the process, to compete on export markets with the products of developed countries. Other industries, particularly those for intermediate goods, could not be established economically in some countries, because of the small market sizes. Import-substituting industrialization had created some new jobs and incomes, in the new industries themselves, which expanded demand somewhat beyond the levels maintained by export incomes (or their inflationary substitutes such as Brazilian payments for stockpiled coffee). But markets were still not large enough for steady balanced growth. Except in Mexico (and even there to some extent), large numbers of peasants and slum-residents remained at incomes too low to make them consumers of many industrial goods. Other reasons, including bad policy, lagging food supplies, continued loss of export markets, and heavy capital intensive development in industry, themselves at least partially rooted in the structure of ownership, may have also played a part in lowering the pace of growth. But in general, it may be said that once substitution for consumer imports reached its market limits, stagnation set in. This process has already worked itself out in Argentina, Uruguay, and Chile. It seems to be happening in Brazil and Colombia. And it remains a potential danger to the transitional countries which are still growing rapidly, such as Peru and Venezuela.

This stagnation of industry has been linked to limited market size through two mechanisms. The first is the existence of economies of scale. These have been documented in a number of studies by the Economic Commission for Latin America, as well as by others. [2, 16, 26] It has been shown in a number of cases that Latin American economies' current consumption could not support an optimal-size plant, with the result that either no plant is built, or that it must operate inefficiently behind a tariff wall. Automobile purchases in Argentina or Brazil are annually slightly fewer than those in Belgium or in the Netherlands. The latter do not produce automobiles; Argentina and Brazil each have several plants, and prices and costs are high. [3] Assuming, as ECLA does, that exports to developed countries will be presented by tariffs, small markets would doom Latin American countries to inefficient production for a long period. But even if there were no barriers to export imposed by developed countries, and rigid economies of scale were not a factor, small markets might still inhibit productivity and prevent exports. David Felix has argued that if markets are small, firms will only grow rapidly for a short period of time before exhausting their market and slowing down their expansion. If, as seems to be the case, learning by doing is a factor in efficiency, the firm may settle down to production at a lower level of efficiency than it would have attained had it undergone rapid growth for a longer period. [11]

In either case, small markets for consumer goods may retard industrial expansion. But the market size for any product is itself a function of income distribution, as well as of a country's population and national income. If the amount spent on some product out of a dollar's increment in income varies between income levels, then making the income distribution by size more or less equal can affect spending. The macro-economic implications of differences between the marginal propensities to consume—to spend on all goods—at different income levels have often been considered. If savings propensities at higher incomes are greater than at lower incomes, greater inequality can increase savings, and greater equality increase consumption. A belief that this was the case once led to the claims that inequality is favorable to rapid capital formation in the early stages of development, while increasing equality is wanted to prevent underconsumption and stagnation at later stages of development. As more recent studies have shown little difference between the marginal propensities to consume of different income groups in the Unites States, and as fiscal and monetary policy have been recognized as other remedies for recession, this macro-economic view has seemed less important. But differences between income levels in propensities to consume specific products, or even light industrial products as a whole, as opposed to consumer durables, foods, and services, may be considerable. The interaction of these with scale factors can significantly affect economic growth.

As an example, consider a hypothetical Latin American country with a million inhabitants, and a per capita income of $300. Assume that income is unevenly divided, so that 20 per cent of the population, with incomes of $900, earn 60 per cent of the income, while 30 per cent earn the national mean, and the remaining half of the population earn only 10 per cent of the income, or $60 each. Assume that at each of these three income levels, consumption is divided among three groups of products as in Table III. The figures in this table are, like the rest of those in the example, very rough approximations of the situation prevailing in a small, moderately developed Latin American state, but they do roughly represent the range of demand elasticities prevalent in the area. The income elasticities for food are considerably less than one; that for automobiles is considerably greater than one; while that for clothing is greater than one at low incomes, and falls at higher incomes. In this situation, the demand for the three types of goods will be $120 million for food, $85 million for clothing, and $95 million for cars.

If income were redistributed so that all individuals received the average income of $300, then consumption of food and cloth would increase, while that of automobiles would decline. If, as is the case with most Latin American cloth or other industries,

TABLE III

Income and Demand in a Hypothetical Latin American Country

Per Capita

Income Level	Number People	Spent on Food	Spent on Cloth	Spent on Cars
60	500,000	50	10	0
300	300,000	150	100	50
900	200,000	250	250	400

Totals (Before Income Equalization)

Income Level	Total Income	Spent on Food	Spent on Cloth	Spent on Cars
60	30,000,000	25,000,000	5,000,000	0
300	90,000,000	45,000,000	30,000,000	15,000,000
900	180,000,000	50,000,000	50,000,000	80,000,000
Totals	300,000,000	120,000,000	85,000,000	95,000,000

Totals (After Income Equalization – 1,000,000 People at Income of $ 300)

Income Level	Total Income	Spent on Food	Spent on Cloth	Spent on Cars
300	300,000,000	150,000,000	100,000,000	50,000,000
Totals	300,000,000	150,000,000	100,000,000	50,000,000
Net Change	0	+30,000,000	+15,000,000	-45,000,000
Percent Change	0	+25%	+18%	-47%

this country had a number of factories each producing a different type or grade of cloth, at the outset several might operate at below full capacity, or in substandard scale plants. With demand increasing by 18 per cent, some might be raised to a more economical level of production, or plants producing several grades might be able to specialize more completely. Engineers estimate that normally an increase in capacity will reduce costs by six-tenths as great a proportion.[3] Economic studies usually show a somewhat smaller, but still measurable effect.[16] In the case of textiles the difference between an efficient plant and a higher-cost unit may be only a matter of an extra two or three million dollars demand for a specific variety of cloth.[26] The textile-producing sector might thus be able to grow after income redistribution. On the other hand, even the pre-redistribution demand for cars would be only for thirty or forty thousand units—far too few to sustain a factory. Diminishing demand will only diminish imports, not productivity. The economy, as well as industry, will be a net gainer, if no decreasing returns elsewhere offset the increasing returns in cloth. To be sure, increased food supply is also required in this model. If income redistribution takes the form of a land reform which raises productivity as well as purchasing power, there is no problem. If not, the decreased foreign exchange expenditure on automobiles could be diverted to food imports, assuming that most of the income in the model came from some export industry not catering to the domestic market.

This hypothetical case is too narrow in its assumptions to be realistic. But it can indicate the sort of mechanism by which narrow markets impede industrialization and growth. The history of industries in specific countries demonstrates the same sensitivity to market size. For example, the Chilean textile industry has alternately grown and stagnated throughout its history. The periods of rapid growth have occurred either when export-based prosperity was widening the market (1878-1883, 1898-1913, and 1918-1929), or during the period of tariff-or-depression protected import substitution (1929-1953).[5, 8] Since the exhaustion of import substitution in the early fifties, however, it has grown only slowly, and profitability has been slight.[6, 9] Throughout their history, the textile-manufacturers have been concerned with wider markets. Until the completion of import substitution, this usually took the form of demands for higher tariffs or for exclusive rights to markets for uniforms, which were often favored for they avoided the problems of multiple varieties.[5] Since the mid-fifties, they have had to seek other markets.

In Chile, this desire has led, to some extent to a willingness to experiment with agrarian reform and other "structuralist" measures.[13, p. 234] In other countries, business-oriented political leaders have stressed similar points. Thus Gustavo Díaz Ordaz, President of Mexico, has stated:

> Capitalization, rather than being based on the reduction of the essential consumption of the lower-

income classes, should be based on the elimination of superfluous spending by the higher-income classes... Without a market, there can be no industry; without purchasing power among the great mass of the population, there can be no market. 1, p. 203

Although Colombia has not shared Mexico's experience with the effects of agrarian reform on development, similar sentiments were expressed by the cabinet minister, and mayor of Bogotá, Virgilio Barco Vargas:

The basis of accelerated development... is increasing production in response to a vigorous demand for goods, which allows savings in costs, lower profits per unit sold, and lower prices to the consumer, which increases his ability to buy other articles... To begin a beneficent process of interaction between agriculture and national industries is the first objective of a national development policy that ought to consist of agrarian reform plus industrialization.. 4, p. 21

A leading Colombian businessman, Rodrigo Uribe Echavarría, president of the COLTEJER textile firm, echoed Barco's remarks from the same platform, when he said that agricultural development permitted the formation of a strong, healthy, and diversified industry, and praised the "meritorious national accord to reform the ruinous structure of land tenure."4, p. 71 These remarks are only a few examples of a frequently held view. Although it would be incorrect to predict that business concern for agrarian reform will rapidly become great enough to insure its effective implementation, the restraints of markets have at least provided something of a readiness to experiment with redistributive measures among some businessmen.

This influence, however, might be weakened by the initial success, or even the thought of, a common market. Although even within such a Free Trade Area or Economic Union, some industries will remain inefficient in scale (or else monopolized if one or two efficient firms are enough to supply the entire demand) unless a wider distribution of wealth broadens demand, enough industries will be freed from their current demand constraints by such a market to reduce their need for redistributive reform. In this sense, regional integration can be a substitute for income redistribution and vice versa. Virgilio Barco Vargas presumably advocates both sorts of program when he parallels his advocacy of agrarian reform with the comment that the "classic process of extending the market to take advantage of efficiencies of large-scale production" is also the force which, "breaking barriers, has moved governments to create common markets undreamed of a few decades ago."4, p. 21 But it will be easy for many industrialists (and, no doubt, American officials) who see the need for markets, yet are somewhat uneasy with the degree of social change involved

197

in income redistribution, to seize on regional integration as a unique solution.

Regional integration should, definitely, be part of the solution for Latin America. But it is not a complete solution. Integration may have backwash effects that increase inequality of incomes in the hemisphere. These effects, and the inequality that already exists, must be fought with other policy weapons, separate from those of integration. That a common market can remove one of the sources of support for redistributive reform makes the struggle for this reform harder. But it is a struggle that must be continued, and it is to be hoped that the advantages of economic integration will not blind us to the need for redistributive social change.

APPENDIX

Two propositions are presented here which may clarify points raised in the text. The first relates factor price equalization in a two-factor model to the difference between average (per capita) incomes of the two trading countries. In each, if w and r are wage and rent rates, and K, L, and Y are aggregate capital, labor, and national income, then

$$Y = wL + rK$$

or, if per capita quantities (assuming population equal to the labor force) are denoted by small letters, then, again within each country

$$y = \frac{Y}{L} = w + r \frac{K}{L} = w + rk.$$

If the countries are denoted a and b, then after trade, if the conditions for factor price equalization hold, $r_a^* = r_b^* = r^*$, and $w_a^* = w_b^* = w^*$. If k_a and k_b, the capital-labor ratios, are unequal, a condition assumed in the factor-price-equalization proof, it follows that per capita incomes in the two countries will also be unequal, $y_a \neq y_b$.

Let $D = y_a - y_b$, where $k_a > k_b$. In the absence of trade,

$$D_o = (w_a - w_b) + (r_a k_a - r_b k_b).$$

When trade is opened, factor price equalization will lead to the replacement of the original rent and wage rates, which we will continue to write with subscripts, with the equalized rates, w^* and r^*. The difference in income per capita will be

198

$$D_1 = (w^* - w^*) + (r^*k_a - r^*k_b) = r^*(k_a - k_b).$$

The change in the difference due to trade will be equal to

$$D_o - D_1 = (w_a - w_b) + k_a(r_a - r^*) + k_b(r^* - r_b).$$

Since $r_b > r^* > r_a$, while $w_a > w_b$, the first term will be positive while the second and third will be negative. In order for $D_o - D_1$ to be positive, and thus for trade to diminish the difference, the original difference in wages must be great enough relative to the difference in rental rates and the capital-labor ratios. In general it cannot be predicted that this will occur. Hypothetical cases yielding the opposite result may easily be constructed. Trade may or may not decrease international differences in income per head.

The second proposition, based on one used by Kusnetz[15] and Swamy[28] in the analogous case of income distribution in an economy with two sectors, agricultural and nonagricultural, holds that the distribution of income by size in an economic union of two countries is affected by the distributions of income within the two countries, their relative sizes, and the difference between their levels of per capita income. If inequality is measured by the Gini coefficient of concentration (C), the ratio of the area between the Lorenz curve and the 45 degree line, to the entire area under the 45 degree line (a measure equal to zero if there is perfect equality and 1 if there is complete inequality), then for the economic union,

$$C = \frac{\sqrt{N_a C_a^2 + N_b C_b^2 R^2 + N_a N_b (R-1)^{2/}}}{N_a \neq N_b R}$$

where C_a, C_b, and C are the coefficients of concentration for country A, country B, and the union respectively; N_a and N_b are the proportions of the combined population resident in A and B respectively; and R is the ratio of per capita income in country B to that in country A. Income is presumed higher in country B. In this case, Swamy shows, the change in overall concentration (C) can be written as the weighted sum of changes in C_a, C_b, N_a, and R. Any increase in the intra-country concentration ratios will increase overall concentration. An increase in the divergence of the ratio between per capita incomes in the two countries will do the same. So will an increase in the population of the richer country relative to the other (an important factor in the model where the richer country is the urban sector which draws population from agriculture). In the case of formation of a common market, even if changes in factor prices made C_a and C_b lower (more equal income), the immediate impact might be to increase R, in which case the overall effect on C would be ambiguous. And if the long-run effects of economic union were a widening of income disparities on the average between regions ΔR or migration to the more developed region ΔN_b, this would further increase C. The net effect of economic integration may thus be an increase in the inequality of the distribution of incomes by size over the entire region.

REFERENCES

1. Alba, Víctor. *Alliance without Allies*. New York:
    Frederick A. Praeger, 1964.

2. Bain, J.S. *Barriers to New Comptetition*. Cambridge:
    Harvard University Press, 1958.

3. Balassa, Bela. *Economic Development and Integration*.
    Mexico: CEMLA, 1965.

4. Barco, Virgilio, Rodrigo Uribe Echavarría, and others.
    Estamos ante una revolución. Bogotá: Tercer Mun-
    do, 1967.

5. *Boletín de la Sociedad de Fomento Fabril*, Chile, 1884–
    1913.

6. Davis, Tom E. "The Rate of Return on Capital in Latin
    American Economies with Special References to
    Chile," U.S. Congress, Joint Economic Committee,
    Hearings on Economic Development in South America.
    Washington, D.C.: 1962.

7. Eckaus, Richard S. "The North-South Differential in
    Italian Economic Development," *Journal of Eco-
    nomic History*, XX:3, September 1961, 285-317.

8. Economic Commission for Latin America, United Nations.
    "Desarrollo industrial de Chile," annex to *Estu-
    dio económico de América Latina*, 1949, E/CN 12/
    164, anexo 1.

9. ___. *La industria textil de Chile*, E/CN 12/622, 1962.

10. Edel, Matthew. "The Limits of Economic Expansion,"
    Studies on the Left, IV:4, Fall 1964, 10-16.

11. Felix, David. "Monetarists, Structuralists and Import-
    Substituting Industrialization: A Critical Ap-
    praisal," *Studies in Comparative International
    Development*, I:10, 1965.

12. Heckscher, E. "The Effect of Foreign Trade on the
    Distribution of Income," in AEA *Readings in the
    Theory of Trade*. Philadelphia: Blakiston, 1949.

13. Hirschman, Albert O. *Journeys Toward Progress*. New
    York: Twentieth Century Fund, 1963.

14. Kusnetz, Simon. "Economic Growth and Income Inequal-
    ity," *American Economic Review*, XLV: 1, March
    1955, 1-28.

15. Kusnetz, Simon. "Distribution of Income by Size,"
    Part VIII of *Quantitative Aspects of the Eco-
    nomic Growth of Nations,* supplement to (Part II)
    Economic Development and Cultural Change, XI:2,
    January 1963.

16. Manne, Alan S. *Investments for Capacity Expansion.*
    Cambridge: M.I.T. Press, 1967.

17. Navarrete, Ifigenia M. de. *La distribución del ingre-
    so y el desarrollo económico de México.* Mexico
    City: 1960.

18. Ohlin, Bertil. *Interregional and International Trade.*
    Cambridge: Harvard University Press, 1933.

19. Ojha, P. D., and V.V. Bhatt. "Pattern of Income Dis-
    tribution in an Underdeveloped Economy: A Case
    Study of India," *American Economic Review,* LIV:
    5, September 1964, 711-20.

20. Rosenstein-Rodan, Paul N. *Latin American Development:
    Results and Prospects,* mimeographed. M.I.T.
    Center for International Studies, 1967.

21. Rostow, W.W. *The Stages of Economic Growth.* Cambridge:
    The University Press, 1960.

22. Russett, Bruce M. "Inequality and Instability: The
    Relation of Land Tenure to Politics," paper
    presented to American Political Science Associa-
    tion, 1963.

23. Samuelson, Paul A. "International Factor Price Equali-
    zation Once Again," *Economic Journal,* LIX, June
    1949, 181-97.

24. __ *Economics: An Introductory Analysis,* 7th ed. New
    York: McGraw-Hill, 1967.

25. Schulman, Sam. *Aspectos sociológicos de la reforma
    agraria.* Bogotá: IICA-CIRA, 1965.

26. Soza Valderrama, Héctor. *Planificación del desarrollo
    industrial.* Mexico City: Siglo XXI, 1966.

27. Stolper, W., and P. Samuelson. "Protection and Real
    Wages," *Review of Economic Studies,* IX:1,Novem-
    ber 1941, 58-73.

28. Swamy Subramanian. "Structural Change and the Distri-
    bution of Income by Size: The Case of India,"

The Review of Income and Wealth, Series XII:2, June 1967, 155-74.

29. Williamson, Jeffrey G. "Regional Inequality and the Process of National Development," *Economic Development and Cultural Change,* XIII:4, July 1965, part II.

Author's note: I have received useful comments from P. K. Bardhan, particularly in the formulation of the appendix, and from J. R. Harris.

CHAPTER **16** COMMERCIAL BANKS AND
LATIN AMERICAN INTEGRATION

By   William H. Bolin, Vice-President
Bank of America

Commercial banks in general, and especially those operating in several Latin American countries, tend to be thrust increasingly into the integration process on a daily working basis.
With intra-regional trade among the CACM nations having increased
almost sixfold and with LAFTA interchange having doubled between
1960 and 1966, new demands have been made on these institutions.

The logic of regional economic integration, which calls
for an expanded market, fosters greater economic specialization
and diversification, and stimulates increased flows of goods, services, and capital among member countries must, of course, be
extended to financial institutions.   In order to take full advantage
of the economic opportunities created by regional economic integration, there must be a viable network of financial institutions
throughout the region capable of providing the necessary financing.
This can be accomplished by allowing banks to establish branches
in the various countries that comprise the region and by strengthening correspondent banking relationships.   While in recent years
there has been progress in creating this financial network, there
is still much to be done. It is, however, encouraging to note that
the Banco do Brasil, S. A. and Banco de la Nación Argentina
have been establishing branches in various Latin American countries and that the Banco Capitalizador of El Salvador has established a branch in Honduras.

Commercial banks serve as sources of information to industry and commerce on the progress of inter-governmental consultations within CACM and LAFTA. Questions range from tariff
bargaining to telecommunications services. Banks serve as the
principal source of information on new trade and investment possibilities offered by economic integration, and provide a means of
communication between buyers and sellers hitherto unknown to
each other.

Finally, they provide the mechanism for payments of all
sorts for intra-regional trade. Businessmen often call upon either
commercial banks directly or indirectly through central banks in
bilateral and multilateral payments arrangements to provide credit
to one or both sides of intra-regional trade transactions. Such financing involves not only the transit of goods between exporter and
importer but also often the allocation of funds for production in
one nation and for ultimate distribution in another.

From this vantage point, several phenomena may be observed in the financial aspects of the integration process, as it has unfolded so far, which perhaps merit more attention.

First the problem of fluctuating currencies which is often cited as a major impediment to intra-regional trade and investment appears to loom somewhat larger in principle than in practice — although it is by no means a negligible factor. Trade among and between the CACM nations and the LAFTA nations is not being hindered nearly so much by the fear of invoicing in the "soft" currency of a neighbor as by many other fundamental deterrents.

Businessmen have been becoming increasingly sophisticated concerning matters of international trade and finance. They have learned to look at economic factors such as economic growth rates, rates of inflation, the development of internal savings, etc. that are more fundamental than simply the current exchange rate. To an important degree, businessmen have learned to forecast for themselves the likely changes in the relative values of currencies. Certainly, the trade flows that already occur among Latin American countries give evidence to this heightened sophistication. In particular, it is possible to point to the extensive trade in wheat from Argentina to Brazil or concrete from Colombia to Brazil, or the trade flows between Argentina and Chile or Colombia textiles to their Andean neighbors.

This is worth mentioning because a great deal of effort has gone into multilateral clearing arrangements, including the creation in Central America of a unit of account in the form of the Central American Peso. In the end, these mechanisms may prove to have been worthwhile steps. Viewed from the working level, however, there appears to be at the present time a number of more urgent problems deserving higher priority.

Some of the problems are: the lack of harmonization of taxes applicable to financial transactions, the delays and complexities of exchange control procedures, the lack of mechanisms for perfection of creditors' security interests in goods, the delays incident to legal redress of defaulted contracts, unpredictable changes in trade parctices such as tariffs and quotas, and violent changes in credit availability in response to balance of payment needs. These are but a few of the financial roadblocks to intra-regional trade and investments which appear to be impeding integration more than currency instability as such.

Certainly there is a great need for more consultation and coordination between governments concerning expansion and contraction of commercial bank credit and other monetary policy matters. For example, I talked with a Chilean industrialist who has made several successful investments in Argentina, thus involving two of the countries having the highest degree of currency instability in recent years. Following the drastic changes in Argentine trade policy last year, he told me he was considering giving up his Argentine interests. He could find ways to hedge against depreciation of his investment and could manage the difficult problem of pricing between affiliates that fluctuating currencies implied. He could not, however, stand the combined effect of sudden tariff changes on his product in Argentina and at the same time drastic restriction of bank credit in Chile.

Tne greatest progress in this area apparently has been achieved over the last five years by the CACM member central banks. They are now consulting very regularly with each other.

Another noteworthy trend arising from intra-regional trade, as viewed by the commercial banks, is the relative shrinkage of short-term supplier credit to Latin America on consumer goods induced by the integration process. While the magnitude of this phenomenon is not yet sufficient to be noticed widely, one can see an interesting pattern beginning to develop along the following lines.

In the Central American Common Market, industry has been the chief beneficiary of economic integration as it has thus far developed. About 86 per cent of the increase in intra-regional trade has been in manufactured goods, such as textiles, clothing and processed foods. Industry has also benefifed from the LAFTA, but in lesser proportion because of the dominance there of Argentine - Brazilian trade in primary commodities.

As intra-regional imports supplant manufactured goods from outside LAFTA and CACM, importers within each country who were formerly able to rely on a substantial amount of short-term supplier credit (either in the form of purchases on open account or by means of documentary collections made through commercial banks) tend to place this burden on manufactured goods exporters within their trade blocs. Sr. Felipe Herrera in his address before the Eighth Meeting of the Board of Governors of the Inter-American Development Bank in Washington, D. C. in April 1967, recognized this problem and stated: "The liberalization of intra-regional trade will also create a demand for additional short-term financing."

As an example, tire-importing firms in Central America had long received 90-120 day terms from overseas manufacturers. When an "integrated" industry was established to produce tires in the area, this same credit was demanded of it, and the result was a considerable potential increase in its working capital credit demanas from local banks. In other words, sales and inventories (which in Latin America constitute a far larger segment of a firm's assets than in the U.S.A. — because of delivery lead times), which were to a great degree financed from outside of CACM and LAFTA, increasingly have to be financed with supplier credit from within these regions. Each product which comes to be produced within the area, and the sale of which is hence financed by bank credit within this area, is that much "float" of working capital in foreign exchange which the area as a whole might otherwise have enjoyed. In the case of a pure "transformation" industry it is true that suppliers' credit on the previous consumer - goods imports may be replaced by suppliers' credit for imported raw materials. (In the aforementioned example, the tire manufacturer might get credit for the part of its rubber needs that it imports.) However, this nearly always is less in value than the goods previously imported (one hopes!), and in addition raw materials often are not available on the same terms as finished goods.

This is best illustrated in the Central American Common Market partly because this trading area is more fully integrated and partly because changes are reflected more clearly in a small economic region. Although definitive statistics are not available, an estimate based on CACM nation trade activity with the United States alone would place the magnitude of worldwide, short-term supplier credit to Central America within the range of $ 50-75 million at any given moment. The demand for such working capital is growing rapidly but the amount of short-term supplier credit from outside is not increasing at a commensurate rate. The scope of the problem is put in perspective when you examine the gains made in intra-regional trade. Of total imports into various Central American Common Market countries, only 7.4 per cent came from other CACM countries in 1961 as opposed to 15.8 per cent in 1966. Many credits which would have been supplied by outside suppliers must now be provided through expansion of credit from local institutions.

Some attention has been given to this problem as far as medium-term credit is concerned. The Inter-American Development Bank (IDB) has extended nine revolving lines of credit totaling $ 30 million to Argentina, Brazil, Chile, Mexico, Nicaragua, Peru, and Venezuela, to assist these countries in financing exports of domestic capital goods within the Latin American area. Under this program the IDB finances up to 70% of the CIF or FOB value of intra-regional exports with loans for as long as five years, carrying interest of 6.5% per annum.

Representatives of Latin American governments meeting recently in Washington recommended expansion and modification of the aforementioned medium-term capital goods export financing program. Specifically, they suggested that the IDB might broaden its program: to cover certain types of manufactures and semi-manufactures other than capital goods (presumably with short-term credit); to offer financing for the period during manufacture as well as after manufacture; to cover medium-term financing of manufactured goods shipped outside Latin America; to provide more financing for periods in excess of five years for both intra-regional exports and extra-regional exports in order to give a competitive advantage to Latin American manufacturers relative to developed nation suppliers.

The recommendation of this Washington working group was presented to the Second Meeting of Governmental Representatives on the Financial Implications of Latin American Integration in May 1968 in Montevideo. That meeting in turn prepared a report for study and action by the Inter-American Economic and Social Council.

At this juncture, and in view of the study being made by the IDB staff of the foregoing recommendations, it is submitted that several of the proposals deserve closer examination for possible alternative courses of action.

To begin, the IDB employs a wide diversity of approaches in support of Latin American economic integration (acting in Sr. Herrera's words, as the "Hemisphere's Economic Integration Bank"), and it is limited in its resources, by both constitutional and financial-market considerations. Thus, it appears proper to explore to the maximum the possibilities for the private commercial banking system to shoulder some of this burden in coordination with correspondents and affiliates outside the region. There is the reasonable probability that private funds from outside Latin America can be employed to finance trade sourced from within Latin America.

A second, related question is that of providing financing for extra-regional exports. The recent Washington meeting of CIES gave attention to this problem by asking the IDB to study it. Here again, at least for the short-term needs, it seems more logical to allow and expect indigenous commercial banks within Latin America to obtain credit from abroad for this purpose or to encourage multinational commercial banks having branches in the area to set up programs to enable Latin American exporters to obtain financing rather than to place a drain on the scare resources of the IDB.

It should be possible for leading commercial banks in Latin America and for U.S. and European banks active within the area to tap resources from developed-nation money markets so as to find together a field of mutual cooperation for meeting the recommendations recently set forth in Washington. The fact that such credits are self-liquidating in international currencies makes them particularly adaptable to the use of foreign bank credit.

Inquiry into this subject should include study as to whether the substitution of new commercial bank credit from abroad in place of the previous (or potential) supplier credit from outside is aided or complicated by the clearing arrangements being set up. At least in a theoretical sense such credits from abroad in dollars or European currencies may be complicated in the future by the growing tendency to invoice intra-country exports in either the currency of the importing country or in a clearing unit.

At an April 1968 meeting in Guatemala of various commercial banks operating in Central America a proposal for creation of a Central American acceptance was formulated. As visualized at this point, suppliers in one Central American country would draw drafts at short-term on importers in other Central American countries and with the "aval" of the importer's bank for the purpose of

207

assuring convertibility. The implications at this stage are that
the acceptance would be denominated in Central American dollars
because of the evident intent that the Central American Clearing
House be utilized. Convertibility at a fixed rate would be guaranteed by agreement between the two central banks and the discount
would be effected for the exporter in his own currency by his own
local bank.

This may well be useful, but it should be noted that the
system still leaves the credit load on the Central American banking system — where (since all of the countries find credit control
necessary for anti-inflation purposes), each acceptance discounted
presumably will mean that much less credit for other productive
purposes. If such acceptances were drawn on the U.S. in dollars
or, if their convertibility to dollars (or D.M. or Swiss Franc)
could in some way be collectively assured by the five central banks
so that equivalent bankers bills could be drawn on major capital
centers and discounted there, then this credit load might be shifted
back outside the area again.

Presumably, the clearing of intra-regional acceptances
would be handled through the Central American Clearing House
which was formally established in July 1961 by mutual agreement
of the five CACM central banks. The Clearing House has been in
operation since 1963. Each of the CACM central banks provided
the equivalent of $US 500,000 to facilitate clearing operations of
its currency by the other four members. In practice, any credits
over $US 500,000 are cleared every two weeks, and every six
months all balances are settled. In August 1963, an additional arrangement was made with Mexico to clear payments between CACM
countries and Mexico. Interest has also been expressed in establishing additional agreements with other neighboring countries.

Although this question has been studied at some length by
the LAFTA countries also, actual progress toward establishing a
meaningful clearing arrangement among the LAFTA countries has
been quite slow. In 1965, most of the LAFTA central banks agreed
to establish a system of bilateral credits. The credits range from
$ 5 million to $ 200,000. Currently the central banks involved will
cover payments up to the maximum amount of the credit agreement
for a period of two months. Every two months a full settlement is
made, and the process of accumulating balances by the central
banks begin anew. Any credits in excess of the maximum agreed-
upon figure are settled immediately. Similar arrangements are
under discussion for the Andean region.

In summary, the most readily available credit in the international money markets for the Latin American countries, and
normally the cheapest, is short-term financing of the movement of
merchandise (with its preparation before export and its distribution following importation). Care should be taken so that, as the
new payments arrangements evolve from Latin American integration, the region continues to tap to the maximum this availability.
Private commercial banks inside the area as well as their corre-

spondent, affiliated or parent institutions in the developed capital centers can continue to provide a valuable "float" of continuous foreign exchange and working capital, if their present and potential role is taken into account in the planning now taking place, and if their efforts are properly coordinated with those of the institutions at work on the problem.

CHAPTER **17** INFLATION AS AN OBSTACLE TO
LATIN AMERICAN ECONOMIC
INTEGRATION

By David Huelin
Bank of London and South America

Inflation is often confused with the restrictive policies
that are normally used to check or eliminate it. Inflation may not
be desirable, but anti-inflationary measures that fail to achieve
their aim undoubtedly make a bad situation worse; restrictions are
the very negation of economic expansion, and they can be justified
from a social point of view only when they are demonstrably the
lesser of the two evils — that is to say when restrictions actually
do check inflation. Restrictive policies are much harder to justify
if they turn out to be not an alternative evil but an additional one
acting as a brake on economic activity but not on prices.

In Latin America there is a great variety of economic
climates, from near-perfect stability to very rapid inflation, and
an equal variety of economic policies. In general terms — and it
must be stressed that all generalizations are sure to be untrue
in part — there is a tendency towards monetary restraint, in differing degrees of severity, intended either to prevent the appearance of inflation where it does not exist already, or to hold it in
check where it is an established phenomenon. In neither case
does monetary restraint solve any structural problems in the economy; on the contrary it may delay or impede remedial action.

This study does not attempt to take sides in the structur-
alist-monetarist controversy; its contention is rather that the
difference in views is irrelevant to reality. Latin America ex-
hibits examples of inflation that are unmistakably of structural
origin, on which monetary remedies have no beneficial effect and
may even be harmful; it also can show striking instances of
purely monetary inflation, caused by indiscipline and misgovern-
ment, in an otherwise sound economy.

The variety of economic climates, ranging from almost
complete freedom to rather rigorous control, makes it evident
that policies in both the domestic and the external sectors are
likely to be extremely disparate and difficult to harmonize; for
example, credit regulations, fiscal policy, labor legislation, and
the social expenditure policy of each government, are inevitably
involved in any move towards economic integration no less than
the more obvious elements in the external sector such as foreign
trade policy and the regulations governing foreign capital. Underlying every attempt at harmonization will inevitably be the question
of inflation, its causes, its nature, its intensity, and the policies

210

to which it has given rise, including structuralist and monetarist attitudes.

This study attempts to examine the origins and course of inflation in Latin America, from which it may be possible to infer the main reasons for the conclusion that the existence of inflations of various types and intensities constitutes an almost insuperable barrier to the harmonizing of economic policies.

*　　　*　　　*

Probably none of Latin America's economic difficulties has been the subject of so much controversy as has inflation: it affects every economic activity and confuses the republics' foreign relations; it is a potent factor in domestic politics, and an element of instability in almost every aspect of the republics' affairs. There is the observed fact that economic growth has been accompanied by rapid inflation, notably in Argentina and Brazil, but not in Mexico; from this stems a debate on whether inflation is an inevitable accompaniment to economic growth; the example of Mexico suggests that it is not, but there are differing views on whether it is the reformed social and political structure of Mexico or the Mexican authorities' pursuit of cautious monetary policies that has prevented the appearance of inflation.

Before the relevance of the debate can be appreciated it will be as well to examine the social and economic context in which inflation has occurred in Latin America, the course that it has taken, and the consequences of the measures used to check it. Inflation in Latin America does not differ from its manifestation elsewhere in the world in being the outcome of an excess of demand over supply and of consumption in relation to savings; it is in the structural reasons underlying these ordinary causes that Latin America has some particular characteristics.

Not the least distinctive feature of the inflationary republics is the attitude of governments and business communities, who from long experience have learned to live with and to some extent protect themselves from inflation. They do not share the European or U.S. view that inflation is an intolerable evil.

SOME INTERNAL CAUSES OF INFLATION

The population of Latin America as a whole is growing at a rate of nearly 3 per cent a year, and the greater part of this growth is occurring in the lower social strata and particularly in depressed rural areas, in some of which the rate of increase exceeds 4 per cent a year. This means, statistically, that unless national incomes increase by more than 5 per cent annually there can be no perceptible rise in the average income per inhabitant.

Average incomes are low; even the comparatively high per capita levels of Argentina and Uruguay are below one-half of the general level of northern Europe, and that of Brazil is barely one-third. Moreover, in most of the republics —Argentina and Uruguay being the main exceptions — the distribution of income is extremely unequal, with wide disparities between the upper and lower social classes and between the urban and rural communities.

This pattern reflects the social and agrarian structure inherited from the nineteenth century; in many of them, including Chile and parts of Brazil, archaic systems of land tenure remain unreformed, with latifundia or plantation agriculture depriving peasant populations of land resources. Even where these conditions are not extreme, domestic agriculture is in general technically backward, under-capitalized and low-yielding; its development has been impeded by poor communications and marketing mechanisms, taxes and price controls, and inadequate credit facilities. Moreover the migration, mainly of young adults, towards the cities has been reducing the human potential in agriculture.

The growth of urban demand, and the failure of agricultural output to keep pace with it, has resulted in shortages and has been a primary cause of inflation. When demand has caused prices to rise, the effect has seldom penetrated through the distributive mechanisms to the producers; at various times governments have imposed price controls on essential food products so as to avoid rises in urban living costs. Rising demand has not been translated into increased production and increased rural incomes; accelerated economic activity in the cities has been accompanied by stagnant or even declining agricultural output, and the disparities between the two sectors have been accentuated.

In Brazil and Chile, for example, the neglect of agriculture has led to these countries' being no longer self-sufficient in food supplies, while Chile was until as recently as the mid-1950's, and their being obliged to spend foreign exchange on imports. Even in Argentina and Uruguay, agricultural countries par excellence, legislation has induced occasional shortages and has to some extent isolated agriculture from urban economic growth.

In the public sector there are other consequences; the depression of agriculture, in conjunction with the population growth and the rising tide of expectations, has attracted many thousands of rural workers to the cities, so that urban populations have been increasing at rates of some 7 per cent or more annually; this has created an ever-rising demand for social services, housing and public works, often exceeding governments' ordinary resources and giving rise to inflationary pressures.

The neglect and isolation of rural populations implies a waste of human and agrarian potential which is one of the major impediments to Latin America's balanced economic growth.

THE PREBISCH EFFECT

The Latin American republics derive from the nineteenth century and from international economic circumstances, a dependence on exports of primary commodities; many of the economies are geared to a single product, such as coffee or copper; few have highly diversified exports, and exports of manufactured goods, which began in a small way in the late 1950's, and showed some promise in the early 1960's, are unlikely to reach a significant scale for some years to come, despite the resolutions adopted at the recent UNCTAD conference in New Delhi.

Most of Latin America's exports are sold either on free world markets or through private commercial channels, and are subject to the price fluctuations generated by changes in the balance of supply and demand. The general trend of prices since the end of the Korean war boom has been downwards, with the result that the contribution of the export trade to economic growth has been declining, certainly relatively to the rate of growth itself, and in some cases absolutely. This has occurred precisely in the period when the social pressures for economic expansion have been greater than ever before.

Dr. Raúl Prebisch, doyen of Latin American economists and Secretary General of the UNCTAD, showed as long ago as 1950 how the mechanisms of free markets and international trade combine to transfer from the industrialized countries to the exporters of primary commodities all cyclical contractions in demand, through falls in prices, but only a part of the rise in prices resulting from cyclical expansion, because of economies in the industrial use of primary materials or a greater use of substitutes. This means that the benefits of technical advances are not passed on to the developing countries.

This process, which has come to be known as the "Prebisch Effect" leads to the rich countries' becoming richer while the expansion of the developing economies is delayed. The various expedients used in Latin America to overcome the worst effects have not proved to be adequate substitutes for export earnings; they have led to balance-of-payments difficulties and to inflationary pressures, as will be shown later.

An additional, and at times significant, cause of shortage of both domestic capital and foreign exchange resources is the deeply rooted tradition among Latin American capital owners of depositing or investing funds abroad. Originally this was done as a safeguard against political instability — a sort of exile insurance — or simply to enable the rich to live in Europe; more recently it has been used as a hedge against inflation or for exchange speculation.

INFLATION IN THE PRIVATE SECTOR

In the more advanced republics where the growth of the urban middle classes dates from before the first world war, reflecting their thriving foreign trade and its allied developments, the social pressures for economic expansion have been constantly at work. Two world wars and the intervening depression emphasized the dangers of relying on overseas suppliers for consumer goods, and on world markets for the export earnings to pay for such goods. This applied especially to Argentina and Brazil with their large Europe-orientated trade.

Immediately after the second world war, in particular, domestic conditions were extremely propitious for industrial development aimed at the substitution of imports. Starved consumer markets were avid for manufactures, and demand was backed, especially in Argentina, by an exceptional increase in the money supply; this was the local currency counterpart of accumulated foreign exchange from exports maintained throughout the war and largely unrequited.

With a strong domestic demand and ample exchange reserves for imports of equipment, industrial growth was extremely rapid. As the former belligerents resumed their normal exports, Latin American manufacturers were able easily to obtain from their governments protective barriers, behind which high costs — and high profits — were no impediment to expansion. There was an accompanying keen demand for industrial labor, and high wages were offered; this accelerated the drift, which is still continuing, of rural workers to the industrial centers; the rapid growth of the labor force — consisting largely of people earning hitherto unheard-of wages and neither acquainted with the idea of saving nor, in the absence of effective mechanisms for the purpose, being encouraged to save — added fresh impetus to the consumer demand, especially for foods, with a consequent tendency for prices to rise.

Attempts by governments to limit rises (because of their impact on living costs) created shortages and black markets, and belated price rises had in the end to be allowed. Cost-of-living indices in Latin America naturally give a heavier weighting to foods than they do in high-income countries; rising indices form the basis of wage claims.

The governments of, for example, Perón in Argentina and Vargas in Brazil, actively encouraged the formation of trade unions to strengthen labor's bargaining power, and frequently gave official support to wage claims, or even decreed general wage increases for the private sector no less than the public. In Chile there was legislation that automatically ordered wage increases of the same percentage as the rise in the cost-of-living index in the previous year. In the highly protected climate in which industry has operated, manufacturers have been able, without fear of competition from imports, to pass increases in costs on to consumers, often in advance of impending cost rises. Thus classical price-wage-cost spirals have been generated.

The inflationary influence of industry has been accentuated by a lack of selectivity in official promotion schemes; there has been excessive duplication among uneconomically small plants. These, being labor-intensive, have helped to improve employment statistics, but the technical shortcomings of their equipment have limited the productivity of the labor employed. On the other hand, the installation of modern capital-intensive plants has in some cases led to the creation of productive capacity far in excess of the market's potential, with consequently high operating costs. The pattern of duplication within each of the national economies is repeated in the regional context, as is mentioned below.

Import substitution gave considerable scope and impetus to manufacturing industries in the early stages, but it has been evident even in the comparatively large markets of Argentina and Brazil that the initial pace of expansion slowed down — in the absence of other outlets — as the process neared completion; since the late 1950's or so growth has been largely dependent on the ordinary expansion of domestic demand. Some further industrial development was achieved, especially in Argentina and Brazil, from about 1960 onwards in substituting imports of capital goods; but the limitations of the market and the large capital investments required have so far prevented any spectacular growth.

The gradual slowing down of the pace of industrial expansion has not, in general, been accompanied by a parallel decline in the rate of increase in industrial wages. The tendency of wage costs to rise faster than output has had obviously inflationary effects.

In all the circumstances outlined, an important role has been played by the inflationary countries' banking systems. In the initial stages of industrialization, when there was ample financial liquidity, large amounts of domestic capital were attracted by the high profits in industry; as the inflationary process advanced the underlying inadequacy of savings in relation to consumption became increasingly manifest in the difficulty experienced by entrepreneurs in avoiding the erosion of their capital by rising costs. Even the extensive capitalization of profits by the issue of new shares rather than cash dividends was not always enough to maintain a company's capital structure. Inflation itself has deterred savings and promoted consumption, especially of consumer durables as a simple hedge, and has thus accentuated the imbalance.

Increasing difficulties in this respect have driven entrepreneurs to rely more on bank credit and loans, not only for working capital but even for fixed capital too. The banking systems have exercised their normal multiplying effect on the money supply, and this, in conjunction with high interest rates, has added further to inflation.

THE INFLUENCE OF THE PUBLIC SECTOR

Governments have felt the impact of rising prices, perhaps even more acutely than the private sector, because of their
less flexible revenue. In most of the Latin American republics
the reform of archaic tax structures has been slow and late, and
collection has been far from efficient; only recently in a few
countries has tax evasion ceased to be respectable and become an
indictable offense; losses through evasion have been as high as
40 per cent of nominal tax revenue. At best, taxes are collected
in arrears on values which in a highly inflationary economy are
soon out of date.

In addition, great pressure has been put on fiscal resources by the social changes accompanying industrialization and
the migration of rural populations to the cities; industry itself
has exercised an increasing demand for the investment of public
funds in energy supplies, communications and similar services.
Also there have been subsidies on certain essential consumer
goods and on imports of vital supplies that have increased steeply
with the growth of cities. There has been, moreover, a great
proliferation of bureaucracy with the creation of new agencies to
deal with new social and economic phenomena; to this must be
added the losses of state-owned public services, state-owned
industries, and the financing by the state of crops, such as coffee.

The combination of sluggish revenue and rapidly rising
costs has resulted in very large deficits in national accounts; on
occasions in both Argentina and Brazil expenditure has been more
than twice the amount of revenue. In an inflationary economy in
which savings are inadequate and interest rates are high, the
ability of a government to finance its deficits by bond issues is very
limited.

Therefore, only two methods of financing fiscal deficits
have in effect been open to governments: borrowing from the
commercial banking system, by forcing the commercial banks to
take up special bond issues or make compulsory deposits with the
central bank, thus diverting resources from the private sector;
or borrowing from the central bank itself. These additions to the
money supply rapidly find their way into the private sector through
government payments to contractors, employees, and the recipients of subsidies; the commercial banking system exercises its
normal multiplying effect, and further inflation ensues.

The structuralists maintain that increases in the money
supply generated in the public sector are a reflection of inflationary pressures caused by structural defects in the economy, which
would appear to be true. The monetarists contend that increases
in the money supply without corresponding increases in production are a direct cause of inflation, which could not continue for
long if monetary expansion were adequately regulated, which
also seems undeniable.

216

THE ROLE OF FOREIGN CREDIT

The Prebisch Effect in Latin America, as already noted, has prevented the rapidly developing republics from deriving from their export trade the domestic capital and the foreign exchange that they needed to maintain adequate investments and imports. The double deficiency has been to some extent concealed, rather than overcome, by foreign assistance in various forms. Long-term loans to governments and official enterprises have contributed significantly to the economic infrastructure, but the private sector has had to rely mainly on private investments and on medium- and short-term credits.

Private investments by foreign industrialists in associated enterprises have made a substantial contribution to industrial development by their introduction of equipment and techniques. It has been argued, however, that some of these ventures, by establishing plants with excess capacity, by using bank loans for installation expenses, and by adding their over-large demands for buildings, energy and other services to already existing demand, have had indirect inflationary consequences.

In default of adequate domestic or foreign investment, industry has made extensive use of credits from foreign banks and suppliers of capital goods. Supplying countries have readily offered these credits as a means of promoting their exports, and Latin American governments have approved this means of enabling industrial expansion to continue without excessive immediate impact on the balance of payments.

The suppliers' credit system has been criticized as being an unsuitable method of financing industrial expansion; not only do such credits cost more to the borrower than investment capital, but they are short in relation to the borrower's needs. Both factors are an addition to the Latin American manufacturer's costs. It is probable that new equipment acquired in this way has enabled some industrialists to reduce costs, at least comparatively; but it is not certain that such reductions have compensated the additional costs implicit in the system; clearly, it is possible that costs might have been reduced still further if industrialists had been able to borrow on longer terms and at lower rates of interest.

The virtually unrestricted acceptance of these credits from the early 1950's onwards eventually led to excessive accumulations of medium- and short-term foreign exchange liabilities; several countries have at various times been obliged to negotiate fresh loans or the postponement of their obligations.

The abuse of the suppliers' credit system has accentuated existing distortions by being merely a transitory substitute for savings and concealing the real deficiency; it has led to additional exchange obligations without creating any export trade; and it has increased the Prebisch Effect by raising the effective cost of imports.

The protective barriers erected by all the industrializing countries have resulted in the excessive duplication of industries in Latin America as a whole, preventing exports of manufactured goods from one country to another, and thus making it impossible for industries to expand their activities beyond their national markets. The Latin American Free Trade Association is attempting to break down this structure, but it is clear that the extensive reorganization of industries in each republic that will be required will take some years to achieve.

Though it cannot be said that the high level of industrial protection common in Latin America is a direct consequence of inflation — it may be more appropriately defined as one of its causes — it seems probable that the existence of inflation and the pressure that it exercises on the balance of payments will make import restrictions necessary for some years to come. The extent to which such restrictions can be liberalized in favor of fellow members of the LAFTA has been shown to be slight, and it is already apparent that industrial protectionism is one of the largest as well as the most obvious of the obstacles to integration; although import restrictions may be kept in force ostensibly or mainly to protect the balance of payments, their nature and incidence are almost inevitably governed by protective considerations.

The only likely way out of this impasse would appear to be an arrangement that would open the markets of the rich countries to the products of the developing countries' industries, thus reducing their dependence on their domestic markets and making competition from a neighbor admissible. It remains to be seen whether the UNCTAD or the Atlantic Free Trade Association — if it ever comes into existence — can achieve some arrangement that will free Latin American industries from the restrictions of each other's protectionism; obviously no attempt at integration can progress very far until this obstacle is overcome.

ANTI-INFLATIONARY POLICIES

Anti-inflationary restrictions of differing intensity and effectiveness have been applied since the early 1950's; in no country has inflation been permanently and wholly arrested, though there have been several notable reductions of the pace. In other instances it is more doubtful whether governments have made very enthusiastic attempts, partly perhaps because of the difficult social and political consequences of recession — as for example in Argentina — and partly no doubt because of governments' unwillingness to curb their own expenditure, as in Brazil before 1964. Although Prebisch has referred to the "false dilemma" of a choice between expansion and stability, a very real dilemma has arisen on many occasions, notably in Argentina, Brazil, Chile, and Colombia, when industrial expansion and inflation have combined to produce a crisis in the balance of payments. It is virtually essential for any Latin American republic in payments difficulties to apply to the International Monetary Fund for a credit; the necessity is dictated by the common practice among other creditors — government or private —of looking to the IMF for a lead and making their loans or credits conditional on IMF approval.

The Fund correctly believes that inflation is an important factor in a country's balance of payments and wishes to ensure that inflation will be curbed so as to avoid the credit's becoming ineffectual through a further deterioration in the payments position, and the borrower's ultimate inability to repay drawings. The Fund normally examines the borrowing country's monetary situation in detail, specifying the precise amount beyond which the money supply should not be allowed to expand, and requiring a letter of intent agreeing to these and other stipulations.

Latin Americans tend to regard these methods as an unwelcome intervention in their domestic affairs, and relations with the Fund have been strained on occasions. The structuralists are critical of the Fund because of its insistence only on monetary restraint rather than on structural reforms. Their case is strengthened by the observed consequences of monetary restrictions vigorously applied, which can be not only detrimental to economic development but actually self-defeating.

IMF doctrine is based on restraint of the money supply, which is intended to curb demand. It does not affect costs, however, and a rigorous restriction of bank credit, on which businesses rely heavily in times of inflation, may cause a slowing down of industrial expansion or even an absolute contraction, with perhaps a rise in unit production costs. It may also affect the distributive trades and lead to shortages of essential supplies. Perhaps its worst effect is the encouragement that it may give to "parallel" money markets, where the cost of borrowing becomes very high indeed; there is commonly an increase in the velocity of circulation that partly neutralizes quantitative restrictions of credit, but does not solve the business sector's problems.

Excessively severe restrictions can lead to bankruptcies, to disinvestments from enterprises that cease to be profitable, and to a general crisis in confidence, often reflected in a flight of capital from the country. The theory that credit restraint will not only discourage the demand for imports but also persuade businesses to borrow working capital abroad, and so give immediate relief to the payments position, has been proved not to be valid if confidence is weakened.

Even in less severe circumstances than these, a falling off of economic activity has reduced government revenues; as it has seldom been possible at short notice to curtail official expenditure to a significant extent without causing social hardship, the governments of the inflationary countries have had to meet their fiscal deficits with inflationary financing, even in times of severe credit restriction in the private sector. Argentina, Brazil, Chile, and Colombia have experienced the double evil of recession with continuing inflation.

CONCLUSION

It seems possible to identify certain causes of primary inflationary pressure in Latin America that are undoubtedly structural and could be eliminated only by structural reforms. The economic and even social isolation of agriculture from urban prosperity has been a basic cause of shortages of essentials; in this context it matters little whether the isolation is caused by inherited patterns of land tenure, by poor communications, by lack of investment or by deliberate policies. The inflationary forces latent in these situations became active when industrial expansion, in response to middle-class urban demand, attracted rural populations to the cities and added to the demand for both foods and manufactures.

Increased consumption was not accompanied by a parallel growth in savings and investment; capital formation has been inadequate both in agriculture and in industry, largely because of social attitudes and the absence of suitable institutions. The public sector has, largely for institutional reasons, failed to match expenditure with revenue, and for social and political reasons has intervened in the private sector with legislation that has tended to encourage consumption rather than to curb it in favor of savings. The various expedients used to overcome the deficiency of domestic capital formation in both sectors — amounting in effect to the creation of money in various ways — may be regarded as causes of a secondary stage of inflation, structural or political in its origin and monetary in its consequences.

The experience of Mexico appears to confirm the structural hypothesis; the basic social and agrarian reforms were achieved before the appearance of the social pressures that have led to inflation in other republics. These reforms included the establishment of a strong and stable government and an efficient administration equipped with the power and the expertise required to eliminate structural inflationary pressures where they appeared and to apply wise monetary and fiscal policies.

At the other end of the wide scale of development in Latin America are republics with small middle classes, small urban concentrations, low national incomes, little industrialization, and no inflation.

The countries that have been most severely afflicted in the past have recently been evolving more balanced monetary policies and modernizing their fiscal and financial administration, so that they are succeeding in checking what might be called a tertiary stage of superinflation from purely monetary causes. The complete disappearance of inflation may have to await the execution of their plans for agrarian reform and agricultural modernization or the emergence of more stable political structures.

When the many basic reforms have been carried far enough for the fear of inflation to have diminished, it will be possible for integration in its widest sense to be studied; the Latin American republics that have avoided or overcome inflationary tendencies naturally have no desire to "import" inflation from their neighbors — that is to say, they will resist moves towards integration if these mean that rising prices in a neighboring country adversely affect domestic values, wage levels, and other key factors. Similarly, no country where there is stability and low interest rates, wishes to lose its domestic capital to neighboring financial centers where interest rates are higher; more important still, perhaps, no country that has achieved or preserved its stability by cautious monetary policies and carefully planned development is going to be willing to abandon such an achievement for the sake of the ill-defined advantages of integration.

The inflationary countries, for their part, cannot possibly afford to adopt the easy-money policies, fiscal lenience, and liberal trade practice of some of the uninflationary, undeveloped, economies; nor would they be able, socially, to impose the kind of restrictions that have been used elsewhere to maintain stability.

Integration, in its broadest sense — which is the only sense worth serious consideration — must remain an unrealistic ideal in Latin America while economic conditions and policies are so various. This does not mean that, as an ideal, it should be abandoned; on the contrary, if attempts to achieve integration lead to improved economic discipline, they will have served a secondary purpose of great importance.

CHAPTER **18** PROBLEMS OF CURRENCY
UNIFICATION IN LATIN AMERICA:
THEORY AND POLICY

By   Ronald A. Krieger
Graduate School of International Studies
University of Denver

POSSIBILITY

The continuing advance of the Latin American integration movement in the past few years has progressively opened up discussion of higher and higher forms of economic union. One of the most advanced possible stages — the currency union — already has stirred many imaginations around the hemisphere and is receiving serious consideration in some policy making circles. Indeed, it is highly possible that the next 10 to 15 years will see the attempted formation of one or more currency unions in Central or South America.

Central America already has moved several steps along the way, although monetary and financial co-operation generally has taken a back seat to removal of trade barriers in Central American integration policy.[1] Nevertheless, as early as March 1963 the five Central American heads of state in a joint declaration indicated their intention to begin work on establishment of a monetary union. Eleven months later the five central banks concluded an agreement to move progressively towards monetary unification by gradually increasing the levels of monetary co-operation and co-ordination of exchange and credit policies. This "Agreement for the Establishment of the Central American Monetary Union" contemplates the eventual development of a common currency and a supranational regulatory authority. It established a Central American Monetary Council, consisting of the five central bank presidents, to carry out the interim steps of consultation, research, and development of specific instruments. A previously organized clearing house arrangement, established in 1961, continues to provide for the unilateral clearing of accounts and the recording of clearing transactions in an artificial unit, the Central American peso, pegged at 1:1 parity to the U.S. dollar.

The Latin American Free Trade Association, of course, lags considerably behind the Central American Common Market in both the forms and the substance of economic integration, and a LAFTA currency union is not a serious possibility in the near future. Nevertheless, two recent developments indicate that the pace of financial co-operation may soon be stepping up among the 11 LAFTA members. The first is the agreement reached at the April 1967 summit meeting of the presidents of the Latin American

222

republics to begin steps in 1970 toward an eventual merger of the CACM and LAFTA, aiming at a full Latin American Common Market by 1985. This perhaps will accelerate the adoption by the LAFTA nations of some of the more advanced forms already contemplated in Central America. The second indication is the recent formation of a development bank for the six-nation Andean bloc within LAFTA, which may well lead to discussions of further forms of regional financial co-operation.

Although complete monetary integration in any part of Latin America obviously is not imminent, the idea already is being advanced in Central American circles that currency unification is a necessary and logical step forward in the process of total economic integration. Examples of this attitude abound, typified perhaps by this statement of a former top monetary official of the region: "The fact that political and institutional conditions are not directly conducive to full monetary integration should not prevent the advancement of a process that, by its own nature, must evolve closely related to the vigorous over-all program of economic integration."[2]

A. U.S. commentator on the Latin American business scene puts it even more strongly: "The hard-nosed bankers and economists, in private conversations, say that the entire Common Market set-up is still badly fragmented and many years will be required before this is resolved. Most are agreed that a single currency is needed for all the Central American countries, and unquestionably this would be ideal. Such a project is in the making with a 'Central American Peso,' but at the moment this unit is only something used by statisticians in preparing reports."[3] Finally, the economic ministers of the five republics, in the August 1967 meeting of the Central American Economic Council, reaffirmed their determination to include monetary integration as part of the advance toward higher levels of economic co-operation. They declared their "determination, within the framework of the Declaration of the Presidents of America, to propel the Central American economic movement toward higher degrees of integration, and to take the actions necessary to bring about as quickly as possible a customs and monetary union...."[4]

Given the ready acceptance of monetary integration as a desirable goal and the enthusiasm which the concept seems to engender, it is not too early to begin assessment of the policy choices open to governments and monetary authorities as they take the first tentative steps down that relatively unchartered road. Is a common currency really "unquestionably ideal" for Central America or for any other part of Latin America, or are there hazards involved that must be taken into account as well? This study will attempt to examine critically the goal of currency unification in the light of certain theoretical considerations and in relation to specific problems of the Latin American area.

Because terminology varies among authors in the field of economic integration, it might be well to begin this section with some definitions of several terms used in a specific manner by the present writer. For purposes of this study, a currency union is a grouping of sovereign states that share the same currency under a single monetary authority. A currency area, similarly, denotes any geographical area — be it a territory, a country or a region — that uses a common currency under a common regulatory authority. These are distinct from what is sometimes called a monetary area, in which participating countries have separate central banks and separate currencies guaranteed freely convertible at fixed exchange rates. A homogeneous area is one in which the great bulk of economic activity centers around production of a single commodity or closely related products. Finally, an economic region will be defined as an area for which productive factors are mobile internally but immobile externally.

The purpose of this section is to examine certain theoretical issues involved in the grouping of territories or countries into a currency union. Although each of the sovereign republics of Latin America now forms a separate currency area, by definition, it does not necessarily follow that each of these politically determined currency areas is economically optimal. The notion of "optimality," of course, depends upon the criteria one is using; for purposes of this study, the criterion for judging the optimal size and composition of a currency area will be the ease and efficacy with which the grouping helps to resolve the potentially conflicting goals of smooth balance-of-payments adjustment, full employment, monetary stability and economic growth.

Various criteria have been suggested over the years for the proper domain of a currency area, and much of the enthusiasm that has greeted the idea of international currency unification has revolved around concepts other than optimum adjustment. Many of the classical economists, for example, were here concerned mainly with the freeing of trade from inconveniences of foreign exchange dealings, and thus considered the whole world to be an optimum currency area. Money in this view is principally a medium of exchange, and as such is most useful when it is universally accepted. [5] A more common interpretation sees the function of currency unification as lubricating the machinery of a common market by overcoming imperfections in commodity and factor movements:

> Under one currency, some of these imperfections
> could not survive, and others would be subject to new
> pressures. The very first consequence of having a
> single currency is, of course, that it allows complete
> freedom of payment by any one place to any other place
> in the union; thus a currency union gives complete liberty
> to capital movements, which under a common market may still be restricted. . . . Even under full

interconvertibility of currencies of countries in the
common market, a change in par values remains a
real possibility, a threat which is finally removed
only by the unification of the currencies. This is
indeed the great advantage of a currency union over
a monetary [area]. [6]

The lubricating function of a common currency is certainly of crucial importance in the advanced stages of economic
integration, but such considerations should not be allowed to over-
ride the essential monetary function of internal and external adjustment. National currency sovereignty, after all, means close
economic regulation in accord with national priorities — domestically through credit policy and note issue, externally through foreign exchange operations. Therefore, the critical issue in deciding whether to alter the domain of a currency area is whether
such alteration would help or hinder the pursuit of such goals as
a high level of economic activity, price stability and external
equilibrium.

A. CASE I: Adjustment Among Homogeneous Areas

A simple two-country, two-commodity model will serve
to illustrate the principal issues involved in currency unification
and the adjustment process. [7] Assume to start that, say, Guatemala and Honduras form a monetary area, each with its own central bank and currency (freely convertible at fixed exchange rates),
and that Guatemala produces only coffee for export, Honduras only
bananas. Prices and wages are inflexible downward, but each
country starts out in balance-of-payments equilibrium with full
employment. The usual Ricardian assumptions hold of internal
factor mobility and international immobility, so both countries
can be considered homogeneous economic regions.

Now suppose there are shifts of world demand into bananas and away from coffee, tending to cause a decline in output
and employment in Guatemala and inflationary pressure in Honduras. A balance-of-payments deficit opens up in Guatemala, a
surplus in Honduras. The domestic monetary policy prescription
is simple enough: Guatemala should take expansionary measures
while Honduras tightens credit. Assuming that both economies
respond readily, full employment can thus be restored to Guatemala and price stability to Honduras. But this will be in conflict
with exigencies of external adjustment policy. Since Honduras is
unwilling to permit inflation and prices and wages are inflexible
downward in Guatemala, the classical prescription — price defla-
tion in Guatemala and inflation in Honduras — cannot be followed.
For external adjustment to take place, Guatemala must permit a
contraction of output and employment that, in the absence of constraints dictated by external policy considerations, probably could
have been prevented by domestic monetary expansion. The demands of domestic stabilization in Honduras have made it impossible for the monetary authorities of the two countries to co-ordinate their efforts. If a large amount of trade takes place between

the two countries, then it is precisely the unwillingness of Honduras to inflate that forces the burden of adjustment onto Guatemalan income and employment.

It might be argued that the adjustment burden could be eased by instituting a regime of flexible exchange rates between the two countries.[8] This is probably true under the restrictive assumption that each country is a homogeneous economic region. Presumably the Honduran lempira would appreciate and the Guatemalan quetzal would depreciate until the surplus and deficit were eliminated. Each country could then follow an independent monetary policy for domestic stability. There might be a slight loss of real income to Guatemala through a deterioration of its terms of trade, but there need be no severe dislocation of output and employment and no inflation in Honduras. Although the adjustment in this case is smooth and facile under the given conditions, it would not be so effective, as we shall see, once the above restrictive assumption is relaxed.

But now let us proceed to the main issue at hand: fuse the two countries into a bi-regional currency area with a supranational central bank. Would this help to ease adjustment? The shift in demand from coffee causes unemployment and a balance-of-payments deficit for the Guatemalan "region" of the currency union. The Honduran region undergoes inflationary pressures and a surplus. If the central bank pursues a full-employment policy for the union, it will expand the money supply to cure the unemployment in Guatemala — and will thereby increase inflation in Honduras. In fact, if interregional trade is high, the Honduran price increases alone could serve both to bring about full employment in Guatemala and erase the payments disequilibrium between regions. Full-employment policy thus imparts a distinct inflationary bias to the corrective mechanism. Such bias would not be present, of course, if the joint central bank were willing to purchase price stability at the expense of unemployment in the deficit region (which also would tend to correct the interregional payments disequilibrium). In other words, in a currency union composed of distinct homogeneous regions a potential policy conflict arises among full employment, price stability and payments equilibrium. Either the deficit regions must suffer unemployment or the surplus regions must undergo inflation.

B. CASE II: Adjustment Among Multiregional Areas

Let us now relax certain assumptions in the direction of reality. For simplicity, assume once again a two-country, two-commodity system, but now let each country have two economic regions, one for the production of each exported commodity. For example, let both Guatemala and Honduras each have a coffee-producing region and a banana-producing region. Again starting from full employment and external equilibrium, what happens if the world coffee market shows a sudden decline while there is a boom in the banana market?

Both countries, we may presume, will tend to suffer unemployment in the coffee region and inflationary pressure in the banana region. If they form a monetary area with separate currencies pegged at fixed exchange rates, each central bank is faced with a dilemma: It can expand the money supply to stimulate full employment in the coffee region[9] only at the expense of introducing inflationary pressures in the banana region (which are likely to spread throughout the economy). On the other hand, if it fails to act it will maintain price stability only at the expense of unemployment in the coffee-exporting region. Each monetary authority will probably choose a compromise combination of "some" regional unemployment and some inflation, perhaps in accordance with its notions of the degree to which each factor inhibits economic growth. To the extent that economic growth might depend upon full employment and price stability, however, some growth will probably have to be sacrificed, one way or the other.

The dilemma is much the same in this case even if the separate currencies are connected through flexible exchange rates. Neither country will necessarily go into external surplus or deficit, but rather only different regions of each country. With bananas booming and coffee crumbling in both Guatemala and Honduras, neither appreciation nor depreciation of the quetzal or lempira offers any solution to the maintenance of domestic stability; external adjustment is irrelevant to interregional payments imbalance.

Now, we may ask, would a currency union offer any way out of this highly typical dilemma? Clearly, a union between the two countries would have no special success. There would be only one central monetary authority instead of two, but it still would have to deal with the same dilemma of unequal pressures on differentiated regions.

C. The Ideal Currency Union and the "Second-Best"

An obvious theoretical solution suggests itself at this point, if Guatemala and Honduras ever could advance sufficiently in political and economic integration to permit it. Ideally, they should reorganize monetarily so as to establish the one successful adjustment pattern identified above (under Case I): flexible or readily adjustable exchange rates between homogeneous economic regions. In our simple two-region model, this would mean combining the coffee regions of each country into one currency area and the banana regions into another. The external values of the coffee and banana currencies would be flexible with respect to each other and to outside monetary units, either on a freely floating basis or with a frequently adjustable peg. Now when demand shifts away from coffee and toward bananas, the "coffee peso" will depreciate and the "banana peso" will appreciate. The coffee central bank and the banana central bank each could then adopt the domestic policy appropriate to its region to insure both full employment and price stability. In this case, the coffee bank would expand the money supply while the banana bank would tighten credit.

To summarize the argument to this point, the ideal currency area is a homogeneous economic region, similar to the simplified "Guatemala" or "Honduras" of Case I. Nevertheless, there is little likelihood in the real world, however integration-minded it may become, of reorganizing currency systems on a strict product-region basis. The costs to world trade, in fact, might be prohibitive, for such a restructuring implies a separate currency area for each internationally traded commodity. This could quickly degenerate into a system of barter.

If the ideal is impractical, then, perhaps a theory of the "second-best" currency area will suffice. Given that the "first-best" homogeneous product-region is barred, a practical second-best alternative might well be the non-homogeneous economic region, producing many commodities but with high internal factor mobility. And, if it is impossible to make over pre-existing economic regions into currency areas, then it may be possible to reverse the process — map out a currency area and then, through promoting factor mobility, make it into an economic region.

To demonstrate how such an arrangement would work, let us once again take Guatemala and Honduras, each with its production areas of coffee, bananas and now, for that matter, any number of other commodities. Let the two countries be joined in a currency union and let labor, capital and entrepreneurship be fully mobile both between the two countries and among the various product-areas (no longer product-"regions"). Further, let the union have a high ability to reallocate resources from coffee to bananas or among any other industries. Now a divergence in the rates of growth of various industries would bring about total internal adjustment through factor movements. The supranational central bank can successfully regulate the level of aggregate economic activity without concern for regional disparities.

As a practical guide to policy, then, any grouping being considered as a potential currency area should have, as the minimum prerequisite, a high potential for internal factor mobility and for flexibility in the reallocation of resources. It should have, in other words, the potential to become a non-homogeneous, unitary economic region.

It has been suggested elsewhere[10] that, although the economic region is an optimum monetary area, it would not necessarily require a common currency and common regulatory authority. However, the above analysis indicates that without a common currency and supranational authority, the independent central banks of a multinational monetary area might well disrupt the adjustment process by pursuing divergent or conflicting monetary policies.

D. Other Prerequisites

The above discussion has served to resolve the theoretical grouping problem in terms of internal and external adjustment.

228

Let us now return to the currency union's "lubricating" function, as defined earlier. If the grouping's potential to become an economic region makes it eligible for candidacy as a currency area, what lubricating factors must be present to turn that eligibility into actuality?

The most obvious need of a lubricator is something to lubricate. That is, the nations involved should already be in the advanced stages of formation of a common market before it makes any sense to unite them with a common currency. Further, there should be a reasonably long and firm history of monetary cooperation among the central banks of the prospective currency union, to assure a transition to supranational regulation with a minimum of dislocation.

Two other prerequisites for a successful transition to a currency union might be suggested for purposes of promoting a widespread distribution of factors of production once factor mobility becomes a reality: no one country should be dominant in too many industries, and all should be at approximately equal stages of economic development. It also would help the trans-national adjustment process if at the beginning some of the leading export industries were shared by more than one country.

E. Currency Relations With The Outside World

A final theoretical question we might touch upon here is the relation of a currency union's common monetary unit to monetary units outside the union: should they be connected by fixed or fluctuating exchange rates? Sohmen, a vigorous advocate of freely floating rates among national states, believes that policy also to be optimal for an economic union vis-à-vis the rest of the world:

> As long as the integrated countries want to determine
> their own economic policies rather than be slavishly
> subject to the pushes and pulls of all random develop-
> ments in the rest of the world, they will have no
> choice but either to prevent the free flow of payments
> with outside countries, or to let exchange rates be-
> tween their currencies and those of other countries
> fluctuate freely. [11]

On the other hand, the effects of a fluctuating rate on a non-homogeneous currency union might not always be benign. In the hypothetical Guatemalan-Honduran currency union, for example, an appreciation of the currency because of a sudden boom in, say, bananas could have disastrous effects on the competitive position of coffee, cotton and other products whose markets might have been comparatively stable at the time.

Another argument against flexible rates — at least for a currency union with substantial trade with the rest of the world — has been proposed by McKinnon. [12] He demonstrates that in a highly open economy, defined as one with a high proportion of

229

tradable to nontradable goods, flexible exchange rates can be extremely damaging to internal price stability. He also notes that for a small union the international liquidity value of the currency will be low if it is not convincingly pegged to a major currency; liquidity fears might then tend to bring about capital export by domestic nationals.

In any event, by the time currency unification becomes immediately relevant for Latin America the issue is likely to have been settled by reorganization of the entire international monetary system, and the argument will be moot.

REALITY

Robert Triffin has suggested a four-step approach to the establishment of a currency union, once the go-ahead signal has been given: (1) legalization of the use of a common unit of account in the writing of contracts; (2) adoption of new national monetary units, still independent but of equal value; (3) free intercirculation of national currencies; and (4) establishment of a single authority in charge of currency areas. [13] To these I would add a fifth, the adoption of specific measures designed to facilitate the free geographic and inter-industry mobility of labor and capital.

Before embarking on that uncertain journey, however, integration officials should have a clear idea of what they are getting into and the prospects for success once the union is consummated. The above discussion of theory should have made it clear that establishment of a currency union is a difficult and risky enterprise, even under ideal conditions. And Latin America, unfortunately, presents for the most part conditions that are decidedly less than ideal for currency unification.

Let us first briefly consider Latin America as a whole. Although it is not unlikely that at some future date the entire zone might be united into some form of a customs union, it is apparent that this disparate grouping of nations could never successfully be united by a common Latin American currency. The primary factor needed for the success of a currency area — full internal factor mobility — is inconceivable in the context of Latin American history and economic geography. The isolated population clusters, the disparate social groupings and the wide range of climatological regions suggest that, if anything, many Latin American countries would be better off subdividing into subnational currency areas than expanding their currency domains across national borders.

The 11 LAFTA nations offer little more hope for successful currency unification than does the hemisphere as a whole. If LAFTA's co-operative ability is uncertain on commercial matters, it is virtually untested in the financial realm. Widely variant histories of financial and exchange stability indicate divergent approaches to internal monetary regulation that would be difficult.

to reconcile under a common supranational authority. The several countries find themselves at widely separated stages of economic development, with some states dominant over a broad range of industries while others are still in the pre-industrial stage. Large areas of many LAFTA countries are nonmonetized and only slightly integrated into the national life, if at all. In sum, the heterogeneity of the LAFTA area, the rudimentary state of its commercial integration and its dim prospects for flexibility of resource allocation and factor mobility make it a decidedly poor candidate for currency unification.

The Central American countries present a more hopeful picture, although even here the road towards a common currency promises to be far from smooth. Yet, all five countries enjoy an enviable record of price and exchange rate stability over a long period, and all five central banks apparently share common notions as to effective monetary policy. The countries have similar histories, and social patterns, while diverse, probably are not so variant as to erect an effective barrier to labor mobility. As a matter of fact, promotion of mobility across borders is now a conscious policy of the CACM. [14] Mobility also could be facilitated by the current location of many important commodities and industries in two or more countries. Although there are laggards and leaders among CACM members, the countries are roughly at a similar stage of economic development and none can claim clear domination in the concentration of industrial opportunities.

On the other hand, interindustry labor mobility is certain to be hampered by the lack of diverse and transferable skills on the part of labor and small entrepreneurship. There is little evidence to indicate that resource reallocation could be at all flexible if adjustment policy required it. Much of the area is still nonmonetized and large groups are not yet fully integrated into the national life. Diverse climatological and geographic areas abound and have traditionally been isolated from one another. As Wionczek has put it:

> It is difficult to believe that economic integration can proceed in the longer run under the conditions exemplified by the following data: only one-third of the population of Central America participates significantly in the market economy, the middle classes do not account for more than one-eighth of the population, and the degree of illiteracy (among people over 15 years of age) varies from 20 per cent in Costa Rica to 70 per cent in Guatemala. [15]

RECAPITULATION

We may infer from the preceding sections that currency unification even in the best of circumstances should not be hurried along without first paying the most agonizing attention to prerequisites. Far from being ideal for all groupings of countries at all times, a currency union is in fact only rarely to be favored over separate national currencies with domestic monetary control. If not entered into under the proper conditions, currency unification could easily be disastrous. By allowing its currency area to widen beyond optimum size, a country might sacrifice sovereignty over internal and external stability and gain nothing more in return than permanent ascription as a depressed area or inflationary hothouse.

The analysis has indicated that the theoretically ideal currency map could emerge only from tight political and economic fusion of areas containing similar homogeneous economic regions — if these regions could thereupon combine across previous national boundaries into finely drawn currency areas. Short of that ideal, currency unification still can be useful if applied to groupings of countries already highly advanced in their progress towards other forms of economic union and possessing excellent prospects for high factor mobility and flexibility in resource allocation.

For LAFTA members, a proper climate for currency unification is not visible in the foreseeable future. Even the Central American Common Market has many hurdles to clear before such a step should be attempted. If the attempt is made too early, before the five economies have attained adequate economic flexibility and before the processes of political and economic integration are sufficiently advanced, the abortive results could set back the entire Central American integration movement. But if the preliminaries can be completed with due attention to all the painful prerequisites outlined in the previous pages, and if proper attention can be given to timing and the fine points of institutional change, currency unification might indeed turn out to be a lubricating oil rather than a monkey wrench in the machinery of Central American economic integration.

NOTES

1. This is true in part because national banking systems have a long tradition of political and administrative independence in Central America, and each of the five central banks has spent years consolidating its position as guardian of national monetary sovereignty. Cf. Jorge González del Valle, "Monetary Integration in Central America: Achievements and Expectations," *Journal of Common Market Studies*, V (September 1966) pp. 14ff.

2. *Ibid.*, p. 25.

3. William G. Gaudet, "Central America," *Latin American Report Newsletter*, XXXV(June 1967), p. 1.

4. Quoted in "Revisión de la estrategia del Mercado Común Centroamericano," *Boletín de la Integración,* September 1967, p. 490.

5. See discussion in Robert A. Mundell, "A Theory of Optimum Currency Areas," *American Economic Review,* LI (September 1961), pp. 657-65.

6. J. V. Mladek, "Currency Unions—Pro and Con," *Finance and Development,* III (June 1966), pp. 93-94.

7. The analysis that follows draws somewhat on insights presented in Mundell,*op. cit.*, and Delbert A. Snider, *Optimum Adjustment Processes and Currency Areas* (Princeton, N. J.: International Finance Section, Princeton University, 1967).

8. Flexible here will be taken to mean either freely fluctuating or on a readily adjustable peg.

9. Although coffee is the only export industry in the region, we assume that alternative employment opportunities are available in services and non-traded goods.

10. Mundell, *op. cit.* In Mundell's terminology, "currency area" denotes what is referred to here as a "monetary area."

11. Egon Sohmen, *International Monetary Problems and the Foreign Exchanges* (Princeton, N. J.: International Finance Section, Princeton University, 1963), p. 25.

12. Ronald I. McKinnon, "Optimum Currency Areas," *American Economic Review,* LIII (September 1963), pp. 717-725.

13. Cited in Bela Balassa, *The Theory of Economic Integration* (Homewood, Ill.: Richard D. Irwin, Inc., 1961), p. 262n.

14. *Boletín de la Integración, loc. cit.*

15. Miguel S. Wionczek, "The Central American Integration Experiment," *B.O.L.S.A. Review,* I (March 1967), p. 136.

PART IV

INDUSTRY

CHAPTER **19** A WELFARE ANALYSIS OF
LATIN AMERICAN ECONOMIC
UNION: SIX INDUSTRY STUDIES

By   Martin Carnoy
SIDEC
Stanford University

The welfare implications of a customs union for potential partners and third countries has been the subject of a number of theoretical and empirical studies. [1]

In the empirical work welfare gains and losses from entering into a customs union are usually estimated in terms of
whether the union brings individual economies closer to or farther
away from an optimal division of labor. However, both Johnson's
and Denison's estimates, which concentrate on the resource allocation effects of reducing trade barriers, show the increase in
growth rates as a result of such gains to be relatively small.

This treatment of customs union theory which necessarily assumes constant or increasing costs of production because
of the perfect competition conditions of the model, fails to deal
with decreasing costs of production within the customs union.
By reducing the cost of products in member countries, tariff
reductions may increase long-run economic growth (and aggregate demand) even though prices of manufactured goods in the
union do not immediately fall to world market prices. [2] In the
case of estimates made for the European Economic Community
it may well be that the market expansion created by European
integration in addition to national market expansion since 1950
did not increase growth rates significantly in those already highly
developed economies. Nevertheless, it seems that in the less
developed industrialized countries, like those of Latin America,
increasing market size through a customs union would have a
direct and important influence on the prices of domestically produced manufactured products. This, in turn, would increase the
efficiency of resource allocation in each economy and in the region.

The purpose of this study is to estimate the welfare effects of a Latin American customs union on the major countries

---

*
The present study is based on a joint study of Latin
American economic institutes under the coordination of Economic
and Social Development Studies at the Brookings Institution.   For
the complete study, see Martin Carnoy, ed., Industrialization in
a Latin American Common Market: Six Case Studies (Brookings
Institution, March 1968), mimeo, in "Estudios Conjuntos de Insti-
tutos Económicos Latinoamericanos (ECIEL)."

of the area. [3] In order to expand the traditional static analysis to include economies of scale, the study turns to space location theory[4] and attempts to estimate the magnitude of welfare gains and losses resulting from union through a series of industry case studies. [5] This approach attempts to determine under certain restrictive assumptions which country or countries within the region have an absolute advantage in producing the products studied. That country is considered the "optimum" location of production in the region, and the supply price from the optimum location is taken as the "customs union" price of the goods. [6] The cost to each member of the union of buying from the minimum cost (optimum) production points within the region is compared with the cost of importing from developed countries or producing the goods domestically. The analysis then goes on to estimate the gain or loss to each country associated with buying the products in a customs union.

THE LINEARIZED PROGRAMMING MODEL

The method of determining the minimum cost location of industry in a given market has been well developed in a number of sources. [7] The present methodology is concerned with the choice of plant location for products which are characterized in all but one case (powdered milk and cheese) by economies of scale in a range of output whose upper limit may exceed the constraint of a purely domestic market. This particular characteristic affords the plants producing these products opportunities for expansion in the much larger market produced by the creation of a free trade area. The constraint on the expansion — and hence on the location of all production in one low-cost production point — is transport costs between the location of production and the ever increasing distance to additional markets. The model used here weighs both types of costs in order to determine how decreasing cost industries should be distributed in the area.

The objective of the model is to find the combination of plants which would supply, at a minimum cost to LAFTA, the fixed demands for a given product at specified locations in the area. The cost minimization depends on the quantity demanded at each consumption point, the cost of production at each production point, and the cost of transportation between each production point and each consumption point. In multi-stage production processes, the costs of transportation between successive stages also enter as variables. The generalized form of the model can be thought of in terms of production points, consumption points, and production-consumption points, the last consuming the output of earlier stages and producing for final consumption and for consumption by plants at the next stage of production. This study treats only single and two-stage production processes largely because of data limitations. Nevertheless, neither the theoretical model nor the algorithm written for the computer is restricted.

In the case of every product, demand is projected to 1970

and 1975. The two projections are made in order to provide a guide to the expansion of production over time, and to test the possibility of changes in the location of production due to changes in the geographical composition of final consumption. As has been mentioned above, consumption is spatially fixed at each point in time.

Transportation costs are estimated in three stages: from the production point to the nearest port or frontier; from the port or frontier to the port or frontier of the consuming country; and from that port or frontier to a "representative" consumption point, or alternatively, as an average transport cost to a number of consumption points in the country. Transportation costs per unit are considered to be constant between any two points. [8] Production costs, on the other hand, are expressed in terms of a fixed and a variable element. The method of cost estimation depends on data available for both the product and the country for which the estimation is made. In some cases, costs of production represent a single plant, and are therefore short-run costs meaningful only up to the capacity of that plant. In other cases, costs are estimated for a number of different size (capacity) plants in the same country, and can be thought of as representing the long-run cost curve for the product in that country. In the long-run case, the fixed element of cost has nebulous meaning. The linear approximation to the long-run total cost curve, however, yields a positive cost when production is zero, and it is this cost at zero production which represents "fixed" costs and generates economies of scale. [9]

The analysis of the six industry groups studied indicates that the effect of economies of scale is significant for a wide range of products in Latin America. The results of the linearized programming model yield the minimum cost location for production of each of the goods studied subject to the limitation of a partial equilibrium model. These "optimum" solutions to the model show that in many of the products the scale effects are important enough to make Latin American regional production competitive with third country imports. Costs of domestically produced goods can be expected to fall in a Latin American free trade area or customs union, and even if there is net trade diversion as a result of union, it will be lower than if differences between Latin America and third country costs (net of tariffs) remained constant. Thus, there could be a net gain to Latin America even in Viner's limited definition of welfare benefits from a customs union. [10]

BENEFITS AND COSTS OF UNION

In the estimates of benefits and costs of union derived from the solutions to the linearized program, the concern is with the cost to the region and to each country of two particular alternatives to the optimum: importing from third countries; national production, or that which would occur if each country presenting

cost   studies developed autarkically and if those which did not
present cost studies imported from the lowest cost source.   The
estimates made here are not really concerned with the trade diversion or trade creation effects of union, but rather the gains
or losses to LAFTA countries from choosing imports from third
countries, domestic production, or imports from   the optimum
location in the region as their source of supply.

These gains and losses are a function of total market demand in 1975, the difference in the delivered price of the goods
at each market from alternative production points, and the elasticity of demand for the goods.[11] Table 1 shows the welfare gains
and losses by country and by product group.   The table is divided
into three parts.[12] In Table 1a, the annual gains of buying from
the minimum cost (optimum) location within the region rather
than importing from the United States are estimated for each
product group.   The import price is the 1965 f.o.b. New York,
San Francisco, or Laredo price plus transport costs to Latin
American markets.   Possible changes in world market prices
between 1965 and 1975 are not accounted for, and in the case of
tractors, European prices for a 50 h.p. tractor are considerably
lower than the price of a U.S. tractor.   In all other goods considered here the U.S. is competitive in the world market.   Table 1b
estimates the annual welfare costs of having plants in a number
of countries (all those for which cost studies are available) rather
than producing only in the minimum cost (optimum) locations.
This alternative compares the welfare gain of union with autarkic
development.

The difference in the national price and the optimum location price reflects differences in scale of production as well as
differences in input prices.   Table 1c estimates the annual welfare cost to consumers of the present tariff structure in LAFTA
countries.   This estimate can be taken as the maximum welfare
cost of national production in 1975, since existing tariffs are assumed to continue to reflect price differentials between domestic,
nationally-oriented production in Latin America and imports.   It
implies that the internal expansion of national markets will not
decrease the price differential between domestic and import
prices.   The types of estimates in Table 1b and Table 1c are not
directly comparable unless it is assumed that the regional optimum location price can be taken as the import price in 1975.
This means that each Latin American country would be levying
present duties without affecting the price of production at the optimum location.   For purposes of comparison, that is the assumption made, and the import price is taken as the optimum location
price.

The annual welfare gain of producing the fourteen products studies in Latin America rather than importing them from
the United States totals almost Ŝ250 million for the ten LAFTA
countries shown.   In relative terms, this welfare gain equals 16
percent of the projected total value of production of the six product groups in 1975 (see Table 2).[13] The total value of production

Table 1a. LAFTA: Total Annual Welfare Gains and Costs of Various Production Decisions Buying from Optimum Location in LAFTA Rather Than Importing from the United States

Six Industry Groups, by Country, 1975
(thousands of simones)

	Methanol and Formaldehyde	Nitrogenous Fertilizers	Tractors	Lathes	Paper and Pulp	Powdered Milk and Cheese	Total
Argentina	313	6,756	15,508	2,608	2,823	40,442	68,450
Brazil	3,198	36,229	24,645	2,916	24,632	8,973	100,593
Chile	125	735	2,666	244	6,073	-3,708	6,135
Colombia	223	3,362	2,512	738	6,972	-1,840	11,967
Ecuador	---	349	107	---	13,756	-637	13,575
Mexico	344	23,048	3,607	2,032	15,995	---	45,026
Paraguay	---	---	413	20	33	-186	280
Peru	158	6,343	668	---	4,350	923	12,442
Uruguay	11	1,646	1,948	---	395	2,087	6,087
Venezuela	67	2,545	---	---	---	-20,379	-17,767
Total	4,439	81,013	52,074	8,558	75,029	25,675	246,788

Source: ECIEL, Martin Carnoy, ed., op. cit., Chap. III

Table 1b.   National Production Rather Than Buying From Optimum Location in LAFTA

	Methanol and Formaldehyde	Nitrogenous Fertilizers	Tractors	Lathes	Paper and Pulp	Powdered Milk and Cheese	Total
Argentina	-316	-1,314	---	-446	-413	-9,817	-12,306
Brazil	-3,191	-7,120	-27,355	-2,163	-3,872	-74,120	-117,821
Chile	-521	-820	---	-20	-936	-227	-2,524
Colombia	-135	-1,575	---	-67	-9,022	-128	-10,927
Ecuador	---	-211	---	---	-9,310	-36	-9,557
Mexico	-653	-9,864	---	-2,453	-19,314	---	-32,284
Paraguay	---	---	---	-2	-5	---	-7
Peru	-239	-293	---	---	-5,225	-778	-6,535
Uruguay	-16	-668	---	---	-77	-29	-790
Venezuela	-42	-1,303	---	---	---	---	-1,345
Total	-5,113	-23,168	-27,355	-5,151	-48,174	-85,135	-194,096

Source: See   Table 1a.

242

Table 1c.   Welfare Costs From Present Tariff Structure

	Methanol and Formaldehyde	Nitrogenous Fertilizers	Tractors	Lathes	Paper and Pulp	Powdered Milk and Cheese	Total
Argentina	-1,351	-73	-33,278	-1,579	-4,604	-75,857	-116,742
Brazil	-5,876	-10,366	-33,714	-1,397	-42,451	-103,390	-197,194
Chile	-562	-820	-4,548	-54	-7,403	-31,161	-44,548
Colombia	-265	-23	-294	-319	-9,675	-6,472	-17,048
Ecuador	- - -	-260	- - -	- - -	-21,459	-2,134	-23,853
Mexico	-524	-13,782	-1,939	- - -	-38,954	- - -	-55,199
Paraguay	- - -	- - -	-598	-5	-63	-990	-1,656
Peru	-318	-1,550	-344	- - -	-5,216	-4,573	-12,001
Uruguay	-22	-1,742	-719	- - -	-940	-5,343	-8,766
Venezuela	-86	-37	- - -	- - -	- - -	-22,091	-22,224
Total	-9,004	-28,653	-75,434	-3,354	-130,765	-252,011	-499,221

Source: See Table 1a.

243

Table 2.   LAFTA: Total Value of Output and Value Added of Product Groups Studies, Minimum Transport Cost Assumption, by Product Group, 1975 (Millions of Simones)

Product Group	Total Value of 1975 Output
Nitrogenous Fertilizers	218
Methanol-Formaldehyde	32
Tractors	263
Lathes	24
Powdered Milk and Cheese	643
Paper and Pulp	292
Total	1,472

244

and transportation of the six groups in 1975 is $ 1.5 billion. [14]
Assuming that the manufacturing sector accounts for 25 percent
of gross domestic product in 1975,[15] that the six industries,
producing approximately 4 percent of gross national product in
manufacturing in 1975, are representative of the manufacturing
sector in Latin America, and that only the manufacturing sector
is affected by the formation of a customs union, the gains of
producing at the optimum locations rather than importing would
imply a gain of 4 percent of GDP in real resources for Latin
America (0.16 times 0.25). Assuming a 15 percent average
rate of return to capital, the 4 percent gain is translated into an
increase of 0.6 percent in the growth rate of the region. If Latin
American producers are not competitive now with U.S. imports
in any of these products, this result means that formation of a
customs union would not only allow Latin America to compete in
the production of manufactured goods, but would free 4 percent
of GDP annually to be used for further investment. Because of
biases described below, this estimate is probably too high, but
even under the maximum transport cost and official rate of exchange assumptions, only two products, powdered milk and kraft
pulp would be imported from the U.S. in the free trade situation. [16]
For many products, then, the market expansion and specialization arguments for a customs union may have important implications for making Latin American producers competitive in world
markets.

The largest gains to the region are in nitrogenous fertilizers, lathes, and paper and pulp. Regional production would
save consumers 44, 33, and 25 percent, respectively, of the
total cost of producing and transporting these goods in 1975.
The countries which gain relatively the most from regional production over importing from third countries are Ecuador, Uruguay, and Brazil. [17]

Table 1b shows that the cost to the area of national production rather than producing at the minimum cost location is
about $ 200 million for the six product groups. It should be re-
membered that the alternative of national production is not available for every country for all products. Since tractor production
costs, for example, are presented in this study only for Brazil
and Argentina (Mexico began production in 1965), national production in Brazil and Argentina is the only alterntive to the minimum
cost location in Argentina. Thus, Brazil is the only country affected by supplying Brazilian 1975 demand with Brazilian tractors and all other countries of the region with Argentine tractors. [18] Similarly, production costs for hard paste and semi-
hard paste cheese and powdered milk are only available for two
countries.

Since it is assumed in this welfare cost estimate that
those countries for which costs are not available buy from the
optimum location, the estimate is biased downward. Not including the cost of production of chemicals in Argentina and
Brazil, paper and pulp in Argentina, and dairy products in Mexico

245

and Venezuela as alternatives to the optimum location price reduces the total welfare cost of national production. Countries with costs of production not represented are generally those which recognize that they have no possibility of being competitive in that product with other Latin American producers.

Using tariff rates as proxies for cost differentials between national production and imports probably gives a much better estimate of welfare cost to the region of national production. The latter would be biased upward by the use of tariffs for revenue rather than protection. The estimate of $ 200 million is 13 percent of the total projected value of production of the six product groups in 1975. Under the same three assumptions outlined above, the welfare benefits of producing at the optimum location rather than nationally imply a gain of 3 percent of GDP in real resources of the area. Similarly, the gains of eliminating current tariffs levied on goods produced at minimum cost locations in the region in 1975 (assuming that the current tariff rates would continue to 1975, and production at optimum locations could expand to projected 1975 levels despite such tariffs) equal 33 percent of the total value of production of the six products in that year. This implies a gain in real resources of 8 percent of GDP. Averaging the "minimum" estimate of the welfare cost of national production from Table 1b with the "maximum" estimate of Table 1c yields an increase of 0.8 percent in the growth rate of the region due to customs union as an alternative to an autarkic development policy.

These estimates, especially the comparison of buying from the optimum location versus importing, imply that as a result of union, costs of production of manufactured goods could fall significantly in the region. Even though trade would be diverted by union to initially high cost production, the expansion of markets caused by the diversion of trade (combined with specialization within the area) would lead to consumer benefits if the real resource cost of regional production falls below the real cost of imports.

This scale effect, yielding welfare benefits to consumers in the region, and the trade diversion effect occur over a period of time rather than at a point in time. Thus, trade diversion to higher cost regional producers would not take place all at once, especially since trade among Latin American countries is currently quite small. Gradually, Latin American consumers would shift to Latin American goods that, because of the elimination of duties, appear cheaper to them. Habits and consumer responsiveness to price differentials would vary the speed of the process from country to country. At the same time, the growth of demand and the specialization of production would be lowering prices in those industries characterized by economies of scale. The gains from union would also be increasing over time as prices from optimum location plants fell relative to national plants (assuming that output of optimum location plants would be increasing relative to national plants) and relative to third country imports net of tariffs.

EXCHANGE RATES

It has already been pointed out that in the maximum
transport cost case official rates of exchange are used in translating local currency costs into simones. In the minimum transport cost case, an approximate "free" rate of exchange is used.
The free rate is set equal to the official rate in countries with no
active black or grey market. Therefore, the free rate used is
not a shadow rate of exchange which would reflect the real price
of foreign currency. Although industry studies demonstrate the
importance of differences between the two rates, only rates in
Argentina, Chile, and Colombia can be varied on the basis of the
free rate—official rate distinction.

In order to go beyond the limited sensitivity analysis of
using two rates of exchange, an estimate is made in each industry case of the "indifference rate" of exchange which would make
any consumption country indifferent to buying from one production location or another. In other words, the indifference rate
is that exchange rate of two currencies which reduces comparative advantage of a given location over a competitor to zero. To
estimate indifference rates in each market for various production locations, it is assumed that total production for the area
takes place at one production location. Thus, comparisons are
being made between delivered costs from each location with the
full advantage offered by economies of scale.[19] It should be
clear that indifference exchange rates are different for the "maximum" set of transport costs and the "minimum" set. The
smaller a_1 and a_2, the smaller the differences in the results
with the two sets.

The indifference rate results show approximately how
sensitive the optimum location estimate is to the choice of exchange rate used. Sensitivity varies from product to product
(see Table 3). For example, in the case of nitrogenous fertilizers for minimum transport costs, Venezuela is competitive
with U.S. imports everywhere in LAFTA at an exchange rate of
3.5 Bs/$\hat{S}$, which implies that a revaluation of the bolivar (Bs) of
20 per cent would still enable Venezuelan nitrogenous fertilizer
exporters to undersell the U.S. products. Similarly, Venezuela
is competitive with Chile almost everywhere in Latin America in
all nitrogenous fertilizers when the Chilean escudo and the bolivar are equal in value. This means that at the official exchange
rate for the escudo, Chile cannot compete with Venezuelan nitrogenous fertilizers in Latin America, but at the "free" rate of
1.22 E^o/Bs, Chile is highly competitive.

In the case of parallel lathes,[20] Chile again is competitive with Argentina and Brazil at the free rate, but the indifference rate of exchange with Argentina is only slightly below
the free rate. Chile cannot compete with either Argentina or

247

Table 3. Example of Comparative Prices (Simones) and Indifference Exchange Rates; Minimum Transport Cost Case, by Product, Country of Production, and Country of Consumption, 1975.

Nitrogenous Fertilizers
Production Points

| | (1) Chile [a] | | | (2) Venezuela [b] | | | |
Country	Ammonia	Urea	Ammonium Nitrate	Ammonia	Urea	Ammonium Nitrate	Ammonium Sulphate
Argentina	55.1	114.0	172.0	54.2	125.9	161.1	194.0
Brazil	65.4	117.7	164.7	67.1	216.0	159.6	197.0
Chile	38.4	84.6	133.2	40.5	95.0	126.7	---
Colombia	---	106.2	154.3	---	102.2	128.7	172.0
Ecuador	---	96.1	138.8	---	99.1	120.5	140.8
Mexico	51.6	87.5	130.3	44.5	89.0	107.2	117.0
Peru	---	103.0	148.1	---	108.8	133.8	162.8
Uruguay	---	86.3	---	---	98.2	---	130.1
Venezuela	46.4	90.2	129.9	31.2	83.4	102.8	125.4

(continued)

Table 3. (continued)

Nitrogenous Fertilizers
Production Points
(3)

United States

Country	Ammonia	Urea	Ammonium Nitrate	Ammonium Sulphate
Argentina	85.2	185.5	248.9	296.5
Brazil	100.4	187.9	252.0	301.1
Chile	88.8	157.0	216.0	---
Colombia	---	173.8	219.1	281.9
Ecuador	---	170.0	206.2	291.9
Mexico	57.8	132.9	132.3	171.8
Peru	---	176.0	218.7	299.6
Uruguay	---	157.8	---	232.6
Venezuela	73.6	149.5	182.1	238.2

(continued)

249

Table 3. (continued)

Nitrogenous Fertilizers
Indifference Exchange Rates

Country	(4) Bs/E°c			(5) Bs/d			
	Ammonia	Urea	Ammonium Nitrate	Ammonia	Urea	Ammonium Nitrate	Ammonium Sulphate
Argentina	0.88	0.99	0.85	2.88	3.06	2.92	2.92
Brazil	0.92	0.96	0.87	3.02	3.02	2.84	2.92
Chile	0.94	1.01	0.86	2.07	2.70	2.66	---
Colombia	---	0.86	0.75	---	2.66	2.66	2.74
Ecuador	---	0.93	0.78	---	2.61	2.61	2.16
Mexico	0.78	0.92	0.74	3.46	3.02	3.64	3.06
Peru	---	0.95	0.81	---	2.79	2.74	2.30
Uruguay	---	1.03	---	---	2.79		2.52
Venezuela	0.60	0.83	0.71	1.89	2.52	2.52	2.38

(continued)

250

Table 3. (continued)

Consumption Point	Production Point		Tractors	Indifference Exchange Rates	
	(6) Argentina f	(7) Brazil g	(8) United States	(9) Pesos/Cr h	(10) Pesos/ i
Argentina	4,671	5,520	5,117	0.062	123
Brazil	4,773	5,418	5,297	0.064	122
Chile	4,734	5,596	5,299	0.062	122
Colombia	5,040	5,861	5,196	0.063	131
Ecuador	5,027	5,873	5,248	0.063	130
Mexico	5,024	5,853	4,802	0.063	140
Paraguay	4,687	5,514	5,131	0.062	123
Peru	5,036	5,881	5,362	0.063	127
Uruguay	4,725	5,489	5,118	0.063	124

(continued)

Table 3. (continued)

Universal Parallel Lathes

	Production Point			Indifference Exchange Rates		
	(11)	(12)	(13)	(14)	(15)	(16)
Country of Consumption	Argentina[j]	Chile[k]	Brazil[l]	Pesos (E^o) [m]	$Cr/(E^o)$ [n]	Cr/pesos [r]
Argentina	2,962	2,775	3,986	33.2	634	19.0
Brazil	3,042	2,860	3,929	32.8	603	18.3
Chile	3,014	2,726	4,042	33.8	651	19.0
Colombia	3,270	3,006	4,264	33.8	625	18.5
Mexico	3,315	3,050	4,297	33.8	620	18.5
Paraguay	2,987	2,806	3,997	32.8	625	19.0

Source: ECIEL, Martin Carnoy, ed., op. cit., Chaps. v-x.

(continued)

252

Table 3.   (continued)

[a] Chile does not intend to produce ammonium sulphate.   Prices in simones based on exchange rate of 5 $E^o/\hat{S}$.

[b] Prices in simones based on exchange rate of 4.5 $Bs/\hat{S}$.

[c] Column (2)/(1) times 0.9 Bs/E^o.

[d] Column (2)/(3) times 4.5 $Bs/\hat{S}$.

[e] Assumes 20,000 unit limit on plant capacity, and that all tractor production takes place at each production point.

[f] 135 pesos $/\hat{S}$.

[g] 1,850 $Cr/\hat{S}$.

[h] Column (6)/(7) times 0.073 pesos / Cr.

[i] Column (6)/(8) times 135 pesos $/\hat{S}$.

[j] 155 pesos $/\hat{S}$.

[k] 5 $E^o/\hat{S}$.

[l] 2200 $Cr/\hat{S}$.

[m] Column (11)/(12) times 31 pesos $/E^o$.

[n] Column (13)/(12) times 440 Cr/E^o.

[r] Column (13)/(11) times 14.2 Cr /pesos.

Brazil at the official rate of exchange between the escudo and peso or between the escudo and cruzeiro. Chile appears as a producer in many of the industry studies, and in all of them the official rate of exchange for the escudo all but prices Chilean production out of the market. Since these cost studies were made, the escudo has been steadily devalued until its official rate has begun to approach the free rate. However, other countries in LAFTA, primarily Argentina, Brazil, Colombia, Peru, and Uruguay, have also devalued their currencies in the face of domestic inflation.

The indifference rates have the advantage of being adjustable for both inflation and devaluation. An attempt is made to do this in the case of tractors. The rate of inflation of tractor prices in domestic currency is available for Argentina in 1964 and 1965. Data are also available for exchange rates in that same period in both Brazil and Argentina. Comparing inflated tractor costs of June 1965 in Argentina (Argentine tractor costs are taken for December 31, 1963) with measured tractor costs in Brazil at that date shows that at official rates, the optimum location of tractor production in LAFTA switches from Argentina to Brazil. [21] Exchange rates at any point in time therefore play a leading role in projecting the distribution of production in a customs union, especially in a region of rapid price changes.

LIMITATIONS OF THE ANALYSIS

In the light of the more general analysis possible with more extensive data, the solutions to the minimum cost model must be interpreted with great care. They are dynamic only in the sense that demand is projected to 1970 and 1975, and the distribution of production for each industry estimated for both those years. Cost functions are estimated using, for the most part, base year relative prices of inputs and it is assumed that the functions are identical in 1970 and 1975. Transport costs are also taken in the base year, but this problem is somewhat "dynamicized" by estimating the optimum (low cost) distribution of production with minimum and maximum values for transport costs. No attempt is made to project changes in wages or to consider changes in the cost of other inputs as a result of changes in the tariff structures of member countries. [22] Nor is account taken of changes in relative exchange rates. It is expected that individual country trade balances will not be the same with a customs union, and exchange rates will therefore be changed to achieve new long-run equilibria.

The solutions to the linearized program, therefore, indicate where production in those industry groups would take place in Latin America assuming a number of variables unchanged between the base year and 1975: (a) The relative prices of different inputs at each location and the relative prices of each input at various locations of production. This implies that lowering tariffs between Latin American countries does not change the production cost curves at each location. The relative effects of technological change are also implicitly equal. (b) The relative exchange rates between Latin American currencies will not vary outside the limits imposed by the "indifference" exchange rates. (c) Transport costs will not change beyond the limits imposed by the maximum and minimum assumption used. (d) External economies or diseconomies are equal at all possible locations of production for each product. (e) The relation between market prices and the competitive equilibrium price will not change.

The importance of these assumptions varies from industry to industry, depending on the effect of changes in the current structure of tariffs on the price of the major inputs entering into the production of the goods. Although the industries studied here were chosen for a number of reasons, especially for the interest that various Latin American institutes had in studying them, the industry cases also happen to represent a variety of production processes. Because of the differences in the nature of the industries, the possible biases in the solutions to the linearized programming model resulting from not using a more dynamic analysis is greater for some case studies than for others.

In four of the six industry groups (nitrogenous fertilizers, methanol-formaldehyde, paper and pulp, and dairy products), the cost of raw materials is crucial in determining the optimum location for production; in these industries the transportation cost of the principal raw materials is high, forcing plants to locate near the source of raw materials rather than final markets. The prices of natural gas, lumber, and fresh milk, which are the main cost items in the production of these products, will probably not be very much affected by changes in the tariff structure of Latin American countries or by free trade among them. New discoveries of resource deposits, or technological innovations in processing and transportation are the primary sources of changes in cost functions for raw material-oriented products. The bias introduced in the optimum solutions found with the partial analysis for this type of industry is probably not great except perhaps with regard to changes in the equilibrium exchange rate.

On the other hand, in two industries studied (tractors and universal parallel lathes) economies of scale and a developed industrial base (availability of skilled labor and parts suppliers) are the most important variables in cost. Transportation of the final product and inputs is a small fraction of production costs, so location of the industry is more flexible. Because such industries depend on the supply of goods from a number of other highly protected industries, a change in the tariff structure could radically influence the production cost curves of the final products. Biases due to a "quasi-static" analysis, then, would probably be much smaller in the raw material-oriented products and more important for the production of machinery and equipment.

255

1. Jacob Viner, *The Customs Union Issue* (New York: Carnegie Endowment for International Peace, 1950). Among the major works which built on the Viner study are:

J. E. Meade, *The Theory of Customs Union* (Amsterdam: North Holland Publishing Company, 1956). F. Gehrels, "Customs Union from a Single Country Viewpoint," *Review of Economic studies,* 1956-1957. R. G. Lipsey, "The Theory of Customs Unions: A General Survey," *Economic Journal,* LXX (September 1960), pp. 496-513. H. G. Johnson, *Money, Trade and Economic Growth* (Cambridge: Harvard University Press, 1962). Bela Balassa, *The Theory of Economic Integration,* (Homewood, Ill.: Richard Irwin, 1961); C. A. Cooper and B. F. Massell, "Toward a General Theory of Customs Union for Developing Countries," *Journal of Political Economy,* LXXIII, No. 5 (Oct. 1965), 460-76.

Major empirical studies are:

Tibor Scitovsky, *Economic Theory and Western European Integration* (London: Allen and Unwin, 1958). Harry Johnson, "The Gains from Free Trade with Europe, an Estimate," *Manchester School* (Sept. 1958), pp. 247-55. Edward Denison, *Why Growth Rates Differ.* (Washington: Brookings Institution, 1967), pp. 260-62.

2. In a separate estimate, Denison shows that national market growth and associated economies of scale explain a large part of the growth rates in Europe in the post-war period (Denison, *op. cit.,* pp. 225-255).

3. Because of lack of data, the estimates are restricted to the Latin American Free Trade Association (LAFTA) countries (not including Bolivia). Nevertheless, the methodology is easily extended to include all Latin American countries.

4. The theory of space location (p. 26).

5. The industry groups include nitrogenous fertilizers, methanol-formaldehyde, tractors, parallel lathes, paper and pulp, and powdered milk and cheese. For the rationale behind the choice of the industries studied, see ECIEL, Martin Carnoy (ed.), *op. cit.*

6. The partial equilibrium approach really estimates which countries are likely to have absolute advantages in producing a specified product under given assumptions. If the country which would produce it under the partial equilibrium estimate of optimum location would have still greater advantages in producing other goods, it might not be the best place in which to locate production of the goods under study. The implication is that the results do not give loca-

tions that can be properly called "optimum," but rather "minimum cost." Obtaining the optimum requires a general equilibrium, including limitations on total resources available in each area and the region as a whole.

7. See especially Thomas Vietorisz and Alan S. Manne, "Chemical Processes, Plant Location, and Economies of Scale," *Studies in Process Analysis,* chap. vi, edited by Manne and Markowitz (New York: John Wiley and Sons, 1963). There is also a short bibliography at the end of their chap. vi.

8. Two sets of transport costs are used. The "high" projection of costs was based on existing freight rates of shipping lines, and the "low" projections were made on the basis of private estimates prepared by a private shipping concern. Similarly, in comparing production costs presented in domestic monetary units, two sets of exchange rates are used to convert into a common unit of account. The "high" rate is the official rate of exchange. (The unit of account in the study is the "simón," defined equal to the U.S. dollar. The sign for the simón is Ŝ The "low" rate is the free, or curb, rate of exchange, when this differs from the official rate.

9. In the long run, there should be no fixed costs, i.e., all elements of cost become variable. The long-run total cost curve should therefore start at the origin. The cost curve used here does not go through the origin and since the approximation to the total cost curve is linear, marginal costs are constant, and only average costs decline. For the purpose of the welfare analysis, resource costs should be taken equal to marginal costs as the welfare gain model below shows. However, marginal costs estimated from linearized total cost curves do not reflect economies of scale, while average costs do. Resource costs are therefore set equal to average costs to represent changes in costs due to increases in market size. At large outputs, differences between marginal and average costs derived from the linear total cost curves are not large. In the case of Venezuelan (minimum transport cost optimum location) production of methanol, for example, the assumed technically maximum output of a plant is 33,000 metric tons annually. At that output, the estimated marginal cost of production and transportation of methanol to Venezuela is Ŝ 74 per ton. The estimated average cost is Ŝ 85 per ton, or 15 per cent more. The use of average cost biases downward the welfare gain of buying from the optimum location versus importing from the United States.

10. The model further indicates that the distribution of production in LAFTA of the fourteen products is not limited to one or two countries. Under the minimum transport cost and "free" exchange rate assumptions, six LAFTA

257

countries participate in producing these products. Under the maximum transport cost and official exchange rate assumptions, production is more dispersed, and seven countries participate. Of the LAFTA countries, Bolivia and Paraguay did not present any cost studies. Ecuador presented a cost study only for paper and pulp, and Uruguay only for powdered milk and cheeses. Other countries are represented by cost studies in at least two product groups. See ECIEL, *op. cit.*, chaps. iii, v-x, for a detailed breakdown of minimum cost location and the cost of alternative solutions to the linearized programming model.

11. For a derivation of the equations used to estimate welfare gains and losses from the minimum cost solution, see ECIEL, *op. cit.*, chap. iv, app. B. The elasticity of demand for all products is taken as unity.

12. All three parts estimate gains and losses based on the minimum transport cost and free currency exchange rate optimum location estimates. Delivered prices of products to markets are, therefore, minimum estimates, which may bias gains in part one of the table upward, costs in part two, upward, and costs in part three, downward.

13. Table 2 shows the value of output (including transportation charges) supplied from the minimum cost (optimum) locations for the six product groups considered. The values equal the cost of filling 1975 projected physical demand for each product for all or most LAFTA countries. In order to correspond to the data in Table 1, the figures in Table 2 are shown for the minimum transport cost and free currency rate of exchange case.

14. The projected value of production of the six groups represents approximately one percent of the projected value of LAFTA gross national product (GNP) for 1975. The GNP estimate is based on Hollis B. Chenery, "Towards a More Effective Alliance for Progress", AID Discussion Paper No. 13 (Washington, D.C., March 1967).

15. See *Economic Survey of Latin America, 1964* (New York: United Nations, 1966), Table 23. Manufacturing accounted for 23 percent of the gross domestic product (GDP) of Latin America in 1964. This percentage has been steadily increasing from 18 percent in 1950.

16. With completely free trade, Argentine tractors would not be able to compete with English imports even under the more favorable assumptions.

17. Ecuador's gain is almost entirely from pulp and paper, but both Uruguay's and Brazil's is spread over the range of products.

18. The limitation of plant size to 20,000 units annually removes any scale effect of eliminating Brazilian markets from Argentine production.

19. Because of the fixed element of costs, this reduces the estimated CIF prices from each production point. Although in some cases, like nitrogenous fertilizers and paper and pulp, the single location assumption is only an approximation to the size of the market that would face any production point, even in those cases, because of plant size limitations, the estimated indifference rates are quite close to those which would prevail under a more complicated distribution of plants. A second assumption is that transport costs, because they are originally almost entirely in simones, could distort the estimates of indifference exchange rates, but do not. The evidence behind this assumption is quite straightforward. The cost of a given product at a given consumption point consists of a production cost in national currency and a transportation cost already in simones. The uncorrected indifference rates shown in chap. iii can be expressed as the ratio of the sums of the two costs (transport costs have been converted to national currency at given exchange rates):

$$R_{12} = \frac{p_1 + t_1}{p_2 + t_2},$$

where the p's are production costs in national currency (converted at given exchange rates) and the t's transportation costs, also in national currency.

Letting a_1 and a_2 represent t_1/p_1 and t_2/p_2, respectively, R_{12} becomes:

$$R = \frac{p_1 (1 + a_1)}{p_2 (1 + a_2)} .$$

Ideally, R_{12} estimated with the exchange rates used to convert t_1 and t_2 to national currency would equal R_{12} estimated with the exchange rate implied by R_{12}. Although this rarely happens, the difference is usually small enough that the difference between R_{12} found by an iterative process is small. Since a_1 and a_2 are only fractions of p_1 and p_2 the difference between R_{12} and the exchange rates used for t_1 and t_2 conversions is considerably reduced when it enters the calculation.

20. The possible bias in the Chilean production costs mentioned earlier in this chapter should be noted.

21. See ECIEL, *op. cit.*, chap. vii.

22.   Prices of inputs used are market prices. This
brings up the issue of possible distortions in such prices,
so that the market price does not equal the socially optimum price of the input. Beyond tariffs affecting the market price, this price may also include monopoly rent (which
could be eliminated by competition from other Latin American
producers once barriers to trade are eliminated) and internal taxes, also changing over time.

20

INTEGRATION PROSPECTS FOR THE AUTOMOTIVE INDUSTRY UNDER LAFTA

By   Jack Baranson
Economic Development Institute
World Bank

The manufacture of industrial products in developing economies poses a basic problem of scale. This is true for a wide range of products and intermediary goods, including automotive products. Even the largest and industrially most advanced of developing economies have experienced rising costs as they have displaced imported goods with local manufacture. In the case of automotive products the proliferation of models and plants have exacerbated the problem of diseconomies of scale particularly in the manufacture of components and parts. The solution to the scale problem is either to expand the extent of the market or to rationalize production in such a way as to increase the length of production runs. The former may be achieved through production for regional or world markets and the latter through a reduction in the range of models and makes or an expansion of interchangeable parts.

Regionalism, as a solution to the problem of the diseconomies of scale imposed by the extent of market encounters the problem of inter-country rivalries and vested commercial interests. A basic problem is the equitable distribution of economic gain to the region and commercial losses to individual firms. Another intractable reality is that in terms of efficient production the total size of the LAFTA vehicle market projected to 1975 would allow for approximately five plants located in the entire region manufacturing five basic vehicles —in place of the more than 70 plants now manufacturing more than 200 different basic vehicle types.

EFFORTS TO LIBERALIZE TRADE IN AUTOMOTIVE PRODUCTS

Under the LAFTA Agreement, tariffs and related restrictions among member countries were to be eliminated on "substantially" all products by 1973. In the seven-year period since 1961, no progress has been made in placing automotive products on the national or common lists for tariff reductions.[1] The LAFTA Treaty does provide for a third mechanism, whereby two or more countries may negotiate the reduction or removal of trade barriers for specific items not yet included on national lists. These are known as complementation agreements. Under these arrangements industries may develop plans to exchange certain components or specialize in given product categories. These plans are then formalized in inter-governmental agreements, permitting parts manufactured in one country to qualify as national content in another. A few such complementation agreements have been negotiated since late 1965 between Argentina, Chile, and Mexico. These bilateral arrangements have been very limited in nature and actually have resulted in overall increased production costs, contrary to the basic intention of the LAFTA Agreement.

Chile and Argentina initiated the first complementation agreement in 1964. Chile was especially anxious to develop its automotive parts industries on a more economic basis, and Argentine firms were looking for opportunities to lower production costs through increased sales volumes in export markets. Two difficulties arose from the outset. One was related to the wide disparity in the relative size of the markets, and the other to differences in the stage of automotive sector development. In 1964, 7,800 vehicles were manufactured in Chile as compared with 166,000 in Argentina. Moreover, production was fragmented among 22 firms in Chile, as compared with 13 in Argentina. Domestic content averaged between 60 to 80 percent in Argentina, as compared with 25 to 40 percent in Chile.

The Chilean Automotive Commission, recognizing the constraints imposed by the limited size of the domestic market, has been the staunchest advocate of LAFTA. They have followed through with bilateral arrangements with Mexico. Beginning in 1967, the Chrysler affiliate in Mexico began shipping 1,000 engines a year to Chile in return for a variety of components and parts. The Mexican engine plant is also shipping a third of its output (10,000 engines a year) to Venezuela. Jigs and fixtures are also supplied to Venezuela from Mexico.

Two-way trading between Argentina and Chile has been extremely difficult for several reasons. Argentina has agreed to allow only a limited interchange of components up to 6 percent by Argentine vehicle value and not more than 30 percent of any one local item. Chile insists upon the development of parts that "contribute to the country's technological improvement." The value of trade must also be equalized in the long run. The difficulty has been that whereas Argentina is able to export a few high-value items (such as engines, transmissions, and rear-axle assemblies), Chile is only able to export a large number of low-value items (such as air cleaners, wire harnesses, hub caps, and various forgings and castings). It has been especially difficult to find items in Chile that come near Argentine quality and price.[2]

Ford Argentina began shipping engines to Chile in 1968 in exchange for 41 different parts from Chilean vendors (ranging from wiring assemblies to brake drums and radiators). Chrysler investigated the possibility of producing automatic transmissions in Chile for the Argentine market, but found it would cost $6 million for a new facility in Chile, as compared with $0.7 million marginal investment in the Argentine installation to manufacture the same output.

Negotiations on lowering trade barriers between Argentina and Brazil began in November 1967, but Argentine manufacturers are fearful of the more efficient Brazilian parts manufacturers. The cost structure is lower in Brazil largely because of lower tariffs and less lag in the exchange rate, rather than because of any significant differences in technical capabilities or market opportunities. It is proposed to initiate interchange at the 15 percent level and move to 30 percent within 5 years (in place of the 6 per cent limit imposed on Argentine trade with Chile). A more ambitious aim is to implement preferential tariff treatment between Argentina and Brazil under the national list mechanism. Vehicle manufacturers are hoping for a 30 percent reduction initially and 100 percent elimination of intra-LAFTA duties by 1973. Large firms in a competitive position have strong incentives to liberalize trade between the two countries because of mounting investment costs. Production facilities are especially costly for the manufacture beyond 40 percent vehicle content, which involves engine and transmission, and sheet metal body work. According to one estimate, investment in a crankshaft and camshaft facility alone (parts valued together at about $15 in a $2,000 vehicle) amounts to $3.4 million. If a complementation agreement can be signed, investment either in Brazil or Argentina can be avoided.

In May 1967, a proposal was made to form a sub-regional Andean group consisting of Venezuela, Colombia, Chile, Peru, Ecuador, and Bolivia. Under the proposed arrangements, there would be a duty-free trade in components and parts under participating governments' approved automotive production programs. In 1965, this sub-region accounted for 28 percent of the productive output of LAFTA, 22 percent of registered vehicles and 17 percent of vehicle production. This two-step approach to regional integration is somewhat analogous to the Benelux grouping within the European Common Market. It also bypasses the complicated machinery of negotiating complementation agreements and sidesteps the problems that have occurred between Argentina and Chile. But at the level of Andean development, Colombia (a late-comer) has balked at signing a final agreement, fearful of overwhelming competition from Venezuela and Chile. [3]

PRODUCTION PROBLEMS IN THE LAFTA REGION

Total demand in the LAFTA group ran to just over 650,000 vehicles in 1967 (less than 3 percent of total production). Most LAFTA countries now have automotive sectors that assemble cars and trucks and manufacture vehicle components and parts in varying degrees. Production was fragmented among eight countries. Brazil, Argentina and Mexico accounted for 82 percent of the LAFTA total. The remaining 18 percent was spread among five other countries including Uruguay, where 1,000 vehicles a year were being assembled.

Programs to manufacture automotive products domestically are part of national efforts by developing economies to save

CAR AND TRUCK PRODUCTION, LAFTA REGION,
1967

	Vehicles	Percent Distribu-tion	Total Number Firms	Firms account-ing for over 80% output
Brazil	228,700	35.1	10	4
Argentina	117,500	27.2	11	5
Mexico	131,200	20.1	8	5
Venezuela	60,300		13	6
Peru	26,300		4	2
Chile	16,400	17.7	19[1/]	11[1/]
Colombia	10,500		2	2
Uruguay	1,000		(n.a.)	(n.a.)
LAFTA Total (1967)	651,900	100.0	over 67	over 35
LAFTA Total (1966)	650,000			
World Total (1966)	23,514,000			

Source: 1967 LAFTA estimates furnished by U.S. automotive manufacturer; other data from McGraw-Hill 1967 World Automotive Market Survey, and Baranson, Automotive Industries (cited below).

1/   1965 figures.

foreign exchange and promote economic growth and employment opportunities. A basic difficulty with import substitution programs has been that as domestic production is phased into the economy, resource costs have risen.

Production costs, even among the largest LAFTA countries, were considerably above c.i.f. import prices. In Mexico, with only 63 percent national content (including assembly) a light truck costs 58 percent above c.i.f. import price. Locally manufactured parts averaged 119 percent above c.i.f. prices. In Brazil, at 99 percent domestic content, costs ran 80 percent above c.i.f. import prices and parts 76 percent. In Argentina, with 83 percent domestic content, vehicle costs were 145 percent above c.i.f. costs and vehicle components averaged 210 percent higher.[4]

COMPARATIVE PRODUCTION COSTS

LAFTA/U.S., 1967

	Dollar Value[1]	Cost Index Entire Vehicle (U.S.=100)	Percent Domestic Content[2]	Cost Index (Parts Only) (U.S.=100)
U.S.	$ 1,660	100	near 100	100
Argentina	4,069	245	83	310
Brazil	2,996	180	99	176
Mexico	2,630	158	63	219

Source: Jack Baranson, Automotive Industries in Developing Countries, World Bank Economic Staff Paper (June 1968).

1/ Converted at official exchange rate January 1967.
2/ Include 15% vehicle value for "assembly."

A major contribution to high costs are the diseconomies of scale in the manufacture of components and parts. Market demand in the largest country was just over 225,000 vehicles in 1967, but there were ten firms manufacturing no less than 40 different models and makes. (As noted below, the optimal scale is reached at about 240,000 units for a single vehicle line.) The situation was even worse in Argentina where 11 firms manufacturing over 50 makes and models produced under 180,000 vehicles in 1967. Chile is a classic case of fragmentation—16,000 vehicles manufactured by 15 or more firms (an improvement over the 7,500 vehicles assembled by 19 firms in 1965).

In addition to the more than 67 vehicle manufacturers now located in LAFTA countries, there are thousands of parts suppliers in each country. One Brazilian manufacturing affiliate, with only 12 percent of the vehicle market, purchased components and parts from 480 suppliers.

A U.S. FIRM'S MANUFACTURING OPERATIONS IN LAFTA, 1967

	Units Produced (nearest thousand)	Number of Vehicle Models	Firm's share of National Market	Number Parts Suppliers	Domestic Content Requirement	Local Price[1]/ (U.S. Price =100)
Argentina	22,000	3	12%	480	90-96%	193-259
Brazil	17,000	2	7%	400	near 100%	197-228
Mexico	24,000	4	18%	220	64%	157-166
Venezuela	14,000	5	27%	65	35%	194-235
Peru	4,000	5	16%	70	12%	208-226
Total	81,000					

Source: Special report by U.S. firm's international division

1/ Advertized delivered price including local taxes. Price differences reflect a composite of differences in production costs, tax incidence, and profit margins. As domestic content requirements rise, costs are bound to increase (see Baranson, Automotive Industries, 37-46).

266

A typical large American firm with manufacturing facilities in 5 of the LAFTA countries produces a total of 81,000 cars and trucks (12 percent of the LAFTA market). Production costs are essentially a function of plant volume, the percent domestic content requirement, the tariff level on the remaining import content, and the overall price structure (including the exchange rate). Prices also reflect profit margins and the tax incidence. Price differentials may be compared to cost differences cited previously— between 57 and 66 percent above c.i.f. in Mexico, 97 to 129 percent more in Brazil, and 93 to 159 percent higher in Argentina.

High investment costs in low-volume fragmented markets has been a continuing problem. Vehicle and parts manufacturers have been forced to duplicate segments of product lines and production facilities in several countries. Within the national framework, efforts have been made to reduce investment and operational costs through a) merger of vehicle and parts manufacturers, b) standardization of major automotive components, and c) narrowing product lines of individual firms. It is interesting to note that the largest producers in the two LAFTA countries (Kaiser of Argentina and Willys Overland of Brazil) have merged with Ford and Renault.

Changes in body and engine design mean additional investments in retooling, which only can be avoided through less frequent style changes. (This is one way in which European producers — with production volumes of one-half to one-third their American competitors—manage to stay competitive.) Body and engine design cycles are at least twice as long in Latin American countries as they are in the United States.

Another basic issue has been over the question of foreign ownership and control. Latin American governments have acknowledged the need for foreign capital and know-how, but there is widespread resentment over foreign ownership and control (particularly in Mexico).[5] Many international firms, however, insist upon majority control chiefly as a device for realizing adequate returns on corporate investments and know-how. The build-up of domestic industries under national programs of protection and import substitution has also left in its wake powerful commercial and political interests that are now difficult to phase out. These vested interests, in turn, contribute to national sentiment opposed to foreign ownership, despite the fact that international corporations are a vital link in the rationalization of production and marketing in the LAFTA region.

OBSTACLES TO FULL INTEGRATION

First, there are price and exchange instabilities. Even if tariffs among LAFTA trading partners were eliminated, there would still be disturbing price disparities due to inflation and lags in the exchange rate. Between trading partners, a unilateral devaluation has the same effect as a one-sided lowering of national tariffs.[6] Hyper-inflation and lagging exchange rates have been chronic problems in Chile, Brazil, and Argentina. A regional Payments Union (with concomitant adjustments in exchange rate policies) would greatly enhance the market viability of LAFTA.

Secondly, vested national interests oppose trade liberalization. Marginal producers are threatened as regional integration proceeds, and the rivalry exists within each country between local vehicle and parts manufacturers. In effect, there are many willing sellers, but few willing buyers. If parallel degrees of vertical integration from vehicle assembly through component manufacture existed between trading partners, losses and gains could be traded off more readily. But this is far from the situation among LAFTA countries.

Thirdly, differences in stages of sector development lead to intercountry rivalries. These rivalries are proportional to differences in national cost structures, which in turn are a function of the relative size of domestic markets and the fragmentation of models and plants. This is why the Andean Group was formed, which in a sense, was a step backward. More advantageous scale efficiencies could be realized in new plants serving the entire LAFTA region, rather than the Andean market which is one-sixth the size. But a two-phase approach to regionalism may be the only way to placate domestic interests in the less advanced countries.

Fourthly, there are the added costs of internal distribution. Transportation and additional handling costs alone raise delivered prices by as much as 20 percent. There are also the internal tariff duties to be paid during the transitional phase of trade liberalization.

AUTOMOTIVE SECTOR OUTLOOK UNDER LAFTA

The rationale underlying LAFTA was that by reducing internal trade barriers and enlarging the extent of the market, substantial increases in production efficiency could be realized followed by subsequent cost reductions. These in turn would lead to a second round of expanded demand in response to price reductions depending upon demand elasticities.[7] But insofar as the automotive industry is concerned, the reorganization of production necessary to achieve meaningful economies of scale does not seem politically feasible within the time horizon set for complete integration in 1973.

Current trends toward sub-regionalism and retrogressive complementarity, if anything, point in the direction of decreased efficiencies. Complementation programs in the form of industry-by-industry agreements have introduced uneconomic barter trade into the region. The general lowering of trade barriers would permit more advantageous trade-offs among industrial sectors. The fragmentation of industry throughout Latin America entails additional investments in roads and power in an area already overburdened in the servicing of its external debt.

LAFTA VEHICLE MARKET, 1967/1975[1]

		1967	1975
ARGENTINA			
	Passenger cars	130,500	190,000
	Commercial vehicles	47,000	68,000
		177,500	258,000
BRAZIL			
	Passenger cars	152,400	320,000
	Commercial vehicles	76,300	25,000
		228,700	345,000
MEXICO			
	Passenger cars	90,500	150,000
	Commercial vehicles	40,700	60,000
		131,200	210,000
PERU			
	Passenger cars	17,200	34,000
	Commercial vehicles	9,100	14,500
		26,300	48,500
URUGUAY			
	Passenger cars	500	8,000
	Commercial vehicles	500	4,200
		1,000	12,200
VENEZUELA			
	Passenger cars	43,500	60,000
	Commercial vehicles	16,800	25,000
		60,300	85,000
OTHERS			
	Passenger cars	10,400	48,500
	Commercial vehicles	16,500	42,800
		26,900	91,300
TOTAL LAFTA MARKET			
	Passenger cars	445,000	810,500
	Commercial vehicles	206,900	314,500
		651,900	1,125,000

Source: US vehicle manufacturer report.

[1]   Projection is based upon an overall average annual
             growth rate of approximately 6.5%.

The LAFTA vehicle market may be expected to double by 1975. This means a market for about 1,125,000 vehicles. From what is well known about motor vehicle production, minimal costs per unit are achieved at somewhere near 240,000 units a year of a single basic vehicle type. [8] This would mean no more than 5 major complexes throughout the LAFTA region. The largest complexes now manufacture from 3 to 5 basic vehicle types totaling from 25,000 to 40,000 units —which means average runs of somewhere around 10,000. As indicated earlier, the cost structure for the 3 largest countries in 1967 ranged between 58 and 110 percent above c.i.f. import prices. As LAFTA content displaces imports valued at international prices, the internal cost structure will rise even higher.

Significant progress under LAFTA arrangements is yet to be made. It is not inconceivable that if foreign enterprise were given wider latitude to reorganize production facilities in the LAFTA region, they would then be in a position to establish manufacturing interchange along the lines of the U.S.-Canadian Automotive Agreement. Under this agreement parts manufacture for export to the U.S. has been expanded considerably along with U.S. investment in Canadian production facilities. [9] Volkswagen and others have already discussed the possibility of assembly and partial manufacture in Mexico for export to the U.S. market.

NOTES

1. Each year members draw up national lists of products on which they seek, or are willing, to grant concessions. Negotiations for mutual concessions are conducted bilaterally and are later extended to all LAFTA members. Under the Treaty, the average tariff within each rate bracket is to be reduced 8 per cent per annum over the 12-year period. Under a second mechanism, members agree every 3 years on a list of products representing 25 per cent by value of intra-LAFTA trade in the previous 3-year period. These tariff concessions do not go into effect, however, until 1973. Although the original intention was to eliminate all barriers on "substantially" all goods, this has subsequently been interpreted to mean 80 per cent of total trade in the last 4-year period.

2. Chilean firms are under pressure to export items even at a loss in order to avoid heavy fines now being imposed for unliquidated trade deficits that have built up from Argentine imports (over $ 1.0 million for a single firm). Pressures to liquidate deficits in Chile force Argentine affiliates to absorb high inventory costs (to stockpile a high volume of low-value items) or suffer the consequences of repeated stop-and-go procurement. One Argentine affiliate of a Chilean firm had to import sub-

standard radiators, which they subsequently reconditioned for resale in the replacement parts market, supplying the Argentine vehicle manufacturer with their own radiator in order to meet quality standards.

3. There are exceptions. One Colombian firm (Forjas de Colombia) produces gray iron forgings which are considered competitive in terms of cost and quality even in the U.S. market. The firm has productive capacity to earn $2.5 million in the U.S. and LAFTA markets.

4. Cost differences depend upon a composite of complex technical and economic factors embedded in market structure. Factors contributing to cost differences are the exchange rate, protective tariffs, internal taxes, and the technical efficiency of vehicle and parts plants (where scale and stage of leanings are critical). See Baranson, *Automotive Industries*, Chap. 5, "Cost Comparisons."

5. On the detrimental efforts of assimilation policies, see Harry G. Johnson, "A Theoretical Model of Economic Nationalism in New and Developing States," *Political Science Quarterly*, LXXX, No. 2 (June 1965), 169-85.

6. For example, the Argentine exchange rate was devalued from about 250 pesos to 350 pesos to the dollar in late 1966. After devaluation, it cost $1.40 to import from Argentina what had previously cost $1.00. The effect is the same as a 40 per cent tariff imposed by the importing country.

7. Opinions differ on price and income elasticities for automotive products. Some have argued demand is relatively inelastic due to the skewed income distribution pattern of Latin American economies and low per household incomes. Others maintain that vehicle price reductions of 30 per cent or more would bring marginal income groups into the car market and lead to faster replacement of vehicles now in use.

8. This assumes investment in a complex of facilities with an output of 60 units per hour, operating two shifts of 2,000 hours each per year.

9. See Baranson, *op. cit.*, p. 79. For additional recommendations on the potential role of multinational corporations, see pp. 87-88.

PART V

LAW AND POLITICS

21 LEGAL ASPECTS OF ECONOMIC INTEGRATION IN LATIN AMERICA

By William S. Barnes
Fletcher School of Law and Diplomacy
Tufts University

The conversion of a policy of integration into an action program for all of Latin America requires legal measures of three types. First of all, there must be between the several states binding agreements which will create the framework for economic integration into a Common Market including both South and Central American nations. Secondly, the movement toward integration leads inevitably to an exercise in comparative law aimed at harmonizing and making uniform the fiscal and commercial legislation of the several states. Thirdly, the contact with other legal systems and the abrasive effect of daily transactions across an international border highlight the inadequacy of legal structures and wear away at national idiosyncrasies. In other words, there are legal aspects of economic integration which are international, comparative, and national. One example of each type will be considered here, and some conclusions and recommendations presented on the basis of this short case study.

Although we begin here with national reform rather than with unifying the rules of private international law, the experience of the Latin American countries is just the reverse. Instead of participating in international conferences on the unification of the law of sales, for example, they have concentrated most of their international activities on the rules of conflict of laws, especially the revision of the so-called Bustamante Code which will be discussed in the final section of this study. Before we consider the provisions which are most relevant to the process of integration, further discussion of general legal aspects may be useful.

Extra-national criticism of internal legislation is distasteful; one way to avoid it is to concentrate on the international issues of working out conflicts between laws in the various countries. One obvious advantage of this approach is that it does not require the laborious technical preparation of reform legislation nor does it involve the difficult and frustrating political problem of getting a reform passed into law. Another advantage is that it keeps from exposing national law to a standard of international relevance and therefore makes it possible for each country to continue to operate in the international field without making any basic reforms in its legal structure. Some doubt might even exist as to whether the present legal systems are sufficiently modern to qualify as such. In the field of tax law, the experience of the World Tax Series would confirm this conclusion. The elaborate outline of all aspects of tax law worked out on the basis of comparative studies of modern tax systems ran up against the fact that few, if any, of the Latin American countries have developed their tax law to cover quite a few of the points in the outline. On the very threshold, there is the question whether a sufficient body of law exists to take care of the problems which would arise under an expanded hemispheric trade pattern. As a survey of the shortcomings which we might expect to encounter in this regard, we will take up here the field of taxation and some of the needs which would have to be met in that field. In those fields where there has been sufficient development (for example, in the law of corporations), the legal problem or "law job" for the integrationalist is to identify those aspects of existing law which would need to be changed or adjusted in order to achieve the necessary harmony. Although uniform law may be more necessary in the commercial field than in the field of corporations, with increased international commercial arbitration, it would seem more appropriate to concentrate on the field of corporations where some harmonization of existing laws will be necessary. The final point we will consider here is the traditional Latin American approach to the problem of conflicts of national legislation, namely international agreement in the field of private international law.

NATIONAL LAW REFORM

Taxation is the field which has been chosen to illustrate the need for basic reform in national legislation before it is possible to consider integration of tax systems. Since August 1961 when the American states adopted the Charter of Punta del Este, reform of tax policies and tax administration has been high on the list of national goals. This effort has been aided by the establishment of a joint OAS-ECLA-IDB tax program. In the publications of this program, most emphasis has been on the conflict between national tax reform and international or regional economic integration. For example, a border tax designed to introduce equality as between foreign and domestic goods subject to sales or excise tax may, in fact, discriminate against the products of fellow members of the Central American Common Market or the Latin American Free Trade Association. In Central America the national tax incentive laws have operated in conflict with each other and have necessitated the introduction of a special treaty to control the reforms which have been introduced to stimulate the industrial development in the several states. The possibility that national tax reform could preclude international cooperation should not be overlooked. In other words, national reform is not necessarily compatible with economic integration and must be undertaken with the larger international goal constantly in mind.

As Latin America progresses from a free trade area to a customs union and finally to a Common Market, the tax considerations will become increasingly important. In a free trade area, the only policy decision for member countries concerns the elimination of tariffs on goods originating in other member countries. When tariffs on goods originating in third countries are unified and a common external commercial policy established, as in a customs union, there is even more possibility of conflicts between national tax systems. Finally, when an effort is made to establish free movement of factors of production and replacement of several markets with a single common market, then the internal tax policy of each country is likely to come under the scrutiny of the organization which is administering the Common Market. Therefore, the shortcomings of each national tax system become increasingly apparent as the region moves toward more thorough integration. National taxation will obviously affect the freedom of movement of labor, capital and business entreprise.[1]

In a free trade area such as now exists in Latin America, imports from third countries are likely to enter the area through the lowest tariff state unless the cost of transshipment is greater than the difference between the tariff at the point of entry and the tariff in the country of the sale. Having different external tariffs causes trade to be diverted and investment in productive facilities misallocated.[2] The distortion of normal trade patterns which might result from entry and transshipment of externally produced products may be alleviated by a proper definition of "origin" as suggested in Article Three of the Montevideo Treaty. The various standards available for determining origin, such as the percentage of the value added to the product within the free trade area, depend upon the existence of the modern concepts of taxation which permit easy identification of these determining factors.[3] If free movement of goods within the area is limited to those which have their "origin" within the area, then the definition of origin will depend upon information which is generally available from well-organized national tax administrations. As Latin America moves toward a customs union, even on a subregional basis, problems of origin will become less important because goods entering the area from outside will be under a common external tariff and, therefore, discrimination would be more likely to result from national fiscal and monetary policies. As Cosciani points out, when the Common Market is established, there would be a common tax with compensatory payments and grants-in-aid as between the several states. The autonomous nature of each state's fiscal competence would tend to disappear.[4]

Export duties are not included in the LAFTA program although they represent an obstacle to intra-regional free trade. Export taxes do exist in a number of Latin American countries, notably Brazil, Colombia, Mexico, and Uruguay. If such taxes were eliminated as between members through international agreement, this would have a profound effect on the trade patterns of the area. Obviously, exports leaving the area would seek out the member country with the lowest export duties. There will also be an economic effect within the area since the producers of raw materials, subject to export taxes, may be forced to sell that raw material domestically at a price which is less than the world price. Thus, domestic manufacture which depends upon that particular raw material, will tend to gravitate toward the country which has the highest export tax.

The price of products within the free trade area is not only affected by differing import duties but also by internal sales and excise taxes. In Latin America these indirect taxes are a significant source of revenue. For example, in 1961 they represented 35% of the total revenue in Mexico, 42% in Chile, and 54% in Brazil. [5] Naturally as import duties are reduced between free trade area members, these indirect taxes will have increasing effect on the trade patterns within the area. Drawbacks and rebates based on the destination principle are usually introduced in order to overcome the fiscal implications of trade within the area. For the purpose of economic planning the calculation of these rebates becomes more difficult and internal taxes become more significant in comparison with import and export duties. The vicissitudes of discrimination may either favor free trade area imports or on the other hand, subsidize exports. [6] It is likely that there will always be some distortion since the difficulty in figuring the tax component of the finished product will naturally lead to computation based on some general average of the incidence of indirect taxes on exported products. [7] If national tax reform attempts to remedy this problem by introducing a tax on the value added, there is still a possibility that it would be shifted backward and continue to operate as an export susidy.

The problem of calculating the influence of internal taxes on prices becomes even more difficult when we consider the taxes on business profits and capital and the extent to which they are passed on in the form of higher prices. If some effort is made to overcome the effect of these "direct" taxes on the prices of goods moving within and out of the free trade area, the more advanced countries are likely to get the greater reward, as their tax structures rely more heavily on direct taxes than on indirect taxes. But if such rebates are only available for indirect taxes, this policy would favor more reliance on transactions taxes and, therefore, tend to discourage tax reform which was moving in the direction of greater income and property taxation.

The Montevideo Treaty requires that the national tax treatment of members of the Latin American Free Trade Association be no less favorable than that accorded to domestic or national goods.[7] If this purpose is to be achieved through providing compensatory duties, then each country will be attempting through its national or internal tax policy to influence the trade within the area and the prices received for products traded therein. The effect is to make the national tax structure of a country importing goods apply to the product as if there were a uniform tax structure throughout the free trade area.

If the member states turn to internal, direct and indirect taxes to solve the problems of trade imbalance or distortion, there will be less pressure for maintaining a free trade area which provides for national tariff schedules. National tax reform may have the effect of requiring more rapid developments of an overall Common Market.

When a customs union is introduced trade within the union becomes competitive and problems caused by differing external tariffs are no longer important. Taxation in the country of origin becomes most feasible at least with respect to certain taxes. Trade patterns and income distribution among member states more nearly reflect relative national productive efficiency and national tax policies. Although monetary and fiscal policy toward capital-exporting third countries and internal development laws and credit policies affect trade patterns, increased attention will focus on revenue considerations. The pressure from producers competing with other member states will attempt to achieve in each state an equal competitive position, at least as far as the tax component of prices is concerned. Governments, on the other hand, will be seeking to provide the maximum tax revenue as a principal goal of tax reform. Each member state will still be free to decide the principle which will govern the imposition of direct taxes. For example, rules may differ according to whether residence or origin is to be the deciding factor in determining jurisdiction to tax. If the principle of territoriality applies, then the tax would be imposed by the state which was the origin of the income and, therefore, it would be better taxwise for an investor to receive income in that state rather than for the income to arise there. Nationals would then invest their capital in other states and receive non-taxable income on their investments. On the other hand, if tax jurisdiction is based on the residence of the taxpayer and on the place of payment, under the destination principle then it would be best to invest capital or generate income in that state and maintain a residence elsewhere. If taxation applies both on the basis of the origin or source of the income and on the residence or nationality of the taxpayer, that is, all income produced or received within the taxing jurisdiction is subject to tax; then investors would probably favor establishing themselves and their business outside of the region.

Another factor in tax reform will involve the introduction of tax on net wealth or property as a new source of revenue when indirect taxes and tariffs produce less revenue. Taxes on improved land, for example, would drive industry to establish in the lowest tax country and make it necessary for the introduction of special concessions or incentives with respect to desirable investments. One other problem which results from the lack of uniformity among the jurisdictional principles adopted in the several states is the possibility of double taxation. Cosciani states that "Simultaneous taxation of the same items (either the income or the net wealth of either the company or an individual) by more than one country because the activities of the company or individual are conducted not merely within the single country but in several at the same time, constitutes a brake on international economic activities or at any rate obliges the operator to misrepresent his own affairs to avoid such excessive taxation."[8] National tax policy must take into consideration the disincentives caused by double taxation of investments of capital from one country in the enterprises of another country. To alleviate the distortion in capital movements which could result from this situation, a national tax system will have to introduce some form of credit for taxes paid in other countries. It has been noted in the United States, which has the advantage of being a federal common market, doing business across state lines subjects the business not only to one or the other of the state taxes but forces it to cope simultaneously with several, for example, corporate income taxes, sales and use taxes, gross receipt taxes as well as taxes on property and special excises.[9] Even if national tax reform eliminates the possibility of imposing income taxes in the country where goods are delivered, at least in the absence of a permanent establishment there, sales and excise taxes may still be imposed on the sale of the item in both the country of production and the country of destination. In one country reliance on sales taxes may impose most of the burden on the consumer, whereas another country may rely principally on manufacturers' excise taxes, so that the original burden will fall on the producer. Obviously, manufacturers will attempt to produce goods in the country with the high sales tax for sale in the country with the high manufacturers' excise tax.

All of these tax policy considerations will come up as the free trade area develops into a regional trading unit. Not only will it be necessary to harmonize tax policies but some effort will have to be made to harmonize tax incentives as in the Central American Common Market.[10]

Not only must national tax legislation provide measures to alleviate the effects of overlapping tax jurisdiction, but cooperation between nations will be needed to assure that there is no "underlapping" of tax systems which would result in international transactions paying no national tax to the detriment of government revenue.

There are five situations in which international activities avoid payment of tax. All of these situations are to be found in the taxation or rather non-taxation of income and profits which could ordinarily be subject to tax if the activities were carried on within one country or within the other. As soon as two countries are concerned, as is usually the case in an international transaction, then there is the possibility of greater or lesser tax collections depending on the tax policy and administrative practice in each of the countries involved.[11]

An enterprise may manipulate its transactions so as to realize a minimun profit in the country of manufacture to provide for most of the manufacturing profit and even part of the sales profit to be realized in a third country, a so-called tax haven, where these profits will be subject to little or no tax. The failure of the two countries to obtain their fair share of the revenue from the profits of international operations is the result of the "underlapping" of tax jurisdictions.

Most of the Latin American countries confine their taxing power to income from sources within the country. The exclusive application of the territorial principle ("el principio de la fuente") may create underlapping even where there is no conflict with respect to the definition of source. A resident, either corporate or individual, of one country who earns income from foreign sources will not be taxed on this income in his own country. Being a non-resident in the country which is the source of the income, the taxpayer may not be taxed in that country either.

National tax reforms should consider three possible solutions: the adoption of internationally uniform source rules; withholding of tax at source of payment in international transactions; and tax policy to include world-wide income with credits for taxes paid abroad.

Recent surveys of tax legislation in Latin America indicate that there has been much activity in the last ten years, especially since the Alliance for Progress began effective operation. Since 1961, the Inter-American Development Bank has published an annual report on socio-economic progress in Latin America including the mobilization of resources.[12] This report shows a definite trend toward the introduction of higher taxes, especially on personal income and consumption. In the last five years, several countries have modernized their tax administration, but it is doubtful whether there is yet sufficient data to undertake a comparative analysis of their effect on economic integration. Although, Brazil, Mexico, Argentina and Paraguay have the most sophisticated systems, recently Chile, Peru and Colombia have introduced significant reforms. The present system of taxation in Bolivia, Ecuador, Uruguay and Venezuela is not sufficiently balanced to be easily converted into part of a harmonized Common Market system.[13] In another survey of recent changes in Latin American legislation, there are only two countries that have any significant developments in the last year. Both of them have had serious political repercussions, and neither of them have gone in the direction of preparing to participate in regional economic integration.[14]

The creation of a Common Market in Latin America by 1985 will require negotiation of a common external tariff, a unified commercial policy and programmed dismantling of internal barriers. This last requirement involves significant changes in the law of taxation and the introduction of some type of tax code to serve as a model in the member countries.[15] In such a code, it would be necessary to establish a balance between three different types of taxes, namely, those on income, wealth, and transactions. If each country put equal emphasis for its revenue on each of these taxes, then it would be possible to make the adjustments necessary to achieve the economic effects described above.

The need for the mobilization of internal as well as external resources to cope with the increasing financial demands generated by the integration effort and the disappointing experience of the last decade with regard to the overall flow of available external resources lead to the prediction that internal tax policy will have to increase revenues without too much regard for international consequences.

Thus in the internal legislative reforms two principal criteria must be reconciled: that these reforms produce the results necessary to maintain and improve the economic development and the social progress of the nation, and that these reforms bring the nation into harmony with other nation members of the regional integration effort by establishing more complete tax systems and by introducing modern provisions which meet international standards.

COMPARATIVE CORPORATION LAW

The Inter-American Juridical Committee included in its agenda for the meeting in Rio de Janeiro in June-September 1968 a study of the problems of harmonization of national laws in two important fields, namely, in the law of corporations (sociedades) and in commercial law. The secretariat of the committee prepared a background paper on the basis of which one can obtain a preliminary notion of the problems and potentialities for introducing common principles in the former field, that is, corporate law. [16] The first volume of this document brings together a summary of the provisions on the incorporation of entities and of societies in general in the various Latin American states. The second volume deals with some of the preparatory work which has been done in other regional integration efforts, especially in Europe. The Central American Institute of Comparative Law has prepared a draft uniform Central American law which could serve as a basis for evaluating the legislation of the various countries. In its investigation of the legal and institutional infrastructure necessary for the creation and operation of multinational enterprises in Latin America, the Institute for the Integration of Latin America (INTAL) is making a comparative study of legislation in the various countries of the Latin American Free Trade Association. The country reports are written on the basis of an exhaustive questionnaire prepared by INTAL.

Although some of the European efforts have related to specific problems of shareholders in countries operating within the European Common Market, there is one report of the Legal Committee of the European Parliament which specifically deals with the harmonization of European corporation law. [17] A series of treaties between member states of the European Economic Community is in preparation; one of these draft treaties would deal with the maintenance of juridical personality in case of the removal of the head office from one country to another.

The necessity for uniformity in corporation law appears indispensable in such a situation since the articles of the corporation and bylaws should qualify the corporation whether its place of business was located in one or another of the member states.

282

As regional integration develops, there is also the possibility of the merger of two companies organized under the laws of different states and again, this would require very close coordination between the two systems. Unless multinational investment opportunities are to be developed by international public corporations, it will be necessary for corporations organized under the laws of one state to be able to merge or work in close cooperation with affiliated corporations in other countries. As the concept of an international regime for multinational corporations develops, there will be increasing need to compare the legislations of the several member states and to adopt a regional law which fits into the laws of the several states.

The classic approach to the problem of corporations organized under the laws of one state doing business in other states has revolved around the recognition of foreign corporations. Here again, the willingness of one state to recognize foreign corporations as qualifying to do business in that state will depend on the degree to which there is uniformity in the two states involved. In the introduction to its preliminary document, the secretariat of the Inter-American Juridical Committee points out that there have been two different views, one that legal personality is a fiction and that the foreign corporation is an artificial creation of law (Savigny) and the other, that recognition is based on the reality of the existence and obvious capacity of the foreign corporation to operate outside of its own country (Gierke). Because of the possibility that recognition of foreign corporations will always be subject to considerations of public order and therefore, more of a political than a legal problem, there are obvious disadvantages in approaching the questions of harmonization from this point of view. The solution to this problem is normally controlled by rules of private international law which are dealt with in the final section of this paper.

The possibility of achieving more uniformity in corporation law in this hemisphere, especially within the countries of the Latin American Common Market is greatly enhanced by recent developments in Europe. For example, the decision of the highest court in Belgium in the Damot Case is an example of the current interest in reconciling problems of corporation law for the sake of adjusting to the reality of the Common Market. [18]

A mere comparison of legislation is not sufficient because scholarly interpretation (doctrina) and court cases (jurisprudencia) are equally important in an international context. Administrative and commercial practices suggest that arrangements are being made in financing and operating multinational concerns without benefit of legal forms.

The possibility of using international public corporations can be approached from two different view points. On the one hand, a group of private companies can agree to work together either through a series of special contracts or by adherence to a common agreement. These international corporations, such as, for example, the Scandinavian Airlines or the Flota Grancolombiana are always organized in one country where they have legal status as nationals. On the other hand, public international corporations which do not depend on the law of any particular country have international status because they are formed under the provisions of an international treaty. Such recent international entities as Eurochemic are examples of this type. The French proposal for a European corporation introduces another variation since it would not be established by governments through international agreement but would rather be subject to uniform regulation by agreement between the governments. Further research will be necessary in order to obtain more concrete results on the possibilities of applying this experience to Latin America.

There has been no development of regional corporation law in Latin America similar to the recent developments in Europe. The Seventh International Conference of American States appointed a commission of experts to draft a project on the juridical personality of foreign countries; the proposal was ultimately approved by only eight countries, including the United States. This delaration simply provided that companies organized under the laws of one of the contracting states which had their seat in its territory would be able to carry on commercial activities in the other contracting states, notwithstanding that they do not have a permanent establishment, branch, or agency in such territories.[19] Since at least some of the Latin American countries would not give adequate recognition of foreign corporations in their domestic laws, an international treaty providing for the incorporation of international, private companies qualified to do business in any other contracting states, may be the only feasible approach. Public international corporations have been organized by agreement between states; for example, the United Nations itself is such an entity. The possibility of national private corporations under public international law is a new concept. Autonomous or decentralized agencies of the national governments which are, in fact, public corporations, with juridical personality, are being recognized as entities by other Latin American states. These public agencies (for example, PEMEX, the government oil agency of Mexico) do, in fact, engage in international commerce.

If an international treaty were developed in the context of a Latin American Common Market, mixed corporations, organized with government capital and private capital, would presumably also qualify as legal entities in all of the states of the region. Since the Treaty of Montevideo makes no reference to this problem, it should be amended along the lines of Article 220 of the Treaty of Rome and subsequent efforts within the European Economic Community to establish mutual recognition of multinational corporations. Bilateral treaties between the countries of the EEC were found insufficient to solve the problem, by the special commission set up to draft the treaty.[20]

Since both types of international treaties, one providing for an international public corporation and the other for the mutual

recognition of each other's corporate entities require thorough
understanding between the member states concerning their present corporation law; the first step in any such effort is to make
a comparative study and to inform all of the member states concerning Latin American legal provisions. This is the aim of the
report which is to be prepared by the Inter-American Juridical
Committee and circulated to the governments as a means of stimulating the harmonization of corporation law. [21]

PRIVATE INTERNATIONAL LAW

The Sixth International Conference of American States,
held in Havana in 1928, approved the code of private international
law drafted by Antonio Bustamante Sánchez. The code was ratified as a treaty by many of the Latin American countries after
the conference; some, such as Chile and Costa Rica, with general
reservations; others, such as Brazil and Venezuela, with limited
reservations; and only six, including Peru and Cuba, with no reservations. Argentina, Colombia, Mexico and Paraguay have not
adhered to the Bustamante Code, but Argentina, Paraguay and
Colombia together with Chile and Peru, have participated in the
so-called Montevideo Treaty of 1889 as revised in 1939-40. Great
interest was expressed in the United States concerning the possibility of adhering to the Bustamante Code, but nothing has been
done. Comparisons between the Code and the law of the United
States would indicate that substantial revision of one or the other
or both would be necessary in order to arrive at agreement on
the rules which govern this field. Since the United States is not
a member of the Latin American Free Trade Association, the
problems of United States adherence are not discussed in this
study.

Since the Inter-American Council of Jurists first met in
1950, there has been considerable interest in the possibility of a
revision of the Bustamante Code so as to achieve greater uniformity in the rules of private international law of the various American countries. The comparative study made by J. J. Caicedo
Castilla, the Colombian member of the Inter-American Juridical
Committee, included the so-called Restatement of the Law published by the American Law Institute as a source of the Conflicts
Law of the United States. This material can be used without considering the special problems of reconciling Latin American rules
with those of the United States. [22] As between the Latin American
countries, conflicts are often settled by reference to European
rules rather than to the Bustamante Code or to the Montevideo
Treaties of 1889 and 1940. [23]

Comparing the development of rules concerning the recognition of foreign corporations under the Montevideo Treaties
and the Bustamante Code and its suggested revision, one can only
conclude that the development of the law has not yet provided a
solution to the problem. The original treaty of 1889 (Article 5)
provided only that corporations and other associations with sepa-

rate juridical personality would be governed by the laws of the country of their domicile. These corporations are recognized as such in the contracting states only to the extent that they exercise civil rights, for example, access to courts. But as to all other activities they are subject to the laws of the state in which the activities are carried out. This was clarified and expanded in Article 8 of the treaties of 1939-40 to recognize their rights to exercise commercial activities in other states; if the activities were regular or habitual, they would be subject to the laws of the state in which they were carried out. The Bustamante Code in its Article 252 provides that corporations constituted in one of the contracting states will enjoy the same juridical personality in the others, except for the limitations of the local law. This same provision is included as Article 200 of Caicedo Castilla's proposed revision. [24]

The approach to the problem of reconciling different laws with respect to corporations and other societies still refers back to the local law to determine what status a corporation will have in each of the contracting states. It, therefore, does not solve the problem of conflicting rules as between the state of the corporate domicile and the state where the corporation is doing business.

In Argentina, under Articles 285 to 287 of the Code of Commerce, as amended, the recognition of foreign companies depends upon the character of their activities within the country. Those which are doing a regular business in Argentina must be inscribed in the public registry and are subject to the rules with respect to publication. In Ecuador, Article 325 of the Code of Commerce states that foreign companies cannot establish agencies in Ecuador without the approval of the commercial court. In Mexico, the rules with respect to foreign companies are more detailed (Article 24 of the Code of Commerce), providing not only that they must register but also that current inventory, balance sheet, and a certificate of having been organized in accordance with their national law must be deposited.

In the field of commercial law and contracts there are many examples of how a uniform set of rules of private international law would still rely heavily on local law especially under the general exception of the "public order." Even though there is merit in the plan to call a Latin American conference to unify the rules governing conflicts of law and jurisdiction, this method of solving legal problems of integration is not sufficient. It will require a combination of all three of the proposed approaches in order to achieve a Latin American legal order, namely, the unification of rules of private international law, the harmonization of legislation, and the reform and modernization of certain sectors of the national legal systems.

APPENDIX

On June 30, 1967, the Joint Tax Program sponsored by
the OAS and the IDB published its Seventh General Report on Tax
Reforms in Latin America, covering the years 1966-67   (Doc.
No.: UP/G. 15/10). Some of the highlights described in this 135-
page report are as follows:

Argentina: Japan signed an exchange of notes on double taxation
in December 1961 with Argentina, which was approved by Law
No. 17035 of November 28, 1966. After the report of a Joint Tax
Program Mission, Argentina adopted an emergency tax reform
in Law No. 17196 of March 6, 1967. As a result, the tax rates
on income in excess of 100,000 pesos were reduced from an average of 30% to an average of 23% and the highest rate was reduced
from 53% to 50%. A one-time tax of 1% on the value of urban and
rural property was adopted. The sales tax was increased to 20%
on certain luxuries, remaining at 15% on all other articles. Rates
on alcoholic beverages were raised from an average of 7 pesos
per litre to an average of approximately 40 pesos per litre. A
new system of export taxes was introduced by Law 17198 of March
13, 1967, which also imposed a one-time tax of 80 pesos per dollar
at the same time as the monetary devaluation from 250 to 350 pesos to the dollar became effective. With this tax the government
recoups the better part of the profits which banks and exchanges
would have derived from their holdings of foreign currency.

Brazil: Amendment No. 18 of the Brazilian Constitution of 1946
was adopted December 1, 1965. The allocation of new taxes as
between the three levels of government was reorganized on the
basis of power to impose, capacity to administer, and distribution of revenue. Some taxes previously collected by states are
now collected by the federal government to be distributed to municipalities and other taxes previously collected by the municipalities are to be collected by the states. A new federal tax on manufactured products based on the value added during the process
of manufacture was introduced. The state sales tax was also converted into a value added tax. The state tax on exports is to be
replaced by a federal tax based on the price of export products.
A thorough reform of the structure of the personal income tax
transforms it into a global or unitary tax at progressive rates
from 3% to 55%. The tax on corporations (empresas) is imposed
on global income at the rate of 28%, its distribution at 7% and
its transfer to reserves or to increases of capital at 15%. A
special withholding tax is imposed on the Brazilian income of
foreign residents and payments to bearer at average rates of
approximately 30%. A rural land tax administered by the federal
government but distributed to the municipalities was introduced
at varying rates beginning at 0.2%, depending on such factors as
improvements, technique of agricultural exploitation, quality, and
total area of each holding.

Mexico: Among many technical changes in the income tax law, the minimum person taxable income was raised from 50,000 pesos to 100,000 pesos. The tax on electricity was raised from 10% to 15% and the tax on cigarettes and cigars to a range of from 15% to 93.5%. Social security taxes were raised so that the employer contributions which represented 50% of the total are now 62.5% and the contribution of the state was reduced from 25% to 12.5%.

Peru: By a series of decrees issued between January 1966 and April 1967, reforms in tax administration were introduced on the basis of reports by a Joint Tax Mission collaborating with the AID/IRS Tax Administration Team. By decree of September 6, 1966, a tax code was adopted which in many points followed the Model Tax Code for Latin America published by the Joint Tax Program.

Venezuela: The Law of December 16, 1966, introduced the basic reforms in the Income Tax Law, providing for a new global system of four taxes: on corporations and business concerns; on mineral and hydrocarbon enterprises; on individuals; and on windfall gains.

The rates of tax on individual income, other than business income, are progressive ranging from 4.25% to 45%. Dividends payable to bearer are taxed at 30% and dividends to nonresidents at 15%. Reforms were also introduced in the tax on inheritances and the alcoholic beverage tax.

NOTES

1. Cosciani, Cesare, "Fiscal Problems of a Common Market," *Fiscal Policy for Economic Growth in Latin America*, Joint Tax Program: OAS, ECLA (Baltimore, Md.: Johns Hopkins Press, 1965), p. 360.

2. Strasma, John, "Reform Finance and a Latin American Common Market: Some 'harmonization' problems in tax policy," paper submitted to the *Latin American Economic Integration: Methodological Essays* project directed by Joseph Grunwald, the Brookings Institution, June 1965 (mimeo, reproduced for comment and criticism), p. 11.

3. Gillim, Marion Hamilton, "Some Fiscal Aspects of the Latin American Free Trade Association," in *Fiscal Harmonization* (New York: Columbia University Press, 1967), p. 544.

4. Cosciani, *op. cit.*, p. 368.

5. Gillim, *op. cit.*, p. 539.

6. Balassa, Bela, *Trade Liberalization among Industrial Countries: Objectives and Alternatives,* Council on Foreign Relations (New York: McGraw-Hill, 1967), p. 63.

7. Cosciani, *op. cit.,* pp. 365-366; Gillim, *op. cit.,* pp. 545-546; Organization of American States, *Treaty Establishing A Free Trade Area and Instituting the Latin American Free Trade Association (Montevideo Treaty) Including the Relevant Protocols and Resolution,* OAS Official Records, Information Document No. 4 (English) rev., June 29,1961. Article 21.

8. Cosciani, *op. cit.,* p. 363.

9. United States, House of Representatives, Special Subcommittee on Taxation of Interstate Commerce of the Committee on the Judiciary, "Recommendations" comprising Chapters 37-43 of Vol. IV of *State Taxation of Interstate Commerce,* Union Calendar No. 399, 89th Congress, 1st Session, House Report No. 952, House of Representatives (Washington, D.C., 1965), p. 1121.

10. Baca Muñoz, Mauricio, "Comment" on Cesare Cosciani's "Fiscal Problems of a Common Market," in *Fiscal Policy for Economic Growth in Latin America,* Joint Tax Program: OAS, IDB, ECLA (Baltimore, Md.: Johns Hopkins Press, 1965), p. 383.

Barnes, William S., "Los impuestos en el mercado común de la América Central," discurso al IV curso de gerencia avanzada de INCAE, 21 de julio de 1966 (mimeo).

11. Barnes, William S., "Tax Policy and Administrative Practice" in M. Kriesberg, ed., *Public Administration in Developing Countries* (Washington, D.C.: Brookings Institution, 1965), p. 103.

12. Inter-American Development Bank, *Annual Reports of the Social Progress Trust Fund, 1961-68.*

13. In the Appendix to this paper, there is a summary of recent reforms based on OEA/BID Programa Conjunto de Tributación, *Informe general sobre reformas tributarias en América Latina,* Doc. No.: UP/G.15/10 (Washington, D.C.: Pan American Union, June 30, 1967).

14. Brazil and Venezuela. See Recent Developments in Latin America, R.C. Allison, ed., in *The International Lawyer,* published by the Section of International and Comparative Law, American Bar Association, October 1967, pp. 282-320.

15. OEA/BID Programa Conjunto de Tributación, *Modelo de Código Tributario* (Washington, D.C., 1967), prepared by Carlos Giuliani Fonrouge (Argentina), Rubens Gomes de Sousa (Brazil), and Ramón Valdés (Uruguay) provides an excellent synthesis of general norms and procedural rules but does not cover any specific taxes.

16. Comité Jurídico Interamericano, *Armonización del Derecho de las Sociedades* (Rio de Janeiro, March 1968), mimeo.

17. Report by Otto Weinkamm (May 1965).

18. Leleux, Paul, *Journal du Droit International* (1967), p. 141.

19. Vries, Henry P. de, and José Rodríguez Novás, *Law of the Americas* (New York: Oceana, 1965).

20. Report of the Berthold Committee, June 1966.

21. Comité Jurídico Interamericano, *Armonización del Derecho de las Sociedades* (Rio de Janeiro, March 1968), mimeo.

22. Comité Jurídico Interamericano, *Textos de los documentos de la Organización de los Estados Americanos sobre la posibilidad de revisión del Código de Derecho Internacional Privado o Código Bustamante,* OEA/Ser. I/VI CIJ-90, September 1967.

23. Inter-American Academy of International and Comparative Law, *Cursos Mongráficos,* VII (1957), 400.

24. CIJ-90, *Textos, op cit.,* pp. 188-89.

22

THE POLITICAL ECONOMY OF ECONOMIC INTEGRATION

By   Anthony E. Scaperlanda
Department of Economics
Northern Illinois University

During the last decade several economic integration schemes have changed economic, political, social, psychological, etc. relationships among nations. Concurrent with these changes an extensive economic integration literature has developed. The policy aspects of this literature usually identify economic development as being the principal motivation of underdeveloped nations participating in integration ventures.[1] However, descriptions of actual economic integration ventures in underdeveloped areas yield evidence that economic integration has not allowed the rate of economic development to be substantially accelerated. This divergence of goal and achievement points up several fundamental questions. First, does economic integration have the potential for allowing changes which will accelerate the rate of economic development? Second, if economic integration has the potential for allowing economic development to be accelerated, what conditions must exist for this potential to be realized?

The components of the answer to the first question are briefly surveyed in this study. The principal focus is on the second question. When developing an answer to this question, a set of criteria are developed which allow one to both identify the fundamental reasons for the present state of an economic integration scheme's progress and estimate the extent to which integration may permit accelerated development in the future.[2] (As these criteria are stated, the reader will note that there is some resemblance to the functional theory of integration.[3]) The conclusion to which this set of criteria or analytical model leads is that in order to have fundamental progress in the economic integration process, it is necessary to have in existence an influential, progressive group of industrialists (either public or private).[4] Further, substantial mechanization is necessary before this group is large enough and cost-conscious enough to exert a progressive influence. Thus, the material contained in this study demonstrates that economic integration is an evolutionary process and that the rate of evolutionary transformation is a direct function of the extent of progressive, technocratic influence which itself is directly determined by the stage of indus-

*The author wishes to thank Lester S. Levy, Robert H. Renshaw, George A. Thoma, and George H. K. Wang for their comments on an earlier draft of this study.

trial development. Data used in developing these points are taken from the experiences of the two Latin American integration ventures.

II

In answer to the first question, if one assumes: that Latin American industrial production is either presently or potentially complementary[5]; that substantial future growth in market size, at least in the Latin American Free Trade Association (LAFTA), is likely; that an appropriate transportation policy will be developed and implemented[6]; and, that when complementarity exists integration will provide considerable preference for member-produced products, emphasis can be placed on the most important development impacts of economic integration — economies of scale and the related external economies. Regarding economies of scale, surveys indicate that significant gains can be reaped as a result of their exploitation in Latin America. Industries often identified as potentially yielding economies of scale include: chemicals, paper and pulp, metals, transport equipment, machinery, consumer durables, cement, synthetic fibers, etc.[7] Since the integration process' enlargement of the size of the market should encourage the exploitation of these internal economies, industrialization should proceed pari passu with integration.[8] If this occurs, external economies, which are primarily a function of industrialization, should also be forthcoming in Latin America. In addition, the author has elsewhere concluded that the LAFTA's implementation (if it fully transpires), "will unleash forces that will profoundly change the 'industrial environment' of the area." Domestic, "institutional resistances, which may otherwise prove insurmountable will be overcome."[9] These changes can be categorized as a type of external economy.

In summing up this section of our study, it may be noted that, if certain factors can be assumed to be present, in general, both Latin American integration schemes have the potential for being "economically" beneficial by permitting the exploitation of internal and external economies.[10] Thus, there seems to be no basic deficiency in the idea that economic integration can permit changes that can result in accelerated economic development.[11]

III

Attention can now be turned to the second question: What conditions must exist for economic integration's development potential to be realized? In developing an answer to this question, the analytical model which is used in developing an answer is first outlined in this section of the study. The model is tested, that is, the answer is developed, in the study's final two sections.

The analytical model used here, developed by Thorstein Veblen and Clarence Ayres,[12] has been synthesized approximately as follows:[13] Economic progress is a function of the institutional resistance to technological change, the dynamic forces inherent in the process of accumulation of technical knowledge, and the appropriateness of raw material resources to the state of technical knowledge. In this study it is assumed that in those large, underdeveloped areas in which economic development is considered possible, resources are sufficiently abundant and varied to permit development. Therefore, in the analysis of economic integration's potential in Latin America, emphasis is placed on the interaction of institutional resistances and the forward thrust of the technological process.

The Veblen-Ayres model is dynamic in the sense that the technological process is a cumulative, dynamic force. However, for analytical purposes it can be adapted to a comparative statics technique. The application of the model creates the possibility of identifying a number of "stages" of development. Given the present concern, it seems feasible to limit the identification and definition of "stages" to four.

Stage A can be identified as a situation in which per capita production is very low, that is, low enough to warrant an identification of "very underdeveloped." The extremely underdeveloped state of development is assumed to be a direct result of relatively primitive technology.[14] As one would expect, the people in such a society are able to "get along" with what is available. This is accomplished by developing domestic institutions (attitude and action patterns) which reflect and relatively efficiently utilize the existing technology. It is not unusual in such societies to find that the economic-political power structure is geared to maintaining the order of the society (status quo). There are few, if any, pressures for improved technology and the consequent institutional change which a change in technique would require.[15]

Stage B is defined as a situation in which a higher and more complex level of technology yields a relatively high per capita product. In an absolute sense, a nation at this stage of development may still be classified as underdeveloped according to the generally accepted per capita income criterion. In this stage consumer goods industries are assumed to exist. Many firms in these industries are assumed to have assisted in their development by some form of protection. Some capital goods production may be beginning to emerge. Further, the domestic institutional environment is in a transitory state. As a result, there are those possessing economic and political power who are resisting change and the possibility of the concomitant erosion of their relative political strength. Others have a vested interest in industrial activities.[16] Assuming members of this group fully understand the economic implications of the industrial process, they would favor expansion of markets for their products.[17] Further, it is assumed that some members of government have been educated to recognize the benefits to be derived from advanced technology (technocrats). Finally, it is assumed that the technocrats together with industrialists are still in the ascent in terms of political power during this stage. They do not dominate. The established groups in the society are assumed to continue to be powerful enough to substantially "moderate" the pace at which technological advances are made.

Stage C is defined as being a situation in which a still higher per capita level of output is achieved. At this stage technocrats are assumed to be more powerful, consumer goods industries more developed, and capital goods industries both more developed and probably in excess capacity. It is assumed that, by the time Period C is well under way, a significant increment in the nation's capital stock has been accomplished. As a result, and as a direct by-product, the number of individuals whose vested interest is connected with the industrial process is much larger by the end of Period C than at the end of Period B. As a result of this technologically-caused change in the relative importance of the factors of production, the political climate is assumed to be more receptive to policies, such as economic integration, which will allow accelerated, efficient industrial development and thereby economic development. [18]

Stage D is defined as a situation in which technocrats and private and public, progressive entrepreneurs predominate politically. At this stage economic integration is taken as given and fully implemented. Rapid industrial advancement is permitted by flexible institutional arrangements. Dynamic economic growth results.

In the above identification and definition of the four stages, it was assumed that an economy's institutional arrangements will not develop in a vacuum. They will be shaped by the prevailing technique of production. Further, the assumption is made that a given level of technology requires a specific institutional pattern if optimal utilization is to be accomplished. Also the term "technology" is often repeated above. Technology is defined in the broadest sense as the sum of rationally derived human knowledge. More specifically, it is the sums of the tools and of the skill to use the tools that have been accumulated over time. Most important for the purpose of this study is technological progress. The general definition allows technological progress to be defined either as a combination of existing technological components which result in a more advanced level of technology, or as an extension or copying of the same level of technology so that the total volume of available technology increases. Having outlined in general terms the analytical framework, it is now possible to employ it to analyze the Latin American experience.

IV

After 1939 various Latin American countries attempted international economic co-operation with neighboring countries.

Beginning in the early 1950's these national attempts to promote trade and/or payments co-operation were superseded by the thrust of the Economic Commission for Latin America's (ECLA) emphasis on economic integration. Although progress at times was sporadic and although the present integration schemes were neither established by ECLA nor conformed to ECLA's desired form, there is no doubt that the intellectual leadership provided by ECLA profoundly influenced the economic integration endeavors being implemented.[19] A fundamental point in ECLA's argument was that Latin American industrialization had proceeded to a stage where the absence of efficient capital goods production was a severe bottleneck to continued development (especially in view of the pessimistic outlook for future expansion of Latin America's capacity to import).[20] Using the analytical framework established above, this situation can be described as one in which technological change had proceeded to a point where it was obvious that larger markets were needed if the technology available were to be used efficiently. Alternatively, it could be said that it became obvious that institutional change (economic integration in this case) was a prerequisite to the optimal utilization of available technology. But the situation was not universally obvious. Indeed in Latin America it was obvious primarily to the ECLA experts and their colleagues employed by national governments. There was not in existence a "grass roots, private" groundswell of support for economic integration (and as will be clearer at the end of this study, there was no reason to expect substantial private support).

Eventually two economic integration organizations were established. Potentially more important is the Latin American Free Trade Association. Presently composed of Argentina, Bolivia, Brazil, Colombia, Chile, Ecuador, Mexico, Paraguay, Peru, Uruguay, and Venezuela, LAFTA was established in Montevideo, Uruguay, in February 1960. After several "false starts" the present Central American Common Market (CACM) treaty was signed by El Salvador, Guatemala, and Honduras in February 1960. Later Costa Rica and Nicaragua joined.

Let us consider LAFTA first. The implementation of the Montevideo Treaty's first stage was to last twelve years. Trade restrictions were to be reduced over this period by annual negotiations, which would result in the placing of goods on National Schedules and by negotiations each three years to place goods on the permanent Common Schedule.[21] This cumbersome negotiating process seemed to yield significant results at first. But the initial restriction reductions had been easy because restrictions on "unthreatened products" were reduced first. At each successive negotiating session fewer of these "safe" products remained. And as would be expected, "... local high-cost industries... exerted pressure to resist (restriction) cuts on their products."[22] As a result in more recent years the restriction reduction process seems to have relatively stagnated. This impression is reinforced by the lack of dynamism in the implementation of complementarity agreements.[23]

LAFTA's lack of vitality resulted in an examination of its functioning and in a set of recommendations which are known as "The Report of the Four."[24] But studies and recommendations (regardless of the excellence of the quality) proved not to be sufficient. At the annual meetings of the Conference of the Contracting Parties[25] in 1965 and in 1966 only token actions were taken on the recommendations.[26] Thus, LAFTA continues to stagnate. Is this its organizational destiny? Before attempting an answer to that question the Central American Common Market experience will be surveyed in an attempt to identify parallels to the LAFTA experience.

Various of the Central American nations participated in a series of co-operative activities during the 1952-57 period. Even though these efforts did not endure, Castillo has stated that this "first phase" both established economic integration as an ongoing endeavor and provided the opportunity, "to gain knowledge and sharpen the issues concerning the common market."[27] But the advances during this period were slow. Thus, the principal economists in El Salvador, Guatemala, and Honduras asked their respective presidents to support a new integration agreement. This was accomplished and, as noted earlier, the new treaty was signed in February 1960.[28]

The new Central American organization reduced restrictions much more rapidly and automatically than the LAFTA process mentioned above. As a result by June 1966, 94 per cent of the items traded (95 per cent of value) were free of duties or restrictions. Nye has described other indications of dynamism and success, but also has noted some indications that little progress has been made. As evidence that integration's impact has been rather "superficial" in Central America, he has cited the fact that most businessmen and labor leaders are unfamiliar with the CACM's institutional apparatus (especially the Permanent Secretariat), that private attitudes continue to be primarily parochial, and that government behavior (aside from the manifestation of flexibility to keep integration "going") continues to be arbitrary.[29]

The position that progress has not been fundamental is supported by the lack of progress in the integration-sponsored allocation of industry among Central American nations. (This is an especially important indicator because this feature has the potential of having a substantial impact on the economic development of the region.) As Nye has put it, "serious coordination (of industrial development) to avoid duplication, and especially any regional allocation of scarce resources, has yet to come."[30] Thus, although Central America has made more restriction-reduction progress than has LAFTA and in spite of the fact that integration should be easier in the Central America area than in LAFTA, the Central American Common Market experience does not indicate to the present author that integration is advancing rapidly enough to substantially and fundamentally accelerate the economic development process in the near future. Economic integration in Central America has the potential for permitting much more industrial development than is currently being manifested. This leads to a question similar to the one stated regarding LAFTA. Will the potential of CACM continue to go unrealized? Additional, specific aspects of the combined experiences of both organizations will now be analyzed in an effort to formulate an answer.

If one assumes that political action (or inaction) is a reflection of the pressures generated by various, national, economic-political pressure "groups," it is not surprising that progress in the two Latin American integration ventures has been far short of potential. [31] As mentioned before the motivation for integration came from above (ECLA) down through national technocrats to national political leaders. In some cases political leaders have gone along with economists' recommendations to pacify them. In other cases, "the técnicos play an important, if not preponderant, role in the policy making process..."[32] However, in other cases actions by national technocrats have been quickly recinded by national political leaders. [33] In general, it is probably not unusual for foreign economic policy to be determined by the president and his staff in most Latin American countries. In addition, experiments and endeavors such as economic integration are likely to be permitted so long as the national, political cost is not high. [34] But one aspect of economic development should involve a relative shift in the distribution of income. If integration successfully permits development, the political cost is bound to be high.

At the time LAFTA began, "support for those technocrats favoring integration came (primarily) from... raw materials producers in the four southern countries of the continent" (South America). These countries sought a device whereby they could discriminate in favor of each other without violating the rules of the General Agreements on Tariffs and Trade. [35] The position of other nations which joined seems to have been that nothing would be permanently lost by joining and some gain might be realized as a result of having access to larger markets. [36] In the Central America area, Nye has noted that, "during the early 1950's many commercial and industrial interests were wary of free trade, which was supported almost exclusively by the technocrats."[37] Thus, for all practical purposes there was, aside from the technocrats, no "fundamental" economic power permanently in support of integration at its inception.

It can be assumed that when integration begins to become effective the present position of landlords, labor leaders, entrepreneurs in protected industries, those fearing foreign domination, some agrarian-military based high political officials and even some of the export-oriented agricultural interests (which originally supported LAFTA's creation) will be threatened. In such a circumstance the political cost of integration rises rapidly. If this cost rises rapidly enough and is not offset, it will at least retard, if not completely obliterate the economic integration ventures.

The fact that the two Latin American economic integration organizations continue in existence is evidence either that the political cost has not been overwhelming or that these costs have been at least partially offset by the benefits derived by others.

The benefits of integration immediately manifest themselves to those engaged in new industrial endeavors (especially heavy industry). These firms are, "... run by a growing class of entrepreneurs who have been educated abroad and are aware of the advantages of large markets and mass production..." Also, it has been noted that it is rather "natural" for commercial banks associated with this kind of industrial enterprise to also favor integration.[38] It is not unusual for new industrial enterprises (again, especially heavy industry) to encounter excess capacity. Since integration should permit the utilization of present excess capacity, this group's vested interest in larger markets is immediately intensified as economic integration possibilities develop.[39]

There seems to be little doubt that the importance and extent of excess capacity in Mexico has made that country one of LAFTA's most progressive members. The policy position favoring economic integration was reinforced by the fact that in Mexico many of the firms in which excess capacity existed were either completely or partially publicly owned.[40] To support this evaluation of Mexico's position, one could identify the fact that Mexico has granted more restriction-reduction concessions on manufactured goods than any other industrialized, LAFTA member and the fact that Mexico has played a leading role in the organization of LAFTA-wide meetings of representatives of various industries as being a manifestation of Mexico's progressive, pro-integration position.[41]

The role of the foreign enterprise in the process of promoting integration is uncertain. It could be held that it is not unusual for firms to prohibit exports from branches or subsidiaries which would compete with the exports of the "parent" firm. This kind of restriction obviously would retard intraregional trade.[42] Alternatively, it can be argued, "... that a considerable proportion of these (Mexico's intra-LAFTA) dynamic exports... are products of industries in which either government or North American interests are strong."[43] Supporting this line of reasoning is the fact that the first two LAFTA complementarity agreements, "... in both cases... affect Latin American branches of foreign corporations almost exclusively and were negotiated upon their initiative."[44] Regardless whether foreign firms will retard or stimulate the integration process, the evidence in support of the latter effect can be taken to support the thesis that those immediately involved in large-scale, modern industry will find integration in their best interest.[45]

Beside a growing, new industrial elite and the international and national technocrats, are other groups likely to support

298

integration? Denton, when examining the situation in Panama, found the middle class (in this context those not associated with new industry), student associations and the Christian Democratic Party in favor of integration. [46] This pattern is probably duplicated in some of the countries presently participating in the integration process. However, these groups are, in general, probably not powerful enough to effect more meaningful integration. Further, and perhaps more important, since they generally have a "political" rather than an "economic" base, they are not likely to increase their influence. Thus, in general, the forward thrust of "upgrading" the economic integration ventures must in the final analysis depend on what may be termed a new entrepreneurial elite. "Technocrats may be able to initiate an integration process... but if the technocrats remain isolated and do not form coalitions with other groups, political leaders soon find that it is more expensive to continue to please them than it is to antagonize them."[47]

Finally the advancement of the integration process is not solely determined by the offsetting forces of pressure groups that resist the accumulation of technical knowledge and the new technology-based new entrepreneurial group that tends to favor the further accumulation of advanced technology. Affecting the Latin American area, the existence of a relatively common language, a common religion, a colonial history of relative unity, a substantial period of political independence, a spirit of "Central Americanism,"[48] etc. all should make integration easier than would otherwise be the case.

V

Although all member nations are not at similar stages of development in LAFTA and in CACM, in general, the description above indicates that currently economic integration in Latin America is just on the border line of what were identified as Stages B and C. At the time integration was first seriously considered the member nations were generally at an earlier point in Stage B. And at an even earlier period (for example, 1920) many of the member nations may have even been near the border line between Stages A and B. This indicates that economic integration, to the extent thus far implemented, could not have transpired at an earlier period.

An extension of this point is that there is reason to think that more complete economic integration will evolve in the future. The key word is evolve. More complete integration will become a reality only as a result of increasing, domestic political pressure in that direction. Within the framework described here, this pressure will develop only as a result of increased industrialization. In the absence of that phenomenon, special meetings, special studies, rewriting agreements, etc. will be of no avail. It follows from the foregoing analysis that when industrialization has proceeded sufficiently so that the new entrepreneurs together with the technocrats predominate, new, more efficient procedures will "spontaneously" blossom into more sophisticated integration organizations.

Having come to the conclusions that in Latin America integration would have been impossible in the recent past, that given the present state of technological development, it is unrealistic to expect that integration would have proceeded further than it has in Latin America, and that it is reasonable to expect integration to make evolutionary progress in the future, it seems desirable to identify sample recommendations, based on the analysis, that would hasten the evolutionary development of the integration process.

It has been stated elsewhere that what is needed to accelerate Latin American integration is: regional planning, a regional financial agency, a regional agency to administer fiscal encouragement to new, high-priority, regional economic activities, a consistent region-wide set of regulations for foreign investment, and a means of compensating less developed nations for the revenue losses resulting from reduced restrictions. [49] But as described earlier, it is estimated here that most of these developments are presently impossible. Nevertheless, as goals, as ideals, they are quite useful now. Nye, for example, has delineated the benefits that may be forthcoming as a result of having the economic integration ideal clearly stated. [50]

Before the ideal (end of Stage C — beginning of Stage D) can be approached, there must be generated in the various member nations a commitment to the use of economic integration as a means of accelerating development. This indigenous commitment, it was concluded earlier, will result primarily from the development of new, modern industry. Thus, an obvious recommendation is that industrialization should be encouraged so that the ranks of the new entrepreneurial elite will be swelled. This industrialization should reflect those factors which dictate the economic feasibility of a particular venture. Wild, unwarranted industrialization must be avoided. Further, if fiscal incentives are used to encourage the new industries, they should be of a variety that can be adapted easily into the integration process.

This national industrialization can be substantially directed into an integration-oriented scheme by international lending agencies. Ideally all gifts and loans to Latin America could be channeled through a single agency (i.e. the Inter-American Development Bank). This agency (ies) should initially develop a basic, regional economic plan relatively independent of national efforts. Having done this, industries could be allocated so that long-run duplication of capacity is avoided. [51] In addition, even though it would be suboptimal in the short-run, it is probably optimal from a long-run perspective to develop excess capacity in the new facilities. This has the result of not just creating supporters of integration, but in addition, there is built into this approach the creation of an immediate urgency to support integration and thereby exploit the existing excess capacity.

And in Latin America the presence of international and national technocrats together with the national existence of trade associations (Cámaras) of various emphases will facilitate the process of marshaling and organizing support for integration among the new entrepreneurial elite. Judging from the progressive position displayed by Mexico at LAFTA conferences, the interaction of these forces seems to have been effective in generating support for integration among the business community.[52]

Finally, it follows from the analysis that the capricious juggling and rejuggling of treaties of which Castillo has warned can be avoided.[53]   Present institutions can be allowed to evolve as needs change.   The evolution will be made easier because assistance in adapting can be expected from the technocrats. And at a time when a fundamental change in institutions is needed and supported, the expertise of these same technocrats will facilitate rapid, efficient institutional development.

In summary it can be noted that, "being both political and economic in nature, it (the economic integration process) will evolve in the thick and thin of conflict, as divergent interests clash."[54]   At times the expansion of economic integration will be retarded and possibly even stopped. However, it is quite certain that so long as modern industry expands in underdeveloped areas, the pressure will grow for increased integration. Thus, assuming the continued expansion of industry in Latin America, it is reasonable to expect continued, evolutionary economic integration progress.

APPENDIX

Given the analytical framework outlined in this study, it becomes desirable to identify a nation's stage of development. This is necessary if a nation's readiness for economic integration is to be judged. Per capita income could be used. An alternative that avoids the numerous problems of comparing incomes is to arbitrarily compare the relevant nations' productions of selected products usually produced early in the industrialization process. Likewise the consumption of strategic industry-oriented products may be compared. This approach has the advantage of establishing a rough estimate of the relative predominance of "industrialists" in a society. If production or consumption per capita is small, one would expect that industrialists are relatively unimportant as a "political" force. Likewise, if the per capita estimate is large, one would judge that a nation is politically capable of being in a more advanced stage of implementing integration (State C, D, or beyond).

Arbitrarily selected here are beer production, cotton yarn production (which also serves well as a proxy for wool and rayon yarn production), sulfuric acid production, and cement production. Energy consumption, commercial railroad traffic, commercial motor vehicles in use, telephones in use, and steel consumption are also identified as being indications of the extent of industrialization. All data are in per capita terms to allow for differences in the size of nations. It is recognized that the size of the market may be a significant variable influencing the extent of industrialization.

Data for the United States and West Germany are included as benchmarks. Not all member nations of the relevant economic integration schemes are included in this survey. "Representative" nations were arbitrarily selected in an attempt to keep the size of the tables manageable. In general (except for railroad traffic), the East Africa area seems least ready for economic integration. Also, Central America seems, in general, to be second least ready. And the LAFTA area is most ready (with the exception of Paraguay). Although it would be difficult to indicate precise dividing lines, there is usually such great difference among the data for various areas that a general estimate can be made with little risk. In fact, it is suspected that these data lead to conclusions which the reader may have already reached on the basis of "general impressions."

Table 1

Per Capita Production of Selected Commodities in Selected Countries, 1965

Country	Population[a] (thousands)	Beer (litres)	Cotton yarn (kilograms)	Sulfuric acid (kilograms)	Cement (kilograms)
Costa Rica	1,433	6.0[b]	n.l.	n.l.	n.l.
Guatemala	4,438	5.1	n.l.	n.l.	52.05
Nicaragua	1,655	6.9	n.l.	n.l.	39.88
Argentina	22,352	11.1	4.4	7.25	147.86
Brazil	*82,222	8.0[c]	1.2	3.53[c]	67.44
Chile	8,567	19.2	3.2[b]	15.18[b]	138.67
Colombia	*18,068	36.7[c]	0.3[c]	0.83	113.67
Mexico	*42,689	24.0	1.2[b]	13.58	101.24
Paraguay	*2,030	3.8	5.2[c]	n.l.	14.29
Peru	*11,650	14.8	1.5	3.35	87.81
Kenya	*9,365	5.3	n.l.	n.l.	51.68
Tanganyka (Tanzania)	*10,179	0.6[c]	n.l.	n.l.	n.l.
Uganda	*7,551	2.5	n.l.	n.l.	n.l.
W. Germany	56,839	118.6	6.8	65.99	600.52
United States	194,572	65.2	9.7	115.82	334.47

Source: United Nations, Statistical Yearbook, 1966.

a) midyear estimate, 1965   b) production data, 1963   n.l. not listed.

*estimates of questionable reliability   c) production data, 1964

Table 2

Per Capita Consumption of Selected Items in Selected Countries, 1965

Country	Energy (a, b)	Railroad Traffic (a, c)	Commercial Vehicles (a, f)	Telephones	Steel (g)
Costa Rica	306	.0216	.0084	.0152	n.l.
Guatemala	182	.0291	.0038	.0056	n.l.
Nicaragua	234	.0079	.0030	.0074	n.l.
Argentina	1,341	.6276[d]	.0279	.0670	114
Brazil	347	.2239	.0120	.0161	39
Chile	1,089	.3059	.0123	.0307	70
Colombia	532	.0493	.0058	.0245	24
Mexico	977	.4294[e]	.0092	.0193	64
Paraguay	126	.0099	.0024	.0069	n.l.
Peru	588	.0552	.0085	.0118	34
Kenya	124		.0012	.0057	
Tanganyka (Tanzania)	55	.1248*	.0009	.0022	6*
Uganda	42		.0008	.0026	
W. Germany	4,234	1.0433	.0152	.1549	540
United States	9,201	5.2915	.0729	.4814	656

Source: United Nations, Statistical Yearbook, 1966.

a) data provisional, 1965
b) kilograms per capita, coal equivalent
c) net ton kilometers
d) consumption, 1963
e) consumption, 1964
f) commercial vehicles in use
g) kilograms
* East Africa
n.l. not listed

304

1. Víctor L. Urquidi, "The Common Market as a Tool of Latin America's Economic Development: A Comment," in Albert O.Hirschman (ed.) *Latin American Issues: Essays and Comments* (New York: The Twentieth Century Fund, 1961), pp. 151-60.

2. It is recognized that a substantial amount of good work has been done on economic integration in underdeveloped nations. The thrust of this study should not be taken as an implication that the author is disparaging previous work. Rather since our theoretical frameworks are still in the early stages of development, the purpose is to complement previous work by offering an alternative framework which to this author's knowledge has not been applied in this context. It is hoped that the comprehensiveness of the model will allow for sound evaluations of the present as well as for reasonable predictions. Finally, it can be noted that this framework is not proposed as the only one that can be useful. Rather, it is proposed as an alternative. If a more reasonable and comprehensive model can be developed, it should be done.

3. Dirk U. Stikker, "The Functional Approach to European Integration," *Foreign Affairs,* XXIX (April 1951), 440.

4. It would be desirable to know the origins of these new industrialists and the forces which enabled them to succeed. A study delving into these considerations would have to be both intensive and extensive if it were to make an important contribution. For the purpose of this study, the emergence of a new entrepreneurial elite was assumed possible and occurring. The study of the history of this emerging group is left for another time. A related question involves the distribution of these new entrepreneurs among member nations and the relationship of this distribution to changes in policy implementation. This question is also avoided here.

5. The reader no doubt questions why agricultural production seems to be ignored. Such is done for several reasons. First, agricultural trade, in general, has been either excluded or subjected to special treatment in most economic integration endeavors. Second, if economic development is to take place, more advanced technology must be introduced in both manufacturing and agriculture. Given this "prerequisite" to development, in fact, agricultural production must be "industrialized." It is assumed, however, that it is politically and socially easier to introduce more advanced technology in the less tradition-bound manufacturing sector (rather than the agricultural sector)

where the labor requirement will expand even though more advanced techniques are used.

6. For a description of what the author considers to be an appropriate transportation policy, reference can be made to: Anthony Scaperlanda, "The Role of Transportation in the Economic Integration of Underdeveloped Areas," *Land Economics,* XLII (May 1966), pp. 205-09.

7. Bela Balassa, *Economic Development and Economic Integration* (Mexico, D.F.: Centro de Estudios Monetarios Latinoamericanos, 1965), pp. 85-105. Sidney S. Dell, *A Latin American Common Market?* (London: Oxford University Press, 1966), pp. 19-24. And, Miguel S. Wionczek, "The Latin American Free Trade Association," *International Conciliation,* 551 (New York: Carnegie Endowment for International Peace, 1965), pp. 46-49.

8. In the economic integration context, Scitovsky has noted other factors which influence investment in new capacity. Tibor Scitovsky, *Economic Theory and Western European Integration* (London: George Allen & Unwin, Ltd., 1958) pp. 113-14.

9. Anthony Scaperlanda, "Economic Integration, Institutional Change and Economic Development," *Duquesne Review,* 11 (Spring, 1966), pp. 65-74. Also see: Howard S. Ellis, "National Development Planning and Regional Economic Integration," *Organization, Planning and Programming for Economic Development,* Vol. VIII (United States Papers Prepared for the United Nations Conference on the Application of Science and Technology for the Benefit of Less Developed Areas). (Washington, D.C.: U.S. Government Printing Office, 1962), p. 41.

10. The factors assumed present may not always be present. In the case of Latin America, various of these factors are not present in either the LAFTA or the Central American Common Market. However, for purposes of this study, it is assumed that the existing deficiencies are recognized and that policies aimed at eradicating the deficiencies are either being planned or implemented.

11. As is often said, the CACM potentially offers fewer benefits. However, sufficient benefits can be derived to make the venture worthwhile. And the possibility of the merger of the LAFTA and the CACM increases the benefits that could be derived by the CACM nations.

12. Thorstein Veblen, *The Theory of the Leisure Class,* Modern Library Edition (New York: Random House, 1934 [first published in 1899]) and *The Theory of Business Enterprise* (New York: Mentor Books, 1958 [first published in 1904]). Clarence E. Ayres, *Theory of Economic Progress* (New York: Schocken Books, 1962 [first published in 1944]).

13. Wendell C. Gordon, *The Political Economy of Latin America* (New York: Columbia University Press, 1965) p. 6.

14. Assuming an efficient distribution process, a society's level of living is directly correlated to the level of production technique utilized. If dramatic increases in the level of living are to be realized, there must occur changes in the productive techniques. More advanced technology must be utilized if substantial increases in output per unit of labor input are to occur.

15. It is realized that Stage A as defined is an extreme situation. In the real world, for example, pressure will be exerted for change both from educated leaders and from the general populace who have been "educated" by way of phenomenon often identified as the demonstration effect.

16. As mentioned earlier, individuals in this category can either be connected with some aspect of manufacturing or with industrialized agriculture. Regardless of the specific affiliation, it is assumed that for this group to be progressive its members must be aware of the advantages of large—scale production.

18. This assumption of responsive government may seem unrealistic to some. It must be recognized that projecting to the end of Period C involves relatively long-run estimates. And it does seem realistic to assume that pressure groups are likely to exert influence on government policy (regardless of the precise form of government) over time.

19. Víctor L. Urquidi, *Free Trade and Economic Integration in Latin America* (Berkeley and Los Angeles: University of California Press, 1962), pp. 129-35. Christopher Mitchell, "The Role of Technocrats in Latin American Integration," *Inter-American Economic Affairs,* XXI (Summer, 1967), 8-9.

20. Plácido García Reynoso, "Mexico's International Trade and Regional Economic Groupings" (speech delivered at the meeting of the Board of Trustees of the Committee for Economic Development, San Francisco, California, November 29, 1962), supplement to *Comercio Exterior de Mexico,* VIII (December 1962), 4.

21. The National Schedules are lists of commodities upon which each country is willing to lower trade restrictions. These restrictions are being reduced annually during the transition period. However, these trade-restriction-reduction concessions can be withdrawn if "adequate compensation" is made. The Common Schedule is the list of products on which all members agree ultimately to eliminate

restrictions. Twenty-five per cent of intra-LAFTA trade
had to be included on this schedule by November 30 of the
third year of the Treaty's operation. Fifty per cent,
seventy-five per cent and "substantially all" of such trade
must be included by November 30 of the sixth, ninth, and
twelfth years respectively. Concessions made on items on
this list cannot be withdrawn. The Common Schedule provides
both a strong incentive for each member to be as "liberal"
as possible in developing its National Schedule and insures
the steady progression toward the end result of the present
phase of the Treaty — a complete or nearly complete free
trade area.

      22. Mitchell, *op. cit.*, p. 21.

      23. The Treaty encourages the entering into agree-
ments on an industry basis which would result in a geographical specialization of the industry's production.

      24. Mitchell, *op. cit.*, pp. 25-26.

      25. The Conference, which is composed of an accred-
ited representative from each member country (each with
one vote), must meet once a year in regular session and at
other times as directed by the Standing Executive Committee.
The Conference is responsible for: taking the steps necessary to carry out the Treaty; promoting the negotiations
concerned with the lowering of the restrictions to trade;
and, dealing with other business of common interest. In
addition, the Conference is implicitly designated as the
judicial organ of the LAFTA.

      26. Mitchell, *op. cit.*, p. 26.

      27. Carlos M. Castillo, *Growth and Integration in
Central America* (New York: Frederick A. Praeger, 1966), p. 80.

      28. Joseph S. Nye, Jr., "Central American Regional
Integration," *International Conciliation*, 572 (New York:
Carnegie Endowment for International Peace, 1967), p. 29.
Nye presents evidence (p. 28) that presidential support was
forthcoming because integration ideas were fashionable, the
presidents thought integration would not be effective, and
the presidents wanted to keep "their economists" happy.

      29. *Ibid.*, pp. 40-48.

      30. *Ibid.*, pp. 38-39. The United States' refusal
to allow the use of U. S. funds in the promotion of monopolies
is identified as, "one of the most important reasons," for
the slow development of industrial coordination.

      31. For purposes of this analysis it is assumed that
a commonalty of interest is sufficient for a functional

"group" to exist and exert influence. It is assumed that there is no need for the members of this "group" to be formally organized as such. However, a formal organization might increase the influence of the "group."

32. Philippe C. Schmitter and Ernst B. Haas, *Mexico and Latin American Economic Integration* (Berkeley: University of California, Institute of International Studies, 1964), p. 12.

33. Charles F. Denton, "Interest Groups in Panama and the Central American Common Market," *Inter-American Economic Affairs*, XXI (Summer, 1967), 49.

34. Nye, *op. cit.*, pp. 33-34.

35. Mitchell, *op. cit.*, p. 10.

36. *Ibid.*, p. 18.

37. Nye, *op. cit.*, p. 33.

38. Wionczek, *op. cit.*, p. 60.

39. The various industries identified earlier in which economies of scale are possible, but not presently exploited, can be the sources of some of the pressures for accelerated integration. Mitchell has noted the relationship between new, heavy industry, excess capacity and pressure for accelerated integration in the LAFTA area. (Mitchell, *op. cit.*, p. 11.) Nye has identified the same relationship for Central America (where excess capacity was estimated to be about 30 per cent in 1962). (Nye, *op. cit.*, p. 33.) And on a national basis, Dell has noted that it had been reported that, "In Mexico, ... most industrial establishments were operating at something like 52 per cent of capacity." (Dell, *op. cit.*, p. 19.)

40. Schmitter and Haas, *op. cit.*, p. 17.

41. *Ibid.*, p. 25, p. 29.

42. Wionczek, *op. cit.*, p. 60.

43. Schmitter and Haas, *op. cit.*, p. 28.

44. Wionczek, *op. cit.*, p. 51.

45. In this particular case the author has a bias that can be expressed as a hope that foreign entrepreneurs will possess less domestic "political clout" than would similar domestic firms.

46. Denton, *op. cit.*, p. 52.

47. Nye, *op. cit.*, p. 63.

48. *Ibid.*, p. 30.

49. Wionczek, *op. cit.*, p. 57.

50. Nye, *op. cit.*, pp. 20-22.

51. The Inter-American Development Bank is presently examining the regional implications of projects it is asked to support when these projects are located near national boundaries. Thus, this aspect of the proposal would just involve an extension of present practice.

Care should be taken to insure that new enterprises are subjected to periodic efficiency tests. But unreasonable requirements that competition per se must exist should not be arbitrarily imposed.

52. Schmitter and Haas, *op. cit.*, p. 13, p. 26.

53. Castillo, *op. cit.*, p. 112.

54. *Ibid.*, p. 177.

23 POLITICAL INTEGRATION IN LATIN AMERICA

By Andrés Townsend Ezcurra,
Secretary General, Parlamento Latinoamericano
Member of Peruvian Senate

From a historical point of view, the movement toward Latin American unity preceded the movement which advocated economic unity. It may further be stated that in the ideology and in the programs of the founders of our countries, the terms national independence and continental unity or confederation represented equivalent and inseparable concepts. This was particularly true in the case of Bolívar. The term "Patria" had then a Latin American implication and scope. A "continental citizenship" existed, de facto during the wars of independence and de jure up until the beginning of the nineteenth century, and attempts were made at various times to rebuild the union. All efforts toward such utopian unionism ended in failure.

Panamericanism, promoted from Washington since 1889, changed the sense of continental unity and built it around the United States and its belief in its "manifest destiny" to conduct the affairs of the Hemisphere. Weakened by the international wars of the nineteenth century and by the increasing emphasis on petty nationalism, Latin American unity ceased to be a political matter and became, at best, an evocative and cultural subject.

"Continental nationalism" emerged again in the second decade of the twentieth century, stimulated by two events which had repercussions throughout Latin America. The first was the Mexican revolution, which brought about reaction of instinctive solidarity in our countries, and which, through some of its spokesmen (mainly Carranza and Vasconcelos), claimed "Ibero American" leadership. The second of such events was the youth movement for university reform, which originated in Córdoba, Argentina, in June 1918. It proclaimed a return to the ideals of Bolívar, and viewed with pride its expansion throughout Latin America.

It was under the influence of both movements that Alianza Popular Revolucionaria Americana (APRA) was founded in 1924. It was conceived by its leader, Haya de la Torre, as a Latin American unionist and anti-imperialist political party. For the first time since independence did an ideology develop that was based on the need to unite the Latin American countries, politically, economically, and culturally. The possibility of an international party committed to a co-ordinated and simultaneous political action in search of unity did not materialize. But APRA's

311

ideas, which spread among the new Latin American political teams emerging in the 1930's formed a common doctrinal background. APRA promoted the idea of a Latin American confederation based upon democratic regimes and programs stressing social justice. The trend of the "popular parties" or of those of the Latin American "democratic left" is to support the integration movement, identifying themselves in various degrees with such a movement. Peru's APRA party, Venezuela's Democratic Action, Costa Rica's National Liberation, Paraguay's Febrerista Party, Bolivia's M. N. R. , Guatemala's Revolutionary Party, and the Dominican Revolutionary Party are classified as members of this group. The first five signed in Lima in 1961 a common declaration in favor of the political and economic integration of Latin America.

Important sectors of some traditional parties of other countries (such as Colombia's Liberal Party, Argentina's Radical Party, the Radical Party of Chile, and Batlle's Party in Uruguay) have accepted the political platform of integration.

The activity of the Christian Democrat parties, particularly in Chile and Venezuela, began to gain public attention in the 1950's. At a continental congress, Christian Democracy defined its position in favor of Latin American integration. Chile's President Frei has been very active in spreading the thesis of integration.

ECONOMIC INTEGRATION

The ideal of the proposed Latin American union did not obtain, with the exception of Peru, sufficient popular support, in spite of the fact that it was adopted by various political forces. Even in modern and advanced parties the limiting influence of the nationalism of post-Bolívar times could be noticed. And in the case of communist or socialist movements, internationalism projected itself to encompass the entire world. Hence, the new drive for Latin American unity originated of necessity in the specialized world of international agencies and in the coincident opinion of the economists. At this new stage, which we are still passing through, the movement, discarding all designations of a political type, chose the new formula of "economic integration. "

Recognition should go to the Economic Commission for Latin America (ECLA) for the role it played as a forerunner during the preliminary period of 1949-1956. ECLA, by the very reason of its existence and because of the nature of the studies in which it was engaged, was in a position to discover the regional pluralism of the modern world and the need to establish a Latin American Common Market. In 1967, the Organization of American States, at the Economic Conference held in Buenos Aires, accepted the initiative of a regional Common Market. The "Panamerican Operation, " sponsored by Brazil in 1958, endorsed regional integration. The founding of the Inter-American Development Bank (IDB), called upon to become, as stated by its President Felipe

Herrera, the "Bank of Integration," represented an important
step from the point of view of the Hemisphere.

Under the stimulus of economic motivation, integration
materialized with the signing of two treaties: the Central American
Economic Integration Treaty, which has been in force since 1963,
and the treaty by which the Latin American Free Trade Association (LAFTA) was created and which was signed in Montevideo in
1960. In 1961, the First Punta del Este Conference, sponsored
by President Kennedy's administration, recommended the "acceleration of integration."

Economic and technical criteria in matters pertaining
to Latin American unity have prevailed since then. The use of
the emotional and historical language peculiar to the nineteenth
century was discontinued, followed by a trend toward the imper-
sonal language of figures and statistics. The subject of political
integration was either dropped or handled with extreme caution,
emphasis being given to the advantages of economic co-ordination.
Latin American unity had been a romantic proposal under the
leaders of our independence. Beginning with APRA and University
Reform it became an anti-imperialist and defensive demand.
From 1956 on it turned into a developmental proposition with a
marked commercial profile.

Such a reaction was undoubtedly necessary and, to a certain
extent, healthy. When the unionists of the nineteenth century
tried to rebuild the Confederation, having gone as far as signing
treaties of a similar or perhaps wider scope as that of the Panama treaty of 1826, they encountered serious difficulties, which
prevented their ratification. No satisfactory explanation was
ever given on the inability to federate a family of nations so obviously similar to each other. Domingo F. Sarmiento alone, with
his typical insight, forecast in 1847 the failure of the Latin
American congresses because — he stated — "we still do not have
common interests to defend."

We do now have common interests to defend in the face
of a world organized into large regional groups, a world of
"pueblos-continente, "to use the expression coined by Antenor
Orrego in defining Latin America. Strangely enough, it has been
established that we recognize these common interests and we
accept economic integration, but we lack what we had abundantly
in the past century: the will to attain political integration.

We maintain that Latin America's economic integration
will continue to encounter almost unsurmountable handicaps, if
an openly favorable attitude toward political integration is not
awakened in the people of these countries and obtained from their
governments.

In the preceding century, political integration without a
sound economic basis represented the dreams of idealists or

the fancy of diplomats. Economic integration now, without political support or leadership, may remain the cold and inoperative thesis of international experts.

FORCES FAVORABLE TO INTEGRATION

The political integration of Latin America is advocated by several forces as listed below:

Political Parties. As already stated, the democratic left (most especially the APRA party), the Christian Democrats, and certain sectors of some of the traditional parties are openly favorable to integration.

Labor Unions. At the Mexico Congress of February 1965, ORIT (Organización Regional Interamericana de Trabajadores) declared itself in favor of Latin American integration. A similar position was assumed by CLASC (Confederación Latinoamericana de Sindicatos Cristianos) representing the Christian Socialist trend, and by some of the unions affiliated with Argentina's CGT (Confederación General de Trabajadores), such as the light and power union.

Entrepreneurial Sector. In January 1968 in Buenos Aires a large group of leaders from the world of business, with entrepreneurs in the majority, attended the foundation of an Action Committee for Latin American Integration, similar to the "Monnet Committee" which operated in Europe in the 1950's. In the Declaration of Buenos Aires, the participants declared themselves in favor of "Latin American integration in all its forms" and maintained that "there will be no development without integration, nor integration without development."

University Sector. The Union of Latin American Universities, founded in Guatemala in 1949, marked the start of a cultural integration and academic solidarity movement, which has been gaining strength. In the 1930's and 1940's, all student congresses ratified the position of 1918 in favor of Latin American unity. The increasing influence of Communist or pro-Communist leadership in the national students' federations has curtailed in recent years this traditional support.

THE LATIN AMERICAN PARLIAMENT

Because the Latin American Parliament is at present the most extensive and open political organization in favor of integration in all its aspects, we wish to point out the principles behind it and to describe its main activities.

The Latin American Parliament held its "Organizing Assembly" in Lima, in December 1964. At the initiative of parliament members from the APRA party, and with the support of all political sectors in Peru, a parliamentary conference was summoned to study the procedures through which the Latin American legislative bodies could meet and participate in the process of integration.

The response was very favorable and showed that the integration development process was further advanced than anticipated. A total of 160 delegates represented the congresses and assemblies of fourteen countries: Argentina, Brazil, Colombia, Costa Rica, Chile, El Salvador, Guatemala, Honduras, Nicaragua, Panama, Paraguay, Peru, Uruguay, and Venezuela. Mexico sent only observers. Bolivia and the Dominican Republic were at the time under the rule of de facto regimes. Neither Cuba nor Haiti was invited.

At the Organizing Assembly a "Declaration of Lima" was unanimously approved. This Declaration states that "the integration of Latin America is a historical process, whose culmination is essential in order to ensure the freedom of our people, the social and economic development of our countries, the attainment of higher living standards for our population, and the presence in the world of a great Community of Nations."

The Latin American Parliament stands as the "democratic institution, of a permanent character, representative of all existing political trends within our legislative bodies; it will be entrusted with promoting, harmonizing and channeling the integration movement."

The Parliament's first regular assembly was held, once again in Lima, in July 1965, at which time the by-laws, the regulations, and the budget were approved. Article 5 of the by-laws, defines the objectives of the organization thus: "To promote and channel the political, social, economic, and cultural integration of the Latin American countries. One of the four permanent commissions of the Parliament is the Political Integration Commission. Each national parliament has the right to a maximum of 12 votes in the assemblies, regardless of any differences as to area or population between the various countries. The delegations should proportionately reflect the various political trends represented within each national parliament."

Following the first few meetings in which there was a tendency to vote with a national criterion, signs were observed of a voting attitude based on ideological affinity.

In April 1967, somewhat belatedly as a result of the dissolution of the Argentine Congress, the second regular assembly met in Montevideo under the auspices of the Uruguayan Assembly.

Inaugurated twelve days after the Presidents' Meeting at Punta del Este, at which the creation of the Common Market was approved (to be fully established by 1985), the assembly endorsed this proposition, at the same time placing on record Latin America's aspiration to reach a trade agreement with the United States to defend the prices of its basic products.

Resolution No. 19 was an important one. It urged national parliament members to promote by all appropriate constitutional and legal means and through the mobilization of public opinion, the conclusion of an international treaty establishing the Economic Community of Latin America.

The same Resolution defines the fundamental bodies having a clear political character which the Community should possess. They are as follows:

a. The Government Council, made up of the Presidents of the Latin American Republics or the Ministers which they may designate;

b. The Latin American Parliament, officially endowed with deliberative and control functions;

c. The Latin American Court of Justice; and

d. The Executive Committee, appointed by the Government Council to carry out the resolutions of said body.

It is recommended that "operational bodies" be established under these higher ones which would report to the Executive Committee, with one "operational body" for each of the following fields: trade, investments, finance, social problems. There would also be a Community Planning Body to structure economic plans with a regional criterion.

The draft treaty, which systematizes these principles, preceded by a "Latin American Magna Charta," was studied in May 1968, at the meeting of the Political Integration Committee held in San Salvador under the auspices of the Legislative Assembly of that country. It was discussed at the third regular assembly held in Brasilia in June 1968.

EXPERIENCES OF THE LATIN AMERICAN PARLIAMENT

It is evident that the organization which we are discussing does not have the same powers as the European Parliament which inspired it. It corresponds more appropriately to the Council of Europe, which preceded the European Economic Community. As was true of the Council of Europe, the Latin American Parliament must create in its leaders an integration awareness, which is essential to adopt the political resolutions which will lead to its materialization. It may be asserted that Latin American legislators have proved to be more daring in the integration approach than the executives.

In accordance with the Parliament's recommendations, several National Congresses have approved or have started discussions on the reforms or laws which advocate integration, political integration included. The Constitution of Uruguay, following its reform in 1967, inserted an article (Art. 6) pertaining to integration. Ecuador took similar action, also in 1967. Several parliaments have considered laws creating the so-called "Latin American citizenship, " which would confer upon the citizens of one country within the Community equal rights in any other member country. In the same way, one of the aims of the Latin American Parliament is to eliminate completely from passports present visa requirements and to intensify integration at a university and cultural level.

In contemplating an inter-American policy at the parliamentary level, an invitation to the United States Congress was approved at Montevideo to hold the First Inter-American Parliamentary Conference in order to discuss the main problems of hemispheric co-operation and to study the possibility of solving them through co-ordinated action.

This invitation, which was to open up a new and promising channel between Latin America and the United States, has not yet been accepted either by the Senate or by the House of Representatives of the United States. The Council of Europe, however, invited the executive board of the Latin American Parliament to discuss at Strasbourg matters of common interest to both continents.

The Assembly of the Latin American Parliament prompted diverse political sectors, ranging from the Conservatives of Colombia to the Socialists of Chile, to define their attitude on the question of integration. However, it has not resulted as yet in legislative measures as advanced or generalized as could be expected. Nevertheless, the Latin American Parliament continues to be the most active source of proselytism in favor of total integration, with special emphasis on political integration.

PART **VI**

COMMUNICATIONS

CHAPTER **24** TRANSPORTATION INTEGRATION:
A VARIETY OF PROBLEMS

By Hampton K. Snell
College of Business Administration
University of Texas

With more than 400 years of history to examine, with
reasonably complete transport integration achieved in much of
Europe and most of North America, the analyst cannot help but
wonder with some degree of pessimism why South America and
Central America are not farther along in the integration of their
transport methods both internationally and among the several
modes.

Reasons galore have been examined and discussed —
historical, topographical, psychological, climatical, regional,
"resourcial," managerial, political, financial, ethnological — to
explain the slow integration in most phases of human development.
Transport integration remains outstandingly meager in South
America, apparently affected by a "variety of major problems."

The Andes, the Amazon, the rugged coastline of Brazil,
the often wrong-way rivers, the deserts, even the Strait of Magel-
lan, have all been emphasized as obstacles to integration.   Yet
other countries and other regions with topography of their own,
notably Switzerland, Japan, and Mexico, have solved problems of
rugged terrain, nationally and internationally.   Possibilities for
development exist and will be mentioned later.

Technology involves not only the development of mechanical devices, such as motive power and kinds of airplanes, road
vehicles and road building techniques, freight handling equipment
at terminals and docks, bulk transport techniques, and a myriad
of other applications, but a co-ordinated application of modern
techniques and a willingness to use them.   The author personally
witnessed in Brazil some of the most advanced and sophisticated
transport almost side by side with some of the most amazingly
obsolete methods and attitudes.

The effects of political institutions and attitudes on
transportation would make a subject of considerable magnitude in
itself, within and between nations.   In almost every country the
author has visited, one or more transport modes were neglected
or possibilities unrealized or deliberately curbed for the benefit
of a government monopoly; or rate structures were so obsolete
or inadequate as to destroy more transportation than they created.
Even preference in equipment purchases by countries created
difficulties, which resulted in poor quality and complex problems

regarding parts and maintenance. Where international relations
or the fancied benefits of national self-reliance are involved, such
simple decisions as a difference in rail gauges can erect a self-
defeating barrier at a frontier or between states within a nation.
The stresses and strains of internal politics, often mixed with
those caused by inflation, can divert attention from such mundane
duties as dredging channels and harbor slips, or lead to overload-
ing the port personnel with political friends or unnecessary labor
forces. Brazil's major ports at least for a time could not possibly perform efficiently enough either to handle the available
traffic competitively or to attract new, much needed business.
The effect of early subsidy decisions on the construction of Brazilian railroads is too well known to need emphasis here, but the
disastrous results have plagued the economy of that nation for
decades and will continue to be most expensive to change to meet
modern demands.

The politics of nationalism, which presently insists that
each nation must have its own airline system or systems, with
heavy subsidies in most instances, or requires that an international passenger stopping over in City A must use the national
airline to fly to City B in the same or neighboring country, does
little to assist transport integration nor to stimulate greater attention to freight traffic.

The author found almost universally among nations whose
steamships or railroads are state-owned and operated a complete
disinterest in "selling" their services to shippers or passengers,
and almost no interest in working with communities or industries
or shippers to tailor service or equipment to industrial requirements or developmental possibilities. The attitude most frequently
encountered was: "The trains are here; if you want to use them,
they are here; if you don't like the service, so what!" How to
stimulate bureaucratic zeal is one of the unsolved problems of
humanity!

Integration makes not only harmonious international co-
operation but also the co-ordination among transport modes, with
the objective of achieving greater efficiency at lower costs. The
United States is slowly engaged in developing containerization and
interchangeable container devices, ship to truck, ship to railroad,
railroad and truck, soon truck and rail to plane, origin to destination without disturbing cargo. It is not the answer to all transport
and shipper problems, but is an immense improvement over
archaic and increasingly expensive multiple handling of freight.
The Houston Chronicle of April 28, 1968, carried the headline:
"Pallet, Not Container is More Feasible in South America." The
Permanent Technical Committe on Ports of the Organization of
American States, meeting in Bogotá, advanced every kind of
reason why containers cannot be used in South America — inadequate rail system, mountain curves, narrow roads, narrow rail
gauges, widely separated shippers, small volume, small cars and
locomotives, bridge clearances, tunnel restrictions, inadequate
numbers of locomotives and cars — the usual negative attitude —

— not "What can we do to start, or where can we use it, " but just negative — let's stay with our present pallets or small non-standard containers. Let us leave to our management experts and behaviorists how now to generate a positive attitude toward bringing water and rail transport up to the needs of developing nations.

The financial experts can dwell at length on the significance of adequate fiscal policies; without credit ratings transport equipment is difficult to obtain, at least on favorable terms. The poor condition and inadequate supply of equipment hobble production and development. Even the necessity of running to national government or state agencies to meet the growing deficits becomes a cumulative restriction or burden on the carrier, and greatly affects its budget, maintenance, equipment purchase, and labor relation plans. It leads to a policy of attrition. The same is true of the regulatory refusal to adjust carrier or utility rates during inflationary binges — and a city may be short a million telephones and a railroad 5,000 cars. Rates consistently too low to even come close to meeting costs may be pleasant politically but tend to destroy the carrier.

The continuing trends in several Latin American nations toward rapid urbanization is creating transport problems, as in the United States. São Paulo is reputedly growing at the rate of a thousand people per day, or over 350,000 per year, and Rio de Janeiro, without benefit of its sister city's better topography, is growing almost as fast. Such cities as Buenos Aires, Santiago, Montevideo, Lima, and Caracas are all attracting a disproportionate share of the total national population. This forces a redirection of transport expenditures, puts emphasis on commuter roads and railroads, city transport and service. The largest Brazilian steel mill, federally owned, was supposed by law to use the federally owned railroad to reach São Paulo. It had to use trucks for a very high percentage of shipments because of inadequate freight rail terminals at destination.

Some benefits of urbanization may derive, however, from the increased need for bulk-handling facilities for grain and other food products, a possible trend to containers and intermodal coordination, the introduction of modern warehousing techniques, and a greater use of electric power for railroads, with consequent saving in scarce fuel.

If Latin American nations can work together toward internationally workable agreements on border procedures, document simplification, and tariff reductions or simplification, trade should be encouraged and increased and transportation systems improved accordingly. The author witnessed in 1965 the dedication of a new international bridge over the Paraná River between Paraguay and Brazil, and much talk and writing accompanied the festivities and ceremony directed toward the concept that the new route to the Atlantic port of Paranaguá, where Brazil has granted Paraguay a free port, soon to be improved with an all-weather pavement, would give Paraguay "free tariff" access to Europe and the United States. The railroad manager, with a wiggly "bonus" line much of the distance, was enlarging tunnels, easing some curves, and planning on more electrification and dreaming of containerization to extend his service westward beyond the end of his rails. He was one of the few integrated-minded managers I encountered; I hope at least part of his plans have developed.

In almost every country that this author has visited for professional purposes, the problem of simplification of "paper work" for exports and imports was observed to be of major importance, from the several months sometimes required to clear goods actually visible on the docks and desperately needed in Indonesia to the entire day — and sometimes more — required of a ship's officer to clear his vessel properly into Alexandria Harbor, with visits to six different offices scattered about a large city. One of the chief obstacles now encountered to containerization revolves about the necessary condensation and reduction of paper work and repeated and generally unnecessary inspections. A shipper and consignee can greatly benefit, in speed of handling, in reduction of transit time and capital costs, in risk of pilferage, in spoilage, in numerous other business ways, by being able to lock his shipment into containers untouched, or virtually so, from end to end of the journey. One can only surmise that the present vigorous opposition comes from vested interests who now profit, justifiably or otherwise, from present slow and uneconomic methods, interests notably such as labor unions and brokers and customs inspectors. Transportation students can still wince at memories of labor unions in Puerto Rico and elsewhere requiring that all truck containers and all rail cars entering their countries be completely unloaded and reloaded, thus nullifying almost entirely any economic or elapsed-time gain from the new method. The critic can only conclude that such restrictions and opposition, in a variety of situations and methods, are among the principal reasons why integration has progressed so slowly in Latin America. When controlling interests decide it is desirable to do something about it, simplicity can be achieved.

The year — obviously too short a time — spent by this writer, and one of his statistically-minded associates, in a large South American nation developed considerable doubt about the accuracy of basic statistical data of several sectors of the economy, including transportation. Much of the information and conclusions were based on sampling processes, and examination at source indicated such sampling was guesswork or worse. For transport, long lists of number of cars and locomotives and similar data endlessly repeated obscured the total lack of efficiency data by which comparable performance could be determined. In airline statistics, manufactured misinformation appeared, in an effort to "beef up" nonexistent performance. Subsequent studies by visiting teams of consultants confirmed these observations and recommended much-needed improvements in statistical and accounting methods and procedures. Since much "planning" in Latin America seemed to be performed by chair-borne economists with a great

324

fascination for the comforts of capital cities and home and family, and dependent upon the uncertainties of statistical accuracy to reach policy decisions, obviously any spurious accuracy must be replaced by genuine data capable of providing valuable information. This still needs to be supplemented by field work and auditing.

While this economist is biased in favor of "field work," his conclusions as to its necessity have been developed by experience; often information reaching offices where decisions are made is incomplete or obsolete or in error. In all countries in which he has worked, including the United States, actual observation of field conditions is vital if problems are to be solved.

In 1965 a Brookings Institution team of Harral and Kuhn, in a study entitled Transport Planning in Developing Countries, concluded (pp. 219-234) that the frequently long time intervals involved in taking projects from inception to completion were discouragements in themselves, involving changes of personnel, shifts in policy by granting agencies such as AID, difficulty even of keeping supporting documents in current files. This consultant found it difficult to uncover the work and conclusions of his predecessors, and if he had not been persistent — and even perhaps obnoxious — in digging for what went before, he would have wasted even more time plowing the same ground as covered by his previous consulting brethren, not to mention what he discovered when previous elaborate studies by able teams were examined for actual accomplishment!

The Brookings study previously mentioned noted project times problems as follows:

> Looking at the results as a whole, the great variations in disbursement patterns are remarkable. The range from loan agreement to first disbursement is from 1 to 41 months, with a questionable average of 10.8 months. The next phase, from the first to the last money disbursement, takes from 5 to 55 months or more; the average for completed projects is 19.9 months, . . . Combined, the 31 projects took between 11 months to 60 months and more from loan agreement to last disbursement.

> Putting all the evidence together, and ignoring the individual characteristics, idiosyncrasies of decision making, and technical features which really make every one of the sampled projects quite unique, some rough general conclusions emerge. It is clear from the evidence that the analyst. . . would count on 2.5 to 4 years from the beginning of the study to the first flow of costs, and on about 4 to 7 years from study commence to 100% project completion. (p. 226)

A general conclusion of the study was:

The frequent failures of national development plans
to live up to expectations may partly be due to the extremely long gestation periods between idea, plan,
decision, action and the harvesting of benefits.

Comparing the average time taken by the various
stages in the investment process, it seems that the
field studies have perhaps been unnecessarily rushed
relative to the deliberation and decision-making
stages. A study period in the field of four or five
months to appraise a $50- or $100 million investment appears far too short. (p. 239)

The analysts then make a series of recommendations
which they hope will speed up the investment and project-comple-
tion process, without impairing desirable checks and analysis.
Critical path diagramming and related analytical techniques should
be used, with some stages being run simultaneously instead of
in sequence, or what they call "one consecutive chain of discrete
investment phases as seems to be the general practice now." (p. 241)

One of the more useful and informative studies of South
American transport integration problems was that by Robert T.
Brown, entitled Transport and the Economic Integration of South
America, (Brookings Institution, 1966). Here are a few quota-
tions from this study.

The first statement serves to emphasize a point that it
is not enough to build some form of transport across a given area
and expect economic development to follow automatically; it is
not necessarily true that transportation comes first and then resource development. Resources must be there, or transportation
can be not only valueless but an actual drag on the economy.

Says Brown, early in his book:

The planner charged with programming transport
investments, whether for a region within a country,
a country as a whole, or for a group of countries,
should ideally have available a detailed economic development plan covering all of the productive sectors.
This plan should identify both the location of new
productive facilities and the precise time when they
should begin operating. The plan should not, for
example, indicate merely that national steel output
will reach one million tons ten years in the future,
but should rather state explicitly both the location of
the new plants to be established as well as the year-
to-year tonnage output. Sectoral targets, such as
wheat production and coal production, are wholly inadequate unless accompanied by information on location and timing.

326

The importance of space and time to the transport planner is far greater than to planners of other sectors. This is because little is gained from talking of transport in the abstract. Slight use can be made of a transport plan composed solely of national targets of gross ton-miles, for example. A transport plan must deal with specific transport media — highways, railroads, pipelines — and must determine the capacity required in specific geographic areas. Thus the transport program must identify which railroad should be built or abandoned, where a highway should be constructed, and how much capacity is required in a specific port.

The transport planner is concerned with time because serious economic losses can occur if the relative priorities to be given to different transport projects are not determined. If transport is not to be an obstacle to growth, transport facilities must be available when they are needed. At the same time, the scarcity of capital in underdeveloped countries makes it undesirable to anticipate transport needs by too great a margin.

. . . The real task of the transport planner, however, is complicated . . . by the fact that investments in transport affect both the pattern and the sequence of growth. Transport plays a dynamic role in the real world, and decisions in this sector affect all other sectors. It is impossible to specify the location and timing of all investments in other sectors unless transport considerations are explicitly introduced throughout the entire planning process.

. . . No development program of any sort exists for South America taken as a whole. Because the national plans that exist in a number of South American countries have given almost no consideration to the possible implications of successful economic integration, it would be impossible to prepare a useful continental plan by aggregating the separate national plans. (pp. 2-4)

Brown then emphasizes that there are three groups of forces contributing to regional development: (1) internal forces, (2) impetus from exports to nearby adjoining regions, and (3) exports to far distant areas. He claims that United States development has resulted chiefly from Number 2, aided by 1 and 3.

Yet in South America, the presently available development plans for individual countries focus nearly exclusively on the first factor, internal boot-strap development, and on the third factor, export to far distant nations. No consideration is given to the growth potential of integrating the various nations into a continental economy.

Furthermore, the economic studies presently available have either examined the South American countries as separate and independent units or have treated all of Latin America as a macro unit with no spatial dimension. It is not possible to find a spatial projection — or even a vision — of a rational or desirable pattern of continental development for South America that relates the separate countries as part of a whole. (p. 4)

Brown then lists some of the principal restraints on such continental plans: (1) the geographical distribution and location and accessibility of resources; (2) present distribution of population and present transport networks, present economic specialization, and present trade patterns; (3) the fact that a few commodities represent a great proportion of total transport, such as iron ore, grains, coal, and other minerals; and (4) the possibility of planning future developments, based in part upon projections of present tendencies.

These projections can then be examined and accepted or rejected. Their rejection implies the necessity of adopting policies that would tend to bring about a different state of affairs from that which would result from a continuance into the future of what has occurred in the past. The formation of the Latin American Free Trade Association represents such a rejection of the past and an explicit desire to change present tendencies in the economies of the member countries. (p. 5)

Regional development, as a logical step or steps toward more complete integration is discussed, drawing upon various sources and tendencies, and the early parts of Brown's study are devoted to grouping the several parts of South America according to factors: education, forestry, nutrition, land reform, taxation, philology, and transport. Regions were affected, in their delineation, by concepts of topography, population densities, economic development, and a feeling of what a structured and developed South America might look like if economic integration should succeed. Brown evolved nine regions, from Region I: The Industrial Heartland (the São Paulo-Rio de Janeiro-Belo Horizonte-Pôrto Alegre area of Brazil and the Buenos Aires area of Argentina) through Region II: Supporting Hinterland (back from the industrial area) to Region VIII: The Amazon Basin and to Region IX: Northeast Brazil. The isolation among these regions and the continued lack of contact are quite apparent. It is doubtful that some of the regions can be successfully brought together.

Brown then points out some of the existing trade patterns among the South American nations:

Several important conclusions can immediately be
drawn . . . First, intra-South American trade has
essentially stagnated since 1948. Although Venezuela's exports to the other . . . nations increased
dramatically, the increase was offset by reductions
in the exports of other countries, most notably Brazil . . .

Second, despite the importance of international trade
in the economies of most of the South American
republics, intra-South American trade is relatively
unimportant. Total intra-South American exports
in 1962 amounted to only $524 million, and three of
the ten nations, Venezuela, Argentina, and Brazil,
supplied 75% of those exports. Of total intra-South
American imports of $602 million, Brazil, Argentina,
and Chile received 77%.

Both the stagnation of intra-South American trade and
its relatively small importance are clear. . In 1962,
the exports of the South American countries to one
another represented only 7.5% of their total exports.
Similarly, imports . . . represented only 10.3% of
their total imports. Furthermore, these percentages
for most countries are even lower than they were in
1948: while total trade of South America with the world
increased significantly between 1948 and 1962, intra-
South American trade was practically unchanged.
(pp. 33-39)

As has this author and critic, Brown then noted the routes
and extent of economic access between South American countries,
listing 45 pairs. He noted only fourteen examples of "relatively
good access," and called the remainder "relatively poor." Brown
shows, within the limits of available statistics, the importance of
access to trade, as between Brazil and Argentina.

The importance of water transportation to South America,
particularly in handling of international trade, is made clear.
Says Brown:

At the present time, ocean and river transport is
practically the sole means by which South America
moves its exports and imports. In 1962, 99.3% of
South America's foreign trade was transported by
this mode . . .

If information were available to break down the data
showing total foreign trade carried by ocean and
river transport between intra-South American trade
and trade between South America and other continents,
it would undoubtedly show that land and air transport
is of more importance within South America than it
is between South America and the rest of the world.

329

At the same time, however, it is most probable that upwards of 95% of even the intra-South American commerce is moved by water. In part, this is due to the fact that more than two-thirds of trade within South America is composed of petroleum, which is transported almost exclusively in tankers. Another important part of total trade within the continent is composed of grains and minerals, which again move almost entirely by water. (p. 44)

Brown's book examines in detail shipping policies of LAFTA. His conclusions are disappointing. He mildly states:

It is unfortunate that neither the LAFTA members nor the United States officials concerned with shipping policy have made a more thorough analysis of the economic effects that the different LAFTA proposals would have were they implemented, as this analysis could aid considerably in reconciling the many conflicting positions. If it could be shown that cargo reserves, for example, could contribute effectively to the economic development of the LAFTA nations, this would go far in softening United States opposition. The three million dollars which could be lost by the U.S. carriers, after all, represent but a small portion of the aid given annually by the United States to the LAFTA republics. It also represents less than one per cent of the annual construction and operating-differential subsidies that the United States gives to its merchant marine.

It is also unfortunate that the attention of the LAFTA members during five years has been dedicated largely to devising a draft convention designed to develop the Latin American merchant fleet instead of solving the more important problem of improving ocean transport service within the LAFTA region. (pp. 112-13)

Brown, quoting extensively from other sources, finds that LAFTA ship conferences seem to suffer from the ills of other ocean conferences — a tendency to be more interested in obtaining high rates than in performing good service, irregular sailings, inadequate equipment, long delays, which they blame upon poor ports and poor port facilities, endless red tape, excessive damage to cargo. This author finds that Brown's conclusions are much like his own during his Brazilian assignment. Says Brown:

Transport along the west coast and between the east and west coasts of South America is reasonably adequate. The most important problem at the present time is the poor service and high rates between the northern and southern parts of the continent. Here, perhaps, a policy of direct subsidies to companies willing to provide regular liner service would make

330

a greater contribution to the problem than an indirect
policy of cargo reserves. On the east coast, the
major difficulty lies in the ports, where cargo handling costs are high and ship turnaround time is slow
. . . .both here and throughout the rest of South
America port inefficiency must be attacked directly.
. . A transport policy based on direct subsidies to
liners plus a massive and coordinated assault on the
port problem might well be the best way to provide
the regular, frequent, and economical ocean transport which the economic integration of Latin America
requires. (p. 161)

Since this is the logical place to say it, my own conclusions, not published nor accepted by either AID or the Brazilian
Government in 1965, were:

1. Do not necessarily increase the number of ships or
the size of the fleet, but launch into a complete modernization
program for ships, with experimentation with roll-on-roll-off
vessels, barge-carrying vessels, railcar-carrying sea-going car
ferries (U.S. Sea Train type), cargo container ships (U.S. Sea
Land type, Matson Pacific - Hawaii service; Trans-Atlantic service); bulk grain carriers, with adequate associated handling on
shore — grain and soy bean silos, bulk handling port equipment,
grain cars on the railroads and grain-bulk-handling bodies on
trucks, bulk storage for such products as rice in the growing and
storing areas.

The author made a brief special study of rice, wheat,
and soy bean handling in Brazil and found such ancient handling
practices as to be almost unbelievable, with costs generally above
world prices, with inevitable requests for government subsidy and
an assist to Brazil's inflation. Much of these high costs could
have been saved, both nationally and internationally, by modernized
bulk handling facilities.

2. A complete overhaul of ports, docks, wharves, channels, storage, labor and manning requirements, port and service
charges, dock and wharf equipment, dredging practices, bulk
handling activities and attitudes, access to docks by rail, truck,
barges, and eventually helicopter-air cargo.

3. Special efforts to co-ordinate water and land transport.
In rice shipping, it was cheaper to move rice to ports in Southern
Brazil and thence to Rio or other more northerly ports, but the
shippers preferred to pay the higher shipping costs by truck,
sometimes for hauls of over 2,500 miles, because of storage and
port delays — 45 to 60 days was possible from the Pôrto Alegre
growing region to Salvador or Recife. Railroad transportation was
virtually impossible, since no through routes existed because of
change of gauge and poor service, so truck it was, in sacks for
rice or wheat. Time was perhaps a week or ten days, sometimes
less, and there was no handling or rehandling enroute.

Because of this situation, and for other reasons, Brazil and probably other countries, are embarked upon a road building program of vast proportions, arguing: it can be accomplished much faster; it is cheaper to obtain a roadbed; even unpaved or only partially complete it can be used by local inhabitants, whereas rail or ocean transport cannot; it assists Brazilian truck manufacturing industry and creates more jobs, whereas rail equipment, especially locomotives, requires foreign exchange; roads are much more flexible and adaptable.

What to do with the internal waterways of South America has intrigued observers and planners for decades. The Amazon is a vast resource, but hardly used for much; it serves relatively few people or industries. The São Francisco flows the wrong way and few people at present live along it. The northern rivers have some use but are not major arteries. The River Plate system has international problems and lacks the improvements to produce real bulk or merchandise movement.

Within the past few years, intrigued with "what to do with such water resources?", intriguing ideas have emerged, mostly related to the Amazon. Typical is an article in Fortune magazine, (December 1967), entitled "A Wild Plan for South America's Wilds."

While various schemes have been suggested, including one which proposes to build a dam of such tremendous proportions that it could flood most of the Upper Amazon Basin, creating a vast inland ocean which would supposedly enable trade between the unflooded fringes, the latest to receive some degree of serious attention includes, to quote Fortune:

> Seven huge artificial lakes . . would be the most conspicuous of the changes wrought on maps of South America by a major new development plan. The lakes would form the heart of a hydroelectric-transportation network that would connect the Amazon, Orinoco, and Paraguay river systems. None of the nine dams required for the total system . . would be more than about 115 feet high, and all would probably be built by local engineers and labor. The largest dam — the one across the Amazon at Monte Alegre — would be an immense dike, over 20 miles long. It might be constructed by using huge boulders to form a leaky wall or weir. Total estimated cost without locks or generating equipment: $125 to $250 million. Although the resulting lake is dwarfed on the map by the immensity of the Amazon Basin, it would be about the size of Montana.

> Before many of the dams are built, a good deal of additional investigation and negotiation will be needed. The project would require agreement and cooperation among as many as eight South American nations that

have never shown much tendency in this direction
before. Among other things, Brazil would have to
flood a substantial portion of its territory to give
land-locked Bolivia access to the sea and foreign
markets. This might be hard to sell to Brazilians,
even though the bulk of the land is quite worthless
at present. Moreover, some of the potential long-
range effects are vast and rather frightening. The
new Amazon Sea might, for example, so change the
heat-moisture balance at the equator that the world's
weather would be markedly influenced. There would
certainly be some effect upon the ecology of the
Amazon-Paraguay-Orinoco basin — an area larger
than the U.S. Stopping the turbid Amazon's dis-
charge of nutrients to the sea might wipe out the
shellfish industry as far north as the U.S. east
coast. (p. 148)

So goes the discussion and conjecture. The ideas and
variations come principally from the Hudson Institute.

This observer of the transport scene would not go quite
so far overboard, but would seriously recommend a more conservative type of development of the interior river system, utilizing the present principal tributaries of the Amazon, and, with
appropriate dams and locks, constructing a waterway between the
headwaters of the Parana - Paraguay system and the Guaporé -
Madeira Rivers to the Amazon. What could be gained by hooking
up with the Orinoco I do not know, since I saw none of that area
except from 35,000 feet altitude at 600 mph.

A properly constructed and developed interior waterway
would possibly, if not positively, open up the Gran Chaco - Mato
Grosso agricultural areas and might encourage a considerable
shift of population. Then as basic transport needs were met, more
sophisticated transport could follow.

With a few exceptions, such as the noted Paulista in Brazil and perhaps some in Argentina and Chile, railroads in Central
and South America are almost relics or anachronisms. The
writer found it difficult to induce his inspection party to ride on
Brazilian railroads, until they encountered the Paulista, which,
however, is fighting, at least temporarily, a losing battle for successful existence. It is a victim of state ownership, low income
from artificially restricted rates, inadequate traffic solicitation,
growing undermaintenance of equipment and roadbed, and unrestricted competition from trucks and buses.

It is difficult for South Americans to visualize what a
modern railroad is or what it can do. New construction is pro-
gressing, at least in parts of Brazil. Extensive reconstruction
was observed in the State of Rio Grande do Sul. In addition, a few
kilometers at a time, the Brazilian Army engineers are building
a fairly modern type of railroad bed through some of the rugged

terrain of Southern Brazil to establish eventually rail routes as short as the highways and with favorable grades and curvature. Unfortunately, in my opinion, the lines are meter-gauge, but are capable of being widened to broad-gauge (1.6 meters), which could allow an integrated rail system through the most productive parts of Brazil and serve, with adequate terminals, signals, and equipment, to give the kind of service modern railroads are capable of.

Something dramatic is suggested between Argentina and Chile, and between the coast of Peru and the Amazon Basin. With tunnel-boring, ground-moving techniques as well developed as the engineers say they are, it is suggested that great tunnels be built through the Andes Mountains, at altitudes below 7,500 feet or whatever is most economically feasible, tunnels perhaps 40 to 60 miles long or longer, for rail and highway traffic, pipelines, electric power lines, or whatever would serve to unite the separated areas. No real use is ever going to be made of the high slopes. Because of weather conditions at high altitudes, surface transport is not dependable. Nor does airfreight transport of minerals seem feasible.

Integration policy should emphasize the necessity of uniform gauges, both internally and internationally. Much of existing equipment is old and delapidated, except for a few modern ore lines. Electrification will be feasible as hydroelectric sources are improved and utilized. Thus the several parts of the heartland and hinterland could be tied together into a truly useful and efficient rail system. Total reliance on ships and trucks will not get the transport job done, nor can air transport do it.

As for air transport, it would be especially difficult to solve the problems of national pride, of equipment, of international regulations, of fare structures, of developmental policies, and of the part freight traffic should play.

If real progress toward transport integration is to be achieved, existing international organizations will have to engage less in discussion and debate and more in action and positive policy.

CHAPTER **25** ELECTRIC POWER INTEGRATION
IN LATIN AMERICA

By H. Leslie Robinson
Elbert Covell College
University of the Pacific

INTRODUCTION

In the European Common Market and in the United States
"common market," interconnections of the various electric power
systems form the backbone of industrial development and integration. In Latin America, on the other hand, there are as yet no
significant electrical interconnections across international borders. In the past this in itself has not really been a fundamental
deterrent to development. As is well known, in very few frontier
areas between Latin American nations are sizable population
clusters to be found that could use any power that might be provided locally nor could the availability of power alone be expected
to lure much migration to such regions. Political borders pass
through forbidding mountains, deserts or rain forests, which are
massive impediments to colonization and to international communication. Most border areas, for these obvious reasons, have always been assigned the least priority in development planning in
each country and have continued over the years to attract few inhabitants.

Today there is increasing justification for giving greater
priority not only to achieving simple trans-border interconnections of existing power systems but also to undertaking cooperative development of multinational river basins to tap their substantial power and other resources. Such projects are more feasible not only because of the growth of population and power consumption in areas to be interconnected but also because of technological advances in high-voltage power transmission. Larger
power transfers can now be made at lower costs and for longer
distances. There are indications that planning for some frontier
interconnection and multipurpose development projects, as in
Central America, between Venezuela and Colombia, Argentina
and Chile, and in the Lake Titicaca and River Plate basins, is
being taken quite seriously indeed by the countries concerned. It
does not seem unreasonable to expect some concrete results from
such planning within the next five to ten years. In fact, some
results are already tangible. Specific projects are discussed
below in terms of advantages that may accrue from them.

ADVANTAGES OF INTEGRATION

Load Sharing

Interconnection of regional power systems provide a number of important cost and other benefits that can help to accelerate development in each nation. Primarily, they permit each generating plant to even out its load diagram by sharing power during off-peak hours with other plants and systems. Advantage is thus provided by variations in hours of maximum consumption in different areas. This makes it possible for plants to reduce appreciably their reserve capacity requirements since emergency situations caused by power failures or unexpected increases in consumption can be instantly resolved with power transfers from other systems. In fact, load diversity even makes it possible to keep installed capacity in a particular region always below anticipated peak demand. The effect of such load sharing is to reduce the cost of electric power to the consumer, not only by decreasing the amount of investment required for new construction in each region but also by lowering operating costs. Increasing utilization of the installed capacity obviously reduces unit costs of generation. On this score, there is much room for improvement in Latin America, where in recent years the average level of utilization (number of hours of gross generation per year for each kilowatt of installed capacity) has been on the order of 41% of capacity, as compared with 52% in the United States and 57% in Canada and Norway.

One of the most feasible and likely applications of the load sharing advantage in the near future will be in Central America and Panama. This is not only because that region has been making the most impressive progress of all Latin America in other aspects of multinational cooperation, but also because distances between systems are not excessive and because recent power consumption growth rates in key cities of the region have been among the highest of the hemisphere. Increases in power sales in some Central American systems have ranged as high as 26% in certain years, as compared to an average of close to 8% annually for all of Latin America since 1960. This growth has been accounted for not only by higher residential and commercial loads but especially by the quickening pace of manufacturing production, heretofore never very significant in Central America but now sparked by the stimulus of the Central American Common Market. Because of this spurt, power demand in the five republics is at least expected to nearly triple within a decade and to be supplied by a generating capacity exceeding 1 million kilowatts before 1975. It is estimated that capacity will then be expanding by 100,000 kw a year. Certainly this prospect should justify the construction of some 530 miles of high voltage lines interconnecting the systems of the five nations. Already well advanced are studies for the integration of the central systems of El Salvador and Honduras; also being studied are plans for interconnecting those two systems with that of Guatemala and for interconnecting Nicaragua and Costa Rica as well as the border areas of Costa Rica and Panama.

In South America, the first modest international power connections have been made since early 1965 between four small border municipalities of Uruguay and Brazil and between the minor networks of Norte de Santander, Colombia, and Táchira, Venezuela. Being considered is the broader integration of the Venezuelan and Colombian systems by the interconnection of Maracaibo and Barranquilla with a 220-mile transmission line extending from the border town of Maicao. Other near-term and even more significant prospects include a Buenos Aires — Montevideo interconnection, with lines either extending directly under the Río de la Plata or crossing the Uruguay River at Fray Bentos, and a 125-mile line between Mendoza, Argentina, and Santiago, Chile. These southern tie-ins would be especially attractive since they would combine large consumer areas of over a million inhabitants on each side of the border. Furthermore, since Mendoza and Santiago are in different time zones, the demand curves of the two cities should mesh very advantageously. There are also time differentials between Colombia and Venezuela.

Economies of Scale

Power integration can also contribute to lower operating costs by enlarging markets and thereby permitting the construction of larger and more economical generating units. This is provided, of course, that distances between systems are not too great in relation to the size of the loads to be connected. In Central America, most power plants are small, since each serves a relatively limited and isolated area, and generating units typically have a capacity of only about 20,000 kilowatts. A plant may have a larger total capacity than this, but each unit in the plant is small because at the time it was installed a larger unit could not be justified considering the small expected increase in demand in the plant's service area. A 1966 study for the Inter-American Development Bank estimated that units of at least 100,000 kw should be feasible by 1972 if the systems are all interconnected by then with high-voltage lines. In any case, as it is frequently pointed out, there is a decided advantage to pressing on with multinational planning of power development. The systems are bound to be interconnected eventually, but integrated planning now can accelerate the process. It can also assure that the greatest efficiency is achieved with connections at uniform and adequate voltage levels and with development of the best power sites first.

To the extent that the new installed capacity is thermal, in Central America or elsewhere, benefits should derive from the greater efficiency of larger units as well as from a savings in foreign exchange in fuel-short countries, for the larger units consume less and cheaper, lower-grade fuel oil. Where supply areas are especially large, as in the River Plate zone, nuclear plants should now be able to supply power even more economically and may well be constructed before long.

337

Further savings in operating costs and in foreign ex - change can be achieved where increasing reliance on hydroelectric energy, which requires no fuel, is possible. Usually it is far too costly to undertake hydro projects where the market to be supplied is remote and limited. To be sure, hydro generation itself is cheaper than thermal generation with fossil fuels; however, hydro power costs to the consumer must also reflect the cost of dam and plant construction, which is much higher than the construction cost of a steam plant of equal capacity, and they must reflect the high cost of power transmission from the plant to the consumer. Transmission costs have been reduced by technological improvements but they are still relatively too high for distances of over 300-500 miles except in cases of very large bulk transfers of power.

As a matter of fact, hydro installations are increasingly the preferred source of electric power throughout most of Latin America, now providing slightly more than half the energy generated. Further, the greater part of all new capacity under construction is hydroelectric. This significant development has been possible in Latin America because the hydro potential has been economically accessible to centers of heavy consumption. Now some hydro sites located in or near international border areas and previously considered too remote or too large for early exploitation, are also becoming increasingly attractive. This is particularly so in Central America, so long as international transmission lines are built so as to broaden the market for the power that would be generated. Also being seriously studied is the joint power development of the Lake Titicaca basin, to benefit Peru, Bolivia, and Chile, and the River Plate basin, to supply electricity to Brazil, Paraguay, and Argentina. In both cases, load sharing, when such projects are finally built, would also be favored by differences in international time zones, which change between Bolivia and Peru, and between Paraguay-Argentina and southeastern Brazil.

While it is true that nuclear energy is now competitive in certain circumstances even with hydro energy, in general the latter is likely to have priority in Latin America for some time to come. This is not only because of the abundance of hydro resources remaining to be developed in the region, but especially because the foreign exchange requirements for constructing nuclear-fueled facilities are said to be much greater than for building hydro installations.

Multipurpose River Basin Development

Multinational exploitation of power sites will in some cases be undertaken as an integral part of multipurpose river basin development. Such projects become feasible much sooner than might otherwise be the case because the cost may be allocated proportionately among the various benefits, such as power, flood control, navigation, land reclamation and irrigation. Following the classic model of the TVA in the United States, these multiple benefits then presumably permit expanded agricultural production in the affected regions and make it possible for the latter to attract new industry. Thereby, industry and population may be decentralized in each nation, or further migration to overpopulated centers arrested, and standards of living uplifted in presently backward areas. At the same time, with frontier areas tied closer together in such joint ventures they should also become more integrated commercially and develop a greater sense of cooperation for working out mutual problems.

There are only three Latin American areas with a fairly dense border population, i.e., the Catatumbo basin of Colombia and Venezuela, the Tulcán basin of Colombia and Ecuador, and the Lake Titicaca basin of Peru and Bolivia. Of the three, only the Catatumbo and Titicaca zones actually appear to have any early prospects of international multipurpose development since preliminary studies for such projects are fairly advanced. Even development of the Titicaca basin would presumably not involve power generation and integration in the initial stages. Irrigation, resettlement projects and road building should logically receive first priority. At a later time, a power site could be created by diverting water from the basin, either west to the coastal area of southern Peru or east to the lower altitudes of the Bolivian interior. Agriculture-based industries might then be attracted to the area, while some power could be transmitted to La Paz, northern Chile and even as far as Lima. There have been some discussions about a possible 280-mile interconnection between Quito and Colombia's Cauca Valley hydro system, but very little enthusiasm seems to have been generated for this project.

Planning for the multiuse integrated development of the River Plate basin has been receiving particular attention during the past three years. It has been given special priority for study and planning by the five nations of the basin as well as by various international agencies, such as the Organization of American States, the Inter-American Development Bank, the Inter-American Committee of the Alliance for Progress, the United Nations Development Program, and the U. N. Economic Commission for Latin America. A preliminary survey of the area's hydrologic resources is now under way.

The possibilities for hydro development in the River Plate basin has inspired special enthusiasm, though navigation, erosion control to combat river silting, and many other benefits are also contemplated. Countries bordered by the Paraná River have long looked covetously at the possibility of joint development of the immense potential of the Iguaçú and Sete Quedas (Saltos de Guairá) projects. The potential of Sete Quedas alone is spectacularly estimated at between 10 and 25 million kilowatts. Brazil would be the chief consumer of power from these projects, since it has the most accessible large markets, but the economies of Paraguay and northeastern Argentina could also receive substantial boosts from the availability of such energy. Paraguay must presently use scarce foreign exchange for its small, high-cost thermal plants. However, it may be at least a decade before these projects receive full attention since Brazil has several more accessible and presently more economic hydro developments under way or on the planning board. In the meantime, Paraguay will meet its immediate expanding needs with a 45,000 kw hydro plant now under construction on the Acaray River, which will produce some excess power for sale to Argentine and Brazilian border areas. Plans are then to increase this capacity to 90,000 kw.

OBSTACLES TO INTEGRATION

Distances Between Populated Areas

Neither in the River Plate basin nor in most of the other large-scale multinational power development projects in Latin America can spectacular results be expected any time soon, for they are necessarily long-term undertakings. Because of their relative remoteness and enormous cost, they must take a back seat to other more pressing needs and more economically justifiable enterprises. And even as development begins it will no doubt be accomplished in many stages extending over several decades. This is particularly so in the case of multinational basins such as those of the Amazon and Orinoco Rivers and rivers of the Guiana Highlands, such as the Essequibo, Courantyne and Marowijne (Maroni), which are lightly populated and remote from major centers of economic activity. By and large, there is still much to be done just to increase consumption and accomplish regional interconnections within most countries in order to make international integration more attractive.

Political and Psychological Barriers

Another obstacle to rapid international power integration in Latin America is the marked tendency for governments to prefer thinking and planning in narrowly national terms and to be suspicious of having to depend on reserves of other countries to supply their own needs. Witness the apparent difficulty of agreement between Ecuador and Peru over the exploitation of the Tumbes River resources. The latter country has made elaborate plans for a multipurpose hydro plant at the site of a falls in its territory, while Ecuador has independently planned tapping the Tumbes upriver from the falls, within its own borders, for water to irrigate farmland not far from the proposed Peruvian project. A more rational and economic joint development of the Peruvian site, for the mutual benefit of the adjacent international areas, has been suggested; however, no serious official consideration appears to have been given to this idea.

Joint Argentine-Uruguayan construction of the Salto Grande project on the Uruguay River was for many years thought to have the earliest prospect for development of any of the major

340

multinational power ventures on the continent. Uruguay's hopes for this were dashed last year, however, when Argentina postponed participation in the development in favor of the entirely Argentine and more grandiose El Chocón - Cerros Colorados scheme in northern Patagonia. Buenos Aires could be supplied with hydro power more cheaply from nearby Salto Grande than from 700-mile-distant El Chocón. Nevertheless, Argentina preferred the Patagonian project because of its potential, through irrigation and flood control, for contributing to the development of the rich Río Negro agricultural valley, and its long-term possibilities, through the provision of power locally, for luring manufacturing investments and thus promoting decentralization of the nation's industry and population. In the meantime, there has even been some speculation that Argentina may abandon plans for Salto Grande altogether and give next priority to the construction of a nuclear plant to supply the Buenos Aires - Litoral area.

Standardization of Equipment and Procedures

Another important obstacle to integration, particularly in the River Plate and Lake Titicaca basins, is the problem of divergent frequencies, voltages and accounting procedures. For example, power in the "southern cone" countries of Argentina, Bolivia, Chile, Paraguay, and Uruguay is generated at the European frequency of 50 cycles per second, while the remaining Latin American countries have the American frequency of 60 cycles. Mexico City, Caracas, Rio de Janeiro, and a few minor systems within the northern countries have been on 50 cycles, but they are now committed to the slow, enormously expensive process of converting to 60 cycles. The Brazilian border state of Rio Grande do Sul is on 50 cycles and will presumably also be converted to the same frequency as the rest of the country, even though interconnections with Uruguay at the old frequency have already begun. The Brazilian variance with Paraguay, Argentina, and Uruguay, and the Bolivian variance with Peru will make more difficult the task of interconnecting loads of differing frequencies since the expensive installation and operation of converters will be required.

CONCLUSIONS

In view of these material obstacles and national inhibitions, no one can logically expect more than slow, piecemeal steps toward integration of Latin American power systems. On the other hand, this slow motion should not itself prove a major encumbrance to progress in other aspects of integration. Common market trade and industrial integration will surely, for a long time to come, continue to take place primarily between and in presently developed areas. Nevertheless, it is the position of this study that an integrated Latin America can most assuredly benefit from integrated power developments and interconnections as they become economically feasible. Even though this will be a gradual process, there is every reason to proceed now, as is being done, with tentative planning programs for the development of entire basins in border areas. In this way, priorities can be established in the most logical and consistent fashion to permit a coordinated long-term development at the lowest cost.

26

INTEGRATION OF LATIN AMERICAN COMMUNICATIONS

By Andrew J. Lipinski
Stanford Research Institute

For almost a decade, because of the efforts of a few dedicated and farsighted administrators, the movement toward integration of Latin American communications has been gathering
momentum. The first definite attempt to co-ordinate development
of an inter-American telecommunications network took place during a meeting of the Organization of the American States in
Washington, D. C., in 1959. In the past nine years, three other
developments have furthered the goal of achieving an integrated
American network: (1) the use of submarine cables and satellites
as a means of long distance multichannel transmission; (2) the
interest of the Inter-American Development Bank in financing
communications projects; and (3) the agreement, in Punta del
Este, by the American heads of state on the importance of early
development of communications as a necessary step in the creation of a Latin American Common Market.

Although integration can mean many things, we propose
to treat integration of communications as a means of achieving
two objectives — (1) developing a better interregional network
than could be achieved by separate national developments and
(2) by the actual effort of creating the network, changing the attitudes of the telephone administrations and beginning an exchange
of skills and experiences.

First, we will examine the sequence of tasks that must
be done to get an integrating process under way and divide them
into four major activities: planning, implementation, operation,
and feedback (Figure 1).

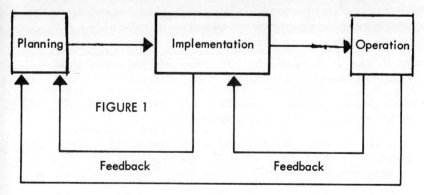

FIGURE 1

After we have examined the tasks included in the four major activities, we will focus on those aspects of the integration process that, given the past history of Latin American communications, may be particularly difficult.

THE PROCESS OF INTEGRATION

Planning

If the objective of integration were to interconnect the South American countries, planning such as described here would not be necessary. However, neither of the two objectives of integration that were mentioned, i.e., the economy of effort and the learning process, would be achieved. For that reason, a review will be made of planning as an essential element of the integration process.

It is helpful to divide the planning of a communications undertaking into the following tasks:

> Setting of objectives (scope, timetable, and performance)
> Decision on resource allocations among different
>   sectors of a national economy
> Definition of work to be done
> Preparation of detailed management and hardware
>   specifications (final staff work)

These tasks are discussed in more detail below.

The Setting of Objectives

To minimize future conflicts of policy and to improve the chances of success of integration, it is desirable that agreement be reached on certain questions.

What relative weight should be given to the need for development of domestic and international communications in Latin America compared with other urgent regional needs such as education, health, transportation, and the development of industry? Also, what relative weight should be placed on the development of domestic compared with international communications?

Table 1 shows the ratio of domestic to international calls for selected countries. It can be seen that the ratio of domestic to international calls is on the order of one thousand to one. Because the charges for international calls are higher, international revenues amount typically to a few per cent of total revenues. The resolution of the above priorities, i.e., communications or other services and the ratio of domestic/international communications will depend on the utility of communications to the decision-makers, on their costs, and on the urgency of satisfying other competitive national needs.

344

TABLE I

RATIO OF DOMESTIC CALLS
TO INTERNATIONAL CALLS
1963

United States	6,000
Sweden	507
Australia	19,300
Argentina	9,450
United Kingdom	1,200

During actual planning, one can approach agreement by first starting with a definite proposal and exploring the consequences of its adoption. For Latin America, we have such a proposal. During 1966, Page Communications Engineers, Inc., completed a feasibility study[1] for the IDB that, among other conclusions, forecast the required investment to build the South American communications network. Page concluded that, in the next decade, an over-all investment of $2.7 billion will be required, four-fifths of which will be needed for the improvement and expansion of local services and one-fifth for long distance services, both regional and international. Page strongly recommended using satellite communications to satisfy the needs for long distance services. Here we have an excellent example of the first "bid." The amount of annual investment suggested is approximately .5 per cent of GNP and the ratio of domestic to international investment is five to one.

In October, 1967, a special meeting of the CITEL (Inter-American Telecommunications Commission)[2] was held in Mexico City to plan the implementation of ITN (Inter-American Telecommunications Network). At this meeting, Dr. Dirceu L. Coutinho, Chief of the IDB mission, informed the participants that IDB expected to complete the feasibility studies required for the construction of the ITN in 1968.

The Decision on Resource Allocations

How can the administrations evaluate the merits of this very desirable investment in communications? If they were only trying to interconnect, each administration could make an independent decision, but to integrate they would have to agree on a joint investment. However, the urgency of developing different sectors of the economy may vary greatly from country to country. As a means of obtaining an agreement and consolidating a decision, it may be necessary to explore the consequences of different levels of investments, to try different cuts at the problem that may provide an insight into the likely quality of the end product and of the product costs for each level of investment, and then to judge whether the results are attractive compared with those of other investments. If this problem of allocations is not faced by administrations, it may have to be faced by the funding agency (IDB).

Figure 2 illustrates the iterative process of comparing alternatives.

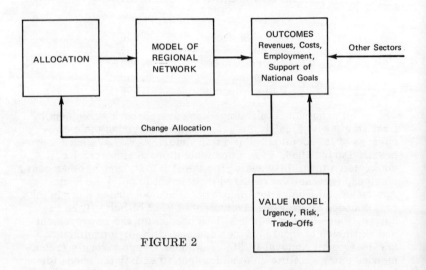

FIGURE 2

Note that someone has to compare the benefits of investments in communications with benefits of investments in other sectors. That someone may be the Economic Council of the Latin American Common Market, IDB officials, or perhaps the Economic Section of CITEL. Whichever it is will have to establish a set of value judgments. But will these value judgments reflect the value judgments of the users of the integrated network? Before we can answer that question, we must ask: Who are the customers of the regional communications network and what relative weights should be given to their needs?

There are several classes of customers: ordinary telephone subscribers (you and I), industry, government departments or agencies (education, transportation, health and welfare, police, fire, armed forces, and security forces), embassies, and trade missions.

Suppose that a decision was reached as to how to weigh the relative importance of the users. Next comes the problem of how to judge the user's acceptance of the services that are to be provided.

How do we judge quality compared with price, i.e., whether to provide large coverage at a lesser quality or a smaller coverage at a higher price, and what are to be the channels by which the customer or customers can influence the decision process in this regard?

If the value judgments as to the importance of communications, the relative importance of different classes of users, and the price/quality trade-off differ among the individual country telephone administrators and their policy makers and also differ among the policy makers of different countries, establishing a consensus may be quite complicated. Yet it should be faced. In Central America, the lack of consensus at a high policy-making level greatly delayed the beginning of the planning of the integrated communications network.

Since objectives cannot be set except by facing up to the larger issue of alternative investments, this choice brings us immediately to the question of: Who are the decision-makers and what are their value judgments?

Assuming however that the issues are gradually resolved, the end of analysis of alternative resource allocations (however imperfect and intuitive) is reached when the marginal utility of communications is just equal to that of any of the other expenditures.

Once the resource allocations have been decided on and (to be practical about it) a co-operative source of funds has been found (not a difficult problem, in my opinion, if the preceding planning has been carried out, but difficult without it), the next planning step toward integration can be taken.

The Definition of Work To Be Done

Once the scope and the timing of the project are agreed on, planners of integration will address themselves to the more detailed tasks of defining the personnel and management needs, constructing a financial plan, defining the hardware plan, and co-ordinating all three. These steps may appear obvious, but every day we see examples of inadequate planning in which one of the above elements is missing. In the Bay Area, we have the Bay Area Rapid Transit system, an example of inadequate financial planning. When expenditures exceed available funds, how long can the lender be expected to extend credit?

When we read in the newspapers about U. S.-financed equipment rotting at the quays, we might imagine that the co-ordination plan failed somewhere. It is interesting to note that of the three planning tasks mentioned above, i.e., management, financial, and hardware, the hardware task is usually given most attention and comes out best probably because, by its nature, it is easy to quantify, it is least subject to uncertainty, and it has the least emotional content. We will review briefly the individual elements, because some of them contain seeds of problems that may grow to threaten the future of the enterprise.

The management task is presumed to determine the future organization that is to run the integrated communication network, accountability, the corrective feedback paths (by which discontent on the part of one or more of the participants in the regional network can be cleared up before the structure falls apart), the division of revenues, the allocation of common costs (such as, for instance, the cost of the satellite space segment), and provision for continuous planning for the future.

The financial task will specify the required structure of rates to be charged, the division of revenues among member states, the foreign exchange needed for the plant, and a schedule of depreciation and loan repayments. If the lending agency requires that sector loans be consolidated on a national basis, the financial task for communications must be developed in conjunction with tasks for other sectors. This consolidation may be of advantage to communications, because of the possible differences in the respective timestreams of revenues and costs among sectors.

The facilities task will optimize the quantity and the quality of service offered for a given level of investment and the timing of expenditures, matching the revenue requirements with the financial objectives. In other words, the revenue-producing capacity of the network must be available at the time required by the revenue-paying customers. It would not be appropriate, for instance, to give a majority of circuits to the military, if the military was not willing to pay for its share of the costs, or to provide network capacity much larger than justified by the demand.

The co-ordination task will establish the measurement points and yardsticks of management performance and will allow for contingency plans, in case different aspects of implementation should go awry.

Preparation of Detailed Management and Hardware Specifications

Preparation of detailed management and hardware specifications is the most tedious, but a very responsible part of the planning process. However, very often it is performed too early, before the completion of the analysis and agreement on objectives or resource allocations. The result of "jumping the gun" is to freeze the concept before anyone in authority has had a chance to think about it, and white elephants often result.

Specifications for the communications equipment must be written in a way that allows several suppliers to participate on equal terms. Some of the countries may have favorite suppliers or their telecommunications may be operated by a private organization that also happens to manufacture equipment. The complexities of communications hardware are such that sometimes a minor phrase of the specification can discriminate in someone's favor. Strong pressure may develop, via the friendly administrators, to void the contracts, should they be in favor of the "wrong" supplier.

Management specifications should foresee the training and

manning requirements needed for the regional network and provide the future flow of talent. In the early phases of network operations, consultants, suppliers' personnel, or other outside help hired on a contractual basis may tide things over but, in the long run, provision of locally trained people is necessary. Because the technical talent in the emerging countries is scarce, competition for it develops among different sectors of the economy. If the telecommunications administration is tied to the civil service salary scales, talented people may leave for other, better paying occupations, and the operation and maintenance will suffer.

At this stage the planning process is completed. There is a general agreement on objectives, resources to be allocated, work to be done, and the detailed plans are spelled out and approved.

Implementation

It is probably unwise to count on the newly emerged regional communications entity to implement the construction of the huge network, even though it was assumed that the learning process is one of the aims of integration. The administrators certainly will learn from their mistakes, but these mistakes may prove too costly and time-consuming, delaying the flow of badly needed revenues. Perhaps it would be wiser to let the suppliers commission the equipment on a turnkey basis and then, gradually, take over the operations stage. Once the network is implemented, the operational phase begins. Planning has decreased in importance, and other tasks must be accomplished:

> Preservation of the technical quality of the network
> Engineering of network changes
> Continuing development of connections; for example, between the domestic and the international network and between the regional communications network and the regional educational network
> Maintenance and upgrading of skills
> Financial record keeping, failure recording, and analysis

The customer's satisfaction with the service should be measured. The quality of service can be measured in quantifiable terms, such as waiting time for a telephone, average waiting time for the dial tone, time required to establish a connection, circuit noise, level, and signal quality. But it can also be judged in more human terms, such as the politeness of the operator and of company personnel and in financial terms by the rates charged. The inventiveness and the enterprise of the regional communications administration in introducing new services, upgrading the plant, and improving performance also can be judged.

The above are the most typical but by no means all the tasks that will have to be accomplished to make integration successful. From this list we will select some tasks that may be problems, using as a guide the recent experience of the early stages of the development of the Central American network.

349

PROBLEMS OF INTEGRATION

The Growth of Central Authority

Communications is a service to the community but is an important part of the command and control network of the individual administrations. Integration cannot but relax the control of any one country over its part of the network, and a successful emergence of the administrative central team inevitably leads to most of the decisions being taken by that team. In a politically dynamic environment, this new class of regional decision-makers may not be welcome. In Central America, COMTELCA, the communications central body, so far has only advisory authority, but several administrations hope that, with the passage of time, this authority may be extended to operational matters.

Resource Allocation Among Different Sections of Regional Economy

There is considerable disagreement among experts as to the effectiveness of different development sectors in expanding the growth of national economy. Much depends on the particular conditions in the individual country. It is therefore unreasonable to expect that every country in a region will make a similar percentage allocation of scarce resources for the integrated regional communications. In any case, in many of the countries a large slice of the available investment will be absorbed by the security services. It is therefore evident that Costa Rica may have more to invest in communications than, say, Nicaragua. Figures 3 and 4 illustrate this point and show how the past rates of growth of telephony in some Latin American countries compare with those rates of growth of telephony and GNP of other administrations.[3]

The Ratio Between Bread and Cake

The needs of the domestic network are for more local plant, such as telephones, small end-offices, exchange carrier, or open wire carrier. There is little glamour in the engineering of the local plant, and the results are unspectacular. A wait for a dialing tone may be reduced from 4 minutes to 1 minute by an expenditure of $1 million. Provincial towns may be able to communicate better.

On the other hand, we have the pride in and the glamour of satellites. Also satellites are a spearhead of U.S. technology and one of the few successful fallouts of our defense spending. We need better communications to Latin America. One of the few places that has excess external communication capability is Panama, where a cable was put as a result of the experience with inadequate communication during the Cuban crisis. As an adviser in the development of Latin American communications and as a probable main financial contributor, the United States may mistakenly believe like Marie Antoinette and suggest cake (satellites) rather than bread (local plant).

350

FIGURE 3

GROWTH RATES OF THE INDIVIDUAL ADMINISTRATIONS
IN THE 1951-1966 PERIOD

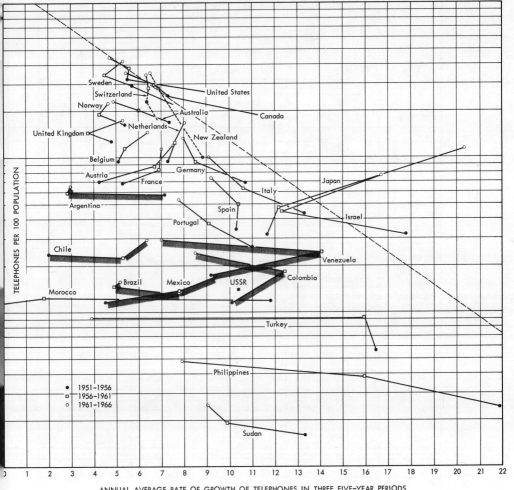

TELEPHONES PER 100 POPULATION

ANNUAL AVERAGE RATE OF GROWTH OF TELEPHONES IN THREE FIVE-YEAR PERIODS

• 1951-1956
□ 1956-1961
○ 1961-1966

FIGURE 4

COMPARISON OF THE GROWTH RATES OF TELEPHONES AND GNP

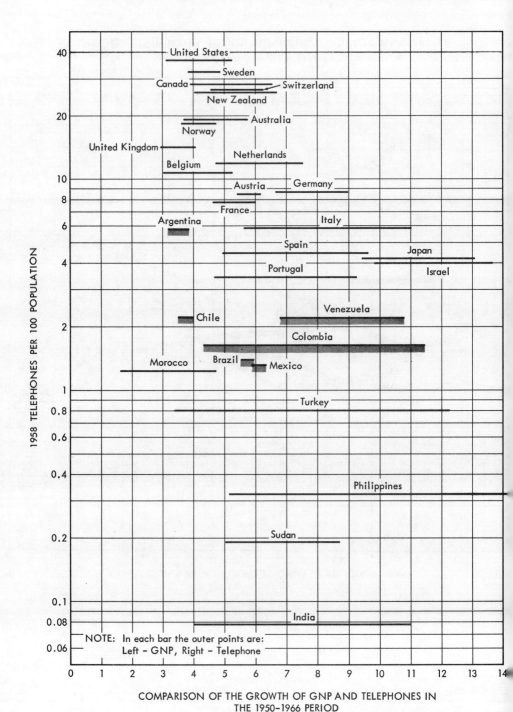

COMPARISON OF THE GROWTH OF GNP AND TELEPHONES IN
THE 1950-1966 PERIOD

Most telephone administrations in the world are well-insulated from the wrath of the dissatisfied telephone customer and force him (at least hypothetically) to overthrow the government as the only means of redressing a grievance for not getting a telephone or for poor quality of service. Or, to put it another way, the issue of communications service is merged with all other issues of confidence in the government — foreign policy, taxes, education, and so forth. Because of this lack of effective feedback, there is a danger in South America that the emphasis may be placed on the spectacular developments (such as intercontinental satellite communications) rather than on the more mundane development of the local network.

Personnel, Management, and Profitability

Deficiencies in management structure are likely to be one of the critical problems that need to be overcome before integration can succeed. Although it is not absolutely necessary, it is highly desirable that the regional network be based on sound and profitable domestic networks. In Latin America, this is far from being the case. We will merely comment on what may be the causes of the present deficiencies — the concept of communications as a government service, a source of employment for civil servants, and a sinecure for political appointees, instead of a concept of self-governing, self-supporting organization. The advocates of the "service" concept point out in its defense that administrations must control communications because of communications' unique importance to the administration and the safety of the state. An additional, and perhaps more compelling argument, is that the allocation of available investment funds cannot be left to the discretion of the general public, which by its desire for a good telephone service may siphon away funds from other national projects that are considered more important by the decision-makers. As an illustration of the possible validity of this argument, in the United Kingdom eight years ago (1961) the structure of domestic communications was changed from the "service" concept to the "agency" concept by the transformation of the Post Office into an autonomous corporation. Service improved, demand boomed, profits rose, and the annual investment level doubled.[4] In the February 1968 budget, however, the U.K. government was forced to cut drastically the proposed expansion of telecommunications plant to help arrest the trade gap. We must therefore be wary of accepting laissez-faire policies, even in the context of a free-wheeling, government-owned authority, as a recipe for instant success. Sooner or later an independent organization of this sort may run up against the problem of national priorities and of investment scarcity.

In Latin America, communications have been an underdog for so long that a change in concept cannot but help. The necessary injection of foreign capital to augment the plant may be conditional on a semi-independent communications administration, otherwise the future revenues (and consequently the loan repayments) will be left in doubt.

Once these fundamental policy decisions are taken, as they have been taken in some Latin American countries (Costa Rica, Colombia, and Venezuela are good examples), improvement in management quality is bound to accompany the new policy. As a result of better management, the domestic network will improve and add revenue support to the regional network.

Technical Manpower

The supply of technical talent may be less of the problem in Latin America than it is in other parts of the world. The experience in Central America is very encouraging. Mexico has a thoroughly modern and efficient administration, and the Costa Rican administrators are also excellent. Whether other telephone administrations can match the success of Mexico's and Costa Rica's administrations may depend on whether they are willing to resolve the underlying basic policy problems.

SUMMARY

A sequence of tasks that must take place in the integration process was described; however, a few of these tasks may prove difficult to achieve in Latin America. Agreement on telecommunications policy, agreement on allocation of resources to communications, and a necessary reformation of communications structure are seen as the prerequisites for a successful integration of Latin American communications.

NOTES

1. Page Communications Engineers, Inc., *Feasibility Study of Space and Terrestrial Telecommunications in South America,* PCE-R-4111-0001 (Washington, D.C., December 1966).

2. Pan American Union, *Final Report of the First Special Meeting of the Inter-American Telecommunications Commission (CITEL), Inter-American Economic and Social Council, OEA/SER, H/XIII CIES/Com X/120* (Washington, D.C., revised November 29, 1967).

3. A. J. Lipinski, "Relative Rates of Growth of Telephone Density in Different Administrations and Their Implication for the Future," IEEE International Conference on Communications, Philadelphia, Pa., 1968.

4. England, Postmaster General, *The Inland Telephone Service in an Expanding Economy,* Comnd. 2211 (London, November 1963).

CHAPTER **27** DEVELOPMENT AND INTEGRATION
OF LATIN AMERICAN
TELECOMMUNICATIONS

By Eitel M. Rizzoni
Page Communications Engineers
Washington, D. C.

INTRODUCTION

Necessary to the realization of economic integration of
Latin America is the ability of the various countries, groups of
interests, and people to communicate with one another rapidly,
reliably, and efficiently. This process is enormously facilitated
by the use of a modern telecommunications network permitting
intercountry, intracontinental and intercontinental communications.

Historically there is an undeniable cause-effect relationship between overall economic growth and telecommunications
development. Correlations between telephone density, national
long-distance calls per capita, international traffic on the one
hand, and economic indices such as gross national product, per
capita income, etc. on the other, have been amply demonstrated.
For example, Figure 1 depicts a least-squares correlation between telephone density and gross national product per capita for
a group of facilitated nations, Latin America, Africa, and Asia.

The Inter-American Development Bank, aware of the
importance of telecommunications and of the insufficiency and
inefficiency of telecommunications in Latin America, early in
1966 embarked on a program of preinvestment studies which
would serve as the basis for the integrated development of Latin
American telecommunications.

This study is a brief report on the work sponsored by
the Inter-American Development Bank and accomplished by Page
Communications Engineers, Inc. , having as its objective the development and integration of telecommunications in Latin America.

SUMMARY OF TASKS

The program of preinvestment studies was divided into
a number of tasks, or phases, which are listed below:

Task 1. Collect pertinent data and carry out a survey
of South American countries to determine the
status of telecommunications, the expressed
needs as well as latent demand, and to develop

355

TELEPHONE DENSITY

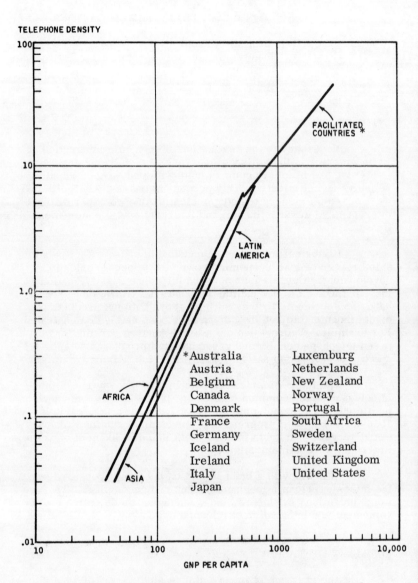

Figure 1. Correlation Between Telephone Density and
Gross National Product (1964)

a telecommunications system plan, technically and economically feasible, which would make use both of terrestrial and satellite facilities.

Task 2. Develop comprehensive technical standards of transmission, automatic switching, numbering, and signaling for the integrated long-distance Inter-American Network (ITN), and lay out its terrestrial and space configuration.

Task 3. Estimate the telecommunications traffic potential arising from economic integration and determine the economic feasibility of the ITN.

Task 4. Study in detail and prepare documentation for implementation of those portions of the ITN that do not exist at present, with a view toward closing the gap and permitting a continuous flow of communications throughout Latin America.

Task 1 was planned and carried out by Page Communications Engineers from April 1966 to March 1967 and resulted in the report "Feasibility Study of Space and Terrestrial Telecommunications in South America," in three volumes and three languages. The report is available from the Inter-American Development Bank.

Task 2 was directed by the Telecommunication Program Management Group (PMG) of the Inter-American Development Bank and executed by Page Communications Engineers from July 1967 to November 1967.

Task 3 was performed by Page under the direction of the PMG and completed in 1968.

Finally, Task 4 is directed by the Telecommunication Program Management Group of the IDB and is being carried out, with the co-operation of ITU, by telecommunication consulting firms and counterpart personnel of Latin American telecommunication organizations. This phase began in 1968, for completion in 1969.

While Tasks 1, 2, and 3 were funded entirely by the IDB, Task 4 was funded jointly by the United Nations Development Program (UNDP), the IDB and individual countries concerned. The IDB acts as executing agency, administering the funds.

DESCRIPTION AND RESULTS OF TASK 1, "FEASIBILITY
STUDY OF SPACE AND TERRESTRIAL TELECOMMUNICA-
TIONS IN SOUTH AMERICA"

Survey

A study of existing and future telecommunications facilities was conducted in 1966 in Argentina, Bolivia, Brazil, Chile,
Colombia, Ecuador, Peru, Paraguay, Uruguay, and Venezuela.

The technical, financial and managerial situation of the
telecommunication organizations in the ten countries was assessed
and a broad-gauge, ten-year technical and economic fundamental
plan was developed for each country. In addition, a system plan
for satellite communications in South America was evolved.

This information enables the Bank to determine preliminary loan feasibility for future telecommunication projects, both
terrestrial and by satellite, in the ten South American countries.
Central American countries were not included in the study as
earlier surveys and feasibility work had been completed under
the auspices of the World Bank. The principal results and recommendations derived from the IDB feasibility study are described
below.

The status of telecommunication was found to be as
follows:

a. The demand for domestic and international telephone
service has been largely unfulfilled. As an example,
Figure 2 shows the expressed unsatisfied demand
for telephone service.

b. For the level of economic achievement expressed
in terms of per capita gross national product, Latin
America as a continent appears to fall behind in telecommunications development, as shown in Figure 1.
Figure 3 depicts the relative position of each country within the continent.

c. Revenues derived from domestic-rate tariffs are
inadequate to make the enterprise self-sustaining,
to say nothing about capital required for expansion.
In general, frequent tariff revisions failed to catch
up with chronic inflation and rising expenditures due
to rising costs and overstaffing. The overall tariff
level and structure for local service was in many
cases found to be so low as to render local plants
either operating at a loss or yielding a rate of return
lower than prescribed by law. The long-distance
telephone rates were found generally comparable to
those in Europe and North America. International
rates are formulated according to rule by the International Telecommunications Union.

358

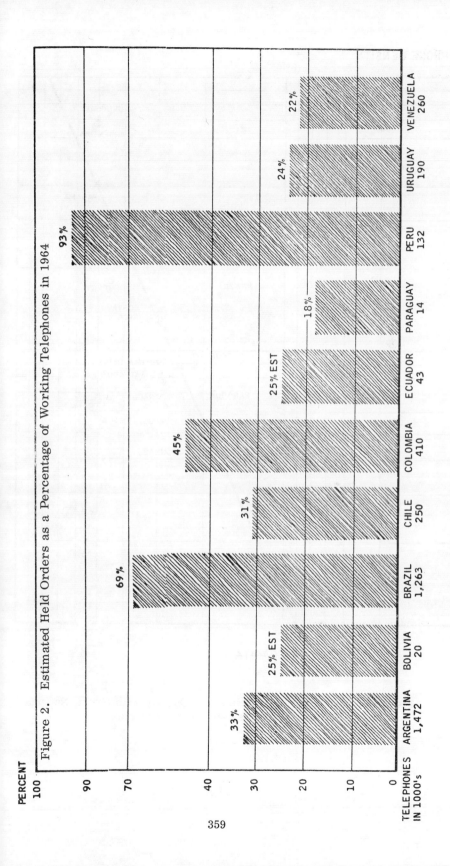

Figure 2. Estimated Held Orders as a Percentage of Working Telephones in 1964

TELEPHONE DENSITY

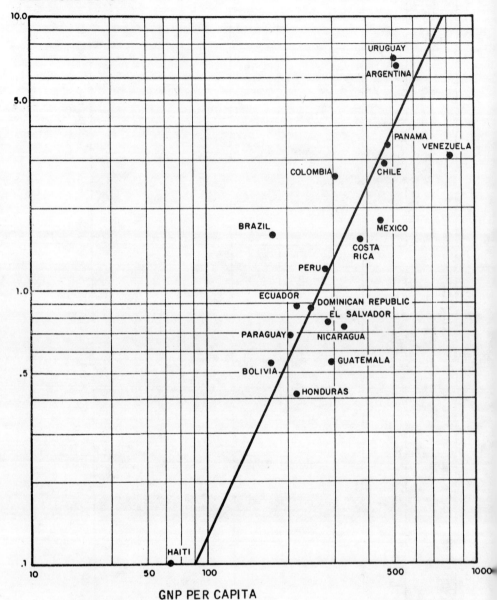

GNP PER CAPITA

Figure 3.   Correlation of Telephone Density with Gross National
Product for Latin American Countries

d.   The telecommunications organization is too often
      under political influence, is not business-and service-
      oriented, and lacks sufficient well-trained employees.

e.   The overall investment expenditure has been inade-
      quate.

To remedy the above situation, the following steps were
proposed in the report:

a.   Clear the held orders situation for local telephones.

b.   Develop short-term and long-term economic and
      technical plans and accordingly provide local cen-
      tral office plant, outside plant, and long-distance
      plant, and give service within accepted standards.

c.   Modernize the existing plants and methods of opera-
      tion with a view toward eventual attainment of direct
      distance dialing.

d.   Co-ordinate transmission plans, maintenance prac-
      tices, rates and routing among the various countries.

e.   Implement earth stations, where economically fea-
      sible, to permit international high-quality commu-
      nication in sufficient volume. The early implemen-
      tation of satellite facilities in Latin America is par-
      ticularly significant, since it will make it possible
      to meet long-standing demand without waiting the
      full (and slow) implementation of the terrestrial
      intracontinental network.

f.   Restructure internal telecommunications organiza-
      tions on a nonpolitical public-corporation basis and
      revise rates and tariffs with a view toward self-
      liquidity.

It may now be interesting to look in some detail into two
aspects of the study, namely, the satellite communications plan
and the telecommunications investments and financing arrangements.

Satellite Communications Plan

The advent of satellite communications truly provides a
new dimension to both intracontinental and overseas communications for South America. A preliminary assessment was made
in the study as to the technical possibility and economic feasibility
of an earth station using a stationary satellite, in each of the ten
countries.

The quantitative results arrived at in this study can serve as an estimate of the order of magnitude for decision-making purposes. A pro forma income and expense profile was prepared, for each nation, for the period of 1969-1978, inclusive. Conservative assumptions were used throughout, as documented in Volume III, Annex I of the report, and each nation was treated as an isolated case without any one assuming the role of regional communication center. Intra-South American traffic involving Bolivia, Ecuador, Paraguay, and Uruguay was excluded, and so was across-the-border-traffic which can be handled with conventional means. Furthermore, only incremental overseas record traffic from 1968 was assumed to be served by satellite in order to avoid disruption of existing arrangements. Intra-South American record traffic and the potential television relay capability were also excluded as revenue source of the proposed earth stations.

The analysis indicates that the installation of earth stations in Argentina, Brazil, Chile, Colombia, Peru, Uruguay, and Venezuela would be profitable, while the profitability of earth stations in Paraguay, Ecuador, and Bolivia would appear to be somewhat doubtful within the study period, under the assumptions chosen.

The present worth (using a nominal discount rate of 6% per annum and expressed in 1967 U. S. dollars) of the cumulative annual surpluses or losses (gross revenue net of national terrestrial connecting costs, space segment charges, loan repayment, and operating and maintenance expenses) was computed. A graphic presentation is given in Figure 4 which summarizes the overall and relative profitability of each country in each year over the study period.

Based on the economic viability of seven earth stations in South America, the proposed South American Satellite Network, to complement and integrate with the terrestrial Inter-American Network, is shown on Figure 5.

The establishment of this satellite communications system neither competes with nor excludes the necessity for the development of the Inter-American Telecommunication Network (ITN). Indeed, these two systems complement each other. Both require long-distance domestic networks and urban telephone facilities that are efficient and adequate, if they are to be economically justified. Satellite communications will make available high-quality intracontinental facilities in sufficient quantity and at reasonable cost without the need for awaiting full implementation of the international interconnections of ITN and will accelerate the development of internal networks of telephone, telegraph, and television programs.

Satellite and terrestrial networks envisioned in the study are summarized in Table I.

362

Table I

Country	Intra-Continental 1968-1976	Inter-Continental 1968-1971	Inter-Continental 1971-1976
Argentina	HF Radio Radio Relay Satellite	HF Radio Satellite	HF Radio Satellite
Bolivia	HF Radio Radio Relay Radio Relay to Satellite*	HF Radio	HF Radio Radio Relay to Satellite*
Brazil	HF Radio Radio Relay Satellite	HF Radio Satellite	HF Radio Satellite
Chile	HF Radio Radio Relay Satellite	HF Radio Satellite	HF Radio Satellite
Colombia	HF Radio Radio Relay Satellite	HF Radio Satellite	HF Radio Satellite

Country	Intra Continental 1968-1976	Inter-Continental 1968-1971	Inter-Continental 1971-1976
Ecuador	HF Radio Radio Relay to Satellite†	HF Radio Radio Relay to Satellite†	HF Radio Radio Relay to Satellite†
Paraguay	HF Radio Radio Relay (Satellite)‡	HF Radio	HF Radio (Satellite)‡
Peru	HF Radio Radio Relay	HF Radio Satellite	HF Radio Satellite
Uruguay	HF Radio Radio Relay Satellite	HF Radio Satellite	HF Radio Satellite
Venezuela	HF Radio Radio Relay Satellite	HF Radio Satellite Undersea Cable	HF Radio Satellite Undersea Cable

* Peruvian ground station

† Colombian ground station

‡ Based on the possibility that an earth station in Paraguay will eventually be feasible as a regional communication center in that land-locked area. If Paraguay is considered as a hub for the development of regional telecommunications integration for the region covering neighboring cities of Argentina, Bolivia and Brazil, the Paraguayan earth station may be justified.

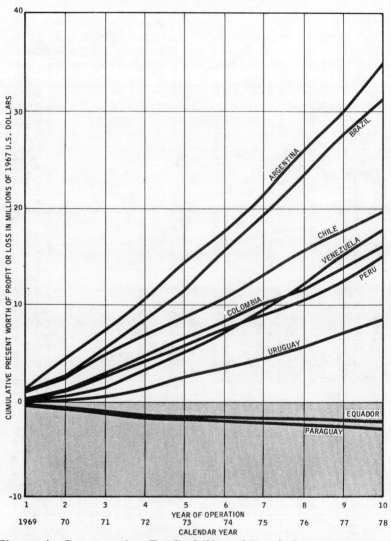

Figure 4. Comparative Profitability of Earth Stations in
South America

364

Figure 5.   Proposed South American Satellite Network 1968-1976

Telecommunications Investment and Financing Arrangements

Capital expenditures for domestic telecommunications plant improvements and expansion in the next decade, based on forecast requirements and evaluated according to each country's individual needs, are summarized and tabulated below in millions of U.S. dollars in Table II.

Additions to physical plant, in terms of telephone additions for the periods 1965-1968, 1968-1976, and the sum total for the next decade, as well as corresponding proposed investments involved for each country, are depicted in Figure 6. In addition, the capital requirement for earth station implementation will be on the order of $50 million for the continent, bringing the total to nearly $2.7 billion. Considering the existing manufacturing capabilities of Argentina, Brazil, Chile, and Mexico, it is estimated that between 80 per cent and 90 per cent of the total required equipment can be manufactured in South America with the assistance of the South American capital market. This would limit the foreign exchange requirement to approximately $300 million to $500 million, primarily for the import of high-capacity microwave equipment, telegraph and voice multiplex, toll switching systems and other specialized materials or equipment, particularly those needed for earth station implementation.

While the cost of additions for each country was evaluated according to individual need, the proposed share in the total investment conforms to the existing distribution pattern of the economic and investment resources in South America. Furthermore, the grand total for the next decade was found to be quite reasonable, if not modest, in view of the neglect and deterioration of facilities in the recent past experience of other countries in varying stages of telecommunication development. Figures 7 and 8 compare the distribution of proposed telecommunication investment with the distribution of gross national product and investment resources, respectively, in South America. The two graphs suggest that the investment share proposed conforms closely to the existing distribution pattern of the economic and investment resources in the continent. The proposed investment per telephone addition is on the order of $560 as shown in Figure 6, which also falls within the range of the historical cost under divergent conditions.

The overall capital need for communication expansion and improvement as recommended in this report is of such a magnitude that a bold and imaginative approach to this problem is necessary. There is a need for certain integration of the capital markets in financing the domestic manufacturing, and for the leading international lending institutions in financing foreign exchange requirements.

The Inter-American Development Bank is in a unique position to finance and co-ordinate the overall activities of international and national bodies concerned with the planning and execution of Latin American telecommunications.

366

Table II

Nation	Proposed Telecommunications Investment				Gross National Product (1964)		Gross Capital Formation (1964)	
	Long Distance	Local Service	Total	Percent of Total	Million Dollars	Percent of Total	Million Dollars	Percent of Total
Argentina	90	587	677	25.8	11,160	23.2	2,455	28.7
Bolivia	19	18	37	1.4	717	1.5	79	0.9
Brazil	200	700	900	34.3	14,100	29.4	1,974	23.2
Chile	36	186	222	8.4	3,920	8.2	470	5.5
Columbia	50	164	214	8.1	5,065	10.6	962	11.2
Ecuador	7	34	41	1.6	1,032	2.1	206	2.4
Paraguay	4	9	13	0.5	394	0.8	63	0.7
Peru	35	163	198	7.6	3,166	6.6	728	8.5
Uruguay	9	71	80	3.1	1,390	2.9	208	2.4
Venezuela	60	180	240	9.2	7,070	14.7	1,414	16.5
Total	510	2,112	2,622	100.0	48,014	100.0	8,560	100.0

367

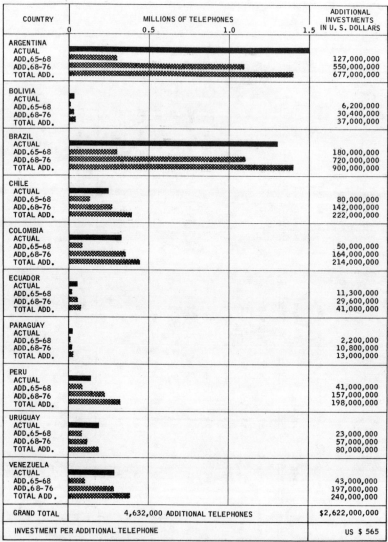

COUNTRY	MILLIONS OF TELEPHONES			ADDITIONAL INVESTMENTS IN U. S. DOLLARS
	0 0.5	1.0	1.5	
ARGENTINA ACTUAL				
ADD.65-68				127,000,000
ADD.68-76				550,000,000
TOTAL ADD.				677,000,000
BOLIVIA ACTUAL				
ADD.65-68				6,200,000
ADD.68-76				30,400,000
TOTAL ADD.				37,000,000
BRAZIL ACTUAL				
ADD.65-68				180,000,000
ADD.68-76				720,000,000
TOTAL ADD.				900,000,000
CHILE ACTUAL				
ADD.65-68				80,000,000
ADD.68-76				142,000,000
TOTAL ADD.				222,000,000
COLOMBIA ACTUAL				
ADD.65-68				50,000,000
ADD.68-76				164,000,000
TOTAL ADD.				214,000,000
ECUADOR ACTUAL				
ADD.65-68				11,300,000
ADD.68-76				29,600,000
TOTAL ADD.				41,000,000
PARAGUAY ACTUAL				
ADD.65-68				2,200,000
ADD.68-76				10,800,000
TOTAL ADD.				13,000,000
PERU ACTUAL				
ADD.65-68				41,000,000
ADD.68-76				157,000,000
TOTAL ADD.				198,000,000
URUGUAY ACTUAL				
ADD.65-68				23,000,000
ADD.68-76				57,000,000
TOTAL ADD.				80,000,000
VENEZUELA ACTUAL				
ADD.65-68				43,000,000
ADD.68-76				197,000,000
TOTAL ADD.				240,000,000
GRAND TOTAL	4,632,000 ADDITIONAL TELEPHONES			$2,622,000,000
INVESTMENT PER ADDITIONAL TELEPHONE				US $ 565

Figure 6. Proposed Investments and Plant Additions

368

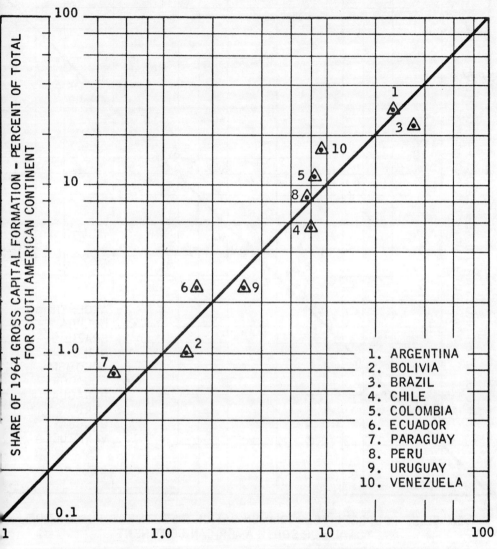

Figure 7. Share of GNP vs Share of Proposed Investment

369

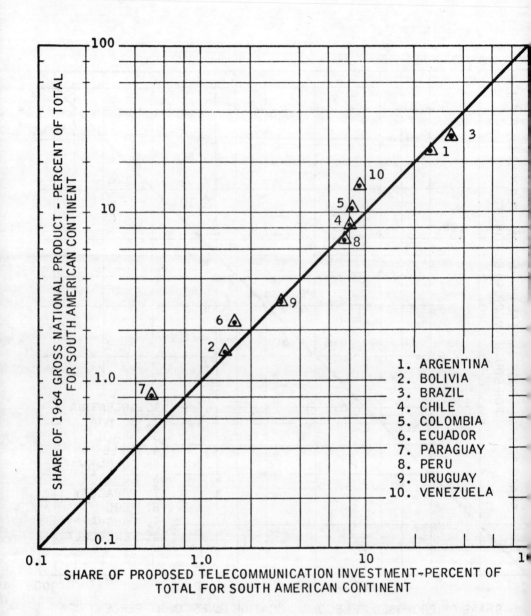

Figure 8. Share of GCF vs Share of Proposed Investment

370

The long-term goal should be the achievement, on the part of the communication enterprises, of self-liquidity, and the capability of generating sufficient internal reserves and of yielding a competitive return that will attract local capital for further expansion.

DESCRIPTION AND RESULTS OF TASK 2, "TECHNICAL STANDARDS AND CONFIGURATION OF THE INTER-AMERICAN TELECOMMUNICATIONS NETWORK"

Technical Standards

The design and implementation of an integrated intracontinental telecommunication network must of necessity be based on a set of common technical standards. Accordingly, the second task of the IDB preinvestment studies included the development of technical system specifications and standards which all the Latin American nations would adopt in planning the ITN.

The Inter-American Telecommunications Network is made up of individual sections, owned and controlled by administrations in the countries of Latin America, but designed to operate as an integrated and fully co-ordinated network. The function of the ITN is to carry international telephone, telegraph, telex, television, and data traffic between the countries of Latin America and between these countries and the rest of the world. In effect, the ITN is a large integrated regional network and as such is part of a world-wide network of telecommunications.

The standards were prepared in the second half of 1967 and presented to the CITEL (Inter-American Telecommunications Commission), which is made up of government experts of the member states of OAS, at a meeting held in Mexico City in October 1967.

Technical standards and recommendations were developed for numbering, switching, signaling, and transmission. The description of these standards, a rather detailed work, can be found in the report, "Inter-American Telecommunications Network - IDB, October 1967" and will not be dealt with here. However, it may be of interest to note that adoption of these standards will eventually permit subscriber dialing from any telephone in Latin America to any other telephone in Latin America or elsewhere in the world connected to the world-wide network. Initially, the Network will permit manual and, later, semiautomatic operations; ultimately, fully automatic operation of the switching network, designed on the economic principle of alternate routing, will be achieved. A modern and efficient signaling system will allow rapid connections to made between all switching centers.

Finally, the adoption of the comprehensive transmission plan will assure satisfactory quality of transmission on any connection, regardless of the route followed, i.e., terrestrial, satellite, or a number of circuits switched together in tandem.

ITN Configuration

The configuration of the ITN can be defined by: the location of the international switching centers; their designation as CT2's or CT3's in the hierarchy of switching centers; the routes between the switching centers; and, an indication of the "size" of these routes in terms of the number of circuits carried.

Within the last few years, the extension of submarine cable systems to Central and South America and the construction of new microwave systems and switching centers in Latin America, either in progress or planned, has affected the configuration of the ITN. However, the most important new influence, one which will profoundly affect the configuration, is the use of satellite links. Earth stations are under construction in Panama, Chile, Brazil, Mexico, Argentina, and Peru. It is expected that earth stations will be implemented in the near future in Venezuela and Colombia. Other countries will follow later on. Communications can be established from these ground stations and through a satellite to points in North America and Europe and later on to Africa where other ground stations are located. Terrestrial extensions make it possible to provide circuits between many points.

Prior to the availability of satellite circuits, it was necessary as a practical matter to depend on HF circuits for communications to and from many points in Latin America. The most important effect of satellites in Latin America will be the availability of an alternative to HF circuits and their limitations. Transmission over satellite circuits is comparable to that obtainable from the better grades of cable and microwave radio systems. Large numbers of high grade channels can be provided. As a consequence of these characteristics, heavy traffic requirements can be met with a good grade of service. Growth in traffic need not be throttled by inability to increase the number of circuits or discouraged by poor transmission quality. The satellite channels are suitable for a full range of services —telephone, telegraph, data, television, etc. — and they have the same potential for handling future new services as do terrestrial systems. The superior transmission characteristics also make it practical to meet the technical requirements of semiautomatic and automatic operation.

The net effect of these factors is to open up the possibility of using more direct-circuit groups among Latin American countries and between Latin American and other countries of the world. This in turn will affect traffic routing patterns and in particular will reduce the volume of traffic which has to be switched at intermediate points.

Satellite channels have a unique characteristic in that the cost of the channel is independent of the distance spanned. This fact makes it possible for a circuit group which cannot be justified on economic grounds over a terrestrial path to be justified over a satellite path. It should be mentioned that a group of channels, or frequency band, transmitted from a satellite is accessible for reception at all ground stations. This broadcasting characteristic of a satellite system opens up future modes of operation quite different from the point-to-point method. For example, a group of channels from a given ground station could be caused to terminate at different distant earth stations by activating receivers, transmitters, and multiplex equipment on a time-sharing basis. This and other arrangements, currently being explored by the many parties concerned with the needs of developing countries, will represent future operating modes of satellites.

One characteristic of a channel through a stationary satellite is that there is a long transmission delay from one ground station through the satellite to another ground station because of the great distance (23,000 miles) of the satellite from the earth. This delay amounts to about 0.3 seconds for one-way transmission and would be 0.6 seconds for two satellite links in tandem. Although these delays might seem small, a definite impairment of transmission is produced because of the subjective effect of the delay on a two-way conversation and an enhancement of the probability of clipping and lock-out of speech due to action of the echo suppressors which must be employed on these long-delay circuits. After consideration of the results of tests of these impairments, committees of the CCITT have recommended that two satellite links should not be used in tandem except under conditions of dire necessity. This restriction has an effect on routing plans and affects the configuration of the network.

The Inter-American Telecommunications Network consists of international transit centers of two categories, designated CT2's and CT3's, and a fabric of international circuits routed between the transit centers.

The configuration is depicted on Figure 9 which shows:

a. The international switching centers, denominated CT's (transit centers) and located in each capital.

b. The proposed terrestrial route of high capacity (in part existing).

c. The proposed terrestrial route of medium capacity (in part existing).

d. The existing telephone submarine cables.

e. The eight earth stations presently under construction.

373

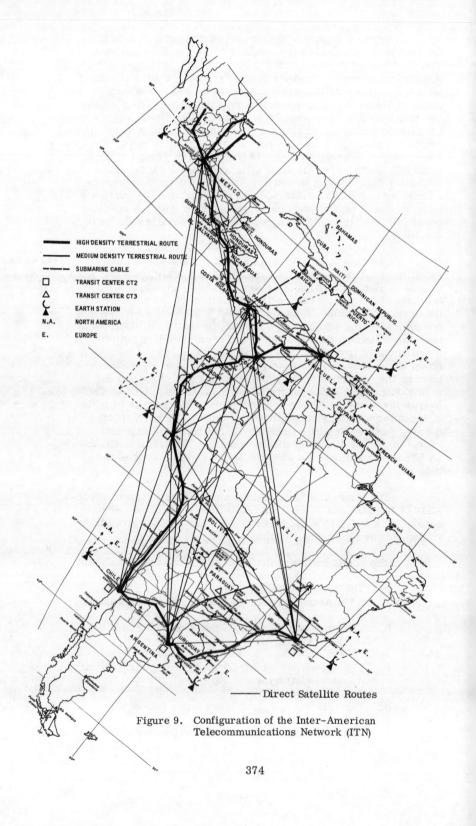

Figure 9. Configuration of the Inter–American
Telecommunications Network (ITN)

374

f.   The possible direct space routes between the earth
      stations.

It is not expected that all earth stations will be connected
together by direct circuits; nevertheless, the map shows all possible satellite links in order to emphasize the great flexibility and
availability of high-capacity direct routes which satellite communication opens up in Latin America.

It is to be noted that the terrestrial system is not yet
continuous as depicted on the map. There exist several important gaps which will be considered in Task 4.

The "size" of the routes shown on the map will vary as
a function of the traffic requirements in each cross section. These
requirements go from a few channels to hundreds of channels and
video bandwidths. This is no problem, however, as the facilities
planned for the main trunks of the ITN are all of the wide-band
type, capable of transmitting video programs and many hundreds
of telephone and data channels. The "size" of the routes is still
under study and will be finalized after completion of Task 3,
described below.

DESCRIPTION OF TASK 3, "ECONOMIC FEASIBILITY OF THE
ITN"

Introduction

Task 3 of the preinvestment studies, presently underway,
deals with the following:

a.   The telecommunication traffic potential resulting
      from economic integration.

b.   The economic viability of the ITN, based on the
      traffic forecast and the configuration of the net-
      work.

Traffic Potential Forecast

Two approaches are being used to forecast traffic.

The first is based on information about existing intra-
Latin American and inter-continental traffic (telephone, telegraph,
telex) obtained from the Latin American telecommunications
administrations and on forecasts of traffic engineering and plant
extension carried out with the aid of traditional methods. However, forecasts based essentially on existing traffic are by
nature incomplete since existing traffic in Latin America is
limited by inadequate facilities rather than by demand. Moreover, there is obviously no traffic where facilities are unavail-
able, although potential demand may exist.

375

The second approach correlates potential traffic to economic indices and their growth. This methodology introduces a sound foundation to what would otherwise be speculation based on historical traffic trends.

In looking, then, at Latin America, its economic activities and the trends of economic growth, we notice that there are two major regional economic groups. The first is the Central American Republics Common Market (CACM). The second is the Latin American Free Trade Association (LAFTA) consisting of almost all of the republics of South America.

A close parallel to this economic configuration is that of the European Common Market of six countries and the European Free Trade Area (EFTA). Our attempt is to correlate telephone, telegraph, and telex traffic patterns with the trade pattern generated by such economic integration and to apply this model to the intraregional traffic of the CACM and LAFTA. As far as intercontinental traffic is concerned, we apply the traffic vs. trade model across the Atlantic basin (i.e., between the U.S. and Western European countries) to the current and projected economic ties between Latin America and North America/Europe. This is not to say that trade alone generates telecommunications traffic. But, rather, it serves a very useful guide in developing traffic volume potential in relation to the direction and volume of trade if services of acceptable quality and at reasonable charges were made available.

Economic Viability

After the traffic volume has been established, the configuration of the ITN can then be finalized to meet the requirements. Here, we are confronted with the problem of traffic routing with the aim of channelling it by the 'least cost' means, especially with regard to terrestrial vs. space communications. Revenue requirements to support the proposed network will be obtained, and appropriate rate level will be recommended. The existing tariff of various countries will be examined and necessary modifications will be noted.

The economic feasibility of the overall ITN system will serve as the fundamental economic justification of the individual segments of border-crossing links. This work constitutes Task 4, described below.

DESCRIPTION OF TASK 4, FEASIBILITY STUDIES OF LINKS CONNECTING BORDERING COUNTRIES

Existing Connections

The existing portions of radio-relay and coaxial cable systems along the route of the ITN are shown in Figure 10 in solid

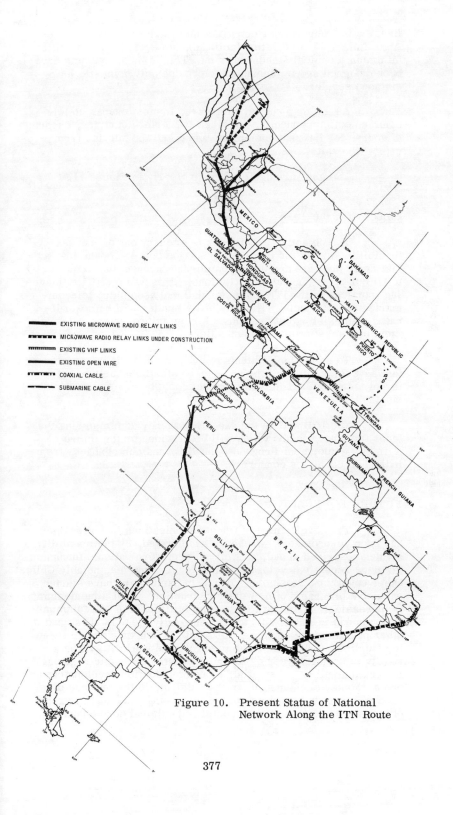

Figure 10.   Present Status of National
Network Along the ITN Route

lines. The routes under construction are shown in dotted lines.
A good many of the existing facilities, however, do not meet the
minimum technical standards of the ITN, as these systems have
been designed and implemented to provide only domestic long-
distance service.

As the map shows, there are, in most cases, no telecommunication connections between bordering countries, except
of course for HF radio-telephone and telegraph service from
capital to capital.

The gaps are depicted more clearly in Figure 11.

Objective of the Task

The objective of this task is to carry out the necessary
feasibility studies for the interconnection between countries, so
that these projects may be accomplished through loan requests
to IDB or other financing institutions. This will facilitate financing portions of the ITN and other national associated telecommunications projects. The feasibility studies will be co-ordinated with existing national plans for the improvement and development of domestic telecommunications.

To solve the problems of such urgency, it is expected
that several studies will be undertaken simultaneously by different teams so that the total project could be completed in nine
months.

The IDB will be the executing agency administering the
funds for these studies which will be provided by the United
Nations Development Program, the IDB, and contributions from
individual countries concerned.

FUTURE FORECAST

The development of telecommunications in Latin America
has been co-ordinated, and hence accelerated, by the feasibility
studies described above, as well as by modern national fundamental plans recently developed by individual countries, notably Chile.
Other countries, Mexico and Brazil in particular, have started
extensive programs of network construction. That a momentum
is increasingly mounting towards the fulfillment of telecommunication needs in Latin America is abundantly clear by these and
other parallel developments. It is not any longer a dream today
to visualize a Latin American integrated network: it will be a
reality in very few years. Its impact on the economic regional
integration will be substantial, as communication development is
one of the key elements, if not the catalyst, in the process of
economic growth and in its role of furthering pressing programs
of mass education as well as social and cultural developments.

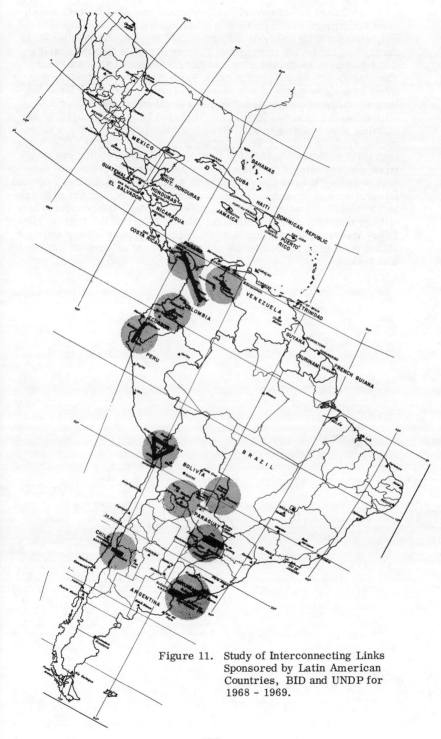

Figure 11.   Study of Interconnecting Links
Sponsored by Latin American
Countries, BID and UNDP for
1968 - 1969.

There is, however, one important and obvious task which must be carried out to further telecommunications development and, concurrently, elevate the industrial level of the region. It is the task of achieving integration and expansion of telecommunication equipment manufacturing and distribution in Latin America. The Page study of ten countries in South America estimated that about $2 billion worth of telephone, telegraph, and telex local and long-distance equipment, out of the capital requirement of $2.7 billion for the next ten years, could indeed be manufactured in the existing plants of Argentina, Brazil, Chile, and Mexico. A more recent study of the Northrop Corporation estimates the Latin American total potential market for telecommunication equipment of all types and associated technical services at over $7 billion in the next decade. It is obvious that, with a market of this size, regional integration and expansion of telecommunication equipment manufacturing and distribution must be achieved and will tremendously benefit the economy and the industrialization effort of the region. The Inter-American Development Bank, again, appears a very well-suited vehicle to stimulate the accomplishment of such an important task.

CHAPTER **28** AN EDUCATIONAL TELEVISION
AND COMMUNICATIONS SYSTEM
FOR LATIN AMERICA

By Jorge Heraud and José Pomalaza
Instituto Geofísico del Perú

INTRODUCTION

The purpose of the ASCEND study (Advanced System for
Communications and Education in National Development) prepared
at Stanford University, was to show that communication satellite
technology has advanced to such a degree that its application to
the problems of national development will provide novel and significant solutions to these problems. It was found that, in the
case of developing nations, these solutions can drastically alter
the whole concept of communications in general, and education in
particular.

It was also found that it is economically feasible to provide communications and educational television on a nationwide
basis, thus attacking two of the most urgent problems faced by
the developing nations:

1. Lack of suitable communications network.

2. Inadequate educational system and high illiteracy
ratio.

In the field of education, television can make the best
teachers in the country available to the majority of the population.
When used within the framework of the existing system, it can
effectively supplement classes presenting new points of view and
material unattainable otherwise, particularly in the sciences,
geography, and art at both primary and secondary levels. Television can also be used as a new information source and focal
point for community development through adult education, training
in agriculture, health and civics, specialized jobs, and literacy.
Perhaps its greatest impact would be in the training of teachers
after school hours. Also, time could be reserved for transmitting commercial TV programs directly to school or to home
receivers for entertainment and news coverage.

In the field of communications, the satellite system is
not only the least expensive means of providing high capacity communications, but, in some regions, it is perhaps the only way to
do it. Also, implementation time is short compared to other networks and it has the added advantage of being flexible enough to
allow multiple solutions to the problem of bandwidth allocation.

During the night time, the capacity can be greatly increased by devoting the ETV channels to the communications mode, thus providing more channels for data, facsimile, and telegram transmission, as well as TV.

A significant advantage of including a communications capability in the proposed ETV system is that it could become a major source of revenue.

The ASCEND study was made specifically for three countries, Brazil, India, and Indonesia. The purpose of this report is to briefly apply ASCEND to the other Latin American countries.

TECHNICAL DESCRIPTION AND COST OF THE ASCEND SYSTEM

One of the major conclusions arrived at in the ASCEND study was that in order to transmit educational television programs to the majority of the population in developing countries, it is necessary to provide both direct broadcast from a powerful satellite to low cost ground stations, and rebroadcast of television programs from a central station to standard VHF receivers. The high power capability needed for ETV was achieved by designing the ASCEND spacecraft using state of the art technology and some devices still in the experimental and development stages. However, the satellite is expected to be well within the advanced technology available by the early 1970's. Table I gives the principal features of the spacecraft.

For the ETV system, two modes of program distribution are used: direct broadcast to low-cost receiving stations, and rebroadcast through local retransmitting stations. The type of mode used in a particular location depends on its population density. Studies have shown that with the ASCEND cost estimates this breakpoint occurs for cities with a population over 200,000. In those cities where rebroadcast is economical, ETV programs are rebroadcast by local VHF transmitters and received by conventional TV sets. The cost estimates for this mode of distribution are as follows:

Rebroadcast station:

Production cost	$ 200,000
Research and Development (R and D)	$ 250,000

Conventional receiver:

21" black and white TV set and installation	$ 100

TABLE I

ASCEND Spacecraft Specifications[1]

Orbit:	Synchronous
Launch:	Atlas–Agena launch vehicle
Lifetime:	Five years
Projected date of launch:	1975

Attitude Control:
Antenna aiming:	0.1 degree accuracy
Control system:	Interferometer and Earth sensors
Stabilization:	Spin stabilized in pitch axis and ion thrusters for roll and yaw axes.

Power source:
Solar panels:	Two 2.10 x 9.0m, flexible rolled up for launch. Dendritic solar cells.
Total DC power:	2.5 kw.

Communications:
Radiated power:	Three 350 watts channels
Transmitter:	Three high efficiency TWT's
Down link:	3.7 to 4.2 GHz, FM modulation
Up link:	6 GHz multiple access capability
Antenna:	Despun parabolic.

Cost:
R and D	$ 63,645,000
Satellite, 1 spare and launching:	$ 23,742,000

The central station where ETV programs will be originated and transmitted to the satellite will cost approximately $3.1
million. This will include: transmitter, 25' antenna, two program studios, and telemetry equipment for control of the satellite.
The cost of R and D is estimated at $1 million.

For the down-link frequency modulation (FM) was chosen,
since this permits an improvement of about 15 dB in signal-to-
noise ratio. The frequency band is centered around 4 GHz. In
direct broadcast areas, the low-cost ground receivers would
consist of a microwave adapter that translates the signal to the
VHF band and provides demodulation to convert the video signal
into a standard AM-VHF signal, and a conventional black and
white TV set. The design specifications for the direct broadcast
adapter are as follows:

Input:	Frequency modulated micro- wave carrier
Bandwidth:	60 MHz (effective bandwidth for one ETV channel: 30 MHz)
Noise figure:	7 dB maximum
Output:	Standard amplitude modulated VHF carrier
Freq. spectrum:	Standard video channel plus audio

The direct broadcast receiver cost is estimated on the
basis of a total production of over 100,000 sets. The total cost
for a 6' parabolic antenna, microwave converter, 21" transis-
torized set and power supply is $ 378, including transportation
and installation.[1] The cost of R and D is estimated at an extra
$1.1 million.

The annual operating costs were estimated considering
a 10-year period and taking the average of the total costs over
this period. Maintenance expenses were considered to be 10% of
the production cost. These estimates are as follows:

Launch and satellite (5 year lifetime)	US$ 5,144,000.00
Direct broadcast receiver	65.60
Central station (where ETV programs are originated)	976,000.00
Rebroadcast stations	20,000.00
Conventional TV receiver	20.00

For communications, each of the three 350-watt transmitters in the satellite is able to handle up to 166 MHz of bandwidth, permitting the transmission of five low power channels of
30 MHz bandwidth each. Since each of these five can accomodate
600 one-way telephone circuits, the capacity of each transmitter
is 3,000 one-way telephone circuits, or five low power TV channels, or any combination of the two. The total capacity of the
satellite is 9,000 one-way telephone circuits, as depicted in Fig.
I. The satellite will be provided with both multiple access and

frequency translation capabilities, permitting point-to-point communications between any two terminals as well as high capacity channels (for TV distribution for instance) from any one terminal to all the other terminals simultaneously. High capacity fixed links would use FM frequency division multiplex on the up-link, while smaller stations and those requiring multiple access would use high power AM-SSB on the up-link and allow the satellite to assemble these transmissions into 600 channel FM signals for the down-link. The communication terminal will be more sophisticated than the ETV receivers. The cost of a 15' antenna, parametric amplifier, 30 MHz phase lock demodulator, multiplex equipment and power amplifier has been estimated at $ 30,000.[1]

OTHER SATELLITE ALTERNATIVES

The International Satellite Consortium has plans to start design and production of its largest communication satellite, named Intelsat IV which would have a capacity up to 8,000 circuits and a radiated power of about one-third that of the ASCEND satellite.[8] There is no schedule yet for delivery of Intelsat IV; however, the 1971-73 period is often mentioned as an approximate date. It is worth mentioning that the intended coverage would be the entire Earth; hence, an actual increase in effective radiated power (ERP) would be achieved if the antenna pattern is modified to circumscribe a particular country or region for domestic use. This is reflected in Table II which compares the capabilities of an ASCEND satellite with an Intelsat IV satellite under the following assumptions:

a. Radiated power for Intelsat IV is one third that of ASCEND.

b. The capability of the ASCEND satellite for Brazil as described in the ASCEND report is considered as unity. This means an effective radiated power of 52.8 dBW which would give a signal-to-noise ratio of 43.2 dB at beam edge (or a grade 1 picture) using a 6' parabolic antenna and a 7 dB noise figure receiver.

TABLE II

Coverage	-3dB beamwidth from synchronous altitude	ASCEND	Intelsat IV
Earth (hemisphere)	19.2° by 19.2°	0.0168	0.0056
Brazil	7.16° by 7.16°	1	0.33
Venezuela, Colombia, Ecuador, Peru, Bolivia	6.3° by 4.2°	1.95	0.65
Peru	3° by 2.7°	6.35	2.11

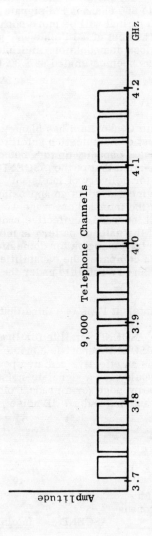

FIG. I-A   Spectrum for Satellite Used Entirely for Communications

Fifteen 30 MHz channels. Each can carry 600
one-way voice channels or one TV channel.

3.2 MHz guard bands between channels.

2.6 MHz guard bands at top and bottom of bands.

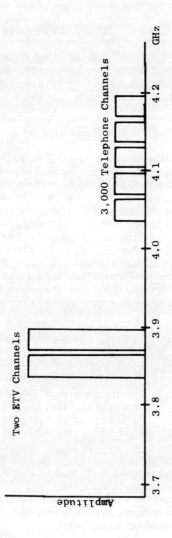

FIG. I-B   Spectrum for Satellite Used for ETV and Communications

Two high power 30 MHz channels for ETV.

Five communications channels each capable
of 600 one-way voice channels or one TV channel.

387

It is not known at this time what arrangements could be made to use the Intelsat IV satellite or what the costs involved might be, but a significant reduction in overall cost (especially Research and Development) could be achieved by using an already developed satellite. It is possible that only the electronics and antenna would have to be replaced to meet the specifications of the ETV and communications system.

The cost for a modified Intelsat IV was estimated to be:

	Cost (US$)
R and D of the modified Intelsat IV	24,850,000
Production cost of satellite and launching	13,440,000
Annual operation cost for satellite and launch	2,866,000

ETV AND COMMUNICATIONS FOR LATIN AMERICA

Most countries in Latin America have substantial demands for an efficient high-capacity communications network and the need for upgrading their educational system. The possibility of several of these countries sharing a satellite to meet both demands is now considered. As will be shown, there are economic advantages in using one satellite to broadcast educational programs to a group of countries, taking advantage of linguistic, historic, and cultural ties between them, and at the same time meeting the future demands for internal communications in each country. This satellite system would also provide high-capacity channels for domestic and intercountry communications and television which could accelerate present trends towards economic integration.

Due to power limitations and the fact that the use of low-cost ground receivers is imperative for the educational system, the satellite power should be used efficiently. When trying to circumscribe Latin America with a possible antenna illumination pattern from synchronous orbit, radiation spillover occurs which is wasted over the oceans. This, and the fact that the power density would be reduced due to the large area to be illuminated, makes the use of one ASCEND-type satellite infeasible for all of Latin America.

For these reasons, it is optimal to group Latin American countries into regions to co-operate in designing their space communications system. One possible solution, taking into consideration an efficient illumination pattern, and assuming that Brazil will have its own satellite, would be as follows:

Region I: Mexico and Central America.
Region II: Bolivia, Colombia, Ecuador, Peru, and
            Venezuela.
Region III: Argentina, Chile, Paraguay, and Uruguay.
Region IV: Brazil.
       (This configuration is illustrated in Figure II.)

FIG. II   -3dB ANTENNA PATTERNS
FROM SYNCHRONOUS ORBIT

Mexico and
Central America

Bolivia
Colombia
Ecuador
Peru
Venezuela

Argentina
Chile
Paraguay
Uruguay

Brazil

389

From the economic and technical point of view, all regions are similar so it is only necessary to consider any one of them in order to arrive at meaningful conclusions. Region II, involving countries which have very similar educational and geographic problems has been chosen for a more detailed study.

From Table II we can determine that this region could use an ASCEND-type satellite to provide:

Six high-power ETV channels, or
Four ETV channels and 6,000 voice circuits, or
Three ETV channels and 9,000 voice circuits, or
Any combination of these.

The most efficient way to use the ETV channels would be transmit programs of common interest (selected upon agreement by the co-operating nations) simultaneously to all the countries in the region. However, in certain aspects of education, as in adult training for specific jobs, or local geography and history courses, it is likely that these nations would want to maintain a certain degree of autonomy. For this purpose, one or more channels could be used on a time-sharing basis to accomodate local programming.

In order to estimate the cost of this space communications system, the following assumptions have been made. First, the date of implementation is taken to be 1975; hence, population and number of schools required in each country have been estimated accordingly. Also, since the number of receivers is within the ASCEND assumptions for low-cost production, costs of the ground and space segments as detailed in the ASCEND study are applicable. Tables III A, B, C, D, and E show initial investments and operating costs for each country in Region II, and Table IV gives the total system cost including the communications terminals.

It should be noted that these cost estimates are conservative and that the revenue obtainable from the communications network has not been considered.

NATIONAL ETV AND COMMUNICATIONS SYSTEM FOR PERU

It is illustrative to compare the costs obtained for Region II with those resulting from the use of a satellite system by one country alone. Peru, as an average country in Region II, is now briefly discussed.

Peru, like the majority of South American countries, has an underdeveloped infrastructure with serious problems in education. In spite of the fact that the Peruvian government spends a good percentage of the governmental budget on education (24.7% in 1963) the progress has been slow, especially in the rural areas.

TABLE III   ETV SYSTEM FOR REGION II

COUNTRY: BOLIVIA

Estimated Population (1975)	5,200,000
Number of students*	1,540,000
Number of schools**	18,600
Educational budget (1963)[4, 6]	$13,500,000
Cities with rebroadcast stations	La Paz

	Quantity	Initial Investment (Million US$)//	Annual Operating Cost (Million US$)//
Receivers in rebroadcast areas	1,740	0.174	0.0348
Rebroadcast transmitter	1	0.200	0.020
Receivers in direct broadcast areas	16,860	6.374	1.106
Central stations for ETV programs	1	3.100	0.976
Share of R and D of the total system		6.445	---
Share of satellite and launching		2.320	0.503
Total		18.613	2.640

Cost Per Student Per Year: US$ 1.72

---

* 1975 school age population taken as 29.7% of total.

** Estimated for 1975 from a 1965 ratio of 83 students per school.

// Totals rounded to nearest thousand dollars.

(continued)

TABLE III   ETV SYSTEM FOR REGION II   (continued)

COUNTRY: COLOMBIA

Estimated Population (1975)	24,200,000
Number of students*	7,700,000
Number of schools**	77,000
Educational budget (1964)[4, 6]	$80,000,000

Cities with rebroadcast stations:			
	Bogotá	Barranquilla	Manizales
	Medellín	Cartagena	Cúcuta
	Cali	Bucaramanga	Ibagué

	Quantity	Initial Investment (Million US$)//	Annual Operating Cost (Million US$)//
Receivers in rebroad-cast areas	20,424	2.042	0.4085
Rebroadcast transmitters	9	1.800	0.180
Receivers in direct broad-cast areas	56,574	21.380	3.711
Central stations for ETV programs	1	3.100	0.976
Share of R and D of the total system		26.700	---
Share of satellite and launching		9.607	2.081
Total		64.629	7.357

Cost Per Student Per Year: US$ 0.96

---

* 1975 school age population taken as 31.8% of total.

** Estimated for 1975 from a 1964 ratio of 100 students per school.

// Total rounded to nearest thousand dollars.

(continued)

392

TABLE III   ETV SYSTEM FOR REGION II   (continued)

COUNTRY: ECUADOR

Estimated Population (1975)		7,060,000	
Number of students*		2,380,000	
Number of schools**		18,500	
Educational budget (1964)[4, 6]		$ 21,600,000	
Cities with rebroadcast stations:		Quito	Guayaquil

	Quantity	Initial Investment (Million US$)[//]	Annual Operating Cost (Million US$)[//]
Receivers in rebroadcast areas	3,695	0.3695	0.0739
Rebroadcast transmitters	2	0.400	0.040
Receivers in direct broadcast areas	14,805	5.596	0.971
Central stations for ETV programs	1	3.100	0.976
Share of R and D of the total system		6.420	---
Share of satellite and launching		2.310	0.500
Total		18.196	2.561

Cost Per Student Per Year: US$ 1.08

---

* 1975 school age population taken as 33.8% of total.

** Estimated for 1975 from a 1964 ratio of 129 students per school.

// Totals rounded to nearest thousand dollars.

(continued)

TABLE III   ETV SYSTEM FOR REGION II   (continued)

COUNTRY: PERU

Estimated Population (1975)	15,820,000
Number of students*	5,140,000
Number of schools**	42,500
Educational budget (1964)[4,6]	$115,000,000
Cities with rebroadcast stations:	Lima-Callao Chiclayo-Trujillo Arequipa

	Quantity	Initial Investment (Million US$)//	Annual Operating Cost. (Million US$)//
Receivers in rebroadcast areas	7,925	0.7925	0.1585
Rebroadcast transmitters	3	0.600	0.060
Receivers in direct broadcast areas	34,575	13.070	2.268
Central stations for ETV programs	1	3.100	0.976
Share of R and D of the total system		14.732	---
Share of satellite and launching		5.300	1.148
Total		37.695	4.611

Cost Per Student Per Year: US$ 0.90

---

* 1975 school age population as 32.5% of total.

** Estimated for 1975 from a 1964 ratio of 121 students per school.

// Totals rounded to nearest thousand dollars.

(continued)

TABLE III   ETV SYSTEM FOR REGION II   (continued)

COUNTRY: VENEZUELA

Estimated Population (1975)   12,160,000

Number of students*   4,010,000

Number of schools**   33,700

Education budget (1963)[4, 6] $197,000,000

Cities with rebroadcast
  stations: Caracas   Maracay
                                   Valencia   Barquisimeto
                                   Maracaibo.

	Quantity	Initial Investment (Million US$)[//]	Annual Operating Cost (Million US$)[//]
Receivers in rebroadcast areas	7,554	0.755	0.151
Rebroadcast transmitters	5	1.000	0.100
Receivers in direct broadcast areas	26,146	9.885	1.715
Central stations for ETV programs	1	3.100	0.976
Share of R and D of the total system		11.685	---
Share of satellite and launching		4.205	0.911
Total		30.630	3.853

Cost Per Student Per Year: US$ 0.96

---

* 1975 school age population taken as 33% of total.

** Estimated for 1975 from a 1964 ratio of 119 students
   per school.

// Totals rounded to nearest thousand dollars.

TABLE IV

COMMUNICATIONS SYSTEMS AND TOTAL SYSTEM COSTS

	Cost Per Student Per Year (US$)	Number of Voice Channels**	Number of Ground Stations //	Cost of Ground Stations*	Capital Investment in ETV System*	Total Capital Investment*
Bolivia	1.72	300	50	3.45	18.613	20.113
Colombia	0.96	3510	230	6.90	64.629	71.529
Ecuador	1.08	420	70	2.10	18.196	20.296
Peru	0.90	1600	150	4.50	37.595	42.095
Venezuela	0.96	2570	115	1.50	30.630	20.113
Intercountry communications		600				
Totals		9000	615	18.45	169.663	188.113

 * Millions of US dollars.

** Assuming 3 ETV channels are devoted to communications, and 600 voice channels to intercountry traffic.

// Assuming Peru will require 150 stations (one in each province plus 15 more) and estimating other countries' requirements according to population.

The Ministry of Public Education (Ministerio de Educación Pública) is the official body responsible for education throughout Peru. In 1950 a ten-year Plan for National Education in Peru (Plan de Educación Nacional del Perú) was started, and in 1957 a National Survey of Peruvian Education (Inventario de la Realidad Educativa del Perú) which has served to complement the 1950 plan, was completed. There are now approximately 20,000 schools in Peru, [4] and it is estimated that 42,500 will be needed to provide education to all school age Peruvians by 1975.

In March 1962, a group of civic minded persons organized the TEPA "Telescuela Popular Americana" in Arequipa, [9] with the main purpose of providing education to a large number of young people in the area, who did not continue studies beyond the first grade of primary school. The enthusiasm and success of TEPA stimulated the Peruvian government to organize the "Instituto Nacional de Teleducación" (INTE) in November 1964, with the purpose of promoting, supervising, and co-ordinating ETV in Peru.

The adverse geographic characteristics of the country have been a major obstacle for the development of an efficient communications system. Even though great efforts have been made in this respect, the capacity of the communications system is still inadequate to meet the actual needs of the country.

Telecommunications in Peru are under the control of the National Telecommunication Agency (Junta Permanente Nacional de Telecomunicaciones) which has made a very detailed study of an integrated communication system and published its recommendations in the "National Plan for Telecommunications" (Plan Nacional de Telecomunicaciones). It considers the planning of communications up to 1975. The estimated capacity for Peru obtained by the above study is 1,464 voice channels at the following estimated costs:

Item	Cost (US dollars)
Network	$ 8,610,000
Long distance terminals	12,720,000
Local telephone terminals, expansion of existing ones	75,200,000
Total	$ 96,530,000

Considering that the angles subtended by Peru from synchronous orbit are approximately 3° x 2.7°, it is possible to increase the ERP to 61 dBW, about 6 times that of Brazil, by using a suitable antenna on the satellite. Then a satellite which has 6 times less power could be used and still obtain the same capacity as on ASCEND. This opens the possibility of using an Intelsat IV satellite which has about one-third of the power of the ASCEND satellite, and still have twice the power needed. This will allow for either reduction of the size of the satellite and therefore its cost, or

397

reduction in the cost of the earth stations by reducing the size of the antenna. The first alternative, which will provide two ETV channels and 3,000 voice channels, has been assumed to estimate the costs of Peru. Table V shows the cost distribution of the ETV system for Peru alone.

TABLE V

ETV SYSTEM FOR PERU

Estimated Population (1975)			15,820,000
Number of students*			5,140,000
Number of schools**			42,500
Cities with rebroadcast stations:			Lima-Callao Chiclayo-Trujillo Arequipa

	Quantity	Initial Investment (Million US$)//	Annual Operating Cost (Million US$)//
Receivers in rebroadcast areas	7,925	0.7925	0.1585
Rebroadcast transmitters	3	0.6000	0.0600
Receivers in direct broadcast areas	34,575	13.0700	2.2680
Central stations for ETV programs	1	3.1000	0.9760
R and D for the entire system (considering a low power Intelsat IV, ERP 49.6 dBW)		27.1900	---
Satellite and launching (including one spare)		13.4400	2.8700
Terminals for communications	150	4.5000	
Total		62.6930	6.3330

Cost Per Student Per Year: US$ 1.23

---

* 1975 school age population taken as 32.5% of total.

** Estimated for 1975 from a 1964 ratio of 121 students per school.

// Figures rounded to nearest thousand dollars.

CONCLUSIONS

The possibility of several countries in Latin America sharing a satellite to provide a system of educational television and internal and regional communications has been discussed. It was found that with the available technology, it is necessary for Latin American nations to group themselves into regions. Under this condition, it would be economically feasible to provide ETV and communications.

The case of a single country, Peru, undertaking alone the task of planning and implementing its own ETV and communications system has also been discussed. This case results in an overall increase in investment of about 53% and an increase in annual operating cost of 38% compared with Peru's share of a regional satellite system. There are also other advantages in a regional system such as co-operation in the enormous task of planning the system as well as programming, operation, and evaluation.

This study should be considered only a first approximation, and, although its findings are attractive, the plethora of problems that might arise should not be forgotten, particularly those of a political and legal nature. Hence, a more detailed study of the use and cost of an ETV and communications system is recommended. The study should preferably be conducted in situ and probably a pilot project to evaluate and design the software would be found to be necessary.

1. Stanford University, School of Engineering, *Advanced System for Communications and Education in National Development* (ASCEND), June 1967.

2. Agency for International Development, *AID Economic Data Book: Latin America* (Washington, D.C., December 1967).

3. United Nations, *Statistical Bulletin for Latin America*, Vol. IV, No. 1, 1967.

4. Pan American Union, *América en Cifras, 1965: Situación Cultural*.

5. Pan American Union, *América en Cifras, 1965: Situación Demográfica*.

6. Pan American Union, *América en Cifras, 1965: Situación Económica*.

7. Inter-American Development Bank, *Feasibility Study of Space and Terrestrial Telecommunications in South America*, 3 vols., prepared by Page Communications Engineers (Washington, D.C., 1966).

8. Sidney Metzger, "The Commercial Communication Satellite System 1963-1968," *Astronautics and Aeronautics*, April 1968, p. 42.

9. UNESCO, *New Educational Media in Action: Case Studies for Planners II*, International Institute for Educational Planning, 1967.

PART VII

SCIENCE AND CULTURE

CHAPTER **29** BIOMEDICAL COMMUNICATIONS:
UNITED STATES AND LATIN
AMERICAN COOPERATION

By Mary E. Corning
National Library of Medicine

To shape the destiny of the Continent, it is first necessary to create a collective consciousness, a way
of thinking, of feeling, and of acting that allows national interests to be pursued in harmony with regional interests .... Relations between countries
should have the same harmony that modern medicine
strives to develop between every human being and
his environment. The difficulty lies in giving practical expressions to policies which, it is generally
agreed, will improve not only the living conditions
of the people of the Americas but also the relations
between the constituent countries and between the
Americas and other regions of the world. *

INTRODUCTION

The United States and Latin American cooperative activities in biomedical communications described in this report are in
their early stages of development. They represent an earnest
effort to meet some immediate and long-range needs, a recognition that existing operational difficulties must not prevent the initial examination and projected resolution of problems, and an
opportunity to develop some regional activities in biomedical communications which could be a model to other areas of the world.

Medical library and information services in Latin America are not able to respond satisfactorily to the dynamic needs
of the professional communities in health research, education and
practice. Libraries are small with inadequate and often out-dated
collections; and staff are limited in number and in specialized
training. Fiscal resources to remedy these basic problems are
not made available nor are they provided within the context of
program and policy plans for medical research and education.

Hence, the libraries are not used and effective information tools are not developed. Some of these difficulties have been

---

* Abraham Horwitz, Director, Pan American Health Organization, "Health and Progress in the Americas," 1966.

met in part by Latin American scientists and institutions requesting services and assistance from the U.S. National Library of
Medicine. However, the fundamental resolution of these problems
in biomedical communications requires action in Latin America.
Individual libraries must be improved; but it would be a duplication of effort and too costly in terms of manpower, material, and
fiscal resources to develop each one irrespective of the needs of
its own specialized users. There are certain functions and services which can be provided by a central resource. Accordingly,
functionally and economically, it is feasible to establish Latin American international/national resources to bolster, supplement and
complement the local institutions and their activities.

As a first step toward these goals, the United States and
Latin America have initiated cooperative efforts in biomedical
communications. They can best be understood by first placing
in perspective the nature and functions of the National Library of
Medicine (NLM), one of the partners in this cooperation.

THE NATIONAL LIBRARY OF MEDICINE (NLM)

The National Library of Medicine is the largest specialized
research library in the world. It was founded in 1836 as the "Library of the Surgeon-General's Office" (Army) and was developed
as a national and international resource by Dr. John Shaw Billings,
Librarian from 1865 to 1895. In 1886, Billings said,

> ... the library, which commenced in a collection of
> those books relating solely or especially to military
> medicine and surgery ... has expanded into a great
> medical library, which is now one of the best practi-
> cal working collections of the kind in the world.
> These collections, then, no longer appertain ex-
> clusively, or chiefly, to the business of one de-
> partment, but belong to the whole profession of
> the United States as a body; and the department
> which has charge of them is managing them from
> this point of view. The influence of the library
> in stimulating research, and upon the quality of
> medical literature, is already very perceptible...
> the utility ... of the library, is by no means confined
> to the medical profession of the United States, for
> the catalogues and indices, which are being issued...
> are of service to medical writers and teachers all
> over the world. *

The Library has undergone changes in name in succeeding
years, but the basic mission and philosophy of domestic and inter-

---

* John Shaw Billings, "Medicine in the United States, and
its Relations to Co-operative investigation." Delivered before the
British Medical Association, 1886.

national service expressed by Billings has been maintained and sustained. In 1956, by Congressional mandate, the Library was renamed the National Library of Medicine and established within the Public Health Service, Department of Health, Education and Welfare "in order to assist the advancement of medical and related sciences and to aid the dissemination and exchange of scientific and other information important to the progress of medicine and to the public health. "

Today, the National Libarary of Medicine is not a traditional library but has become, in recent years, an active force in biomedical communications. This is largely due to the "Medical Literature Analysis and Retrieval System (MEDLARS), " the first computer-based bibliographic system, becoming operational (1964); the passage of the Medical Library Assistance Act (1965); the delegation of authority from the White House for a Toxicology Information Program (1966); the transfer of the Public Health Service Audiovisual Facility to the Library to become the National Medical Audiovisual Center (1967); the designation of the Francis A. Countway Library, Boston, as the first Regional Medical Library (1967); and a new directed program of research and development in biomedical communications (1967).

MEDLARS, which provides bibliographic control of the world's biomedical literature, is a computer-based reference storage and retrieval system. It revolutionized the technique of preparing publications and providing bibliographic services to the individual in the form of specialized publications or demand searches. The Medical Library Assistance Act provided a framework for the Library (through a grant and contract program) to strengthen facilities and resources at local medical library levels, train professionals in biomedical communication, develop new techniques for communicating, support publications and research and development, and develop a system of regional medical libraries.

The Library, therefore, is an international resource, provides services, strengthens regional or local library resources through special support programs, performs and supports research and development in biomedical communications, and may draw upon any or all of these functions in order to meet specialized information needs or to aid in the continuing education of the practicing physician and dentist. The Library interrelates with the Federal and non-Federal libary community, other government institutions, professional scientific groups and specialized users.

The Library is thus unique and is the recipient of ever-increasing attention from abroad. Functionally, the international activities of the Library include: the traditional acquisition, exchange and service functions; an agreement with the Agency for International Development for provision of specialized services; Public Law 480 programs in abstracting, indexing, translating and critical reviews; cooperative projects involving the computer-based information storage and retrieval system (MEDLARS); and the development of institutional relationships in the broad and fundamental aspects of biomedical communications.

Geographically, the international activities of the Library are widespread: the United Kingdom, Sweden, Japan, Poland, Yugoslavia, Israel, India, South America through the Pan American Health Organization, Mexico, and potential programs in Australia and Canada. We are also developing programs with the World Health Organization and the Organization for Economic Cooperation and Development. Many of these programs are of a cooperative nature whereby funds are not spent outside the United States.

U. S. NATIONAL POLICY STATEMENT ON INTERNATIONAL BOOK AND LIBRARY ACTIVITIES

In 1967, the President of the United States issued a National Policy Statement on International Book and Library Activities and a Directive to Government Agencies for Implementation of the National Policy Statement. This policy states that it was essential that "... all agencies of Government concerned in any way with international book and library programs assign to these a high priority." For implementation, agencies were directed to work with developing countries in activities such as:

... (8)   supporting a program of library development in cooperation with the U.S. publishing industry, U.S. libraries, library organizations and institutions, to include:

   (a)   assistance in adapting to local conditions and needs the most advanced library technology;

   (b)   overall collection development programs by cooperating institutions in the U.S. ;

   (c)   counseling on library development;...

(9)   initiating a major training program for library personnel, to include:

   (a)   strengthening of existing national and regional library schools, plus refresher and in-service training and selected work-study training in the U.S. ;

   (b)   development of additional regional library schools, with provision of scholarship funds;

   (c)   instruction in the application of modern technology to library practices...

E. To encourage closer liaison between American
    and foreign libraries, greater exchange of ref-
    erence and bibliographical information, and
    closer collaboration in the development of in-
    formation storage and retrieval and computer
    utilization programs. "

The National Library of Medicine welcomed this policy
statement and directive and is developing international cooperative
programs consistent with these stated policies and goals.

LATIN AMERICA

The programs specifically described in this paper are
our cooperative efforts with the Pan American Health Organization for South America, with the Gorgas Memorial Laboratory in
Central America and with the Ministry of Health in Mexico. Each
of these programs has developed in a specific way in response to
demonstrated needs. They are at various levels of development
and may use different mechanisms, but the ultimate objective is
improved biomedical communications to advance medical research,
education, and practice.

Emphasis on these three programs in this brief report
does not signify a lack of awarenes or appreciation of efforts made
by others, for example the Rockefeller Foundation, Ford Foundation, Milbank Memorial Fund, Kellogg Foundation,and Agency for
International Development. These organizations may sponsor programs which are communications-related but they are primarily
directed toward specific areas in medical research, medical education, strengthening of institutions,and provision of health services. The Pan American Union Library Development Program of
the Organization of American States has concerned itself with library
development and training of librarians for libraries ranging from
public through specialized research libraries. Provision of textbooks and establishment of local publishing houses have been stimulated by the Franklin Book Programs.

These specific project and program-level activities are
distinct from the national/international resource building, which
is the basis of the NLM/Latin American cooperation. The
approaches which are being applied should reinforce each other
because the problem of communications should be examined at all
levels: individual, institutional, country, international, and within
the requirements of research, education, and practice.

The Pan American Health Organization (PAHO) since its
establishment in 1902 has concerned itself with specific disease
problems, health services, research, manpower, education, and
science policy. It has more recently taken positive action on the
matter of biomedical communications, recognizing its interrelationships with strong programs in research, education,and services. It approached the National Library of Medicine for advice

407

and consultation on these matters in 1965. The Library was eager to be responsive because we have had a long-standing interest in Latin America. We have an extensive program for acquisition of current and historical Latin American biomedical literature by purchase, exchange, and gifts in order to make it available to our U.S. health community. We send to 19 Latin American countries approximately 319 subscriptions in exchange for 126 subscriptions. Of the 2,288 journals indexed in Index Medicus, 86 are Latin American.

Argentina	16
Brazil	34
Chile	6
Colombia	2
Ecuador	1
Mexico	14
Peru	3
Uruguay	5
Venezuela	5
Total	86

We also provide extensive library services to our Latin American colleagues; 45% of approximately 25,000 international services (reference, interlibrary loan, demand searches) are made to Latin American countries.

A. Regional Medical Library for South America (RML)

In 1965 PAHO began examining biomedical communications in South America using the National Library of Medicine in a technical and advisory capacity. There were meetings of experts concerned with problems of Latin American medical education, biomedical research, and international health, and a study team examined South American medical libraries. The net conclusion reached by these groups was that Latin American medical libraries had not kept pace with the needs of biomedical researchers, educators, students, and practitioners, and that the problem should receive immediate attention on a regional basis.

The PAHO Advisory Committee on Medical Research recommended the establishment of a Regional Medical Library in South America under the joint sponsorship of PAHO and the Pan American Federation of Associations of Medical Schools with technical backstopping by the National Library of Medicine. The site selected for the Library was the Escola Paulista de Medicina, São Paulo, Brazil. The policy for the Regional Medical Library would be established by a Board of Governors appointed by PAHO.

The Regional Medical Library (RML) is in its very beginning stages and the current and projected status is described here. One very interesting aspect of this library is the multiple cooperation which exists between the PAHO, the Ministries of Education and Health in Brazil, the Escola Paulista de Medicina in São Paulo,

the Commonwealth Fund, and the National Library of Medicine.
PAHO has organizational and administrative responsibility for
the RML which provides it with international status. Funds are
being provided by the Ministries of Health and Education in Brazil,
the Pan American Health Organization, the Commonwealth Fund,
and also by the National Library of Medicine under the President's
National Policy Statement on International Book and Library Activities.   Staff and buildings have been made available by the Escola
Paulista. National Library of Medicine excess credit rights at
the U. S. Book Exchange are being used by the Center to build a
core collection. Currently, PAHO is recruiting for a Director,
the collection is being enlarged in scope and coverage, training
needs of current staff are being identified, and an assessment is
being made of present resources projected against the current and
potential functions and goals of the RML.

Once the collection has reached adequate strength, services in the form of handling reference questions, performing
bibliographic searches, and providing interlibrary loans will
begin, probably in July, 1968.   Cooperative programs with other
libraries will be developed to eliminate duplication of effort and
to draw on each other's resources.   Training will be provided by
the NLM for MEDLARS Search Specialists so that they may perform search preparation and formulation to answer specific requests from scientists.   The computer processing can be done at
the National Library of Medicine.

Potentially, the RML will become an institutional base
on which to build, strengthen local institutions in the various
countries, provide medical information through the use of modern
methods to scientists, educators and practitioners in the health
fields, and provide a unique opportunity for training librarians
and information specialists.

B. Proposed Regional Medical Library for Central America

In 1965 following discussions in Panama with officials of
the Gorgas Memorial Laboratory, the Pan American Health Organization, and the Government of Panama, the Director of the National Library of Medicine was asked to discuss the concept of the
development of a Regional Medical Library with the Ministers of
Health of Central America. The reception to the concept was
highly favorable.

Follow-up actions in Panama have been principally concerned with acquisition of land to construct a building for the
establishment of the Regional Medical Library in Panama for
Central America. The site is in the process of being acquired by
the Gorgas Memorial Laboratory.

Detailed plans for the physical plant, collection, staff, and
services have yet to be developed. In the interim, the National
Library of Medicine has been assisting the Gorgas Memorial Laboratory in the strengthening of its collection through our sending

duplicate books, journals, and through the use of our excess credits at the U.S. Book Exchange.

C. Mexican National Center for Medical Bibliographic Information

In 1967, the Surgeon General of the U. S. Public Health Service indicated his willingness to assist the Ministry of Health and Welfare in Mexico in its establishment of a central focus for medical library development and liaison with the National Library of Medicine. Subsequent discussions between the Minister of Health and Welfare and the Director of the National Library of Medicine have led to the Ministry taking steps to initiate a National Center for Medical Bibliographic Information with the cooperation of their National Academy of Medicine, the Social Security Institute, and the National Autonomous University of Mexico.

The Ministry of Health is establishing the initial nucleus which will be housed in the National Academy of Medicine with library and documentation back-up provided by the Social Security Institute and the National Autonomous University. The National Library of Medicine agreed to respond to requests for material or information not available in Mexico and to provide specialized training for staff. Dr. Luis Marcial, Office of the Undersecretary of Health, has been identified as the Director of the new Center; and he is currently undergoing comprehensive and broad training at the National Library of Medicine. Training will subsequently be given for an individual to become a MEDLARS Search Specialist so that requests for computerized bibliographic and reference services may be formulated at the Mexican Center with the search and response provided by the National Library of Medicine.

The initial plan in Mexico is for an information referral center and clearinghouse, but the ultimate goal is an organizational entity resembling a national library of medicine.

CONCLUSIONS

The U. S. /Latin American cooperation in biomedical communications is in the developmental stages. Only through diligent and constant effort will they succeed. They represent an approach which is regional, but one where the interdependency rests on a "service network" rather than on formal organizational or physical networks.

The programs are planned in successive stages with basic steps being taken first in terms of training people, strengthening resource collections, initiating services in response to demon - strated needs, and stimulating in general an increased awareness of the utility of these resources. When appropriate and timely, advanced technologies can and will be introduced. This does not mean that one will achieve a homogeneous entity which can be called "integrated Latin American medical information services." Instead, one can achieve the knowledge of what resources exist where, and how and by whom they can be utilized.

There is an increased understanding in the United States that biomedical communications interrelate with medical and health research, education and practice. Communications in the health area may include communication between researchers; the researcher and the clinical investigator; the researcher, clinical investigator and practitioner; and with the cycle providing feedback to the researcher.

Some of the communications problems facing Latin America are similar to those which we are attempting to solve in the United States and which are receiving world-wide attention. The fundamental problems are the volume and worth of material, the organization of information, and identifying and satisfying user needs.

These NLM/Latin American cooperative programs are constructed with special care so that they are not simply a transplantation of what now exists in the U.S. to another locality. Full participation of our foreign colleagues in the development of a truly cooperative effort is required. In many cases there is no transfer of funds; in some cases there are funds provided by both the U.S. and by the host government and institutions.

These programs can only be successful if they are closely tied to demonstrated needs and to the cultural and educational scene. This means that one begins and develops activities with full appreciation of the immediate needs and resources of the locale but keeps in mind the ultimate objective of a sophisticated modern communications center. The progress of each one of these efforts is under both informal and formal periodic review. We recognize that this is only a beginning, but we also believe that the implications for the future of research, education, and service are exciting and far-reaching.

BIBLIOGRAPHY

Health in the Americas and the Pan American Health Organiza-
tion, prepared for the Committee on Government Operations,
United States Senate and its Subcommittee on Reorganization
and International Organizations. Washington, D.C.: 1960.

"Health Manpower and Medical Education in Latin America; Report of a Round Table Conference," *Milbank Memorial Fund*
Quarterly, XLII, No. 1 (1964), 11-66.

Horowitz, Abraham. *New Dimensions in Health: A Report on*
International Health Work in the Americas. Washington,
D.C.: Pan American Health Organization, 1964.

____. *Health and Progress in the Americas.* Washington, D.C.:
Pan American Health Organization, 1966.

Pan American Health Organization. *Science Policy in Latin*
America: Substance, Structures, Processes. Washington,
D.C.: 1966.

____. *Annual Report of the Director, 1966.* Washington, D.C.:
1967.

Pan American Union. *Science Information in Latin America.*
Washington, D.C.: 1961.

____. *Guide to Latin American Scientific and Technical Period-*
icals: An Annotated List. Mexico City: Centro de Documentación Científica y Técnica de México, 1962.

____. *The Publication of Scientific and Technical Journals in*
Latin America: A Statistical Analysis. Mexico City:
Centro de Documentación Científica y Técnica de México,
1962.

____. *Round Table on International Cooperation for Library and*
Information Services in Latin America, Vols. I-II.
Washington, D.C.: 1966.

CHAPTER **30** A ROLE FOR THE UNIVERSITY
IN THE INTEGRATION OF
LATIN AMERICA

By Winthrop R. Wright
Department of History
University of Maryland

Traditionally, Latin American universities have been
manifestations of a closed society. No longer, however, do all
institutions of higher learning in Latin America serve an intellectual, social, and political elite at the exclusion of the majority.
Within the last decade an increasing number of universities have
played an active role in the integration movement of Latin America
as agents of social and economic change. As integration is not
merely an economic problem but has psychological ramifications
as well, the universities are important instruments for creating
an awareness of a greater Latin America. By serving as forums
of debate of the movement and as centers for the dissemination of
information concerning integration, the universities can help effect
an integration mystique, or encourage a commitment to the social
and political integration of the area among an increasingly broad
sector of the Latin American public.

The purpose of this study is to stimulate discussion about
a role that universities can play in the integration movement.
More specifically, it is to suggest that universities seek a positive
role in the movement through the introduction of Latin American
studies programs into their curricula. For that reason much of
the study will be devoted to a critique of a pilot program that was
begun at the Universidad de Oriente (UDO) in Venezuela in 1966,
with the hope that it will serve as one example of the position that
Latin American universities are ready to take as activists in the
integration movement.

THE REFORM OF 1918

Few observers of Latin American universities would deny
that the University Reform that began in the Rio de la Plata in 1918
has been aborted. What started as an attempt to broaden the social
base of the university and ultimately change society at large failed
because the reformers and their followers were swept up by the
vortex of political activity. Curricula changes were made, many
incompetent professors were dismissed, and autonomous campuses
were set up, free from the threat of police or military intervention,
but the reform was circumscribed by universities that continued to
presume the privilege of maintaining a political and social elite
and by students who made a mockery of university autonomy through
irresponsible political behavior. Since the thrust of the University

413

Reform was aimed against the structure of society rather than toward the improvement of higher education, it must be considered a failure; until recently the old regimes have continued to rule in most nations and the universities have continued to isolate themselves from the mainstream of national development. [1]

Students of the University Reform in Argentina have often overlooked the involvement of its leaders in the resuscitation of the continental system once advocated by nineteenth-century political theorists. As Gabriel del Mazo, one of the staunchest supporters of the Reform, later stated, the Reform was "a vast undertaking aimed at organizing and unifying Indo-Spanish America on ethical-social bases, transforming its states through the inspiration and effort of the genius of its soil and people."[2] To a large degree the University Reform was an integral part of the resurgence of continental nationalism that swept Latin America during the first three decades of the present century. Men like del Mazo, Alfredo Palacios, and Manuel Ugarte, whose book La patria grande gave currency to the concept of a patria grande throughout Latin America, were Yankeephobes who sought to counterbalance the power of the "Colossus of the North" in the western hemisphere.[3] In so doing they popularized the anti-Yankee aspects of the University Reform movement.

As the University Reform became identified with a growing political and social revolution that was aimed against the unholy alliance of foreign imperialists and indigenous oligarchs, it was readily accepted by students in all parts of the hemisphere. By 1921, enough interest had been generated among student leaders for them to hold an international congress in Mexico during that year.[4] Representatives of student organizations from all Spanish American universities attended the congress and openly debated common educational problems. Consequently, a broad social program was adopted which was aimed at restructuring Latin American society through the creation of autonomous universities.[5] As noted above, the ultimate failure of the University Reform was due in large part to the political involvement of its student organizers. Furthermore, its contribution to inter-American co-operation, was short-circuited by the rise of economic nationalism in the individual Latin American states after 1930 that destroyed immediate hopes of fulfilling the Bolivarian dream of building a grand nation of republics. Nonetheless, the student congress of 1921 exemplifies a fifty-year-old commitment to integration that university groups have held, and illustrates the potential role of universities as agents of reform and integration.

REFORMS OF THE 1960'S

An important link between the University Reform of 1918 and subsequent reforms undertaken during the 1960's is found in the faith that supporters of both movements have placed in an integrated Latin America. In both instances universities have been urged to take an active role in uniting Latin America. The link is important because, although the ends of both are similar, their means are different. Whereas the former was predominantly student-led, the reforms of the past decade have been instigated by university administrators, often against strong student opposition. Furthermore, while autonomy was a by-product of the Reform of 1918, the new reforms are directed against the traditional definition of university autonomy in an attempt to eliminate the campuses as sources of chronic political insurgency. According to the new philosophy, the university must serve the nation, not the student; its primary function is to train technicians to solve the many pressing problems that retard the improvement of the standard of living of the whole citizenry. [6] One solution has been to create regional universities that are dependent upon the state for funds and direction, and whose charters explicitly deny them territorial autonomy, in the hopes that such institutions will serve as tools of national integration while preparing individuals to administer an increasingly industrialized society.

Typical of the new breed of Latin American universities are the Universidad de Oriente (UDO) in Venezuela, the Universidad Veracruzana in Mexico, the Universidad del Valle in Cali, the Universidad de Huamanga in Ayacucho, all state universities, and the private Universidad de los Andes in Colombia, and the Instituto Tecnológico de Monterrey, Mexico. These universities, along with institutions like the universities of Costa Rica and Rio de Janeiro, comprise a representative body of institutions that are attempting to prepare their graduates to cope with national problems by providing them with adequate training in the fields of science and in the social sciences.

The above-mentioned universities are working towards integration on several levels in Latin America. On one plane the administrators are integrating the universities themselves by setting up departmental rather than professional school organizations in order to do away with the assemblage of separate but equal faculties, whose over-all efficiency has long been doubted. The new universities have also become instruments of integration within their respective nations. In many cases they are the first institutions of higher learning to serve interior or remote regions of Latin America. Because they are apolitical they attract increasing numbers of students from other regions of the nation who desire to pursue their education without the frustrating interruptions of student strikes and violent political activity that constantly disrupt the academic process at the autonomous universities. [7] Regions that had previously been barren in the field of higher education now benefit from the prestige of responsible universities and for the first time these previously neglected areas are operating in the mainstream of national development. [8]

It has long been held that "Necessity is the mother of invention." Through international commitments necessitated by demands of developing viable universities, the new institutions have been forced to take a prominent position in the movement to integrate Latin America. Previously, Latin American universities were little more than a series of "cultural archipelagoes," operating in self-imposed isolation, cut off from each other and from society.[9] Since the end of the Second World War, however, there has been a marked increase in the dialogue between Latin American universities, both on national and international levels. Organizations like the Unión de Universidades de América Latina, now under the capable direction of Efrén C. del Pozo, have encouraged co-ordinated activities between Latin American universities. Concomitant developments have led universities to consider the feasibility of establishing regional programs by which students from several nations could attend common graduate programs in specialized fields that otherwise could not be supported by any one institution or nation. This latter possibility has itself touched off debate about establishing a uniform credit system by which students from one university could easily transfer to another, or even enter a foreign university, without sacrificing years of previous study.[10] International co-operation in the field of higher education is in itself a manifestation of Latin American integration aimed at alleviating the economic strain of developing first-rate institutions in an emerging area of the world. Anti-Yankeeism appears as a motivating factor in the establishment of international training programs; Latin American educators hope to stop the serious drain brain whereby promising young Latins remain in the United States or Europe upon completing their advanced degrees rather than return to the frustrations of their home lands.[11]

LATIN AMERICAN STUDIES

One reason that international co-operation between the universities has been slow to develop is that Latin Americans still have much to learn about each other. Although most of the new universities are highly cosmopolitan, owing to the large number of foreigners on their faculties, only a relative handful of Latin Americans comprise a well-informed elite who can speak with any authority about the area at large. The majority of Latin Americans, including the university students, know little or nothing about the culture and history of their immediate neighbors, let alone more distant Latin American nations, and the masses hardly understand the existence of their own nation. Yet most Latin Americans feel they have something in common. In general a citizen feels he is both a member of his respective nation and of a larger Latin American community. This concept is shared by most informed Latin Americans, who will react in common against an overt act of the United States or will join together as one to cheer a Latin American football team in a World Cup soccer match against a European opponent. At such times there is a fine line between national and continental identity. Yet the fact remains that, in spite of a Latin American mystique, there is an appalling lack of understanding and knowledge between individuals of the republics that comprise contemporary Latin America.

Most attempts to define what is meant by the generic term, Latin America, have failed. Confusion about the patria grande exists in the minds of the best informed native and foreign observers of Latin America. A classic example is found in the widespread misunderstanding that resulted from Luis Alberto Sánchez' ¿Existe América Latina?[12] To Sánchez the title contained an interrogation — rather than a negation — for he accepted Latin America as a unit and described its many common characteristics along with its regional and national differences.[13] Many distinguished readers, however, both in Latin America and the United States, have understood his work to be a negation of the existence of one Latin America, and have cited it as an argument against treating Latin America as a unit.[14]

To this day there are very few intellectuals who can provide a mutually-acceptable definition of the term. But more serious is the ignorance of the general population of Latin America. If pensadores cannot satisfactorily define the total, what must be the confusion of the average Latin American who cannot see the tree for the woods? While Bolívar and San Martín are universally acclaimed, twentieth-century poets, artists, and statesmen are not as a rule well-known and are hardly understood outside of their respective nations, though there are notable exceptions. Of relevance to this study is that when one turns to discussions of comparative economics, natural resources, political systems, sociological patterns, and related topics, it is soon apparent that the Latin American's knowledge of his neighbor is superficial.

The introduction of Latin American studies into the curricula of Latin American universities is one means of correcting popular misconceptions held by an influential segment of the populace. To be most effective, any Latin American studies program should work within an educational framework that covers at least three areas. First, a primary goal should be to make undergraduates aware of their Latin American environment and heritage by familiarizing them with the history and culture of all Latin American nations, not just their own. Second, the program should be extended to the communities surrounding the university through extension courses that involve a broader base of society in the integration movement. Third, there should be concern for the dissemination of information to the general public by means of the modern communication media, including educational television where the facilities exist. Related to this final undertaking is the influence that serious study of Latin America may have upon primary and secondary school curricula, holding that ultimately the trickle-down theory will apply and that reforms will be made in the curricula of the latter institutions.

Obviously the merits of establishing Latin American studies programs at Latin American universities is subject to serious questioning. Perhaps one is justified in asking whether it is like "carrying coals to Newcastle" to offer such programs to Latin Americans. Although this charge has been answered above in discussing the mutual ignorance of Latin Americans about each other, a comparable criticism could be made of urban studies at New York University or any other urban campus. And to any professor who has suffered through a survey of U.S. history with American freshmen, it is self-evident that most nationals know very little about themselves, let alone foreign nations, except what they learn from highly nationalistic textbooks.

Of greater significance is the support found among Latin American educators who have recommended the introduction of Latin American studies into the curricula. One, Luis Manuel Peñalver, Rector of the Universidad de Oriente, and a member of the advisory council of the BID-sponsored Instituto para la Integración de América Latina (INTAL), stands out in this regard; he personally established a department of Latin American studies at his university. The involvement of Luis Alberto Sánchez in encouraging similar projects is well known, and more lately Ramón de Zubiría, the former president of the University of the Andes in Bogotá, is among the educators who have gone on record in support of Latin American studies programs.[15] According to Zubiría, the introduction of Latin American studies into the curricula of Latin American universities is an urgent necessity.[16] These men, and others like them, are attempting to use the universities as a means of breaking the straitjacket of modern nationalism. For instance, secondary school children in Venezuela are taught the following about Pan Americanism:

> Our patriotism should not be closed but rather broad
> and generous. We must realize that at our side and
> throughout the world live people whose countries have
> realized glorious achievements, and these are worthy
> of admiration and respect... Venezuela, who gave
> her blood to liberate four countries, has always been
> a generous and co-operative nation. Admiration,
> respect and a spirit of collaboration create a feeling
> of solidarity between people that leads to mutual aid,
> thanks be to God. Certainly there are more oppor-
> tunities to understand each other and to give aid be-
> tween neighboring countries of the same culture;
> for that reason they celebrate pacts. Thus the Or-
> ganization of American States was organized.
> ...Every year on the 14th of April, they celebrate
> Pan American Day, or the Day of the Americas. On
> this occasion official ceremonies, cultural events,
> and civic displays are held. All of this is to mani-
> fest the mutual glories, the virtues of the heroes,
> and above all, to exalt the figure of Bolívar, the
> Father of Liberty and the creator of Panamericanism.[16]

It is readily obvious that Venezuelan attitudes towards integration are warped by primary and secondary school history and civics courses that teach little more than the adulation of Bolívar and the acceptance of the patria as the center of the universe. In eastern Venezuela, where a recent survey has shown that nearly two-thirds of the school age children do not complete four years of schooling, it is almost impossible to convey the concept of the role Venezuela plays in the Latin American system to the public at large. [17] Students who do complete their secondary school courses and enter universities comprise a small percentage of the population. Therefore it is doubly important to re-educate them in regard to the inter-American movement, for, although this group is no longer following the path of previous student elites toward political involvement, they will comprise a professional elite who will have an increasingly important role as decision makers in Venezuela.

THE DEPARTMENT OF LATIN AMERICAN STUDIES AT UDO

It was in light of the emerging nature of eastern Venezuela that UDO's Department of Latin American Studies was conceived during the summer of 1966. Employing guidelines set by INTAL in 1965, the UDO project set the three following objectives for its initial program. [18] The new department's primary function was to be in the area of curriculum reform. The original plan called for the preparation of a course in Latin American studies that could be introduced into a revised basic courses curriculum that all entering students would take during their first year at the university. The purpose of offering all new students an interdisciplinary course about Latin America was to provide them with a basic concept of a common Latin America. Second, the department was charged with organizing a series of post-graduate seminars for professional persons and interested citizens of the major cities of the Oriente section of Venezuela. [19] The seminars, based on the theme of integration, were seen as a means of encouraging broader participation in the integration movement. It was felt that persons involved in courses concerning integration would more readily become involved in the movement itself. Third, the department was given the important responsibility of serving as a communication medium with other Western Hemisphere universities through publications and exchange of personnel. Since UDO had no television facilities, it was not practical to plan to use that important medium, but in the future it is conceivable that a consortium of Latin American universities could undertake an exchange of documentaries aimed toward enlightening a large audience.

As might be expected, the first phase of the program has been the most difficult to implement. A number of diverse reasons explain the lack of success in this undertaking, but the major obstacle was a reluctance on the part of many university officials to give the program their full-fledged support. UDO, like other new universities, is suffering from growing pains. In the past nine years it has established a school of basic sciences, a school of agronomy, maintained a school of medicine, staffed an oceanographic institute, begun a school of social sciences, and is presently constructing a technological institute patterned after MIT and Cal Tech. In a University of California-like fashion, UDO is scattered over four separate campuses in eastern Venezuela, and is planning to develop another campus within the next few years. [20] As a result of what might be considered over-expansion in any other context, university officials were hesitant to tie up much-

needed funds in any project they considered to be non-essential
to the primary objectives of the university. Therefore the growth
of programs not directly involved in the process of training technicians has been limited by official control of the purse strings.
This, along with a propensity to plan but not implement, has retarded the growth of Latin American studies and relegated the
curricula changes to the drawing-board stage.

On the positive side of the ledger, experimental courses
given to a small number of students were well received by the
latter. Student opposition to changing the curricula was minimal,
and in many instances the students openly encouraged the work of
the Department of Latin American studies. Working in conjunction with the School of Science and the School of Social Sciences at
the Cumaná campus, classes on Latin American culture were offered during two semesters between August, 1966, and May, 1967.
Admittedly, the courses were disjointed endeavors, treating in
general terms such topics as political systems, social change,
literature, and indigenous populations in the Western Hemisphere.
We were handicapped by a shortage of personnel: the department
consisted of an Ecuadorian lawyer-educator, steeped in the literature of geo-politics, and a North American historian, whose field
is Latin America. A further handicap, but only for a short time,
was the lack of adequate library facilities. This problem has
been resolved in part by gifts from several organizations, including INTAL. A result of our preliminary classes were positive
plans for future courses, stressing the necessity of an interdisciplinary approach in order to cover a broader spectrum of Latin
American institutions in an introductory-level course. One conclusion was that it was essential to include adequate instruction in
the fields of political science, economic geography, sociology and
anthropology, and literature as well as history to assure the success of the course in Latin American culture as we conceived it.
Instructors in those disciplines were available at UDO but were
not freed from other teaching responsibilities in order to participate in our project. For that reason UDO can undertake a broader
program of Latin American studies at once if it is willing to allo-
cate more money and manpower to its development. The situation
could be alleviated by support from outside foundations and U. S.
universities, as long as the latter do not treat UDO as a satellite.

Several important lessons were learned from the courses
offered during the department's first year of tenure at UDO, that
might be of aid to organizers of similar programs at other Latin
American universities. First, there is much to be gained by establishing an international faculty; there is no better way to explain the difference between Venezuela and Ecuador than to have
an Ecuadorian mestizo lecture to young pardos of eastern Venezuela about the Indians of the Andes. A cosmopolitan faculty offers
flexibility and provides a living example of the integration movement. Another consideration, already noted above, is that courses
at any level will be more effective if they are interdisciplinary.
At UDO, for example, over 90 per cent of the students enter scientific or technical professions. For that reason it is imperative

that they receive a broad exposure to disciplines that they would not ordinarily study in the normal pursuit of a degree in their major field. A dangerous trend in the new reform movement is its emphasis upon scientific knowledge at the expense of the traditional humanities. In other words, Latin American studies should be treated as supplementary material in the education of young scientists and technicians, whose primary concern is to embark on a crusade to rectify the living conditions of their respective nations.

The accomplishments of the second phase of the department's planning, the engineering of extension courses for the public, are of a more positive nature; at least on a short-run. Several short seminars were presented, since these could be quite effectively staffed by a few professors and needed little financial support. Initial response to the program was encouraging, and attendance at seminars included members of the military, the church, the judiciary, the legal profession, along with several teachers, and a few medical doctors. Because enrollment was restricted to individuals with university degrees or the equivalent, there is no way of judging what response there might have been among the merchant class of the same cities. Informal surveys of Cumaná, Barcelona, and Puerto la Cruz, however, indicate that a large number of the middle class would participate in extension courses if they were made available for credit toward a degree, but it is still too early in the department's existence to contemplate such a formal move, again, owing to the lack of funds and personnel.

Through trial and error we tried to develop a seminar that would encourage open but orderly debate about the integration movement. As is often the case, the first attempt was a disaster. Inadvertently the course was extended over a thirteen-week period, meeting on a twice-a-week basis in order to give what was thought to be a thorough treatment of literally every aspect of the integration movement. Enrollment fell from fifty to two loyal students within the first eight weeks, hardly a testimony of Latin American patience! The next two endeavors owed their success to the failure of the original program. The content of the course was drastically reduced to the bare essentials, and organized around the contention that economic integration of the area was impossible unless it was preceded by a general desire for the political and cultural integration of Latin America. In a two-week seminar, meeting five evenings a week, the department presented an interdisciplinary treatment of many related facets of integration. Members of other departments brought new insights into the discussion through formal lectures. Participants were stimulated by the lectures and ensuing discussions, and many admitted that they had acquired a new awareness of the implications of the integration movement. Several began to read about economic integration, including works by Herrera and Prebisch. Among this group was an officer of the Guardia Nacional who previously had owned a copy of one of Herrera's books but had never read it.

The participants of the seminars were not the only ones

to benefit from the seminars. An important side-effect of the course was to draw UDO closer to the communities which it served by providing a stimulating public service. Individuals came to the campus who had known very little about the university's activities, although it must be admitted that the majority were previous friends of the university. Nonetheless, it was proved that the university could serve the interests of the community; mutual benefits accrued as an increased number of citizens became more attuned to the integration movement, while the university took a step toward becoming an integral part of its environment. Through this process UDO is working to end the "ivory tower" isolation of the traditional university.

In its third area of endeavor, as an information gatherer and disseminator, the impact of the Department of Latin American Studies at UDO has been negligible. Two volumes of a new publication, <u>América Unida,</u> have been issued and distributed to universities and other interested institutions in the Western Hemisphere and in Europe. The department has instituted a series of colloquia on the various Latin American republics; Germán Arciniegas, then serving as the Colombian Ambassador to Venezuela, gave the first lecture. By taking advantage of visiting scholars and dignitaries to Venezuela, the department hopes to provide a continuous forum for the public discussion of Latin American integration. Parallel to the series of visiting lecturers will be a program of local participants, drawn from UDO's cosmopolitan faculty. Because native Venezuelans are reluctant to leave the comforts of Caracas to work in the isolated eastern interior states, the faculty at UDO comprises representatives of practically every Latin American nation, along with several North Americans, Europeans, and Asians. For that reason there is a reservoir of talent to draw upon in presenting colloquia about individual republics of Latin America.

In summation, the Latin American studies program at UDO is comparable to a diamond in the rough. More plans have been made than implemented. Yet the university now stands ready to participate in the integration movement and is actively working to spread the idea throughout Latin America. As a direct result of the work at UDO, two similar projects are being contemplated at universities in Ecuador. There are people at UDO who are desirous of participating in broader Latin American undertakings, like the frequently discussed Salzburg-type seminar for Latin America that has yet to be organized. Now the university is prepared to venture forth in the positive quest of means by which Latin American integration can be brought about.

NOTES

1. For a discussion of the political involvement of Latin American students see John P. Harrison, "Learning and Politics in Latin American Universities," *Economic and Political Trends,* Proceedings of the Academy of Political Science, Vol. XXVII, No. 4 (New York, May, 1964), pp. 23-24. Also see Paulo de Goes, "The Significance of University Reform in Brazil," Inter-American Development Bank, *Higher Education and Latin American Development: Roundtables* (Asunción, Paraguay, 1965), pp. 38-39. Hereafter the latter will be referred to as *Roundtables.*

2. As quoted by Arthur P. Whitaker and David C. Jordan, *Nationalism in Contemporary Latin America* (New York, 1966), p. 164. For additional information about the University Reform movement see Julio V. González, *La reforma universitaria* (Buenos Aires, 1927) and documents published in Gabriel del Mazo, *La reforma universitaria,* 3 vols. (La Plata, 1941). Also read the latter's *Reforma universitaria y cultura nacional* (Buenos Aires, 1955). For a brief synopsis of the University Reform in Argentina, read Risieri Frondizi, "Old and New Argentine Universities," *Proceedings of the Inter-American Conference on Intellectual Interchange,* Institute of Latin American Studies of the University of Texas, 1943. A Peruvian point of view is found in José Carlos Mariátegui, *Siete ensayos de interpretación de la realidad peruana,* 10th edition (Lima, 1965), pp. 90-139.

3. Ugarte's writings are said to have influenced the Peruvian leader of the integration movement, Víctor Raúl Haya de la Torre. Other works by Ugarte include *Mi campaña hispanoamericana, El porvenir de América Latina,* and *El destino de un continente,* all written before 1917.

4. Harrison, p. 24, and Mariátegui, pp. 110-111.

5. Autonomy, as used in this study, means the privilege enjoyed by most Latin American universities before 1960 by which their campuses were placed outside the jurisdiction of the police and the military.

6. As David Burke recently pointed out in a report to the Senate Foreign Relations subcommittee, greater attention must be given to the student movements by Latin American governments for "at both the high school and university levels [they] are one of the continuing sources of insurgency in the hemisphere." (Quoted in the *Baltimore Sun,* January 14, 1968.) Three types of action have been taken to put an end to student politics. In Argentina and Brazil, repressive measures have been put into effect to limit students' academic freedom, but no major reforms have been implemented. In Venezuela the government has attempted

423

to use moral persuasion to urge academic reforms, although it, too, has used troops to intervene on the campus of the Universidad Central in Caracas. Nonetheless, the positions taken by spokesmen for the governing party, Acción Democrática, regarding changes in university autonomy have been positive, and have carefully emphasized the need to maintain campuses with strict academic freedom, as in the United States, while curtailing political activities that are detrimental to the educational process. The most extreme action, however, has taken place in Cuba, where the sacred cow of autonomy has been sacrificed upon the altar of the revolution. Now students in the Cuban university system who do not pass their courses are flunked out; attendance at classes is compulsory, and time limits have been placed upon a student's tenure at the university. Of far more importance, student participation in university administration has been eliminated. As John Harrison observed ". . .about the only thing in common between the Cuban and Cordovan way for universities is the belief that they should be free and that the cost of living scholarships should be available " (Harrison, p. 32). As recorded by the *New York Times* on April 7, 1968, "The military, which now has control of discipline at the university, banned beards, mustaches, long hair, and narrow pants. Military leaders told students that though such wear was not against the law, it is incompatible with the new military conditions.

"It is all part of a tightening up in Cuba on customs and manners that goes with the militant message that all youth should be a combination soldier-student-worker, a sort of ROTC guerrilla. It used to be said that Cuba was Communism cha-cha-cha. Now, it is Communism by the numbers, 'Fall in. 1-2-3-4.'"

7. Statistics for the Universidad de Oriente are not available to the author at this writing, but there are close to three hundred students from Caracas on the main campus at Cumaná, and a large number of students from western Venezuela, too.

8. The growth of the city of Cumaná, Venezuela, since 1960, when UDO was established there, has been nothing short of phenomenal. Its population is approaching 100,000, it is now only eight hours from Caracas by a new highway, and its economy has been expanded greatly by the millions of bolívares that the university has spent for salaries and for construction. Natives of the oriente section no longer refer to Cumaná as a sleepy little town. In fact, the first eight-story building in eastern Venezuela was recently constructed in Cumaná, indicative of the good times that UDO has brought to that long-neglected area of the nation.

9. Goes, p. 32.

424

10. For a brief description of this process see Andrew M. Torres, "Plan KUUDO: An Experiment in a New Dimension of University Responsibility," *AAUP Bulletin*, Vol. 54, No. 1 (March, 1968), pp. 88-89.

11. Ramón de Zubiría, "Contribution by Latin American Universities to the Solution of National and Regional Development Problems," *Roundtables*, pp. 101-120. For a typical criticism of graduate training outside of Latin America see Goes, p. 38.

12. Mexico City; Fondo de Cultura Económica, 1945.

13. As a result of widespread misunderstanding of his book, Sánchez clarified his position in the prologue to the second edition which was published in 1962 under a new title as *Examen espectral de América Latina* (Buenos Aires, 1962).

14. See Lewis Hanke, *South America* (Princeton, N.J.: Van Nostrand, 1959), p. 9, and Frank Tannenbaum, "Toward an Appreciation of Latin America," in Herbert Matthews, ed., *The United States and Latin America* (Englewood Cliffs, N.J.: Prentice-Hall, 1959), p. 46.

15. Zubiría, p. 113.

16. *Moral y cívica*, Quinto grado (Caracas, 1961), p. 57.

17. The study referred to was made during 1966 and 1967 by James Mudra of UDO's Central Planning Office at Puerto la Cruz. Mudra's findings shocked university officials into questioning the role of the university in fostering improved elementary education programs. For a general, but dated, study of education in Venezuela see George I. Sánchez' *The Development of Education in Venezuela* (Washington, D.C., 1963).

18. Banco Interamericano de Desarrollo, Instituto para la Integración de América Latina, *Primera memoria anual* (Buenos Aires, 1965). The original UDO plan has been published in *Américas Unidas*, Vol. 1, No. 1 (Cumaná, 1967).

19. The oriente section of Venezuela comprises the states of Anzoátegui, Bolívar, Monagas, Sucre, and Nueva Esparta, plus the Orinoco delta area and the rich Guayana. Its major cities are Cumaná, Barcelona, Puerto la Cruz, Ciudad Bolívar, Maturín, Porlamar, and the new Ciudad Guayana complex on the Orinoco.

20. For a concise description of UDO see Barbara Waggoner, *The Latin American Universities in Transition*, Occasional Publication No. 5, Center of Latin American Studies, University of Kansas, 1965, pp. 17-21.

CHAPTER **31** LATIN AMERICAN
BRAIN DRAINAGE

By Frank T. Bachmura
Department of Economics
Indiana University

"Full many a gem of purest ray serene
The dark unfathom'd caves of ocean bear ..."
Thomas Gray

Economists, policy makers, and journalists in Latin America as well as elsewhere appear to be giving increasing attention to the so-called brain drain problem. [4][9][22] This development follows upon public scrutiny of similar problems in Western Europe, particularly Britain, [16][17][40] and Canada. [17][26] Although some differences exist in the precise nature of brain drainage, particularly in terms of the permitted domestic price response to effective international demand, [17] we may, for our purposes, consider a brain drain to be an export of educated manpower. The general presumption is that such exports are "unfavorably balanced" in a manner similar to an unfavorable balance of trade of commercial accounts. [19][34] Naturally there are differences in the export composition of such educated manpower by specialty, but the term typically ignores lower than university educated manpower, although nurses and medical technicians are often included.[22] Thus, there is no consensus as to the cut-off point of number of years of schooling necessary to qualify a worker into the brain drain category. Within Latin America, Argentina,[15][21][28] Chile,[14] Colombia,[2][32] and Uruguay[27][29] have manifested most concern about the brain drain problem.[34] In general, however, the problem affects all of the Latin American and Caribbean countries.[22](chap. 2) [38](app. A) Within Latin America, Venezuela appears to be a significant importer.[6] An up-to-date and useful general bibliography will be found in Robert G. Myers' article on brain drains. [20]

The general tendency is for professional migration to the United States and Canada to constitute an increasing proportion of all immigrant workers, [34](p. 482) and for developing countries such as those in Latin America to provide an increasing proportion of all professional workers. [34](p.487) This tendency, abstracting from crisis immigration from Cuba, appears to hold for Latin

I acknowledge with thanks helpful discussions with two of my colleagues, Franz Gehrels and H. Scott Gordon as well as the assistance of two of my graduate students, Gary Burrell and Richard Donnelly. Responsibility for the paper is fully mine, of course.

America as well.[34](p. 487) The numbers of Latin American professionals emigrating to the United States appear to be increasing.[22](p. 6) New immigration legislation coming in to full effect
at mid-1968 probably will reinforce these tendencies.

Little is known in a systematic way about intra-Latin
American brain flows.   Available U.S. data has generated most
of the current Latin American[2] discussion.[15 25 27 28 29 32]
Attention also focuses upon both perverse and remedial aspects of
United States technical assistance programs.[23]

THE GENERALIZED NATURE OF THE BRAIN DRAIN PROBLEM

International manpower transfers, of which educated manpower may constitute a part, necessarily figure in the determination of a nation's foreign economic policy. As such, they fit into
comprehensive economic integration endeavors such as the Latin
American Free Trade Area and the Central American Common
Market as well as other proposals. There is no established nor
commonly approved method for recording the economic value of
movements of people as economic assets. However, the omission
of human asset transfers from the balance of payments record
limits its usefulness for the totality of economic integration problems. More significantly, failure to account for human asset movements in economic terms has distracted the attention of economists
from significant aspects of international economics. Given the
present day emphasis upon capital investment in the human agent
involving a new approach to the economics of labor,[16](pp. 6-7)
the omitted statement of the economic value of human assets moving internationally can be less easily justified than in the past.[3] [18]
To include money capital flows and flows of capital goods, but to
exclude the value of human beings, including the capital embedded
in them, serves to distort analysis and consequent economic policy.
True, between free societies the human asset flows cannot be conceived in terms of payments, but a comparable statement of inflows
and outflows of human asset values as an adjunct to the conventional
balance of payments would be informative. It would provide more
comprehensive economic information leading to superior economic
analysis and to more knowledgeable policy decisions.

A special characteristic of international flows of human
assets is that they involve, almost necessarily, expatriation as
well as transfer of assets. That is to say, there is no international
quid pro quo. They are thus unilateral transfers of national assets
initiated and determined by the individuals themselves. Although
there is the possibility of returns to the "mother" country in the
form of personal remittances or in the form of an advanced technology freely available to the exporting country,[17] these connections appear to be, at best, tenuous and uncertain. Private capital flows are, of course, not necessarily productive of counterflows
of interest and dividend flows nor of repayments. Nonetheless,
there is far greater probability of repatriation for such capital
flows. A migrant with considerable native equipment and capital

427

investment within him may be compared with a personally less favored migrant who takes considerable amounts of non-human assets with him. He truly acts as "a very considerable capitalist" [16] engaged in making judicious investment decisions.

Human assets moving internationally, then, have an economic dimension, hitherto largely neglected, which relates to other assets so moving whether they be commodities or economic factors. Neither the fact of expatriation nor the absence of an explicit payment constitute a justifiable exclusion of migration from international economic accounting. Even if it should be shown that present-day preoccupation with brain drainage is misplaced or misconceived, the attention it creates provides a useful focus for policy determination well beyond the international dimension alone.

IMPERFECT CONCEPTION OF THE PROBLEM

Much of the preoccupation with the brain drain problem is indeed misplaced and misconceived. Discussion proceeds from an unfortunately meager empirical base. Not only are there few facts, but the nature and availability of existing data lead to exaggeration and perhaps to reversed conclusions. By definition, but unfortunately not by consistent definition, brain drainage necessarily includes only part of a much broader human asset problem. For Latin America, the available facts and existing definitions reinforce and make more rigid a view of non-reciprocity or even victimization by the Colossus.

The common misconception of the brain drainage problem has at least five facets:

1. It conceives of "brains" as existing only among the highly educated. Although even illiterates do have mental ability contributing to their economic worth, the important point here is that any arbitrary cut-off leads to a less than comprehensive view of the international asset transfer problem. The only solution is to include, and properly evaluate, all flows of human assets.

2. The human asset flow is often inadequately valued. It conceives of these flows essentially as direct costs of production, that is to say, in terms of educational costs. This view ignores broader value connotations, particularly the concept of value added by education, as well as excluding certain aspects of indirect cost in terms of foregone income. From our point of view, the relative scarcity of educable persons in any society creates an asset value which is essentially a rent. Further, the probable length of future productive life of the migrant is not considered. Recognition of the broader concept carries with it both analytical and political consequences as well as a more comprehensive accounting of costs of production.

3. Characteristically, there is no comparison of human capital flows with other capital flows.

4. Characteristically, the flows considered are gross flows rather than net flows. The purview thus includes only one side of population transfer accounts.

5. The temporal focus is extremely short run, particularly when we recognize that career decisions are generally lifetime decisions and that former large importers may now be exporters. It is significant, for example, that Argentina, one of the greatest proportional recipients of imported human assets in world history, [41] (tables iii-5,iii-6) should be a focus of criticism about brain drainage. [4] [9] [22]

Other distortions of our knowledge of the brain drainage problem stem from the nature and incompleteness of available demographic information with respect to international migration. Demographic information is, by its nature, physical rather than economic. It provides us with numbers, and sometimes, characteristics of migrants. The characteristics constitute a series of taxonomies. We have age and sex classifications which can be formed into a population "pyramid." We have educational attainment or occupational classifications which can be summarized graphically in the form of a "tree." Although these and similar classifications can be useful to economists, they are no substitute for economic evaluation. For other areas there are some economic rather than physical estimates of human asset flows, but for Latin America such information is not available.

The relative national availability of demographic information also produces distortions. Because the United States provides more detailed information about the demographic characteristics of entrants, much of the brain drain discussion takes the form of a polarization of movement as between the United States and the rest of the world, with the United States viewed as the brain importer. Return flows are usually unknown even for Great Britain. [34] (pp. 504-6) Viewed in the Latin American context, such a focus tends to submerge intra-Latin American movements and to neglect the possibilities of mutually advantageous two-way movements between Latin American countries. They neglect the economic advantages of specialization and the international economies of educational scale within the region.

IMPLICATIONS OF CAPITAL MARKET IMPERFECTIONS FOR THE BRAIN DRAIN PROBLEM

Were capital markets perfect, both internationally and domestically, both in the human agent and in artifacts, then the resolution of the brain drain problem would be much simpler. As it is, we know that capital markets are far from perfect. Virtually all countries in Latin America are lacking in capital relative to the United States. There are variations also as between Latin American countries. With more perfect capital markets, we would expect net capital flows to the capital-shy countries. The brain drainage problem raises the possibility that capital flows for human asset values may be in the opposite direction from that expected to lead to factor market improvement, [34] (p. 479-80) and therefore to be perverse in their economic effects, serving to intensify rather than moderate the intensity of the capital scarcity problem in the exporting country. For this reason, the brain drain problem is intimately tied to national investment policy, whether in the human agent or not, and to the development problem. Because educational investments are life-long in their effects, non-migratory adjustments operate largely through a career-long pattern, into which new entrants come and out of which departures occur through death and retirement. At the higher levels particularly, transfers from professional specialty to specialty usually require additional capital investment through retraining. This may shorten gestation periods and hasten adjustment, but probably disinvests through disuse some of the value of the earlier profession-specific assets.

Investment policy is, of course, an integral component of national development policies. If only because investments in the human agent are competitive with other investments, educational investments also have development significance. These policies relate educational investments vis-à-vis other investments, as well as to the mix of educational investment. By influencing the mix, brain drains clearly relate to the national payoff for educational investment. Although we shall not prejudge the case at this point, it is important for us to recognize that in a context of market imperfection, brain drains, if they exist, have pervasive relevance for domestic policy. Still further, because of the per capita income criterion commonly used to measure success in development, a selective export of capital intensive human assets with relatively high productivity and income will tend to depress per capita growth rates, suggesting the non-maximizing allocation of scarce investment resources within an admittedly imperfect factor market.

Abstracting from other components of human asset value and concentrating for the moment simply upon the investment component, it behooves us to examine investment alternatives in further detail.

Mobility characterizes human agent investment relative to other investment. This is true whether the investment is public of private. Public other investment is particularly likely to be immobile in view of the generally accepted role of the government, in Latin America as well as elsewhere, for providing infrastructural investments. This implies that if investments in the human agent yield returns to the investor, public or private, which are made smaller or less certain by migration or the possibility thereof, the attractiveness of investment in the human agent is reduced. This implies a reduction of the attractiveness of human agent investment if migration, or the possibility of migration, reduces the flow of returns to the investor or makes them less certain.

A further characteristic of the principal human agent investments is their identification with a particular individual. This

attribute is particularly distinct from infrastructural investment
in which personal beneficiaries may not be identifiable because of
the diffused nature of the benefits. The identifiability of the beneficiary or at least of the vehicle for human investments raises
political questions with respect to the freedom of the individual to
move and the degree of inalienability of property values vested in
him.

POLICY RESPONSE TO THE MARKET IMPERFECTION AND MO-
BILITY PROBLEMS

One way to respond to the reduction of the migration-in-
duced investment in the human agent is simply to prohibit external
migration. The Soviet Union, which is reported to have realized
sizable returns on educational investment, has done just this. By
prohibiting migration regardless of the degree of investment, the
entire value of the human asset is "captured" and there is no uncertainty in human-nonhuman investment alternatives attributable
to external migration. Because the State makes the investment
and the proceeds remain within the country, many of the uncertainties in the capital markets in private or mixed economies do not
exist. This method for the reduction in uncertainty for basing allocative decisions achieves its gains at a considerable social cost—
a cost unacceptable to Latin American countries, even including
Cuba.

In mixed economies the general solution to the imperfection problem has been to finance all or part of the educational investment publicly. This then has the effect of reducing some of
the imperfections for individuals in families which cannot meet the
direct costs of education, but which can meet incidental increased
maintenance costs, and which can forego the income that the student would otherwise have earned during the instruction period.
Families which undervalue educational investments may be forced
to underwrite some of the costs of education through a compulsory
education law. The realizable foregone income can be reduced to
zero through child labor legislation. In some cases, the student's
family might be compensated for the child's foregone earnings by
public payment. Generally, however, the educated person in Latin
American countries represents an asset in which investment expenditures are a bundle of private and public costs. [7]

Should private and public investments in the human agent
be distinguished for economic policy? In most Latin American
countries, despite considerable public investment in human assets,
inadequacies and foregone opportunities are obvious. High rates of
both absolute and functional illiteracy, systematic de facto exclusion from educational opportunity by income class, residential sector, and otherwise suggest that public investment has gone only a
short way in the direction of eliminating the major imperfections
in human asset investment. These conditions lead to a general conclusion that the private sector should absorb a larger amount of the
financing problem than it now does.

What might be the process for requiring greater private participation in the human investment financing problem? Although compulsory education and child labor laws stimulate private investment in some cases, such policies may be unenforceable for many low-income people and might create great hardship for others. Another possibility is to charge a fee for the available public education facilities. That is to say, to enforce a needs test in combination with a compulsory education law, ideally using the proceeds to broaden educational opportunities to people in poorer classes.

Another possibility is to base all public education upon an implied fee system. Compensation to the public would be expected of those who did not pay the fee at the time of education, but no one would be excluded if he did not pay. Repayment would be made in subsequent years either explicitly or by residence, presumably as a productive taxpayer. Residence in the country for a given time period would extinguish the fee on a pro rated basis. This would entail an indenture [25](p.1073) which would inhibit migration without compensation to the public for its investment. As such it constitutes a restriction upon the individual's freedom, but it is removable by him, the receiving country, or by a private lender in either country. Modified programs of this type which finance education but require some degree of service exist in the United States— the Health Professions' Educational Assistance Act of 1965 (Public Law 88-605) for example. This suggests some compatibility of indentures with human freedom.

The fact that human investments are financed privately rather than publicly does not erase the effect of movement upon the international balance of asset flows. A country may wish to prohibit or severely limit private investment abroad. Thus, it might in terms of self-interest require some degree of compensation from the receiving country for the educational investment in the migrant, and even for other aspects of the economic value of the expatriated human asset. Such a proposal for an international quid pro quo for human asset movements does, of course, modify the absoluteness of the individual's equity in himself — a political step with important implications. Although such a step constitutes an abridgement of a person's freedom, it can alternatively be viewed as introducing an enhanced degree of reciprocity in the international exchange of all assets, which may conduce greater economic as well as political freedom for yet others.

An important part of the imperfection in the capital market with respect to human investment arises from the relative imperfection of knowledge inherent in minors. This aspect of the imperfection normally diminishes with maturity, prior educational investment, and general experience. To this extent, then, the case for resolving educational investment imperfections through "universal" free public education and compulsory education laws becomes weaker for each population cohort as it moves toward adulthood and with each increment of formal education. For these persons the imperfections in terms of the uncertainty of payoff through death or disability can be viewed in terms of an insurable risk, and educational loans become significant market oriented, yet possibly publicly funded, means for resolving capital imperfections. A very large proportion of the domestic investment in higher education in Latin American countries is publicly supported, "universal," subsidized education. It is specifically this facet of the overall problem which bulks so large in brain drainage discussion.

FULL ECONOMIC ACCOUNTING FOR HUMAN ASSETS

Although recognizing the composite nature of the economic value of a human asset, my emphasis to this point has rested upon the investment in the human agent rather than other capitalizable human asset components. In other words, the economic justification for the existing mixes of publicly supported professional and other higher education is weak to begin with. Migration of substantial proportions of those professional graduating classes simply intensifies the problem.[22](p. 28) Moreover, it is precisely this investment component of human asset value which can most readily be treated in economic terms rather than in political terms of the inalienability of human rights.

Should the educational (or other) investment in the human agent be compensated in terms of the original cost of production or in terms of the properly computed value added by production (education)?[7] Generally the latter is larger than the first. Should not the individual acting as a "considerable capitalist" and entrepreneur receive this as a reward for his effort and that he reimburse the investor for the cost of production including interest? Such a view would reinforce the role of the individual as a free agent rather than as a creature of the State as well as provide a reinforcement for achievement incentives.

There are, though, at least three other components of human asset value stemming from the individual's productive efforts. They include the basic value of the person as an economic asset independent of capital investment within him. In addition, there is differential value reflecting an individual's differentiated educability.[3](pp.61-6) Not every one can absorb a physician's education, for example. This differential value is frequently obscured in educational analysis partly because only a minor portion of even the most educable persons in Latin American countries have the opportunity to be educated to their potential. Indeed, "Full many a flower is born to blush unseen, and waste its sweetness on the desert air." We know, however, that potential for education, or educability, is not uniformly distributed, so that part of the return to an educated person's work is explained by his educability. In this process, the educational system acts as a discoverer of talent—utilizing the grading process, trial and error, and testing services. I believe that a case can be made for compensating the provider of the discovery service by awarding him a "finder's fee." Compensation ethically could be required in a manner analogous to that for the basic educational investment.

433

Furthermore, a part of the relative differential in earning capacity in these countries is attributable to de facto restriction of entry to educational opportunity on fortuitous or ascriptive grounds, not to educability nor effort. To some extent this restriction creates an artificial value operating to benefit the actual recipient of the educational service even though there are others who are equally capable within the system who, because of continuing imperfections in the capital market, do not have access to the opportunity for superior income flows. In this case, a compensatory scheme can be justified even in the absence of a brain drainage problem.

The really difficult political and ethical question is strongest in terms of the basic, "pre-investment" component of human productivity. Here, as well as in the basic distribution of native ability, we are confronted with a specification of national policy toward its basic human assets. Do human beings by birth constitute part of the value of a nation's wealth and is the wealth vested in the State? Although my ethical penchant is to urge these basic values to be vested in the individual, there is a basis upon which there may be some compensation to the exporting country which will still leave the individual better off economically. Non-human resources which have a "place of birth" are commonly subject in Latin America to a severance levy or an export tax, even when the asset is sold on a quid pro quo basis, for example Venezuelan petroleum and Chilean copper. There is, of course, no similar necessary national quid pro quo for human assets vis-à-vis their birth places.

GAINERS AND LOSERS THROUGH MIGRATION

To this point I have written as though there were no question that the net export of human assets was contrary to the national interests of the exporting country. It will behoove us, however, to look at a considerably broader picture than this. Six groups will be identified— the migrant, members of the profession with whom he competes in the new country, members of the profession with whom he ceases to compete in the old country, the general citizenry of the new country, the educational discriminee, and the general citizenry of the old country. One could easily construct a more detailed taxonomy, of course.

For the time being let us view the migrant as one who moves voluntarily in response to economic stimulation rather than in response to political crisis. On this basis no worker would move unless he expected to improve himself and reverse or third country movement would be a continuous possibility, so that we regard the migrant as one who quite obviously is made better off by the process. The movement of non-working women and dependent children may constitute a partial exception to this statement, as does the movement of the political refugee.

The competitors in the new country would be losers and the erstwhile competitors would be gainers, under most circumstances. It is quite possible that shifts in the supply schedule would

434

have no perceptible effect upon income, particularly in the exporting country where prices may be administered by the government or quasi - governmental agency. Quite clearly there are some groups made worse off by the migration in the very nation which reputedly reaps brain "gains." Quite obviously it is not an economic transfer which makes everyone better off, even apart from the gift of tax receipts.[17](p. 302)

The general citizenry in the new country would gain; it would be a recipient of a new asset, providing a service at a no higher price. The exporting citizenry would lose assets for which they would receive no compensation and would face increased prices for professional services.

To some extent this loss might be modified by personal remittances and contributions to the world level of technology which is conceivably of benefit to the exporter,[17](p. 306) but this is not likely for the small, low-income country.

There remains one other significant population component— the educational discriminee, probably found in both countries, but I shall emphasize those in the exporting country. Educational discriminees are those excluded from subsidized educational opportunities open to other nationals of the same level of educability. Exclusion in such cases may be fortuitous or systematic, including rationing through family inability to cover indirect costs of childhood education, geographic isolation and rural residence, ethnic, linguistic, and racial patterns, and possibly sex.

The precise individuals made worse off by educational discrimination cannot be identified; the best we can do is identify groups. Nonetheless, there can be little doubt as to their deprived position. Even without migration, domestic remedial programs are called for to make fuller use of the country's available talent. With educationally selective migration, their foregone loss through restriction of entry rises in two ways — the expatriation of the migrant and the effect of reduced supply upon the costs of professional services. Under such circumstances, it would be consistent for the discriminees to "present their bill," before the migrant left the country. Presumably those remaining professionals would be expected to pay larger amounts to offset the discriminee's disadvantages also.

RECIPROCITY IN HUMAN MIGRATION

Even with the recognition of the ethical values involved, is there not a sense in which an ethical onus does rest upon the net benefit receiving country quite apart from the ethics of individual liberty? Does not the benefit receiving country have to share the ethical burden? Are there not some gains from migration which are ethically capturable from the beneficiaries?

Would economically motivated migration occur if compen-

sation were required for unrequited investment in the migrant, a
finder's fee, and a discriminee's bill? The answer must be yes.
It would occur if the adjusted income receipts were enough larger
in the new country. Basically the higher reward would reflect the
scarcity relative to other factors of the basic human endowment
and differential educability. However, there are at least three additional possibilities conducing mutual gains even where the adjusted
income increments are no larger. They are increased professional
longevity, lower cost of production in the exporting country, and
differentially higher occupational status in the new country.

Increased professional longevity, particularly through
longer life expectancy, constitutes a clear case, and for some Latin
American countries this difference may be considerable, even
though professionals enjoy superior life expectancies in almost all
countries.

Lower cost of production in the exporting country also is
a possibility although obscured by quality differences. Quite clearly,
foregone income costs, ususally privately absorbed, are lower in
the exporting country. Alternatively, education abroad, with home
country foregone income adjusted by the international differential
in personal maintenance costs, also yields an advantageous alternative. It explains at least some of the non-returning student
phenomenon.

Some societies ascribe higher status to occupations than
others. Even with complete elimination of pecuniary advantages
under those circumstances, migration would be advantageous for
that occupation. It is sometimes held that British engineers and
Chilean nurses [5] (p. 312) face relatively low status in their home
countries.

FEMALE PRODUCTIVITY

Although lifetime earning profiles constitute powerful
instruments for human investment analysis, the pecuniary productivity of women is probably not an accurate index of their economic
worth. The problem stems from the exclusion from national income accounting of the home production of household services.
This exclusion raises important social considerations with respect
to the basis for the education of women in underdeveloped countries.
Using conventional market criteria alone, the education of women
would be inhibited. This reasoning flows from the generally much
reduced volume of the potential income flow. Ironically, however,
such a policy would systematically eliminate about half the highly
educable people from the possibility of labor force participation in
line with their full potential.

From the economic point of view, a narrow interpretation
of female labor force productivity could lead to extremely distorted
education patterns by twentieth-century standards. Yet for educational planning purposes alone, it is necessary to equate the returns

436

to female education with those of male education. There seems to be no escape from the conclusion that it will be necessary to establish some "shadow" or "pro forma" price for female household services for the basis of calculation. This does not imply that men make no family contribution other than that encompassed by the market, nor that they and women alike may perform other unpaid community services of high social value.

Failure to give proper and complete accounting for the education of women can produce untoward results. From the point of view of the market alone, an illiterate mother and housekeeper is the economic equal of the educated mother and housekeeper. Moreover, rates of economic growth are statistically stimulated by the growth of female labor force participation which is not offset by the value of the erstwhile home services.

THE EMPIRICAL RECORD FOR LATIN AMERICA

The vociferous and sometimes polemical public discussion of the "brain drain" which has lead us to broader problems is founded on a meager, incomplete, and thus, as we have seen, inadequate basis.[22] [34] [35] [36] [39] United States records of entrants who declare their professions promote a polarized rather than a "matricized" view of Latin American "brain" flows. Economic valuation of the one-way flow is usually known only in direct educational cost terms. Adjustment of even these data to human capital and related lifetime income profiles is a rarity, even for European countries with better statistical information than Latin America.

We know, however, that human asset flows are internationally significant. For Canada, we have a peak estimate of 13 per cent of U. S. merchandise imports for scientists and engineers alone.[34](p. 485) We know, too, that large proportions of Latin American medical school graduates emigrate to the United States.[22](p. 28)

The brain drainage problems lead us to the "tremendously integrative power"[16](p. 7)of the human capital concept and with it a recognition of the interrelationship of all human assets. From the migration point of view we know that only a small proportion of migrants are "brains." Yet information for Latin American international human asset flows are demographic rather than economic. Moreover, even the demographic information is meager and sporadic (Table I). For purposes of interrelationship to LAFTA or CACM integration efforts, data are inadequate.

Brain drainage problems then lead us to domestic investment policy, particularly in education. Carnoy has developed an earnings profile and human capital returns analysis for Mexico,[7] but little other empirical information seems to be available. Adelman's heuristic model for Argentina provides arbitrary shadow prices for education products. [1](p. 406)In addition she gives some

TABLE I

Availability of Latin American International Migration Data 1919-1966

Country		Classification A	B	C	D
Argentina	E	1920, 1929-43		1923	1924-26, 1948-54
	I	1919-26, 1930-43 1960-1965			1948-1954
Brazil	E	1936-37	1940-44	1922, 1935	1918-19, 1935, 1939
	I	1936-37, 1960-62	1939, 1945-47		1918-21
Chile	E				
	I	1962-64			
Colombia	E	1930-37, 1944-47 1960-65		1925-29	1938-43, 1948
	I	1930-37, 1944-47, 1960-65		1925-29	1938-43, 1948-54
Costa Rica	E				
	I	1960-65		1925-27	
Cuba	E				
	I	1919-35			
Dominican Republic	E	1960-63			1937-47
	I	1960-63			1937-47
El Salvador	E		1941-43, 1945-47		1934-40, 1948-50 1952-53
	I		1941-43, 1945-47		1934-40, 1948-50 1952-53

Country	E/I	A	B	C	D
Guatemala	E			1924-38, 1941-47	
	I	1928-47, 1960-65		1924-38, 1941-47	1920-36, 1948-52
Mexico	E				
	I	1925-47, 1960-65			1948-52
Nicaragua	E	1937-47			
	I	1937-47			
Panama	E				
	I	1960-65			
Paraguay	E				
	I		1922-23, 1926		1918-21, 1924-25; 1927-42, 1945-47
Peru	E	1961			
	I	1960-64			
Uruguay	E		1920-42		
	I		1920-42		
Venezuela	E				1936-47
	I				1936-47

Symbols:
E - Emigration
I - Immigration

A - Age and Sex
B - Age & Sex (Not in Combination)
C - Children & Adults (With sex for adults only)
D - Sex alone

Sources: (35, 1954, pp. 634-681; 1966, pp. 641-700)(36, Vol. 11, Table I)

attention to the economics of female education by introducing a "leakage to housewifery" term.[1](p. 343) Blitz[5] provides some female productivity information for Chile. Estimates of human asset value being as rare as they are, it is no wonder that other concepts such as the discriminee's bill, the finder's fee, and return to educability are still unknown. The significant thing, however, is that they are not unknowable given the work done elsewhere. It is, therefore, appropriate for those in both regional and national development to support and to further research and data collection in these areas.

One specific symptom of misguided public policy appears in the record. This has to do with the proportion of graduating professionals leaving the country taking the state-provided education with them. For Haiti to export 48 per cent of its physicians to the United States seems perverse and would continue to be so even if returnees and inaccurate statistics were to reduce this by half. Most of the Central American countries apparently are important losers as are the Dominican Republic and Colombia. Except for Colombia, the principal vocal countries (Argentina, Chile and Uruguay) are not significant losers.[22](p. 28)

SUMMARY AND CONCLUSIONS

The issue of the brain drain in Latin America is an important one both for domestic and foreign policies including programs for regional economic integration. Unfortunately, the force and polemic with which some positions are held are not supported by adequate information nor comprehensive analysis. The problem is viewed in terms of a gross flow to the United States, largely because of the availability of more detailed, yet still inadequate, demographic data for the United States. Intra-regional flows are imperfectly known. Typically the problem is conceived of in isolation from other flows of human assets as well as in isolation from other asset flows from country to country. Moreover, the problems are viewed in extremely short run rather than long run terms. From the point of view of international economic policy as well as for domestic educational and investment policy, vastly more information is needed. As a starting point even information of a demographic nature, taxonomically organized, will be useful. Ultimately, the computation of value figures attributing value contributions to the education investment, the talent discovery function, and the intrinsic economic value of the human asset differentiated by educability will be required. Although these estimates require complex analysis, there can be little justification in further delay — either in collecting data or refinement of research given the goals of maximizing economic advantages, including rates of growth. The regional integrating associations in Latin America, as well as the individual countries in their own individual interests, can reasonably expect fruitful results from such efforts. The associations should minimally arrange for standardized collection of data and simultaneously move to comprehensive intra-association coverage. There also is a remarkable opportunity for association support for in-depth analysis and more refined collection. These endeavors would lead both symbolically and substantially to a more cooperative posture for the associations and bring with them the promise of sizable returns.

REFERENCES

1. Adelman, Irma. "A Linear Programming Model of Educational Planning: A Case Study of Argentina," pp. 385-411 in Irma Adelman and Erik Thorbecke, eds., *The Theory and Design of Economic Development*. Baltimore: The Johns Hopkins Press, 1966.

2. Arias Osorio, Eduardo. "Emigración de profesionales colombianos," *El Tiempo*, Bogotá, October 16, 1966.

3. Becker, Gary S. *Human Capital*. New York: Columbia University Press, 1965.

4. Beijar, G. "Selective Migration for and 'Brain Drain' from Latin America," *International Migration*, IV, No. 1 (1966), 28-36.

5. Blitz, Rudolf C. "Some Observations Concerning the Chilean Educational System and Its Relation to Economic Growth," pp. 303-313 in C. Arnold Anderson and Mary Jean Bowman, eds., *Education and Economic Development*. Chicago: Aldine Publishing Company, 1965.

6. Buitrón, A. *Las inmigraciones en Venezuela: sus efectos económicos y sociales*. Washington, D.C.: Pan American Union, 1956.

7. Carnoy, Martin. "Earnings and Schooling in Mexico," *Economic Development and Cultural Change*, XV, No. 4 (July 1967), 408-19.

8. Council on International Educational and Cultural Affairs. *Some Facts and Figures on the Migration of Talent and Skills*. Washington, D.C.: Department of State, March 1967.

9. Economic Commission for Latin America, United Nations. "The Training of Human Resources in the Economic and Social Development of Latin America," *Economic Bulletin for Latin America*, XI, No. 2 (October 1966),1-57. Also known as *Document UNESCO/MINEDECAL/9*.

10. Grubel, Herbert G. "The Brain Drain: A U.S. Dilemma," *Science*, December 1966, pp. 1420-23.

11. ——. Letter to the Editor, *New York Times*, April 14, 1968, p. E17.

12. Grubel, Herbert G., and Anthony D. Scott. "Determinants of Migration: The Highly Skilled," *International Migration*, V (1967), 127-39.

13. ——. "The International Flow of Human Capital," *American Economic Review*, LVI, No. 2 (May 1966), 268-74.

14. Gutiérrez, S., and J. Riquelme. *La emigración de recursos humanos de alto nivel y el caso de Chile*. Washington, D.C.: Pan American Union, 1965.

15. Horowitz, Morris A. *La emigración de profesionales y técnicos argentinos*. Buenos Aires: Instituto Torcuato Di Tella, 1962.

16. Johnson, Harry G. "The Economic Approach to Social Questions," *Economica*, XXXV, No. 137 (February 1968), 1-21.

17. ——. "The Economics of the 'Brain Drain': The Canadian Case," *Minerva*, III, (Spring 1965), 299-311.

18. Kiker, B. F. "The Historical Roots of the Concept of Human Capital," *Journal of Political Economy*, LXXIV, No. 5 (October 1966), 481-99.

19. Mondale, Walter F. "How Poor Nations Give to the Rich," *Saturday Review*, L, No. 10, 24-26.

20. Myers, Robert G. "'Brain Drains' and 'Brain Gains'," *International Development Review*, IX, No. 4 (December 1967), 4-9.

21. Oteiza, Enrique. "Emigration of Engineers from Argentina: A Case of Latin American 'Brain Drain'," *International Labour Review*, December 1965, pp. 445-61.

22. Pan American Health Organization. *Migration of Health Personnel, Scientists, and Engineers from Latin America*. Washington, D.C.: PAHO, Scientific Publication No. 142, September 1966.

23. Perkins, James A. "Foreign Aid and the Brain Drain," *Foreign Affairs*, July 1966, pp. 608-19.

24. Phillips, H. M. "El capital humano," *El Correo*, UNESCO, Año XVII (October 1964), 11.

442

25. Schultz, T. W. "Efficient Allocation of Brains in
     Modernizing World Agriculture," *Journal of Farm
     Economics,* XLIX (1967), 1071-82.

26. Scott, Anthony. "The Recruitment and Migration of
     Canadian Social Scientists," *Canadian Journal of
     Economics and Political Science,* XXXIII (1967),
     495-508.

27. Selser, Gregorio. "El drenaje de los técnicos,"
     Marcha, Montevideo, January 13, 1967.

28. ——. "¿Se van o nos roban? La succión de técnicos lati-
     noamericanos por Estados Unidos," *Inédito,* Buenos
     Aires, December 21, 1966.

29. ——. "La succión de técnicos en América Latina," *Marcha,*
     Montevideo, December 23, 1966.

30. Shearer, John C. "In Defense of Traditional Views of
     the 'Brain Drain' Problem," *International Educa-
     tional and Cultural Exchange,* Fall 1966, pp. 17-25.

31. Sutherland, Sir Gordon. "The Brain Drain," *The
     Political Quarterly,* XXXVIII (1967), 51-61.

32. Thiesenhusen, William C. "Help for the Brain Drain,"
     The Progressive, XXXII (March 1968), 30-32.

33. ——. "How Big is the Brain Drain?" *LTC* (Madison:
     University of Wisconsin, Land Tenure Center), No. 29,
     mimeo, January 1967.

34. Thomas, Brinley. "The International Circulation of
     Human Capital," *Minerva,* V (Summer 1967), 479-506.

35. United Nations. *Demographic Yearbook.* New York: U.N.
     Department of Economic and Social Affairs, 1953, 1966.

36. ——. *Population Studies.* New York: U.N. Department of
     Social Affairs, Population Division, 1953.

37. United States Advisory Commission on International
     Educational and Cultural Affairs. "The International
     Migration of Talent and Skills; A Selective Bibliog-
     raphy," *International Education and Cultural Exchange,*
     Summer 1966, p. 67.

38. United States Congress, House Committee on Government
     Operations. *The Brain Drain of Scientists, Engineers,
     and Physicians from the Developing Countries into the
     United States.* Hearing, 90th Congress, Second Ses-
     sion, January 28, 1968. Washington, D.C., 1968.

39. ___. *The Brain Drain into the United States of Scientists, Engineers, and Physicians*. Staff Study, 90th Congress, 1st Session. Washington, D.C., 1967.

40. Wilson, James A. "The Emigration of British Scientists," *Minerva,* IV (Autumn 1966), 20-29.

41. Woodruff, William. *Impact of Western Man*. New York: St. Martin's Press, 1966.

42. Worsnop, Richard L. "World Competition for Skilled Labor," *Editorial Research Reports,* I, No. 23 (June 21, 1967).

CHAPTER **32** THE PROSPECT AND PROBLEMS
OF LATIN AMERICAN CULTURAL
INTEGRATION

By William C. Atkinson, Director
Institute of Latin-American Studies
University of Glasgow

To speak of the prospect and problems of cultural integration in Latin America as seen from Europe carries the implication that there is such a thing as a European viewpoint, and
this the further implication that in Europe cultural integration has
already been achieved. The painful and so far frustrated attempts
not of Europe but of western Europe over the last decade to achieve
a measure of economic integration make for caution. Two world
wars, each fought in the conviction that it was a war to end wars,
the gigantic strides of modern technology towards control by man
of his environment and ultimately of his destiny, these, far from
bringing to realization that happy concept of one world governed
by reason wherein all mankind would pull harmoniously towards
common goals, have uncovered new tensions, multiplied divergences, sundered allies into opposing camps, decried affinities
and exalted incompatibilities to a point where the would-be citizen
of the world no longer knows where his true allegiance lies.

European culture had its unity when it meant the culture
and civilization of Greece. Later it meant those of Rome, en-
riched by the Greek heritage and carried now to the confines of
empire. Altered in kind and degree, it was still a unity throughout the long centuries of mediaeval Christendom, and might have
continued so through the Renascence and after had not that movement of intellectual emancipation—in which, be it noted in passing, the discovery of the New World played a role no less significant than the rediscovery of the Old—invaded the domain of
dogma from which the play of rational enquiry had till then been
warded off, and spawned the Reformation. This makes the great
divide, with Protestant, more specifically Anglo-Saxon, on the
one slope and Catholic, more specifically Latin, on the other:
each obscured in his vision, and hence in his comprehension, of
the other by the doctrinal schism, each readily persuaded that,
since matters of eternal truth were at issue, the honest thing was
to fight it out.

Initially, to the extent that the culture of Latin America
derives directly from that of the Iberian Peninsula, there might
appear to be no problem of integration, at most a minor problem
of reintegration, of the correction of incidental or accidental
fissiparous tendencies. Over the formative period of the New
World there was no questioning the cultural unity of Spain and
Portugal, that Iberia of the Greeks, Hispania of the Romans,

that nature had always intended to be one. Differences of ethnic strain there were indeed, notably the pronounced Celtic element in the west whose stamp remains clear till today; differences too of vital experience, a Reconquest lasting for some eight centuries in the one, for a century and a half in the other, a nation of sea-farers here, responding to the challenge of ocean, of landlubbers there, no less ready to challenge any land-mass with its armies. But their culture, their system of attitudes, resting on a common faith and common belief in a divinely appointed mission and destiny, were as one. Across the ocean there would be rivalries and a concern with lines of demarcation, there would be the nuances of literary heritage and of the language in which that heritage was enshrined; but culturally there seemed every reason to believe that the Peninsula had simply added a new, a not merely vast but illimitable, dimension to its horizon.

The factors that gave the lie straightway to this flattering prognostication are, with hindsight, familiar to us all. There is first the consideration that we are what we are in respect partly of heredity, of the genes that carry their predispositions from generation to generation, but partly also in respect of environment. Man is man in his circumstantia. The exaggeration is manifest in the statement that the man of the Old World, once come to and settled in the New, became a new man; but in the coming to terms with a new life, set in a whole new frame of reference unimaginable to those who stayed behind, there could be no relying on that earlier system of attitudes whose intelligibility, coherence and efficacity novel experience now called in question. Vested interest in maintaining the system could not have been stronger: all the resources of Church and State were bent to that end. But one recalls the early discovery of the Jesuit fathers in Brazil, eager to preach the true faith to the indigene in his own tongue, that while Tupí had words for "father" and for "son" it had none, nor any discoverable way of signifying, "Holy Ghost," and the Trinity had perforce to decline in their teaching to a binity. And the even more disturbing discovery of a new heresy fast spreading among the faithful of their own race, now so far removed from effective authority, the indulgent doctrine that "south of the Equator there is no sin."

With the eternal verities thus called in question on two fronts and the daily invalidation on the more immediate material plane of the assumptions underlying an earlier way of life that was fast becoming but a memory, the New World that Spaniard and Portuguese fondly imagined themselves to be fashioning in the image of the Old was steadily refashioning them. And refashioning them not in one new distinctive mould but in many. For by environment is to be understood, as well as the actual physical setting, the whole play of attendant circumstance. The Peninsula as patria had been extensive enough to allow many patrias chicas. How to look for unity of response, and resulting unity of attitudes, to a life now pinpointed anywhere between New Mexico and Cape Horn, between sea level and the summit of the Andes, between fertile plains and desert wastes, between an agricultural and a

446

mining economy? This was no colony, it was an empire, a continent and a half, one-sixth of the earth's surface, whose extremes lay farther one from the other than either did from Europe. "The most shattering fact to be established in the 19th century" — so a scientist has recently described Darwin's demonstration, in <u>The Origin of Species</u>, that man was a part of nature. It was, appropriately, his experience in South America that led Darwin to the discovery of a truth that had lain there, awaiting his formulation, for over three centuries. Man must needs partake of and be shaped by his physical setting.

As for attendant circumstance, that impinged immediately, and most forcibly, in the shape of the peoples already in possession. In the flat regions, notably the River Plate area, they allowed themselves, still nomads, to be pushed back as the white newcomers demanded more and more of their territory — and this is perhaps the only significant resemblance to be found between any part of Latin and Anglo-Saxon America. For the rest they stood their ground, fought, were defeated, but still stood their ground; and the white man, having to come to terms with them too, was doubly affected and in the process doubly differentiated still further alike from his fellows back home and from his fellows in other parts of the New World. Firstly, in the infinite variety of the cultural panorama he so unexpectedly encountered. Tribes there were of extreme primitiveness, though none so primitive that there was nothing to be learnt from them. But others had passed far beyond the tribal to achieve not merely stable complex societies, but civilizations as advanced in their different ways as that of Europe. This was the surprise of surprises, the dawning realization that there could be other civilizations, a surprise so shocking in its impact that he set himself instinctively to destroy what he could of them. But affected by them he was, and the new societies he shaped could no more escape their imprint than he could escape the need to devise a pattern of co-existence with new variants of the human species.

Which brings in straightway the secondly, the mingling of blood. The ifs of history are infinite, and infinitely intriguing; few more so than the thought that had Spaniard and Portuguese crossed the Atlantic with their womenfolk, and with thereby their own social sufficiency, as the Pilgrim Fathers were to in the north, the whole subsequent history of Latin America would have been vastly different. Instead, from the moment of arrival they consorted with the native women, raised up a new generation of half-breeds, and Latin America was cast in the act for a new role as the mestizo New World, its culture a mestizo culture, its destiny inevitably far removed from what might have been looked for from a mere projection overseas of Peninsular sway and civilization. The second element in this commingling of genes being anything but a constant, and the proportions likewise with each new generation, there could patently be no hope of a continuing unity, and still less of keeping alive the Peninsular cult of <u>sangre limpia</u>. The offspring of Spaniard and Aztec, Spaniard and Inca, Spaniard and Araucanian, Portuguese and Tupí: how much could they have in common when Spaniard and Portuguese too now had to be re-defined for each region? Add in the further ingredient of African blood, and the permutations and combinations become endless. There will still be the River Plate, the endless rolling plains of Argentina where the Indian pulled out and the African was never significantly brought in. Alberdi's "Gobernar es poblar" provided the catalyst here, and today the population of an all-white Argentina is more Italian than Spanish.

While authority was still exercised from Madrid and Lisbon, one could cling to the belief, or at least keep up the pre-tence, of a Spain, a Portugal beyond the seas, legislate and ad-minister by remote control, decree what might be produced and imported, what might be written, printed, read or taught. The cultural history of the New World during the colonial period, as it finds expression in the printed word, can be made to appear one more chapter in a familiar story; "Vivimos tan lejos los crio-llos," not repudiation of an alien master-race and all it stood for—one could not hope to get that into print—but lament for the dis-tance, the time-lag, the faintness of the prospect of a respectful hearing. The printing press came to America, to some few fa-vored corners of the vastness, but it came to serve the purposes of authority, never to encourage creative, independent thinking and the free flow of ideas. The university came to America, to serve the same purposes and ensure the steady output of clerics, lawyers, administrators necessary to the perpetuation of the status quo. The "University Reform" of Córdoba in 1918 is to be seen as a long-delayed, too long delayed, reaction to the policy—a Bourbon as well as a Habsburg policy—of "No conviene ilustrar a los americanos." But, in the measure in which the literature of those three centuries represented experience and not an imitative literary cult, its keynote was the immediate, the local and hence the differential; the forms, like the language, were perforce of the Old World, the content was of the New, and exotic to readers in Old and New alike outside of the writer's own territory.

With independence the trend was doubly reinforced. Cul-tural ties with the mother country, seen now as the tyrant, the oppressor, were violently shattered—witness the sentiments ex-pressed in the national anthems of the new republics—the France of "liberté, égalité, fraternité" filling the void for those who still owned or sought a European allegiance in this sphere. But inde-pendence had brought too political fragmentation, in recognition that Latin Americans no longer felt themselves members of one great family, and Bolívar ploughed the sea in his refusal to ac-cept here the inevitable. To stay independent one had to feel in-dependent, to respond to a new loyalty based on the conviction that one's country had now a clearly defined separate existence alike from Spain or Portugal and from the other new country across a still often ill-defined frontier. The terms came later, those strange yet natural concepts of chilenidad, peruanidad, mexicanidad and the rest; but the feeling was already in the air, a deliberate if still instinctive policy of cultural differentiation, soon to be reinforced as the clash of national interests set its

dubious seal on the growth of nationhood with wars and rumours
of wars, Argentina against Chile, Chile against Bolivia and Peru,
Peru against Ecuador, Bolivia against Paraguay, Paraguay
against Brazil, Uruguay, and Argentina. The language was still
the same; the religion, at least nominally (how nominally among
mestizo and indigenous populations the traveller in Latin America
can remark for himself); the colonial heritage the same; but cultural unity was now but a fond and distant European illusion.

And from Europe came specific urges to make certain it
should remain so. Suiting example to precept, Bello found new
possibilities for the descriptive muse in singing the bounty of a
new mother nature, for the heroic muse in exalting the prowess
of the heroes of a new independence. Olmedo, remembered for
two heroic poems, points the dilemma from another angle. The
"Oda a la victoria de Junín" is vibrant with American pride at
seeing the might of Spain humbled to the dust, a pride in which
Inca can join hands with Bolívar. The "Oda al vencedor de Miña-
rica" again celebrates a triumph, but a bitter-sweet triumph in
a squalid civil war that is already turning to ashes the rejoicings
of yesterday. If the heroes of independence are so soon to throw
away their victory, reverting to the same old Spanish tradition of
wantonly squandering achievement that had delayed the mediaeval
Reconquest by two and a half centuries, does it matter so greatly,
is it not in fact appropriate, that one should sing them in a form
still wholly European? Something of all this could have been in
Echeverría's mind when to his urging on writers the choice of
native American themes he added the injunction that the distinctive
new literature they sought to create should be distinguished no less
by a deep sense of moral purpose. Freedom only becomes meaningful with definition. Freedom, what for? is the question.
Spaniards and Portuguese had created a society of privilege, a
culture, however fragmented, resting on an only too clearly defined system of attitudes. To dispossess them and leave the system meant no gain at all to the underprivileged, the vast majority.
And to change attitudes is an undertaking infinitely more formidable than to change the façade of government, since it hinges on
the most formidable factor of all, human nature.

Echeverría's own contribution, La Cautiva, pointed
the way to a fruitful half-century of literary striving throughout
Latin America to awaken the social conscience on the fundamental
problem of race. The mester de gauchería, the Indianist novel,
grapple manfully with this issue of how white stands to mestizo,
mestizo to Indian, Indian to both. With literacy still the preserve
of the infinitesimal minority, this was merely a leavening, but the
leavening had to work from the top. And it was perhaps meritorious rather than vital that the lead should have come from Argentina, a country relatively, if still only relatively, free from racial
complications. For on this matter of culture and attitudes one can
read a much deeper significance into the same author's briefer
tale of El Matadero. The present writer can still relive the shiver
of horror that went through him when, more than twenty years ago,
he first saw in a Buenos Aires museum a banner of the dreaded

Rosas tyranny with its lemma "Mueran los salvajes unitarios. "
One's political opponent—ran the creed—was ipso facto infra-
human, a wild beast, and wild beasts existed to be killed. This
from the self-styled federalist, notoriously the greatest unitarian
of them all, whose monument is to have debased not alone the
sacred name of freedom but the whole art and science of politics.
And this was white against white: another Spanish civil war under
American skies with nothing learnt in three hundred years. Echeverría lifted the curtain from a corner of the dread scene. Sarmiento saw the issue in all its starkness: civilization and barba-
rism fighting for the soul of the new-born independent republic.
Other countries were spared their Rosas, few their tyrants and
their tyrannies, one would have ten civil wars before the century
was out, many came to accept violent uprising as the normal way
of changing government.

Where, in all this, did culture come in, and what could
be the prospects of a common culture on a continental scale? Sarmiento thought he saw the answer, or at least the first step to an
answer. It lay in education. The "No conviene ilustrar a los
americanos, " if it had not led to Rosas, had made a Rosas possible. An informed public opinion should make impossible a
second. Teach the masses to read for a start; and of all his
forty books none gave him greater pride and satisfaction in old
age than the Gradual Reading Method thanks to which, it was
reckoned, two million children throughout Latin America had
become literate.

A century has passed and we see now how much more
complicated the problem is, that of literacy for a start. In spite
of the Gradual Reading Method, in spite of UNESCO and Pátzcuaro,
in spite of the Alliance for Progress with education as its priority
number one, in spite of the notable level of educational achievement in some few countries, Latin America is an area still crip-
pled in its every attempt to pull itself into the twentieth century
by this dead hand of illiteracy. The facets are many: the population explosion that defeats by sheer pressure of numbers, economic stringencies that continue to make teaching the Cinderella
of the professions, large indigenous groupings posing the prior
dilemma of the language in which they are to be taught, lack or
distrust of the specific inducement of better job and career prospects for the educated, a secular apathy that is often the despair
of the educator. It is unlikely that we shall witness another such
head of steam as was built up for a mass onslaught on the problem
in the name of the Alliance for Progress—the ten-year program,
scheduled to solve it once and for all, launched in 1961; the half-
way stocktaking of 1966 brought only gloomy prognostications of
one defeat more.

Perhaps the problem is insoluble. But, even supposing
the contrary, supposing universal literacy one day achieved,
where do we go from there? In teaching the child, or the man,
to read we have not taught him to reason, and a wholly literate
population can still be prey to superstition and prejudice, to mass

suggestion and hypnosis, to exploitation by the crook, the advertiser, the politician. It is this fact that gives first the censor, then the dictator, his opening, underlining the truism that democracy is not the automatic cure for a society's ills, nor the necessarily desirable form of government at any given stage of its development. Is higher education for the few the answer, the multiplication of universities, the opening wider and wider of their doors? This is perhaps the most prominent feature of the educational landscape in Latin America today, and the onlooker pays willing tribute to the enthusiastic pursuit of intellectual objectives, the level of scholarship, the genuine concern with social problems, the urge to be off with the old and on with the new, that characterizes them.

The same onlooker, if he be from Europe, will be conscious too of a strange feeling that no European institution transplanted to the New World has suffered a more striking sea-change. The university too, in spite of the notion of universality implicit in the term, is the university in its circumstantia. The present phenomenon of a student body bent seemingly on taking over the institution lock, stock,and barrel, and the degree of seeming acquiescence this can compel from authority, consort oddly with the status pupillaris and with the responsibility, intellectual, and social, that is their mentors'. Doubtless it reflects a less than divine dissatisfaction with the present injustices of the body politic, the realization that after a century and a half of sovereign independence, the square deal for all, the social integration, that was to be its first fruit still lies over the horizon. That the true purpose of a university and its relationship to society are being so violently called in question are already provoking their own reaction in the founding of new private universities where these fundamental questions are being thought out anew. But inasmuch as the university, old or new, is a basic repository and channel of culture and this student upsurge, being largely common to Latin America as a whole, has brought its universities into increasingly close touch one with another, we can recognize here one important factor capable of making, consciously or unconsciously, for that cultural integration that is our theme.

What are the others? Ease of communication in the modern world, if not the guarantee against misunderstanding or divergence of interests that the one-language enthusiasts pin their faith to, does at least rule out the prospect that Castilian, as once Latin, may disintegrate throughout the erstwhile empire into a cluster of related but independent tongues. A Chilean novel published in Argentina may need its glossary of localized names for things, the pronunciation of ll or s may place the speaker; but the language of ideas continues uniform and—over the air or in the flesh—Spanish American may still speak to Spanish American anywhere and be understood. Nor, given that language will always be plural, could the effort necessary to bring the Brazilian into the dialogue be easier of acceptance.

The channels of cultural communication are open. The

question is rather what flows along them. Is there a lively desire among cultured minds in each country of the twenty to know what is happening among the other nineteen, to savour and appraise their achievements, to analyse, for purposes of contrast or of comple- ment, their values, to study this whole large question of whether there exists, or can exist, or desirably should exist, a common system of attitudes to life? The writer has been bold on occasion to assert that Latin American literature can be better studied in Glasgow—better still, needless to say, in any of a dozen centres in the United States—than anywhere in Latin America, Peruvian literature in Peru, Paraguayan in Paraguay, but do the resources exist, or the interest, to study Brazil in Guatemala or Guatemala in Brazil? How many of these countries can be relied on to keep even their own classics in print (an objective this, let it be said in parenthesis, much more worthy of the attention of UNESCO than the promoting of the odd translation into English)?

The reply to a remonstration on this score made to a leading Brazilian bookseller, that of every four books he sold three were translations, casts its own light on this aspect of the problem. The Brazilian reader, still a microscopic minority of the Brazilian people, is more concerned to keep in touch with Europe and the United States than with his own country or own continent. In the technical sphere, in an age of technology, this is understandable, inevitable. In the cultural sphere, the Latin American reader doubtless turns to European literature, not of the Peninsula, for the same reasons of exotic appeal, enlarge- ment of experience, intelligent curiosity that draw the European reader to the masterpieces of New World writing. But there comes in, too, another consideration that is part aesthetic, part intellectual. It was a painful discovery of the new nations of a century and a half ago that political independence, like patriotism, is not enough; and they have been struggling ever since to achieve that economic independence from the Colossus of the North that would alone make of the other a reality. And economically they are still underdeveloped countries, standing only on the thresh- old of their potential. Can the same be said of them culturally? The gifted individual, the genius, is a law unto himself; the Nobel prize-winner can emerge, in poetry as in physiology, with scant reference to his background. The general level of culture is very much a matter of background. If this does not provide the stim- ulus, and the response, the artist must seek them elsewhere, and his art will be derivative in consequence and addressed to a so- phisticated, minority public. If, likewise, he does not come of a long cultural tradition he must perforce go to school, in matters of craft and artistry, under alien masters, and again his signifi- cance and his recognition at home will be in question.

Herein lies, perhaps, the fundamental dilemma of Latin American culture, to which neither Bello nor Echeverría was fully alive. There was a period, after the half-century of delib- erate differentiation that followed on independence, when the poets of Latin America recovered the sense of one-ness and, professing the same ideals, sang with the same voice. Rodó spoke for the same generation in prose, defining explicitly as they implicitly a stance, an attitude that, against the cult of materialism he sought to identify with the Anglo-Saxon north, would commit Latin America to the pursuit instead of values aesthetic and spiritual. Intelligible, coherent—to recall Ortega's three requirements for the "system of attitudes to life" that can constitute a culture—yes. Efficacious? There lies the rub. A culture for escapists from the materialism of existence must leave broadly untouched a society where the material demands of existence are still unmet. This specious cultural integration in an atmosphere so rarified soon produced its own reaction. "Tuércele el cuello al cisne": R. I. P.

What of the novel? The reasons why drama, the other outstanding field of literary achievement of Mother Spain, has made so little impact, and has so little to show, in the New World are again social rather than literary, and stress anew the complexities in this cultural context of the social structure wherever we look. But the novel is the Latin American kind par excellence, and precisely because it has, over a century and more now, drawn its sustenance from the soil, concerned itself with real people and real problems at once localized in their setting and universal in their significance, and achieved this with an intuitive mastery of the craft in all three aspects—story-telling, character portrayal, philosophic undertones—that goes straight back to the founder, Cervantes himself.

"Circumstantial realism and psychological depth" have been postulated as essential to the revealing of this New World to itself, as to the observer from without. We live in an age of dissolving values, of aesthetic experimentation in every direction, of a suspect internationalism that to the older among us can seem, far from promoting unity, to threaten total cultural disintegration. Poets are a prey to isms as never before and have seemingly less and less to say to us. Novelists forsake the elements of their craft and turn pseudo-philosophers writing pseudo-philosophy in the void. The need for Latin American writers, the hope for Latin American culture, as it seems to this European, is not that they should set themselves to sink or swim in the wake of every European current but that they should come to grips honestly with the social, the vital challenges that confront them. When Latin America has become a just, a fair New World for every Latin American, then cultural integration too can be a reality.

CHAPTER **33** LATIN AMERICAN UNITY:
A SOCIO-ECONOMIC OVERVIEW

By Hugh Fox
Department of American Thought and Language
Michigan State University

To the "outsider" Latin America can easily be considered as one single, socio-economic unit. After all, ostensibly all the Latin American countries stem from a common heritage, they all are formed out of the former Spanish empire, they have a common language, common religion, some common folkways. Beneath this superficial semblance of unity, however, from the very beginning of their independence from Spain, Latin American countries have fought among themselves with as much ferocity as they ever fought against the Spaniards — or the Spaniards fought against them. The letters of Simon Bolivar, the Liberator of South America, who more than any other single individual was responsible for freeing Latin America from Spanish domination, are filled with disillusioned statements regarding the disunity of the new republics at the beginning of the nineteenth century. As soon as they were liberated from Spain wars began within Chile, Mexico, Guatemala, Venezuela, Ecuador, Peru, and then, in the 1820's and 1830's these conflicts spread and Colombia was fighting Venezuela, Peru invading Ecuador, planning on invading Colombia, Buenos Aires threatening to invade Bolivia. These wars continued on through the nineteenth century into the twentieth century and created deep-rooted enmities between most Latin American neighbor republics: Peruvians against Chileans, Ecuadorians against Peruvians, Bolivians against Paraguayans, Chileans against Argentinians, and so forth.

War, however, was not the only cause of "differences" between the Latin American republics; the differences go much deeper. Racially, for example, there are vast differences between the Negro-based countries such as Venezuela and Cuba and Indian-based countries such as Bolivia and Peru. Temperamentally the Peruvian or Bolivian does not feel "comfortable" in Venezuela, does not understand — or want to understand — the quicksilver and volatile nature of Venezuelan character. Other countries like Argentina have made a grand to do of their racial "purity, " and look with a disparaging eye at those mestizo countries that surround them. Sometimes, even within one country these racial differences make themselves strongly felt such as in Ecuador where a city like Guayaquil, hot tropical, with a Negroid racial substratum, is totally different from the cold, introverted, Indian-derived highlands of Quito.

Indeed, these differences within countries are often more marked than the differences between countries. The Peruvian Indian from Cuzco has much more in common with his racial-cultural counterpart in Bolivia (or the north of Argentina or even in some remote mountain areas in Chile where some watered down remnants of the Inca system still exist) than the inhabitants of Lima, near the Peruvian coast. In Venezuela the whole coastal mystique is totally different from that in Mérida.

At times these regional differences actually break one country into a series of de facto cultural groups which often have long histories of independence or semi-independence. For a long time during and after the wars of independence it seemed that the east of Venezuela was going to be a separate country under a separate ruler with its own congress and its own laws. Quito, it seemed, was going to set itself up as an independent city-state, and the same is true for Guayaquil. In the literature of the early nineteenth century no one talks of Argentina, but merely Buenos Aires—and even today there are still two Argentinas, Buenos Aires and "the rest."

These differences, in fact, can often be traced back to colonial times where the divisions of the Spanish Empire created very distinct and independent political units. The centers, of course, were Mexico and Peru and consequently the two viceregal capitals, Mexico City and Lima, were the most "Spanish" of all Spanish America. This "Spanish-ness" of Mexico City was destroyed by the Mexican Revolution, but there was no analogous revolution in Peru and so Lima, the City of the Three Kings, still retains its touch of baroque grandeur. As Fernando Belaúnde Terry, the former president of Peru pointed out in numerous books and articles, the Spanish were coastally-oriented, looking back to Spain and Spanish trade and supply lines, and consequently for the most part abandoned the interior of South America which in the case of Peru represented a complete historical reversal, because in Inca times the country's backbone had been cordillera and its heart, the ancient capital of the Incas, Cuzco. Three hundred years of colonial rule successfully split Peru into her two distinct contemporary socio-economic units, and it may take another three hundred years before any real national unity can be restored. Those areas outside the power of the viceroyalties were for the most part neglected, and their hispanization was at best rudimentary and scant. The seeming "Spanish" homogeneity of Latin America is, in truth, incomplete and spotty and half (or more) of Peru still speaks Quechua, most of Bolivia still speaks Aymara and Quechua, much of Guatemala still speaks Quiché, and Paraguay is still fundamentally a culture based not on Spanish, but Guaraní.

In some respects the old pre-Columbian cultural units still hang on. Peru and Bolivia are two countries, but the old Inca Cuzco-centered world that spread out into the Bolivian highlands still preserves its basic unity. In Mexico, Yucatan is still Maya, and the Maya cultures move down across national borders

455

into Guatemala, Honduras, and British Honduras.

The republics in Latin America are not based on geographical or ethnic logic, but are to a great extent arbitrary Spanish colonial divisions which were set down primarily with the ease of administration from Spain in mind. There was a kind of pre-Columbian logic based on tribal areas, the Incas, the Mayas, Toltecs, Olmecs, the Araucanians, the Chimus..... the Conquest occurred, the units were imperfectly fragmented and rearranged, and it has been this imperfect arrangement that has carried down to the present, because one of the principles upon which the new republics were based was that they should be created not out of the pre-Columbian socio-economic but rather the Spanish colonial administrative units. And so it is that the myth of common language, religion, or folkways is really more myth than reality, and the consideration of Latin America as a unit has been more the result of the thinking of non-Latin Americans than it ever has of Latin Americans themselves.

The fact that Latin America has been under the scrutiny of the United States and of both the Communist power centers (in the early sixties Russia, and increasingly now China), has exerted a cohesion-producing force on Latin American diversity and begun to force many Latin Americans to think of themselves not solely as Chileans, Peruvians, Colombians, and Argentinians, but also as participants in a cultural unit which others are convinced should be considered as a whole. The simple most impressive result of the Alliance for Progress on the one hand and of Communist subversion and the spread of Castro-directed guerrilla movements on the other has been the beginning of a formation of over-all unity which has begun to reverse the historical developments not of centuries but of millennia.

The U.S. Information Service, our system of bi-national centers throughout Latin America in every major city and most smaller towns, the "invasion" of Peace Corps volunteers, the stepping up of educational exchange programs by the United States, Moscow, and Peking have forced the Latin American for the first time to see himself as others see him. Whether the supposed "sameness" of all Latin Americans has any objective validity or not is unimportant. The net effect, however, is important—and meaningful. Anticipating and antedating possible future economic integration, a great deal of cultural integration has already taken place, the proof of which is amply demonstrated by the fact that for the first time all Latin American intellectuals know each other, know what they are producing, thinking, and hoping for. There are a number of inter-American magazines and movements such as Eco Contemporáneo (Argentina), Cormorán y Delfín (Argentina), Corno Emplumado (Mexico), Nueva Era (Colombia), Pájaro Cascabel (Mexico), Haravec (Peru), Cuervo International (U.S.), or Ghost-Dance (U.S.) which are based on a total inter-American "awareness" which did not exist even ten years ago. Traditionally the Latin American has thought in terms of his own national literature. The Peruvian had read Ricardo Palma (but not Gallegos), the Venezuelan had read Gallegos (but not Palma). Now all Latin American intellectuals read Raquel Jodorowsky, Dukardo Hinestrosa, David Valjaló, Miguel Grinberg, Mario Vargas Llosa, Julio Cortázar, Gabriel García-Márquez, Ernesto Cardenal. Such a unified total culture-view is entirely new and presages a unification movement that is now moving into economic and commercial areas. It might also be added that this same external pressure that has unified Latin American awareness has by the same token placed Latin America in another category, that of the Third World (underdeveloped and uncommitted to the United States or to the Communist World); one finds Latin American poets like Miguel Grinberg publishing regularly in African literary journals. This whole movement is beautifully summed up in an editorial by Ariel Canzani in Cormorán y Delfín (February, 1967) in which he says: "Cormorán y Delfín was born as an international review of poetry [and] we have seen that many reviews in Latin America have begun their tasks inspired by the same ideas." Previously Latin Americans had been involved with groups, and sects, but now there is a new kind of "Planetarism," committed to the ideas of "internationalness."

Economic and political institutions, which always change last in terms of historical development, in the last few years have begun to reflect this Latin American-internationalist view expressed by Canzani.

In 1958, the Central American Common Market (CACM) was set up, comprising Costa Rica, El Salvador, Guatemala, Honduras, and Nicaragua. In 1960, the Latin American Free Trade Association (LAFTA) was established, including Argentina, Brazil, Chile, Mexico, Paraguay, Peru, Uruguay (and later Colombia, Ecuador, and Venezuela). In April, 1967, at Punta del Este in Uruguay, there was a meeting sponsored by the Organization of American States which proposed setting up a Latin American Common Market, aiming toward 1985 as the latest acceptable target date for complete economic integration of the Latin American republics. In September, 1967, at the meeting of LAFTA in Asunción, Paraguay, the first immediate subgrouping within LAFTA was set up—that of the Andean Group consisting of Colombia, Chile, Ecuador, Peru, and Venezuela.

The theory behind this entire move toward integration is that industrialization and subsequent economic development in Latin America are hampered primarily by the fact that there is an insufficient market within individual countries to justify the establishment of the kind of mass-production designed industrial plant that seems so integral a part of "modern times." As Gabriel Valdés of Chile said at the Asunción meeting, the formation of the Andean subregional group: ". . .means the creation of a market, or even better, an economic 'nation' of some 55 million inhabitants and a combined gross national product greater than that of Brazil."

457

It remains to be seen, however, whether the creation of an economic "super-state" automatically will stimulate industrialization, although certainly it will facilitate the movement of non-manufactured goods and raw materials. In other words, if non-industrial Peru abolishes all her trade barriers with non-industrial Ecuador, how is this going to produce alarm clocks?

What very well might happen is that countries that are already producing manufactured goods (such as Chile) will definitely benefit from an expanded market, but that what benefits the manufacturing nation will have no benefit whatsoever on the non-manufacturing nation and might very well be detrimental. Peru, instead of importing alarm clocks from Austria, say, now begins to import them from Chile. Chile, because of her inflation-crippled economy and because she is merely in the initial stages of industrial development produces an alarm clock slightly inferior to the Austrian alarm clock in quality and twice as expensive. The net result is that Peru spends more money for slightly inferior goods.

Besides, how do the "poor" benefit from this kind of trade manipulation? The highland Peruvian could not afford an alarm clock from Austria in the first place. He remains totally untouched by any supranational change as long as the internal economy within Peru remains essentially the same.

Even if traditional grudges and enmities, and radically different national characteristics could be subordinated to the interests of the larger issue of common "progress," no meaningful progress can be accomplished unless all the participating countries move simultaneously toward industrialization, and increases in the Gross National Product are accompanied by a democratic betterment of the lot of the Latin American lower classes. The great tragedy would be that the already-industrializing countries would become more industrialized at the expense of their neighbors, and that in both industrial and non-industrial countries the "progress" would affect only the managerial and entrepreneur classes.

Colombia, Ecuador, Peru, Chile, and to a lesser extent Venezuela, are all controlled by a small oligarchical class which may very well benefit by increases in Gross National Products while the lot of the poor remains unchanged.

Gunnar Myrdal in his classic study Economic Theory and Underdeveloped Regions, in speaking of the economic integration of developed and developing areas, makes the important observation that "the play of forces in the market normally tends to increase, rather than to decrease, the inequalities between regions." What this means in Latin America is that certain industrial centers may arise essentially at the expense of the non-industrial. Certainly foreign investment, which is often offered as the quickest and surest way to industrialization in underdeveloped areas such as Latin America, may turn out to be little more than exploitation—where the profits of the industrialization accrue to the original investors, who are not "nationals" in the exploited country. If any industrial complex is introduced into a country by international interests without massive national participation, it makes little or no difference where the industry is located because the profits are not plowed back into the national economy. And, as industrial automation increases, the number of jobs created within a given country is not a significant factor in raising the over-all national living standard.

CONCLUSION

The terms "progress" and "development can cover a multitude of partial truths. The U. S. is presumably the most developed country in the world, with an enviable record of industrial progress, but in 1963 we were suddenly informed that 35 million Americans belonged to families earning less than $3,000 a year. In Latin America the majority of the people lived in a state of slavery or semi-slavery during the whole colonial period, and in the 150 years since independence, conditions have not appreciably changed. Venezuela is oil-rich and semi-industrial, but the city of Caracas is ringed with hills that are covered with makeshift shanties housing the poor. Chile has great industrial promise, but from the lower middle class down meat is a luxury. It is possible, as demographer Raymond Ewell predicts, that by the 1980's Latin America will be hit hard by massive famine and Lima, Caracas, Asunción, and Santiago will be filled with the starving homeless as is the case in contemporary India. Certainly population control is just as important as industrialization, and widespread industrialization just as important as industrialization confined to a few already-industrializing areas. Foreign private direct investment capital must be carefully watched and controlled—further economic colonization must be discouraged. And, most important of all, internal, individual programs of social justice must go hand in hand with programs of supranational economic development, or "development" can come to be regarded solely in economic terms without the slightest consideration of the common weal.

"Progress" and "development" cannot be measured solely in terms of GNP growth. Progress must mean total progress, progress for everyone and progress not merely considered from the point of view of per capita income, but rather the total economic and human gains in the lives of the individuals involved in development programs. Economic development in itself is a very incomplete and deformed thing if not accompanied by a larger spiritual and human development well distributed over the total population. Latin American economic integration may very well contribute to this sense of development in a larger sense, but it is only one among many programs that must be initiated if "progress" and "development" are to have any viable meaning in relation to over-all socio-economic reality.

CHAPTER **34** THE CHURCH AND LATIN
AMERICAN INTEGRATION

By Jack Anthony Licate
Department of Geography
University of Chicago

INTRODUCTION

Latin America is the most Catholic of continents. For
almost five centuries Roman Catholicism has been the most active
religious force in Latin America; it now claims at least ninety
per cent of the continent's 275 million inhabitants. Before the
end of this century, Latin Americans will constitute well over
half of the world's Catholics and nearly half of its Christians.
The Roman Catholic Church, in which every Catholic holds membership, is the oldest and most widespread institution in Latin
America. It is impossible to speak of the history and formation
of the culture which we call Latin American without speaking of
the Church. So many of the spiritual elements which bind that
culture together have either emanated from or been encouraged by
the teachings and activities of the institutional Church. This is
not a denial of the existence of culture traits, particularly political and economic ones, toward which the Church has been either
neutral or opposed. The point which is significant is that the institutional Church has been most important in the formation and
direction of a great part of the cultural complex of Latin America.
Indeed, any discussion of the people of Latin America which does
not consider their religion and its Church would be a truncated one.

With the present process of disintegration, or at least
reorientation, of its traditional and tribal societies, Latin America
is undergoing its most fundamental and rapid cultural change since
the sixteenth century Conquest. Not only are social, political, and
economic institutions experiencing changes in structure and function, but more importantly so are the values which underlie and
bind them. The latter is of particular concern to the Church, the
institution which has traditionally been interested in the formation and maintenance of cultural as well as religious values. In
addition to the concern over the challenge of "modernization" and
all that it implies, the Church is being swept by the most rapid and
fundamental changes she has experienced since the sixteenth century Counter Reformation.

Both the process of "modernization" and "aggiornamento"
are now taking place more in Latin America than anywhere else.
Actions taken by the Latin American Church in the realms of
spiritual and cultural values will have a profound affect on the continent's future and important ramifications for the rest of the world.

It is the purpose of this study to offer a glimpse at some of the attitudes of the Church toward the development and integration not only of Latin America, but also of the Latin American Church itself. No attempt will be made to explain or interpret some recent controversial events involving Latin American Catholics, or the activities in Latin America of Catholics from other areas.

THE INTEGRATION OF LATIN AMERICA

Particularly since the reign of Leo XIII (1878-1903), papal encyclicals and Catholic teaching in general have been increasingly concerned with the development of a body of social teaching relevant to the modern world. Until recently these teachings have been most applicable to the highly industrialized areas of Europe and North America. However, since the reign of Pope John XXIII (1958-1963) and the sessions of the Second Vatican Council (1961-1965), an increasing concern has been shown for the underdeveloped world and its coming transformation. Encyclicals such as John's "Pacem in Terris" (Peace on Earth) and "Mater et Magistra" (Christianity and Social Progress), Paul VI's "Populorum Progressio" (On the Development of Peoples) along with conciliar decrees on the nature of the Church, the Church in the modern world, religious liberty, the missionary activity of the Church, and ecumenism have added to this body of teaching. Particularly important for Latin America were the 1965 Council decree "Gaudium et Spes" (Pastoral Constitution on the Church in the Modern World) and Paul's 1967 "Populorum Progressio" because their principles underly many of the resolutions adopted at the 1966 meeting of the Consejo Episcopal Latinoamericano (CELAM) in Mar del Plata and the 1967 publication of the Consejo's "Conclusiones de Mar del Plata." Here Latin America's Roman Catholic bishops fully embraced the "ideal of integration" as fundamental for the development of the continent and the continental Church. We shall dwell on these "Conclusiones" for some length.

Paul VI declared to CELAM that after considering the gravity of what he thought the two greatest questions of our time, the promotion of progress everywhere and the prevention of war in all its forms, and considering the importance and value of international organizations which seek to answer these questions for the betterment of mankind, that

> ...the Church can contribute valuably to the diffusion of the ideal of integration, awakening in Christians the conviction that national goals will be only attained within an international community forming a supranational consciousness. (CELAM, Presencia, p. 17).

More specifically, the "Conclusiones" of Mar del Plata state:

> The integration of Latin America is an on-going process

of an irresistible character. It constitutes an indispensable instrument for the harmonious development of the region and marks a fundamental stage in the movement for the unification of the human family. In the present circumstances of crisis and the consolidation of political, economic, and social relations, integration is an essential contribution toward world peace. Manifesting itself as a "sign of the times," the integration of the Latin American continent arouses an attitude of service on the part of the Church, not only in view of the positions derived from the Second Vatican Council and the words of Paul VI to CELAM, but also as a consequence of a matter of conscience for Christians who live this historical reality (Ibid., pp. 17-18).

This commitment to the "ideal of integration" is the basis and goal of the various programs suggested by the bishops. In addition, it also serves as the grounds from which the Church wishes to launch a "doctrine capable of orienting the process of integration" of the entire Latin American continent (Ibid., p. 21).

Although the Church feels that it is not within her "capacity or competency" to directly advance the necessary social, political, and economic reforms, "it is her concern to orient toward the betterment of man in all his dimensions and toward the complete integration of marginal populations " (Ibid., p. 21). The imbalances which exist between various national social and economic sectors, between regions of a country, and between the developed and underdeveloped countries must be considered as grave threats to world peace. To alleviate these threats, basic structural reforms are necessary "in the socio-economic life" along with "a conversion in mentality and mode of being" (Ibid., p. 20). "The structures of society must have as their goal the development of the whole man and of all men. As such, they should be at the service of the human person and not at the service of themselves" (Ibid., p. 20). Since many existing economic, political, social, and cultural structures do not permit the participation and integration of the Latin American population, and there are great masses of people who remain on their margins, they should, in the light of this new mentality and mode of being, be reorganized.

The process of socialization, the necessity to order a dynamic production and just distribution in this new organization, obliges a thorough review of the structure of associations, and of the State (Ibid., p. 21).

More specifically referring to basic structural reforms, CELAM has encouraged its member national Episcopal Councils (national councils of bishops) to promulgate several important pastoral directives.

462

While safeguarding the natural right to private property, following the teachings of the Church, it is necessary to treat the following points: the fundamental right of all to the use of material goods comes before private property; that it is necessary to correct, with wisdom and firmness, the accumulation of property in the hands of few; that the State — bearing in mind the common good and social justice — has the right to determine the limit to which proprietors may freely administer their goods (Ibid., p. 21).

As for associated structures, it will be necessary to promote

enterprise systems which institute a just distribution of the common product and the responsibility of all participants of the enterprise; a free syndical organization of external pressure groups which determine the attainment of their ends; an organization of the sectors of production, based on the equal participation of workers and employers; a cooperative organization which loans the necessary services to producers with the object of increasing the productivity of their work (Ibid., p. 22).

And as for the increasing role of the State, it will be always necessary in Latin America

to stand in favor of associations and persons within the limits of the common good. Thus, it is necessary to plan the economy with the cooperation of the community, and to modify structures of democratic power and public administration so that they are able to play their economic and social part with major efficacy and with major participation of the community in the means of their organization (Ibid., p. 22).

Agrarian reform is of seminal importance here. Latifundia and minifundia are grave problems in Latin America which contribute to the continent's imbalance. Thus, it is necessary to establish a policy of land redistribution. Again, the notion of the common good should come before the idea of the rights of private property. In all of agrarian reform, basic education (Educación de base, mainly adult education) is indispensable for the formation of personal incentive and a sense of community.

For this, it is necessary to contribute to the raising of the rural population's standard of living giving Church properties an effective social function; contributing to the creation of a rural middle class capable of participating in the social, economic, cultural, and political life of each country;

contributing to the raising of the productivity of the
land, helping in the propagation and adoption of
modern techniques of production; stimulating fundamental education especially utilizing audio-visual
aids; assuring, through competent organisms, official and private, an ample program of technical
assistance and financial credit   (Ibid., p. 23).

But these are mainly economic and political reforms
deemed necessary by the bishops. Latin America now is beset
also by social problems which need solution.

Apparently the Church feels that while it does not have
the "competency or capacity" to directly foster necessary economic
and political structural reforms, it does so in areas needing social
reform. While recognizing the State's "rights and obligations" to
deal with its population problems, such as social and family legislation, rural to urban migration, or the provision of information
about the situation and needs of the country, no policy suggestions
similar to the ones made above are made to the State in these
areas. However, CELAM suggests the continental promulgation
of a broad range of pastoral programs and reforms dealing with
the problems of population, urbanization, and internal migration.

Specifically dealing with "population" the Mar del Plata
"Conclusiones" suggest the establishment on a continental level
of technical organizations which stimulate an awareness of the
gravity of the problem, warn society and Christians against easy
solutions which will hinder human dignity and which are at the
same time socially insufficient. They suggest programs which
will investigate the causes and sources of the solution of the
problem. They also suggest the intensification of pastoral programs, especially in "fluctuating groups," concentrating and
orienting themselves toward the family. This includes increasing
the number of family apostolates with emphasis on the dignity of
love, human generosity, and a sense of parental responsibility
to children, society, and the Church as well as the psychological,
cultural, and spiritual dimensions of Christian matrimony—mainly
through courses before marriage   (Ibid., p. 23).

For a program aimed at the solution of the problems of
urbanization, CELAM suggests to its member Episcopal Conferences the study and creation of urban pastoral programs which
will be dynamic, adaptable, fruitful, open to the participation and
colaboration of all, and which go beyond present static and routine
ones. Also suggested is preparation and adoption of new norms
for the distribution and co-ordination of clergy to come more into
focus with urban life; the intensive recruitment of the laity, and
the mobilization of all Church forces into integrating the work of
evangelization; and the revitalization of sacramental and liturgical
programs designed to promote the formation of a lay community
and the formation of missionary groups within the city. As for
the great masses of people pouring into Latin American cities,
CELAM suggests the acknowledgment of the problem, the creation

of special pastoral programs for immigrants, the promotion of centers which will plan the settlement of migrants, and the encouragement of ideas for the decentralization of economic and social resources from large cities to areas in the country. The last will, with the creation of "poles of development," alleviate pressures on the great cities (Ibid, p. 28).

INTEGRATION OF THE CHURCH

In addition to its concern with the problems facing Latin American society in general, the Church is faced with a host of problems of its own. The late Manuel Larraín E., Bishop of Talca, Chile, for example, has outlined four "areas of deficiency" which call for immediate attention: "the absence of proper evangelization; an excessive devotion to the sentimental rather than the doctrinal; a lack of adequate structuring of pastoral programs; and a scarcity of clergy" (Larraín, p. 217). More specifically on the "religious situation" Cardinal Suenens notes

> the long traditions now imperfectly understood, the customary Catholicism, the flashes of true heroism and generosity, the patience and simplicity of the poor, the fiestas — little more than an emotional release — the fervent practice and the social inertia, the cultured piety, and the superstition (Suenens, p. 345).

Houtart and Pin quote a 1958 estimate that 3.5 per cent of male and 9.5 per cent of female Latin American Catholics attend Sunday Mass—compulsory for Catholics (Houtart and Pin, p. 166). My own calculations indicate Latin America's priest-laity ratio of 1:4851 (one priest for 4,851 Catholics) was in 1966 about a quarter of that of the rest of the Church. Despite these problems, Latin America remains, "in some mysterious way," to quote Suenens, overwhelmingly Catholic. Any attempt to solve these internal problems and remedy the causes they signify must be massive and involve a great deal of the Church's organizational structure.

A start toward a solution was made in 1955 with the foundation of the Consejo Episcopal Latinoamericano (CELAM). This organization is both unique in the Catholic world and in Church history, since it is the first and only continental organization of bishops. The purposes of CELAM are to

> Study the problems of interest to the Latinamerican [sic] Church in order to find their adequate solution; obtain an opportune coordination of Catholic activities of the continent in order to assure efficiency; promote and sustain projects that, directly or indirectly, present a common interest; make available to the national Episcopal Conferences the pastoral and technical services that respond to the real needs of the Church; prepare for the Latinamerican Epis-

465

copal Conferences, when the Holy See convokes
them and at the same time concern itself with
the problems that the Holy See refers to it
(CELAM, Latinamerican, p. 5).

CELAM is made up of delegates and alternates elected
by each of the 21-member national Episcopal Conferences (national organizations of bishops). A delegate or alternate must
hold the office of bishop. CELAM has no formal authority to
implement policies, its role is purely one of "contact, collaboration, and service " (Ibid.).

To fulfill its purposes, CELAM has a dozen specialized
departments dealing with pastoral programs, liturgy, faith,
missions, vocations, seminaries, education, university apostolates, social action, lay apostolates, social communication, and
ecumenism (Ibid., p. 14). While the General Secretariat of CELAM
is located in Bogotá, specialized departmental headquarters and
staff are scattered across South America, the president of each
department may be — but sometimes is not — in the same country
as his department. The departments also prepare special institutes in their respective fields. Apparently once held an institute acquires a specialized staff and continues as an educative
organ. Thus, mainly through the work and co-ordination begun
by CELAM, the Latin American Church has committed — or will
commit — a great deal of its resources to its "ideal of integration."

As a testament to this commitment and so that others in
Latin America will follow its example, the Church has begun the
integration of all its facilities on all levels, parish, diocesan,
national, continental, and intercontinental. This amounts to a
monumental task involving in Latin America 352 dioceses with
17, 213 parishes, 43, 756 priests, 7, 689 seminarians, 29, 585 men
religious (brothers), 136, 394 women religious (sisters), 14, 808
schools with 3, 987, 267 students (National Catholic Almanac, 1968)
and countless thousands of "associated structures" such as Catholic Action groups, labor unions, political action groups, family
movements, co-operatives and so forth. It also involves the co-
operation and aid of the Church in other areas, mainly North
America and Europe. For example, about 40% of the clergy in
Latin America now is foreign (Labelle, p. 168); the United States
will have about 10% of its clergy in Latin America by 1971. The
Holy See evidently feels that the "ideal of integration" in Latin
America is so important that it established the Pontifical Commission for Latin America in 1958 to deal specifically with that
problem in the area.

Ultimately all levels of the Church in Latin America will
be committed to the "ideal of integration" of not only the Church
itself, but also of the continent. If need be, there will be the
"creation and adoption of structures, services and movements
within the Church which contribute to the integration of the continent, " there will be the "approval and giving favor to organizations which are engaged in Latin American integration, " and the

"ideals of integration and development" will be dispersed to all
Church educational institutions. "It is necessary to explain and
fortify a Latin American consciousness... for socio-economic,
political, and cultural unity, and for an effective consciousness
of a Christian community on the continent" (CELAM, Presencia,
p. 18).

CONCLUSION

Obviously the material considered here has as many interpretations as there are readers to read it. Mountains of pages
already exist seeking meanings or motives from the statements of
the recent Council, from CELAM, and from the words of Paul VI
in his "Populorum Progressio." What strikes this author, a
cultural geographer by craft, is that Latin American Roman
Catholicism joins other religions of the "third world"—Islam,
Buddhism, Hinduism, and the thousands of messianic cults everywhere—in their reaction to the spread of northwestern European
and Anglo-American technological and industrial innovations.
While each reacts in its own way, all show a vitality and determination to cope with and indeed alter the processes of industrialization and "development." Roman Catholicism in Latin America
seems determined to "orient" the development of the continent
toward its "ideal of integration" based on the Christian humanistic
concept "the whole man and all men." If successful in the formation of a "Latin American consciousness" necessary for this
orientation, the results will be profound, not only for Latin America
and the Latin American Church, but also for the rest of the world.

BIBLIOGRAPHY

Consejo Episcopal Latinoamericano (CELAM). *Latin-
american Episcopal Council.* Bogotá: CELAM, General
Secretariat, 1967?.

___ . *Presencia activa de la Iglesia en el desarrollo y
en la integración de América Latina.* Salvador,
Bahia: CELAM, Departamento de Acción Social, 1967.

Considine, John J., ed. *The Church in the New Latin
America.* Notre Dame, Indiana: Fides Publishers,
Inc., 1964.

___ . *The Religious Dimension in the New Latin America,*
Notre Dame, Indiana: Fides Publishers, Inc., 1966.

___ . *Social Revolution in the New Latin America: A
Catholic Appraisal.* Notre Dame, Indiana: Fides
Publishers, Inc., 1965.

D'Antonio, William V.,and Frederick B. Pike, eds. *Religion, Revolution, and Reform: New Forces for Change in Latin America.* New York: Frederick A Praeger, 1964.

Houtart, François, and Emile Pin. *The Church and the Latin American Revolution.* Trans. Gilbert Barth. New York: Sheed and Ward, 1965.

Labelle, Ivan, and Adriana Estrada, compilers. *Latin America in Maps, Charts, and Tables, No. 2: Socio-Religious Data* (Catholicism). Cuernavaca: Center for Intercultural Formation, n.d. (1964?).

Larraín E., Manuel. "Latin America and the Universal Church," pp. 214-222 in John J. Considine, ed., *Social Revolution in the New Latin America.* Notre Dame, Indiana: Fides Publishers, Inc., 1965.

Mecham, J. Lloyd. *Church and State in Latin America: A History of Politico-Ecclesiastical Relations.* rev. ed. Chapel Hill: University of North Carolina Press, 1966.

National Catholic Almanac 1968. Paterson, N.J.: St. Anthony's Guild, 1968.

Pike, Frederick B., ed. *The Conflict between Church and State in Latin America.* New York: Alfred A. Knopf, 1964.

Shapiro, Samuel, ed. *Integration of Man and Society in Latin America.* Notre Dame, Indiana: University of Notre Dame Press, 1967.

Suenens, Leon Josef Cardinal. "Latin America and the Universal Church," pp. 337-52 in Samuel Shapiro, ed., *Integration of Man and Society in Latin America.* Notre Dame, Indiana: University of Notre Dame Press. 1967.

PART **VIII**

REGIONAL STUDIES

CHAPTER

35

THE STATUS OF "LESSER
DEVELOPED" COUNTRIES
WITHIN A LATIN AMERICAN
COMMON MARKET

By Walter Krause   and F. John Mathis
    Department of Economics   State University of
    University of Iowa   New York, Brockport

*Regional economic groupings, integration or
other forms of economic co-operation should be
promoted among developing countries as a means
of expanding their . . . trade and encouraging
their economic growth . . . .*

United Nations Conference on
Trade and Development, 1964

*If integration is to succeed, all the countries
must have . . . equal opportunities to profit
from the establishment of the common market.*

Felipe Herrera, et al

Economic integration — the joining together of separate
countries to form a more or less unified economic entity — has
moved forward dramatically in Latin America during recent years.
Long an esteemed ideal, the process of translation into reality
found its triggering force in a mounting developmental urge during
the post-World War II era. Repeated conferences, dwelling on the
imperativeness of development, focused attention increasingly on
the potential role of integration. And as familiarity and tactical
know-how grew, the scene in due course proved conducive for concrete action. This action came with the close of the 1950's — with
the formation of, first, the Central American Common Market
(CACM)[1] in 1958 and, second, the Latin American Free Trade
Association (LAFTA)[2] in 1960.

The ensuing years witnessed considerable progress as
tariffs and related barriers to trade were lowered among members
of the two groups of countries. Intraregional trade rose in volume,
significantly altering the split between the intraregional and extra-
regional components of total trade. Moreover, investment showed
important reorientation, ostensibly stimulated in given directions
by the prospects of enhanced market opportunities within a rede-
fined market framework. Between the two trends — greater intraregional trade and augmented investment of priority types — development received a decided boost. Certain accompanying
problems aside, the growing impression was one of integration
providing a hopeful means of development inducement and
acceleration.

Thus matters stood by 1967. In that year, a monumental further step occurred. The setting was Punta del Esta, at a meeting convened under auspices of the Organization of American States and attended by, among others, the "heads of state" of all member countries.[3] The issue, once again, was development — only this time with the stress placed squarely on integration as the intermediary. The gist of deliberations was that Latin America should seek to form a single "common market," a Latin American Common Market; that the target date for realization of such full, area-wide integration should be envisioned as no later than 1985, inviting allusion thereafter to the 1970's as "The Decade of Integration." Indeed, adding to an unmistakable aura of deliberateness and determination, the President of the United States, in an on-the-scene address, gave the goal his blessing as he pledged this country's support.[4]

To be sure, no one expects area-wide integration in Latin America to come about free of all resistance, or even of unbargained-for setbacks. Just as CACM and LAFTA met with problems, so a more expansive movement seems destined not always to enjoy smooth sailing. True, the important matter of who (i.e., what organizational entity, or entities) should spearhead the big drive appears to have been pretty well resolved; LAFTA and CACM are being viewed as providing the base upon which, and via which, to build. But many other matters remain and will need to be dealt with. Indeed, one among them looms especially large (so large, in fact, that overall success or failure may well hinge on it): the status to be accorded the "lesser developed" countries of the region.

NATURE OF THE PROBLEM

Latin America has cohesive qualities about it. Despite the number of countries, similarities among them — in culture, in history, in economic attributes — offer a basis for considerable meaningful generalization. Perhaps most basic of all, the countries are linked by the circumstance of underdevelopment. All the countries are underdeveloped, though by no means equally so.

Relative to degrees of underdevelopment, we note that per capita income in Latin America, everywhere vastly lower than in the United States, spans a considerable range: over $500 in Argentina, Uruguay, and Venezuela; under $200 in Bolivia, Haiti, and Paraguay. And while income levels differ, the environments from which income stems also differ widely. The geographic size of Brazil stands in sharp contrast to that of, say, the Central American countries. Similarly, the population of Brazil (over 80 million) dwarfs that of most other countries (under 5 million in roughly a dozen and under 2 million in three). And, of course, some of the countries are well beyond the elementary stages of development, avidly concerned with an emergent industrial complex, while others are less far along, still concerned basically with the traditional raw-materials sector or with the preconditions of infrastructure.

The fact that the countries differ widely in ways such as those mentioned entails interesting implications for development in any event, and especially so when regional integration comprises an integral part of the environmental framework. Within a regional context, competition among countries automatically is accorded greater scope for play — and competition tends, characteristically, to work to the advantage of the "stronger" countries. It is these countries — of best endowment, or simply farthest along developmentally — that stand to benefit most (barring action to the contrary); indeed, some of the benefit that then accrues to them derives, somewhat ironically, from the very participation of countries less well-situated or less far along developmentally.

All the while, the spirit of nationalism is on hand to affect thinking. Basically antagonistic to regionalism, this nationalism is sometimes joined, at times strongly reinforced, by a variety of pressures rooted in narrow self-interest. Given such forces, it is to be expected that the matter of "split of benefits" should not go unnoted; there is an awareness of how regional integration tends to favor some countries over others, and the response — on one basis or another — frequently is one of outright opposition or of calculated delay.

Thus, three major ingredients, all intertwined, are on the scene. (1) Economic disparities exist among the region's countries. (2) The competition generated under integration favors the stronger countries. (3) Nationalism and self-interest being what they are, integration does not always appear attractive. Given this context, some fundamental questions emerge. Why should a "weaker" country go along with integration? Why, indeed, when it is the growing industrial complexes of countries like Brazil and Argentina that are strengthened — in part through support from the "Bolivias" of the region. If the "weaker" countries need to go along, what reasons can the more-favored countries cite to induce the desired co-operation? What, in fact, do the "Bolivias" of the region stand to gain?

Obviously, there is a problem: the problem of the projected status of the "lesser developed" countries. Unless this matter can be satisfactorily resolved, the co-operation among countries upon which successful integration action hinges can hardly be expected. In terms of our direct interest here, the matter represents the basic determinant of the fate of the movement toward a full-scale Latin American Common Market.

Before focusing on what might be done to resolve the foregoing matter in the interests of a LACM, let us survey briefly what preceding integration movements — CACM and LAFTA — have tried to do about it. Perhaps there are lessons in the past that can be brought to bear on future decisions.

EXPERIENCE OF THE PAST

Because the CACM and LAFTA experiences differ some-what, at least in particular respects, it seems well to consider them separately.

CACM

CACM embraces five small Central American countries (Guatemala through Costa Rica) — all relatively underdeveloped (as compared with, say, Argentina or Brazil), and all rather poorly situated to promote development unilaterally. Given the uniformity of situation among these countries, there is a basis for considerable cohesion (and, conversely, relatively little basis for a direct conflict of interest). With unilateral action lacking in force, the possibility of greater impact through unison in action readily acquires appeal — the foundation, in fact, of regional integration.

CACM's intended spur to development was seen as linked to reductions in impediments to intraregional trade, which reductions, in turn, might prompt greater intraregional trade and the greater investment undertaken in anticipation of greater trade generally. Progress proved gratifying — to an extent that, by the second year of operations, the initial goal of ten years for attainment of free trade within the region could be advanced to just five years. By 1967, some 94 per cent of all items listed on tariff schedules stood free of duty and other trade restrictions. Concurrently, the magnitude of intraregional trade advanced — by over 300 per cent (in value) between 1960 and 1965, with the upward movement continuing; alongside of this, intraregional trade as a proportion of total foreign trade rose — more than tripling between 1960 and 1965 (or from about 6 per cent to roughly 20 per cent). All the while, investment in new industry was rising significantly, the requisite financing stemming from both indigenous and foreign sources.

Of course, more than just tariff liberalization was responsible for the progress shown. Beneficial impact derived also from (1) the movement to a common external tariff, (2) the introduction of a zonal payments system, and (3) the decision to support special "integration industries." Relative to (1), the goal, by 1970, of uniform duties on imports originating outside the region was substantially attained by 1967, at which time imports so treated exceeded 80 per cent. A co-effect of encouragement of intraregional trade at the expense of imports of extraregional origin was the further buttressing of incentives for investment in new industry within the region.

Relative to (2), new arrangements were instituted to assist the clearance and settlement of trade balances among countries of the region. [5] Supplementary arrangements were concerned with the harmonization of monetary and credit policies among countries of the region, preparatory to eventual movement to full monetary union. [6]

Relative to (3), the problem of individual countries being too small to sustain many types of industry was countered with the idea of "integration industries": the selection for establishment within the region of specific industries, each to enjoy a monopoly-like status,[7] and each placed geographically, per plan, so as to give every country some industry. Success for such industries was regarded likely by virtue of (a) free access to a unified five-country market area, (b) sheltered from external competition by the presence of a common external tariff. Despite a slow start, projected action in this vein pointed to a more substantive future.

LAFTA

A crucial factor in the success generally ascribed to CACM was the extent of harmony among its members, a harmony helped by high similarity of situation among them. A like environment was never the case for LAFTA. There it was a matter of big countries alongside small countries; of relatively far-advanced countries alongside countries still quite undeveloped; of Brazil, Argentina, etc. alongside Paraguay and Ecuador.

That the successful merger of countries so diverse would require special provisions was recognized in LAFTA from the out-set. In most basic terms, member countries were classed in three categories in accordance with similarities of developmental status: (1) the most developed countries (Argentina, Brazil, and Mexico), (2) countries in an "insufficient market" state (Colombia, Chile, Peru, Uruguay,[8] and Venezuela[9]), and (3) the relatively less developed countries (Bolivia, Ecuador, and Paraguay[10])[11]. Supplementary to this, forms of special treatment for "weaker" countries were cited, covering (1) the implementation of reductions in tariffs and other trade restrictions, (2) the amelioration of balance-of-payments difficulties, and (3) the introduction or expansion of specific productive activities.[12] Thereafter, as LAFTA has pushed forward, each resolution of major substance has continued to reflect a concern for those countries confronted with inhibiting circumstances.

The basic rationale of LAFTA, as in the case of CACM, was that of reductions in tariffs and other barriers to trade between member countries in the interests of greater intraregional trade and, along with it, greater investment, output, etc. The intent was that of progressive reductions in barriers to intraregional trade, resulting in "free trade" within the region[13] by the end of twelve years.[14] Concurrently, in the hope of smoothing the path of trade liberalization, the intent was for a closer co-ordination among countries of planning effort[15] and of actions generally.

While the over-all intent unmistakably was for swift trade liberalization, circumstances and situations were such as to seem to warrant the retention of a number of important "loopholes." Always the alternatives posed for LAFTA were (a) to try to compel a similar response by every member, whatever its status, and thereby perhaps give some member no choice but nonparticipation, or (b) to try to provide a livable avenue for the member with a "special" problem and thereby assist it in participation to the best of its capacity. Given the alternatives, LAFTA leaned to (b). Thus, relative to items of intraregional trade on the so-called "national list" (on which duty reductions of no less than 8 per cent per year were contemplated, all such reductions normally generalized thereafter via most-favored-nation treatment), member countries retained the discretionary right under an "escape clause" provision to withdraw concessions[16] in the event of balance-of-paments difficulties[17] or of serious threat to output vital to national well-being[18]; or, under circumstances of pressure, remained eligible to request approval for release from even the commitment to enter into an annual round of reductions.[19] Further, relative to items on the "common list" (to which list 25 per cent of all items in intraregional trade were to be added every three years, resulting in virtually all such items being on the list by target-year 1973), disproportionately heavy adjustment pressure expected to fall upon some members in the course of compliance with planned duty reductions was cited as justification for a slower pace in reductions in particular instances, such as in the case of certain agricultural products of dominant importance to the lesser developed countries.

In another respect, relative to "complementation agreements" (which aim at immediate free trade between two or more countries in a specified product or group of products, chiefly in the industrial sector), little or no success has been had in helping the lesser developed countries. The early expectation that such agreements would help to attract major industrial investment even to small otherwise-poorly-situated countries (since resultant output, however limited its market at home, then stood free of barriers in its movement to the partner countries, where the major market presumably lay) simply has not proven out in practice. In fact, sentiment in the lesser developed countries has turned critical on grounds that complementation agreements may, as they have been used, actually contribute to a further polarization of industry in the already more advanced areas.[20]

Similarly, the principle of "margin of preference," introduced with the lesser developed countries in mind,[21] has not proven a success in its translation into practice. The intent, of course, was to assure the lesser developed countries of favored treatment (i.e., a margin of preference) in the scheduling of tariff reductions in the hope of achieving (a) greater substitution, within these countries, of domestic output for customary imports and (b) improved access externally (in the market of better-situated countries in LAFTA) for domestic output. Yet, little was accomplished in this direction — though "pro" sentiment in the lesser developed countries, always strong, proved a factor in evoking renewed consideration of the matter more recently.[22]

Data are on hand, to be sure, to shed light on the extent of success, over-all, in expanding intraregional trade. Intraregional trade has been rising within the LAFTA area (though not as dramatically as within CACM) — in index terms, intraregional trade rose from 100 to 222 between 1961 and 1966, while extra-regional trade rose from 100 to 126; intraregional trade as a pro-portion of total foreign trade roughly doubled (from about 6 per cent to almost 11 per cent). A major portion of the increase un-questionably should be ascribed to tariff cutting, though, as in the case of CACM, improvements in payments arrangements,[23] etc., surely also contributed in this direction.

In short, trade liberalization, reinforced with other ac-tions, resulted in the significantly greater intraregional trade that had been sought in the interests of developmental promotion. How-ever, as intraregional trade increased over-all, gains at the in-dividual-country level did not necessarily accrue as intended or expected. Actually, the distribution-by-country of intraregional trade changed little during the period; the more developed coun-tries (especially Argentina and Brazil) continue to dominate intra-regional trade, while the shares of lesser developed countries re-main small and have even decreased for some (e.g., Ecuador and Paraguay).

CURRENT STATUS AND FUTURE PROSPECTS

As the foregoing reveals, LAFTA has encountered prob-lems far more formidable than has CACM. This has been the case not so much because of any difference in diligence of effort, but more directly because of a difference of environment. Unlike CACM, comprised of countries of roughly similar status, LAFTA has had to work with countries of assorted status. Indeed, the contrast in the two experiences has provided a lesson: diversity invites disunity — which situation, unless countered, impairs the very basis for successful integration.

The problems of LAFTA within a ten-country context are a matter of record. Looking ahead, it seems only reasonable to expect similar problems, on a grander scale, within the context of all of Latin America as the movement to a full LACM proceeds. The big problem, rooted in diversity, does not, of course, rest fundamentally with the more advanced countries; these countries are moving ahead, and stand to move ahead even faster as the benefits of integration accrue. The problem rests, rather, with the lesser developed countries. There can be no true regional in-tegration without these countries; yet, co-operation on their part presumes "adequate" benefits for them as well as for the more ad-vanced countries.

Thus, the thesis here is that the leaders of integration, as they push to hasten the shift to a LACM, should be concerned — probably even more concerned than in the past — with the status of the lesser developed countries. In this connection, four areas of potential activity seem especially to merit attention: (1) subregional integration, (2) sector integration, (3) intraregional financing, and (4) the exercise of leadership (apropos the role of the Council of Ministers of LAFTA).

SUBREGIONAL INTEGRATION

The rationale for subregional integration is simple: to ease the transition to region-wide integration, integration can advantageously be pursued first within smaller blocs (within subregions, each fairly homogeneous and, hence, fairly conducive to progress), leaving until later — to a time when substantial headway has been made at subregional levels — the final drive to all-out amalgamation. Actually, the CACM area comprises such a subregion;[24] and, more recently, a further subregional movement of note has taken hold: the so-called Andean Group, linking Bolivia, Chile, Colombia, Ecuador, Paraguay, and Venezuela.[25]

To illustrate with the Andean Group, the participating countries seemed to have much in common that might facilitate immediate progress. All were "lesser developed," relative to, say, Argentina and Brazil. If within the same framework as the more advanced countries, competitive forces threatened to retard development within them; but if joined together in an arrangement somewhat apart from the more advanced countries, prospects seemed improved for autonomous development (involving, say, investment in the industrial sector) somewhere within their confines. Accordingly, steps were taken to initiate a working arrangement that might result in, first, greater co-ordination in the over-all policies affecting development and, second, some amount of tangible action yielding immediate development. As evidence of work during several official meetings, the Andean Group has proven instrumental in (a) the formulation of agreements for the joint development of the petro-chemical and machinery industries and for the integration of the automobile industry, (b) the acceptance of a schedule of accelerated tariff reductions within the subregion, (c) the establishment of a pattern for a common external tariff, and (d) the creation of a mechanism intended to ease the settlement of trade accounts among the participants.[26]

Given the immensity of the task involved in moving to a LACM, the merits of subregional integration as an intermediary step would appear to warrant careful consideration. In all this, the Andean Group, a major movement of considerable area-coverage, would seem a "model" worth watching (capable of providing important insights alongside lessons already on hand via the CACM "subregional" arrangement). Possibilities clearly exist for further subregions, as well as for revised combinations of countries within subregions — even as, with experience, more activities come to be accepted as properly within the scope of whatever subregions are on the scene.

SECTOR INTEGRATION

Just as the impediment inherent in diversity-among-countries stands to be breached when integration effort is applied somewhat selectively in terms of a smaller area (subregional integration), so a sectoral approach (sector integration) — under which integration is aimed not at all products at once or at random, but at one product or at one group of products at a time — stands to ease the pangs of the integration process. However difficult across-the-board integration may be (and difficulties aplenty are usual), some integration, involving only some lines of activity, may nevertheless prove an immediate possibility — and, hence, merit serious consideration.

Little has occurred thus far in Latin America in the realm of sector integration. True, LAFTA has given attention to three important sectors: iron and steel, petro-chemicals, and paper and cellulose; however, only the first two have appeared even likely for area-wide treatment. Nor has much been accomplished with the closely-related procedure of complementation agreements (under which two or more countries can establish immediate free trade in covered items, sheltering them from outside competition with a common external tariff). In fact, sentiment in the lesser developed countries has turned somewhat critical of the sectoral approach, whatever its form. All too often the impression has been that intraregional sector linkages work in favor of the stronger producers, generally situated in the more advanced countries rather than in the lesser developed countries.

Yet, the technique(s) would seem to hold potential for the lesser developed countries, and, therefore, merit further consideration as to possible successful application. Certain circumstances are imaginable under which a lesser developed country might well carve out a role: (1) multi-product producers might find advantages in dispersing some portion of their production capacity; (2) components of a product might be produced in quite a number of locales, in anticipation of shipment to a major locale for final assembly; and (3) dissimilar phases of production in a multi-stage production process might be carried out in widely-separated locales, with final assembly or processing centered in some major locale.

INTRAREGIONAL FINANCING

Many associate heavy financial outlay with a program of integration: not only are projects costly in the aggregate, but the seriousness of effort itself depends on the adequacy of backing. Others, in fundamental agreement as to probable costliness, go on, however, to contend that financing poses no immediate constraint; sufficient financing to service current activity is available, they suggest, or can be made available through existing arrangements — through, say, the Inter-American Development Bank (IDB) or like institutions.

Yet, even if financing seems adequate in some over-all sense, can it be regarded as adequate also in terms of the needs of the relatively less developed countries? Is it not possible that available financing will, in the absence of special arrangements to the contrary, simply come to be applied very largely in the

479

countries already more developed? If such is a strong likelihood, is there not then a case for evolving supplementary procedures that can give the lesser developed countries a better prospect for new production facilities? Needless to say, not only is there reason to believe that something further along these lines is in order to place the lesser developed countries more nearly on a par with better-situated countries, [27] but a body of thought already exists as to the form this support might take.

One approach, perhaps best thought of in terms of initial application solely within the LAFTA area (where diversity among countries is currently felt most keenly), is to establish a special "integration fund" on behalf of development in the lesser developed countries. Contributions could come from all members — computed, say, as a small percentage of current GNP. Eligibility for financing — on a loan basis — could extend to projects in lesser developed countries, and to those multi-country projects involving directly one or more of the lesser developed countries. Administration could be by the IDB, already widely referred to as the "Bank for Integration." [28]

Ostensibly, two main advantages could derive from an arrangement of the suggested type. First, lesser developed countries could reasonably envisage enhanced developmental potential for themselves, and, hence, could afford to feel greater enthusiasm in their over-all participation. Second, all countries would stand to be drawn together more closely, thereby strengthening the basic integration spirit.

INTEGRATION'S LEADERSHIP

What will happen with integration depends, in important measure, on how responsibility is exercised in the initiation and implementation of action. With LAFTA a critical component within the total context, attention of necessity is directed to its Council of Ministers. There, however, good cause may exist for some second thought.

Weak initially because of no provision for executive power at the ministerial level, LAFTA was subsequently provided with leadership in the form of a Council of Ministers. In practice, the Council has been composed mainly of Ministers of Foreign Relations, not of representatives from more-directly-concerned, or more-powerfully-situated, economic ministries — e.g., Ministers of Industry or Commerce — as true in the case of CACM's counterpart. The major problems of integration have been, and remain, economic, not diplomatic — thereby suggesting that a changed composition, to assure a different type of talent and outlook, is in order.

Not only is there question as to the Council's representation, but also as to its administrative procedures in the handling of work. Unlike CACM, which aims at all but final agreement on agenda items prior to the convening of a formal meeting, LAFTA, in its practices to date, is prone to see a considerable amount of early-stage work come before the formal meeting itself. Preferable, seemingly, would be a greater thrashing out of preparatory matters at the "working level," sparing the Council excessive detail and possible diversionary debate when it does convene.

THE BIGGER PICTURE

Admittedly, more can be done in Latin America to prod integration — which, if to prove successful, has to assure all countries, including the lesser developed countries, of benefits. Yet, not everything that is germane to the success of integration lies within Latin America's power. What Latin America can do is much affected by the greater environment — by what happens outside the region, as well as within. Many elements are involved: the extent of global well-being, economically and politically; the nature of the rules that govern international trade; the status of capital flows, public and private. If, however, this greater environment is reasonably favorable, Latin America seemingly has every reason to expect decided gains from her own efforts in perfecting the course of integration.

NOTES

1. The CACM members are Costa Rica, El Salvador, Guatemala, Honduras, and Nicaragua.

2. LAFTA's initial seven countries — Argentina, Brazil, Chile, Mexico, Paraguay, Peru, and Uruguay — were later joined by three others: Colombia, Ecuador, and Venezuela.

3. Appraisal of the significance of the meeting was reflected in the tone of labels quickly attached: "Summit Conference," "Chiefs of State" meeting, etc. The formal sessions occurred during April 12 - 14, 1967.

4. The "Declaration of Presidents" that followed from the meeting stated as follows: "The President of the U.S. of America, for his part, declares his firm support for this promising Latin American initiative." The President's address, in full, appeared in *Department of State Bulletin,* May 8, 1967, pp. 707-712.

5. Introduced in 1961, the Central American Clearing House was, by 1965, handling over 90 per cent of all transactions between members. Creation of a Central American peso further facilitated the clearance process; used in the settlement of intraregional balances, its effect was to lessen the need to draw down scarce external reserves.

6. The Central American Monetary Union, introduced in 1964, was expected eventually to absorb the Clearing House.

7, Because monopoly conditions readily invite abuse, certain control tactics — all indirect — were outlined.

8. LAFTA's Council of Ministers, during its 1967 sessions, reclassified Uruguay as "lesser developed" for the period up to 1972.

9. Though provided for by LAFTA as indicated, Venezuela continued, as of early 1968, to occupy an "intermediate" status, short of full-fledged membership. On the other hand, Bolivia, classed by LAFTA as a relatively less developed country, had not as yet moved beyond introductory phases in the acquisition of membership.

10. Relative to non-LAFTA portions of Latin America, probably rating categorization under (3) also are the CACM countries, along with the island countries of the Caribbean plus Panama.

11. Resolution 71-III (of the Contracting Parties of LAFTA) expressed the intent of "a just distribution of the benefits. . . [of integration]" for countries having "insufficient markets" or being "lesser developed."

12. Under Article 32 (of the Treaty of Montevideo, which established LAFTA).

13. While CACM aimed for a "common market" (free trade within the region, but with a common external tariff relative to imports of extraregional origin), LAFTA was intended to yield a "free trade area" — free trade within the region, but with each member country remaining free to fix its own tariff levels on imports of extraregional origin. Following the Punta del Este meeting (April 1967), however, LAFTA's goal was advanced from simple free trade to that of a full-fledged common market — with a LACM envisaged as the product of a merging of CACM and LAFTA.

14. By 1973.

15. Expressed, if not enforced.

16. From the national list.

17. In the absence of other balance-of-payments support (say, an IMF-type of support), the alternatives open to a country quickly reduce to (a) withdrawal from a concession or (b) outright non-participation in LAFTA.

18. Countries invoking the escape clause (relative to a limited number of products) have included Chile, Colombia, and Uruguay.

19. A prerogative exercised by, for example, Ecuador and Paraguay.

20. Four major complementation agreements had been concluded by 1966; statistical machines (Argentina, Brazil, Chile, and Uruguay); electronic tubes (Argentina, Brazil, Mexico, and Uruguay); household electrical appliances (Brazil and Uruguay); and electronic and electrical communication equipment (Brazil and Uruguay).

21. Resolution 53 - II (of the Contracting Parties of LAFTA).

22. By LAFTA's Council of Ministers at its 1967 meeting, where a proposal for a three-category regimen of preferential margins was advanced.

23. LAFTA is evolving a zonal payments system, based on a network of bilateral agreements between central banks. Initiated only in 1966, early experience indicates multilateralized compensation arrangements embracing something over 30 per cent of potentially coverable transactions.

24. The procedure of "subregional agreements" as a transitional tactic in integration first gained recognition within LAFTA during a 1964 meeting in Bogotá. Though CACM had earlier origins, its identification as a subregion-in-fact came only with the cited meeting.

25. The Andean Subregional Group, in process of formation over several years, was joined most recently, during 1967, by Bolivia. Formed in anticipation of compliance within the framework of LAFTA's over-all rules, the Andean Group had not as yet, by mid-1968, acquired legal status under LAFTA; still pending was the requisite action by LAFTA in agreeing on the compatibility of the Andean Group's statutes with the Treaty of Montevideo. While thus continuing short of formal endorsement under LAFTA, the Andean Group nonetheless proceeded with the formation of organizational substructures of its own. Most important, the Andean Development Corporation (ADC) was introduced; patterned along lines of the Chilean Development Corporation, the role envisaged for ADC related to the financing of preinvestment and investment needs within the area, in essence providing the member countries with their counterpart of the CACM area's Central American Bank for Economic Integration.

26. The arrangement under (d), standing beyond the ADC "regional bank" concept, bears strong similarities to the CACM area's "Cámara de Compensación Centroamericana."

27. The reasoning ordinarily associated draws upon factual material such as the following: the IDB, while committed in principle to favorable treatment of lesser developed

countries, nevertheless is responsible primarily to all of
Latin America; the ADC is committed to service the Andean
Group, not lesser developed countries, per se; the Central
American Bank for Economic Integration is committed to ser-
vice the CACM area, not lesser developed countries, per se.
In sum, no one of the major prevailing institutions bears
an all-out responsibility toward, expressly, the lesser
developed countries.

        28.   While the IDB can (and does) service multi-
country projects of the type cited (encompassing lesser developed countries or these countries and more advanced
countries), the suggested "integration fund" would be "self
financed" — by Latin America, for the lesser developed
countries of Latin America (or, in the case of LAFTA, by
LAFTA countries, for the lesser developed countries within
LAFTA) — unlike the IDB procedure, which extends beyond
Latin America in its reliance on "foreign" participation
(e.g., co-operating funds of United States, and other-
country, origin). In sum, the suggested "integration fund"
involves something beyond what currently prevails.

36

THE DYNAMICS OF THE
SUBREGIONAL AGREEMENTS
WITHIN THE LAFTA MOVEMENT

By Francisco Orrego Vicuña
Department of Legal Affairs
Pan American Union

PROBLEMS AND DIFFICULTIES WITHIN THE LAFTA MOVEMENT

The process of integration of the Latin American Free Trade Association after an initial spurt of energy in its immediate objective of trade liberalization, entered a period of stagnation caused primarily by a disagreement among its members regarding improvements in the institutional mechanisms. To consolidate its achievements, a free trade area must necessarily proceed toward a customs union and a common market, as was foreseen by the Montevideo Treaty. [1] This need became manifest once again in the LAFTA case. In order to overcome the growing stagnation, the member states sought a high-level political decision which would definitively solve the question of whether LAFTA would evolve toward those more advanced stages.

Highlights of the search for a political decision were: the letter which President Frei of Chile sent, in January 1965, to Raúl Prebisch, Felipe Herrera, José Antonio Mayobre, and Carlos Sanz de Santamaría, requesting their specific proposals for the improvement of LAFTA; their reply, published in April 1965, under the title "Proposals for the Creation of the Latin American Common Market"; [2] the meeting of the Ministers of Foreign Affairs of the LAFTA countries, in November 1965; and the creation of the Council of Ministers as the highest organization of LAFTA. All these initiatives helped to define the mechanisms necessary to push LAFTA forward. These mechanisms included the automatic unencumbering of trade, as contrasted with the current mechanism of negotiations; a common external tariff; the co-ordination of economic policies, as foreseen by Resolution 100 of the LAFTA Conference; and the subsequent establishment of the Latin American Common Market. In a parallel way an institutional readaptation was foreseen, so as to create a high-level political institution — the Council of Ministers — and a regional or community-type insitution — the Technical Commission — which would, through their decisions, promote the integration process. A mechanism for the settlement of disputes would provide suitable legal safeguards. The labor and management sectors would be duly represented. Other mechanisms, providing for liaison between national parliaments and the free transit of persons, would complete this framework.

This process culminated in the Declaration of the American Presidents in April 1967 promising to improve LAFTA, through the automatic disencumbrance of trade, a common external tariff, the co-ordination of economic policies, the co-ordination of laws and other important mechanisms, and, by linking LAFTA and the Central American Common Market, the creation of the Latin American Common Market. Nevertheless, and as was predictable, the disagreements previously noted continued. The second meeting of the Council of Ministers of LAFTA, held at Asunción in August-September 1967 did not reach an agreement for implementing any of the essential mechanisms provided by the Declaration of the Presidents for the improvement of LAFTA; its Resolution 191 only entrusted the Standing Executive Committee with the preparation of additional studies on the automatic disencumbrance, stand-still mechanisms, unencumbering of the common list, establishment of a margin of preference within the zone, common attitudes toward nonmember countries and international organizations and establishment of the common external tariff.

On the other hand, the organic and balanced institutional system which had begun to be organized was implemented only in its intergovernmental aspects; the community-type approach was abandoned. Thus, the Council of Ministers was established; the mechanism for the settlement of disputes was also established upon traditional bases; liaison between the labor and management sector and the integration movement, as well as the free transit of persons were also set up in a limited way, [3] but the Technical Commission— the community-interest organ— and the liaison between national parliaments were abandoned. The development of the integration movement is basically a process of political maturity among member states, and obviously this maturity has not yet been attained in an homogeneous form within the LAFTA framework. The traditional and classic concept of sovereignty is still present in many of LAFTA's approaches to economic integration. As long as this maturity is not attained, the improvement of LAFTA will continue to be the subject of profound disagreements.

ORIGINS OF THE SUBREGIONAL PROCESS

A group of LAFTA member countries acquainted with this basic reality and whose position with respect to the improvement of the integration process had been similar to a certain extent, initiated the search for mechanisms which, within the general framework of the Montevideo Treaty, would permit the acceleration of the integration process among them, at the same time strengthening their position in relation to the more developed members of LAFTA. In this sense the principle of harmonic and balanced regional development would become a reality, and facilitate the creation of a Latin American common market. In August, 1966, at the invitation of the Colombian President Carlos Lleras Restrepo and on the occasion of his inauguration, there was a meeting in Bogotá of the Presidents of Colombia, Chile, and Venezuela, and the personal representatives of the Presidents of Ecuador and Perú. At the close of this meeting the "Declaration of Bogotá, " was made public. This document, in addition to stating the position of the Presidents on international, regional, and LAFTA problems, established the basis for the formation of a Subregional Agreement among the Andean countries. Bolivia joined the Andean group in 1967. The program of action of the Declaration of Bogotá contemplated important steps to be undertaken at the subregional level, principally, the liberalization of trade, the co-ordination of industrial development, the establishment of multinational enterprises, the substitution of imports from countries not belonging to LAFTA, agreements on air and sea navigation, the interconnection of telecommunications systems, professional training and the establishment of dual nationality for the citizens of these countries residing in another one of them. To carry out this program the Presidents agreed to establish national secretariats, a joint commission (Comisión Mixta), a development corporation (Corporación de Fomento), and other mechanisms.

The organization of this subregional group encountered serious obstacles at the outset. On the one hand, and as a consequence of the traditional approach that has often characterized relations among Latin American countries, the rapprochement of the Andean countries was interpreted as pursuing the formation of blocs within the LAFTA ambit, an interpretation which was rejected by the Chilean Foreign Ministry and by Colombian officials, who stated very clearly that subregional agreements sought only to facilitate the integration process.[4] However, doubts arose regarding the compatibility of such agreements with the Montevideo Treaty, particularly in relation to the most-favored-nation clause. As will be seen, these doubts were answered in the Declaration of American Presidents and in LAFTA resolutions.

GENERAL REGULATIONS OF THE SUBREGIONAL AGREEMENTS

Commitments were assumed in the Declaration of Bogotá to undertake joint action within the LAFTA framework so as to obtain suitable treatment for the less developed countries and those having insufficient markets. Likewise, in the program of action, there were commitments for immediate action at the subregional level. The signatory governments therefore began consultations to create a subregional common market, within the Montevideo Treaty. The first result of this joint action was in the Declaration of the American Presidents. They instructed their respective Ministers of Foreign Affairs to implement the following decision: "To promote the conclusion of temporary subregional agreements, with provisions for reducing tariffs within the subregions and harmonizing treatment toward third nations more rapidly than in the general agreements, in keeping with the objectives of regional integration. Subregional tariff reductions will not be extended to countries that are not parties to the subregional agreement, nor will they create special obligations for them." (Chapter I, No. 2, d.) Further on it adds: "The countries of relatively less economic development will have the right to participate and to obtain preferential conditions in the subregional agreements in which they have an interest."[5] All these provisions, by decision of the Presidents, are to be understood within or based upon the Treaty of Montevideo.

In compliance with these instructions, the second meeting of the Council of Ministers of LAFTA, by means of its Resolution 202, established the basic principles to which the Subregional Agreements should be adjusted. These principles were detailed in Resolution 222, adopted by the Seventh Ordinary Conference, held in Montevideo in October - December, 1967. This resolution defines the Subregional Agreements as: "... those through which the LAFTA countries that subscribe to them may promote the process of economic integration in a balanced and more accelerated way than the one derived from the commitments assumed within the framework of the Treaty of Montevideo."[6]

Upon examining these provisions, one realizes that the system of subregional agreements within the LAFTA framework has the following principal characteristics: The subregional agreements must be compatible with the Montevideo Treaty and the resolutions of its institutions, as well as with the pertinent provisions of the Declaration of the Presidents. At the same time, as we shall see further on, the legal order of LAFTA complements that of the subregional agreements, so that in cases not foreseen by these the LAFTA provisions will be applicable. The subregional agreements are of a transitory nature. Subregional agreements must contain provisions for the disencumbrance of trade and the establishment of a common external tariff in a more accelerated way than the general commitments of LAFTA; thus, when the commitments of LAFTA, in its evolution towards a common market, attain a degree of disencumbrance or tariff harmonization with respect to third nations more advanced than that of the subregional agreements, the latter will no longer operate since its principal purpose would no longer be fulfilled.[7] Subregional tariff reductions will not be extended to countries that are not parties to the subregional agreement, nor will they create special obligations for them. In this sense another exception has been admitted with regard to the most-favored-nation clause contained in Article 18 of the Montevideo Treaty.

Nevertheless, these agreements have certain limitations. Tariff reductions must be general and not restricted to specific sectors, as their purpose is to accelerate the fulfillment of the goals of the Montevideo Treaty, that is, the general disencumbrance of trade. This disencumbrance must not affect the commitments already assumed by the parties in the Agreement through their national lists, special lists or common list with respect to the other members of LAFTA. The complementarity agreements within the subregional process are regulated by the general system of LAFTA, that is, they are open to any LAFTA member that wishes to join, provided that it gives suitable compensation in accordance with Resolution 99 of the LAFTA conference. The Declaration of Bogotá contemplated the possibility of complementarity agreements for the exclusive benefit of the subregion, but this was not accepted by LAFTA. Each subregional agreement must receive the approval of LAFTA's executive committee, by the favorable vote of two-thirds of its members, and there must be no negative vote; this veto is absolutely unjustifiable, and might create arbitrary obstructions. The progress of the agreements will be examined annually by LAFTA institutions. The provisions for becoming a party to the agreement must also be compatible with the goals of the Treaty of Montevideo. These provisions have not yet been established because of the existing disagreement on their scope. Each subregional agreement will be conducted and administered by its own institutions.

THE DYNAMICS OF THE ECONOMIC MECHANISMS

The regulations that have been described have a general character, applicable to any subregional agreement worked out within LAFTA. The subregional agreement of the Declaration of Bogotá also rests upon specific bases and regulations, prepared by the joint commission and approved by Resolution 203 of the second meeting of the Council of Ministers of LAFTA. In accordance with these bases, the objectives of the agreement are to facilitate a more suitable participation of the countries which are parties to the Declaration of Bogotá within the integration process of the Montevideo Treaty, through a substantial expansion of their markets by means of a transitory subregional agreement which contains more accelerated commitments for the conversion of LAFTA into a common market.

In order to attain these objectives, an internal program for trade liberalization was set up, with the following characteristics:

a. Total and immediate disencumbrance of the products included in the common list of LAFTA's liberalization mechanisms, as well as of those products which are included later on;

b. total and immediate disencumbrance of manufactured, agricultural and mining products which are not currently produced within the subregion;

c. automatic and accelerated disencumbrance of products not included in the aforementioned categories, with certain exceptions that we shall comment upon further on; this liberalization would be completed

489

for numerous sectors approximately in 1975-1976, and in any case before 1985, the date established by the Declaration of the American Presidents for the full functioning of the Latin American Common Market;

d.   the industrial sectors of basic metallurgy, nonmetallic minerals, chemistry and petrochemistry, wood, cellulose and paper, mechanical manufactures, electronic industry and foodstuffs industry, will be disencumbered through the mechanisms set up by the respective complementarity agreements;

e.   this program will not be applicable to a limited list of exceptions, which will be disencumbered through LAFTA mechanisms; and

f.   a special regime is established for Bolivia and Ecuador, due to their condition of being relatively less developed countries.

The bases also contain provisions for the establishment of a common external tariff, which will be applicable to imports from outside the subregion; provisions for the co-ordination of economic policies, including those of development, monetary and foreign exchange, fiscal, external trade and investments; and other provisions on origin, safeguard clauses and administration. A committee of experts and the joint commission are preparing the final instrument that will guide the subregional process.

One may note that these mechanisms constitute a profound innovation with regard to the general system of LAFTA. In the first place, the disencumbrance of the products included in the common list will be undertaken immediately if this obligation exists within LAFTA only at the end of the transitional period (1972) and if the initiatives for advancing this date have failed; in the second place, all the disencumbrance mechanisms are automatic as a general rule, an initiative that has not succeeded within LAFTA; in the third place, a "stand-still" commitment is also ensured, which likewise has not been attained in LAFTA; the same might be said with regard to the co-ordination of policies and the establishment of a common external tariff. Even in the case of the complementarity agreements, which are regulated as indicated by the LAFTA system, those that are being drafted within the subregional framework — as the one in the petrochemical sector, for instance — take advantage of mechanisms that have never been utilized until now by the complementarity agreements in effect, as the common external tariff, co-ordination and orientation of investments, localization of industries, harmonization of the treatment of foreign capital and establishment of multinational enterprises in the respective sector, all of which is permitted by Resolution 99 of the LAFTA conference. Other mechanisms, such as the establishment of a common air-freight line, the co-ordination of shipping policies, the establishment of a clearing institution (Cámara de Compensación), the creation of multinational enterprises, the establishment of a fund for the financing of exports, agreements on double taxation, and many others in the process of being studied or drafted, demonstrate that this agreement creates a real subregional common market.

THE DYNAMICS OF THE INSTITUTIONAL MECHANISMS

The institutional aspects of this subregional process promise to be equally dynamic. As was said before, the Declaration of Bogotá provided for certain basic institutional mechanisms. The joint commission, formed by representatives of each government, first met in 1967. It agreed upon the establishment of the following institutions: the joint commission itself, a national technical secretariat in each country, a standing consultative committee, an executive secretary of the joint commission, and a technical group of high quality. This scheme, as we shall see, was subsequently modified. It is also worth noting that the employer sector has formed a businessmen's committee (Comité Empresarial) for the subregional agreement, which has been recognized as a consultative organ by the joint commission; liaison with the labor sector has also been agreed upon.

At its fourth meeting, the joint commission instructed a committee of experts to draft the final text of the subregional agreement to submit it for the approval of the joint commission. The committee of experts met in Bogotá in 1968 and drafted the text. The joint commission, due to certain difficulties arising in the private sector of Venezuela, has not yet concluded its revision, but the institutional aspects proposed by the experts have been almost entirely cleared.

The first conclusion at which the experts arrived in the institutional field is of extraordinary importance: the subregional agreement is only the general legal framework of the subregional integration process, establishing its great principles and objectives, but entrusting its application, development and adaptation to the institutions set up by the agreement. This is a typical "traité-cadre."

The joint commission will be the highest organ of the subregional agreement and will be empowered to adopt all the decisions required by the fulfillment of the objectives of the agreement. Its general voting system will be by two-thirds of the member countries, except for those matters in which the agreement expressly stipulates a requirement of the two-thirds of affirmative votes and the nonexistence of a negative vote. It may be observed that this system inverts the voting mechanism of the LAFTA conference: there the general rule is the veto and the exception the qualified majority, and here the general rule is the qualified majority and the exception the veto. Nevertheless, Bolivia, Ecuador, and Peru have reserved their acceptance of this mechanism.

The standing executive board is defined by the draft agreement as "the technical and community-type institution of the subregional agreement." This institution will be given executive powers and those for introducing proposals. In addition it will provide the required secretariat services. In those matters specified by the agreement and those delegated by the joint commission, it shall possess its own powers of decision. This organ is formed by three members, appointed by the joint commission; they shall be responsible to the joint commission and in the exercise of their functions they shall represent the community interest. As a general rule decisions are adopted unanimously.

This scheme of institutional balance, in which both the governmental interest and the community interest are represented, in which the institutions share in a certain way in the decision-making process, in which the executive powers are entrusted to the community-type organ, and in which the latter enjoys autonomy and independence, constitutes an improvement of the highest importance, demonstrating once again that this subregional agreement is on its way to solving in its own ambit the problems that afflict LAFTA. [8]

THE DYNAMICS OF THE ANDEAN DEVELOPMENT CORPORATION (CORPORACIÓN ANDINA DE FOMENTO)

A very important mechanism within the subregional agreement is the Andean Development Corporation; the agreement (convenio constitutivo) establishing this institution was signed in Bogotá in 1968. This institution, contemplated in the Declaration of Bogotá, has as its objectives the development and stimulation of subregional development, especially with regard to the expansion and reconversion of industries, financing and orientation of investments, support of multinational enterprises, and research and strengthening of money markets, with the right to issue various kinds of bonds, obligations and guarantees. Its authorized capital is 100 million dollars and the subscribed capital 25 million dollars. This capital is divided in shares of series "A," corresponding to member governments; in shares of series "B," corresponding to governments and other public institutions, with the right to transfer up to 40% of the shares assigned to each country to legal or natural private persons; and in shares of series "C," which may be issued for the subscription of legal or natural persons from outside the subregion.

The first plans were to establish this institution as a multinational private corporation, governed by the laws of Venezuela, where its headquarters have been located. But difficulties arising from that legislation and other difficulties regarding the participation of Peruvian public entities in such corporations determined that it be definitively established as a legal entity of public international law; its agreement is subject to ratification. This requirement of ratification was certainly not necessary; within the LAFTA framework several public entities have been

492

established by more dynamic means, and this example could have been easily followed. [9]

This is not the occasion to analyze the structure of the Andean Corporation. Nevertheless, a synthesis of its most dynamic features will give an idea of its importance. This corporation has the peculiarity of combining elements of an international organization with those of a private corporation, particularly of a stock company, which enables it to qualify as a public multi-national enterprise of a special nature. Among the first elements worthy of note are: its character as a legal entity of public international law, with the agreement subject to ratification; the provisions for its entry into force; the regime of privileges and immunities; the conditions for becoming a contracting party; its objectives and functions and, as a consequence of its character as a legal entity, the special and preferential rights recognized in the series "A" shares. Among the second elements worth noting are: the structure and denomination of the organs — assembly of shareholders, board of directors and president —; the provisions for voting, quorum and convocation; the system for dissolution and liquidation; the provisions on capital structure and issue of shares; the financial term and balance; and others.

The examination of the agreement leads to two definite conclusions: with regard to the instrument itself we are once again in the presence of a typical "traité-cadre," which establishes the basic principles, orientations and mechanisms, entrusting its development, improvement, and adaptation to the autonomous competence of its institutions. And from the point of view of the entity as a whole it is possible to conclude that it is a typical "communitarian" institution. These conclusions are sustained by the following dynamic features:

a. The system to dissolve the corporation, by simple accord of the extraordinary assembly of shareholders, constitutes an innovation with regard to the traditional international techniques, particularly important since accords are reached on a majority basis. On the other hand, the traditional denunciation has been converted into a special withdrawing right of the shareholders of series "A," of special legal effects since the shareholders what withdraw may always join again in accordance with the conditions determined by the assembly.

b. The power given to the extraordinary assembly for modifying, by majority vote, the agreement in any administrative or procedural matter is typical of a community-type institution. Furthermore, it may also modify the structure of the board of directors and adapt pertinent provisions of the agreement, with the requirement in this case of the favorable vote of the six shareholders of series "A," and the majority of the other shares represented at the meeting; this is the only case in which veto is contemplated. This system reminds one of the ECSC Treaty and its famous "Petite révision."[10]

c. The system of voting by majority, applicable to every organ, is another dynamic feature. The veto has been completely eradicated, except in the case just mentioned. The quorum is also very flexible.

d. The binding force of decisions for every shareholder, even for those who do not attend an assembly, reveals a direct link between them and the legal order of the corporation; this applies to governments and public entities as well as to legal or natural persons.

e. The general system of sanctions that has been established is very drastic. It is worth noting, for example, that the shareholders who are in default in the payment of capital will not have a right to vote; that the shareholders of series "A," that is, governments and public entities, that are very delinquent in fulfilling their obligations might be suspended and after a certain time will automatically cease to be members — expelled —, being unable in the meantime to exercise any of their rights except the one to withdraw; and that for the acceleration of the ratification process sanctions exist in the sense of dispensing with the nonratifying countries, adapting the agreement, and changing the headquarters in the event that the country appointed for such headquarters does not ratify within a certain time.

f. The power given to the board of directors for solving any matter not foreseen in the agreement and for interpreting such agreement is also typical of a communitarian system. Nevertheless it would be more suitable to give the interpretation powers to a jurisdictional institution.

g. The arbitration system for the settlement of disputes, with binding jurisdiction and unlimited competence, is another dynamic aspect worthy of note.

h. Among other aspects which sustain the aforementioned conclusions attention should be given to the direct participation of the private sector, which may be a shareholder and thus may elect directors and exercise other rights; to the residual competence of the executive president, who may decide and be in charge of every matter not expressly assigned to the other institutions; and to the power of the board of directors for establishing subsidiary institutions.

This community-type nature of the corporation might be

technically defined in a still more precise way, with the conclusion that it is a supranational organ. When we are in the presence of a system of majority voting, which makes decisions directly binding upon governments and individuals and whose effectiveness is guaranteed by drastic sanctions, we are in the presence of specific supranational powers.

Finally, may we add that this corporation is closely linked with the political and community-type institutions of the subregional agreement.

RELATIONS BETWEEN THE SUBREGIONAL LEGAL ORDER AND THAT OF LAFTA

The relations and links between the legal order of the subregional agreement of the Declaration of Bogotá and the legal order of LAFTA pose various interesting aspects. For the appraisal of the exact nature of these links it is necessary to recall that the essential objective of the subregional agreements is to promote the economic integration process among its members in a balanced and more accelerated manner than that originating from the commitments assumed within the framework of the Treaty of Montevideo. This objective, in turn, must be related to two principal characteristics of the Montevideo Treaty: its "traité-cadre" character, which permits its constant adaptation and projection, and the minimum character of all its commitments, which permits their amplification so that the final stage of customs union and common market may be attained as foreseen by the treaty itself. [11]

From this point of view the subregional agreements constitute, with respect to their members, an amplification of the commitments established within LAFTA, bringing them closer to the indicated final objectives within the basic framework of the Treaty of Montevideo which, in this case, is the subject of specific development applicable to the subregion. Since they constitute a special improvement of the framework of the treaty, the compatibility of these subregional agreements with that treaty has been admitted without reservation by the Council of Ministers of LAFTA. [12] This has been possible only because of the "traité-cadre" nature of the Treaty of Montevideo.

The subregional agreement is based upon its own legal order, which establishes both the rights and duties of the participant states and the rights and duties of such states with regard to the general legal order of LAFTA. This legal order of the subregional agreement has the following principal characteristics: it is derivative, special, transitory, and dynamic.

   a.   Its derivative nature means that it is derived from the general legal order of LAFTA, as a specific application to the subregion. In this sense the basic provisions to which the agreement must adjust itself have been established by the LAFTA institutions, and the original instrument of the agreement must receive the approval of the pertinent institutions of LAFTA. This characteristic is important in that this legal order is derived from that of LAFTA and, thus, being a part of the framework of the Montevideo Treaty, it does not require parliamentary approval or ratification, which thereby accelerates its entry into force, functioning, and adaptation.

b. Its special character signifies, as was said, that it constitutes a special application to the subregion of the general legal order of LAFTA, from which important consequences arise. In the first place, as a special legal order, its provisions prevail, with respect to the subregion, upon the provisions of the general legal order of LAFTA, vesting them with a suppletory character, that is, they will only be applicable when the subregional agreement is silent or when it expressly reverts to them; this has been expressly stated in Resolutions 202 and 222 of LAFTA. In the second place, the subregional legal order must be compatible with the general legal order of LAFTA. Its provisions should not be permitted to affect the rights and duties arising from the Treaty of Montevideo, the resolutions of the institutions, and other instruments of the association. For the same reason the provisions for becoming a contracting party must be compatible with the Montevideo Treaty. These principles also permit the solving of cases of conflict between both legal orders, with the need to determine whether the provision of LAFTA's legal order is a basic principle of the association or not. In the event that it does constitute a basic principle of the association — as, for example, the provisions of the Montevideo Treaty, and of Resolutions 202 and 222 of the conference — the conflict will be solved very definitely in favor of LAFTA, since the provisions of the subregional agreement cannot alter the basic and general framework from which they are derived. On the contrary, if LAFTA's provision does not constitute a basic principle, the conflict will be solved in favor of the provisions of the subregional agreement, which prevail by reason of their special character. Finally, it is worth noting that, also as a consequence of this special character, the disencumbrances agreed upon at the subregional level will not be extended to countries that are not parties to the subregional agreement, nor will they create special obligations for them. As was said, this is a very justified exception to the most-favored-nation clause.

496

c. The transitory character of this legal order is a
    double one. On the one hand, the subregional agree-
    ment must establish the date of entry into force and
    its duration. On the other hand, the subregional
    agreement will only be applicable as long as its com-
    mitments are more accelerated than those deriving
    from LAFTA's legal order, and will no longer be
    applicable when the latter reach the same level. The
    bases of the agreement underline this transitory char-
    acter, stating that "those special regimes will no
    longer be applicable when they identify themselves
    with the more general commitments assumed within
    LAFTA for achieving the common market. "[13]

d. Its dynamic character has already been commented
    upon, with emphasis on its "traité-cadre" features,
    institutional balance, and the dynamics of the Andean
    Development Corporation.

This subregional legal order is a source of LAFTA's law
limited to the subregional ambit, while the general legal order of
LAFTA is also a source of the subregional agreement. A sche-
matic classification of these sources is given in the following chart:

SOURCES OF LAW OF THE SUBREGIONAL AGREEMENT

Direct Sources

Primary
Sources
- Treaty of Montevideo (general framework)
- Basic pertinent resolutions of LAFTA (202, 203, 222)
- Subregional agreement
- Statutes of the Andean Development Corporation
- International Agreements
- Special decisions of a political nature
  - Declaration of Bogotá (1960)
  - Declaration of the American Presidents (1967)

Secondary
Sources
- Protocols of complementarity agreements
- Certain International Agreements
- Acts of the Institutions of the Subregional Agreement
- Acts of the Andean Development Corporation

Supplementary Sources

- Legal order of LAFTA

- Legislative provisions and regulations of the
  member states

497

CONCLUSIONS

The preceding comments allow one to conclude that the subregional agreement of the Declaration of Bogotá is the most important step undertaken within the framework of LAFTA in its evolution towards a customs union and the Latin American Common Market. This subregional agreement creates a common market among the participating countries. By means of the general disencumbrance of trade, the removal of obstacles to the circulation of capital and services, the common external tariff, the coordination of economic policies, the establishment of development institutions as the Andean Corporation, the presence of community-type organs within a balanced institutional system and other mechanisms that have been analyzed, the conditions for the establishment of a single economic area at the subregional level, together with the necessary common and uniform treatment with respect to third nations, will be created. As previously indicated, the subregional agreement has overcome in its ambit the basic problems that still afflict LAFTA within its own ambit, both in the field of the economics mechanisms as well as in the institutional one.

This subregional agreement, through its dynamics, will certainly constitute a powerful stimulus for the general integration of Latin America. Just as Benelux has been acknowledged as "the laboratory of European integration," this subregional agreement is the laboratory of the Latin American Common Market.

NOTES

1. The aspiration of attaining the customs union stage is stated in its Article 15; that of attaining the common market stage is stated in the Preamble and Article 54.

2. Both the letter of President Frei and the above-mentioned document have been published by the IDB, 1965.

3. The protocol establishing the Council of Ministers was signed on December 12, 1966, with Chile signing on April 12, 1967. The protocol establishing the mechanism for the settlement of disputes was signed on September 2, 1967; a provisional mechanism was established by Resolution 165 (December 1966) and regulated by Resolution 126 of the executive committee. The protocol on the transit of persons was signed on December 12, 1966. A consultative Commission on Labor Affairs and another on Employer Affairs were established by Resolutions 74 and 75 of the executive committee. All these texts have been published in Spanish by the LAFTA secretariat. An English compilation, prepared by the Inter-American Institute of International Legal Studies is being published by OCEANA Publications.

4. "Declaración oficial del Ministerio de Relaciones Exteriores de Chile, del día 26 de julio de 1966" and statement of Joaquín Vallejo, *El Tiempo,* Bogotá, July 17, 1967.

5. The English text of the Declaration of the American Presidents has been published by the OAS. OEA/Ser.C./IX.1. Extract. 1967.

6. Unofficial translation prepared by the author of this study.

7. One may note the similarity of this mechanism with the one of Article 233 of the EEC Treaty, which admits the compatibility of Benelux and of the Economic Union of Belgium and Luxemburg (UEBL) with EEC, as long as the goals of these integration movements are not attained by the Treaty of Rome. Article 94 of the Benelux Treaty contains similar provisions with respect to UEBL.

8. The thesis of the need of institutional balance within LAFTA has been vigorously supported by the studies of the Inter-American Institute of International Legal Studies. See *Problemática jurídica e instituticonal de la integración de América Latina.* Washington, D.C.. 1967 (especially chapter ix). This thesis has been specifically applied in the case of this subregional agreement.

9. Among others, this is the case of the agreement of clearing and reciprocal credit between the central banks of LAFTA countries, which entered into force with approval of the Council of Finance and Monetary policies, and the case of the protocol on transit of persons, which only requires "acceptance."

10. Article 95 of the ECSC Treaty. Similar provisions are contained in the instruments of other multinational enterprises, as FUROFIMA. See: Carlos Fligler, *Multinational Public Enterprises,* International Bank of Reconstruction and Development, 1967, pp. 77 and 116 note (2).

11. On these characteristics see: Inter-American Institute of International Legal Studies, *op. cit.,* chapter xiv, and Francisco Orrego-Vicuña,"Developments in the Latin American Free Trade Association," *Proceedings of the American Society of International Law,* April, 1967.

12. See: "Compatibilidad de los Acuerdos Subregionales con el Tratado de Montevideo," Delegación de Chile. ALALC/CM-II/VI-E/doc.32. August 24, 1967.

13. Bases of the Subregional Agreement of the Declaration of Bogotá. Annex of Resolution 203. CM-II/VI-E/ September 2, 1967. Unofficial translation by the author of this study.

CHAPTER **37** A HISTORIAN'S VIEW OF
CENTRAL AMERICA: ECONOMIC
INTEGRATION AND POLITICAL
UNITY

By   Bruce B. Solnick
Center for Inter-American Studies
State University of New York, Albany

Of all the countries and regions that collectively are
Latin America, in many ways Central America is the best area
to use as a case study for economic integration and moves toward
political unity. Its history, summarized below, provides a basis
for the nations of the region to move toward integration and unity.
This small segment of Latin America, often ignored in favor of
larger, more dynamic, or more colorful parts of the New World,
can be viewed as having, in microcosm, all the problems found
anywhere in Latin America, and a number unique to Middle America.

Central America today includes the nations of Guatemala,
El Salvador, Honduras, Nicaragua, Costa Rica, and, sometimes
Panama. In the colonial period, the first five nations were part
of the Captaincy-General of Guatemala, while Panama was administered from Peru. But the geographer undoubtedly would draw a
northern boundary for Central America across the Isthmus of
Tehuantepec. It is now in Mexico, though for much of the colonial
period this region was part of the Captaincy-General of Guatemala.
Panama's history has been more closely associated with mainland
South America than with Central America, and it gained independence almost two-thirds of a century after the other Central American nations. Since independence, Panama has been more closely
associated with the United States, for a longer period of time,
willingly or otherwise, than any other Latin American nation.

The site of one of the major high cultures and civilizations of pre-Columbian America — the Maya, whose descendants
still are a major population factor in some Central American
states — Central America was "discovered" by Christopher
Columbus on his Fourth Voyage early in the sixteenth century.
The first expedition to colonize the region left Spain in 1508, and
its remnants were joined by a second group of conquistadores in
Darién, from whence, in 1513, Balboa crossed the Isthmus to the
Pacific. The Panama colony prospered while other Spaniards
sailed the Caribbean, and touched the Central American coast. By
the mid-1520's no less than three expeditions — from Cuba, Mexico, and Panama — tried to conquer Central America proper. The
region was added to the Spanish Empire, and the conflicting claims
of the conquistadores settled. The benefits of Spanish civilization
soon were extended to this region of the New World. The first
audiencia in Central America was authorized for Panama in 1535,

but not until 1570 were jurisdictional disputes settled. One audiencia, for all of Central America from Chiapas through Costa Rica, would sit in Guatemala City. Panama was assigned to Peru. And the lesser administrative units — the provinces — ultimately would become the other Central American nations — El Salvador, Honduras, Nicaragua, and Costa Rica. The Catholic Church, brought to the area by Spain, paralleled the secular administration. Bishoprics were set up in all the provinces except El Salvador, which remained subject to Guatemala, not raised to the dignity of an archiepiscopal see until 1743.

The apparent unity and stability of colonial Central America after the Conquest had ended and the Spanish had institutionalized their control of the region, remained undisturbed until the eighteenth century. The Spanish Bourbons, after 1700, began a series of reforms for and in the New World that reached even the Captaincy-General of Guatemala. Economic experiments designed to increase trade and commerce through monopolistic trading companies were applied to part of Central America early in the eighteenth century. The Honduras Company was a failure. In 1785-86, the new administrative structure of intendancies was set up for all of Central America except Costa Rica and Nicaragua. But these efforts at modernization were only a few surface signs of a deep-seated failure of the Spanish colonial system and the government of Central America to successfully superimpose a "regional" loyalty for the local and particularistic sentiments that the colonial period had produced in the majority of the inhabitants of Central America. The urban traditions of the Spanish heritage meant that Central America was dotted with towns and cities, many of early foundation, that vied with one another for power and influence. Moreover, in the age of the jet plane it is easy to forget the difficulties of communication of an earlier era. From Guatemala City to San José or Cartago in Costa Rica was a long, hard, and not lightly undertaken journey. Each cluster of settlement tended to develop differently, in response to local needs, the population patterns of indigenous Indians and Spanish and other immigrants, and the differing uses to which land could be put. By the end of the colonial period Central America had clearly defined local units whose inhabitants put their own needs and desires before those of the larger unit—the Captaincy-General of Guatemala. In fact, if there was any unifying factor to be found in the provinces, it was a hatred and fear of Guatemala—the center of Spanish authority.

Central America was far from the center of Spanish America. But it had to be kept part of the Spanish Empire, for in Spanish hands, its coasts protected the treasure fleets that sailed the Caribbean Sea. Yet by the middle of the seventeenth century Englishmen were found along the coasts, engaging in logging and other less respectable activities. During the age of the buccaneers raids were made up the San Juan River and into inland Central America. And from these beginnings came the colony of British Honduras, and problems for Spain and the successor Central American states that still have not been resolved to the satisfaction of all. Though it may have been a backwater of the Spanish Empire, Central America had a university at Guatemala, many other institutions of learning, some printers, and an awareness of the world at large. Before the close of the eighteenth century the Central Americans knew about the intellectual trends —so conveniently labeled "The Enlightenment" —that were sweeping the Western World.[1]

In spite of the American and French Revolutions, it was not until events in Europe upset Spain that Central America reacted. Delegates were elected to the Spanish Cortes and signed the Constitution of 1812. In Guatemala the Captain-General and the Archbishop joined forces to maintain Spanish authority. One or more uprisings were put down in 1811, 1812, 1813, and 1814. The restoration of Ferdinand VII in Spain helped to calm the Central American area, but those who wished freedom became active again in 1820, after news of the Liberal revolution in Spain reached the New World. As the provinces and cities of Central America moved toward independence during 1821, there was increasing pressure to join the new Mexican Empire of Agustín Iturbide. The numerous local entities in Central America attempted to choose between independence and union with Mexico — a choice made meaningless by the arrival of Mexican troops at Guatemala City in June, 1822. Mexican authority was enforced, but Iturbide's fall early in 1823 set Central America free (but with the loss of Chiapas to Mexico).

A Constituent Assembly, which had been called earlier, finally convened in June, 1823, discussed, debated, and completed a constitution in November, 1824. It attempted to meet the demands of all political factions, and established the Provincias Unidas del Centro de América. Those who favored a unitary state and those who favored a federalist country found provisions in the constitution to justify their political viewpoint. Though the United Provinces of Central America survived as an entity until 1839, it never really functioned in a way satisfactory to either major political grouping. Not only was this Central American state not economically viable, but the constitution divided powers of taxation, so that the states were unwilling to permit the central government the necessary funds for it to function properly. Aside from the obvious unpreparedness of the Central Americans for self-government, the removal of Spanish authority opened the way for the imposition of a new master — in the economic sense, if not the political. · Central America would spend the remainder of the nineteenth century as a virtual economic colony of Great Britain —a situation not unfamiliar to the rest of Latin America. Moreover, and conveniently for the Central Americans, the long-term British agent in the area, Frederick Chatfield, has been blamed not only for the failure of union in Central America, but for virtually all of the region's problems. Chatfield served in Central America from 1834 to 1852. Regardless of his position on the question of union, and what he did or did not do to preserve or destroy the United Provinces of Central America, it seems clear that the forces of provincialism really doomed a union that the Central Americans, lacking political sophistication, were unable to make work and, in any case, probably were unwilling to make the sacrifices to local autonomy or sovereignty necessary for a successful central government. Chatfield has been virtually universally condemned by Latin American writers and Anglophobes, though a recent monograph has viewed his work in Central America more charitably.[2]

The United Provinces of Central America had collapsed by 1839. The five successor states — Guatemala, El Salvador, Honduras, Nicaragua, and Costa Rica — were cast adrift, and have continued as independent nations to the present. The remainder of the nineteenth century can be viewed only with dismay. War was an endemic disease, as the little nations of Central America were ruled by dictator after dictator in typical caudillo fashion. And when a strong leader emerged, he would try to gain control of the neighboring states, by force if necessary, and often with the justification that he wished to re-establish some sort of Central American union. This is the only trend clear in this muddled period. Almost every political leader paid at least lip service to the concept of Central American union. No sooner had the United Provinces been dissolved, than calls were issued for a meeting to be held to set up a new confederation. And the catalogue of meetings for this purpose is almost as dreary to recount as is the list of battles fought in the name of union.[3] The British retained the role of overseer and controlled what economic life there was. British Honduras was assured a form of legitimate existence in a series of diplomatic maneuvers that the Guatemalans condemned. And the expansion of the United States westward led to a few temporary flurries of interest in Nicaragua and Panama (then still part of Colombia) in the late 1840's and 1850's for purposes of isthmian transit.

With a new century — the twentieth — came a new nation in Central America — Panama — and a new extraregional power to "oversee" the small, backward countries. Great Britain voluntarily withdrew from its hegemonic position, and was replaced by the United States, now a Great Power, and flexing its imperialistic muscles. Little seemed changed in the early years of the century, though there were signs of a settling down by the Central American states. Some observed constitutional forms, and changed governments by election rather than revolution, but they tended to change constitutions with some frequency too. In other cases there were long-term rulers who brought stability of a kind. For Central America feared its Colossus of the North — Mexico — then in the last years of rule by Porfirio Díaz. Efforts to form some sort of Central American union had not ceased with the turn of the century. An Arbitration Tribunal was agreed upon in 1902, but by July, 1906, with another Central American war in progress, President Theodore Roosevelt of the United States, with the support of Mexico, forced the Central American nations to send delegates to a meeting held on an American warship off the coast of El Salvador. The war was stopped. After meetings in Central America later in 1906, a Central American Peace Conference met in Washington in 1907 and agreed to a number of steps to lessen tension in the region. A

Central American Court of Justice was to help keep the peace, and other agencies, which also functioned for a number of years, were set up by the co-operation of the Central American nations. Though thoughts of union were ever present in Central America, no federation was possible. The Bryan-Chamorro Treaty, signed in 1914 and ratified in 1916, led to objections by Costa Rica and El Salvador to the terms Nicaragua had granted the United States. The Court decided against Nicaragua, but that nation and the United States ignored the Court. Efforts at co-operation and peaceful settlement of disputes had been thwarted by one Central American nation, and by the extraregional "overseer." Central America survived the First World War, and again tried to form a union in 1921. Nicaragua was opposed, but Honduras, El Salvador, and Guatemala adhered to it. Then, as had been the case so often in the past, Costa Rica balked. A revolution in Guatemala created a recognition crisis in which the United States reversed positions it had taken earlier. Finally, in 1922, a second Washington Conference was held. Mexico, a co-sponsor in 1907, was ignored, and the United States ran the meeting. Among the many agreements were a new document on recognition and a new kind of tribunal. The United States clearly was entering a period of paramount and open exercise of power in Central America. Federation, so long desired, at least in theory, by the Central Americans was ignored.

American political influence in Central America had followed and not preceded economic penetration. The growth of a banana industry had seen the emergence of the United Fruit Company. [4] There had been other American investment at the end of the nineteenth century and in the early years of the twentieth century, some of it at the request of the government in Washington. These "requests," however informal, were made by both Republican and Democratic administrations. But American investment in Central America, dating back to the 1880's never was so important a segment of the total American foreign investment as to twist the government of the United States to its own purposes. Yet it undoubtedly influenced policy in the years before 1933, years when American power often was represented by Marines serving as Legation guards, and sometimes as troops in the field. While Nicaragua serves as the best example of what was wrong with American policy for Central America in the years between the two Roosevelts, Panama, by virtue of the canal and its treaties with the United States remained a virtual American protectorate.

The years of the Good Neighbor Policy that all too soon were overtaken by the Second World War did little to alleviate the problems of the Central American nations. The Good Neighbor Policy ended the overt political influence of the United States in the region and worked to change attitudes. But the aftermath of the American military and political presence in Central America was a series of long-term rulers, who, if they seemed to have too much sympathy with the totalitarian enemies of the United States, might be forced out of office. Central America still was an economically dependent area where the century-old frustrated desires for a federation could not be quelled. From time to time, some

504

new aspect of co-operation among the nations of the region would be inaugurated. But neither political union nor economic integration seemed possible. The Good Neighbor Policy had provided a ray of light during a major, world-wide depression that seriously affected the foreign sales of Central America's agricultural products. But, of course, the masses in Central America were far removed from the problems of international economics. And the Second World War, mobilizing as it did all the resources of the New World Republics against the enemy, helped Central America.

The early post-war years, during which the United Nations was established, the Pan American Union restructured into the Organization of American States, and early moves made toward a kind of economic restructuring of western Europe, helped to reinforce Central America's traditional "drive" toward union. It must be reported, however, that in these years the Central American nations seemed as willing as ever to use force to achieve their aims. Nevertheless, by late 1951, meetings were begun that led to the establishment of the Organization of Central American States (the abbreviation, ODECA, is taken from the title in Spanish). Formed on the basis of the eighteen articles of the "Charter of San Salvador," the five Central American nations ratified the document, which included the usual statement about re-establishing a Central American political union, and also invited Panama to join. ODECA began to function only in 1955 and, for some years thereafter, moved cautiously. The possibilities for political union inherent in the organization were not overlooked in a time of rapid and sometimes violent political change in Central America. From an early date ODECA began to set up and spin off subsidiary organizations. Numerous meetings were held; training schools for public officials (Escuela Superior de Administración Pública para la América Central, 1954, San José, C. R.) and technicians (Instituto Centroamericano de Investigación y Tecnología, 1956, Guatemala City) were established. Co-operation in many areas other than political union and economic integration was not unusual for the Central American nations, and the creation of the ODECA opened a new route to such joint ventures. Unfortunately, co-operation has not always meant achievement. Nevertheless, Central America was active, and at least partially successful in programs in these "fringe" areas, while the ODECA survived the political storms.

The path to economic co-operation and integration was partially opened by the Economic Commission for Latin America (ECLA) of the United Nations. It conducted a series of basic surveys and studies of the economy and resources of Central America. Its experts presented a series of recommendations. By the 1950's, Central America still produced three major export crops, i.e. bananas, coffee, and cotton. There had been some industrialization, but it was unevenly distributed not only from country to country within Central America, but within each country. Central America no longer was as backward economically as it had been at independence, but the strides forward in a century and a quarter had been very short ones. In the eighteen months preceding the end of 1960,

the Central American nations signed eight trade agreements that
at least partially implemented the recommendations of the consulting economists. Three ratifications by June, 1961, made effective the Mercado Común Centroamericano (MCC). By late
1962 the other two Central American nations had ratified the agreement for the Central American Common Market.

In many ways the task of the historian ends with the creation of the Central American Common Market. It is too new, and
the details of its struggle for a successful existence too recent,
for the historian to comment on it meaningfully. Moreover, these
moves in the economic sphere toward an effective economic integration of Central America seem to be within the province of the
economist. It is true that the problems faced by MCC are not
solely economic ones, and that political attitudes born of historical precedents have not made the implementation of MCC easy.
Nevertheless, the historian can suggest that economic integration
for Central America, whether or not the geographic definition includes Panama, and whether or not the integration takes place
under the rubric of MCC, or some other agency, is not a panacea
for the problems of Central America. More than three centuries
of colonial rule and over one hundred years of frequently turbulent
independence have left Central America with a heritage not easily
cast aside. Perhaps more importantly, not only does Central
America not exist in a vacuum, but the solutions to the region's
problems seem to be in the hands of extraregional power centers.
Thus, the long-term prospects for success of a Central American
Common Market and some kind of economic integration for the
region are dependent on support from without the region. Whether
or not the nations of Central America are willing to make the effort to lessen the political, social, demographic, and resource
differences that have served to pull them apart and keep them
apart may, ultimately, be less important for the success of MCC,
etc., than continued support from without the area, and pressure
upon it to meet the goals MCC has set. Moreover, the Central
American Common Market must in some way come to terms with
other efforts within Latin America to promote economic integration.

Prognostication on political matters for Central America
is perhaps even more dangerous than predicting the future path of
economic development. Certainly Central America's long tradition of and continuing interest in union cannot be denied or ignored.
Nevertheless, since the collapse of the United Provinces of Central America in 1839, it has not been possible to get all the nations of Central America to agree on a workable plan for union.
Time after time a conference has been held and a draft constitution
presented, and then, at the last minute, one or more of the Central
American nations would not ratify the agreement. On more than
one occasion, a government for a united Central America actually
began to function but expired from lack of support. All efforts at
union have failed. One sometimes wonders whether politicians
in Central America ever seriously consider the re-establishment
of a federation for the region, or whether this is just some sort of
necessary tribal rite. But over the years the Central Americans

have invested too much time and energy in abortive plans for union
for this to be an exercise in futility. Perhaps the co-operation in
economic areas, preceded as it was by co-operation in all kinds
of useful, but not vital aspects of existence in Central America,
may yet lead to a climate of opinion that is favorable to still one
more attempt to establish a political union. It must not be forgotten, however, that Central America is in a period of rapid change,
only partially brought about by the moves toward economic integration. Demands for social change, and the political upheavals
that often accompany them, seem to indicate that important changes
in the political outlook of the Central American nations may be at
hand. Any radical change on the domestic political scene in any
given Central American country may well mean a re-evaluation of
the traditional commitment to a Central American federation.
There is no assurance that contemporary governments in Central
America will continue to look with favor on the old tradition, never
brought to fruition, of union.

NOTES

1. See John Tate Lanning, *The University in the
Kingdom of Guatemala* (Cornell University Press, 1955) and
*The Eighteenth-Century Enlightenment in the University of
San Carlos de Guatemala* (Cornell University Press, 1956).

2. Mario Rodriguez, *A Palmerstonian Diplomat in
Central America: Frederick Chatfield, Esq.* (University of
Arizona Press, 1964).

3. A careful history of the pull to federation is
Thomas L. Karnes, *The Failure of Union: Central America,
1824-1960* (University of North Carolina Press, 1961).

4. See Stacy May and Galo Plaza, *The United Fruit
Company in Latin America* (Washington, D.C.: National Planning Association, 1958).

38

THE COMMON MARKET'S
CONTRIBUTION TO CENTRAL
AMERICAN ECONOMIC GROWTH:
A FIRST APPROXIMATION

By   Donald H. McClelland
Agency for International Development

INTRODUCTION

The Central American Common Market (CACM) became
a fully functioning economic force during 1962. The purpose of
this study is to endeavor to determine how much of the considerable increase in the rate of growth that has taken place in the
Central American economy since the advent of the Common Market is attributable to the Common Market. As befits the nature of
the data, no very elaborate model has been employed. In general,
the approach has been, first, to examine the functioning of the
economy, starting in 1950, both in terms of trends and sector interrelationships. Then, against this background, the analysis
endeavors to quantify the importance of the main forces contributing to the rates of growth, and variations therein, in the period
prior to the Common Market (1951-61). These relationships are
then applied to the period 1962-65 to analyze how much of the
growth they appear to explain. The additional growth forces which
appear to be attributable to the CACM are then analyzed with respect to the "unexplained" portion of this growth. Since this approach has required a series of judgments about the functioning of
the Central American economy, considerable descriptive material
has been included to provide a basis for evaluating those judgments.
And, since the outcome of the quantitative analysis necessarily depends in part on a series of analytical judgments, the analysis has
been presented in considerable detail to enable the reader to decide for himself the validity of these judgments. No effort is
made, in this study, to assess the desirability or longer-run effects of the individual Common Market forces; it is for this reason,
even more than the limitations of the data and the methodology,
that this study is labeled a first approximation.

Major changes have been occurring in the Central American region in the roughly six years since the Central American
Common Market (CACM) became a fully functioning reality. [1]
Over this six-year period, the population of the region has increased by more than a fifth; the Gross National Product (GNP),
by more than two-fifths; and manufacturing output, by about three-
quarters. This rapid growth has been accompanied by major
changes in the structure of the economy and in the level and pattern of foreign trade.

The recent rate of economic growth in Central America stands out in comparison with the rest of Latin America. The per capita growth for Central America, 1962 to 1966, is 3.3 per cent per year. This compares favorably with the Punta del Este goal of 2.5 per cent, and very favorably with the rate of 1.5 per cent for the rest of Latin America.[2] (It is also very favorable when compared with the Central American average of only 1.2 per cent for 1950-61.) Viewed in a different way, three of the five Central American countries (Guatemala, El Salvador, and Nicaragua) were among the first six of all 19 Latin American Republics, and Honduras and Costa Rica both had growth rates above the Latin American average. Despite the serious limitations of the statistics,[3] it seems clear that the sustained Central American per capita growth rate of some 3.3 per cent per year, or more than 6.5 per cent for total GNP, is an impressive performance.

An analysis of this favorable performance would be of interest in any case. It is particularly so, given the widespread interest in economic integration, because the period of rapid growth has coincided so closely with the period of actual operation of Central American economic integration.

From a look at the long-term movement of GNP alone, one might conclude that the increased growth rate was almost entirely attributable to the Common Market. Even the most cursory examination of attendant circumstances, however, shows that at the same time there was also a rapid growth in export receipts. When one recalls that exports have been, to use the ECLA phrase, the "traditional engine of growth" in Central America, and notes that the favorable growth years in the 1950's were associated with high exports, one might conclude — as some have — that the Common Market has really been almost an appendage. The more usual informed view is that the truth lies somewhere in between. But just where in between? It is to this question, basically, that this study is directed.

An answer to this question is complicated by the fact that, during the 1962-65 period, several major growth factors were moving strongly in the same direction. In addition to the rapid growth in exports from the region, regional trade has grown at a phenomenal rate, leaping from $51 million in 1962 to more than $200 million in 1967.[4] Foreign private investment, even on a net basis, increased substantially, with the increase in gross foreign investment being even greater. And value added by manufacturing, which had had a relatively stable rate of growth for a decade, rose sharply. (Some downturns in the rates of growth have appeared, however, in preliminary 1966 data; for 1967, some information suggests that these may have been intensified, while other sources suggest the possibility of some upturns.) With these growth factors all moving together, we shall not be able wholly to unravel their complex interrelationships — nor their relative importance. But a careful examination from varying points of view of the information which has by now become available should enable us to make some meaningful judgments as to what lies behind the favorable GNP growth rates.

It should be noted that this analysis will deal only with what has happened to GNP and why. We have omitted consideration of the extent to which the forces causing these changes have been "desirable," (e.g., the cost at which more rapid industrialization has been bought or the degree to which increased regional trade has been trade diversion); or the question of whether these changes are likely to hamper or stimulate future growth, (e.g., the extent to which land suitable for cotton has already been converted to that use, the degree to which greater tariff protection may interfere with ultimate international competitiveness, or the extent to which the external economies of scale already being achieved may add to the momentum already gained under the CACM). These elements are set aside at this point, not, obviously, because they are unimportant but as a subject for separate subsequent consideration.

SOME MAIN ECONOMIC DEVELOPMENTS SINCE 1950

Economic movement in Central America from 1950 through 1965, the years for which reasonably complete and comparable data are available, falls into three distinct periods. From 1950 to 1957, GNP was moving almost continuously upward, averaging 5 per cent a year. The years 1958-61 were ones of relative stagnation, with total GNP annual growth at 3.5 per cent, and declines occurring in some areas. Beginning in 1962, the upward movement was resumed, this time at an accelerated rate. These main trends, by period and main sectors, will be examined in the paragraphs and table that follow.

Central America has been a dual economy, consisting of a domestic (originally subsistence) sector alongside an export-oriented sector, from colonial days. Following the mid-1800's, coffee supplanted the earlier dyestuffs and precious metals as the region's main export. Soon after, bananas became important. Aside from some temporary reversals resulting from contracted markets during the Great Depression, and shipping problems during World War II, coffee and bananas maintained their dominant role, in both exports and the economy, up through the 1950's. Cotton became an important export during this decade.

From 1950 through 1957 — except for 1954 which was the worst crop year in the 18 years for which data are available — GNP grew at rates of more than 5 per cent each year; value of exports of coffee, bananas and cotton each climbed steadily, with total exports growing at 6.5 per cent per year. These and related developments are summarized in the first part of Table 1.

In 1958, however, there was a sharp reversal of trend. Over the period 1958-1961, GNP growth dropped to 3.5 per cent per year. Value of exports actually declined in absolute amounts, reflecting drops in the prices of bananas and coffee by 15 and 20 per cent respectively in 1958, a further fall in coffee prices of 18 per cent in 1959, and also a drop in cotton production, which had

TABLE 1

SOME MAIN ECONOMIC CHANGES, CENTRAL AMERICA, 1950-1965

(amounts in millions of dollars)

	1950	1957	1950-57 Total 7-year Change	% per Year	1961	1958-61 Total 4-year Change	% per Year	1965	1962-65 Total[3]/ 4-year Change	% per Year
GNP[1]/	1,788	2,496	708	5	2,886	390	3.5	3,892	902	7
Exports (coffee, bananas, and cotton)	283 (235)	445 (396)	162 (161)	6.5 (7.5)	415 (326)	-30 (-70)	-1.5 (-4)	624 (451)[4]/	211 (125)[4]/	11 (11)[4]/
Regional trade	8	17	9	11	37	20	22	136	99	38
Manufacturing	221	340	119	6.5	411	71	5	572	195	11
Commerce[2]/	634	911	277	5	1,047	136	3.5	1,009	281	8.5
Foodgrains	106	110	4	.5	128	18	4.5	160	32	5.5
Utilities and transport	80	144	64	8.5	172	28	4.5	294	81	8.5
Government	92	151	59	7.5	190	39	6	230	22	2.5
Construction	52	95	43	9	78	-17	-4	100	14	4

SOURCE: Primarily JPM (in 1962 prices) thru 1961 and AID (in 1965 prices) thru 1965.

1/ GDP 1950-61
2/ Including services thru 1961
3/ Related to 1961 in the same source rather than the 1961 figure shown here.
4/ Through 1964 only.

leveled off earlier, of 30 per cent in 1958-59. Total exports declined by 3 per cent in 1958, and a further 6 per cent in 1959. By 1961 there had been only a slight recovery. Interestingly, trade among the five countries of the region began to show a major increase during the period. Although the amounts were still rather small, the percentage increase was impressive.

Beginning with 1962, the trends in all the main sectors were upward. Exports outside the region resumed a rate of growth considerably higher than they had been in the 1951-57 period. Regional trade continued to grow at an even higher rate than in the previous period, with a rate of 38 per cent per year, and reached a level where the absolute amounts as well as the rate of growth were impressive. Manufacturing moved from its rate of about 6 per cent in the previous decade to a rate of nearly double that. Just as all of the forces had been adverse in the 1958-61 period, they now all became favorable in the period from 1962 through 1965. These, and the related sectoral movements, are summarized in the last part of Table 1.

MAIN SECTORS AND INTERRELATIONSHIPS

This section will examine the main sectors of the Central American economy and analyze the salient relationships among them. The focus will be upon a determination of which elements in the economy have been the dynamic ones and which the more passive, as related specifically to Central America.

Exports

In terms of the major sectoral components of the Central American economy, exports of course come first. They have been the traditional "engine of growth."

The export sector coincides closely with commercial agriculture. As noted above, the main crops are coffee, cotton, and bananas. All have world market prices almost completely independent of any Central American influence. And all have been subject to wide variations in the value of their exports in the period under consideration.

The general trend in coffee production has been definitely upward, having more than doubled since 1950. Coffee prices have fluctuated widely, reaching peaks in the mid-1950's, although, with the International Coffee Agreement coming into effect in 1964, they have tended in recent years to be somewhat more stable.

Bananas, a dominant element in the Honduran economy, has been showing much less growth — until quite recently — with the major fruit companies meeting their growing world demand largely from areas outside of Central America.

512

Cotton has been the real wonder crop. Exports went from only $4 million in 1950 to nearly $150 million in 1965, almost half the gain accruing to Nicaragua. But for cotton also, the road has not always been smooth; sharp declines in production in the late 1950's having had serious adverse effects.

These wide changes in export receipts — due in large part to factors external to the Central American economy — have had major repercussions on the economy's rate of growth. In part, this is due to their sheer magnitude: net changes from year to year in export receipts have constituted as much as 1.5 per cent of the total GNP. In addition, however, one would expect them to have a large multiplier effect. A major part of these gains have not been at all at the expense of the rest of the economy (nor have resources released by declines been needed by the rest of the economy). This is clearly true of price changes. But it is true to a considerable extent of increases in output as well, particularly in the short run. Much of the increase has been through fuller utilization of existing land and labor, along with the application of improved techniques, rather than through drawing factors of production from other sectors. Thus, the added export earnings over the period have in the main represented a net addition to purchasing power, without at the same time seriously impinging on the means of increasing supply, and can therefore be expected to have had a large second- and subsequent-round effect on the rest of the economy. [5] This expectation of a major multiplier effect will be examined empirically below.

Manufacturing

Also of large and growing importance is the manufacturing sector. While manufacturing has been largely of the "traditional" variety and artisan work has played an important but decreasing role, some shift to more complex industries is taking place.

Manufacturing is of particular importance in this study in that it was here that the immediate effects of the Common Market were primarily centered; and it will be the developments that have taken place in manufacturing that will serve as the main area in measuring the relative importance of the Common Market on the economy's growth rate.

Even prior to the Common Market, manufacturing had been growing steadily at a pace appreciably faster than the rest of the economy. Under the Common Market, it has been growing even faster. Compared to average annual growth rates of 6.5 per cent during 1950-57, and 5 per cent in the subsequent depressed period, there has been an average annual increase of 11 per cent over the period 1962-65.

The great upsurge in manufacturing output is not, of course, entirely accounted for by the introduction of the Common Market; but it appears clear that the widening of the market and other forces associated with the CACM have had a major impact

513

in stimulating industrial production. Collaterally, it seems clear that the CACM forces were, in the first instance, most important in the manufacturing sector where economies of scale and of specialization are greatest.

Much of the impact is seen immediately in the dramatic increase, primarily in manufactured goods, which has taken place in intraregional trade, stimulated by the virtual elimination of tariff barriers between the countries. However, this increase in regional trade represents only a portion of the total increase in manufacturing attributable to the formation of the Common Market.

In addition to the widening of the market, the Common Market has either created or given effectiveness to a number of other economic forces that have encouraged growth in manufacturing. The increases in levels of protection accompanying the creation of the CACM, whether or not desirable in the long run — a question which will not be examined here — certainly were a stimulus to further industrialization in some fields. Similarly, the very substantial industrial lending through the Central American Bank for Economic Integration (CABEI) and the individual industrial lending institutions was made possible primarily, either directly or indirectly, by the CACM.[6] The same may be said for much of the increased private foreign investment, although it can be argued — but again, not here — that some of this may have been misguided. Finally, the individual country industrial incentive programs, while perhaps going too far, in the concessions granted because of their highly competitive nature, owed that competitiveness and most of their effectiveness to the fact that they were competing for a regional, rather than just a national, market.

Also to be taken into account in measuring the increased growth attributable to the Common Market are the secondary effects that the CACM-stimulated growth in turn has had on the economy. The multiplier effects of increases in manufacturing are likely to be as great as those for any other sector, and much greater than for some — to take the extreme case, increases in subsistence agriculture — because of the direct stimulus to commerce, construction, and utilities and transport. In addition, most of the same factors considered with respect to the increased production of export crops are also operative here. The increased manufacturing output that became profitable because of the external force (i.e., external to the individual country economies) of the widening of the market and attendant CACM forces has been achieved with relatively little of it being at the expense of output elsewhere in the economy. This is the case since labor has generally been in surplus (although not, of course, skilled labor) and capital has appeared to be generally available for profitable activities. These same characteristics of expandability in the economy have permitted the expanded demand arising from increased manufacturing—whether directly, as in the commerce sector, or more indirectly throughout the economy —to be met by expanded output rather than resulting in higher prices.

It remains to be determined, of course, how much of the recent upsurge in manufacturing was due, not to the CACM, but to the very great expansion in the value of exports. This question will need to be one of the central ones in the analysis.

Agriculture

Agriculture for domestic consumption is a major sector which accounts for probably about one-fifth of GNP and a very much higher proportion of employment. Unlike the predominantly commercial agriculture for export, much of the food production is on small, even subsistence, farms. Plainly a sector of this size is important to our analysis. But the data are so incomplete that the underlying forces, and indeed the elementary question of what in fact happened, are far from clear.

Data on grain production, the basic staples, appear to be fairly complete. They show a period of virtual stagnation, subject to year-to-year fluctuations, through 1957 and a rather steep upward trend averaging some 5 per cent per year starting in 1958.[7] But there is no wholly satisfactory explanation for this sharp change in trend. The undertaking on a piecemeal basis of price-support programs in some of the countries may have contributed. The most frequent explanation is that more land has been brought under cultivation. The highway program, which reached a peak in the mid-1950's, was probably a factor. But much of the really new land is said to have gone into cotton, and it is known that cotton has displaced corn on some of the best land in Central America. While much of this recent favorable trend shown in the statistics is probably real, one cannot escape the suspicion that a part of it is a reflection of more extensive reporting. With more of the activity moving into the monetized part of the economy, and with greater public attention being given to the nonmonetized sector, it seems likely that the level of recording of foodgrain production has been rising along with the level of production itself.[8]

Our treatment here of domestic agriculture will be the unsatisfactory one of leaving it largely out of the analysis of what is cause and what effect. Where the movements are sufficiently pronounced to be reasonably certain, as in the actual decline of total agricultural production in 1954, the general conclusions will be modified to a degree, but no effort will be made to make specific quantitative adjustments.

Commerce

Commerce, including banking and insurance, is the largest sector in the economy (given the division here of agriculture into two sectors, domestic and export). It has generally accounted for about a quarter of GNP. Its increase of $281 million in the four years 1962-65 is substantially greater than the increase in either exports or manufacturing and accounts for more than a quarter of the total increase in GNP, the causes of which we are seeking to analyze. Although there may be, as our earlier tables suggest, a slight upward secular trend in the role of commerce, there can be little doubt that the vast preponderance of increase in the output of this sector are induced increases. Growing demands for marketing of exports, imports, and industrial products, and the growing service demands from other sectors, whether direct or in themselves induced, plainly account for most of this portion of the increase in GNP.

Other Sectors

Other sectors noted in the tables above are utilities and transport, government, and construction. Although these give some evidence of being "leading" sectors in the 1950-57 period, they were probably less so than they appear. Their growth was very large in percentage terms, but each of these sectors is relatively small. Perhaps more important, the terminal year of this period, 1957, was the peak year of investment in the Inter-American Highway program with resultant total investment in highway transportation that year estimated at $87 million.[9] The impact of this on the growth shown in these three sectors in this particular time period is evident. This is not to say that these sectors had no dynamic effect on the economy — the effect of the road program on opening up land for cotton production, for instance, has already been noted. But the role of transportation and construction during the 1950's was at least in part due to special circumstances. And, throughout the whole period considered here, the role of government expenditures has not been a particularly dynamic one.

Investment

It will have been noted that in laying the groundwork for an analysis of growth factors nothing has been said about rates of investment. In Central America the data show only a very limited relationship between investment and changes in GNP — and almost no relationship on a year-to-year basis. Increases in investment rates often follow periods of growth as well as accompanying or preceding them. Total investment has been in the range of 12 to 14 per cent of GNP for most years in the 1950-65 period despite wide variation in growth rates. Stated alternatively, the incremental capital-output ratio, which for the whole period (using a one year lag) was 2.7, a reasonable ratio, varied from 2.4 in 1950-57 to 5.6 in 1958-61 to 2.0 in 1962-65. This, of course, is not to say that investment is unimportant but, rather, that so far as one can tell from the data for the period, investment seems to be more in response to other changes in the economy than a cause of such changes. It is not clear to what extent this lack of apparent positive causal relationship is due to deficiencies in the data and how much of it is the result of more basic causes. In either case, there appears to be little guidance here for why the economy changed and grew.

516

We thus emerge from this examination of the main sectors with the not unexpected conclusion that exports and the Central American Common Market, the latter operating primarily through the manufacturing sector, are the main dynamic elements in the economy of the region. The largest sector, commerce, is essentially passive with some other sectors having some elements of dynamism in their own right and transmitting expansionary (or contractionary) forces received from exports and the CACM to commerce, the other sectors, and each other. Investment in the private sector appears to have been generally available where needed but to have been less cause than response, and the role of government expenditures has not been a major one. Both of these latter structural characteristics, of course, are ones that are not necessarily inherent in the system and may well change, possibly with rapidity, as the developing regional economy continues to emerge.

QUANTIFICATION OF THE CAUSAL FORCES

It is against this background that the growth effects of the Central American Common Market are assessed.

As the description and analysis above suggest, the variation in growth rates in Central America have been principally due to forces that were in large part external. Historically, export earnings have played the principal role. This was plainly true in the 1951-61 period, and they have been important since. It seems equally clear that in recent years the CACM has also been an expansionary force. The phenomenal growth in regional trade, primarily in manufactured goods (which, by now, is important in absolute amounts as well) is the most striking evidence of this. However, as already indicated, the increased regional trade in manufactures reflects only a part of the CACM impact, and a more comprehensive measure of the total impact can be obtained by tracing it as it has affected manufacturing. The other elements in the economy — except, of course, for crop variations due largely to weather — have in general followed these leading sectors. [10] Thus it has seemed reasonable to postulate that the recent rapid growth in the Central American economy can be accounted for primarily in terms of either increased export earnings or the advent of the Central American Common Market.

Given these interim conclusions on the primary role of exports and the CACM as the two dynamic forces for increasing the over-all growth rate, the remaining questions to be answered are how much of the variations in growth have been due to them and what is the relative importance of each.

We start with the previous findings that during the period 1950-61, the only force with major multiplier effects has been increased export receipts and, by definition, the growth to be used as the base from which to measure variations is the growth that would have taken place had increased export receipts not had a multiplier effect. Similarly, in the 1962-65 period, the base would be the growth that would have taken place without either the multiplier effects of increased export receipts or the effects of the CACM. For convenience, we are labeling this base "minimum-normal" growth. Using this concept, we shall estimate, for 1950-51, the individual importance of both minimum-normal growth and the multiplier effects of export receipts on (1) the yearly changes in value added by manufacture, and (2) the yearly changes in gross national product exclusive of value added by manufacture. Equipped with these relationships, we can then deal with the questions: How much of the 1962-65 above-normal growth in GNP exclusive of manufacturing was due to the multiplier effect of the rapid increase in export receipts? And how much of the above-normal increase in manufacturing was due to this same force? Combining the answers should yield a reasonable estimate of the total effect of export increases on the total economy. Subtracting the export-induced increase in manufacturing from the total above-normal increase should yield a reasonable estimate of the total effect of the Common Market on manufacturing. An estimate of the total effect of the Common Market on the total economy will require, in addition, an estimate of the indirect effect of the Common Market through manufacturing on the rest of the economy.

The technique employed in relating the causal forces and the observed variations in growth is both less refined and less formal than regular regression analysis. In essence, it examines the likely limits for the values for the minimum-normal growth rates, the coefficients of the indirect effects of changes in exports, and, for 1962-65, the coefficient of the indirect effect of the Common Market on the nonmanufacturing economy and endeavors to determine which are the most probable true values. Hypothetical yearly changes in growth were then calculated and plotted against the observed yearly changes. The values used here as the best estimates for the minimum-normal growth rates and the coefficients of indirect effects were those that provided what was considered to be the "best fit" between the observed and the calculated data, with the relative "goodness of fit" being judged in part intuitively. This included consideration of deviations in other variables such as agriculture that are known to be significant in certain years but are not amenable to statistical definition, and major deviations for wholly unknown reasons. [11]

Turning to the concept of minimum-normal growth — that exclusive of the predominantly external forces — this represents the growth that might be expected from population increases, opening up of new land, "normal" investment, the adoption of improved techniques, etc. While the use of such a concept over a long period of time would beg a number of important questions, it appears to have a considerable usefulness in the medium-term context in which it is here applied.

A simple inspection of the rates of change given in Table 2 (some of which are also reflected in Figure 1) provides some basis for estimating these minimum-normal growth rates

in the base period 1951-61. Giving only a minor weight to two
years, 1951 and 1954, that plainly are not "normal," taking into
account the uncertainties of any individual year-to-year change,
and focusing primarily on the period 1958 to 1961, when changes
in exports varied between definitely negative and nearly neutral,
it appears that the minimum-normal growth rates were at least
4.5 per cent for manufacturing and 3.5 per cent for the rest of the
economy; and that these will serve as good starting points for the
quantitative analysis.

We begin with the crucial relationship between exports
and manufacturing. To the minimum-normal growth rate of 4.5
per cent for manufacturing suggested as the starting point, there
is to be added the appropriate portion of the multiplier, or indirect, effect of changes in exports on manufacturing growth. The
initial trial used a coefficient of 0.3. That is, for every million
dollar change in exports, there would be a $0.3 million induced
expansion in manufacturing, to be added to the minimum-normal
growth in manufacturing to arrive at the "calculated" growth in
manufacturing. [12] Neither this value of 0.3, nor the first trial
value of 4.5 per cent as the minimum-normal growth rate, provided a best explanation. The closest correspondence between the
actual annual changes in value added by manufacture and the calculated ones was found to be that obtained with a minimum-normal
rate of 5 per cent plus an addition each year equal to 0.2 of the
dollar change in exports. These values are plotted in Figure 2.

As can be seen from the chart, these values for minimum-
normal growth for manufacturing and the multiplier effect of
exports on manufacturing provide a reasonably good explanation
of the actual changes except at the ends of the total period. There
is no known explanation for the oddities of the relationships in
1951 (for which year the subsequent relationships are abnormal
as well). The explanation might be simply that a major error was
made in the GNP estimate for that year. (For these earlier years,
such a possibility is difficult to check.) In any case, the effect is
partially offset by the sharp movement in the opposite direction
the next year. For the deviation in 1960 and 1961 there is a reasonable rationale; the Common Market, which had already gotten
under way to some degree with the ratification of the 1958 agreements, was beginning to have an effect. This is clearly indicated
by the fact that regional trade went from $17 million in 1957 to
$37 million in 1961. In any case, it appears clear the bulk of the
annual increases in value added by manufacturing is attributed to
the multiplicity of forces making up "minimum-normal growth"
rather than to variation in export earnings, although the latter
have obviously had an important influence on the year-to-year
changes.

A similar process was carried out for GNP exclusive of
the value added by manufacture, to account for the amount of
year-to-year changes attributable to (1) minimum-normal growth
and (2) changes in export receipts. Here again, the initial trial
value of 3.5 per cent for the minimum-normal growth rate proved

TABLE 2

KEY TIME SERIES AND GROWTH RATES, CENTRAL AMERICA, 1950–1966

(amounts in millions of dollars)

	GNP*			Value added by manufacturing			GNP exclusive of manufacturing			Exports (outside region)		
	Amount	Change	Rate	Amount	Change	Rate	Amount	Change	Rate	Amount	Change	Rate
1950	1,788			221			1,567			283		
1951	1,840	52	3%	230	9	4%	1,610	43	2.5%	324	41	14.5%
1952	1,960	120	6.5	250	20	8.5	1,710	100	6	349	25	7.5
1953	2,082	122	6	265	15	6	1,817	107	6	370	21	6
1954	2,110	28	1.5	281	16	6	1,829	12	.5	391	21	5.5
1955	2,217	107	5	294	13	4.5	1,923	94	5	401	10	2.5
1956	2,343	126	5.5	317	23	8	2,026	103	5.5	416	15	4
1957	2,496	153	6.5	340	23	7.5	2,156	130	6.5	445	29	7
1958	2,598	102	4	354	14	4	2,244	88	4	425	-20	-4.5
1959	2,676	78	3	364	10	3	2,312	68	3	399	-26	-6
1960	2,774	98	3.5	385	21	6	2,389	77	3.5	405	6	1.5
1961	2,886	112	4	411	26	6.5	2,475	86	3.5	415	10	2.5
	2,990			377						413		
1962	3,189	199	6.5	406	29	7.5	2,783	170	6	459	46	11
1963	3,428	239	7.5	456	50	12.5	2,972	189	7	514	55	12
1964	3,636	208	6	523	67	14.5	3,112	141	4.5	565	51	10
1965	3,892	256	7	572	49	9.5	3,320	207	6.5	624	59	10.5
(1966)**	(4,119)	(227)	(6)	(621)	(49)	(8.5)	(3,498)	(178)	(5.5)	(663)	(39)	(6)

SOURCES: As in Table 1

* GDP for the earlier years

** Preliminary and incomplete

520

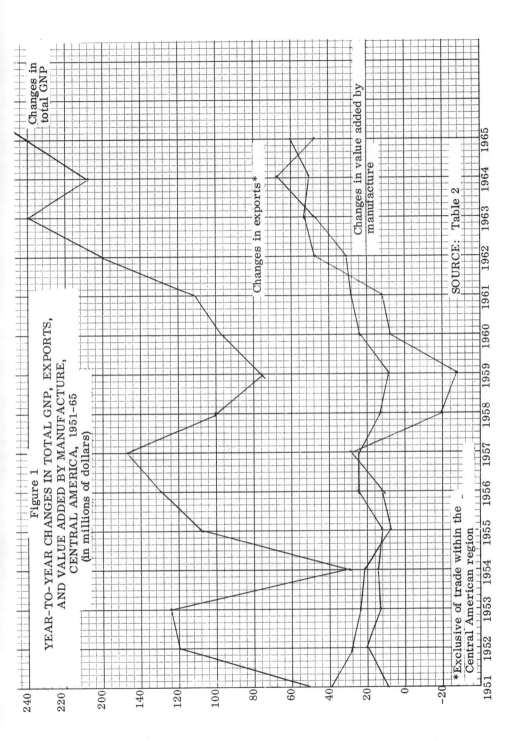

Figure 1

YEAR-TO-YEAR CHANGES IN TOTAL GNP, EXPORTS,
AND VALUE ADDED BY MANUFACTURE,
CENTRAL AMERICA, 1951–65
(in millions of dollars)

Changes in
total GNP

Changes in exports*

Changes in value added by
manufacture

SOURCE: Table 2

*Exclusive of trade within the
Central American region

521

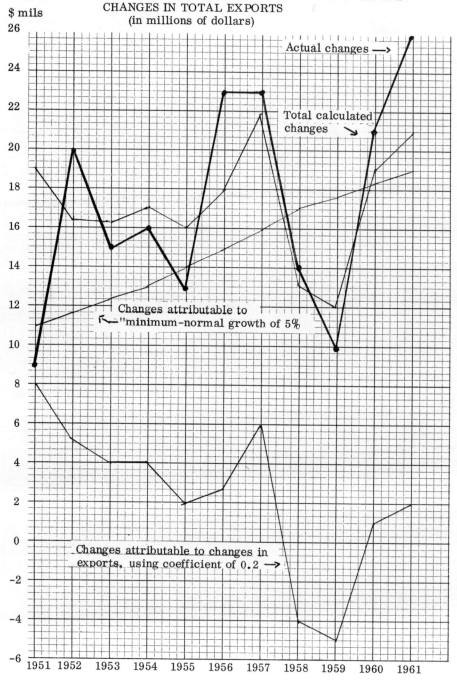

Figure 2
YEAR-TO-YEAR CHANGES IN VALUE ADDED BY MANUFACTURING,
CENTRAL AMERICA, 1951-61, COMPARED WITH CALCULATED
CHANGES ATTRIBUTABLE TO "MINIMUM-NORMAL" GROWTH AND
CHANGES IN TOTAL EXPORTS
(in millions of dollars)

$ mils

Actual changes →

Total calculated
changes →

Changes attributable to
← "minimum-normal growth of 5%

Changes attributable to changes in
exports, using coefficient of 0.2 →

522

to be too low. In successive trials, it was found that a rate of 4 per cent, combined with a coefficient of 1.0 for the indirect effects of export changes provided the best approximation to the actual values.[13]

These values are plotted in Figure 3. Again there is a large divergence for the year 1951 for which there is no readily apparent explanation. For the other years, a part of the changes in the annual rates of growth that are not accounted for by changes in export receipts is very likely due to changes in agriculture. The very low rate of growth in 1954 is certainly due in part to this cause: the only available series shows this to be by far the worst agricultural year in the whole 18-year period with an actual decline in total agricultural output of about 2 per cent. (For the export part of agriculture, the effect was partly offset by peak prices for coffee.) For 1960 and 1961 a part of the difference may be due to some lag, or continuing effect, from the decline in exports of the late fifties, which is not reflected in the analysis.

All in all, the approximation of calculated to actual changes provided by this part of the analysis is hardly one to inspire great confidence. But, more broadly, the value used for normal growth and the indirect effects of exports do appear to account for most of the growth in GNP and the variations therein.

With these estimates of relationships for the 1951-61 period, it is now possible to estimate the effect of new forces in the most recent period. These new forces are taken to be those associated with the creation of the Common Market. As explained above, these appear to have had their effect primarily through the manufacturing sector, initially accounting for the additional growth in manufacturing which in turn may be expected to have had a multiplier effect on the rest of the economy.

All of the values needed for this final step of the analysis can be calculated from the analysis above except for the multiplier, or indirect, effect of the CACM-stimulated increase in the value added by manufacturing. It seems likely a priori that this multiplier would be fairly large. Since value added by manufacturing in Central America is less than half of the total value of manufacturing [14] (with only a relatively small part of the remainder, in the case of the traditional industries, being imports), increased activity in the manufacturing sector would substantially increase demand in other producing sectors of the economy. Also, increased manufacturing would be expected to have a sizable impact on the commerce sector. It is reasonable to assume that the additional manufacturing activity resulting from the Common Market would have a multiplier effect on the rest of the economy of the same relative magnitude as changes in export receipts, i.e., indirect effects of 1.0 of the direct effects. This value was used for the first trial. However, the application of this coefficient to the data, when combined with the other explanatory factors already analyzed, produced a calculated amount of growth greater than that which had actually occurred. If we accept the other relationships,

Figure 3
YEAR-TO-YEAR CHANGES IN GNP EXCLUSIVE OF VALUE ADDED
BY MANUFACTURE, CENTRAL AMERICA, 1951-61, COMPARED
WITH CALCULATED CHANGES ATTRIBUTABLE TO "MINIMUM-
NORMAL" GROWTH AND CHANGES IN TOTAL EXPORTS
(in millions of dollars)

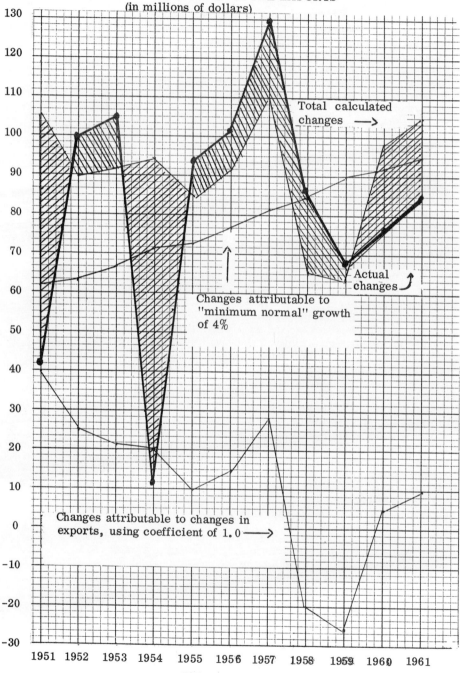

it is necessary to reduce the value of the indirect effects of manufacturing to 0.5 for an explanation consistent with the data. If, on the other hand, we keep our hypothesis that the value of the coefficients for the indirect effects of the two forces could be expected to be about the same, and divide the necessary adjustment between the two, the value for the two coefficients that best explain the annual changes is 0.9. There is no way to determine from the data which alternative most nearly approximates reality. Although the first alternative, with the value of 0.5, is plotted in Figure 4 as being more consistent with the general methodological approach, it should be viewed as something of a lower limit; there is a distinct probability that some higher value might be more nearly correct. [15]

Using the values plotted on the chart, the causal forces here attributed to the Common Market (i.e., the additional value added by manufacturing and its multiplier effect) account for $97 million of the total $902 million increase in GNP over the four-year period. The Common Market is thus estimated to have accounted for about 11 per cent of the total growth over the period. Stated alternatively, of the average annual growth of 6.7 per cent, the estimate shows that these forces accounted for about 0.75 of one per cent. If the alternative approach to determining the indirect effects of the CACM is used, the total effect is estimated to be about 0.9 of one per cent.

If 1962 is dropped from the calculation, the values change somewhat. This year has been included as part of the most recent period, since it is definitely one of the high-growth years. But plainly the effects of the CACM were less then than subsequently. This is to be expected. Time was required for structural changes to be undertaken, and Honduras did not join completely until May 1962 and Costa Rica until 1963. [16] The relatively smaller CACM effect in 1962 is reflected in Chart 4 where it is shown to be only $2 million. Excluding 1962, the estimated growth induced by the Common Market is $95 million out of a total of $701 million, or 13.5 per cent. In terms of growth rates of the average annual growth for the three years of approximately 6.8 per cent, the estimated contribution of the Common Market is about 0.9 of one per cent. Using the alternative approach to indirect effects, it becomes about 1.2 per cent.

Before settling on these estimates and discussing their significance, a few qualifying and supporting points merit exploration.

Even if the above interpretations of the data and relationships are all taken to be reasonable, the question naturally arises as to whether other reasonable interpretations might have yielded substantially different results. In addition to alternatives already considered, we will explore two more.

We started with the assumption that the indirect, or multiplier, effects of exports and CACM-induced increases in manufacturing might be expected to have about the same force.

Figure 4
YEAR-TO-YEAR CHANGES IN TOTAL GROSS NATIONAL PRODUCT,
CENTRAL AMERICA, 1962-66, * COMPARED WITH CALCULATED
CHANGES ATTRIBUTABLE TO "MINIMUM-NORMAL" GROWTH,
THE COMMON MARKET, AND CHANGES IN TOTAL EXPORTS
(in millions of dollars)

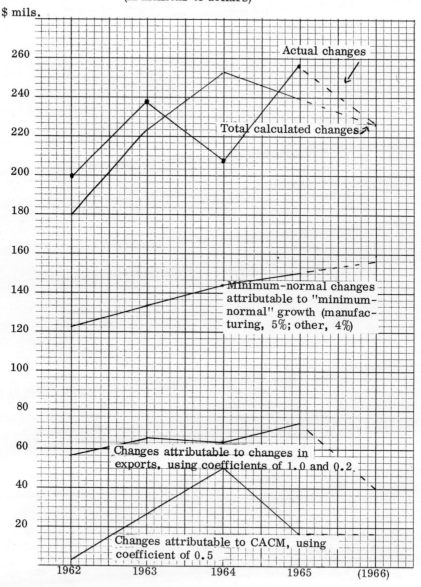

*Data for 1966 are incomplete and preliminary.   They have not
been used in the calculation in the text.

526

Initially, the latter was reduced, to adjust to the data. As an alternative, the original assumption was returned to, with the needed adjustment divided between the two. However, it is entirely possible from our general knowledge of the economy that the coefficient of indirect effects for the CACM-induced portion of manufacturing may be greater than that for exports. If we set the value of the export coefficient at 0.8 (a level which gives a less satisfactory explanation in the 1951-61 period, but not a totally unreasonable one), and the remainder of the GNP growth is assigned to the CACM, the CACM effect would be nearly 1.1 per cent for the four-year period and 1.4 per cent for 1963-65.

As a further alternative, if we were to postulate that the minimum-normal growth rates were 5.5 per cent for manufacturing rather than the 5 per cent estimated, and 4.5 per cent rather than 4 for the rest of the economy (changes that are hardly consistent with the 1951-61 data, but are not patently unreasonable), the amounts to be explained by exports and manufacturing would fall correspondingly. For example, the CACM contribution to 1963-65 growth, estimated on the basis of 0.9 for both coefficients, at 1.2 per cent, would fall to about 0.9 of one per cent.

None of these individual figures, of course, is to be taken too seriously. But they do serve to indicate something of the limits of a reasonable range. [17]

Finally, a supplementary method of appraising the expansionary effects of the CACM may also be considered briefly. This is an examination of the great increase in regional trade. The effect of regional trade on growth is not subject to analysis of the detailed sort we have just carried out. [18] But a mere examination of this spectacular growth in trade within the region does contribute something to forming a judgment about the role of the CACM.

In 1957, this trade was almost negligible, amounting to only $17 million. [19] By 1961 it had grown to $37 million, presumably in large part under the stimulus of the earlier phase of the CACM. This was followed by a succession of very large increases:

	Increase	Total
1962	$14 million	$50 million
1963	22	72
1964	34	106
1965	30	136
1966	40	176

There seems no reason to doubt that most of this increase was due to the Common Market. Not all of this, of course, represents an increase in regional GNP. A part of the trade is certainly the reflection of greater specialization in individual countries within the region. And a significant part of the value of trade in manufactured goods is made up of raw materials and components

imported from outside the region. Even so, the sheer size of
these increases, particularly in percentage terms, certainly indicates that major changes were occurring.

By 1966, regional trade was still only about 5 per cent
of regional GNP, but its increase was equal to 12.5 per cent of
the increase in GNP. Regional exports were only about a quarter
of the exports to the rest of the world, but the increase was equal
to more than half the increase in external exports. While these
movements in regional trade do not argue for any particular figure
for the contribution of the CACM to growth, they do support a
judgment that that contribution was not a negligible one.

CONCLUSIONS AND EVALUATION

We are now in a position to state our quantitative conclusions in a fairly definite form. Rounding our numbers, to pay due
respect to their roughness without doing violence to the magnitudes, we can conclude that the analysis shows that of the roughly
7 per cent per year annual growth in regional GNP in Central
America from mid-1962 through 1965, around 4 per cent was due
to minimum-normal growth, 2 per cent to the increase in export receipts, and 1 per cent to the expansionary effect of the
Central American Common Market and related forces.

An addition of one percentage point to the rate of growth
might not at first glance seem very impressive. But put in the
relevant context, it has a considerable importance. For most
purposes, including the obviously important one of what happens
to people, the growth of per capita GNP is much more relevant
than the over-all growth rate. Compared with the estimated per
capita Central American growth rate of 3.3 per cent, even an increase of a single percentage point looms large. Taking the 2.5
per cent Punta del Este target growth rate as a benchmark, or the
1.5 per cent performance in 1962-66 of the rest of Latin America
(or 2.5 per cent exclusive of Argentina and Brazil), the importance of this increment stands out sharply.

We can conclude, then, that growth in the past few years
in Central America would, without the Common Market but with
the very favorable increase in exports, have been well above that
for the rest of Latin America; and about the same as, or a little
less than, the Punta del Este target or Latin America exclusive
of Argentina and Brazil.

The fact that actual growth was substantially above either
the Punta del Este target, or the achievement of the rest of Latin
America exclusive of Argentina and Brazil, appears to be attributable to the added stimulus of Central American economic integration.

This conclusion must be qualified, however. Although
we can logically add the effect of the CACM to the effect of exports,

it is not necessarily true that we can assume that these effects would have occurred in the absence of those exports increases. The increase in manufacturing, which was the principal dynamic effect of the CACM, required large imports of capital equipment. While there was doubtless some net import-substitution in the manufacturing sector, it is very doubtful if it would have released enough foreign exchange to finance the capital imports. In the absence of increased export receipts, it would therefore be necessary to postulate an increase in capital inflows and/or a considerably different use of foreign exchange in order to conclude that all of the growth induced by the Common Market would in fact have taken place.

Perhaps more important qualifications are those noted at the outset, which gave rise to our labeling this study a first approximation. Although, to stretch the "engine of growth" metaphor, Central America has now become a twin-engined craft, the longer-term efficiency of the newer engine is still untested. And neither of these forces which have produced the recent rapid growth can be counted on to continue at anything like their level of recent years. Should either or both of them falter, it will be increasingly important to strengthen such other sources of growth as improving the structure and competitiveness of the economy — particularly for diversifying exports, increasing savings, developing a more dynamic government sector, and moving more rapidly down that long, difficult road of improving skills and institutions. The fact that it has not been necessary to pay more attention in recent years to these sources of growth — and the fact that they have, consequently, received little attention in this study — is not an indication that they can be overlooked in seeking to maintain the momentum of growth which the Common Market has thus far helped to generate.

Annex I

A NOTE ON THE DATA

The two main sources used in this study have been the Central American Joint Planning Mission (JPM), now a part of the Central American Common Market Secretariat (SIECA), for the earlier years covered, and Agency for International Development statistics for the more recent ones. Where practicable (in general, since the mid-1950's), these were checked against published and unpublished data of the international agencies and, in a few cases, individual country sources. These two sources are not always specifically cited, but the occasional other sources used are.

The basic original sources of the data are the Central Banks and the statistical offices of the five Central American countries. The fact that some of these organizations were created only within the last decade or two suggests that the basic data may on the average have even greater deficiencies than is the case for the less developed countries in general. A part of this problem has been rectified by the work of the JPM which, assisted by experts from outside the region, devoted much of its early efforts to working with the individual countries both in revising past series and in improving current techniques. While some of the corrections in past series seem to have been overcorrections, and some apparent elements of incomparability remain, there is now available as a result of the JPM effort a reasonably consistent set of national accounts for the region for the period 1950-62. Although the need for almost exclusive reliance in the present study on a single source for the earlier part of the period may have occasioned some errors, the data are judged to have sufficient validity to bear at least most of the analytical weight placed upon them.

Fortunately, these limitations of the data become much less important when year-to-year changes, rather than absolute levels, are involved. Undoubtedly there still remain disparities from country to country in definition, methodology, and extent of coverage, which might seriously affect the validity of the summation of the country statistics. Yet even great differences in the measurements need not invalidate their use when stated in terms of year-to-year changes. Unless there are sharp revisions in the definitions or methods used, which would ordinarily be revealed by sharp, unexplained changes in the data, the differences in coverage would be constant over time and the changes would have considerable comparability. Gradual changes in definitions, of course, might go undetected and the differences might pose other problems. One would not have the same confidence in the yearly changes in intercountry comparisons as one would if the base data were more nearly comparable; but they can be expected to give an acceptable indication of the direction of change and, very possibly, a reasonably accurate indication of the relative magnitude of changes between countries. For the present purposes, where we are concerned almost wholly with changes over grouped time periods for the region as a whole, with virtually no need for intercountry comparisons, it is believed that the limitations of the data are not too serious.

Agricultural data present special problems. In addition to random variations due to weather, there are several other difficulties. Much of agriculture is subsistence farming on the fringes of, or entirely outside of, the monetary economy, with the measurement of output necessarily being difficult. A more general problem is that the crop year does not coincide with the calendar year, but the timing of the harvest of different crops varies enough from year to year that this is not easily adjusted for. For example, coffee exports (reflecting at least in part the time of harvesting) from Guatemala dropped from $22 million in the fourth quarter of calendar year 1961 to $20 million in the first quarter of 1962. However, the relation for the same quarters two years later was sharply reversed, a rise from $15 million to $26 million. In addition, the "two-year" cycle in coffee production — good years alternating with poor — introduces distortions. While it is regular enough to be established as a general pattern, the individual country patterns can be broken by a sequence of two poor years in succession. Finally, the analytical approach used has added to the problems; exports, primarily the output of commercial agriculture, are treated separately in the analysis, but output of these crops cannot readily be deducted from the agricultural series that do exist. In short, the analysis would have been much improved had it been possible to develop a series for agriculture for domestic use that accurately reflected the underlying changes free from these chance variations.

One very favorable aspect of Central American economic data is that the problems of deflating the series are not very formidable. Inflation has not been rampant as in much of Latin America. The 1966 cost of living index (1958 = 100) stood at 99 and 100 for the two largest countries and ranged from 107 to 115 for the remaining three. This has made it possible to move from one source to another, even when stated in constant prices for different years, without appreciably affecting the size of the year-to-year changes. It has also made it seem reasonable, where it was analytically useful, to compare changes in exports in current prices with changes in GNP in constant prices. Also, the relatively small difference between Gross National Product and Gross Domestic Product has made it possible to link the series where only year-to-year changes are needed. One other aspect that has been a real convenience is that Central American accounts are officially kept in Central American pesos, which are officially equivalent to the U.S. dollar.

Finally, one further limitation of the data needs to be noted. Much of it is quasi-published, i.e., available only in mimeographed form. While the printed page is not necessarily free from error, mimeographed material is more likely to contain clerical or typographical mistakes. The fact that several errors have been discovered by the researcher suggests that others may well have gone undiscovered here.

On the whole, it is believed that, despite the serious deficiencies noted, the statistics are sufficiently valid that changes in direction shown in the time series are presumably always correct (although the precise turning point may not be) and that the magnitudes of changes shown can be taken to be reasonable guides. Although the use of decimals may well in some cases portray a fictitious accuracy, the main trends that show up in the data are probably real enough. Accordingly, it is believed that the main conclusions of this study, although necessarily qualified by the limitations of the data, are by no means invalidated by those limitations.

1. The Common Market, of course, did not come into being all at once. The important technical studies underlying its creation, largely carried out by ECLA, date back to the early 1950's, as does the formal creation of the Organization of Central American States (ODECA). The Multilateral Treaty on Free Trade and Central American Economic Integration of 1958 eliminated tariffs within the region on a sizable number of commodities. The most important single date, however, is June 1961, when the General Treaty for Central American Economic Integration became effective after ratification by three of the governments. Its full economic effect was of course not felt immediately because of the time required for basic economic adjustments, and also because formal ratification by Honduras was delayed until April 1962 and Costa Rica did not adhere to the General Treaty until September 1963.

For most purposes, in the present study, the period 1962-65 will be taken as the period for analysis of the effects of the CACM. Illustratively, however, 1962 is dropped in some cases since the CACM was not fully effective during all of that year. On the other hand, preliminary data for 1966 and, in some cases, for 1967 are noted where they seem to be helpful, but are not yet firm or complete enough to be included in the basic statistical analysis.

2. The data used here have been taken from a U.S. Federal Reserve Staff Economic Study, "Economic Trends in Latin America in the 1960's" by Yves Maroni (September 1967). Data prepared by the Agency for International Development (AID), which are available in greater detail and are used for this period for much of the remainder of the present study, although not identical in every respect, yield very similar conclusions.

In evaluating the Central American performance, it is of interest that even if the distorting effect of the low performance of heavily-weighted Argentina and Brazil is removed, as the Federal Reserve study does for illustration, the average for the remainder of Latin America is only 2.5 per cent.

3. For some general comments on this subject, see the annexed note on the data. Although the comments apply specifically to Central America, they are believed to have some validity for much of the rest of Latin America.

4. In general in this study the term exports is used to refer to exports from Central America to the rest of the world; regional trade refers to the total of exports from each Central American country to the other four.

5. This is less true of cotton than of coffee and bananas, both because the changes have been almost entirely in output rather than prices, and because land in cotton generally has more productive alternative uses. Consequently, the total effect of cotton may be proportionately less, but even here the external element of a virtually unlimited market has certainly been an essential one.

6. These were financed in large part by external assistance. The increase in total external assistance, however, is less during this period than might be expected, primarily for three reasons. There was a large earlier aid program for the Inter-American Highway and related transportation programs: in a nine-year period, mostly in the 1950's, grants for transportation investment exceeded $100 million and loans, largely from the Export-Import Bank and the IBRD, almost reached this amount. Second, the servicing of these earlier loans has significantly reduced the amount of net aid received in more recent years. And, finally, there has, as always, been a considerable lag between the increase in loan commitments and the increase in disbursements. Taking all of these into account, it does not appear that an overall increase in external assistance became large enough to be a major force in growth, as compared with the base period 1951-61, until perhaps 1965. Most of what increase there has been in the CACM period is attributable in large part to the CACM, what with the loans to CABEI and the Central American Integration Fund being specifically related to the integration movement. While it will be important to assess the effects of larger external assistance, and the portion that may be attributed to the CACM, as the analysis is extended over time (i.e., the inclusion of 1966, 1967 and later years), it is not believed to have been a major additive force except, perhaps, in the industrial sector in the 1962-65 period as compared to 1951-61.

7. The basic grains are corn, rice, and, for this purpose, beans. Data on other food production, primarily animal products, fruits, and vegetables, which have a substantially greater total value than foodgrains, are much more fragmentary, but seem to point in a similar direction.

8. The problem of dealing with agriculture for domestic consumption, as discussed in greater detail in the statistical annex, is complicated further by the fact that the crop year and the calendar year do not coincide, that the nature of the allocation pattern varies from crop to crop, and that even for a single crop, special weather conditions may cause a considerable difference in the allocation pattern from year to year.

9. From the Central American Transportation Study, a report prepared for CABEI, 1964-65: Vol. I, p.124. For purposes of comparison the comparable amounts for some

other years are: 1955, $54 million; 1958, $86 million; 1960, $65 million; and 1962, $54 million

10.   Another element that may be of considerable importance in measuring the full impact of the CACM is not included in the analysis because there is at present no way of even crudely approximating its quantitative importance. The creation of the Common Market may certainly be expected to have begun to produce a new set of attitudes, particularly in creating a more alert and imaginative entrepreneurship, but not necessarily limited to this area. The more that is learned about the development process, the more convincing it becomes that changing attitudes (as well as values) are a key variable. It is certainly possible that the more out-ward-looking attitudes that must have been engendered to some degree by the Common Market may be an important and con-tinuing force for development.

11.   As explained in more detail in the annexed statistical note, some of the individual year-to-year vari-ations are greatly affected by unsystematic changes in the relationship among crop years, export years, and calendar years, although these disturbing variations tend to cancel out in most cases over a two- or three-year period. More-over, at least two years are known to need adjustment, but by an unknown amount. To deal with these factors, a sub-jective weighting is judged to be preferable to the alter-natives of ignoring them or trying to assign specific values. In any case, it is fairly easy to judge from the graphic presentation how good the "fit" is and, since the basic data are all given and the arithmetic is not very extensive, the concerned reader can experiment for himself as to whether a fit that is appreciably better is possible.

12.   The general term "multiplier effect" has been used here in the usual sense of referring to the indirect second-round, and subsequent-round, effects. However, since it is analytically useful to divide these effects in various ways — in the present case, to separate the indirect effect of exports on manufacturing — it will be convenient at some points to refer to the specific values employed simply as coefficients.

From an analysis made of the relative impor-tance and interrelationships among the sectors (with some, such as rental income, which is constant throughout the whole period at around 5.5 per cent, omitted entirely), it appeared that about one-fifth of the total indirect effects of export receipts was applicable to manufacturing. But it was not possible simply from an inspection of the data to determine what the total indirect effects were likely to be.

An initial trial assumed that changes in ex-ports, in addition to their direct contribution to GNP, would have an indirect effect on the rest of the economy of one and one-half times the amount of the change. With one-fifth allocated to manufacturing, this would mean 0.3 of the annual change in exports would represent the effect of exports on value added by manufacture.

13. An initial trial with a coefficient of 0.8 (which would be consistent on the basis of the findings noted in Note 12 with the coefficient of 0.2 used for value added by manufacture) was too low. On the other hand, a coefficient of 1.2 was too high, providing a somewhat better fit for the years where the fit was already reasonably good, but increasing by a slightly larger total amount the divergences where they were already large — 1951, 1954, 1958, 1960, and 1961.

14. 1962 Census of Central American Industry

15. In either case, there remain substantial year-to-year divergences. Once again, variations in agriculture, presumably due to weather, seem to provide a part of the explanation. The only readily available series is not wholly comparable with the data in Chart 4; it is for all of agriculture, thus involving some double counting since the chart already includes export crops which have been considered separately, and is in current rather than constant prices. Even so, it may provide a partial explanation. The increase reported for agriculture for 1964 was $55 million and that for 1965 was $87 million. (It might also be noted that some values based on preliminary, incomplete data for 1966 are also plotted on Chart 4. Although they are not included in the other calculations, it will be noted that they are consistent with the relationships shown for the earlier years.)

16. The fact that these two countries lagged behind the other three in the acceleration of their growth rates, although probably due primarily to other causes than their late accession to the CACM, is certainly not inconsistent with the general conclusion that the CACM made a major contribution to growth.

17. As a rough check on the validity of the general approach in explaining the growth for 1962-65, we can examine again some of the magnitudes shown in Table 1 for this period. Of the total cumulative increase in GNP of $902 million, increases in exports of $211 million and increases in value added by manufacturing of $195 million directly account for 47 per cent. Commerce accounts for more than a quarter, and in the case of commerce the multiplier effect of increases in exports and manufacturing is clear, both from the point of view of increasing the demand for this sector and because the supply of the services of commerce is readily expandable even in the short run.

Thus, even if the multiplier effect were judged to be negligible on some or all of the smaller sectors, the over-all explanation would have considerable validity.

18. This, in turn, although not very sophisticated, may still be somewhat more elaborate than the underlying data will readily support.

19. In Central America, the convention is to use the term regional trade to represent exports or imports among the five countries (which, in principle, are the same amount) rather than the total of the two as is done in some areas.

CHAPTER **39** THE CARIBBEAN IN RELATION
TO THE INTEGRATION OF
LATIN AMERICA

By Sir Harold Mitchell
Geneva, Switzerland

Diversity characterizes the Caribbean of today; its history is largely one of nonco-operation between the different territories. Although Spain retained its foothold long after it had lost its other American colonies, the build up of British, French, Dutch, and later U. S. influences in the Antilles implanted different European cultures. From these beginnings stems the fragmented Caribbean trade and politics of today.

Political rather than purely commercial considerations have traditionally motivated the major powers in their approach to the area. The pattern has continued. The expenditure of the United States on military bases and on political intervention may well have exceeded any commercial benefits from trade. Similarly Russia at great cost keeps afloat the economy of Cuba. Notwithstanding the collapse of the West Indies Federation, Great Britain, hard pressed financially, continues a measure of support. France likewise bolsters up the economy of its overseas Caribbean departments. Canada with little political concern in the area has assumed Britain's declining role, at least in the economic field.[1]

The attitude of independent Caribbean countries differs basically from that of these outside powers. With a deep sense of history and conscious of the colonialism of the past, the island governments are extremely sensitive to any infringement of their sovereignty. Their other major concern is the necessity of economic expansion to meet the employment demand resulting from an annual population increase of at least 3 per cent. However, nationalism is an obsolete luxury; continentalism is the modern ideal. It has become fashionable to regard the merging of small countries as an end in itself, but diversity and not homogeneity still remains the reality. As the United States encourages the integration of its southern neighbours, which incidentally suits the large U. S. industries seeking ever wider markets, Washington will continue to encourage Antillean integration. An obvious comparison is the vital part played by the United States in the establishment of the Central American Common Market.

At the Punta del Este Conference of American Presidents, the incorporation of other countries of the Latin American region into the existing integration systems was envisaged.[2] Not only therefore does the Latin American Common Market foresee the union of the Latin American Free Trade Association and of the

537

CACM, but also of the Caribbean region.[3] The "Declaration of the Presidents of America" revealed that the CACM Presidents had committed themselves to seeking closer ties with the Caribbean. Already in 1966, rumour of the possible extension of membership of the CACM to the Dominican Republic had circulated.[4]

In 1967 the support given to the establishment of the Andean Development Corporation representing Colombia, Chile, Peru, Ecuador, and Venezuela illustrated the significance of subregional bodies within the Latin American Common Market.[5] Should the Caribbean islands form some sort of Common Market amongst themselves, this body might in turn become such a subregional body of the LACM.

A long-term view may well point to the need for intensifying trade relations between the Caribbean and Central and South America. At present, trade between the Commonwealth Caribbean and Latin America remains minimal. Its low level generally is due to competing production in primary products and light manufactures.[6] Any agreements or compromises on trading policies may be achieved only through the co-operation of two large units: a Latin American and a Caribbean Common Market.

Political inheritance and trade patterns have led to the belief that wider types of association at least initially were practicable only within the confines of the Commonwealth Caribbean. As late as the Punta del Este Conference in April 1967 the Caribbean Governments had never considered the hypothetical results of integral economic relations with the LAFTA or with the CACM even in a preliminary way.[7]

The history of Caribbean co-operation has in the past lacked success. However, with political independence, has come the realization at least of a need for intra-co-operation to achieve economic survival. This may be a significant breakthrough since previously encouragement for internal co-ordination has come from outside and not from within the Caribbean territories themselves.

Since the first attempt at some form of co-operation when the Caribbean Commission was instituted in 1946 by the United States, Great Britain, France, and the Netherlands to develop their independencies, political developments have led to further structural change. In 1961 the Caribbean Organization was established, but because of limited membership and excessive reference for decisions to the metropolitan powers, it became a pawn in international relations and likewise failed.[8] Economic weakness contributed to the failure of the West Indies Federation, formed in 1958.[9]

The first Conference on economic co-ordination in the Caribbean sponsored by the Caribbean Economic Development Corporation was held in 1965 at San Germán in Puerto Rico. The formation of this body, the phoenix from the ashes of the Caribbean

Organization, constituted Puerto Rico's contribution towards regional co-operation. At the Conference emphasis was placed on the informal nature of this new approach. Support for a Caribbean Economic Community has continued to grow in the past four years.

Late in 1965, Guyana, Barbados, and Antigua had reached agreement over the setting up of a Caribbean Free Trade Area amongst themselves. The idea of a Commonwealth grouping on a wider scale was encouraged by the successful Commonwealth Caribbean-Canada Conference in Ottawa in July 1966. However, this new Free Trade Area, called CARIFTA, already had its problems for Guyana's opposition leader, Dr. Cheddi Jagan, protested strongly against any limited trading bloc which did not include Cuba and all Commonwealth and non-Commonwealth islands.[10] Nevertheless, CARIFTA came into force in April 1967. In October 1967, at a conference of the heads of the Caribbean Governments, possibility of membership was extended to other Commonwealth territories. It was agreed that free trade among the Commonwealth Caribbean countries should be established by May 1, 1968, and after much controversy Guyana was selected as the site for the Regional Secretariat. Both Britain and Canada agreed to participate in the setting up and financing of a Caribbean Development Bank. The United States undertook to make it a development loan and Puerto Rico also promised co-operation.[11]

CARIFTA envisages something not far short of a revival of the economic concept of the West Indies Federation. The eleven territories with a population of more than three and a half million, need very heavy capital investment to develop their economies and maintain their relatively high standard of living.[12] Together they form a not inconsequential market. However, it is frequently pointed out that even amongst the Commonwealth Caribbean many of its leaders are too inward looking to make co-operation possible.[13] The recent situation in Anguilla affords an example of these attitudes.

Trinidad and Togabo firmly supports the concept of a Caribbean Common Market. At the time of its entry into the Organization of American States, Prime Minister Eric Williams stated "Trinidad and Tobago's position is simple. It has been and it is that we stand ready to sit down and discuss with our colleagues in the West Indies — from Guyana to British Honduras — the establishment of a large Caribbean Free Trade area which would not be inconsistent with membership in the OAS."[14] However, boundary disputes might impede the entry of Guyana or British Honduras into closer co-operation with the OAS or its associated bodies, an obvious possibility of nationalism disrupting international progress.

Jamaica, on the other hand, although agreeing in principle with the setting up of a free trade area, has some reservations.[15] The island is still very conscious of the desirability of becoming an Associated Overseas Territory in the event of the U. K. going into the EEC. However, like other Commonwealth

countries it is also aware of the necessity of trading outside
Britain and West Europe. During Prime Minister Hugh Shearer's
1967 European tour, one of the topics discussed with European
leaders was the compatibility of membership of the OAS and membership as an AOT of the EEC. Jamaica may feel that membership in the OAS might necessitate a too strict adherence to the
decisions of that area. [16]

Jamaica disagreed with the decision taken at the Conference to establish the regional secretariat of CARIFTA in Guyana.
Barbados also had reservations, recalling the disagreements
prior to the choice of capital for the West Indies Federation in
1958. Moreover, should the Opposition come to office after the
next General Election, the course of Guyanese politics might be
altered. Guyana was, however, most anxious to hold the secretariat and was prepared to trade the location of the Development
Bank in return for the support of the smaller territories to this
end. Trinidad and Tobago in order to gain support for an early
Customs Union was also willing to give way to Guyana.

During the Barbados Conference, there was considerable
disagreement over the role of the Development Bank. The smaller,
less developed, islands felt that funds should be devoted almost
exclusively to projects in their own territories. Trinidad and
Barbados, both members of the OAS, and thus with access to the
Inter-American Development Bank, were less concerned over
this point. Guyana too, with considerable U.S. support to keep
Prime Minister Forbes Burnham in power, was prepared to give
way to the smaller islands. On the other hand, Jamaica with no
present facilities for obtaining soft loans and liable for contributing one-third of the total equity, the largest single contribution,
felt that the role of the Bank was of paramount importance.

The basic agreement to establish free trade among the
Commonwealth Caribbean countries came into effect on May 1,
1968. Jamaica, in spite of former diffidence and a withdrawal
from the proposed Regional Development Bank, joined CARIFTA
on August 1. Although it is early to see many positive results,
trade between the member territories—particularly Barbados,
Trinidad, and Guyana—has increased. Should any degree of international investment result from CARIFTA, the opening up of
the interior of Guyana might follow.

Nationalism and parochial attitudes are by no means
limited to the Commonwealth Caribbean. Trinidad has attempted
to discuss with non-Commonwealth territories the possibilities of
economic association, but political difficulties arose since Puerto
Rico was disinclined to be associated with the French Antilles,
whilst the French in turn disliked the thought of associating with
Puerto Rico on account of U.S. influence in the background. Moreover Surinam wished to exclude both Puerto Rico and the French
Antilles and thought in terms of an association which included
Surinam, Guyana, Trinidad and Tobago, and Jamaica. [17]

Both Haiti and the French overseas departments present difficulties in regard to Caribbean economic integration. Haiti exists in isolation under President François Duvalier, supported by the Tonton Macoute. To lift its pitiful economy would be a herculean task for the other Caribbean countries. Nevertheless, any attempt by Haiti to co-operate with its neighbours might well attract U.S. support.

The French islands of Martinique and Guadeloupe, together with Guyane, are organized as French overseas departments. Their ties to the metropolis are much closer than those of Surinam or the Netherlands Antilles to the Netherlands. At the San Germán conference on economic co-operation in 1965 the absence of a representative from the French Government was interpreted as a sign of its unwillingness to support Caribbean co-ordination. The crucial factor for the French overseas departments is that they are constitutionally parts of France and in consequence receive substantial benefits from the metropolis, including entry to the EEC. [18]

An obvious outsider in Latin American economic integration is Cuba; at the signing of the Montevideo Treaty in 1960, creating the Latin American Free Trade Association, Cuba announced its intention of applying under Article 58 for membership. However, the members of the LAFTA were unwilling to accept a fellow Latin American state whose economic orientation seemed incompatible with the Treaty. [19] The Castro Government as a result inevitably turned more and more to the Iron Curtain countries. Castro's interest in Latin America has been political rather than economic. However, the Soviet Union became increasingly reluctant to support Cuba's promotion of guerrilla warfare in Latin America. [20] Despite limited trade with Canada, West Germany, France, Britain, and Spain, Castro depends on the Soviet Union for his existence. Sugar remains his country's most vital export, and not even the Soviet bloc can begin to replace the lost U.S. market.

These obstacles to economic integration are not necessarily insurmountable. Import substitution has to some degree already been adopted by many of the islands and if carefully organized on a regional basis particularly in the agricultural sector could greatly benefit the whole area. Hard currency saving would result and funds thus become available for development projects in the member countries. On the industrial level, attention must be given to the selection of the right industries. The regional distribution of new industries was carefully considered during the setting up of the CACM and will similarly play an important part in the preliminary stages of the LACM.

Air and shipping services between the Caribbean and the rest of the world, particularly with the advent of the tourist, are often more frequent than those between the territories themselves.[21] Letters from the area may reach London and New York quicker than those from Port of Spain to Kingston or Georgetown to San

Juan. Telephone communications are often indifferent and sometimes deplorable within a territory; and they may defeat inter-island communication. Accelerated and improved air, harbour and customs facilities remain a prerequisite for more effective interisland commerce. In addition the amalgamation of overseas diplomatic representation would not only economize in the use of trained staff but would also help to present a united Caribbean point of view, from the commercial as well as the political angle.

Despite arguments in favor of regional integration, the creation of a Caribbean Common Market, even of a limited kind, can only be part of the answer. The progress of the EEC and of the CACM and the potential of the LACM is not necessarily indicative of success for other groupings. The countries forming the EEC already traded extensively one with another; those forming the CACM are linked by historical, social, and cultural bonds which do not exist in South America let alone in the Caribbean. Trade within the EEC and within the CACM takes place overland, whereas in the case of South America and of the Caribbean communications are over thousands of miles of sea and are difficult and costly.[22]

The Caribbean seeks to develop far more quickly than did the EEC; this necessarily involves rapid industrialization which is no simple matter.[23] Capital must be obtained from foreign countries and if a common market existed in the Caribbean, there would have to be no competition amongst members for foreign funds.

Should the establishment of a common market lead to its becoming a subregional body of the LACM, long standing ties between its components and metropolitan powers might have to be severed, in return for an uncertain and new market. If not broken, the Caribbean countries might find it increasingly difficult to reconcile the two resulting in loss of markets. Should they have to surrender a measure of national sovereignty they may not be sufficiently compensated economically. Moreover, some relatively wealthy countries in the Caribbean would have to subsidize the poorer ones.

Few Caribbean countries would be prepared to integrate in order to promote intra-Caribbean or inter-Latin American trade at the risk of losing existing markets. They at present supply the four largest markets in the world: the U.S., the Commonwealth, the EEC, and in the case of Cuba, the Soviet bloc. The need for integration is on the supply side.

West Indian politics are to a large extent still influenced by the idea of constitutional advancement, sometimes at the expense of the general economic good of the country. The universities, the intellectual elite, are well aware of the problems facing the area as a whole; the man in the street is less convinced. His thinking tends to be more insular, and yet in countries where elections are free, it is he who puts the Government in power.

The intellectuals must not make the mistake of overlooking the ignorance of the ordinary man and woman nor must they simplify the problems as a result.

The United States, leading the world in business management and technological development, has set up a pattern of penetration into Europe both in the EEC and in countries outside, such as Britain. The pace may be slowed down temporarily due to the difficulties affecting the U.S. balance of payments in 1968. However, the restrictions affecting U.S. citizens are tempered in the case of Latin America and the Caribbean countries. It is highly probable that an investment pattern of U.S. domination of markets will emerge. The penetration of the EEC has taken place notwithstanding the existence there of local industries relatively much stronger than those in Latin American countries.[24]

Outside pressure to federate, particularly from the United States, on whose tourist dollar so much of the Caribbean depends, may bring some form of unity of government. Evidence of U.S. support of Central American integration is comparatively recent and based on a recognition of the importance of stability and prosperity not only to the countries themselves but also to the United States.[25] It now firmly supports the succesful outcome of the LACM.[26] Undoubtedly it would prefer to deal with a single Caribbean, as with a single Latin American bloc. At present, achievement of this goal seems to be remote.

Like the United States, Canada would find it easier in terms of trade, aid and immigration, to deal with one large rather than several small units. Canada has shown particular interest in fostering economic co-operation between the countries belonging to the Commonwealth. This was emphasized by the success of the Commonwealth Caribbean-Canada conference at Ottawa in June 1966. Subjects discussed included the setting up of a free trade area and possible membership of the participating countries in the OAS.[27] The first meeting, early in 1967 at Castries, St. Lucia, of the Canada-Commonwealth Trade and Economic Committee, set up at this Conference, stressed closer co-operation.[28] In February 1968, Prime Minister Lester B. Pearson stressed to graduates of the University of the West Indies the special relationship existing between Canada and the West Indies. Influencing that relationship were geography, tourism, migration, and a "sympathy for each other's complex position in a changing world."[29]

Canadian tourists continue to flock to the Caribbean aided by direct Canadian air services.[30] Canadian investment has increased and diversified. Canada has expressed its willingness to accept immigrants from the Commonwealth Caribbean on a nondiscriminatory basis. However, despite this, West Indian immigrants remain relatively few, since only skilled labour is desired.

Canada's attitude to the Caribbean has been partly affected by the successful establishment of the EEC which has introduced an important new factor to Caribbean economic affairs. The EEC is committed to a policy of self-sufficiency in the promotion of sugar, dominantly manufactured from sugar beet.

Great Britain grows a limited amount of sugar beet. It also provides a major sugar market for Commonwealth producers, including those in the Caribbean. Should Great Britain eventually succeed in its endeavours to enter the EEC, a goal supported by all of its political parties and by all members of the EEC except France, the result would be extremely serious for Commonwealth producers. [31] Sugar and its by-product rum might also suffer. At present, 84 per cent of the sugar produced in Commonwealth Caribbean countries is sold at preferential prices in the United Kingdom and Canada. [32] However, the negotiated price quota agreement with Great Britain continues until 1974, a contract which the British Government has emphasized that it will fulfill. [33]

The long term outlook remains uncertain: the EEC sugar policy is not yet detailed into its final form. Each country in the Community will have a sugar quota. [34] Should Great Britain and its partners in the European Free Trade Association enter the EEC, it would become a significant deficit area in sugar production. At the same time, production of sugar beet in Great Britain under an EEC quota, at a price far above what Britain now pays for home production, might well expand. The British Government has however stressed the need to protect Commonwealth sugar production by negotiating within the EEC for some continuing quota. A Conservative Government would also regard this as a high priority. Such a policy would be facilitated by Commonwealth Caribbean countries obtaining AOT status with the EEC. This status would seem likely to benefit other Caribbean agricultural production including bananas, [35] citrus, pimento, and, in the case of Jamaica, coffee.

While bauxite enters the EEC duty free, there is a 5.5 per cent duty on alumina. Norway and Sweden import alumina from Jamaica and Guyana. Without AOT status, these two countries would be seriously handicapped in the face of competition from Surinam.

On balance it would seem that for most Commonwealth Caribbean countries, particularly Jamaica, the case for seeking AOT status may be strong. [36] Trinidad depends less on sugar; its major product, oil, would not be competitively affected compared with other producers.

Time is not on the side of those small countries with their limited natural resources and swelling populations. Despite a lack of statistics, clearly the pressures of unemployment are increasing and may become intolerable. Emigration appears to be drawing to a close. Even thinly populated neighbours such as British Honduras are becoming aware that an extensive agricultural policy linked to mechanization is more attractive than the traditional small settler clearing his own little farm in the bush. [37] Today the pioneer is the heavy tractor and its mechanical allies. Emigration to developed counries becomes increasingly restricted, usually limited to the skilled minority which comprises those citizens whose loss can be least afforded. [38] How long, for example, France and the Netherlands will continue to accept citizens from these Caribbean territories with which they are politically linked remains a matter for speculation. Population movement from the Caribbean to Latin America on a substantial scale seems improbable at least in the foreseeable future.

The Antilles must rely mainly on themselves. Their long-established trading connections have greatly helped their economies. In the eighteenth century, the islands were on occasion exploited by the colonial powers; in later times, the fear of losing markets may have held back a developed country from encouraging proper industrialization in a "colony."[39]

The production of sugar cane and raw sugar probably employs more persons in the Caribbean than any other occupation. The industry would face a grave crisis at the present time but for the agreements with foreign countries, mainly those of North America and Europe, who purchase at prices normally above the world price. [40] To the majority of underdeveloped countries, including those in the Caribbean, price stabilization for the principal agricultural products would be of major importance.

Yet even agricultural employment is threatened. Cutting of sugar cane by hand is doomed: within two decades, probably less, no cane for export will be cut by hand. Those areas which are too small or too accidented, will simply go out of production. Alternative crops sometimes exist, but often they may prove more speculative. The Caribbean can, however, increase its production of foodstuffs for home consumption. Better marketing and refrigeration will also help. Supplies of locally grown fresh fruit and vegetables, under hygienic conditions, to hotels would reduce the loss of foreign exchange caused by the importation of foodstuffs from the developed countries. In addition the diet of islanders would be improved. Exports of vegetables and flowers at certain times of year to North America may well increase.

The creation of an effective Caribbean Common Market embracing most of the area seems far off, whether or not it formed part of an integrated Latin American unit. It is not easy to see clearly the economy involved in unifying the trade of this fragmented area, so closely strung and yet on a string of enormous length. On occasions there may be commercial advantage from preliminary sacrifice, but the area of gain should be approached with caution.

Different languages, laws, measurements and currencies compound the isolated nature of these Caribbean countries. Time will bring greater standardization but rapid advance on a wide front is unlikely. For example, public opinion in the Dominican Republic would be shocked at the idea of entering any effective political or economic association with Haiti, notwithstanding that they share a single island and that their combined population is more than twice that of the former West Indies Federation. Bitter memories of events both in the present and past centuries have engendered mutual distrust which language increases. Any association of the two Spanish-speaking islands which flank Hispaniola — in their different ways two of the most effective Caribbean countries — appears to be equally remote in present-day terms. Formidable personalities including Fidel Castro, Dr. Duvalier, General de Gaulle, and the U.S. President all exert influence on the Caribbean but of a centrifugal character.

Tourism is the industry with the brightest potential in the Caribbean. It is this which may well prove the most unifying factor. Its expansion in recent years has been phenomenal and is likely to continue. The U.S. dollar has replaced the Piece of Eight and has gained general acceptance. The Bahamas have illustrated that tourism almost unaided can lead to comparative prosperity. More and more tourists from Canada and the United States flock to the Islands.

In the short term, therefore, it seems unlikely that many Caribbean countries will embark on an economic policy which could weaken any of their existing trade links. In the long run, politics may turn the scale in favour of greater integration. The United States clearly regards the whole region as a vital part of its strategic defense.

Historically, of all areas, the Monroe Doctrine has been applied most forcibly in this region. The new slant given to the doctrine — whether it bears the name of Monroe or Johnson — suggests that the Caribbean remains a vital area to the United States.

The diversity of the past presents the challenge of the future. The orientation of different areas of the Caribbean towards overseas countries often continues to provide an economic life line to the struggling agriculture of these small communities. However, some Caribbean territories are now hesitating between the strengthening of their overseas links with developed countries or integration with the mainland of Latin America. Bearing in mind the weak economic position of most of these countries, aggravated by heavy unemployment which is likely to continue, economic aims are of paramount importance.

Realities must be faced in the Caribbean and it is easy to gloss over the many problems. Despite growing pressures of larger trading blocs in other areas, including Latin America, which may compel some movement towards unification, it would be rash to speculate as to how long this might take. So far economic forces alone have not been sufficient to emphasize the need for unity. Able political leadership capable of rising above national interest, over-coming linguistic and religious barriers and embracing the wide and varied traditions of each island is required to supply the necessary drive to clear the way for unity. A loose federal solution may provide the answer. More than a century ago Switzerland faced the same problems and successfully solved them. Undoubtedly the price some Caribbean countries must pay to achieve a degree of co-operation will be to sacrifice part of their own individual independence. The problem remains — how to put across the message that a measure of political unity alone can secure economic progress. Such is the challenge facing the Caribbean; on the solution hangs its effective relationship with Latin America.

NOTES

1. Prime Minister Lester B. Pearson, the Royal Commonwealth Society, Montreal, May 25, 1966.

2. *Declaration of the Presidents of America,* Punta del Este, April 1967.

3. Lincoln Gordon, "Punta del Este Revisited," *Foreign Affairs,* July 1967, p. 627.

4. *Visión,* September 16, 1966, p. 23; Joseph S. Nye, "Central American Regional Integration," *International Conciliation,* March 1967, pp. 48-49.

5. Anthony M. Solomon, "The Economic Integration of Latin America," *Department of State Bulletin,* October 23, 1967, p. 537.

6. Alister McIntyre, "Aspects of Development and Trade in the Commonwealth Caribbean," *Economic Bulletin for Latin America,* October 1965, pp. 149-50.

7. Havelock Brewster and Clive Y. Thomas, *The Dynamics of West Indian Economic Integration,* Studies in Regional Economic Integration, Vol. I (Jamaica: Institute of Social and Economic Research, University of the West Indies, 1967), p. 5.

8. Sir Philip Sherlock, "Prospects in the Caribbean," *Foreign Affairs,* July 1963.

9. Sir Harold Mitchell, *Europe in the Caribbean,* (Stanford: Hispanic American Society, 1963), pp. 63-75.

10. *The New York Times,* December 31, 1966.

11. *Heads of Caribbean Conference in Barbados* (London: West India Committee, 1967). Jamaica, Trinidad and Tobago, Guyana, Barbados, British Honduras, and the Cayman Islands were all represented, as were Great Britain, the United States, and Canada. The Universities of the West Indies and of Guyana, the Economic Commission for Latin America and the CODECA were also present.

12. Estimated at the incredible sum of £1,525 million. See John Crocker, "Can the West Indies get together again?" *The Observer Foreign News Service* (London), November 7, 1967.

13. Sir Arthur Lewis, *The Agony of the Eight* (Bridgetown, Barbados: Advocate Commercial Printery, n.d.), p. 38.

14. February 3, 1967.

15. *The Sunday Gleaner*, Kingston, editorial, March 3, 1968.

16. *The Daily Gleaner*, Kingston, September 30, 1967.

17. Eric Williams, *Reflections on the Caribbean Economic Community*, reprinted from *The Nation* (Port of Spain, September 14 to November 12, 1965), p. 32.

18. However, the Mayor of Pointe-à-Pitre pointed out that the inhabitants of his island were anxious for cooperation amongst the Caribbean territories. *Official Records*, Conference on Economic Co-ordination in the Caribbean, San Germán, Puerto Rico, May 17-19, 1965, p. 65.

19. Sidney Dell, *A Latin American Common Market?* (Oxford University Press, 1966), pp. 46-47.

20. J. Halcro Ferguson, "Latin America: bad year for revolutions," *The Observer*, December 24, 1967; also Sir Herbert Marchant, "Cuba hamstrung by economic troubles," *The Times*, London, February 8, 1968.

21. S. de Castro, *Problems of the Caribbean Air Transport Industry*, Studies in Regional Economic Integration, Vol. II (Jamaica: Institute of Social and Economic Research, University of the West Indies, 1967), p. 16.

22. In 1959, before the setting up of the LAFTA, 83 per cent of the traffic among the seven original signatories of the Montevideo Treaty moved by water. Joseph W. Reidy, *Strategy for the Americas* (New York: Foreign Policy Research Institute, 1966), p. 16.

23. Sir Harold Mitchell, *Contemporary Politics and Economics in the Caribbean* (Ohio University Press, 1968), pp. 312-15.

24. Jean-Jacques Servan-Schreiber, *Le défi américain* (Paris: Denoël, 1967), *passim*; and Sol M. Linowitz, "The Road from Punta del Este," *Department of State Bulletin,* May 29, 1967, p. 724.

25. John R. Hildebrand, "The Central American Common Market," *Journal of Inter-American Studies,* IX, July 1967, pp. 388-89.

26. "A prosperous Latin America, dedicated to the pursuit of higher living standards, will prove a powerful ally in the struggle for a better world order," Jacob K. Javits, "Last Chance for a Common Market," *Foreign Affairs,* April 1967, p. 459.

27. *Final Communiqué,* Commonwealth Caribbean-Canada Conference, Ottawa, July 6-8, 1966, pp. 70, 72.

28. "Canada-Commonwealth Caribbean Trade and Economic Committee," *External Affairs* (Ottawa), XIX, March 1967.

29. Mona, Jamaica, February 17, 1968.

30. In 1966, the greatest percentage increase (36 per cent) of tourists to Trinidad and Tobago was from Canada. *Economic Survey of Trinidad and Tobago* (London: Barclays Bank, April 1967).

31. *The Commonwealth Caribbean and the E.E.C.* (London: West India Committee, December 1967), pp. 3-7; and "Sugar and the Six—not so sweet," *The Financial Times* (London), February 14, 1967.

32. The overall quota is 900,000 tons, of which 725,000 tons is a negotiated price quota. The NPQ price is at present £47, 10s. 0d. per ton.

33. W. D. Roberts, "Sugar's position in the Common Market," *The Daily Gleaner* (Kingston), October 7, 1967.

34. Prices for white sugar are likely to be about £87, 10s. 0d. a ton.

35. About 96 per cent of the Commonwealth banana exports are sold in the United Kingdom at a price preference equivalent to an ad valorem tariff of 15 per cent. See "New Light on the Common Market," *The Daily Gleaner* (Kingston), October 11, 1967.

36. During Prime Minister Hugh Shearer's European tour in the autumn of 1967, reassurances of support for Jamaica's entry as an AOT should Britain succeed in entering the EEC were given not only by the United Kingdom, but by Germany and the Netherlands. See *The Guardian* (London), September 27, 1967; *The Daily Gleaner* (Kingston, Jamaica). October 6 and 7, 1967; *Mededeling voor de Pers,* Ministerie van Buitenlandse Zaken, The Hague, October 5, 1967.

37. *Report of the Tripartite Economic Survey of British Honduras* (London: Ministry of Overseas Development, 1966).

38. The Cuban situation is a special one based on the U.S.-Cuban ideological quarrel, though here too the pattern of skilled immigration may be observed.

39. Charles Vanhecke comments on the delay in establishing the refining of sugar and the establishment of a cement factory in Guadeloupe, an island where industry employs only 3,000 persons and accounts for only 5 per cent of the internal gross domestic product. "La Guadeloupe dans l'incertitude," *Le Monde,* Paris, December 20, 21, 22, and 23, 1967.

40. It should be borne in mind, however, that the world market for sugar represents only a small percentage of the sugar produced, which accentuates price fluctuations. See Mitchell, *Contemporary Politics and Economics in the Caribbean,* p. 301.

40

LAFTA AND PARAGUAY: ECONOMIC AND SOCIAL DEVELOPMENT

By   John R. Hildebrand
Latin American Studies Center
Michigan State University

Paraguay was one of the seven countries signing the Montevideo Treaty on February 18, 1960. The Montevideo Treaty, establishing the Latin American Free Trade Association (LAFTA), became effective as of June 2, 1961. The first tariff reductions negotiated were effective as of January 1, 1962. The gradual elimination of most trade restrictions was to be completed within twelve years of the effective date of the treaty. The Association has now expanded to eleven members composed of Mexico and all of the South American countries except Guyana, French Guiana, and Surinam. The development of the Latin American Free Trade Association into a common market was enthusiastically agreed upon by the Presidents of the American States in their April 1967 meeting at Punta del Este. The Central American Common Market is expected to join upon completion of their integration plans. By 1985 most internal tariffs and many other barriers to trade will hopefully be reduced to zero while simultaneously establishing a common external tariff around the entire Latin American Common Market. A common external tariff plus free movement of labor and capital converts a free trade association into a common market and avoids the difficult problem of ascertaining the origin of an item traded internally except to the extent that special tariff concessions are granted to less developed countries as is the case for Paraguay.[1] A common market creates bonds that are not likely to be severed in later years. An analysis of a number of general and specific problems or opportunities facing Paraguay provides a basis for policy recommendations as to how Paraguay may more fully enjoy the potential gains and more fully contribute to the general productivity and welfare of the approximately 200 million people residing in the present common market area.

SOVEREIGNTY

"The progressive surrender of sovereignty is the work of an advancing civilization." So stated British Prime Minister Harold Wilson in a recent debate on the European Common Market.[2] Yet, the frightening and emotive phrase "surrender of sovereignty" serves as the major obstacle preventing or delaying economic and associated political integration in Latin America and throughout the world. Nevertheless, economic and some associated political integration is now widely recognized as one of the prerequisites for achieving the intermediate goal of economic and social development which will help move a society up the path toward the ultimate goal of a better life for its people.

In response to critics, Prime Minister Wilson chose to attack the issue of sovereignty boldly and directly in an effort to prevent the traditional sovereign nation-state concept from interfering with the basic requirements for an advancing civilization in the jet-atomic-space age. Clearly, the traditional national framework of small independent countries is not suited to effect the necessary changes required for the movement toward more efficient production units, with their massive capital, research, and market requirements. For Paraguay, with a population of only about 2 million, a per capita income of about 200 dollars, and a gross national product of about 400 million dollars, the local markets are woefully inadequate for efficient production in numerous fields.[3] To solve many problems of the modern world it must first be recognized that there are no adequate solutions within the framework of the traditional sovereign nation-state.

Instead of a direct attack on traditional sovereignty, Mr. Wilson might have chosen to speak of co-operation, collaboration, partnership, or even of the exercise of sovereignty, i.e., the right of a sovereign people and their government to make agreements and establish whatever national or international institutions they may think to be conducive to the general welfare. In this framework, economic and associated political integration is not radical at all but merely a continuation — though perhaps at a more rapid pace as technological changes are moving more rapidly — of the age-old process of developing trading, cultural, and political relations among people. In long historical perspective these relations have of course produced political units expanding from the family, to the clan, to the tribe, to the feudal kingdom, to the city-state, to the nation-state, and now, hopefully, to economic and political integration in varying degrees of nation-states on a subregional, regional, continental, and global basis as may be suited to the new environment of each tomorrow. Clearly, the task for today is that of taming the disruptive force of some aspects of nationalism.

Perhaps most obstacles to progress are man-made. The traditional concepts of sovereignty and associated attitudes were created by man and therefore can be and will be changed by man when the compelling need is recognized. Consequently, a widespread discussion of economic and associated political integration would be desirable to ascertain and understand the extent of the current changes needed. Any government interested in change needs substantial support from politically prominent citizens. A significant task of any government interested in progress is the development of a dialogue leading first to an understanding of the issues and then to consent and support for forward-looking programs. The analysis in this report suggests that the Latin American Common Market is a forward-looking program and that the Paraguayan Government and people should make a firm and vigorous commitment to the Common Market.

Likewise, if the Declaration of the Presidents at Punta del Este is serious, various U.S. missions might appropriately place on their staff a high-ranking economic integration officer. As a further step, an institution something like the Regional Organization for Central America and Panama (ROCAP) could be developed for LAFTA in order to promote more effectively the larger regional points of view. If this is to be the age of integration, country economic missions, implying the narrower nationalistic point of view, should be transformed into regional units working closely with the various regional integration offices and programs.

Recommendation number one calls for an extensive educational effort leading to a re-examination of the traditional sovereign nation-state concept by all parties concerned in order to achieve more understanding and support for adjustments meeting the economic integration needs of the second half of the twentieth century. Assistance of the United States should be more oriented toward encouraging economic and political integration in Latin America. An expansion of support for supranational decision-making bodies is clearly called for. Some assistance programs should be contingent upon or attached to such international units. Experience gained under the Marshall Plan in promoting the European Common Market should be helpful. More co-ordination of assistance programs carried out by international agencies, by the United States, and by other countries could provide additional support for the integration and development goals of the Latin American countries.

A LESS-DEVELOPED COUNTRY

The LAFTA Treaty recognizes Paraguay, Ecuador, and Bolivia as less-developed countries meriting special assistance. According to the thesis of Raúl Prebisch, Paraguay would be on the periphery, having been bypassed by industrialization, and tends automatically under a market system to receive adverse treatment from the industrial centers.

The concern here is not this particular thesis but simply recognition that a problem does exist and that policy measures need to be devised to assure that Paraguay will share fully in the process of economic growth associated with the Latin American Common Market. Also, it is in the general interest to avoid a disruptive schism in the Common Market between countries at different development levels.

Several avenues should be used to resolve this problem. But first, the problem can be clarified and better solutions devised if it is recognized and agreed that the really basic objective here is that of reasonable equality in income distribution rather than the popular, emotional, and antieconomic phrase of equal industrialization. In extreme antieconomic form, equal industrialization may take the shape of "each his own steel mill" which may be translated as a "costly national monument" that destroys the primary objective of the Common Market, which is increased efficiency resulting in a higher standard of living for all. Yet, this point should not be overstated, because there may well be some industrial ventures economically suited for almost any area. Nevertheless, in part by chance and in part for economic reasons, the "industrial Ruhr" of the Latin American Common Market countries developed mostly in the larger capital cities and ocean-port areas. Now the part of economic wisdom appears to be to take advantage of the fact of centuries of tremendous capital accumulation in certain industrial centers as policy measures are devised.

Three basic avenues should be used to resolve the problem of the inferior income position of the Paraguayan in the Latin American Common Market. One avenue is identifying and attracting industry that would have a sound economic basis for locating in Paraguay. A second avenue is assisting the geographic and occupational mobility of Paraguayans as a proper route to higher incomes. In fact, a common market is devised in large part to support both routes leading to greater efficiency by endeavoring to remove the restrictions on the mobility of both capital and labor. Around the world in country after country there is a successful precedent for both measures. Poverty is reduced and total output increased when efficient industry comes into a low-income area and likewise when excess labor moves out of low-income areas to better opportunities in industrial centers. In any developing country around the world, industries do not and economically cannot move to some poverty-stricken centers of population; but rather, it is more economical for people to move to the centers that are ideal for the location of industries. In this manner, additional equality of income distribution and expanded productivity are promoted simultaneously.

Family planning, a third avenue of significant help in overcoming pockets of poverty, in both advanced and less-advanced countries, deserves serious attention. Though the population crisis is not quite as severe in Paraguay as in some other less-developed countries, a voluntary family-planning program should be encouraged as one of the avenues of great relevance to reducing the disparities in income levels and to attaining the higher per capita income goals of both the Alliance for Progress and the Latin American Common Market. To President John F. Kennedy, belongs much of the credit for gaining acceptance of voluntary family planning as a practical policy meriting the support of modern progressive governments. A modern high-income society appears to require a substantial reduction in the high pre-industrial birth rate. Today, the tremendous capital requirements for infrastructure, factories, and training to assure productive employment for each new worker makes a low-birth rate a necessity if the quality of life now desired by people throughout the Americas is to be achieved.

Recommendation number two follows. For less-developed countries, provisions for special tariff concessions and special funds, in line with the economist's case for short-run support of potentially efficient infant industries, should be further developed and utilized. Free mobility of capital and labor within the Common Market should be vigorously encouraged. A program of voluntary family planning merits substantial support — before poverty leads to violence and Castro-type agitation.

ADJUSTMENT ASSISTANCE

Opposition to change, especially when some personal financial loss is involved, becomes a major obstacle to progress in any society. There is increasing recognition that society as a whole should share a part of the cost of readjustment. This feeling prevails on grounds of equity, but also as a basis for speeding economic and social development. For example, in the European Common Market economic integration meant that a number of inefficient coal mines would be closed. To diminish opposition and speed the shift to more productive use of labor and capital, European community funds were established to cover part of the adjustment costs involved for owners and employees. A program for the retraining and redeployment of labor was developed. As another example, in the Kennedy Trade Expansion Act, there is a provision for U.S. Government funds to assist factory owners and employees to readjust to new lines of production if the firm is in serious difficulty as a result of increased imports.

Recommendation number three is that funds and programs be developed to assist Paraguay and other Common Market countries to overcome the adjustment difficulties involved in establishing a Common Market. In the allocation of infrastructure funds, special attention should be given to the mobility needs of an agricultural country such as Paraguay.

BALANCE OF PAYMENTS

Paraguay has an excellent record of exchange-rate stability over the recent decade. Monetary and fiscal policy measures have apparently contributed to this end. Serious inflation has been avoided. During the last decade, a number of Common Market countries have had serious problems of inflation and of inadequate foreign exchange, leading to repeated devaluations of their currencies. A general shortage of foreign exchange is a major problem of developing countries where imports of capital goods and advanced technical skills are always far short of development needs.

Among the Common Market countries, balance of payments problems and abrupt distortions of trading relations by currency devaluations may be eliminated if support for a common currency really takes root and grows. The Central American Common Market is certainly moving in this direction. Its successes and failures should be studied as a possible guide.

In preparation for the future, recommendation number four calls for encouraging studies concerning a common currency. An understanding of appropriate measures to be taken in establishing a common currency may well be of practical value in a real policy sense in the not-so-distant future.

TAXATION

About 60 per cent of Paraguay's revenue comes from taxes on exports and imports. In less-developed countries it is common to rely heavily for revenue on taxes placed on the flow of trade across national frontiers. The customs house always seems to have been an early arrival on the scene of government. Adjustment in Paraguay's tax structure will be required as free trade is established among member countries and as a common external tariff is established around the Common Market. Though the changes in tariff rates and trade flows are not definitely known, revenue will probably decline somewhat because trade from major trading neighbors will eventually enter duty free. A helpful offsetting factor is the higher tax revenue expected from many sources as incomes rise with integration. Tax revision is also of great importance so that the tax structure will promote economic development rather than merely serve revenue needs. Administrative skills must be developed to meet the heavy demands of a society interested in progress.

Recommendation number five is that the development of other sources of revenue and associated administrative skills be initiated now in anticipation of a probable loss in revenue from customs. Administrative efficiency and enforcement skills, which are certainly needed now in view of the delays in customs and the extent of contraband activities, will be even more necessary later because new taxes will present added difficulties in administration. It is recommended that study and initial steps be taken toward the eventual establishment of an effective and efficient civil service system throughout government. Finally, support should be given for a tax structure that encourages, not consumption, but savings, investment, and exports. Imports of capital equipment conducive to an enlarged and more efficient production as required by development opportunities should not be discouraged by import duties unless efficient domestic production of those items is anticipated.

MARKETS

The potential gain for Paraguay is tremendous as she achieves assured access to a Common Market of about 200 million people with a generally higher per capita income. The gross national product of the eleven member countries adds up to a little over 80 billion dollars compared to about 400 million dollars for Paraguay.[4] In addition, under the stimulus of the Common Market, a more rapid rise in per capita income may be expected. In economic terms, access to any market means a willingness and capability to produce at a competitive price. If economic efficiency and higher standards of living are desired, the merits of an opportunity and obligation to compete need to be widely recognized.

Resources and markets do not properly fit national boundaries, and the logical unit changes as technology advances. The rewards of a single large market in Latin America should be clear to consumer and producer alike. The pace of economic expansion in any existing nation would undoubtedly have been hindered had that nation been broken up into compartments separated by numerous restrictions on the flow of goods, capital, people, and had it been afflicted with the complications resulting from different currency systems. Latin America needs a rebirth of a sense of unity — a sense of unity to some degree existing in the colonial past and certainly shared by many of the great leaders at the time of the independence movement.

A large market is needed for economic efficiency — not for maintaining full employment. Full employment at low levels of productivity cannot produce a high standard of living. The problem is to utilize resources as efficiently as possible. Since great promise lies in the enlarged market and in joint action, scarce resources should not be scattered in an unco-ordinated, uneconomic fashion among isolated countries. Multinational projects serving to tie together the enlarged Common Market area should have a high priority.

Recommendation number six, in recognition of the importance of market size, calls for high priority for infrastructure and industrial projects that will serve to tie countries together in a mutually beneficial manner and to create solid support for developing and maintaining the enlarged market. Multinational transportation and river-basin development projects are excellent candidates for support and are of great significance to Paraguay's economic progress.

MULTINATIONAL CORPORATIONS AND JOINT VENTURES

The assurance of a large Common Market in Latin America, even though still small in current total income compared to the European Common Market or the United States, should serve as a substantial incentive for outside capital to move into the Common Market area. Paraguay can expect to share in this capital inflow in the form of new business establishments. These establishments will now have access to a large enough market to justify locating in a small country like Paraguay whenever the resources of Paraguay are suited to a particular operation.

A particularly desirable form of that investment would be joint ventures in which Paraguayan businessmen team up, in financing and management, with businessmen from other Latin American countries or from any of the more developed countries around the world. Another excellent possibility is to promote the establishment of plants by the large multinational corporations with production units scattered around the world. These firms typically have advanced technological and management skills plus a most valuable accumulation of experience in international production and marketing. An effective vehicle for transferring ideas, skills, and organizational patterns from one place to another is an obvious requirement for rapid economic and social development.

These two devices, not necessarily mutually exclusive, of multinational corporations and joint ventures provide two major advantages. First, they offer an excellent pipeline for carrying capital, modern technology, and know-how to less-developed areas. The literature on economic development suggests that these three factors of capital, technological improvement, and above all, improvement in the education or know-how of the human agent are crucial items for economic and social development. Second, these devices serve effectively as a vital force leading to economic integration by tying together the economies and businessmen of various countries in a more productive manner. The increase in productivity and the rise in the standard of living become apparent and create a firm base for popular support of economic integration.

The multinational corporation is a modern concept designed to meet modern requirements. Likewise, economic integration is a modern concept designed to modify the very old-fashioned idea of the traditional sovereign nation-state. The complexities of the modern world demand the building of bridges across national frontiers. The multinational corporation is playing a significant role in the up-dating of economic and political organization. Roger Blough, Chairman of the Board of the United States Steel Corporation, has stated, "the multi-nation corporation may ultimately prove to be the most productive economic development of the twentieth century for bringing the people of nations together for peaceful purposes to their mutual advantage; and it can thus provide the adhesive which will do more to bind nations together than any other development yet found by man in his pursuit of peace."[5]

Recommendation number seven, therefore, asks for increased support in a financial and educational manner for stimulating investment in the form of joint ventures and multinational corporations.

ENCOURAGING NEW INDUSTRY

One of the first avenues to study is the possible expansion of existing industries. The fact that these industries have been in operation over a period of time may well indicate their suitability to the economic environment. More elaboration and processing of existing products appears to be a likely development. As the movement toward a Common Market takes place, a sizable expansion in many of these business firms should be considered. The removal of trade barriers will provide opportunity for the expansion of Asunción as a major distribution and commercial center serving a multinational geographic region.

There is also need to identify new industrial opportunities and induce prospective business firms to look over existing possibilities. The officials of business firms will often pass information on to other interested businessmen, even though they themselves may not find just what they need in the Paraguayan economy.

As Paraguay is an agricultural country, with about 60 per cent of the population working in agriculture, one of the first places to look for additional development is in the agricultural sector. Firms connected with the lumber industry should be aggressive and watch for profitable opportunities to expand lumber production and processing. With more efficient production, processing, and marketing, the cattle industry could be expanded substantially. Likewise the fruit and vegetable industry could probably be expanded as is indicated by the recent opening of a new processing plant. In a sense, a new agricultural industry could be established with the development of commercial poultry and hog production. Associated grain production, and the storage and processing that supports meat production would mean a sizable expansion of industry. With a higher value per pound, these meat products may be able to overcome the costly transportation hurdle Paraguay faces. Expansion of fiber production and associated processing is another common possibility for less developed agrarian countries. Products related to agriculture are not homogeneous with respect to type, location, or timing for market. Therefore, mutually beneficial trade is clearly possible between similar agricultural countries and most especially along national frontiers.

With respect to more advanced industrial production, component parts, or some assembly work may appropriately be carried on in Paraguay to fit in with other units located throughout the Common Market region.

To explore and develop the various possibilities for new industry, recommendation number eight calls for additional emphasis and support for developing on a national and local level Paraguayan committees of businessmen to serve as development boards. With firsthand knowledge of the economy and relevant statistics, Paraguayan businessmen, selling the merits of their community for plant location to outside businessmen, can be effective in promoting economic integration and development. The business contacts in themselves perform a valuable integrative and developmental function. The development boards should

provide for the collection and wide dissemination of up-to-date
Common Market information, with suggestions for exploiting
Paraguayan production possibilities to take advantage of the enlarged marketing opportunities which now exist beyond national
boundaries. The business community should seek the co-ordinated
support of research, extension, credit, marketing, and educational institutions to assure a firm base for new or expanded production. These auxiliary institutions will need strengthening to
perform the needed services.

CONCLUSION

There is no once over and perfected adjustment. Reform
is a continual affair in any society. Perfection is always out of
reach. Goals are also continually refined. In effect one can only
move down the road toward the horizon. One never reaches it. It
now appears that economic integration is never a completed thing.
In fact, that most famous of all common markets known as the
United States of America is still involved in the process of economic integration. Basically, Latin America needs a commitment
to a process — not a commitment to a specific result. The eight
recommendations listed here should be viewed in general as items
in need of continual attention. As new evidence appears, continual
re-examination and modifications are necessary. The extreme
scarcity of capital, both external and internal, calls for a continuing effort to improve the allocation of such a scarce resource
to the most critical of the many important projects.

Perhaps the really difficult problem is the political
problem, i.e., generating the political will, the support and the
skill to carry out an economic integration program without government crises. Confidence in a high degree of political and
economic stability is essential for development. A most difficult
problem facing governments everywhere is that of coping with
claims of special interest groups for protection from competition
borne by the winds of change — especially when that competition
comes from beyond the national frontiers, from those one is
always psychologically disposed to view as outsiders, i.e.,
foreigners. In the arena of battle, military progress requires
soldiers to face death; in the arena of economic integration, economic progress only requires business groups to adjust production in line with economic efficiency criteria. In a dynamic,
developing society such adjustments are a continual necessity,
and competition becomes a healthy force inducing these needed
changes.

As incomes rise, all countries share in an expanded and
mutually profitable international trade. Low-income communities
can buy little from anyone. An institutional improvement such as
economic integration that leads to increased productivity is analytically identical to an internal technological improvement such
as a new piece of machinery that also leads to increased productivity. There can be no progress without a willingness to adjust

560

to improved technological and institutional conditions, even though on occasion such adjustments may be painful.

Consequently, a major challenge of statesmanship today in Paraguay and elsewhere is to point out effectively the common interest of all in increased productivity made possible by economic integration and to develop a strategy for promoting that common interest — a strategy to make possible that which is necessary. In the interest of the general welfare, ways and means must be found to rise above narrow, divisive, short-run national interests in order to harmonize policies and to create the common institutions conducive to economic and social development. Fine words must be accompanied by action if the aspirations of the peoples of Latin America as expressed at Punta del Este are to be achieved.

The inescapable lesson of our century, inscribed in contagious suffering around the world, is that our home is the planet. Therefore, may every sub-unit, including the Latin American Common Market, be also outward-looking and aware of worldwide common interests.

NOTES

1. For an analysis of the 4,955 items for which concessions have been granted to Paraguay, see chapter iv of *Paraguay en la Integración: Cinco Años en la ALALC* by the Paraguayan ambassador to ALALC, Dr. Delfín Ugarte Centurión, Montevideo, February 1967. Also, see chapter ii for additional background information.

2. See page 3 of the February 20, 1967, issue of the *European Free Trade Association Reporter* published by the EFTA Washington Information Office.

3. For one series of estimates, see page 41 of the April 10, 1967, issue of *International Commerce* published by the U.S. Department of Commerce.

4. *Ibid.*

5. Roger Blough, *The Tie That Binds,* United States Steel Corporation, 1964.